For
D.M.O.

Church and Society
in Late Medieval England

Church and Society
in Late Medieval England

R. N. Swanson

Basil Blackwell

First published 1989

Basil Blackwell Ltd
108 Cowley Road, Oxford, OX4 1JF, UK

Basil Blackwell Inc.
432 Park Avenue South, Suite 1503
New York, NY 10016, USA

British Library Cataloguing in Publication Data

Swanson, R.N. (Robert Norman)
Church and society in late medieval England.
1. England. Society. Role of Christian church – history
I. Title
261.1'0942
ISBN 0–631–14659–8

Library of Congress Cataloging in Publication Data

Swanson, R. N. (Robert Norman)
Church and society in late medieval England / by R.N. Swanson.
p. cm.
Bibliography: p.
Includes index.
ISBN 0–631–14659–8
1. Catholic Church—England—History. 2. England—Church history—
Medieval period, 1066–1485. 3. England—Social conditions—
Medieval period, 1066–1485. I. Title.
BR750.S83 1989
282'.42—dc19   88—31863
CIP

Typeset in 10 on 12pt Baskerville
by Hope Services (Abingdon) Ltd.
Printed in Great Britain by
T. J. Press Ltd, Padstow, Cornwall

Contents

Preface

The first necessity with this book is to excuse its title. To talk of 'church' and 'society' in pre-Reformation England as though they were two separate entities is blatantly anachronistic. A distinction between them could be made only when denominational pluralism and post-Christian atheism spawned the view of the church as only one element in a social system, and an identifiably distinct entity. That did not apply before Henry VIII's reign, or for years later. Medieval society was implicitly Christian, even if there were conflicts between the ideal and the reality. Equally, the medieval church and its religion were explicitly social, catholicity defining its membership rather than its beliefs. The traditional tripartite division applied by contemporaries – between those who prayed, those who fought, and those who worked – was not just a statement of social relations. Fourteenth-century English sermonizers used the same categorization within the church, because the church was society: social obligations reflected religious and ecclesiastical interconnections as well as others.[1]

Despite this, there was obviously an institution – 'the church' – which was in some respects set apart from that broader church which was society. At times, indeed often, in what follows, the relationship between 'church' and 'society' has to be viewed as a relationship between these two different aspects of the church, as well as reflecting contrasts and conflicts between the ecclesiastical institution and other authorities. The aim is especially to emphasize the social element rather than the 'ecclesiastical', although the concern throughout is with 'the church'. While I have tried to indicate the wider contexts, it has not been possible to deal with them in great detail: the wider background against which and to which the church reacted is therefore to a great extent assumed rather than stated. The book is explicitly not about the church's administration, nor about Christianity

[1] Owst, *Literature and pulpit* [632], pp. 550–4.

in medieval England – although both will be touched on where appropriate, and are often assumed or subsumed in the discussion. The book is about a morality, an ethic, and the institution which was created to maintain and expand that view, about the individuals who acted on its behalf, and those over whom it claimed authority – their acceptance or rejection of its demands and dictates, and the institution's ability to maintain its stance. Aspects of the relationship between 'church' and 'society' have often been tackled as though they were quite independent of other features; my aim is to attempt a synthesis which demonstrates some of the complexity of the complete picture.

The final version has ended up rather longer than originally proposed, yet I am well aware that much more could have been included. I have generally limited consideration to the period from 1350 to c.1540: essentially between the Black Death and the Reformation, although drawing illustrations from outside those time limits when necessary. The Reformation stands as an obvious terminus; the Black Death is less obviously justifiable, except as a Significant Event With Repercussions – and some starting-date has to be accepted. Its adoption makes the span manageable, and avoids discussion of some of the trends which were altered as a result of the plague's visitation.

The compression needed to keep the volume within publishable limits means that in some areas matters are rather summarily treated. I am, again, well aware that almost every positive statement made could be qualified virtually out of existence. Much more work remains to be done to reveal the mechanisms of some of the processes in full, and the nature of some of the relationships; but a summary of how things appear to stand at present is no bad thing.

The approach adopted is thematic, falling into three main themes. First comes the church itself, dealt with in two parts. The first seeks to place the institutional church in England in focus, discussing its structure and integration into the wider church of western Europe under the papacy. Attention then turns to the church's personnel, the clergy, especially considering the forces which created ecclesiastical careers and exploited clerics and the church as aspects of a wider social structure. The second 'theme' turns attention to English society. The relationship between church and state is considered first, at the theoretical and practical levels, and in terms of the demands of central administration and local rulership. The legal relationships are then tackled, the church's disciplinary claims both conflicting with and complementing the jurisdiction claimed by the royal courts, producing a sometimes tense dualism which was in a constant state of attrition between the two laws as they competed for competence and customers. Then follows a consideration of economic activity, as the church sought to impose its own morality on economic arrangements, whilst actively embroiled in economic relationships by its landholding, and because its institutional and spiritual demands generated and stimulated exchanges, with potentially massive consequences. The third part of the book considers spiritual activities, both orthodox and unorthodox, seeking to establish how people related to the church and the religion which it offered them. On the one hand there is the acceptance of the orthodox, on the other the rejection by those characterized as Lollards, and the challenges of reform movements which in due course became a Reformation.

Any synthesis is necessarily highly dependent on the work of others, a dependence which is mirrored in the bibliography. A case could be made for not including a bibliography, but here I feel that it is an integral part of the whole book, even though restricting it to works cited (with a few accidental exceptions) means that there are omissions – some of them glaring. I have, however, sought to avoid total dependence on earlier writers, including new material derived from work on manuscripts. Many of the references are to the diocesan archives of York and Lichfield, because of their quality and because they are the two with which I am most familiar. Other archives have been scoured in varying degrees of depth, sometimes admittedly no more than toe-wetting exercises, and I make no claims to have surveyed the full range of possibilities. Nor have I really investigated in any depth the considerable flow of theses which remain unpublished: to do that would have been impossible. Simply keeping up with the printed material is hard enough – when (as one colleague commented to me) the current publishing on *Piers Plowman* alone is so prolific that even specialists on that one text feel overwhelmed, I hope my own lapses will be forgiven.

Where counties are identified in the text, I have followed the customary practice and given the locations as they were prior to the great re-organization of 1974.

Writing a book incurs many debts. First and foremost, I have to acknowledge the financial assistance which made it possible. The Wolfson Foundation made a generous grant which enabled me to engage in archive-hopping, and the University of Birmingham also provided funds for travel and research. A British Academy grant for microfilms of Lichfield episcopal registers made dealing with them easier than would otherwise have been the case. The second main category of debts must be to the archives and libraries without whose resources the book could not have been written. The archives are listed in the bibliography. For printed works I have exploited the Birmingham Reference Library, Cambridge University Library, the Bodleian Library at Oxford, and the British Library in

London, but the principal debt under this heading is to the Birmingham University Library, whose Inter-Library Loans office requires particular mention.

The debts which it is most pleasant to recall are those to individuals – in this case far too many to list individually. Conversation, suggestions, and accommodation have been freely offered, and much appreciated. The book has been a long time developing, having germinated way back during my days as an assistant archivist at the Borthwick Institute in York. Since moving to Birmingham numerous students have helped to consolidate and stimulate my ideas, whether in seminars for the option of which this is the book, or in discussions on topics being dealt with for undergraduate dissertations: I hope they will feel it was all worth while. There are some debts which must be particularly acknowledged. In the first place, I am grateful to Philip Carpenter and Virginia Murphy at Basil Blackwell for having the courage of my convictions and agreeing to take on the book. Chris Wickham and Guy Lytle read through a complete draft text, while various portions have been read by Chris Dyer, Valerie Edden, Gervase Rosser and John Thomson. Their comments have led to many improvements. My wife Heather has provided constant support and assistance in developing and challenging my ideas, has read and commented on the complete text, and allowed me to cite her unpublished work. I have finally to thank Dorothy Owen, who also read a full draft and suggested valuable emendations. To some extent the whole book owes its existence to her, for it was she who introduced me to English ecclesiastical archives. I am one of many who have profited over the years from her guidance and friendship, gaining more than can adequately be acknowledged, let alone repaid. This book is for her.

Note on References

For printed works I have used a short-title system throughout. On the first citation in each chapter the title is followed by a number in [ ], which is the number assigned to the work in the Bibliography, where full details of publication are to be found. Cross-references are indicted by chapter and section, usually to appropriate notes (e.g. see 6/4 at nn. 118–20).

The following abbreviations are used to identify record repositories in the notes:

BIHR	York, Borthwick Institute of Historical Research
BL	London, British Library
Bod.	Oxford, Bodleian Library
BRL	Birmingham Reference Library
Cant.	Canterbury, Cathedral, city, and diocesan record office
CCCO	Oxford, Corpus Christi College
CRO	Carlisle, Cumbria County Record Office
CUA	Cambridge University Archives
CUL	Cambridge University Library
DRO	Exeter, Devon Record Office
EDC	Cambridge University Library, Ely Dean and Chapter Archives
EDR	Cambridge University Library, Ely Diocesan Records
ECL	Exeter Cathedral Library
GL	London, Guildhall Library
HCA	Hereford Cathedral Archives
HCRO	Beverley, Humberside County Record Office
HWCRO	Worcester, Hereford and Worcester County Record Office
LAO	Lincoln, Lincolnshire Archives Office
LJRO	Lichfield Joint Record Office
LPL	London, Lambeth Palace Library

NRO	Norwich, Norfolk and Norwich Record Office
PRO	London, Public Record Office
SRO	Stafford, Staffordshire County Record Office
WAM	Westminster Abbey Muniments
Windsor	Windsor, St George's Chapel Archives
WSL	Stafford, William Salt Library
YML	York Minster Library

I

Ecclesia Anglicana

The church in medieval England was closely integrated into the life of the nation. It was also a distinct institution, with its own organizational structure, which needs some consideration. It was, additionally, part of a supra-national whole which was the catholic church, and which necessarily affected the structure within England and the relationship between the church and society within the realm.

Although the English Reformation introduced a lengthy period of spiritual turmoil in England, little in the fundamental administrative system of the Anglican church was actually altered. Henry VIII admittedly increased the number of dioceses, altered the statutes of several cathedrals, secularized the monastic cathedrals, and transferred various papal powers to himself or the archbishop of Canterbury; but in essentials the church's administrative structure remained that of the medieval institution. If a date must be sought for the great organizational upheaval, it would have to be in the nineteenth rather than the sixteenth century.

Like its modern equivalent, the English medieval church was geographically divided into dioceses. England contained seventeen: Canterbury, Carlisle, Chichester, Durham, Ely, Exeter, Hereford, Lincoln, London, Norwich, Rochester, Salisbury, Winchester, Worcester, York, and the two double-headed bishoprics of Bath and Wells, and Lichfield and Coventry. To these must be added the four Welsh sees of Bangor, Llandaff, St Asaph, and St David's, which were jurisdictionally subject to the arch-bishopric of Canterbury, but fall geographically outside the limits of this book. The Welsh bishoprics had sought independence from Canterbury in the twelfth century, and claimed it again during the rebellion of Owen Glyndŵr in the early fifteenth, but they were usually firmly integrated into the province of Canterbury, until the present century. The diocese of

Whithorn or Galloway in Scotland might also be added to the total, as nominally subject to York. This persisted until the erection of the archbishopric of St Andrew's in 1472, but the links had effectively ended in the 1350s, which witnessed the last English consecration of a bishop of Whithorn.[1]

The geographical extent of the individual dioceses varied enormously. The largest were York, Lincoln, and Lichfield, each containing several counties. At the other extreme were the bishoprics of London, Ely, and Carlisle. The diocesan boundaries were unchanged throughout the later medieval period. Wolsey suggested the creation of additional bishoprics in the late 1520s, but nothing came of it; changes came only when implemented by Henry VIII after the break with Rome.[2]

The main geographical sub-divisions of the diocese were the archdeaconries, attached to offices which had been territorialized during the twelfth century.[3] As the dioceses varied in size, so the number of archdeaconries each contained also differed; the vast see of Lincoln had eight, but those of Carlisle, Canterbury, Ely, and Rochester had but one each. Sometimes the territory of the archdeaconry corresponded to a county; sometimes it overlapped county boundaries; sometimes it contained only part of a county. All three types were contained in the diocese of Lichfield. There, the archdeaconries of Stafford and Derby corresponded to the appropriate county; the archdeaconry of Chester included all of Cheshire, southern Lancashire as far north as the Ribble, and a few fragments of Welsh counties; while in the south the archdeaconry of Salop contained only the northern half of Shropshire, and the archdeaconry of Coventry accounted for a vaguely triangular chunk of Warwickshire. Like the dioceses, the archdeaconries varied considerably in size.[4]

The third level of the pyramid was provided by the rural deaneries – in some cases termed deaneries of Christianity. These deaneries grouped parishes, varying in number, into a local administrative unit for a variety of ecclesiastical purposes. They were frequently coterminous with hundreds and wapentakes, but this was not a universal rule. The deaneries dealt with local inquisitions into such matters as patronage of benefices, provided a machinery for discussion and promulgation of episcopal orders, and formed what might once have been the lowest level in the system of ecclesiastical courts. The rural deaneries often derived their name from one parish within the grouping; but there were many exceptions to that

---

[1] Williams, *Welsh church* [912], pp. 3–7, 222–4; Haddan and Stubbs, *Councils and documents* [327], 2/i, pp. 63, 66–7; Watt, 'Papacy and Scotland' [886], pp. 123–5.
[2] Ordnance Survey, *Monastic Britain* [617], and map 1 opposite; Brewer, *Letters and papers*, vol. 4 [87], iii, nos. 5607–8; Scarisbrick, *Henry VIII*, [747], pp. 512–14.
[3] Thompson, 'Diocesan organisation' [823], pp. 163–4.
[4] ibid., pp. 165–7.

detached portions of
Canterbury diocese

jurisdiction of St Albans

•••••• frontier between provinces
of York and Canterbury

Key to detached areas and major exempt jurisdictions

B	Bury St Edmunds	**R**	diocese of Rochester
Ba	diocese of Bangor	**S**	diocese of Salisbury
D	diocese of Durham	**W**	diocese of Winchester
E	Evesham	**Wa**	jurisdiction of Waltham
Ex	diocese of Exeter	**Y**	diocese of York
H	diocese of Hereford		

Deaneries of royal free chapels

1 Penkridge
2 Wolverhampton
3 Tettenhall
4 Bridgnorth
5 St Buryan

MAP I: The dioceses and quasi-dioceses of medieval England and Wales.

generalization. Unfortunately, little evidence survives for the detailed functioning of the rural deaneries: what little notice they receive in the main administrative records, the episcopal registers, concentrates on the individual dean's activities, and then almost exclusively in his role as a minor factotum. The deaneries have left few independent records, and it may be that by the Reformation they were virtually moribund in many areas.[5]

If the normal administrative pyramid of the medieval English church had the diocese as its local apex, then its base lay firmly on the parish, the smallest geographical unit with the exception of the chapelries, which were segments of parishes with incomplete juridical autonomy. The total number of parishes in England and Wales (which have to be counted together now, as they were then, for administrative purposes) was rarely properly appreciated in the late middle ages. In 1371, when introducing a novel scheme for taxation to be organised by parishes, Parliament assumed that there were 45,000 parishes – an absurdly high figure which was rapidly reduced to about 8,600 when the tax was actually assessed. Even so, in *c.*1529 Simon Fish, whilst venting his anti-clerical spleen, offered a figure of 52,000 parish churches. However, in 1535, when the great survey of the *Valor ecclesiasticus* was carried out, the commissioners were hard pressed to identify many more than 8,800 parishes. In fact, the number of parishes had probably declined during the preceding centuries, for varied reasons. How many parishes existed in 1350 is not recorded officially, and cannot accurately be assessed: the *Valor* of 1535 is the only national survey which is in any way reliable. Another taxation survey listing the benefices had been drawn up in 1291, but there are massive difficulties involved in the interpretation of these lists. Nevertheless, the 1291 survey provides a basis for guesswork, suggesting that there were then about 9,500 parishes.[6] An overall drop in numbers of some 7 per cent over two centuries does not seem particularly dramatic, but its impact would be difficult to determine: much would have depended on the regional variations.

As with the higher units in the church's administrative and geographical structure, parishes were not of uniform size. In rural areas, much depended on local physical considerations. In remoter parts of Yorkshire, for instance, sparse population and long valleys produced parishes having immense areas, or extremely elongated: Romaldkirk covered almost 90 square

---

[5] ibid., pp. 172–3, 179–84, 186–9, 192–4; Scammell, 'Rural chapter' [745]. For evidence of continued activity within the deaneries, see Dunning, 'Rural deans' [239]; for the deaneries in Carlisle diocese e.g. CRO, DRC.2/7–8.

[6] Moorman, *Church life* [591], pp. 4–5; Thomson, *Transformation of England* [831], p. 260; Furnivall and Cowper, *Four supplications* [289], p. 2; Knowles, *Religious orders* [484], ii, p. 291. For the problems of the 1291 taxation, Graham, *English ecclesiastical studies* [309], pp. 281–300.

miles, while the parishes of Wykeham, Allerston, and Kirkdale (to name but three) were fingers of territory almost 10 miles long, but scarcely 1 mile wide.[7] Other parishes, particularly in urban areas, could be tiny. Some towns – notably Norwich, York, and Exeter – had disproportionately large numbers of parishes for both their size and their population, some containing barely more than a few acres. The number of parishes bore no relation to population concentration. Some of them reflected a fossilization of ancient organization, their churches often being successors to pre-Conquest private and local chapels which had acquired parochial status as the parochial system was itself established. In consequence, in those towns with many parishes, these were not only small, but frequently poverty-stricken. It can be no accident that one of the first effects of the Reformation in York was a drastic programme to reduce the number of parishes by consolidation. Conversely, the fossilization of the parochial structure meant that the developing towns of the later middle ages were not sub-divided as their needs increased: Leeds and the booming wool towns of the fifteenth century often possessed but one parish church. While the episcopal administrations had a procedure for reducing the number of parishes, usually because of financial pressures which rendered continued independence unviable, the procedure for establishing new parishes was rarely applied after the thirteenth century. It was not totally extinct: St Mary's, Lichfield, was converted from a chapelry of the extra-mural St Michael's into an independent vicarage in the 1530s (although burial rights remained with the former mother church); and in several instances after 1350, chapelries appealed to the papacy for grants of parochial rights because of problems of access to the mother church. However, although many such grants were made, they rarely created autonomous parishes: the churches remained technically subject chapelries, and often had to acknowledge some lingering obligations to the mother church.[8] The creation of these quasi-parishes might well compensate for the apparent reduction in the number of parishes derived from a comparison of the figures drawn from the surveys of 1291 and 1535.

This hierarchy of administration, from diocese to archdeaconry to rural deanery to parish, seems remarkably simple. But it is very much a simplification, ignoring several distortions. These distortions apply both to the organization within England, and to the placing of the English church within that catholic church whose existence was proclaimed in every recitation of the Creeds. The issues raised by the latter perhaps demand the

---

[7] For parishes see the maps in Humphery-Smith, *Phillimore atlas* [427].

[8] Godfrey, *Anglo-Saxon England* [303], pp. 315–24; Brooke, 'The missionary at home' [96], esp. pp. 70–8; Palliser, 'Union of parishes' [634]; Bassett, 'Medieval Lichfield' [47], p. 115; Kitching, 'Church and chapelry' [480], pp. 279–84.

more urgent consideration: in precisely what ways can the church in England be considered a specifically 'English' church before the Reformation?

Limiting discussion of the church's administrative system to the diocesan unit excludes two higher stages of the church's organization. These integrated the local English organism into the catholic whole, into a church which spread throughout western Europe in a jurisdictional pyramid headed by St Peter's successor at Rome. For English ecclesiastical geography, the most immediately relevant unit was the province, co-terminous with the archbishoprics of York and Canterbury. That two distinct provinces existed within the one realm challenges the very concept of an 'English' church: how far can we speak of such an entity when there were in fact two autonomous provinces, each with its own customs and provincial structure (despite some overlapping), each with its own system of synods and convocations, individually answerable to the crown and papacy for taxation purposes, and with no procedure whereby the two could normally come together in any national church council? Even if Canterbury's precedence over York was being increasingly recognized in the fourteenth and fifteenth centuries, the only forum in which the 'English church' might normally claim united representation was not ecclesiastical at all, but in Parliament. And even there, clerical involvement was steadily declining as time passed.[9]

The two churches of York and Canterbury were separate institutions. Each archbishop was a primate – and the semantic distinction between York's primacy of England and Canterbury's primacy of *all* England did not affect their jurisdictional relationship. Moreover, each archbishop was *ex officio* a papal legate within his archdiocese, a *legatus natus*. The only way in which one archbishop could overrule the other was by a direct papal commission as *legatus a latere*, thereby superseding all other forms of legatine or ordinary authority. But such overriding authority would be granted by any commission of a legate *a latere*, whatever his ecclesiastical status.[10]

Above the provinciality of York and Canterbury lay the proclaimed universality of the whole 'Roman' church. The regional church in England cannot be divorced from the international body of which it was a member. In delimiting the jurisdiction exercised by the archbishops of Canterbury, the four Welsh bishoprics have already been listed among the subject sees, their subjection revealing some of the difficulties in identifying an 'English' church. If the 'English' church is to be defined as those areas immediately subject to York and Canterbury, other territories also need to be included. From the late fourteenth century the archbishops of Canterbury had some

---

[9] Thomson, *Transformation of England*, pp. 305–6; see also 3/2 at nn. 48–52.
[10] Paro, *Papal legation* [642], pp. 87–102.

rights on French soil, exercising ecclesiastical authority over the March of Calais which was retained (apart from a gap from 1420 to *c*.1440) until the sixteenth century. Although the Scottish bishoprics had in fact rejected subjection to York from the mid-fourteenth century, *de facto* rule might still be established over some territories during the recurrent Anglo-Scottish wars. Problems also arose with the Channel Islands, which were jurisdictionally part of the Norman diocese of Coutances. They were only detached in 1496, when Alexander VI linked them to the bishopric of Salisbury. In 1499 they were again transferred to the diocese of Winchester.[11]

The frontier works against the 'Englishness' of the church in England, a process further aided by other indications of internationality. Admittedly, the mobile episcopate of the twelfth and thirteenth centuries, when Frenchmen occupied English sees with some frequency, was long past; but foreigners continued to gain a few English benefices. The later middle ages saw occasional foreign bishops, such as Lewis of Luxembourg, Cardinal-Archbishop of Rouen and holder of the see of Ely in plurality from 1438 to 1443 – receiving the see partly in reward for his loyalty to the English conquest of Normandy. The reigns of Henry VII and Henry VIII witnessed a minor flurry of foreign bishops, for the most part Italians, but including the Spanish confessor of Queen Catherine of Aragon as Bishop of Llandaff from 1517 to 1537. Foreigners also occasionally held lesser benefices. Cardinals often appeared among the cathedral dignitaries until the end of the fourteenth century, and even in the fifteenth and sixteenth, Italians, Scots, and others sometimes received archdeaconries and rectories. They might also act as notaries public within episcopal households. Admittedly, the number of foreigners active in England had probably decreased in the early fifteenth century following legislation against papal provisions (with perhaps a minor resurgence in their holdings with the arrival of Italian humanism and humanists in the early sixteenth century), but the important point is that foreigners were not completely excluded from holding benefices within the *Ecclesia Anglicana*.[12]

Equally significant, English clerics were personally as much part of the universal church as the country was geographically, and were eligible to seek advancement abroad. Most obviously, the English tenure of Normandy between 1415 and 1450 provided opportunities for English clerics like Alan Kirketon, who acquired canonries and benefices in the Norman

[11] Churchill. *Canterbury administration* [144], i, pp. 508–19, ii, pp. 219–21; Storey, *Reg. Langley* [781], i, no. 96; Hill, *The English dioceses* [388], p. 313.

[12] For foreign bishops, Fryde et al., *Handbook of British chronology* [286], pp. 229, 244, 251, 274, 280, 294, see also 1/2, at nn. 26–7; foreign prebendaries in cathedrals are identifiable from Le Neve, *Fasti* [509]. For foreigners beneficed in England in the fifteenth century, see e.g. Allmand, 'Some effects' [7], pp. 186–7; Harvey, 'Benefice as property' [361], pp. 162–3, 167–71. For a foreign notary public, Horn, *Reg. Hallum* [411], nos. 65, 466, 858, 864, 923, 1009.

cathedrals. Foreign marriages, such as Philippa of Lancaster's to King John I of Portugal, also opened continental benefices to the possibility of English occupation.[13] Career prospects at the papal curia also meant that English clerics could establish their careers there, either permanently or temporarily. Thus, in the mid-fourteenth century Englishmen acted in the major papal tribunal as auditors of the Rota; while perhaps the most obviously successful English cleric at Rome was Christopher Bainbridge, who attained the cardinalate in 1512. The medieval church was, truly, an international church, its internationality aided by the use of Latin as the international language. English clerics might study at Bologna or Pavia as they could at Oxford or Cambridge (although, admittedly, in smaller numbers), just as Portuguese or Italians could attend the English universities as well as their own.[14]

The church's universality is also revealed in the titles of some of the bishoprics acquired by Englishmen during these years. They were often not real bishoprics, but titular sees – although Thomas Wolsey battled to establish himself in the bishopric of Tournai, and was for a time nominally Bishop of Badajoz in Spain; and both he and Christopher Bainbridge were considered potential candidates for the bishopric of Rome itself.[15] But the nominal sees provide the best show of internationality. The medieval church had no system whereby suffragan bishops held titular sees within the diocese of the bishop whom they were assisting. One diocese, one spiritual father, remained the basic rule. However, this did not prevent the employment of bishops from defunct or unapproachable sees as assistants in the exercise of episcopal power. They relieved the diocesans of much of the work associated with the power of orders. During vacancies, in exempt peculiars (such as the jurisdictions of St Albans and Bury St Edmunds), and during periods of a diocesan's non-residence, they assumed responsibility for the continuity of episcopal sacramental activity. The sees 'held' by these suffragans were usually in parts of the world considered to be *in partibus infidelium* – whether those infidels were Christian Greeks or Moslem Saracens was irrelevant – and provided the titles for a

---

[13] Allmand, 'Some effects', pp. 180–2; Allmand, 'Alan Kirketon' [6]; Russell, *English intervention* [723], p. 543.

[14] Ullmann, 'Decision of the Rota Romana' [856], pp. 465–7; Chambers, *Cardinal Bainbridge* [134], pp. 72–130; Aston, 'Oxford's medieval alumni' [18], pp. 21–3, 25–6; Aston, Duncan, and Evans, 'Medieval alumni of Cambridge' [20], pp. 33–6; Mitchell, 'English students at Bologna' [584]; Mitchell, 'English students at Ferrara' [585]; Parks, *English traveler* [640], pp. 624–40.

[15] For Tournai, Cruickshank, *English occupation of Tournai* [181], pp. 143–70, 176–87; Wilkie, *Cardinal protectors* [901], pp. 88–91, 93–5; for Badajoz, Eubel, *Hierarchia catholica* [258], iii, p. 266 (erroneously giving Bainbridge's name). For Bainbridge and Wolsey as papal contenders, Chambers, *Cardinal Bainbridge*, pp. 43–4; Chambers, 'Cardinal Wolsey' [133].

number of individuals, who, in the fourteenth century, were generally members of the mendicant orders. To them the diocesans delegated the drudgery of touring the diocese to carry out the more menial episcopal duties. Hence the appearance in England of English-born bishops of Christopolis, Selymbria, Sevastopol, Sultaniyeh, and other outlandish places. Some were probably unsure precisely where their sees were – even modern historians are uncertain in some cases, so that their Latin titles are generally retained in the historiography, as with William Northburgh, Bishop *Pharensis*. They would not be expected to visit their dioceses, and therefore could be used elsewhere.

Despite their importance, the suffragans remain largely unknown; there is not even a full list of those active in England during the period. Initially the diocesan was responsible for the episcopal spiritual functions within his bishopric, but might for short periods grant authority to a visiting bishop to perform certain tasks, notably ordinations. The exempt peculiars also used diocesan bishops (preferably not their own, lest that appear a concession of jurisdictional recognition) to act within their territories. But with only one bishop per diocese, having everything done by the diocesan or a visitor was obviously too much. From about 1350 the previously *ad hoc* arrangements for suffragans (vagrant Welsh and Irish bishops were most used) were transformed, as bishops of the titular sees were increasingly employed. Penurious Irish bishops still took on suffragan duties in the English dioceses, and sometimes Irish titles were deliberately given to intended suffragans. Occasinally this caused confusion, with multiple appointments being made to some sees, and the rivals working contemporaneously in England. During the Great Schism, similarly, the rivalry of the papacies, and their rival recognitions by England and Scotland, allowed the creation of two successions in some Scottish sees. The bishops recognizing the Roman popes often worked as suffragans in English dioceses: Oswald, Bishop of Whithorn, for example, was active within York diocese for several years.[16]

The titular bishops remained important through to the Reformation, when England's secession from the catholic community was marked by changes in the arrangements for their titles, while the abolition of the religious orders forced changes in their personnel.[17] Their presence certainly eased pressures on the diocesans; but their wanderings also caused difficulties. How certain could the local administration be that someone claiming to be a bishop of some unpronounceable place was actually of

[16] Thompson, *English clergy* [824], pp. 48–50; Smith, 'Suffragan bishops' [766], pp. 17–22 (also lists those active within Lincoln diocese); Knowles, *Religious orders*, ii, pp. 373–5, iii, pp. 494–5, 497; Haddan and Stubbs, *Councils and documents*, 2/i, pp. 64–5.

[17] *Statutes* [776], iii, pp. 509–10; suffragans with foreign titles apparently remained active after 1534: Smith, 'Suffragan bishops', p. 27.

episcopal status? If he could show papal bulls, so much the better; but in at least one instance doubts arose. William, Bishop *Bellenensis*, acted for slightly under a year in Lichfield diocese in 1375–6, performing all the recorded ordinations. However, his status was questioned, and eventually all his ordinations were repeated conditionally, just in case he was not really a bishop after all.[18]

When considering bishops *in partibus*, the reigns of Richard II and Henry IV provide the only instances of the relegation of English diocesan bishops to such sees. These moves were politically motivated: the successive translations to St Andrews of Alexander Neville (from York in 1388) and Thomas Arundel (from Canterbury in 1397), and in 1399 the relegation of Thomas Merks from Carlisle to the see *Samastrensis* reflected the ebb and flow of contemporary factions.[19] Finally, among these bishops, the apparent contradiction in terms of non-diocesan bishops must be mentioned. Episcopal orders were indelible, even though a bishop might resign (or lose) his see; such bishops then enjoyed a status which emphasized the catholicity of the church, being styled Bishops of the Universal Church. Such individuals appear occasionally in late medieval England, especially during the fifteenth century.[20]

The integration of the English provinces into the universal church in the late middle ages is evidenced by two other features. First, there is the revived English presence among the cardinals. After gaps in the early fourteenth century and first quarter of the fifteenth, there was an almost continuous English representation in the membership of the Sacred College through to the Reformation – and beyond (see appendix 1). The numbers might have been greater, but England's kings would not always permit the absence which such promotion entailed: John XXIII, soon after his accession, named both Thomas Langley (Bishop of Durham) and Robert Hallum (Bishop of Salisbury) as cardinals, but neither actually received the red hat. Equally, the popes might resist pressures to increase English representation within the College. Despite the support of Richard III the then Bishop of Durham, John Shirwood, never did receive the hoped-for promotion. In the fourteenth century, cardinals like Simon Langham and Adam Easton were actually expected to move to the papal curia. In the next century this changed, and the English cardinals appear almost exclusively acting in England, whether as diocesans or politicians, as with

---

[18] Wilson, *Reg. Coventry and Lichfield, book 5* [916], pp. 296–308 (original ordinations), 313–14, 318–19, 321–2, 324 (conditional reordinations), see also BL, MS Harley 2179, f. 44r–v, and Smith, 'Suffragan bishops', pp. 21–2.

[19] Jones, *Policy of Richard II* [448], pp. 56–7, 83–4; Salter, Pantin, and Richardson, *Formularies* [732], i, pp. 182–5; Swanson, *Reg. Scrope* [796], ii, no. 868.

[20] du Boulay, *Reg. Bourgchier* [233], p. xliv and refs.

John Kemp, and most notoriously, Thomas Wolsey. However, Christopher Bainbridge spent all his cardinalate in the Papal States, and earlier Cardinal Beaufort had participated in papal actions against the Bohemian Hussites, and would probably have led a crusading army against them, had it not been diverted to the English war effort in France.[21]

Finally, there is the unimportance of international boundaries to individual religious establishments. From the Norman Conquest, several French abbeys had had possessions (including churches) within England, which they enjoyed with, admittedly, diminishing freedom, down to the fifteenth century. These alien priorities were something of a thorn in the flesh for the English: their French inmates rarely got on well with their English confrères and neighbours, and during the Anglo-French wars were regularly distrusted as potential spies. Nonetheless, they were there. Similarly some English houses had foreign possessions, such as Durham's ownership of the priory of Coldingham in Scotland. The abbot of Fécamp and the archbishop of Dublin even exercised ecclesiastical jurisdiction within England, through their respective holding of royal free chapels at Steyning (Sussex) and Penkridge (Staffs.). Perhaps the most distant connection between an English church and a foreign religious institution affected the rectory of St Andrew, Chesterton (Cambs.): from the early thirteenth century it belonged to the Italian abbey of Vercelli, a relic of the presence of the legate Guala in England following the Magna Carta crisis. The church remained linked to the abbey – which drew not unreasonable revenues from it – right through to the 1440s, when it passed into the possesison of King's Hall, Cambridge. Even so, Vercelli did not forget the links, and was seeking repossession as late as the reign of Mary I.[22]

1.2 ENGLAND AND ROME

As part of the international body, the English church necessarily had to maintain relations with the papacy, and participate in the centralized system which placed the pope at the summit of earthly authority. This participation is vital for, whatever the medieval *Ecclesia Anglicana* may have been, it was definitely not the Anglican Church as now understood.

---

[21] Chambers, *Cardinal Bainbridge*; Storey, *Langley and Durham* [782], pp. 28–9; Holmes, 'Cardinal Beaufort' [409], pp. 721–42; Emden, *Oxford* [255], iii, p. 1692.

[22] Knowles, *Religious orders*, ii, pp. 161–6; Foster, 'Church of Chesterton' [280]; Cowan and Easson, *Medieval religious houses: Scotland* [169], pp. 55–6; Denton, *Royal free chapels* [200], pp. 71–5, 105–6; for the archbishop of Dublin at Penkridge see e.g. LJRO, B/A/1/8, f. 13r–v.

The spiritual headship belonged not to the successor to St Augustine, but by the heir to St Peter and Vicar of Christ; and at virtually every level the papacy and its officials had a role to play. For, whatever a bishop might claim to do within his diocese, the pope could also do: grant authority for ordinations, ordain, grant dispensations, order succession to benefices (including bishoprics), demand taxes, hear court cases, and so on. The pope was at the pinnacle of the numerous administrative hierarchies which made the western, Latin, church – and, as the head, his authority often exceeded that of his minions. Thus, the papacy could grant more extensive indulgences than bishops, and could grant dispensations for more serious offences or disabilities than were within the episcopal remit. Because of this greater scope of papal authority, there never was a time, up to the Reformation and its formal rejection of papal authority, when members of the church in England willingly ceased recourse to Rome. Although there were occasional clashes between England and Rome – or between the king of England and the pope – they are too easily over-emphasized, obscuring the extent to which the papacy remained a focus of loyalty. Complaints against papal interference in benefice administration, against papal provisions of bishops, and against the blood-sucking ways of the curia were traditional; but Rome remained a pilgrimage centre, and the papal curia retained an attraction as a source of spiritual benefits and access to ecclesiastical privileges.

Whilst the relationship between the king and the papacy did change during this period, and the church in England became increasingly identifiable as a national entity (thus matching the development of national churches elsewhere in Europe), much more striking is the sheer volume of contacts between England and Rome for the most mundane matters. The printed volumes of the *Calendar of papal letters*, despite their many drawbacks, give some indication of the variety of this business.[23] They demonstrate only a fraction of the English exploitation of the possibilities of papal patronage: there are other, uncalendared, registers, and many now lost which must have contained relevant entries. Many papal provisions, the provisions *in forma pauperum* (which did not grant a specific benefice, but merely assisted queue-jumpers) were simply not recorded. Other business must have similarly escaped notice; while perhaps the bulk of the dispensation material and minor licences remains to be gleaned not from the specifically papal registers, but from the records of the chief penitentiary – records now lost for the fourteenth century (except when referred

---

[23] Boyle, *Survey of the Vatican archives* [84], pp. 110–14: further volumes of the *Calendar* have been published. The Ecole française de Rome is calendaring the surviving Avignon registers, see ibid., pp. 123–7: further volumes have since appeared.

to in surviving episcopal registers, or stray originals), and as yet un-exploited for the later centuries.[24]

The variety of business conducted between England and Rome (or, before 1378, Avignon) was considerable. Dispensations for marriages, privileges of portable altars or to choose a private confessor, licences for clerics for non-residence for a variety of reasons, dispensations for clerics to receive (or be confirmed in) orders despite illegitimacy, to allow them to celebrate despite their involvement in violence, or to receive benefices in plurality, grants of indulgences, and a host of other documents all streamed from the papal bureaucracy, usually in response to petitions – more than could ever be granted – which reached the curia from England. Legal issues which had been appealed to Rome were debated and settled there, or returned for consideration in the localities by judges delegate.[25] All this activity – to which, in the fifteenth and sixteenth centuries, should also be added the growing formalization of diplomatic practices – necessitated permanent English representation at the papal court and a constant stream of short-term visits. At the lower levels, the permanent residents would be the proctors who assumed responsibility for much of the day-to-day business: representing their principals in court cases, arranging for the issue of privileges, of dispensations, and provisions. A constant series of such individuals (both Englishmen and foreigners) has been established for the period 1305–78, while a representative indication of their activities can be gleaned from the surviving letter book of one such proctor, William Swan, active at Rome in the early fifteenth century.[26] At higher levels, the supervision of English interests could be conceded to official agents, such as the succession of Italian bishops of Worcester – Giovanni de'Gigli (1497–8), Silvestro de'Gigli (1499–1521), Giulio de'Medici (1521–2), and Geronimo de'Ghinucci (1522–35) – who received the fruits of their bishopric in return for overseeing matters relating to England. Before the break of the 1530s, Henry VIII was assiduous in maintaining his contacts with Rome. He received a variety of dispensa-tions, including the ill-fated permission to marry his brother's widow. Like his father, he gained several papal favours, among them the title of 'Defender of the Faith'. Following his father, he maintained a succession

---

[24] ibid., pp. 92–3, 117–21, 128–30, 135–48, and at pp. 152–3 for the possibility of recovering unregistered material from the registers of supplications; Tihon, 'Les expectatives' [840], pp. 58–9; SRO D593/A/1/32/19.

[25] Generally, Pantin, 'The fourteenth century' [638]; du Boulay, 'The fifteenth century' [235]; Thomson, ' "The well of grace" ' [832]; Cooper, 'Papacy and Lichfield' [167]. For delegacy (although early), Sayers, *Papal judges delegate* [739]; for curial procedure, Mollat, *The popes at Avignon* [588], pp. 294–305.

[26] Zutshi, 'Proctors for English petitioners' [939]; Jacob, *Later medieval history* [440], pp. 58–72; Parks, *English traveler*, pp. 343–76.

of cardinal-protectors of English interests in Rome, adding a particularly English presence in the early years of his reign in the person of Christopher Bainbridge, Cardinal and absentee-Archbishop of York.[27]

The consistency with which the English proclaimed their hopes of benefiting from links with the papacy was matched by the fact that the church's central machinery was rarely totally incapable of fulfilling those aspirations. The greatest obstacle was a papal interregnum, but even that was not insuperable. The papal penitentiary, whose department issued the majority of the common dispensations for marriages, illegitimacy, and suchlike, remained in office during a papal interregnum, so that there need be no break in the processing of such basic privileges unless the intended recipient specifically desired a papal grant. The administration of justice might be interrupted by a papal death, but where the dislocation looked like being considerable, a remedy might be created: during the Council of Constance, when technically there was no pope from March 1415 to November 1417, the assembly established its own judicial machinery to deal with cases, and also appointed judges delegate.[28]

Of course, the administration did not always work smoothly, nor was the relationship between England and the papacy static right through to the Reformation. Quite clearly, things did change. Royal interference with papal rights of provision in the fourteenth century virtually abolished papal involvement in the granting of benefices, despite rearguard action by energetic popes like Martin V (1417–31).[29] By 1450 the only aspect of the system which remained normally operative was papal provision to bishoprics, and that was usually done only on royal nomination, transforming the arrangements into a system of collusive exploitation of the English church. The drama of the clashes on provisions rather overshadows the more mundane obstacles to the effectiveness of papal activity. The sheer mass of business to be transacted at the curia caused problems – rival papal provisions to the same benefice, contradictory concessions, inertia, and delay; and the constant danger that the pope might die, thereby invalidating some hard-sought privilege or concession. Occasionally, such instances appear from a subsequent confirmatory document; at other times the impact on individual lives could be quite catastrophic. In 1481 a couple from York diocese, having been reported for consanguinity at visitation, were ordered to separate (they were not divorced: their

---

[27] Burns, 'Papal gifts and honours' [109], pp. 177–97; Wilkie, *Cardinal protectors*; Chambers, *Cardinal Bainbridge*, pp. 22–71.

[28] Crowder, 'Four English cases' [179]; for a delegacy from the council, Archer, *Reg. Repingdon* [8], iii, no. 406.

[29] Jacob, *Reg. Chichele* [438], i, pp. xlii–xlvii; for a different perspective, Davies, 'Martin V and the English episcopate' [193].

marriage remained binding, but they were no longer to maintain conjugal relations). At a later visitation, in 1483, they said that they were trying to obtain the necessary dispensation from the curia to permit them to resume their previous state. The usual procedure in such cases was not to grant the dispensation immediately, but to commission a local authority (usually the bishop) to investigate the matter and, if appropriate, issue the grant. When the couple were reported at a third visitation, in 1485, they handed over the commission from the penitentiary. Unfortunately for them, the pope in whose name it was issued (Sixtus IV) had since died, the commission therefore lapsed, and the unlucky pair were again ordered to separate.[30]

In this instance, time effectively obstructed papal authority; but there were other obstacles to the efficiency of the church's hierarchical structure. While the papacy headed the jurisdictional structure, beneath him there was a considerable problem posed by the fragmentation of authority, by conflicting jurisdictions, and by the existence of enclaves which compounded the administrative and jurisdictional complexities, and provided material for many of the major internal clashes of the period. Generally, the problem is one of the geographical fragmentation of authority, especially within the bishoprics. But it operated on other levels as well. With some of the religious orders, especially the friars, membership conferred personal immunity from episcopal authority in several respects. Moreover, although the papacy unified the church(es), it might voluntarily fragment its own authority; and in the developments of the fifteenth and sixteenth centuries – viewed with post-Reformation hindsight – this fragmentation of papal authority appears as one of the major unconsidered factors in the development of the national churches, especially in England.

Apart from the problems facing papal authority whenever a pope died, there were two other ways in which the papacy's power might be, not circumvented, but undercut. Both derive from the availability of papal privileges outside the curia itself. On the one hand papal nuncios and legates – particularly legates – exercised an authority within their assigned territory which was often all but papal itself. For the nuncios, those powers derived from specific commissions, with great lists of them being issued whenever a nuncio was sent. Papal legates, especially legates *a latere*, had more extensive authority, being little less than a papal *Doppelgänger*, bringing with them their own miniature curia, including a penitentiary. This system of legates, infused with an apostolic authority of their own, reached its peak in England with Thomas Wolsey, whose legatine commission, extraordinarily for life, would have accustomed the English to a sense of independence from Rome. His court, his dispensations,

[30] YML, L2(3)c, f. 55r; Swanson, 'Papal letters' [794], no. 43.

would have prepared England both emotionally and institutionally for a Reformation settlement which effectively transferred papal legatine powers to the archbishop of Canterbury and the king's viceregent in spiritual matters. Wolsey's precursors as papal representatives in England were less dramatic, but still represented a fragmentation of papal authority. It was on this basis that Pileus de Prato, legate and nuncio in England, in 1383 permitted members of the University of Cambridge to be non-resident from their benefices for three years: other grants (before and after) were made by the popes themselves. In 1448 a similar licence for non-residence was granted by Peter de Monte, apostolic protonotary and papal collector and nuncio in England, to the vicar of Soham (Cambs.), under his commission from Pope Eugenius IV.[31]

The delegation of papal authority to its representatives was usually limited, rather than general, but by 1400 was also routine. In 1411, on being appointed nuncio, Anthony de Pireto received a variety of limited powers, including authority to issue sixty matrimonial dispensations for consanguinity. Bishops often received equally limited delegations of authority. Thomas Langley of Durham (1406–37) was at his appointment granted powers to issue various dispensations and appoint a number of notaries public; while Archbishop William Courtenay of Canterbury (1381–96) obtained what amounted to the delegation of the right to make papal provisions when he received authority to appoint to canonries throughout his province. A similar delegation of the right to make provisions to canonries was extended, in admittedly limited terms, to King Richard II by Pope Urban VI in 1379 – but that the delegation was made nevertheless represents a breach of the papal armour.[32]

1.3 COMPLEXITIES IN ENGLAND

Delegations of papal authority counteracted the centralization of the church, and the centrality of the papal curia in the granting of the privileges (even though the delegation was itself a privilege granted by the central authority). Such *ad hoc* arrangements also represented an assault on the local authority of the diocesan. Within the specific context of the English church, it is also necessary to consider two further threats to

---

[31] Sayers, *Original papal documents* [738], pp. 57–8; CUL, MS Mm.I.48, pp. 17–18; CUA, Collect. Admin. 9, pp. 307–8; Meech and Allen, *Margery Kempe* [579], pp. 351–2 – the dating clause is obviously incomplete.

[32] Twemlow, *Calendar of papal letters, 1404–1415* [849], pp. 170–1 (with a resultant dispensation at Horn, *Reg. Hallum*, no. 1009); Storey, *Reg. Langley*, nos. 213–14, 216 (and, for their implementation, nos. 217–21); Wilkins, *Concilia* [902], iii, pp. 173–4; Rymer, *Foedera* [724], vii, pp. 215–17.

episcopal authority. First, episcopal power was challenged by the status of certain of the religious orders. Although not requiring detailed individual treatment, the role of the religious orders within the church was of considerable importance. Yet they were to a great extent administrative anomalies. This especially applies to the orders exempt from normal jurisdictional rules, and thus beyond the control (and, to some extent, the comprehension) of their non-regular clerical counterparts.

The existence of the exempt religious orders, dependent on the papacy for their exemption and legitimization, was a significant breach in the completeness of episcopal authority within the diocese. It was perhaps the friars – the Carmelites, Austin hermits, Franciscans, and Dominicans – who provoked the greatest opposition. With their papal privileges, their jurisdictional independence for their persons and their houses, and their wandering habits, they were considered a major threat to the secular clergy, and as subverters of episcopal authority. For many clerics the mendicants' threat was essentially financial, diverting revenues from the parish church and clergy to their own institutions; but the threat was also disciplinary, as their claims to preach and hear confessions ignored the normal disciplinary procedures over the laity, undermining episcopal diocesan jurisdiction. Many of these problems were overcome in the decree *Super cathedram*, originally issued by Pope Boniface VIII, which limited the financial diversions to the mendicants, and brought their confessional activities under episcopal licences. But the friars remained rivals to their secular brethren, and occasional clashes broke out later; while apart from the stipulations of *Super cathedram* they remained exempt from episcopal jurisdiction.[33]

The non-mendicant exempt orders posed less significant problems. But these orders – the Cluniacs, Premonstratensians, Gilbertines, Carthusians, and Cistercians, and the military Order of St John – were similarly beyond episcopal jurisdiction. Their houses and possessions, together with the houses and possessions of a few exempt Benedictine houses, formed islands of immunity within the bishoprics. While bishops frequently intervened in the activities of the non-exempt orders, especially the Benedictines and the Augustinian canons, the exempt orders could not be controlled, and the existence of what might prove to be enclaves of irresponsibility could be a degenerative influence. Even though these exempt orders were supposedly organized in centralized systems, with their own checks against corruption, the control exercised by the central establishments over the insular houses was itself limited, especially when the former were in France, with which England was often at war, and even

[33] Williams, 'Mendicant friars and secular clergy' [908]. For text of *Super cathedram*, Richter and Friedberg, *Corpus iuris canonici* [697], ii, cols. 1162–4.

more significantly during the Great Schism of 1378–1409, when England
and France officially recognized different popes. Then, Europe's division
into rival obediences meant that the English Cistercians, Cluniacs, and
Premonstratensians were cut off from their central institutions (the Hospitallers managed to retain some contacts), and had to establish their own
administrations. Nevertheless, they were unwilling to forego their jurisdictional exemption from episcopal authority.[34] Like the friars, they maintained their personal exemption from the bishop's control, so that, for
example, their members could be ordained without letters dimissory –
that is, without needing a licence from their own bishop when being
ordained in another diocese.

If the exemption of particular orders and the disruption which that introduced into the church's otherwise straightforward hierarchical arrangement
can be considered as essentially 'personal' – that is, although the orders'
houses were exempt from visitation, the exemption of the individuals
derived solely from membership of that order, rather than from any other
qualification – the second main threat to ordinary authority can be considered as essentially geographical. Within virtually every diocese in
England, the hierarchy of jurisdictions – bishop, archdeacons, rural deans,
parishes – represented an ideal. In reality, the picture was very different,
with the pyramid being disrupted by widespread fragmentation. This
produced considerable challenges to administrative coherence and efficiency
with the existence of 'peculiar jurisdictions'.

The origins of many of the peculiars are obscure. For the most part,
they may well represent relics of the pre- and immediately post-conquest
system of proprietary churches, or *Eigenkirchen*. This certainly seems the
case with the detached portions of the archbishopric of Canterbury, with
the Durham peculiars within the archbishopric of York, and with some of
the royal free chapels – perhaps the most peculiar of all jurisdictions.[35]
However, the pattern of peculiar jurisdictions was not static, and was
being added to even in the fifteenth century. The extent to which any
individual jurisdiction was independent of the local diocesan's authority
varied: several peculiars were in fact subject to episcopal visitation, but
little more; some, however, were totally exempt, and effectively constituted
miniature dioceses (but without their own bishops). Laity in the houses of
the exempt religious orders, and the lands of those orders, also seem to

---

[34] Knowles, *Religious orders*, i, pp. 85–112, ii, pp. 161, 167–70, 204–18, iii, pp. 62–86. For
characteristic printed visitations of religious houses, see Thompson, *Visitations of religious
houses* [817]; Heath, *Blythe's visitations* [371].

[35] Denton, *Royal free chapels*, pp. 134–8 (see also Denton, 'Royal supremacy' [201]);
Barlow, *Durham peculiars* [39], pp. viii–xvii, 56–9; Churchill, *Canterbury administration*, i,
pp. 62–3.

have been totally exempt, but the exercise of spiritual authority within them remains somewhat problematical.[36] Although almost every peculiar jurisdiction had its own courts, their competence could vary enormously: in some the powers amounted to little more than oversight of probate matters; in others they were the final resort below papal or archiepiscopal courts (the latter qualification probably applying especially within the province of Canterbury). The effect of this multitude of jurisdictions on the ecclesiastical map was considerable.[37] With the exception of the royal free chapels, where royal authority was occasionally so extensive that the king's position within them has been equated with that of both pope and bishop,[38] the peculiars were exclusively in ecclesiastical hands – and even some of the royal free chapels were in fact held by ecclesiastics.

The many forms of these peculiar jurisdictions defy succinct summary. At the highest level there were a number of 'mini-dioceses'. One of the clearest statements of such independent quasi-episcopal jurisdiction is provided by the issue of letters dimissory. The power to issue such letters reveals exemption from episcopal visitatorial authority; they were thus granted by (amongst others) the exempt abbeys of Waltham, Evesham, St Albans, and Bury St Edmunds – and by the archbishop of York for his Gloucestershire jurisdiction of Churchdown and his Northumberland peculiar of Hexhamshire.[39] Such exercise of 'episcopal' functions naturally subsumed the exercise of archidiaconal jurisdiction within the peculiars; elsewhere, whilst the local diocesan retained the exercise of episcopal spiritual jurisdiction, the holder of the peculiar jurisdiction regularly exercised the equivalent of archidiaconal functions. Corporations such as the abbey of Glastonbury, or the deans and chapters of cathedrals, thus could not grant letters dimissory, and remained subject to their

---

[36] The problem partly derives from the scattered nature of the properties, especially those of the Hospitallers. Compact estates, as at Keele (Staffs.) could be organized as quasi-parochial peculiars (Studd, 'A Templar colony' [790], pp. 8–9) but other properties, such as the 'manor' of Batley (Yorks.) consisted of scattered individual houses, whose inhabitants could be subjected to peculiar jurisdiction for probate purposes, but probably not in many other respects (Crossley, 'Testamentray documents' [178], p. 67 n. 3). Lay inhabitants of Cistercian properties also fell under separate jurisdiction – for testamentary jurisdiction of St Mary Graces abbey, London, see Madox, *Formulare Anglicanum* [570], p. 441.

[37] Many (but not all) peculiars are marked on the Ordnance Survey map, *Monastic Britain*. See also the maps in Gibson, *Wills and where to find them* [297], and Humphery-Smith, *Phillimore atlas*. For royal free chapels, Denton, *Royal free chapels*, after p. 174.

[38] Denton, 'Royal supremacy', p. 302.

[39] Swanson, *Reg. Scrope*, ii, p. 111 – John de Waltham (Waltham); Parry, *Reg. Trillek* [643], pp. 486–599, *passim* (Evesham); ibid., pp. 479, 512, 515, 524 (Churchdown); Riley, *Registra abbatum* [700], ii, pp. 67–8 (St Albans); Johnson, *Reg. Hethe* [444], ii, pp. 1153 – Walter Raulyn, 1165 – John Skinner (Bury St Edmunds); for Hexham, below, n. 47. For the extent of authority in an exempt jurisdiction, Sayers, 'Papal privileges for St Albans' [740], pp. 75–8.

bishop for visitation (although the extent of the subjection was often disputed, especially by the secular cathedrals) and for the exercise of the episcopal power of orders; but within their territories were relieved of the archdeacon's oversight. Instead, archidiaconal functions devolved to the peculiar holders, who therefore carried out visitations and suchlike, as well as some of the non-spiritual functions of a bishop, such as supervising successions to benefices.[40]

The creation of the miniature dioceses in this pattern essentially reflects the extension of exemption after 1050. By 1300 this process was virtually completed; although there were occasional later attempts at extension – some of them successful – there was nothing like a repetition of the thirteenth-century moves which sought totally to relieve some dioceses of archiepiscopal oversight. Nevertheless, the pattern of exemption did change. At least one bishop, Thomas Hatfield of Durham (1345–81) secured a papal bull of exemption for his see, which caused problems with the archbishops of York for a while. Several religious houses also sought to free themselves from episcopal surveillance. In the 1340s Chester abbey secured exemption from the authority of the bishop of Lichfield. Although that bull was rescinded in the 1360s, the exemption was renewed by Pope Boniface IX (1389–1404), and remained until the Dissolution. In the early fifteenth century Leicester abbey similarly sought exemption from the bishop of Lincoln, but the privilege was apparently as short-lived as the abbot who obtained it. Other houses, such as Burton-on-Trent, occasionally claimed exemption, but were unable to substantiate their claims. Perhaps the most dramatic conflict over exemption in this period occurred between 1395 and 1410, when Oxford University claimed freedom from archiepiscopal visitation according to a bull issued by Boniface IX in 1395. Unfortunately, their adversary was Thomas Arundel, never one to surrender what he considered his rights. When the university opposed his visitation, he unleashed the full range of canonical censures, with royal support. The university eventually renounced its claims and abandoned the bull – although the exemption seems to have been renewed later. As late as the 1480s new exempt peculiars were still being created: the collegiate church of Middleham in Yorkshire then secured immunity from archidiaconal and archiepiscopal jurisdiction.[41]

Even though the exemption movement did not make any startling

---

[40] See e.g. Timmins, *Reg. Chandler* [841]. For the detached deaneries of Canterbury, Thompson, *English clergy*, p. 68; for Glastonbury, Sayers, 'Monastic archdeacons' [741], pp. 183–5.

[41] Davies, 'Alexander Neville' [191], p. 95; *VCH, Cheshire*, iii [868], p. 139; Thompson, *Abbey of Leicester* [825], pp. 57–8 (against his wariness, LJRO, B/A/1/8, ff. 19v–20r); Kibre, *Scholarly privileges* [470], pp. 311–12; Atthill, *Documents relating to Middleham* [22], pp. 10–12, 82–4, 87–9.

progress during this period, it was not dead. Moreover, even for older exemptions, the precise nature of the exemption could be subtly altered, as occurred with the Cluniac houses within the kingdom. Originally exempt by reason of their relationship with the mother house of Cluny, as that link weakened and the English houses became increasingly independent, they maintained their exemption by placing themselves directly under the papacy.[42]

The process of exemption, and the creation of a number of quasi-episcopal authorities, gives some indication of the fragmentation of the jurisdictional map of ecclesiastical England at the time; but it cannot provide a sufficient outline of the overall complexity, ignoring as it does the other non-exempt peculiars. No one diocese contained the full gamut of peculiarity, but the diocese of York perhaps comes closest to providing such a picture and, with its annexes, reveals most of the possibilities.

Until Henry VIII juggled with its geography the diocese of York was one of the largest in the country. Besides all of Yorkshire (apart from some minor indentations on the frontiers) it contained all of Nottinghamshire, parts of Westmorland and Cumberland, and Lancashire north of the Ribble. The jurisdictional organization of the diocese was exceedingly complex, only royal free chapels being conspicuously absent among the range of peculiars. However, since the late eleventh century the archbishops of York had controlled the royal free chapel of St Oswald in Gloucester, making it (with the annexed liberty of Churchdown) effectively a detached part of the see of York.[43]

Among York's peculiar jurisdictions the most significant was that of the archdeaconry of Richmond. Due to its size and remoteness (it covered the north Yorkshire moors and the territory west of the Pennines) it had developed its own quasi-diocesan administration, with its own registers, and with vicars-general ruling in the absence of the archdeacon. Such independence almost excluded the archbishop's diocesan authority, except through control of the succession to the office of archdeacon itself. The archbishop retained some rights of visitation, and responsibility for executing papal commissions to authorize dispensations; but little more.[44] In its turn, the archdeaconry contained several lesser peculiar jurisdictions, usually (like the peculiar of Masham, dependent on a prebend in York Minster) elements of those found elsewhere within the diocese. The college at Middleham gained exemption from the archdeacon's authority

---

[42] Knowles, *Religious orders*, ii, p. 161.

[43] Denton, *Royal free chapels*, pp. 52–7, 141–2; for a church within the county of Gloucester and diocese of York, CUL, MS Ll.1.18, ff. 111v–112r.

[44] Hill, *The labourer in the vineyard* [390], pp. 9–11; Thompson, 'Registers of Richmond' [819]; Thompson, 'Register of Richmond' [821].

in the 1480s. More significant was the jurisdiction of Ripon, a peculiar held by the archbishops of York, and linked to their liberty of Ripon.

The other peculiar jurisdictions in York diocese fall into several distinct groups. Besides Ripon, the archbishop controlled other groups of parishes which formed deaneries exempt from archidiaconal influence, such as the deaneries of Otley and Sherburn (in Yorkshire). The dean and chapter of York Minster exercised corporate jurisdiction over several parishes, like Hornby, Aldborough, and Burton Leonard (in the archdeaconry of Richmond), and Bubwith, Bishop Burton, Weaverthorpe, and Helperthorpe (in the archdeaconry of the East Riding), and over many of York's city parishes. In addition there were the individual jurisdictions of the dignitaries and prebendaries, including places like Masham, Cawood, Pickering, and Market Weighton, scattered throughout the diocese. Occasionally the parishes were clustered, but such groups would not necessarily be controlled by one prebendary. These areas had their own administrations, their own courts. The dean of York regularly carried out his own visitation of the capitular and prebendal peculiars, and the courts maintained by the individual prebendaries were increasingly subjected to supervision by the capitular courts. To some extent, this supervisory role suggests the relationship which within the diocesan structure was that between rural deanery (the individual prebendal peculiars) and the archdeaconry (the corporate capitular oversight). Nevertheless, the jurisdictional frontiers created by these divisions remained an important obstacle to the effectiveness of ecclesiastical correction: boundary-hopping was a readily available means of evading punishment. Southwell Minster similarly had its peculiar jurisdiction. The rights claimed by the provost of Beverley Minster over the group of East Riding parishes under his jurisdiction were almost diocesan in character – but appear to have been in some ways a leasing of archiepiscopal powers.

Peculiar authority was also exercised by other religious houses and institutions, such as the Order of St John. Selby abbey, with its cell of Snaith, had virtually exclusive rights in a patch of territory in south Yorkshire. Although the archbishop participated in elections and had rights to visit the monastery, the abbey enjoyed privileges similar to those of the prebends of York Minster.[45] The bishopric of Durham and the convent of Durham priory had rights within parishes in York diocese which undermined episcopal authority, provoking occasional clashes with the archbishop over such matters as visitation. Most of these problems

---

[45] Brown, *Reg. Greenfield* [101], pp. xxvi–xxviii; Brown, *Courts of York Minster peculiar* [100], pp. 4–16; Leach, *Memorials of Beverley Minster* [500], i, p. xlvii, ii, pp. 307–8; Knowles, *Monastic order* [487], p. 631; Fowler, *Coucher book* [282], i, pp. 291–2, ii, p. 115; the jurisdiction is entered among the peculiars in the archiepiscopal registers, e.g. Swanson, *Reg. Scrope*, i, p. 103.

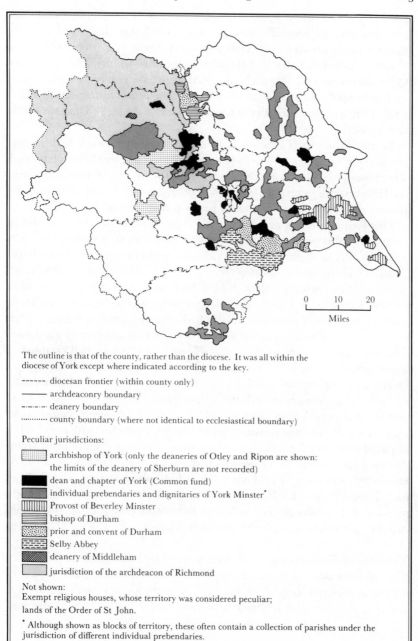

The outline is that of the county, rather than the diocese. It was all within the
diocese of York except where indicated according to the key.

- - - - - diocesan frontier (within county only)

——— archdeaconry boundary

–·—·—· deanery boundary

·············· county boundary (where not identical to ecclesiastical boundary)

Peculiar jurisdictions:

▦ archbishop of York (only the deaneries of Otley and Ripon are shown:
the limits of the deanery of Sherburn are not recorded)

■ dean and chapter of York (Common fund)

▨ individual prebendaries and dignitaries of York Minster*

▥ Provost of Beverley Minster

▤ bishop of Durham

▨ prior and convent of Durham

▦ Selby Abbey

▨ deanery of Middleham

▢ jurisdiction of the archdeacon of Richmond

Not shown:
Exempt religious houses, whose territory was considered peculiar;
lands of the Order of St John.

* Although shown as blocks of territory, these often contain a collection of parishes under the
jurisdiction of different individual prebendaries.

MAP II: Ecclesiastical jurisdiction in medieval Yorkshire.

had been settled before 1350, although without fully integrating the affected parishes into the archidiaconal structure. The areas concerned were the distinct jurisdictions of Allerton and Allertonshire (in the north of the diocese), and of Howden and Howdenshire (in the south). They continued to be mentioned in the archiepiscopal registers, testifying to lingering archiepiscopal rights. The parish of Crayke, however, is not mentioned: as a relict *Eigenkirche* it was effectively an enclave of the see of Durham within that of York.[46]

Reciprocating such relationships, the archbishop of York had his own peculiars in other sees. Churchdown (Glos.) has already been mentioned. There was also a territorial enclave within the diocese of Durham, based on Hexham, for which he granted letters dimissory and delegated his powers of orders to a suffragan of his own nomination.[47]

This basic system of peculiar jurisdictions could be paralleled in almost every other diocese, although perhaps not quite in such complexity. The archdeaconry of Richmond had its closest approximation in the archdeaconry of Chester within the diocese of Lichfield, although the archdeacon's rights were less extensive than those of Richmond. Other forms of peculiar jurisdiction could be found, whether quasi-diocesan or non-exempt. Thus, some of the great Benedictine abbeys had acquired quasi-episcopal rights; others were less successful but still achieved various degree of autonomy from the diocesan system: Burton-on-Trent, for example, had established a territory in Staffordshire and Derbyshire which came close to exemption. Deans and chapters of secular cathedrals, and the priories in monastic cathedrals, could easily match the jurisdictions exercised by York Minster and its members. Yet the frontiers were rarely static: new peculiars were created – and old ones might collapse. In the fifteenth century a number of parishes within the diocese of Canterbury formerly exempt from archidiaconal jurisdiction by being within the archbishop's collation lost their immunity, and merged back into the archidiaconal system. All in all the ecclesiastical map of England at this time was a complex, and still relatively unelucidated, patchwork of conflicting and overlapping jurisdictions, easily capable of confusion, and ever apt to be exploited.[48]

This multitude of jurisdictional entities frustrated the simplistic hierarchy from bishops down to rural deanery and parish; no single diocese could ever be considered 'typical' or 'average'. In each, not only did geographical size and the extent of disruption by peculiars vary, but the nature and

---

[46] Barlow, *Durham peculiars*, pp. 53–115, for Crayke esp. pp. 85–8, 115.

[47] Raine, *Priory of Hexham* [687], i, pp. xxxii–xxxiv, xliv–xlvi, lxxxvii–lxxxviii, cxiii.

[48] Heath, 'Archdeaconry and bishopric' [370]; *VCH, Stafford*, iii [872], pp. 209–10; Woodcock, *Medieval ecclesiastical courts* [919], pp. 21–5.

responsibilities of the different levels of the hierarchy changed. By the later fourteenth century the administrative machinery within the dioceses was basically the same, but there were major differences in the nature of some of the posts. By 1400 the bishoprics were effectively (and, usually, efficiently) managed by a range of officials: sequestrators, vicars-general, officials principal, registrars, and others, whose task was to keep the system going, and frequently to relieve the shoulders (to varying degrees, sometimes totally) of those who were nominally responsible for the actual administration, most often the bishops and the archdeacons. Such bureaucrats, however, had no formally defined place within the church's jurisdictional hierarchy: they were merely assistants; their offices, although customary, were not legally institutionalized. Although this bureaucracy underpins the whole of the late medieval church, it requires no detailed analysis here.[49] What does need consideration is the dioceses' territorial organizational structure, and the officials who were supposedly responsible for the individual segments. While there was obviously some similarity in jurisdiction between archdeacons, or between rural deans, the arrangements for their appointments in different dioceses could vary enormously. Indeed, in terms of powers, this applied even to bishops: the authority of the prince-bishop of Durham cannot be equated with that of the bishop of Rochester, whose position was to a great extent a dependency of the archbishopric of Canterbury. Equally, Winchester's authority differed from that of the bishop of London, with his special function in the provincial structure as viceregent of the archbishop of Canterbury.[50]

In the bishoprics, perhaps the most significant difference was between the monastic and secular sees. Of the English cathedrals, those of Worcester, Canterbury, Durham, Norwich, Ely, Rochester, Winchester, and Hereford were Benedictine monasteries, as were Bath and Coventry in the 'double' sees of Bath and Wells and Lichfield and Coventry. Carlisle was staffed by Augustinian canons. The remaining bishoprics had chapters of seculars, of canons and prebendaries. This meant that relations between the bishops and their officials in the monastic sees were necessarily rather different from those elsewhere; just as the distinction necessarily imposed differences in the whole arrangement of diocesan government.

But the distinction between types of government is not a simplistic one between monastic and secular cathedrals. The organizational structure also differed between the secular cathedrals, not merely in the number of prebendaries, but in their powers and their relations with the lower clergy within the cathedral. Even relationships with the bishop varied: only at Salisbury was the bishop formally integrated into the cathedral chapter as

[49] Storey, *Diocesan administration* [784], pp. 3–9; Thompson, *English clergy*, pp. 47–56.

[50] Churchill, *Canterbury administration*, i, pp. 279–87, 355–9; Lapsley, *Durham* [496], esp. pp. 31–76.

a prebendary (at York, attempts to achieve this were violently resisted by the chapter). At the archidiaconal level, there were also noticeable differences in the precise nature of the office. In some cathedrals, the archdeaconries were considered as benefices – that is, freeholds, with their own annexed sources of revenue. Elsewhere they were not, the income being derived mainly from fees, or from another post (usually a cathedral prebend, not annexed to the office, which could be held in plurality). In the former case, such as held in York diocese, the archdeacon could be an independent actor, with little real episcopal control, since he could not easily be dispossessed. In the latter case episcopal interference and control was probably greater, appointments to the post being less subject to the vagaries of royal or papal patronage, or indeed to the private career aspirations of individual clerics.[51]

Similar comments might apply lower down the scale, to the rural deans. The procedure for their appointment again showed considerable variety from see to see. Usually the dean took his office from his benefice: having acquired the benefice from which the deanery was named, or to which it was traditional attached, he also assumed the responsibilities of the office. But this did not always apply. Sometimes a rural dean might be unbeneficed, deriving his income from a stipend or fees, and the appointment being by episcopal nomination. Elsewhere, the bishop might nominate one of the benefice-holders within the deanery; or, as happened at Bath and Wells, the deanship would circulate among the rectors of the deanery on an annual basis. The office might even be elective, with the rectors choosing one of their own number for the post.[52] To some extent, because of the relatively menial nature of ruridecanal duties, the distinctions between methods of appointment are not particularly significant; but they do indicate the dangers of assuming that all the dioceses would follow an identical model.

Such differences between institutions sharing the same nomenclature, when added to the fragmentation of authority, and the fact that England was only one region of the universal church (into which it remained strongly integrated), complicate any attempt to define precisely what the English church was, and what it was like. Nor did the institutions exist in isolation. This complex structure was only one element in the totality of contemporary England. The church's organization provided a mechanism to be exploited by clerics, by laity, and by the secular government, to create the overall relationship between church and society in England between Black Death and Reformation.

---

[51] Generally, Edwards, *English secular cathedrals* [247] (pp. 108–9 for the bishop of Salisbury, pp. 246–8 for the archdeacons); Swanson, 'Arundel and York' [795], pp. 255–6.

[52] Dunning, 'Rural deans', pp. 208–10; Thompson, 'Diocesan organisation', pp. 189–92, and pp. 192–3 for the situation in 1535.

2

Clerics and Careers

2.1 TOWARDS THE QUESTIONS

The personnel of the late medieval church were the agents integrating the institution within its society. The clergy were responsible for overseeing attempts to maintain the Christian view of society, and as agents of the institution had the duty to protect its property and rights. They could engage in a variety of specialized careers – such as lawyers and administrators – alongside their responsibilities for cure of souls and the spiritual welfare of their parishioners. As mediators between God and man, they were also the principal agents, through the celebration of masses, for the redemption of souls from Purgatory: like St Peter, they held the keys of Heaven and Hell.

Although the medieval clergy have been extensively studied,[1] the church's personnel remain extremely enigmatic. Traditionally, there is an imposed distinction between the recipients of the highest offices – the wealthiest rectories, the prebends of collegiate and cathedral churches, and the bishoprics – and those lower down the scale, the 'mere' rectors and vicars, and the amorphous group of chantry priests, annuellars, and others who are sometimes lumped into a 'clerical proletariat'. The separation is artificial: to identify 'career clerics' in opposition to 'the rest' makes a false distinction. Nonetheless, the divide does have some reality, not in terms of aspirations but of attainments: many might hope for office – any office – but only few would achieve it. If the medieval clergy must be divided, the distinction has to be between the beneficed and the unbeneficed – effectively dividing those with 'tenured' appointments from those without –

---

[1] The main general surveys of the clergy are Heath, *Parish clergy* [369]; Bowker, *Secular clergy* [77]. Thompson, *English clergy* [824] mainly considers institutional aspects, but has much useful additional information on individuals and their careers. On the religious orders, Knowles, *Religious orders* [484].

rather than between 'higher' and 'lower' echelons. Career prospects within
the medieval church were influenced by a multiplicity of factors, any
combination of which might apply to any individual case. Whilst in theory
a cleric might experience the whole range of ecclesiastical employment
and eventually rise to an archbishopric (or even higher), reality was
rather different. It is the influences affecting that reality which demand
attention while seeking to identify just who these medieval ecclesiastics
were, and what was expected of them.

Unfortunately, virtually nothing is known about most of the medieval
clergy. The principal sources for the administrative history of the period,
the episcopal registers, give little more than a record of the administrative
contacts between the diocesan and the secular clergy under his charge.
Crucially, the register records the acquisition of rights and status: clerical
status, with attendant powers, in the ordination lists; property rights, with
the acquisition, resignation, and exchange of benefices; status acquired by
overriding canonical defects through dispensations; privileges affecting
income with licences for absence and study, or to celebrate private masses;
and more. The register is mainly a record of episcopal relations with the
secular clergy; of the mendicants and monks, the former appear only
rarely – in ordination lists, receiving licences in accordance with the papal
constitution *Super cathedram*, as suffragan bishops, and (very rarely) in
receipt of benefices. Monks appear slightly more often, particularly if
not exempt from diocesan authority. Thus, they again appear in ordination
lists, and occasionally in receipt of dispensations; they also appear receiving
benefices with perhaps surprising frequency. Individuals are also mentioned in records of the elections of new heads of houses; while the houses
themselves receive attention in documents concerning appropriations of
benefices to them, or in records of visitations (which are sometimes
collected into separate volumes), or where the house acts as a patron.

Obviously the registers are not exclusively records of relationships
between bishops and clergy: the variety of business which any register
might contain is considerable; while to say that there is such a thing as a
'typical bishop's register' begs numerous questions.[2] But, taking a random
(albeit manageable) example in the register of Robert Hallum, Bishop of
Salisbury from 1407 to 1417, the concentration of material fleshing out the
careers of the secular clergy is immediately apparent.[3] Of the 1,147 entries
in the calendar, thirty-one (covering thirty-nine printed pages) are ordination lists, 694 deal with benefices and their acquisition, and 321

---

[2] For surviving registers, Smith, *Guide to bishops' registers* [765]; for contents Owen, *Bishops'
registers* [629]. A 'formulary' approach is adopted in Offer, *The bishop's register* [614], printing
examples of several types of document derived from a variety of registers.

[3] Horn, *Reg. Hallum* [411].

are entered in the section for 'licences, letters, and commissions'. Admittedly, some 150 of these are not immediately linked to clerical careers, being grants of licences to hold services in private chapels and oratories, grants of indulgences, and documents concerning tithe disputes and the sequestration of revenues; but a considerable number do mention clerics (especially the financial matters), and several of the rest relate to clerical careers. Of the remaining 250-odd entries in Hallum's register, twelve deal with testamentary business (six wills being those of clerics), sixty-nine concern royal writs and their execution (some dealing with benefice holding, pensions, and elections of heads of religious houses), and nineteen deal with judicial business (apart from cases entered elsewhere), several of the issues involving clerics.

With the multiplicity of potential references to be extracted from episcopal registers and other sources, it should be possible to give a relatively complete picture of secular clerical careers in the middle ages. Had the church then been totally meritocratic, and the bishops had complete and effective control, it might have been possible to describe a standard career pattern, as individuals progressed through the system, each finding his appropriate level until the most deserving reached the heights of episcopacy. Unfortunately, neither criterion applies. Promotion was rarely meritocratic, either in the spiritual or administrative spheres: many more calculations were involved in advancement than mere suitability for the job. Clerical career patterns during this period reflect a complex equation in which virtually every component is a variable. The supply of priests is but one element, with its own determinants in the society as a whole; the demand for clerical services is another, placing its own restrictions on the shape of individual careers; and the possibility of securing the 'right' type of job is a third, dependent on the opportunities for guaranteed employment, itself a reflection of changing patterns of benefices and of altered patronage forces within the church – all factors affected by and reflecting changing economic and social patterns. In attempting to work out the practicalities of clerical careers in late medieval England all these factors have to be juggled with, but cannot all be treated fully. Some basic questions are unavoidable. Who were these clergy, how many were there, and where did they come from? Once committed to the church, how did they organize their own careers? A number of specific factors also need investigation. The machinery and operation of ecclesiastical patronage demand attention, patronage being a ubiquitous but often shadowy force. Education has to be considered: it might make individual clerics more attractive to potential patrons. Generally the clerical career structure was beyond the control of the individual cleric – it was controlled wholly by third parties, who had to offer him employment. It is also necessary to consider the forces which affected relationships between clergy and their

parishioners, and which determined their attitudes towards their benefices, assuming that they did actually receive a benefice. In all the consideration of clerical careers, one major determinant cannot be overlooked
– death. Death and the fear of its aftermath provided much of the income
for the unbeneficed; while for all clerics, death provided career opportunities.
Ecclesiastical careers were essentially a matter of seeking dead men's
shoes, and their revenues. No matter how many people aspired to be
bishops, until 1540 there could only be twenty-one diocesans in England
and Wales at any one time, of whom only two could be archbishops.
Similar considerations applied at all ranks of the church: the numbers of
archdeacons, of prebendaries in cathedrals and collegiate churches, of
rectors, were all strictly limited. Over time some of the figures might
change, with changing patterns of benefice creation or erosion, especially
in the lower ranks. The critical factor, however, was that the job had to
exist, and be vacant, before it could be filled.

2.2   NUMBERS AND ORIGINS

Among the many unknowns affecting the medieval clergy, one of the most
significant is uncertainty about how many there actually were. Admittedly,
their contemporaries were equally ignorant. John Wyclif simply thought
there were too many, who were a burden on the country; while in *c.*1529
Simon Fish estimated that clerics comprised 1 per cent of the adult male
population, or 0.25 per cent of the total.[4] One possible guide to clerical
numbers is provided by the number of parishes. If there were about 8,800
in England and Wales *c.*1500, then a multiplier of three per parish (not
unreasonable if including parochial assistants, chantry priests, and scattered stipendiaries and household chaplains) suggests a total for seculars
of about 26,500. The addition of regulars would boost the total to about
33,000 (suggesting in fact that Fish had considerably underestimated).
This would not be a static figure: numbers would fluctuate over time, but
cannot be given any greater precision by this method. The only set of
formal national 'statistics' for the clergy derives from the returns of the
clerical poll taxes of 1377–81. Other sets of diocesan figures can be
constructed from later quasi-poll-tax assessments, especially Wolsey's
impositions of the 1520s, but these have so far received little attention, and
their comparability with the poll-tax evidence awaits assessment.[5]

---

[4] Workman, *Wyclif* [927], ii, p. 112 n. 3 and refs.; Furnivall and Cowper, *Four supplications*
[289], p. 4.
[5] The totals of enrolled poll-tax returns tabulated in Russell, *British medieval population*
[722], pp. 134–7. The multiplier of three is a guess. For the thirteenth century Moorman
(*Church life* [591], pp. 52–5) suggests a multiplier of four to five. For later averages,

The figures for 1377–81 are difficult to deal with properly. Generally, only the enrolled totals of the accounts survive: while several detailed lists remain, there are many gaps. But even the available totals are clearly incomplete, with considerable differences between the numbers of clergy returned in successive assessments. Further doubts emerge, moreover, when enrolled totals are compared with the detailed lists. In the arch-deaconry of Chester, for instance, the recorded total of under 300 in 1379 is revealed as wildly inaccurate by surviving lists which detail over 500 individuals. Again, the turnover in the clergy indicated by comparing the 1379 return and the (incomplete) list of 1377 suggests an under-recording in 1379 of 20 per cent or so. Other regions of the country still need detailed treatment, so that the Chester results cannot be extended; but the warning bells ring loud. Regardless of the problems, these poll-tax returns remain the only national totals which can be given any credence. They suggest a clerical – or, rather, priestly – population of some 24–25,000 seculars, comparable with the figure derived from multiplying the parishes. Depending on allowances to be made for under-recording, however, this figure would need some increase.[6]

The poll-tax assessments provide only static figures. Yet, depending on the relative trends between rates of entrance to major orders (those which involved a commitment to the church), and general changes in the level of national population, so the percentage of clergy in the population would alter. Overall changes in the clerical population can only really be assessed from the ordination lists which record admission to the ranks of clergy. Here, there are major problems with the sources and their interpretation. The overall population trends of the period also have to be borne in mind, with their effects.

The problems posed by ordination lists are not uncommon. Generally, material is missing. In Lincoln, one of the largest dioceses, records are lost from mid-1363 to late 1398, from mid-1409 to mid-1420, and from late 1425 to mid-1431; between early 1436 and 1472 records survive only for 1450–2. Norwich ordinations are missing before 1413; whilst Carlisle retains no record after 1388.[7] Even when ordination records survive, their

McHardy, 'Ecclesiastics and economics' [558], pp. 130–1 (surveying evidence from clerical poll taxes in the 1370s – ranging from 2 per parish to over 8); Zell, 'Clergy of Kent' [936], p. 517; Bowker, *Henrician Reformtaion* [80], p. 124 (early sixteenth-century Kent and Lincoln diocese – under 2 per parish). For printed lists from 1526, 'The Fallow papers' [263], pp. 244–52; 'East Riding clergy' [245], pp. 63–80; Salter, *Subsidy collected in Lincoln* [729].

[6] Bennett, 'Lancashire and Cheshire clergy' [56], pp. 22–8; Bennett, *Community, class, and careerism* [57], pp. 98–9; Russell, 'Clerical population' [721], p. 179. See also Kirby, 'Two tax accounts' [476].

[7] Smith, *Guide to bishops' registers*, pp. 114–25, 152–3, 255–8 (Norwich lists are again missing after 1486, with rare exceptions – ibid., pp. 153–7).

completeness is frequently questionable: odd lists are absent, confusions arise from scribal error. Moreover, assessment is complicated by problems in correlating the several orders. Theoretically, it was illegal to obtain a minor and major order on the same date, or two major orders together. It should, thus, be possible to trace a steady progression up the ladder, from acolyte (usually the earliest recorded order) to subdeacon, deacon, and priest. However, possibly in reaction to the Black Death, one of these restraints apparently disappeared: from at least the 1380s, many candidates were clearly being ordained both acolyte and subdeacon at the one ceremony. Where all stages of the progression to priesthood are recorded, this problem of double ordination could be eliminated from the calculations; but in some dioceses (York stands out) it is likely that the receipt of the lesser order was simply subsumed in the registration of ordination as subdeacon – consequently, that those recorded as becoming acolytes were only those whose advancement was to be delayed, if not halted. Such double ordinations were probably common throughout the country between 1350 and *c*.1450, but perhaps died out before Wolsey's time – precisely when remains to be determined. They were restored, after a fashion, by a papal bull of 1516.[8]

With all these caveats, to which can be added the disruption in the figures caused by individuals moving between dioceses for ordination by virtue of letters dimissory, what can be said about trends in late medieval ordination patterns? Few dioceses provide sufficiently complete records to allow accurate trends to be deduced with any accuracy, but those for the diocese of Coventry and Lichfield are among the most complete extant lists, and can be taken as representative, especially when used in conjunction with evidence from elsewhere.

The Lichfield lists run almost unbroken from 1300 to 1532, but only full collation of individual entries would establish just how defective they are. After the Black Death there are complete breaks in 1350, 1431, 1445–6, and 1502. Several other years have obvious or probable omissions, which reduce the resulting annual totals, but are unlikely to introduce serious distortions. It is not realistically possible to compensate for such omissions, given the multitude of individual variables which might affect any particular ceremony.[9] One further difficulty with the Lichfield lists occurs in

---

[8] Johannes de Burgo, *Pupilla oculi* [108], 7.3.B; the first identifiable double ordinations in Lichfield lists occur in 1384 (LPL, Reg. Courtenay, f. 347v); Bellamy, *Criminal law and society* [54], p. 138.

[9] I therefore reject the averaging process adopted in Moran, 'Clerical recruitment' [594], p. 21. The Lichfield ordinations for the years 1300–1532 are recorded in the following main sources: LJRO, B/A/1/1, ff. 92r–141v, 143r–216v; B/A/1/6, ff.140r–158v; B/A/1/7, ff.1r–v, 212r–236v; B/A/1/8, ff.45r–54v; B/A/1/9, ff.205r–243v; B/A/1/10, ff.5v, 105r–115r; B/A/1/11, ff.4r–6v, 97r–117v; B/A/1/12, ff.5r–6v, 178r–291r; B/A/1/13, ff.112r–123r, 129r–130r,

1414–15, where the ceremonies cannot be allocated to a proper chronology. Despite the archival problems, the Lichfield evidence permits some general statements about overall trends in ordination patterns – and thus, in patterns of recruitment to clerical ranks – between 1350 and 1532. In raw figures, the surviving lists for major orders contain some 70,000 individual entries, suggesting that over the period a minimum of *c.*24,000 males committed themselves to a clerical career. This figure makes no allowances for omissions and incompleteness, nor for movement between dioceses. However, it may be a reasonably accurate representation of the total number from the diocese as a geographical unit, if various factors cancelled each other out. Rough-and-ready calculation over fifty-year periods suggests that some 6,000 candidates were ordained between 1300 and 1349, about 4,000 in 1350–99, a mere 2,700 or so between 1400 and 1449, *c.*5,000 in the next fifty years, and in the final period (restricted by the records to 1500–32), some 5,300. The striking contrast is between the pre-plague total of 6,000 (which is probably rather lower than the reality), the nadir of 1400–49, and the staggering rise which occurs towards the end of the fifteenth century to produce the pre-Reformation peak. These raw figures so far include both seculars and religious: as ordinations of the latter fluctuated little numerically, this only emphasizes the changes in ordination patterns among the seculars.

An obvious break in secular ordination trends occurs in 1349, with the Black Death. The gap in 1350 precludes any assessment of the immediate reaction to the crisis, which elsewhere produced emergency ordination procedures to compensate for losses amongst the clergy, and in York resulted in a massive immediate peak in the number of priestly ordinations which was to be the highest annual total recorded among the surviving pre-Reformation lists.[10] The beneficed clergy were clearly hard-hit by the pestilence, with some places losing a succession of incumbents during the crucial months (although admittedly not all of these deaths would be caused by the plague); and subsequent outbreaks similarly affected them.[11] The Lichfield lists do indicate one immediate effect on clerical recruitment: a two-thirds drop in ordinands when comparing decades on either side of

136v–138r, 171r–189v, 198r–v, 258r–297v; B/A/1/14ii; B/A/1/14iii, ff.4v–5v; LPL, Reg. Courtenay, ff.347v–348r, 351r–353r; Reg. Kempe, ff.335v–338r; Reg. Morton i, ff.154v–155r; Wilson, *Reg. Coventry and Lichfield, book 4* [917], pp. 159–396; Wilson, *Reg. Coventry and Lichfield, book 5* [916], pp. 12–13, 15–16, 18; Jacob, *Reg. Chichele* [438], iii, pp. 327–34 (these were not the only ordinations performed within the diocese; for letters of orders issued following a ceremony held in Chester abbey in 1481 by an abbot of that exempt house in his capacity as bishop of Sodor – but not as a suffragan of Lichfield – see Eeles, 'A fifteenth-century York missal' [248], pp. 9–10).
[10] Moran, 'Clerical recruitment', pp. 22, 26.
[11] ibid., p. 26; Russell, *British medieval population*, pp. 220–2.

the dividing line for which figures survive (1337–48, and 1351–60). The figure is seemingly characteristic of English dioceses, presumably reflecting the immediate reaction to the plague, and the reduction in population pressures which might, before its arrival, have had a major influence in encouraging males with poor expectations to embark on a clerical career.[12]

In the next fifty years, Lichfield figures slowly recover, but never to pre-plague levels. This probably links in with the response among the general population as plague became endemic. In the first couple of decades, the decline in numbers of secular ordinands was countered by population recovery; but further plague outbreaks increased the population slack. At Lichfield, when plague struck, ordination figures fell: in the 1360s therefore the apparent recovery was brutally checked. Elsewhere, however, the plague may have stimulated clerical recruitment: at Carlisle it possibly produced a major change in the organization of ordinations, although this could be no more than the idiosyncratic response of a new bishop in a border bishopric.[13]

During these years to 1399, Lichfield's ordination figures for all three major orders peak in the 1370s, a feature shared with other dioceses, before dropping to a plateau in the 1390s. Here there is a contrast with the northern province, where the drop in recruitment was delayed until the end of the century; with research on York diocese suggesting that repeated plague outbreaks encouraged entry to orders.[14] Precise annual totals fluctuate, sometimes quite wildly, but it is the general trend which matters. In the next half century, to 1449, this turns quite definitely downwards at Lichfield. Whereas, even after 1350, priestly ordinations had occasionally exceeded a hundred (in the 1370s), and usually exceeded fifty, this now changed. Between 1400 and 1449 priestly ordinations were fifty or more in only twelve years, the highest figure being the seventy of 1411. Lesser orders were similarly in the doldrums. Occasionally, incomplete recording and missing years affect the figures, but the overall impression is that a clerical career was no longer particularly attractive, despite the demand for priestly services. Again, evidence from elsewhere, such as York and London dioceses, suggests that Lichfield reflects national trends.[15] The decline in figures probably cannot be attributed totally to overall population

[12] Moran, 'Clerical recruitment', pp. 22, 32. In Carlisle the drop was especially severe, but it could be compensated for by increased movement outside the diocese by use of letters dimissory: Rose, 'Priests and patrons' [710], p. 210.

[13] Rose, 'Priests and patrons', pp. 211, 217; Storey, 'Recruitment of English clergy' [785], pp. 294–5, 308.

[14] Storey, 'Recruitment of English clergy', pp. 294–7; Moran, 'Clerical recruitment', pp. 37–9.

[15] Storey, 'Recruitment of English clergy', pp. 301, 308–9; Moran, 'Clerical recruitment', pp. 39–42.

trends: they were fairly static, but the population was probably not low enough to explain this deep trough in the ordination figures. Presumably opportunities within the wider economy, both agricultural and industrial, were more tempting than the salaries and other benefits available to the clergy, relatively high though they might be; while the general laicization of bureaucracies had removed a major imperative which had earlier directed individuals towards an ecclesiastical career.[16]

The forces which reduced clerical recruitment between 1400 and 1449 were more than adequately countered in the next fifty years. This is no guide to the quality of the recruits, but any problem about maintaining numbers disappeared. In most years, priestly ordinations in Lichfield diocese again exceeded fifty. The change is dramatic: 1449 was a peak year for the preceding period, and although secular priestly ordinations waver in the following decade, they usually (perhaps always) exceeded forty, while in lesser orders there were under fifty candidates in only two years (both probably incomplete) among the subdeacons, and in four years (two incomplete) among the deacons. Indeed, the figures generally climb, with all three orders in 1483 exceeding a hundred for the first time since 1377. This position was roughly maintained throughout the later fifteenth century, although incomplete recording causes occasional drops. Totals sometimes approach 200 among the lesser orders, but were usually 150–70. Nevertheless, 1498 saw 218 secular priests ordained, the highest recorded figure since 1336. Generally, the last two decades of the century indicate a return to the pre-plague position among the seculars. In other dioceses, York shows a similar rise to pre-plague levels (ignoring the extraordinary figures for 1349–50), and others indicate a general rise in recruitment in the later fifteenth century. Clerical careers were again popular, although precisely why is not immediately clear. Certainly the general population was increasing at this time, while the overall economic position may have been getting worse. These years mark the start of the major concern with vagrancy and vagabondage which produced the Tudor Poor Law; presumably therefore economic pressures – enclosures and suchlike – were forcing people from the land; while if the urban position was as drastic as some of the evidence suggests, a clerical career might appear relatively attractive.[17]

The figures for Lichfield ordinands continued buoyant. Between 1500 and 1532, candidatures for all three major orders remained high, usually well over 100, occasionally over 200. The consistency of the trend is remarkable, leading to the virtually inescapable conclusion that the recruitment crisis caused by the Black Death had been completely overcome.

[16] Storey, 'Recruitment of English clergy', p. 304; 3/1 at n. 38.
[17] Moran, 'Clerical recruitment', pp. 22, 45, 47–9, 52–3.

Nevertheless, warning signs were visible. The Lichfield evidence is inconclusive, given its terminal date, but this relative attractiveness of a
clerical career was perhaps again declining in the 1520s. In the last year
for which complete figures survive for Lichfield, 1530, ordinations in all
three orders were under 100 for the first time since 1496 – and that had
been an incomplete year. The impact of the Reformation, changing the
demands made of a priest, abolishing the chantries and masses for souls,
and releasing onto the clerical labour market a large number of religious
all competing for benefices, perhaps pricked a balloon which was already
deflating. The Reformation changes in ordination procedures added further complexities, especially in trying to secure titles for ordination.[18]

Even so, on the eve of the Reformation the available evidence indicates
that, numerically, England's clerical population was doing well. Having
been decimated by the Black Death, both by deaths and by reduced
pressures obliging males to undertake clerical careers, recruitment had
been influenced by the depressed state of the population and economy,
sinking to the depths of the period 1400–49. Thereafter – and especially
from about 1470 – there was a remarkable recovery, continuing until the
Reformation loomed. The clerical percentage of the overall population
remains hard to calculate; but the increased numbers from 1480 doubtless
made the clergy more obviously visible, and visibly more numerous,
perhaps encouraging anticlericalism. In any event, the recruitment of
secular clergy had obviously fluctuated, with its own repercussions for the
role of the church within its society.

Tracing trends in numbers entering the clerical profession reveals little
about the clergy as people. Precisely who were they, rushing to engage on
this career; and what made them seek clerical employment?

Such questions are largely unanswerable. Usually the only evidence
about individuals becoming clerics is provided by ordination lists, giving
little more than names. Those for whom families and social rank can be
identified are, by definition, the exceptions. The main task is to determine
whether the clergy were essentially of gentry stock, as has been claimed, or
whether there was a strong peasant element, as others have argued.[19]
There is clear evidence for both social extremes: gentry and nobility in
people like Henry Beaufort, bastard half-brother to Henry IV, and James
Langton, of an influential Lancashire family; or serfdom in the case of
John Hody, a fifteenth-century chancellor of Wells cathedral. But evidence

---

[18] Swanson, 'Titles to orders' [800], pp. 244–5; Bowker, *Henrician Reformation*, pp. 39–40,
124–6.
[19] Bennett, *Community, class, and careerism*, pp. 137–8; Hilton, *Bondmen made free* [393], p.
212.

of family status is infrequently provided by the episcopal registers – ordination lists rarely mention manumission, although some Exeter registers provide references. Even rarer are explicit statements of gentry birth, although Baldwin Mountford is explicitly identified as a knight in a Lichfield ordination list. Occasionally other documents provide hints, such as the penitentiary dispensation noting that Edmund Constabile was illegitimate child to Sir Roger Constabile; while wills often indicate other relationships.[20] Much of the evidence is miscellaneous in character, and therefore difficult to assimilate. The only hope therefore is for vague generalization, rather than a real conclusion.

Canon law provided two obvious starting-points for defining the clergy's position: ordinands had to be free-born, and legitimate.[21] However, these were purely technical limitations, easily circumvented by manumission for serfs and papal or penitentiary dispensations for bastards.

Evidence of former serfs among the clergy is limited. As freedom was a preliminary requirement even for minor orders[22] (which are only rarely recorded in ordination lists) the identification of the ex-serf is fortuitous. Much depends on quirks of individual registration. Nor is it generally possible to work from the other end, from manumissions recorded in manor court rolls: the time-lag before receipt of recorded orders and the need to correlate material work against the identification of the unfree would-be cleric among those entered in ordination lists.

Quantifying the percentage of medieval clerics with servile origins is therefore a forlorn hope. Possibly, with the gradual decay of serfdom after the Black Death, the numbers became insignificant (perhaps they had been insignificant throughout). Much would depend on the determination of the individual lord to retain his seigneurial rights, or his readiness to sell freedom at a suitable price. Manumitted clerics probably derived from the economically active families within the servile grouping: the acquisition of a penitentiary's dispensation by Simon Baldewyn of Cottenham (Cambs.) in 1416 to secure his manumission and promotion to orders would suggest his wealthy background. Those manumitted were probably also from the sector of rural society most susceptible to pressure from their lords, who would ensure that their freedom was actually purchased rather than simply assumed through default. But it is clear that manumission for

---

[20] Dunning, 'Patronage and promotion' [240], pp. 173–4; Hingeston-Randolph, *Reg. Brantyngham* [399], ii, pp. 777, 794, 799, 829, 849, 854, 856–7, 862, 866; LJRO, B/A/1/11, ff. 115v, 116v, 117r; Swanson, *Reg. Scrope* [796], i, p. 61; Tanner, *Church in Norwich* [810], pp. 25–8.

[21] LJRO, B/A/1/1, f. 134v; Richter and Friedberg, *Corpus iuris canonici* [697], ii, cols. 135, 141–2.

[22] Except in very specific circumstances: Dewindt, *Liber gersumarum* [209], p. 37 no. 191 and n. 13.

ordination could not be widely exploited as a means of evading servility. It almost certainly required payment – perhaps hefty payment – to the lord. Moreover, the loophole had been foreseen, and blocked. At Bury St Edmunds under Abbot Curteys (1429–46), manumission to orders became fully effective only when the orders were acquired, some cases imposing short time-limits for their receipt. Some individuals clearly did take orders before manumission: a York instance frees two serfs (who were probably brothers) who are described as already chaplains; while another chaplain was presented before the bishop of Ely's court as a fugitive serf.[23]

The numbers joining the clergy argue against the majority of them being gentry; sheer probability argues against them being from the lowest sections of society. The vast majority of clerics must have fallen between the two extremes, probably deriving from the middling families, the yeomen and richer peasants in the country, the practitioners of the more profitable crafts in the towns. It seems likely that the chief determinant of initial likelihood to enter the church was not birth, but wealth, and the family's economic standing. The 'titles' to which candidates were ordained were meant to indicate guaranteed financial independence and security; if they did so they should show the minimum level below which individuals would be ineligible for an ecclesiastical career. This may have been about 40s. a year, although penetrating the obscurities in the title system is difficult, and the 40s. may represent salaries for household chaplains. But it could reflect landed income, either inheritance or assignments. In the context of future definition of the political classes (the forty-shilling free-holders) and contemporary formal social stratification in Acts of Parliament, the figure may be significant. If it does reflect landed income, this might account for the low numbers of ordinands between 1400 and 1450, with trends in candidatures reflecting changes in rental levels.[24] It seems quite likely that only the wealthier ranks of the peasantry would have sent their sons for the church – and they alone, if serfs, could have afforded the manumission fees. It would have been no accident for Chaucer to make his Parson the brother of a ploughman (among the wealthiest of peasants) although in some of the literary works of the period the ploughmen themselves look down on lesser-born clerics.[25] In towns, the evidence perhaps confirms the general picture. Among the York craftsmen, a clerical career seems to have been seen as one way of breaking out of the industrial

---

[23] EDR, G/2/3, f. 38r–v; Hilton, *Decline of serfdom* [392], pp. 51–2; BL, MS Add. 14848, ff. 20v–21, 102r, 142r, 349r; YML, M2(5), f. 169v; EDR, E1/16, for court of Saturday after St Etheldreda, 30 Henry VI.

[24] Swanson, 'Titles to orders', p. 244; Hilton, *English peasantry* [394], p. 25; for rent levels, see 5/2, at nn. 23–8, 44–8.

[25] Robinson, *Works of Chaucer* [703], pp. 21–2, ll. 476–541; on ploughmen, Hilton, *English peasantry*, pp. 21–3.

structure, possibly being associated with aspirations of upward social movement. Some 14 per cent of the York craftsmen who claimed the city's freedom by inheritance between 1387 and 1534 were identified as clerics, and presumably are only some of the sons affected. Their fathers' crafts cover the whole spectrum of urban employment, but concentrating on the wealthier occupations in the urban pecking order, with butchers, drapers, and tanners being well represented.[26]

One further aspect of the general question of social origins remains. It would be useful to differentiate between clergy of rural and urban origins; but unfortunately the sources do not allow it. Ultimately we know – and can know – little about the origins of most of the later medieval English clergy. The clerical population included gentry, nobility, townsmen, and countrymen, but in exactly what proportions is anyone's guess.

Apart from social status, clerical origins can also be investigated in terms of birth status. Episcopal registers contain a multitude of dispensations for defects of birth – effectively, the legitimization of bastards, allowing them to receive orders and acquire a benefice. By 1350, the common law recognized all bastards as free born, but they remained canonically ineligible for orders unless dispensed. Dispensations were accordingly obtained, in fairly large numbers, many of them being entered in episcopal registers. Below the subdiaconate, the bishop could grant the dispensation; but for holy orders proper recourse had to be to the papal penitentiary, the pope himself, or one of the bishops or papal agents (legates and nuncios) who received limited powers to grant such dispensations in England.[27] As with manumissions of serfs, correlating the dispensations with the listed ordinands is often difficult. Some individuals may have obtained their dispensations before they were fully committed to a clerical career, leaving a gap of some years between receipt of the dispensation and the ordination: if the John Venables whose dispensation was processed in Lichfield diocese in 1417 was the John Venables ordained in that diocese in 1449, the gap could be extremely long. However, it could also be very short: most recipients of such dispensations in York diocese between 1398 and 1405 were soon ordained, in one case only the day after the dispensation was passed. Perhaps the dispensations were not always sought by the candidate: the four Venables bastards all dispensed on the same date (including the above John) in 1417 are unlikely to have opted voluntarily for the church, assuming (as seems reasonable) that they were brothers. It is impossible to quantify the bastards among the late medieval

---

[26] Swanson, 'Craftsmen and industry' [944], p. 453.

[27] Hyams, 'Proof of villein status' [432], p. 746; Lyndwood, *Provinciale* [539], p. 27 gloss i; compare Hingeston-Randolph, *Reg. Brantyngham*, ii, pp. 763–4, 766, 769–70, etc.; the explicit references to curial dispensations ibid., ii, pp. 754, 773, etc.; see also LJRO, B/A/1/9, f. 160v.

English clergy – and some certainly sought to conceal their defect, and were perhaps successful – but it is unlikely that there were very many. Usually their social status is indefinable: the parents are rarely identified, although their marital status is generally noted. Many recipients are identified as being themselves the offspring of priests.[28] Perhaps the clergy adopted the policy of putting their sons into the church; perhaps the gentry also saw an ecclesiastical career as suitable for their bastards; but no valid generalizations can be made.

2.3 JOBS

The motives for entering the church were many and varied, and doubtless changed with time. The economic context and its pressures cannot be ignored; but cannot have been the only factors. Some would have had private motivations, even vocations; others might have been pushed unwillingly into ecclesiastical careers. Some probably sought job security; others saw the church as a milch cow. One possible trend, especially contrasting the two halves of the fourteenth century, is a delay in the point of commitment to the church, reflected also in the laicization of bureaucracies. As education spread to the laity, so administration no longer demanded clerkly status, removing that imperative towards a clerical career. Ordination could then become a real choice, rather than just the logical step in general career calculations.

Identifying the point when an individual committed himself to the church is difficult. Again, the ordination lists might provide clues, although there are massive problems with collation. Formally, there were age restrictions for the individual orders: the first tonsure was conferred in youth, the minimum age for an acolyte was fourteen, and for the later orders of subdeacon, deacon, and priest respectively seventeen, nineteen, and twenty-four. For promotion as a bishop the canonical age was thirty.[29] The distribution of appearances in the ordination lists should, therefore,

---

[28] LJRO, B/A/1/8, f. 29v, B/A/1/10, f. 108r (the later reference is to the ordination as subdeacon, identifying him as a dispensed bastard. No one of that name appears on intervening ordination lists, or had a bastardy dispensation registered in the intervening years); Swanson, *Reg. Scrope* – compare the bastardy dispensations, listed under 'bastardy' in index, with the index of ordination lists (John Russell was dispensed on 23 May 1399, and ordained subdeacon, and presumably acolyte as well, on 24 May, ibid., i, p. 73, ii, p. 100; see also the case of John Fryston, ibid., i, p. 65, ii, p. 78). Heath's strictures (*Parish clergy*, p. 107 n. 1) against using the *Calendar of papal registers* for discovering priestly bastards as priests are perfectly valid, but ignore the point that the majority of bastardy dispensations, even for sons of priests, originated with mandates issued by the papal penitentiaries, and were included in registers not dealt with by that series.

[29] Johannes de Burgo, *Pupilla oculi*, 7.4.A.

indicate age at some point, even if only a minimum, permitting some comment on the way in which ordinands elected for a clerical career.

Unfortunately, it is not that straightforward. Identification proves most difficult in the early stages of ordination; later the title will usually assist the process of collating references, but this does not apply with lower orders. Moreover, ordination to first tonsure (and in certain circumstances, as acolyte) was apparently considered a fairly routine task, and not always registered. At Exeter in the early fifteenth century the first tonsure seems to have been administered by the suffragan during an annual tour of the diocese connected with the distribution of chrism, and a similar pattern may have prevailed elsewhere. Numbers receiving the first tonsure were surprisingly large, if the scanty surviving evidence provides any real guidance. For the years which provide evidence of the annual tour of Exeter diocese during the episcopate of Edmund Lacy, recipients of first tonsure always considerably exceeded those entering holy orders; but the 900-odd who obtained their first tonsure in 1381 must have been abnormal.[30]

First tonsure – the receipt of clerical status – was a fairly common rite of passage, although precisely why so many received it remains unclear. To assess how many of those possessing it advanced further requires a rigid collation of the material where it survives. Unfortunately, there are large numbers for whom there is no evidence of such advancement, and an equally large crowd for whom there is no obvious evidence of receipt of first tonsure, so that proportions cannot be assessed. Some of the absences must be due to the lengthy gap between first tonsure and 'proper' orders. Some may be due to individuals receiving all their minor orders up to and including acolyte on the same date (a practice for which evidence does exist), with the first tonsure being subsumed in receipt of the higher order – even though this raises questions about ordination practices.[31] Incomplete registration probably accounts for the majority of the omissions.

The gap between first tonsure and ordination as acolyte (the highest of the non-holy orders) was variable. Those receiving both orders on the same day, or within a matter of months, had presumably only recently determined on a clerical career, with at least one university master delaying

---

[30] Dunstan, *Reg. Lacy* [241], iv., pp. 68–257, esp. 68–71, 95–6, 108–14, 145–8, 154–5, 157, 163, 172–3, 177–8, 187–8, 196–7, 202, 213–14, 219–20, 230–2, 240, 256–7; Hingeston-Randolph, *Reg. Brantyngham*, ii, pp. 820–33.

[31] Dunstan, *Reg. Lacy*, iv., pp. xxiv, 218, 224, 226, 228–9, 234. The index, ibid., v, details progress through orders. Some absences can be explained by incomers with letters dimissory, and regulars perhaps ordained elsewhere without needing them. Numerous seculars have no record prior to acolyte; not all can be accounted for by a long gap between receipt of first tonsure under the previous bishop and later orders, which might be covered by the first eight years or so of any episcopal register.

even his first tonsure until after graduation. But a delay of seven or eight years seems not uncommon – such was the case with Thomas Cokkesheade and Stephen Byttebeare in late fourteenth-century Exeter – although identification problems again hinder precision. The twenty-year gap between the appearance of Henry Ambrose in the first tonsure lists in January 1421 and his apparent ordination as acolyte in September 1441 seems rather excessive, and may conflate two different individuals, especially as later advancement was speedy. Equally, from the opposite direction, had the William Andrewe ordained acolyte in May 1442 received his first tonsure in 1427 or 1439?[32]

Some time might also elapse between ordination as acolyte and as subdeacon (in Cokkesheade's case seven years)[33] but in general it seems that, at least from about 1350, advancement beyond acolyte occurred fairly quickly. This speedy ordination pattern suggests that the commitment to a career in the church was being made later than had been the case before the Black Death. Admittedly, without a dispensation (for which examples exist) it was illegal to receive orders under age.[34] But the age limits were minimal, and the crucial one would be twenty-four, to obtain the priesthood. From the mid-fourteenth century, candidates normally received successive major orders at successive ceremonies. They could thus rise from laity to priesthood within about six months if they were promoted at the normal intervals. With a governing age of twenty-four, this represents formal commitment to a celibate career at about twenty-three at the earliest.[35] Before the Black Death, promotion in Lichfield diocese seems to have been more leisurely, possibly indicating commitment at a slightly earlier age.[36] It is, admittedly, difficult to be sure of this, or of its significance: without clear evidence for ages from other sources, precise age at ordination cannot be determined.

Commitment to orders could also be delayed by short-circuiting the system. By using the several small ordination ceremonies which took place in addition to those on the Ember Days, an individual might advance to the priesthood in little over a month, as Thomas ap Ho[wel] did in 1508, becoming subdeacon on 18 March, and priest on 22 April, something of a record for 'normal' advancement. Dispensation allowed further short-

---

[32] Hingeston-Randolph, *Reg. Brantyngham*, ii, pp. 786, 812, 840, 844, 874; Dunstan, *Reg. Lacy*, iv, pp. 70, 109, 173, 183–6.

[33] Hingeston-Randolph, *Reg. Brantyngham*, ii, p. 876.

[34] Twemlow, *Calendar of papal letters, 1471–1484* [850], pp. 426, 581, 610, 708; Haren, *Calendar of papal letters, 1484–1492* [346], nos. 347, 739. Powers to grant such dispensations (or to dispense from the defect after the orders had been received) were also accorded to papal agents: Twemlow, *Calendar of papal letters, 1471–1484*, pp. 2, 200.

[35] See the progression through orders in Dunstan, *Reg. Lacy*, v, index; Swanson, *Reg. Scrope*, ii, pp. 56–124.

[36] Robinson, 'Ordinations of secular clergy' [702], p. 7.

cuts, by reception of two orders on one day. Whilst this uncanonical behaviour was apparently condoned, with people being ordained acolyte and subdeacon at one ceremony well into the fifteenth century, other combinations of holy orders are virtually unknown until Wolsey's legation. He issued several dispensations allowing reception of two orders at once, whether acolyte and subdeacons (thereby emphasizing the return to canonical practice elsewhere), or deacon and priest. Such dispensations permitted the extremely rapid advancement of George Planckney: ordained subdeacon on Saturday, 21 September 1527, he received both diaconate and priesthood on the following day. Few others are likely to be found moving so rapidly from lay to priestly status, although some bishops progressed through the holy orders with great speed. Thomas Arundel was made deacon and priest on the very day of his consecration as bishop of Ely in 1373, and also needed a dispensation for his uncanonical youth.[37]

One corollary of a decision to enter the clergy later in life may be that those entering the late medieval church had made a conscious and deliberate decision. Indeed, some seem to have waited until their careers were guaranteed before they actually decided. Fellows of university colleges not infrequently delayed ordination until their ecclesiastical prospects seemed assured; and a similar habit of deferring ordination until a career was guaranteed also appears among the non-graduates. Thus, John Thower, registrar to Bishop Hales of Lichfield, apparently did not contemplate orders until after his appointment, made when he had only the first tonsure. But by 1500 it was possible to have an 'ecclesiastical' career without taking orders: other episcopal registrars were married laymen.[38] More generally, most parishes employed a parish clerk to assist the clergy and as general church caretaker. Whilst such employment may have been part of the normal route to orders, this perhaps changed in the fifteenth century. There is then growing evidence of married parish clerks, and their position seems to have become more stable. Indeed, they actually gained recognition as a profession in London, their fraternity of St Nicholas developing into a livery company.[39]

Having decided on an ecclesiastical career, and secured orders, most clerics aspired to a benefice, and thereby a freehold income, with its obligations. A benefice could be obtained prior to ordination as priest – rectories and sinecures (but not usually chantries) could be obtained with only the first tonsure – but most clerics obtaining benefices would have to become priests eventually. In determining ecclesiastical career prospects,

---

[37] LJRO, B/A/1/14ii, ff. 45r, 47r, 175r, 190r, 193v, 204r–v; Emden, *Oxford* [255], i, p. 52.
[38] Swanson, 'Universities, graduates, and benefices' [799], p. 53; LJRO, B/A/1/12, f. 278r; Bowker, *Secular clergy*, p. 37.
[39] Heath, *Parish clergy*, pp. 19–20; Adams, *Parish clerks of London* [2], esp. pp. 13–19, 21–8.

however, various factors conspired to affect the situation. Essentially, clerical careers were dictated by laws of supply and demand, although not in a straightforward duality. Whilst there was always the fluctuating supply of clerics, their demands and the demands of those seeking to employ them might well differ. Here, the major changes are apparent in the changing distribution of benefices during the later medieval centuries.

Parochial benefices were not a static feature of medieval ecclesiastical geography. There was frequently some uncertainty as to the identification of a parish, and about the independence of individual churches. Several court cases thus hinged on questions of parochial status *vis-à-vis* another church, usually with one claiming not to be incorporated in or subject to another.[40] Other forces were also at work. Initially, all parishes had been rectories; but following the establishment of new religious orders in the twelfth century, and the creation of the sinecures of prebends, this situation changed. The system of appropriations – whereby the benefice's main revenues would be taken by a religious house or sinecurist, a small portion usually being reserved for a vicar who would assume responsibility for the spiritual tasks – clearly reduced the status of many incumbencies. These appropriations continued throughout the fourteenth century and into the fifteenth, with considerable impact on the ecclesiastical map. Between 1291 and 1535 the number of appropriated churches in England and Wales rose from under 2,000 to over 3,300, their revenues being transferred mainly to religious houses or (a feature of the fifteenth century) to newly founded colleges at Oxford and Cambridge.[41] The change in the benefice's status affected more than the incumbent's income: whereas a rector could exploit his revenues whilst non-resident, vicarages were different. From the thirteenth century permanent residence was an established require-ment; and as a vicar was personally obliged to maintain the cure of souls, he also had to be a priest from the start.[42] As usual, however, theory and practice diverged: the fifteenth century suggests increasing non-residence among vicars, as more of them became pluralists enjoying short-term papally licenced unions of benefices (whose impact has so far been virtually unnoticed) and receiving dispensations to hold offically incompatible benefices.[43]

The change from rectories to vicarages was just one element affecting the parochial map at this time. Economic changes provided a second main

[40] E.g. BIHR, CP.F.60.

[41] Swanson, 'Universities, graduates, and benefices', pp. 35–6 and refs.; see also Thompson, *English clergy*, pp. 109–16.

[42] Wilkins, *Concilia* [902], ii, pp. 5–6.

[43] For unions, see e.g. Fuller, *Papal letters, Alexander VI* [287], nos. 42, 513, 609, 615, 797, 913, and for dispensations for incompatibility, see index under 'Benefices' (at p. 831); Swanson, 'Universities, graduates, and benefices', p. 57 and n. 125.

force. Between 1291 and 1535, it seems likely that the number of parochial benefices – those with cure of souls – dropped by some 7 per cent to just over 8,800, largely due to economic factors. Rural agricultural changes, especially enclosure and the transfer from grain to sheep, sometimes left churches stranded and effectively deprived them of their congregations. In 1519, for instance, the parish of Higham Gobion (Beds.) had only one inhabitant. The desertion of villages made their churches pointless, and deprived their incumbents of their incomes. Tithing and land-holding complexities further complicated the picture. A frequent outcome was that bishops had to authorize amalgamations of benefices. Sometimes this was a natural development: before 1300 many rectories had been divided into portions each constituting a separate benefice. Appropriation and economic necessity gradually reintegrated several of these churches over succeeding centuries. Other amalgamations reflected unions of totally separate entities. In 1488, for instance, the Dorset rectory of Ringstead and vicarage of Osmington were united, their individual incomes being insufficient to maintain two incumbents, and their parishioners in consequence not receiving their due services. Similar unions occurred in towns. Thus, at Norwich, some seven parishes disappeared as independent rectorial benefices after 1370; at Warwick the town's several intramural parishes were united under the church of St Mary by 1400; and similar developments occurred in Winchester.[44] The churches did not necessarily disappear, nor were there fewer jobs; but former freeholds now became merely stipendiary chaplaincies, much less profitable and secure than before.

Other types of benefice were also available in the later middle ages, the fruits of two contemporary movements. First, there was the chantry movement: the creation of small, independently endowed posts for priests to sing masses for the souls of the founders and their nominees, as well as all the faithful departed. The chantry movement provided most newly created benefices in late medieval England, probably accounting for the majority of the transfers of real property to clerical hands in mortmain. (Chantries could also be established informally, thereby avoiding the mortmain requirements; but these did not constitute benefices as recognized by the church.)[45] Precisely how many supposedly perpetual chantries were established is unknown, and a full census would be impossible. Although intended to be permanent, many did not last; unions were frequent, as in late fourteenth-century London, as revenues declined or became alienated.

---

[44] Jones, 'Bedfordshire' [447], p. 179; Wright, *Reg. Langton* [928], no. 470; Tanner, *Church in Norwich*, pp. 3–4; *VCH, Warwick*, viii [874], p. 522; Keene, *Medieval Winchester* [461], i, pp. 116–18.

[45] Below, at n. 62; see also 6/3 at n. 112.

No matter how splendid the original foundation, it would almost inevitably decay. Thomas Holme's chantry in St Mary, Castlegate, York, established in the 1380s (and itself re-endowing a chantry originally established in the 1330s by another York merchant) was still quite wealthy in the 1420s; but by 1547 was a shadow of its former self.[46] Nevertheless, such chantries could provide freehold employment, and independent incomes. But they had their disadvantages: with their special requirements about services, non-residence was not normally possible, and they were perhaps subject to fairly close surveillance from their lay patrons.[47]

The second main movement saw an increase in the number of collegiate churches. These foundations, like Newarke in Leicester, or Hemingbrough in Yorkshire, endowed groups of priests, sometimes supplanting a rectory and taking over parochial responsibilities. A chantry element was common, but not entirely necessary. A member of such a college, having a freehold benefice but no formal cure of souls, could usually engage in other occupations or hold other benefices, even if not actually non-resident.[48]

The number of benefices was still clearly insufficient to employ all the clerics. Even without pluralists collecting benefices, there would always have been a surplus of clergy. But the relationship between supply and demand affecting priests was complex, and at times there are even signs of shortage. The reasons for this lie outside the benefice structure, in the demand for clerics to occupy insecure short-term posts among the stipendiaries.

Most clerics never obtained a proper benefice, and were therefore dependent for their survival on less secure forms of income. Even a successful cleric probably had to wait some time for his benefice, waiting in the knowledge that queue-jumping would be rife, and that he would quite probably be unsuccessful. Where the evidence has been assessed, delays of ten years and more between ordination and institution are not uncommon.[49]

Filling the gap, or simply existing, was done with short-term posts. Although every parish had only one formal incumbent, nevertheless every parish probably needed more than one cleric, and usually more than one priest. Liturgical requirements meant that the priest needed assistants,

---

[46] Hill, '"Chaunterie for soules"' [391], pp. 244, 250; Swanson, 'Thomas Holme' [797], pp. 3–5.

[47] Wood-Legh, *Perpetual chantries* [921], pp. 84–9.

[48] Thompson, *English clergy*, pp. 84–5, 147–58; Edwards, *English secular cathedrals* [247], pp. 295–9. These are distinct from the parallel movement in cathedrals, grouping together the lesser clergy (vicars choral and chantry priests) in colleges, which were entirely disciplinary or administrative developments: ibid., pp. 273–85, 299–301.

[49] Hair, 'Mobility of parochial clergy' [338], pp. 169–70; Bennett, 'Lancashire and Cheshire clergy', pp. 16–17. Zell estimates that only 10–12 per cent of the clergy received benefices: 'Clergy of Kent', p. 322.

acting as subdeacon and deacon during the services. Such liturgical assistants might actually be in priestly orders, possibly being involved in other capacities within the parish. In several parishes, priests were needed for the dependent chapelries, either part- or full-time. (Incumbents often sought to shed these responsibilities, as they usually had to pay for the chaplains; resulting disputes with the parishioners were often taken to the church courts.) The 'part-time' chaplains were not necessarily underemployed: John Dounham's agreement with Ely priory in 1465 combined two posts – on Mondays, Wednesdays, and Fridays he celebrated in the chapel of St Mary (receiving 66s. 8d. a year), and on Tuesdays, Thursdays, and Saturdays in the almonry chapel (for which he received a corrody in kind).[50] A third group of stipendiaries was important for the liberty they gave to their employers. In rectories, despite the cure of souls, the incumbent could be non-resident, provided that due provision was made to continue the services. Thus those wishing to study at university, or serve a patron, or even go on pilgrimage, would usually be rectors. During their absences they had to employ a priest to undertake their cure, acting as vicar or parochial chaplain.[51]

These parochial stipendiaries are largely unknown quantities, leaving little evidence of their conditions of employment or income. Parish subdeacons and deacons are particularly obscure. However, perhaps some special provision was made for them: there are occasional indications that at least the deacon had an allocation of tithe for his support.[52] Most were probably hired, perhaps on relatively low wages (which might be supplemented by other occupations within the parish, but outside the parochial structure). In 1402–3 the chapter of Hereford employed two deacons and two subdeacons (as well as two vicars) at Diddlebury (Shrops.), paying 43s. 4d. a year to the deacons, and 30s. a year to the subdeacons – respectively three-quarters and half of the annual stipends of the vicars.[53] For full chaplains the position is more complex. The actual parochial chaplains were probably hired – in the early sixteenth century about £4 was the standard salary in Yorkshire – but those taking on chapelries sometimes were given specified parts of the receipts. Officially the payments were limited by statute. After some upward drift, the rates were fixed under Henry V at 8 or 9 marks (£5 6s. 8d. or £6) for the parish priest, and 7 marks (£4 13s. 4d.) for other chaplains – reduced if this

---

[50] Timmins, *Reg. Chandler* [841], no. 288 (the role of deacon merges into that of parish clerk, causing some uncertainty – see Heath, *Parish clergy*, pp. 20, 84–5); Swanson, *Reg. Scrope*, i, nos. 486, 557–8; EDR, G/2/3, f. 27v.

[51] Rodes, *Ecclesiastical administration* [705], pp. 160–2.

[52] Timmins, *Reg. Chandler*, no. 71 (at p. 35) – unless this is payment for his role as parish clerk.

[53] HCA, R.462.

included board and lodging. This would have been just sufficient to live on for most of the period, although the Tudor inflation would have eroded the real value.[54] Precisely who paid the chaplains sometimes caused discord, especially if the church had been farmed out and the lessee had to provide the chaplain. Such a dispute erupted in 1519 over the chapel of Sandbeck in Maltby parish (Yorks.), between the prioress of Arthington and the abbey of Roche (as farmers). It is perhaps testimony to the availability of priests that one was found while the case was in progress to act as temporary chaplain there.[55]

Most chaplains were probably employed on an annual basis, although this would not preclude renewal of the agreements and therewith lengthy tenures. Other arrangements suggest greater stability of tenure, and probably greater continuity, as with the arrangements made by Selby abbey for the care of the chapels of Selby and Snaith (Yorks.) in, respectively, 1399 and 1401. Selby was leased to John de Blakewell, chaplain, for twelve years. He was to receive the oblations, lesser tithes, and obventions and mortuaries (with some exceptions, compensated for by a payment of 13s. 4d.); but from these he was to pay 7 marks to the abbey. He had to supply all the necessities for the services – bread, wine, lights, incense, etc. He effectively assumed full pastoral responsibility for the chapel, including finding a replacement if he was ill or unable to act. He was to lead a good life, paying a fine of 60s. to the abbot and convent for each conviction for misbehaviour. Roughly similar arrangements were made in the grant of Snaith to William de Croft, this time for ten years, or so long as he was capable of acting as chaplain. He received the oblations, obventions, and small tithes from four townships, with the tithes of hay from three of them (those of the fourth being covered by a payment of 8s. from the tithe-farmer there). However, mortuaries were excluded from his receipts. Outgoings (apart from the necessities for the services) included £10 to the abbey kitchener, 10s. for Peter's Pence and, after the first year of his tenancy, repairs for the chaplain's house. There was again a clause requiring good behaviour. In both cases, the chaplains had to find guarantors for their fulfilment of the agreements; for Snaith two individuals entered a warranty of 40 marks; while with Selby the chaplain and two companions provided a bond of £20.[56]

Outside the parish framework there were many opportunities for short-term clerical employment funded by the laity, so that the distribution of unbeneficed clergy may provide a rough guide to the distribution of lay

---

[54] 'The Fallow papers', pp. 247–51; 'East Riding clergy', pp. 71–9; Bowker, *Episcopal court book* [76], pp. 38–9; BIHR, CP.F.82; Heath, *Parish clergy*, pp. 22–4.

[55] BIHR, CP.G.93.

[56] BIHR, CP.F.82; Fowler, *Coucher book* [282], ii, pp. 382–3; Hingeston-Randolph, *Reg. Stafford* [398], pp. 115, 251; BL, MS Cotton Vit.E.xvi, ff. 145v–147r.

wealth.[57] Some remained in a sense parish-based; in certain cases, parishioners clubbed together to pay their local chaplain, if they felt the distance to their mother church was too great. Such arrangements were always rather insecure: the chapel's licence might be revoked, or the money run out. In 1473 the inhabitants of Haxby (Yorks.) complained that, although they had hitherto provided a chaplain at their own charge, they were now 'so constreyned with grete poueret' that they would need assistance to maintain the services.[58] Household chaplains might also contribute to parochial care. After 1350 the evidence suggests a great upsurge in the employment of domestic chaplains, with some episcopal registers containing runs of licences for private oratories and chapels. Sir Thomas More later complained that new ordinands generally found employment as such chaplains, ignoring the real demands of the church. Quantifying this sort of employment is impossible: the nobility must have employed several – the fifth Earl of Northumberland had eleven – while lesser mortals would have made do with one. They might share in parochial duties, especially if serving in a proper chapel, rather than just a room in a house. When it was rumoured that William de Sewardeby was constructing a chapel at his home at Sewardby (Yorks.) in 1414, the prior and convent of Bridlington sought to restrict him lest the local inhabitants should cease attending at Bridlington church, although Sewardeby's witnesses said that sometimes, in bad weather, they already used his existing chapel. Employment conditions for these household chaplains are obscure. Salaries in the Percy household – presumably including board – were 40s. for non-graduates, and 5 marks (66s. 8d.) for graduates. (Other specified clerics received different salaries, but these were the staple.)[59] The sum set for non-graduates is particularly intriguing. The tax rates established by the Canterbury convocation in 1419 ordered that chantry chaplains and the unbeneficed should contribute 6s. 8d. if their stipends exceeded 7 marks, or 40s. with food. Many of these last were presumably household chaplains. The 40s. figure is that frequently cited in titles for ordination in the early fourteenth century, either as patrimony or as pensions from laity. Possibly some of these represent household chaplaincies,

[57] McHardy, 'Ecclesiastics and economics', pp. 132–6.

[58] YML, L2(3)c, attached to f. 15v. For short-term episcopal licences for chapels where the chaplain was to be paid by the parishioners see Wilson, *Reg. Coventry and Lichfield, book 5* [916], pp. 6, 12, 42, 62–3, 70, 81, 83, 88: these might be revoked (the revocation at p. 70 seems to refer to the grant at p. 63).

[59] Heath, *Parish clergy*, p. 17; possibly the best series is contained in Lichfield registers of the later fourteenth century: Wilson, *Reg. Coventry and Lichfield, book 5*, pp. 6–89; LJRO, B/A/ 1/6, ff. 122r–137r, B/A/1/7, f. 124r–127r, 139v–159v, 195r–204r – later registers are less comprehensive in their recording; Mertes, 'Household as religious community' [581], p. 124; Percy, *Regulation and establishment* [651], pp. 47, 244, 311; BIHR, CP.F.66 (for another attempt to prevent the building of a chapel, EDR, F5/32, f. 75r–v).

thereby explaining why patrons sometimes refer to the ordinands as 'their' clerks.[60]

Other non-parochial employers of chaplains included guilds and fraternities, who needed priests for their religious purposes as collective chantries. Whilst some guilds were linked to chantries which were full benefices, such as those controlled by the guilds of Newark (Notts.), others were less definite, stipendiary appointments. One such group were the priests maintained by St Mary's guild in St Mary's chapel, Lichfield (Staffs.), probably on annual appointments.[61] Similar to these, or to the household chaplaincies, would be the unofficial but semi-permanent chantries, sometimes being based on property held by trustees, who paid an annual salary to the priest. Again, these cannot be quantified – concealment was integral to their foundation, to avoid the expenses imposed by the mortmain laws – but they could have been increasing in number between 1400 and 1540, to compensate for the apparent decline in the foundation of formal chantry benefices then.[62]

Finally, there come the mass of temporary chantries, established by individuals in their wills to provide prayers for their souls for limited period, as long as the money lasted. These, with other casual employment, may have provided the staple income for many of the unbeneficed clergy; they would also increase the numbers of clergy available as parochial auxiliaries. These chantries also provided an indirect way of increasing the church's endowment, as the testators were apparently expected to provide the necessities for the priest to celebrate with, as well as his salary.[63]

The scope for clerical employment was extensive, and the career ladder a long one. But clerical careers were not just there for the taking. Numerous forces affected them, and had to be taken into account by the would-be benefice-holder, because those forces would ultimately determine the level he reached in the ecclesiastical hierarchy.

2.4 CAREER PRESSURES AND PATRONAGE

The uncertain employment possibilities and fluctuating clerical recruitment created several tensions within the clergy's overall career structure.

[60] McHardy, 'Clerical taxation' [556], pp. 184–5; Swanson, 'Titles to orders', p. 244; for presentations of 'my clerk' see BL, Cotton ch.v.38, Cotton ch.xi.75, Add. ch. 19836. Some of the 'all found' clergy would be like the parish clergy of Bishop's Lynn (Norfolk), who received a cash stipend plus board in the priory of St Margaret: Owen, *Lynn* [630], p. 126.

[61] LJRO, D.30/XVIII, ff. 15v, 19r (the names of the unbeneficed clergy – as well as the guild chaplains they include parochial chaplains and other stipendiaries – scarcely change over the year gap between these two references); Thompson, *English clergy*, p. 134 n. 1.

[62] Kreider, *English chantries* [489], pp. 73, 76–84; Ives, *Common lawyers* [435], p. 430.

[63] Burgess, ' "For the increase of divine service" ' [105], pp. 51–4, 59–60, 62–4.

Lay involvement in the equations, bringing their own concerns, added further complications. One immediate tension arose between the bene- ficed and the laity as potential employers of the unbeneficed. The beneficed parochial clergy depended on the unbeneficed to ease their own burdens and to allow them to be non-resident. But the laity would be equally (if not more) anxious to exploit the unbeneficed, particularly to get their own souls out of Purgatory. The problems created by this competition were most apparent in the century immediately following the Black Death. Then, while the pressures forcing individuals to join the clergy may have been slackening, and recruitment levels dropped to their lowest point for the whole period, the demand for priestly services was almost insatiable. Contemporary piety is marked by an awareness of mortality, of the transitory nature of earthly existence, and a fear for the afterlife. Purgatory loomed large, demanding masses and prayers to liber- ate the trapped souls.[64] In such circumstances, the demand for chantry priests naturally burgeoned, perhaps especially as short-term appoint- ments. Given the fall in the supply of priests they could sell their services to the highest bidder – although not with total freedom. The chaplaincies and chantries would therefore have to pay more, provoking a reaction in attempts to limit the salaries which could be demanded. Such moves were ineffective. Complaints against greedy priests persisted, and for a while in the fifteenth century bishops sometimes forced unwilling priests to take lesser posts within the parishes (whether to assist the incumbent or replace him is not altogether clear). Pressures for wage increases for chantry and unbeneficed priests nevertheless continued: despite the legis- lation, the shortage of priests to satisfy demand inevitably caused salary increases, and by the 1450s testators were offering stipends of 10 marks or more to priests to pray for them. Such wage levels further increased the pressures on the lesser-paid posts, perhaps encouraging the process of amalgamation of both parishes and chantries.[65]

Some of these pressures doubtless declined as time passed, especially as the supply of priests improved from the 1480s. But the demand for their services remained high, and if those pressures had reduced, other changes still influenced career patterns. Economic factors perhaps necessitated the continued use of compulsion to ensure that under-paid jobs were taken, with several such orders appearing in Hugh Oldham's Exeter register between 1505 and 1519.[66] More important was the immense increase during the later medieval period in lay control over clerical careers. The

[64] See 6/1 at n. 4, 6/3 at nn. 110–15.
[65] Putnam, 'Maximum wage-laws' [678], pp. 17–32; Storey, 'Recruitment of English clergy', pp. 300–2; see also EDR, F5/32, f. 16v.
[66] DRO, Reg. Oldham, ff. 131v, 133v, 135v, 144v–145r, 151v, 163r.

opportunities for non-parochial clerical employment were mainly provided by the laity, in household chaplaincies, through foundation of and appointment to chantries established for both short and long term. Lay influences on the stipendiary chantries was probably more oppressive than on the benefices; but even they were under potentially strict supervision, reinforced by legal sanctions to ensure performance of obligations on pain of loss of endowment.[67] Whilst such lay involvement was increasing, clerical career prospects were being adversely affected by several other forces. The supply of benefices and their ability to sustain the clergy was being reduced; while increasing competition for benefices, and individual greed, allowed some clerics to exploit the tensions to their own advantage.

The forces affecting the ability of the benefices to sustain the clergy were mainly economic. The balance of tithes altered, requiring adjustments in provisions for vicarages, and undercutting some rectories; whilst reduced population lowered receipts from incidental income on which most stipendiaries to some extent depended. Changes in rent levels also affected receipts from glebe and benefice-farming. In some areas, depopulation and other changes even threatened to make the old parochial system irrelevant, leading to amalgamations of benefices, and a decline in employment prospects. Apart from the impact on the parishes, there was almost certainly a reduction in the number of 'perpetual' chantries: they fell into abeyance, or were moved, or wasted away. New foundations also declined, in favour of less formal arrangements outside the benefice system, under greater lay control and with less security of tenure.

Other institutional forces within the church were also affecting careers. The concern of religious bodies to maintain their economic standards, and of university benefactors to safeguard their foundations, contributed to the spread of appropriations during the period, with rectories being reduced to the status of vicarages.[68] Even more dangerous to individuals were two other movements – the growing demand for pensions levied on benefices,[69] and the spread of pluralism. The first was perhaps tolerable within the confines of an individual career: at least the benefice was there, with its freehold occupancy, and the pensioner might not enjoy his privilege for long. Pluralism, however, was more insidious, as it reduced the number of tenancies available by concentrating what there were into fewer hands.

The impact of pluralism on the medieval church was considerable, but hard to quantify. The accumulation of benefices by individual clerics had

---

[67] Farr, _Wyclif as reformer_ [267], pp. 104–9 (for a case, Thornley, _Year books, 11 Richard II_ [837], pp. 72–5).

[68] Above, at nn. 41–4.

[69] See at nn. 80–3; Emden, _Oxford_, i, pp. 176–7, 423–4; Fowler and Jenkins, _Reg. Sudburia_ [283], ii, pp. 164–5.

been noted for some time: in the thirteenth century Bogo de Clare gained an unenviable reputation for his collection of wealthy appointments; in the fourteenth William of Wykeham amassed a considerable number; while in the fifteenth Fulk de Bermyngham was castigated by Thomas Gascoigne for various offences, including his insatiable collecting of profitable benefices. Finally, just before the Reformation, the ringing titles of Thomas Wolsey provide a record of pluralism at the highest level, with his archbishopric of York (1514–20), successive commendatory bishoprics of Bath and Wells (1518–23), Durham (1523–9) and Winchester (1529–30), and commendatory possession of the abbey of St Albans (1521–30).[70] Such pluralism, however, was rarely universally excused. Whilst certain cases were considered less serious than others – where provision for parishioners and the cure of souls were unaffected, when restricted to sinecures like prebends in colleges and cathedrals – nevertheless it was still felt to be wrong. Pluralism (except where involving sinecures) required papal dispensation, and from John XXII's bull *Execrabilis* of 1317 action was taken against indiscriminate and unlicenced pluralism, culminating in an inquisition in 1366 which listed pluralists throughout the country.[71] But pluralism continued, at all levels, occasionally allowing one individual to corner virtually all the appointments in a church. In 1390 Richard de Rodyngton was not merely prebendal vicar of Sawley (Derby.) but also cantarist of St Mary in that church and the prebendary's vicar choral in Lichfield cathedral.[72] Individually, these posts probably paid little, but together they presumably provided a reasonable standard of living.

Attention is not usually directed at such low levels. Pluralism among the higher posts was more significant. Cardinals were the leading accumulators in the fourteenth century, taking advantage of their influence in the papal curia. Cardinal Annibaldo Gaetani (d.1350) at one point held the archdeaconries of Nottingham and Buckingham, the prebends of Corringham and Fittleworth (respectively in Lincoln and Chichester cathedrals), and the churches of Maidstone (Kent) and Grinstead (Sussex), all farmed for a total of 785 marks (£523 3s. 8d.). English clerics accumulated similarly profitable groupings. Alexander Lee's benefices in the late fifteenth century, worth 800 marks a year according to his opponent in a court case, included canonries and prebends in Howden Minster, York Minster, St Paul's London, St Stephen's Westminster, Lincoln cathedral, and Salisbury cathedral, with the rectories of Spofforth (Yorks.) and Houghton

---

[70] Fryde et al., *Handbook of British chronology* [286], pp. 242, 277, 283; *VCH, Herts.*, iv [869], p. 415; see also 1/1 at n. 15.
[71] Analysed in Godfrey, 'Pluralists in Canterbury' [302].
[72] LJRO, D.30/Hh4.

(Dur.) and the mastership of Sherburn hospital, Durham.[73] Such collections clearly curtailed the career opportunities of aspirant clerics, perhaps especially for prebends in cathedral churches and major collegiate institutions.

The propensity to pluralism is difficult to determine. Papal dispensations abound, but much depends on their implementation. In the fifteenth century, the extension of pluralism to vicarages and chantries, by dispensations to hold incompatible benefices, or by temporary unions of benefices by papal decree, would have removed many of the former safeguards against such multiple holdings and their impact on parish life.[74] Work on the years c.1490 to 1539 suggests that about 25 per cent of benefices were actually held by pluralists who represented only 10 per cent of the beneficed clergy.[75] The status of pluralists – usually men with good connections, royal employment, or (low on the list) university graduates – would again restrict the opportunities for the ordinary cleric.

Pluralism, and changes in benefice organization and occupancy, meant that the prospects of guaranteeing (or even securing) a stable ecclesiastical career were being steadily undermined. There is thus a contrast between the end of the fourteenth and fifteenth centuries. In 1400 there was a massive demand for clergy, unmet because of the lack of recruits, so that the career restrictions among the secular clergy, although obvious, were not particularly onerous. In 1500 the demand for clergy remained, but increased recruitment gave greater scope for the employers, and the chances of a secure career with a decent income were reduced by the economic problems confronting the church.

Once a cleric was beneficed, opportunities for relocation also affected his overall career. Pluralism and the possibilities of non-residence obviously affected how much the parishioners actually saw of their incumbents, but here the crucial point is the length of nominal tenure of a particular post. Perhaps there was less movement than might be supposed. Nominal tenures in three deaneries within the diocese of York (Buckrose, Craven, and Nottingham) where dates and reasons for successive institutions are discernible indicate a rough 50:50 split at the ten-year mark, with shorter tenures dividing roughly into thirds after two and five years, and tenures exceeding ten years dividing at the twenty-year point. The calculation is rough, and as it stands undoubtedly overstates the case for the lengthier tenures. Some correction reduces the tenures over twenty years to 18 per cent – a drop which still leaves a substantial number of the

---

[73] PRO, C270/17/20/7; BIHR, CP.F.288; see also Heath, *Parish clergy*, p. 51; for a similar accumulation, Thompson, *English clergy*, p. 122 n. 2.

[74] See n. 43.

[75] Lipkin, 'Pluralism in pre-Reformation England' [943], p. 164.

clergy with remarkably long stable service. Overall, the calculation indicates average tenure around fourteen years (see appendix A2).

Actual mobility depended on the aspirations and pressures affecting the individual cleric. The availability of an alternative post was self-evidently a major consideration. Those wishing to stay in a particular place would not need to move; those wishing to be non-resident and suitably beneficed would face no difficulties provided that the income was sufficient and the necessary licence was obtained. But if they had to move, to get closer to family and friends (as is sometimes suggested by comparisons of surname and place-name or by explicit statement), or local circumstances made movement expedient, or if they needed a different benefice to be non-resident, then transfer was possible, often by exchange. Consequently, alongside the evidence for stability of tenure stand indications of relatively frequent movement, reflected in the short tenures of some incumbents. Of course, short tenure need not mean movement: of the six appointments to the vicarage of St Mary, Nottingham, between 2 April 1347 and 14 March 1352, two (possibly three) followed deaths, although the others were exchanges. Some exchanges were quite complex, as individuals worked towards their desired goals. In 1417, for instance, John de Fridaythorp gradually manoeuvred himself from Sutton le Marsh (Lincs.) to Fridaythorpe in Yorkshire. He first exchanged his Lincolnshire benefice for Bradley (Derby.), whose patron was the dean of Lincoln. Within months, he further exchanged Bradley for the prebendal vicarage of Fridaythorpe. Each movement generated its own bureaucratic procedures, in three different dioceses.[76]

Although not evident in Fridaythorpe's case, monetary considerations doubtless played a part in many of the exchanges between benefice-holders. Rectories and vicarages varied considerably in value, and in their potential uses. Some of the recorded exchanges may effectively be sales: the financially embarrassed holder of a wealthy benefice exchanging for something poorer, but receiving a lump-sum payment to ease his predicament. Real evidence for this is virtually non-existent, although some exchanges did involve financial arrangements, with temporary sharing of pooled income, or compensation being paid to the man relinquishing the more valuable benefice.[77] There is, moreover, evidence of a fairly active market in benefices, sometimes organized through brokers known as chop-churches. Their trade smacked of simony, and incurred the wrath of bishops through to the sixteenth century. Nevertheless it was considered

---

[76] Storey, 'Ecclesiastical causes' [783], p. 245; Thompson, *English clergy*, pp. 107–9 (see also p. 76 n. 1); Train, *Clergy of central Nottinghamshire* [844], ii, pp. 28–9; LJRO, B/A/1/8, f. 10r–v.

[77] Storey, 'Ecclesiastical causes', p. 246; Heath, *Parish clergy*, pp. 45–7.

sufficiently honourable in the fifteenth century to serve as a trade qualification for identification purposes in legal documents.[78] The existence of so active a market makes the wariness which clerics sometimes reveal when receiving promotion or engaged in exchanges perfectly understandable: whilst anxious for advancement they were chary about accepting a non-existent vacancy, or of being cheated in exchanging for a fraudulently over-valued benefice. Their protests that they would return to the former benefice if thwarted, and their attempts to annul fraudulent exchanges, cast a disconcerting light on contemporary attitudes to benefices.[79]

Money issues also arose in resignations which were not exactly exchanges. Fifteenth-century incumbents often resigned and received a pension reserved from the benefice. Evidence for this is especially noticeable in Thomas Bourgchier's Canterbury register. Such a practice could be beneficial for the church: an individual wealthy benefice could support an additional cleric, while the problem of posts being ill-served by decrepit clerics could also be circumvented (although bishops might avoid that difficulty by appointing coadjutors to share the duties). The pension arrangements were not left purely to chance: negotiations preceded the resignation, and given the possibility of a conditional resignation, or even of its future retraction, the prospective incumbent – not to mention the pensioner – would wish to secure his position before taking any irrevocable steps.[80] Pensioners may sometimes have continued parish work, the retired incumbent remaining to assist his successor.

Not all pensions reflected such sensible arrangements. The possibility of securing a pension on a benefice invited exploitation without pluralism: when the income was obtainable without incurring responsibilities, why actually hold the benefices? Such considerations may have motivated M. John Topcliff and Thomas Dobson, rectors of Kirby Underdale (Yorks.)

---

[78] Storey, 'Ecclesiastical causes', pp. 246–9; see also Bishop Longland's condemnation of the benefice market in Blench, *Preaching in England* [68], pp. 239–40.

[79] For protests from victims of fraudulent exchanges, see Legge, *Anglo-Norman letters* [506], pp. 32–3; Fisher, Richardson, and Fisher, *Anthology* [276], no. 128. See also EDR, F5/32, ff. 81v–82v, F5/35, f. 177r; LAO, FOR.2, f. 15r; NRO, Will. Reg. Coppynger, f. 70[q]v. Bishops were probably equally wary about accepting a presentation which might be challenged: for an obligation to indemnify the bishop in the event of a challenge see LAO, FOR.3, f. 123r. (Not all protests reflect fraudulence, see also LJRO, B/A/1/2, f. 94v.)

[80] du Boulay, *Reg. Bourgchier* [233], pp. 220–1, 226–7, 247, 251, 255–6, 259, 269, 287, 341–2, 345–6, 351, 353, 355; Heath, *Parish clergy*, pp. 183–6; for the prior and convent of Ely as guarantors of a pension, EDR, G/2/3, ff. 72v–73r. While bishops licensed negotiations about pensions (e.g. DRO, Reg. Oldham, ff. 132r, 133v–134r, 135r, 139r, 144v–145r, 147v, 151v, 154r, 156v, 157v, 162v–163r, 165v; LAO, Add. Reg. 7, f. 118v, Bps Accts. 7, ff. 10v–11r) they also issued commissions to ensure that resignations did not involve simoniacal arrangements between an incumbent and his successor: CUL, MS Add. 7802, f. 36r; Hingeston-Randolph, *Reg. Brantyngham*, i, p. 165.

respectively in 1489 and 1531. Topcliff held the post for less than five months, Dobson less than four – but both secured pensions from the revenues when they resigned. One clear exploiter of pensions was Alan Percy, brother of an Earl of Northumberland. He resigned the vicarage of Giggleswick (Yorks.) in 1517, with a pension of £8 a year for life. Successive incumbents to such burdened benefices presumably took such pensions into account when deciding about accepting them – which meant that diocesan registrars would need to keep their records up to date. In 1553 Percy sought the arrears of his pension, unpaid since 1547. John Newell, the then vicar, asserted that the knew nothing of the pension, and had not been told of it by the registry (a possibility admitted by his opponents). In this instance, the situation was probably obscured by Giggleswick having been appropriated to a now-defunct religious house, with all the resulting upheavals of the Reformation. Nevertheless, the case illustrates the possible problems with pensions, and the exploitation of the pensioned benefices by long-lived pensioners. Percy survived until 1560; he could have extracted about £340 from Giggleswick, giving nothing in return.[81]

These pensions considerably distorted the real value of benefices, and affect comments on career patterns. The effect could be extreme: in 1525–6 two prebends at Howden and Beverley were quite worthless to their occupants (unless they received the fruits of residence), the whole income being diverted in pensions to previous incumbents. Elsewhere in Yorkshire at that date, pensions could well exceed the incumbent's share of the revenues – he being left with the burden of collection, and liable to distraint and other legal processes to secure payment. At Brainsby, the rector received £4 8s. 6d., while the pensioner took £10; and at Cherry Burton the rector had £8 while the pensioner took £12. Pensions were perhaps more commonly less than the incumbent's portion. In the 1520s, at South Cave, the vicar and pensioner received £3 each; at Mappleton the vicarage was worth £4, against the pension at 26s. 8d.[82] The processes establishing these pensions need further research, as holders of wealthy benefices with patronage connections could exploit those contacts at the expense of the growing numbers of recruits to the clerical profession, all anxious for security of tenure even at a reduced income. There were considerable differences among the incomes of the beneficed, and possibly considerable poverty. On average, parochial benefices were apparently not well paid: the majority were worth less than the £10 which has been assessed as providing a reasonable income, and which would confer a social position among those recently identified as the 'parish gentry'. The financial rewards of service were not, therefore, likely to encourage the 'best' men to seek parishes; but the multiplicity of variables in the calculations preclude any certainty. But poor benefices did not necessarily mean poor priests: many had additional sources of income and wealth, including inherited lands and goods. Clerical involvement in leasing (perhaps especially their farming of rectories and vicarages) could more than compensate for the apparently low incomes produced by their official posts.[83]

The abilities and quality of the clergy also need to be assessed, matters which vexed contemporary laity and ecclesiastical authorities as much as later historians. Unfortunately, it is not absolutely clear just what was required of would-be clerics. The pre-ordination examinations which are known to have occurred yield few indications of what was demanded, or how effectively the candidates were assessed. The monitions issued to ordinands specify only technical qualifications: they should be free-born, legitimate, unmarried, not bigamists (not have married twice, or have married a widow), not be homicides, not be seeking advancement by simony or fraud, and have sufficient title (means of support) or appropriate letters dimissory if being ordained outside their native diocese. There is no mention of ability or vocation. Commissions to examine, and grants of letters dimissory, occasionally refer to *scientia* (knowledge) in the examination of habits and character, but this adds little to the overall picture. The levels remain vague; and technically, beyond the status qualifications (many of which might be circumvented by dispensation), all that was required was a good reputation in the neighbourhood.[84] Some degree of literacy was essential – Latinity was a clear requirement as the language of liturgy and ecclesiastical administration – and was tested, as bishops sometimes ordered individuals to receive further instruction. But the process could be outflanked by giving false (or ignorant) statements about age, birth, and status, or by collusive action to present a fictitious title. Some received orders almost accidentally, joining the queue during the ceremony and receiving promotion. The church's precise attitude to examination is hard to elucidate; many of those who cheated at ordination are known because they were found out and confessed; and the authorities were certainly anxious to ensure that clerics were properly ordained, checking credentials at visitations and occasionally chasing up those

[83] Heath, *Parish clergy*, p. 173; Zell, 'Economic problems' [937], pp. 33–5; Pound, 'Clerical poverty' [669]; for 'parish gentry' Given-Wilson, *English nobility* [300], pp. 71–4.

[84] LJRO, B/A/1/1, ff. 134v, 136r, 174r–v; EDR, F5/32, f. 14v, F5/35, f. 169r; Richter and Friedberg, *Corpus iuris canonici*, i, col. 87; Johannes de Burgo, *Pupilla oculi*, 7.ii.G; Boyle, 'Aspects of clerical education' [81], pp. 19–20; Swanson, 'Titles to orders', p. 240.

whose status was uncertain. Yet it remains unclear how seriously the responsibilities of examination were shouldered; the authorities may have preferred to leave the ordination examination to others (at least, whilst there was a shortage of priests), saving detailed checks on quality for those seeking institution to benefices. Nevertheless, if standards had slipped in the fifteenth century, the exhortations to improvement in the pre-ordination sermon delivered *c.*1510 by William Melton, Chancellor of York Minster, may reflect a concern among catholic reformers to restore some strictness to the demands of the ordination system.[85]

But what happened after ordination? Most clerics remained unbeneficed, and therefore avoided further detailed examination by the diocesan officials. Those presented to benefices were subject to examination, partly a technical examination of qualifications at the inquests into vacancies and patronage which are sometimes found in episcopal registers; but also formal examination of learning and theological abilities.[86] The mass of the unbeneficed clerics pose the greatest problem, with their sporadic appearances in the records. It was probably for them, as they shouldered responsibility for much of the parochial work, that the succession of manuals for clergy were written, in English and Latin, in the fourteenth and fifteenth centuries, together with the series of sermons which could be drawn on throughout the year, typified by John Mirk's *Festial*.[87] These are rather basic works, but the demands on the unbeneficed were not essentially theological. Their main function was pastoral, caring for the parishioners and the benefice; and also supplicatory, offering the masses to ensure repose for the dead and security for the living. There would be little reason to demand high levels of education and theological awareness from most of the clergy. As usual, however, the available evidence is inconclusive. Whilst there is considerable support for the denunciation of the clergy's intellectual attainments, there is equally evidence of learning, if the books listed in their wills provide any guide. Unfortunately, in the early sixteenth century (which provides so much of the condemnatory evidence) the demands made on the clergy were changing: perhaps the complaints then reflect not a lack of ability, but a lack of malleability, and a failure to adapt to the demands of reforming catholicism, or the changes in emphasis which came with Protestantism. The general clerical outlook may have been outdated, and inadequate for the changing world, but in the

---

[85] E.g. Marrett, *Reg. Wakefeld* [575], p. xxv and refs.; Robinson, *Reg. Melton, vol. 2* [701], no. 164; EDR, F5/32, f. 15v; BIHR, DC/AB.1, f. 233r; Swanson, 'Titles to orders', pp. 239–41 (but see EDR, F5/32, f. 14v); William de Melton, *Sermo exhortatorius* [580].

[86] Swanson, 'Learning and livings' [801], pp. 11–12 and refs.

[87] Pantin, *The English church* [637], pp. 195–218; Erbe, *Mirk's Festial* [257]; see also Fletcher, 'Unnoticed sermons' [278].

circumstances that is a comment on relative speed of change, not an absolute judgement on quality.[88]

The late medieval clergy were most often attacked on moral and practical grounds. Suitability for office tended to be viewed in terms of character rather than intellectual ability. Visitation and court reports thus deal with neglect of services (sometimes by spending too long in taverns), with sexual misdemeanours, and with non-residence, rather than theological inspiration. Accusations regarding sexual activity crop up with depressing regularity. In such cases one recidivist makes more impact than those only once accused (and whose guilt cannot be taken for granted); and they in turn are more obvious than those not charged with anything. Nevertheless, many clerics clearly found it impossible to maintain their vows of celibacy; evidence of clerical paternity is widespread, with all ranks from parish clergy to bishops fathering offspring.[89]

Non-residence and its possible attendant ills, either the neglect of services, or the provision of unsuitable vicars, was perhaps more serious for souls. It was the non-provision of a vicar for his prebend in Westbury-on-Trym college (Glos.) in 1366 which brought John Wyclif to the attention of the church authorities; and concern with similar neglect appears in virtually all the sources. Whilst prepared to license non-residence, the bishops regularly recalled unlicensed incumbents to their benefices. Yet non-residence was something of a necessity, allowing the bureaucrats to do their jobs, providing maintenance for university students, and freeing the dependents of the great to attend their masters, let alone covering absence on pilgrimage, for health reasons, and a variety of other justifiable causes. Occasionally clerics needed to be non-resident to escape local difficulties: an early fourteenth-century Berkshire incumbent sought a non-residence licence for study not for any love of learning, but to escape an overweening patron. The problem of casual unlicensed non-residence may have been growing towards the Reformation, with some of the authorities turning a blind eye to the resultant abuses; but its occurrence also reflected the church's economic difficulties. The abilities demanded of the locum clergy were probably not particularly great (and if they were hired by benefice-farmers, their acceptability possibly depended more on demanded levels of payment than pastoral qualifications), being restricted to saying the services and basic pastoral care of the parishioners. If they also played football with the villagers, this need not be a cause for concern, unless linked with other faults.[90]

[88] Tanner, *Church in Norwich*, pp. 35–42; Moran, 'A "common-profit" library' [596]; Heath, *Parish clergy*, pp. 73–5, 87–9, 91–3.

[89] For Wolsey's offspring, Pollard, *Wolsey* [663], pp. 306–12; for other bastards, Heath, *Parish clergy*, p. 106, and generally ibid., pp. 104–12, 115–19. For charges against clergy, see e.g. Purvis, *Mediaeval act book* [676]; Wood-Legh, *Kentish visitations* [922]; Windsor, XI.K.6.

[90] McFarlane, *Wycliffe and non-conformity* [547], p. 14; Heath, *Parish clergy*, pp. 49–69, 111;

However, the ecclesiastical authorities were worried for the clergy's status, and maintaining the 'dignity' of their orders. They therefore ordered clerics not to treat their vicarages as taverns, not to engage in rural occupations like digging, and not to entangle themselves in medical matters (especially matters gynaecological).[91] The laity may have been more concerned about quality than status. Founders of chantries sometimes wrote into their foundation deeds what they required of the priests. They specified not only services and prayers, but also general levels of conduct. Thus, at Bolton on Dearne (Yorks.) in 1400, any degeneracy by the chaplain, or neglect of his duties for eight days, would be the basis for legal proceedings, resulting in deprivation if he had not reformed within a month. Even more precise were the ordinances for the establishment on the bridge at Wakefield (Yorks.), as laid down by the Duke of York's charter in 1398. This again demanded maintenance of services (unless with justifiable excuse), threatening deprivation for failure to maintain the goods of the chantry, criminal activity, irregularity, bodily deformity, moral laxity, and participation in unworthy or forbidden activities.[92]

Going beyond the precepts to actuality is another matter. Occasionally – but rarely – unfit priests were deprived of their benefices; but there were obviously difficulties in implementing this procedure. A freehold right would not be extinguished without opposition, and those responsible (ecclesiastical authorities or, in some cases, lay overseers) were probably reluctant to expel a priest except on very strong grounds. The rulers of Beverley (Yorks.), responsible for Kelk's chantry, had some difficulties with John Esthorp, one of the foundation's two chantry priests, from 1439 to 1452. At one point he seems to have been replaced, for undeclared reasons, but was soon reinstated. Later, he received a third warning: any further trouble would mean dismissal. Yet, scarcely a year later, when that further trouble arose (its nature unstated), he suffered merely a temporary loss of income, and was apparently still serving the chantry at his death. Similarly, when the vicar of Driffield (Yorks.) was before the dean and chapter of York in 1469 on charges which included his unsuitability to serve his cure, an inquisition found him definitely unfit (*inhabilis*) but it is doubtful if anything came of it. Once in a benefice, removal was difficult, although some clerics may have gone by arranged resignations rather than enforced deprivations.[93]

Bowker, *Secular clergy*, pp. 87–103, 105–9; Hill, 'Berkshire letter book' [389], p. 19; Zell, 'Clergy of Kent', pp. 520–1.

[91] LJRO, B/A/1/14ii, f. 18v; BIHR, DC/AB 1, ff. 69r, 195v; YML, M2(1)f, f. 42r; LAO, FOR.2, ff. 23v–24r, FOR.3 f. 32v.

[92] Swanson, *Reg. Scrope*, i, nos. 186, 249.

[93] EDR, F5/32, f. 31v; du Boulay, *Reg. Bourgchier*, pp. 278, 283, 287, 316; Heath, *Parish clergy*, p. 114; HCRO, DD.BC/II/7/1, ff. 34v, 36r, 69v, 74v, 106v; BIHR, DC/AB.1, ff. 192r, 193v; BL, MS Add. 14848, f. 185r–v.

While the complaints about the quality of the clergy were sometimes directed at the beneficed, the main target was probably the unbeneficed, those now traditionally lumped together as a 'clerical proletariat'. Their identification is to some extent a matter of definitions. One false lead is the existence of the criminous clerks. As few of these criminals were actually in holy orders, and many may have been foisted on to the ecclesiastical authorities by the secular judges, they are really outside the scope of the discussion. Obviously, there were some criminal clergy (deficiencies among the records of the secular courts prevent proper judgement); but they were probably few in reality, and in a sense which contemporaries would have judged criminal: in York records of criminous clerks between 1450 and 1532, only six out of sixty-two offenders whose occupations are stated were actually clerics.[94] The definition as a clerical proletariat might be based on overall status: the drifting lower levels of the church, living if not from hand to mouth, then from death to death, literally singing for their suppers as one series of post-mortem masses followed another, or collecting whatever funeral doles were going. It could also be a definition of abilities, a comment on their capacities for the priesthood, and level of education. It is this definition which has recently been challenged in terms of its applicability to the chantry priests surveyed in the 1540s. Whatever the definition, the existence of an economically depressed group, living on casual incomes (if they had any livelihood at all) can hardly be denied. The unbeneficed included a pool of clerics available for short-term hire outside the normal patronage structure. London was one of the centres – perhaps the centre – for such short-term hiring, with the Pastons for example seeking a temporary caretaker for their vicarage of Oxnead (Norfolk), and another priest being hired in London in the 1460s on a one-year contract as a stipendiary chantry priest in York. Complaints of ecclesiastical authorities against the trading and labouring activities of certain clerics, and occasional tantalizing references to clerks in industrial records – such as the appointment of the chaplain John Edwyn as searcher of the bowstringmakers' craft at York in 1484 – suggest that many clergy may have supplemented or substituted clerical incomes from more worldly sources.[95]

A crucial stage in any cleric's life was old age. Resignation documents often make the point that, unless given a pension, the quondam incum-

---

[94] Heath, *Parish clergy*, pp. 127–8; see also 4/3 at nn. 1–29.

[95] The parishioners of St Mary, Dover, complained in 1512 of the uncertain presence of their priest on Wednesdays and Fridays 'if there be any minde within the toune where oure curate may get a grote' (Wood-Legh, *Kentish visitations*, p. 132 – but he may just have been greedy); Scarisbrick, *Reformation* [748], p. 167; Davis, *Paston letters* [197], i, p. 184; Neilson, *Year books, A.D. 1470* [603], pp. 164–5; Swanson, 'Craftsmen and industry', p. 287; see also n. 91.

bent would be reduced to beggary. Even allowing for exaggeration in such declarations, the decrepit unbeneficed clerk would clearly be in a potentially parlous position: should he become incapable of earning a living, for whatever reason, he would sink into poverty without other means of support. The existence of hospitals specifically for decayed clerics, such as St Mary's Bootham, York, testifies to an awareness of this problem; while its existence is manifest in Westminster in the 1520s, where vagabond clerics were amongst those accommodated in the hospital of St Mary Rounceval, almost literally being taken in off the streets.[96]

Judging the quality of the late medieval clergy is complicated by the varied demands made on them. A cleric was a normal person – and as such possibly responsible for patrimonial and other property, with all its cares – but with particularly clerical duties. These were primarily spiritual, and the cleric with cure of souls was expected to care for his parishioners. Moreover, if he was beneficed he had a major obligation to the benefice itself, as a piece of property to be transferred intact to his successors. The moment of transfer of benefices was frequently a period of anxiety, with disputes over possession being not infrequent, with accusations of cheating in fraudulent exchanges, and conflicts over the state of the property with claims for dilapidations against the previous incumbent or his representatives. Failure to maintain the property was also a concern of the church authorities: if the incumbent or his farmer did not make repairs when ordered to, the revenues might well be sequestrated until he did.[97]

The benefice, whatever its form, integrated the incumbent into his locality, and necessitated contacts with his neighbours. These contacts could all too easily become conflicts, over property or income. Property disputes might well lead to violence, several clerics being forced to secure papal dispensations in consequence. Hugh Martill, rector of Tollerton (Notts.), obtained such a dispensation in 1399 for his part in the death of John Smytheman of Ruddington, which had resulted from a fight between them over some land belonging to the church. Even without a death, the case might still go to court. In 1528 a smouldering row over property at Tickhill (Yorks.) exploded, with the chaplain, Nicholas Kendall, violently assaulting one of his parishioners. His supposed words to his victim clearly reveal the source of the trouble: 'False horeson, thou shall not commande me to make hegges or gappis, nor thy maister. And if thou dar tare me thow shall abye.' Small wonder in such circumstances that relations between incumbent and parishioners could be fragile; although the

---

[96] See n. 80; *VCH, Yorkshire*, iii [877], p. 345; Heath, *Parish clergy*, p. 186; Orme, 'A medieval almshouse' [621]; Rosser, 'Vill of Westminster' [716], pp. 108–9.

[97] BIHR, CP.F.125; EDR, F5/33, f. 25r–v; Heath, *Parish clergy*, pp. 140–1; Timmins, *Reg. Chandler*, p. xxix and refs.; Horn, *Reg. Hallum*, no. 1093.

thanks reportedly expressed to his parishioners for their support during his lengthy incumbency by Leonard de Hedon at Hinderwell (Yorks.) in 1403 suggest that hostility was not inevitable.[98]

Alongside the responsibilities of property, there were often other obligations. Chantries especially tended to have additional duties imposed on their incumbents, such as schoolmastering or care for almshouses.[99] These produced their own financial pressures, and demanded different forms of pastoral care. If engaged on domestic bureaucracy, the demands of such service would also need to be taken into account. Rarely, indeed, could an incumbent concern himself solely with his religious obligations, and the manifold tensions in his position were often irreconcilable. That his income often derived from tithes placed the parish priest in an invidious position: his main weapon to enforce payment was excommunication, but was such action reconcilable with his pastoral responsibilities and duties? The incumbent would also have to worry about providing chaplains for dependent chapelries (and defend himself against attempts by parishioners to force him to provide more chaplains than were required), and generally act to maintain and defend his property. He would need to worry about his relationships with his parishioners and their lords, and his rivalry with other clerics – especially any who intruded into parts of the parish and attempted to claim quasi-parochial autonomy. At Kirby Overblow (Yorks.) the vicar, Richard Pole, thus had to act against Simon Paw after he started celebrating at Righton chapel without any justification (a case which Pole won). Similarly, Thomas Parcor intruded at Whitwell Luge in Slaidburn parish (Yorks.) in the late fifteenth century, costing the rector of Slaidburn a considerable sum in lost tithes as Parcor sought to create an independent rectory with himself as incumbent.[100] Additionally, an incumbent would also need to consider his family responsibilities. Hospitals were perhaps particularly vulnerable to their wardens' kinfolk; Graystoke college (Cumb.) certainly suffered from them.[101]

Insecure as life was among the unbeneficed, their universal aspiration must have been to gain the freehold right and secure tenure of a benefice. Achieving this was no easy matter. Much depended on connection; indeed, the all-pervading force was patronage. As there were, obviously, fewer patrons than aspiring protégés, gaining a patron was a major consideration.

To some extent, ecclesiastical positions were available to those who could afford them. A striking feature of the late medieval English church is

---

[98] Swanson, *Reg. Scrope*, i, no. 492; BIHR, CP.F.11, CP.G.137.

[99] Kreider, *English chantries*, pp. 59–68.

[100] BIHR, CP.G.240, CP.G.870; see also EDR, F5/32, f. 88v.

[101] BIHR, CP.F.180.

the role of money in changing tenurial patterns. For all incumbents, actually obtaining a benefice involved paying fees to the diocesan administration, to those involved in arranging the institution and induction, and presumably to others responsible for the documentation. What evidence there is suggests that institution and induction would cost at least 6s. 8d. each, possibly as much as 13s. 4d. Whilst not hefty sums, they were not inconsiderable, especially if other demands were also made of the new incumbent.[102]

The fees may be regarded as the acceptable face of benefice-hunting, but other payments were more dubious. The cleric who paid a friend 6s. 8d. to recommend his appointment as a parochial chaplain may not have committed simony; but the transaction which obtained the rectory of Wigan (Lancs.) for Oliver Langton in the 1450s raises suspicions. His brother and precursor as rector bequeathed a piece of plate to the patron of the living, on condition that Oliver succeeded as rector or received a pension. Admittedly, there was a let-out clause: if Oliver was unsuccessful, the patron still got the piece, but should pay £10 for it. Even more dubious are some of the other transactions which suggest trafficking in benefices; especially resignations which might have been purchased. The activities of chop-churches must have been close to the limit, at times reducing the benefice to an economic rather than spiritual unit. Exchanges and resignations in return for pensions also approach the frontier. Some of the discussions about pensions may have been illicit, as is suggested for Hinderwell in the early fifteenth century. But formal accusations of simony are rare, although William Curtèys, abbot of Bury St Edmunds, had to issue a public defence of his predecessor against charges of selling the nomination to a benefice for £40. Admissions of simony were even rarer.[103]

Simony could be interpreted in more than monetary terms. If the benefice was seen as an end in itself, rather than a post with responsibilities, then for the moralistic deliberate exploitation of the patronage system might be equivalent to a simoniacal purchase. In one of his anecdotes, the author of Dives and pauper (written about 1410) told of two parsons receiving their Last Judgement. One was condemned for paying £40 to have his church; the other was similarly condemned even though he had not paid money, but had served the patron for seven years 'in hope & in comenaunt to han þin chirche' – earning a living was just as bad as buying one.[104]

---

[102] For general comment, Heath, *Parish Clergy*, pp. 42–3.

[103] BIHR, CP.F.11, CP.F.82; CUL, MS Mm.I.48, pp. 8–9 (the transaction involving Thomas Cromwell and the benefice of 'Danam' [Ches.] mentioned in Dowling, *Humanism* [228], pp. 87–8, also arouses suspicion); Rodes, *Ecclesiastical administration*, pp. 118–19; BL, MS Add. 14848, f. 106r; Heath, *Parish clergy*, pp. 36–8; see also n. 80.

[104] Barnum, *Dives and pauper* [41], 1/ii, pp. 193–4.

The extent of such quasi-simony is unassessable. Moreover, with the absence of any impersonal system to secure promotion for the worthy within the church, to condemn such arrangements was simply unrealistic. There were – with few exceptions – no other ways of obtaining a benefice than securing a patron's notice; and a patron was unlikely to grant a benefice to a particular individual for purely altruistic motives.

One possible way to evade this bottleneck might have been by education, especially at university. It would be pleasant, but invalid, to see the flocks of students converging on Oxford and Cambridge (as well as those receiving education abroad) as evidence of love of learning for its own sake, to be briefly nurtured before the recipients went out to raise the cultural consciousness of their compatriots. But education, learning, degrees, were not an experience to be taken lightly, and rarely for anything as ethereal as moral improvement. Career patterns, career prospects, could be influenced by education and the connections established at university; and it was doubtless as a means to that end that most students – and their parents and sponsors – viewed the years spent in study. At the same time, however, the truly academic retained an ambivalent attitude. For they, too, needed patronage – and as they convinced themselves that their studies were beneficial to the church, so they considered themselves entitled to some sort of pre-emptive right to its benefices, demanding patronage rather than receiving it passively.

Between 1350 and 1430, such aspirations were rudely shattered. For several reasons it seems that the universities experienced a crisis of patronage: it was much more difficult for their members either to obtain the type of benefice which would permit non-residence for continued study, or to re-enter the patronage structure after their university experience to obtain their first benefice. The evidence requires further analysis, but in the fifteenth century graduates were seemingly in competition with others to secure even fairly lowly places in the ecclesiastical hierarchy. Although they continued to dominate the higher ranks, and may have improved their position there as a result of administrative changes in the century, with the increase in lay education and the secularization of bureaucracies breaking the connection between state service and clerical careers, they were probably less likely than before to gain immediate employment as rectors. Graduates now had to work their way up from posts as vicars, preachers, chantry priests, and parochial curates. Their relative position paradoxically appears to have improved towards the end of the fifteenth century, despite the increased recruitment into the church: perhaps then education was considered a positive benefit.[105]

---

[105] Swanson, 'Universities, graduates, and benefices', pp. 31–60; Swanson, 'Learning and livings', pp. 98–9.

Whatever the fate of the graduates, how far was it due to their being graduates? The qualities which made an individual attractive to a patron were many, and to take one – education – out of context is to mistreat the evidence. Any general attempt at perspective is doomed by the individuality of each specific appointment, and the failings of the evidence. Usually, all that is revealed is that someone presented a candidate to a benefice; the underlying motives are scarcely ever indicated.

Yet patronage was ubiquitous. Nothing worked without it, however obtained. But its workings need not be obvious, and may not appear in surviving records. Its force was most evident when an individual obtained a benefice; but there were many other opportunities for its operation.

Most would-be clerics first confronted the obstacle of patronage at ordination. For a serf the lord's goodwill (or cupidity) was needed even before ordination to secure manumission to take orders, bastards needed connections to obtain the necessary dispensation, and everyone needed a title. That need for a guarantee of financial security frequently involved third-party support, usually financial. Anyone able to underwrite such an income would clearly be an influential force in the subsequent career. The few surviving lay letters of presentation for orders (from the early fourteenth century) sometimes refer to the candidate as the sponsor's own clerk, while the ordination lists and other material occasionally show that the individuals concerned were being patronized by the assignment of a livelihood (or possibly a promise of employment as a domestic chaplain). Less expensive patronage might consist of letters of recommendation, such as those issued by a Berkshire cleric in the early fourteenth century, or use of influence in favour of ordinands which William Melton condemned around 1510.[106]

After ordination, employment needs again made patronage a prime consideration, often perhaps continuing connections established earlier. The increasing foundation of private chapels by the gentry and others clearly made them very important potential employers, and thus effective patrons. The surviving material on these private chapels, even where apparently full, may seriously understate the scope of such extrabeneficial patronage.[107] There were in addition all the other short-term or

---

[106] Swanson, 'Titles to orders', pp. 239–40, 243–4; Hill, 'Berkshire letter book', pp. 15–17, 22; Melton, *Sermo exhortatorius*, Aii^v.

[107] In BIHR, CP.F.66, witnesses, asked how long William Sewardeby had had his private chapel, gave replies suggesting anything between fifteen and fifty years, but with no explicit reference to documentry evidence. The licences for Lichfield diocese reveal gaps which are probably due to unregistered renewals. Sir John de Gresley thus received two-year licences for named oratories in 1372, for all oratories in 1378, and for all oratories in 1384. The years apparently unlicensed are unlikely to have seen a cessation of services (Wilson, *Reg. Coventry and Lichfield, book 5*, pp. 61–2, 74, 88).

unendowed clerical posts, where connections might again come into play. Testators sometimes ordered that when prayers for their souls were being arranged the employment should be given to a named individual, presumably already well known to them.[108] Not all owners of private chapels were patrons of fully-fledged benefices, but they did provide an entree to a nexus of connections which could eventually result in a benefice. Especially with the development of feoffment to uses, and shared patronal rights via guild membership or parochial organizations (which often controlled nominations to chantries), such individual connections could bring the aspirant incumbent into contact with those capable of giving him a benefice, and possibly providing 'further references' to support his claims.[109] Household employment might also be a springboard for transfer to another patron with greater patronage resources, or a move to the administrative classes at Westminster, and access to the fund of royal patronage.

The mechanics of patronage were straightforward. Usually the patron presented the candidate for the benefice to the bishop, who, being satisfied of his suitability, and the legality of his presentation, would then institute and order the induction. Where the bishop was patron, immediate collation would take place; while if the patron failed to present within a certain time, the bishop gained the patronage for that turn by lapse.[110] However, the neat theory contrasted with the complexity of reality, thus complicating any detailed consideration of patronage in operation. For the patronage of ecclesiastical benefices is inseparable from other forces operating in late medieval England, involving considerations of bastard feudalism, of papal power, of growing monarchical power, as well as changing attitudes towards the benefice itself. Ownership of advowsons was an important prop for local political power, making their exploitation as significant as any other force in establishing local dynasties.[111] Clerical patronage cannot be separated from the patronage operating throughout medieval society, and the clientage relationships which permeated lay society. Patronage was a commodity, transferable between patrons, whilst reflecting links between clients and their protectors. For the king, its use, whoever it rewarded, was just like the grant of any other honour – and perhaps rather cheaper than a secular privilege. Elsewhere, the Earl of Stafford's 'good lordship' towards Sir John Stanley found expression in 1433 in his support of Stanley's candidate for the rectory of Winwick (Lancs.), pressuring the Bishop of Lichfield to recognize what amounted to usurpation, and parallel-

---

[108] E.g. Dobson, 'Foundation of perpetual chantries' [214], p. 37. For an alternative, the bequest of an annuity until beneficed, Zell, 'Clergy of Kent', p. 523.

[109] E.g. Hill, 'Berkshire letter book', pp. 15–16.

[110] Barnum, *Dives and pauper*, i, p. 354.

[111] E.g. Hosker, 'Stanleys of Lathom' [414], pp. 214–27.

ing any other statement of 'bastard feudal' relationships.[112] Consequently, those with patronage were themselves open to importunity and aggression. The prior and convent of Durham throughout the period received numerous letters advocating the appointment of the senders' clients to the abbey's benefices. Such pressures might be difficult to spurn; and even if the demands could be played against each other, might still seriously reduce the patronage available for the house's own adherents. This correspondence reflects complex relationships and connections. Thus, a letter of Richard III to the Bishop of Lichfield about the next vacancy of Northenden (Lancs.) was seemingly written on behalf of Sir Randolph Brantingham – the king's own clients latched on to his power to invade the patronage resources of third parties.[113] The religious institutions and their patronage were probably most affected by such machinations: faced with growing threats to the patronage which they controlled directly, the lay gentry perhaps sought to appropriate the patronage of the religious corporations for their own use. In this sense fourteenth-century opposition to papal provisions, although reflecting clerical concerns, and although formally constructed by the crown, equally reflects gentry determination to exclude from the patronage system a competitor (the pope) whose canonical powers gave his protégés precedence over all others, and limited the gentry's ability to satisfy their own dependants. However, the squeeze on patronage was not restricted to religious institutions: similar correspondence was also addressed to lay patrons.[114]

The patronage system changed considerably between 1350 and 1540. Papal patronage was virtually extinguished as an independent force, with a corresponding expansion of royal patronage so that by the end of the period the crown was undeniably the most significant individual patron. During these years patronage also became more obviously a marketable commodity, and the notion of 'corporate patronage' by religious institutions may well have collapsed. The opportunities for exploiting ecclesiastical patronage for purposes other than gaining a benefice also apparently increased. It may have been treated more seriously than before as a piece of property and collection of rights, and given the developing tensions within society possibly became more a cause of conflict, leading to cases in both secular and ecclesiastical courts. Only the type of person patronized may not have changed. Those most likely to acquire a benefice remained

---

[112] Lytle, 'Patronage patterns' [540], pp. 115–21; Hosker, 'Stanleys of Lathom', pp. 220–3, 227–9.

[113] Halcrow, 'Position and influence' [340], pp. 79–86; Donaldson, 'Sponsors, patrons, and presentations to benefices' [226], esp. pp. 173–5 (see also Dobson, *Durham priory* [216], p. 163); Horrox and Hammond, *Harleian manuscript 433* [412], i, pp. 61–2; Hill, 'Berkshire letter book', pp. 17, 22.

[114] Wood-Legh, *Perpetual chantries*, pp. 73–4.

those with connections: the gentry appointed their own relatives to the family living – nepotism remained a strong force – while the well-born cleric could virtually command patronage. Those likely to benefit their patrons were also promoted: the bureaucrats, and the lawyers. Usually, however, we cannot even guess why individuals were promoted; but particular careers and individual patrons do suggest the forces at work well enough.[115]

During the fourteenth century the English church remained, like the rest of the church, open to papal intervention in the succession to benefices. From about 1250, the papacy had claimed a developing right to provide its nominees to benefices, emphasizing the pope's status as 'universal ordinary'. The claims were not unopposed, with complaints from individuals like Robert Grosseteste, or the greater Parliamentary protests at Carlisle in 1307. But little practical was done in England until 1343. An ordinance of that year, with the Statute of Provisors of 1351 and other later legislation, severely curtailed papal provisions to benefices.[116]

The mechanics of papal provision depended on the type of benefice involved. Provisions *in forma speciali* actually named the benefice, being usually used for appointments to cathedral prebends and equivalent offices. Provisions *in forma pauperum* (giving the grantee precedence over other candidates for a benefice in the gift of a named patron) were much more common, but generally less effective. In England, a crucial point was that provisions did not apply to benefices in lay patronage: the pope only claimed to pre-empt religious institutions. Where a provision was granted for a benefice in lay patronage, the grant would not operate.[117]

Although theoretically the pope could provide anyone he chose to a benefice, exposing the English church to exploitation by foreign clerics, in fact foreign interests were limited. There were, of course, some foreigners – Italian and French cardinals were relatively common cathedral prebendaries in the 1300s; and some (like Cardinal Annibaldo Gaetani) held substantial collections of benefices.[118] In 1379 the cardinals supporting the antipope Clement VII lost their English benefices, but the popes recognized by England continued nominating Italians to benefices, creating curial successions markedly different from those accepted in England.

[115] E.g. Dunning, 'Patronage and promotion'; Jack, 'Ecclesiastical patronage' [436]; Heath, *Parish clergy*, pp. 27–36.

[116] For papal provisions in England, Lunt, *Financial relations* [534], pp. 324–56, 381–408, 418–28, 430–2, 441–2; on legislation, Cheyette, 'Kings, courts, cures, and sinecures' [140], pp. 320–30; see also Swanson, 'Universities. graduates, and benefices', p. 45.

[117] Tihon, 'Les expectatives' [840], esp. pp. 57–95; for *in forma pauperum* provisions in Lincoln diocese, Lunt, *Financial relations*, pp. 324–5; for provisions and lay patronage, ibid., pp. 409–10; Lunt and Graves, *Accounts* [535], pp. 103, 111, 113, 137, 151, 200, 299, 368, 374–5, 380, 391, 505; *Rotuli Parliamentorum* [717], ii, p. 184.,

[118] Above, at n. 73.

After Martin V's election in 1417, however, the nomination of cardinals to English benefices virtually ceased, unless specifically permitted by the king, as happened under the early Tudors. But foreigners could still receive English appointments by royal licence and representations to English patrons, thereby evading the restrictions on provisions.[119]

Despite the foreign element, most papal providees in England were Englishmen, probably using grants *in forma pauperum*. The system of petitioning for such grants was virtually standardized by 1350, with major patrons – the royal family, the universities, the archbishops – sending lists of candidates to a new pope on his elevation, and naming the institutions whose patronage was to be usurped. For those enrolled, a papal provision could provide the entrée to the beneficed classes, although their effectiveness remains uncertain. Enrolment was perhaps especially important for university members. Whatever patronage arrangements they had may well have been disrupted by their studies and would need reconstruction, with the rolls being one element in that process.[120] The rolls also provided a relatively painless form of patronage: the provisions would be fulfilled by another party, leaving the advocates' own patronage available for cases judged truly worthy of reward; but they would still be acting as patrons and thus maintain prestige.

Although the effectiveness of the rolls is unquantifiable, they did sometimes work, as with an Exeter benefice conferred following a roll sent to Urban VI by the dowager Princess of Wales in 1378. When, in an undated transaction, one T. de K. renounced his right to the chantry of St Andrew in York Minster in favour of a papal provisor (Master T. de B.), he was clearly acknowledging the priority of claim conferred by a papal provision. But many provisions failed. Powerful rival patrons such as the crown could prevent their implementation. The surviving fourteenth-century accounts of papal collectors in England recite long lists of provisions inoperative for varied reasons. Sometimes litigation resulted, as when M. William de Selby sought the vicarage of Knaresborough (Yorks.) against Roger Faukes in 1385. Others would have been blocked at an earlier stage: technically the papal letters were merely commissions to the executors to examine the grantee, and allow the provision to operate if he was judged suitable. Other provisions would have been annulled by the false information on which they were based, or by simple failure to seek their enforcement.[121]

---

[119] Le Neve, *Fasti* [509], *passim*; Swanson, 'Papal letters' [794], no. 15 and n.; Thompson, *English clergy*, p. 11 n. 1; Lunt, *Financial relations*, p. 424; Harvey, 'Benefice as property' [361], pp. 168–70.

[120] Cooper, 'Papacy and Lichfield' [167], pp. 87–103; Jacob, *Conciliar epoch* [439] pp. 231–9; Swanson, 'Universities, graduates, and benefices', pp. 40–2.

[121] Hingeston-Randolph, *Reg. Brantyngham*, i, p. 211; EDR, F5/32, f. 83r; Lunt and Graves, *Accounts*, *passim*; Lunt, *Financial relations*, pp. 364–8; BIHR, CP.E.143.

Papal provisions were disliked by the religious patrons because they
limited their ability to act independently as patrons (some arranged for
their clients to receive provisions to benefices within their patronage in
order to get round the difficulty). They also incurred the hostility of those
who wished to pressurize the religious patrons, but were pre-empted by
papal claims. Fourteenth-century statutes effectively abolished the system. Obviously the papal prerogative of provision could not be eliminated; but the opportunities for English candidates to seek provisions
could be restricted by making access to Rome subject to royal licence and
obstructing the operation of bulls of provision. The last known English
rolls were sent by the universities in 1404, although they continued to
advocate that procedure for some years after, seeking its reinstatement
following the reunification of the church under Martin V. By then,
however, the system of rolls was decaying throughout Europe, the English
decline being by no means unique.[122]

Although effectively excluded from influencing English patronage patterns, the papacy retained a nominal involvement which was exploited to
secure bishoprics for royal candidates. The debate over papal involvement
did not die: an Oxford writer in 1467 steadfastly upheld papal rights,
asserting that lay patrons acted merely under a generous concession by
the pope. That papal authority was merely in abeyance was shown in the
1520s when Wolsey, as *legatus a latere*, exploited his status as local pope to
intervene in the distribution of benefices. Moreover, although provisions
almost disappeared, this did not annihilate papal influence on patronage:
the papacy remained (either directly, or through its local agents) the
source of dispensations affecting an individual's qualifications to hold
benefices, and where these removed certain disabilities (such as age or
illegitimacy) doubtless heightened the tensions within the clerical career
structure.[123]

The void in the patronage system created by the papacy's removal was
filled by the crown. The expansion of royal control – especially over
benefices in the gift of religious institutions – was a relatively slow and
insidious process, but ultimately effective. The crown possessed several
advowsons in its own right; and intermittently held others as a result of
feudal accidents – wardship of minors, escheats when holders died without
heirs, and forfeitures for treason. The claims expanded in the fourteenth
century, and implementation increased. The regalian right to nominate to

---

[122] Harvey, 'Benefice as property', pp. 172–3; Lunt, *Financial relations*, pp. 327–8;
Swanson, 'Universities, graduates, and benefices', p. 45; Jacob, *Reg. Chichele* [438], i. p. clv;
Watt, 'University clerks' [885], pp. 223–4.

[123] Lytle, 'Religion and the lay patron' [541]; pp. 71–2; Heath, *Parish clergy*, pp. 29, 33;
Pollard, *Wolsey*, pp. 204–6. A legatine provision was cited against Wolsey in the Praemunire
accusations of 1529: Baker, *Notebook* [34], p. 59.

benefices vacated during the vacancy of a bishopric or abbey which fell under royal control – essentially extending secular feudal incidents to the church – greatly augmented such accidental possession of advowsons. The concept of patronage as a piece of property, subject to processes in the royal courts, also aided the changes, with the crown's lawyers ruthlessly extending their master's patronal rights, by use of writs of *Quare impedit* (why does he impede?) and *Quare non admisit* (why does he not admit?). The decisions that, in patronage cases, 'Time does not run against the king' and that 'Plenarty [occupancy] is no plea against the king', removed all protection for those whose tenure was their sole title: if the king's precursors had not filled when they could, he retained the right to nominate, and would so do. Edward III could thus nominate to benefices vacated during the reign of Edward I, recovering his rights against those 'usurpers' who had got in first. By 1400 a royal nomination was almost irresistible. If pushed to extremes, the royalist view would have completely undermined the independence of ecclesiastical patrons.[124] Practically, royal power could not be ignored. Kings, or those acting in their name, expected obedience, and the concept of the king as patron paramount could only encourage a proprietorial attitude to benefices, especially those worth having. In Exeter diocese, successive monarchs wrote to influence decanal elections, usually (but not always) achieving the desired effect. Other magnates showed equally proprietorial attitudes. In the early sixteenth century the Earl of Northumberland was especially high-handed in his treatment of Staindrop hospital (Dur.), forcibly ejecting one master and installing his own nominee without reference to the appropriate ecclesiastical authorities. Perhaps the most dramatic expression of such attitudes is provided by the induction of Dominic Civi's proctor to South Ockendon church (Essex) in 1504. Although the usual commission had been sent to the archdeacon, the actual grant of corporal possession was effected by Sir Thomas Tirell, acting on a mandate from the Earl of Oxford. He apparently broke into the church in the process, causing considerable damage.[125]

Ecclesiastical patronage was also used by kings to patronize their lay subjects, by granting them the right to nominate to a benefice in royal gift.[126] A rather similar system became prevalent in transfers of patronage in the fifteenth and sixteenth centuries, as a result of which it could be argued that the virtual elimination of papal provisions allowed more

---

[124] Pantin, *English church*, pp. 30–2; Cheyette, 'Kings, courts, cures, and sinecures', pp. 306–18, 325–6.

[125] *HMC, var. coll.*, iv [401], pp. 85–6; Thomson, 'Two Exeter elections' [833] (I am grateful to Dr Thomson for allowing me to consult a draft of this article); BIHR, CP.G.125; see also Heath, *Parish clergy*, pp. 38, 200–7.

[126] E.g. Brewer, *Letters and papers, I* [88], i, p. 474 no. 21, p. 705 no. 13.

effective lay exploitation of the patronage held by religious institutions. Trafficking in patronage rights, artificially separated from the lands to which the advowson (the right to present a candidate to the bishop for appointment) was attached, was common in pre-Reformation England. Officially, advowsons could not be alienated as abstract entities, being inseparable from the ownership of the lands which they accompanied.[127] This restriction was evaded by alienating the advowson only for a single vacancy or term of years. Such grants proliferated in the fifteenth century. Any financial element in such transactions is hidden, but not impossible. What resulted, however, was even greater obscurity in patronage relations: the grant of the presentation for a single turn was itself an act of patronage, or a reaction to pressures on the individual or corporation concerned. Patronage thereby became a transferable commodity, with some grants changing hands two, three, or four times before being implemented, by grant or by will.[128] At times the reasons for such alienations appear straightforward, as when the nomination to a chantry at Middleton (Lancs.) was granted to an inhabitant of the parish, the true patron living in Essex; or when Lewes priory granted the presentation to several Yorkshire benefices (in this instance for ninety-nine years) to Robert Waterhouse of Halifax, probably a member of the family which farmed the house's hands in that area. Here the distances involved would have caused problems for the patrons, so the presentation was presumably being granted to caretakers, which did not exclude the true patrons from arranging for the succession before any vacancy occurred. Some grants were probably made under pressure – Richard III wrote a number of such letters, sometimes with the transfer of the presentation having conditions attached which effectively meant that demands on royal patronage would be satisfied when the vacancy occurred. Others are less obviously explicable; a financial consideration is not inconceivable, both in the original grants, and their implementation.[129]

[127] BL, MS Cotton Cleo.D.iii, f. 197r,includes the advowson, as does HCA, 1580. BL, MS Harley 2179, f. 112v, is a lease of a cottage and advowson, terminating on the presentation. For leases excluding the advowson, see e.g. HCA, 1180, 3167.

[128] A grant of next presentation to Burnsall (Yorks.), originally made to Sir Robert Tempest, passed first to Sir William Gascoigne, jr, then to James Thompson, Laurence Bayre, Richard Tenaund, and George Bawne, and finally from them to Richard Paver, Bernard Paver, and John Paver (BIHR, Cav. Bk. 1, f. 45r – dating from slightly after the Dissolution). For a transfer by will, see Lawrance, *Fasti parochiales: Buckrose*, p. 29 n. 5. For a grant transferred to the crown to ensure the success of a presentee, see Horrox and Hammond, *Harleian manuscript 433*, ii, pp. 198–201. See also comments of Zell, 'Clergy of Kent', p. 527.

[129] LJRO, B/A/1/8, f. 45v; BIHR, Cav. Bk. 1, ff. 35r–36r (for John Waterhouse as farmer of priory lands at Elland, in Halifax parish, in 1513, see BIHR, CP.G.3378); Horrox and Hammond, *Harleian manuscript 433*, i, pp. 61–2, ii, p. 139; Thompson, *English clergy*, p. 109.

These grants of next presentation greatly complicate the patronage equations. Further obscurity is added by grants of mere nomination. Without formally alienating the advowson patronage was still being transferred, by means which would probably escape registration, as the official patron would still make the presentation. Thus, in 1530, Lewes priory granted the nomination to Halifax vicarage (Yorks.) to the Duke of Norfolk and the Earl of Suffolk for one turn, but retained the presentation; six years later Peterborough abbey granted the nomination to Southeby (Notts.) to Thomas Bedell, Archdeacon of Cornwall.[130]

These procedures produced what can only be called a fragmentation of patronage rights. Monastic houses were probably most affected by the pressures to make grants, and may effectively have been deprived of the patronage of many of their benefices. Certainly, the grants could create queues, for individual grants of second and subsequent presentations are not unknown. At the Dissolution there were long lines of grant-holders: alienations made by Malton priory operated for some years after the Reformation, and several grants of presentation were confirmed before the Court of Augmentations.[131]

Even if the religious houses retained patronage, their degree of independence remains unclear. There is no knowing what tensions hide behind the bland statements of their presentations: pressures from outsiders, evidenced by letters advocating candidates, and pressures from insiders, as individual monks sought to be patrons themselves. Similar considerations apply to secular institutions as patrons, although for the dean and chapter of Lichfield the façade can be partly broken down. An agreement made in chapter in 1456 settled the arrangement of patronage for chantries within the cathedral: in exchanges, the chapter would let the exchangers arrange things themselves, and act in a nominal capacity. In other instances, however, and whatever the formalities might record, corporate activity was abandoned. Rather, a rota was established based on seniority among the canons residentiary, to ease disputes, and allow the individual canons in turn to be active patrons. Under these rules the first nomination was made by the dean, arranging for a kinsman (who also was an Oxford BA – which was the more important consideration?) to receive a chantry.[132] The difficulties of analysing patronage relationships are highlighted by occasional instances where the supposed patron clearly

[130] BIHR, Cav. Bk. 1, ff. 42v–43r (repeated at f. 48r–v), 49r; see also Windsor, XV.7.10, and Wright, *Reg. Langton*, nos. 156, 226, 319, 355, 461.
[131] For Augmentation confirmations, BIHR, Cav. Bk. 1, ff. 44v, 58r–v; for post-Dissolution implementation of grants by religious houses see Lawrance, *Fasti parochiales: Buckrose*, pp. 7, 18–19, 28, 35, 51, 61. Canterbury evidence suggests a massive alienation of patronage in the Dissolution years: Zell, 'Clergy of Kent', p. 527 n. 1.
[132] CUL, MS Mm.I.48, pp. 14–16; see also Swanson, 'Learning and livings', p. 92.

knew little or nothing of the candidate. Royal or other pressure could result in the issue of a blank letter of presentation, with the name of the future incumbent being entered by his nominator. In 1356 William le Botiller actually revoked a presentation issued in his name. Having been 'deluded and deceived by the fraudulent assertions and insistent entreaties of certain persons' into believing that John de Par was suitable, he had presented him to Warrington (Ches.). Now, 'better informed of his unworthiness and unsuitability', the presentation was to be retracted.[133]

Exchanges were one area where active patronal involvement would not be expected, given the general speediness of their completion. But the patron might yet claim the last word, as Leonard de Hedon discovered in 1403–4. After twenty-four years as rector of Hinderwell (Yorks.), he organized an exchange for a chantry in St Martin, Micklegate, York. Unfortunately, the arrangement totally ignored the formalities: Hedon assumed the chantry without securing either presentation, institution, or induction (he claimed, wrongly, that the ordination of the chantry rendered these unnecessary); and appears simply to have introduced Henry de Clitherow as his successor at Hinderwell. Even more unfortunate, Hinderwell was now a rectory patronized by turns, and the patron for that turn had his own candidate, William de Gaunton (who had probably been eyeing the rectory for some time). Peter de Mauley's legal presentation of Gaunton effectively negated the exchange of the chantry, which Clitherow seemingly resumed. Hedon was not so easily restored, and apparently had to fight his case to Rome.[134]

The complex machinations involved in the exercise of ecclesiastical patronage provided a fruitful source of potential conflicts. Although burdensome, patronage was precious, and had to be defended. Accordingly, legal actions were frequent. Sometimes right had to be defended against an intrusive papal providee. Early in 1389, for example, John Macer claimed the chapelry of Lyonshall (Hereford.), in the patronage of Wormsley priory, under a provision granted by Urban VI *in forma pauperum*. The precise events are obscure, but Macer and the nominal patrons were soon engaged in a bitter conflict for possession of the chapelry, the implication being that the priory was quite ignorant of his promotion, whether real or fictive.

Better documented is Thomas Sotheron's disputed attempt to acquire Mitton church in 1368. His provision was clearly to that church, alleging negligence by the official patrons (Cockersand abbey) so that the collation devolved to the pope. His intrusion was vigorously opposed, the abbey

---

[133] Heath, *Parish clergy*, p. 29; SRO, D593/A/1/35/2.

[134] BIHR, CP.F.11; for Clitherow's institution to the chantry, Swanson, *Reg. Scrope*, i. no. 197.

both appealing to Rome, and taking the matter to the royal courts.[135] Patronage cases abounded in the secular courts, with parties disputing rights, and challenging episcopal rejections of presentees. The legal system limited a bishop's ability to reject the nominee of a true patron; but frequently whether the presenter was the true patron was precisely the point at issue. Although bishops frequently held inquests into the patronage of vacant benefices, and would act on the results, this could still be challenged by a writ of *Quare impedit*. The resulting arrangements might be quite complex, as revealed by the vacancy at Milton Damarel (Devon) in 1385. The formal patron was Sir Richard Stapyldon, whose candidate was John Sergent. Stapyldon, however, was outlawed, so that in consequence the king claimed the presentation, issuing a writ of *Quare impedit* to enforce his rights. Meanwhile, Stapyldon's outlawry was quashed, so he recovered the presentation – but by then the vacancy had lasted so long that the collation devolved by lapse to the bishop (if the king had won, of course, it would not have lapsed). Bishop Brantyngham of Exeter collated the living to Sergent. Effectively, therefore, Stapyldon remained the patron, but only through the generosity (equivalent itself to patronage) of Brantyngham.[136] How many court cases were serious patronage disputes, and how many merely obstructive actions started with the intention of producing a settlement, is an indeterminable aspect of such disputes. But such time-consuming cases, grinding down the legal holders of the advowson, could produce a sort of victory for the claimant, especially if he had crown support. Selby abbey faced that problem with the benefice of Adlingfleet (Yorks.), being forced to defend its claims in a case lasting from November 1369 to Christmas 1373, and only then terminated by payments to end the drain on abbey resources – payments of £50 to the king, and of £66 13s. 4d to his nominee, John de Haytfeld, 'pro expensis suis'.[137]

Not all challenges to patronage rights, or patronal abuses, proved successful. Ralph Bulmer fought vigorously against his ejection from Staindrop college (Dur.) in 1522, where he had been replaced by the Earl of Northumberland's nominee. Even the king could be outflanked. The elections to the deanery of Exeter in 1509 illustrate both acquiescence and resistance. Early in the year, when Henry VII demanded promotion for his nominee, the chapter delayed the electon until the royal candidate could comply with the cathedral statutes. In October, with the deanery again vacant, and the new king Henry VIII still settling in, the chapter

---

[135] HCA, 2928, 3220; McNulty, 'Thomas Sotheron' [568]; Cheyette, 'Kings, courts, cures, and sinecures', pp. 334–5.

[136] Heath, *Parish clergy*, p. 41; Hingeston-Randolph, *Reg. Brantyngham*, i, p. 165; Hingeston-Randolph, *Reg. Stafford*, p. 256 (see also Bennett, *Reg. Fleming* [58], no. 235; Davis, *Paston letters*, i, pp. 183–4).

[137] BL, MS Cotton Vit.E.xvi, f. 112r.

opposed his nominee, stood by their statutes, and elected their own candidate, apparently with no royal reaction.[138]

Patronage directed towards the actual acquisition of a benefice was only part of the career process, and only a fraction of the patronage relationship as a whole. Patrons could be useful in many ways, including the secular field. It was only by having the support of Lady Margaret Beaufort, mother to Henry VII, that Robert Fisher managed to stop a concerted attack on him and his adherents in the lay courts, in a dispute over receipts from prebends in Howden Minster;[139] and good lordship was as important a calculation for ecclesiastics as for others. But in the ecclesiastical sphere itself, patronage operated also for the exploitation of benefices and religious institutions beyond the mere obtaining of a benefice. It helped, for instance, when making arrangements for pensions, either to supplement benefice income, or to provide income until a benefice was gained. The latter was probably the more important, appearing most regularly in the sources. Most bishops could demand pensions from religious houses in their dioceses when new heads were appointed, pensions which they used to maintain their clerks until they secured promotion (from the house). The crown also claimed such pensions from religious houses and bishoprics over which it had regalian rights. The religious clearly resented these payments, leading to court cases either to secure their extinction (on behalf of the house) or satisfaction of arrears (on behalf of the pensioner). Patronage also operated when pensions were being arranged for retiring clergy: sometimes the benefice's patron joined in the preliminary negotiations, writing in support of the request to the bishop to allow the pension to be paid.[140]

For the beneficed, the possibilities for non-residence, in order to study or serve a patron, depended on episcopal licence; but obtaining that licence again was easier with supporting letters. Obviously, those seeking absence for magnatial service would receive support from the magnate; but patronage also affected the other reasons. Several licences for non-residence for study were issued following representations from the prospective student's patrons, although such support is not always explicitly recorded. Such sponsorship had a double advantage: it helped secure the licence,

---

[138] BIHR, CP.G.125; Thomson, 'Two Exeter elections', pp. 37–42.

[139] BIHR, CP.F.288.

[140] Swanson, *Reg. Scrope*, i, nos. 116, 281, 367, 665; Heath, *Parish clergy*, p. 28; Sayles, *Select cases in King's Bench* [742], p. 186; Brewer, *Letters and papers, I*, i, p. 647 no. 16; Legge, *Anglo-Norman letters*, pp. 454–5; Pike, *Year book of Edward the Third* [659], pp. 380–3, 406–7; *La premiere part Henry le VI* [495], 19 Henry VI, p. 54; *Syntomotaxia* [805], 34 Henry VI, p. 50 (the claimant actually being ineligible to receive a benefice as he had married since the grant); *Reports Edward V* [511], pp. 31–2; EDR, F5/32, f. 37v.

and might also induce the ecclesiastical authorities to waive (or at least reduce) their demand for fees.[141]

The threads which linked patrons to clients are usually too subtle to be properly revealed, generally because so little is known about individual clerics. One group, however, can be studied in some detail precisely because of their promotions: the bishops. Obviously, they are atypical – those who reach the top always are – and there is no 'standard', with considerable variation in individual characters and careers. Some fall out of consideration here: the foreigners and the religious who occupied bishoprics at various points.

Some 180 bishops occupied England's episcopal thrones in the years

The clerical Booths of Barton

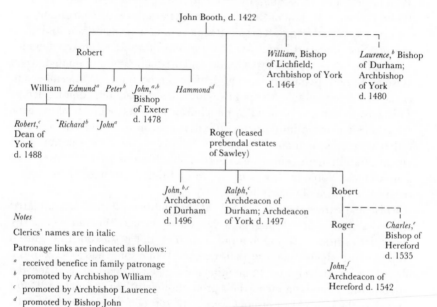

Notes

Clerics' names are in italic

Patronage links are indicated as follows:

[a] received benefice in family patronage
[b] promoted by Archbishop William
[c] promoted by Archbishop Laurence
[d] promoted by Bishop John
[e] promoted by Archdeacon John (d. 1496)
[f] promoted by Bishop Charles

Several other clerics of the same surname who were relatives cannot be fitted into the pedigree (* = position uncertain)

This chart takes no account of relatives through the female line who were also promoted as a result of family connection

– – – – illegitimate

[141] BL, MS Cotton Galba.E.x, f. 88v; LJRO, B/A/1/2, ff. 11r, 13r–v, 14v–15 (for a slightly different linkage in a similar chain, Hill, 'Berkshire letter book', p. 19); Heath, *Parish clergy*, p. 60 n. 6.

between the Black Death and the break with Rome.[142] They must be treated as individuals, for the English church in this period lacked any sense of episcopal dynasties. There was episcopal dynasticism, with the bishops seeking to promote their families within particular localities, but that is slightly different. Only the Booths of Barton appear to break the rule, providing four bishops during the period, two of them Archbishops of York. But even the Booths were not truly dynastic: they were affected by complex patronage relations, their eventual success being more a matter of luck than planning. Nevertheless, the bishops' concern to promote their relatives does show the importance of connections.[143] The rise of the Booths represented considerable success for a relatively unknown gentry family – especially for the illegitimate son who became an archbishop. But bastard bishops were not especially rare, the fifteenth century witnessing (apart from Laurence Booth) Henry Beaufort at Lincoln and Winchester, and John Stafford at Canterbury, while a second episcopal Booth (Charles, Bishop of Hereford from 1515–35) was also illegitimate.[144]

Bishops' social origins varied. Beaufort was a prince's son and half-brother and uncle to kings, Wolsey the son of an Ipswich butcher; for many the evidence is obscure. Gentry and aristocrats predominated, royal kinsmen being especially notable in the fifteenth century. Then membership of the bench tended to reflect political loyalties and factional dominance.[145] This aristocratic involvement in the church suggests elements of dynasticism, but it is essentially aristocratic dynasticism exploiting the church, rather than episcopal families using the church as their main power-base. During the fifteneth century most non-noble bishops were apparently of gentry stock. Noble birth was not a precondition for promotion, although connections were obviously useful.

Episcopal career patterns reveal the possibilities. All had accumulated and worked their way through a succession of benefices (but not necessarily parochial positions) before gaining their sees; but it was not this church employment which enhanced their careers. While some had worked more obviously for the church than others, in general councils and for the papacy, the main dynamic in their promotion was their contact with, and service to, the state. Most bishops were some sort of civil servant: diplomats, members of the royal household, lawyers. Experience of the church councils perhaps increased the diplomatic representation somewhat between

---

[142] On the episcopate, see Rosenthal, *Training of an elite* [711]; Highfield, 'English hierarchy' [387]; Betcherman, 'Making of bishops' [59]; Davies, 'The episcopate' [194].

[143] For the family, see Axon, 'The family of Bothe' [25], pp. 36–82.

[144] For Stafford, Rosenthal, *Training of an elite*, p. 8; Thompson denies Laurence Booth's bastardy (*English clergy*, p. 25 n. 1), but see Axon, 'Family of Bothe', pp. 49–50; for Charles Booth, Fuller, *Papal letters, Alexander VI*, no. 319.

[145] Rosenthal, *Training of an elite*, pp. 7–12.

1420 and 1470, but it was state service which really counted. Royal patronage was therefore crucial, whether through personal contacts, or through the institutional structure which gave the bureaucrats access to patronage as one of the perks. But the point and level at which individuals broke into the ecclesiastical career structure varied considerably. The well-connected Richard Courtenay was receiving prebends whilst officially under-age, because of his birth; usually it took longer, prebends being obtained only some years after a run of rectories. Most bishops were practiced pluralists before their promotions – but would automatically vacate most of these posts on promotion to the episcopate. The pope might allow their retention if the new see was poor, but such dispensations could be voided by action in the royal courts. When Henry Chichele was promoted to St Davids in 1408, he was allowed to retain his earlier benefices, but lost the prebend of Chauntrey in Salisbury cathedral by secular process. The papal dispensations could usually be implemented only by royal licence.[146]

Promotion as a bishop involved a multitude of patronage issues, not all clear in any one case. By 1350 the notion of free election was effectively dead in England: chapters appointed under crown instructions. Support from the king, or from his controller, was therefore vital. However, avoiding free election required papal complicity to provide the king's nominee. Occasionally a pope might resist the crown – it took some time for William of Wykeham to acquire Winchester in the 1360s, and under Henry IV the papacy occasionally opposed royal nominees.[147] But the crown had its own ripostes to papal obstruction, and might prevent the appointment of a papal nominee in its turn.

Generally speaking, the bishops were of a good standard. There were occasional moral lapses, but some accusations, such as the rape charges levelled against Henry Wakefield of Worcester in the 1380s, were clearly fictitious.[148] The great danger was of non-residence, particularly acute in the fifteenth century. John Catterick of Lichfield scarcely entered his see, being almost continuously abroad at the Council of Constance. Thomas Wolsey neglected his archbishopric of York for the politics of London, while his predecessor, Christopher Bainbridge, spent all his pontificate at Rome. Others gained poor reputations for neglecting their ecclesiastical duties.[149] Even so, their educational and administrative capacities were considerable. Most bishops were university graduates – generally either

---

[146] ibid., pp. 19–51; *Reports Henry IV et Henry V* [510], 11 Henry IV, pp. 37–9; see also Horrox and Hammond, *Harleian manuscript 433*, i, pp. 34–6.

[147] Highfield, 'Promotion of William of Wykeham' [386], pp. 39–41, 44–5; Davies, 'After the execution' [192], pp. 46–70.

[148] For the accusations, Sayles, *Select cases in King's Bench*, pp. 53–4.

[149] For John Kempe at York, Thompson, *English clergy*, p. 43.

lawyers or theologians – so that William Booth's appointment, with his training as a common lawyer and no university degree, was considered scandalous by Thomas Gascoigne. Few bishops were major writers during the period, until the Reformation at least; but some had reputations as sermonizers, and apparently took their diocesan duties reasonably seriously.[150]

The bishops were subject to many pressures. As potential patrons, they were pressurized by would-be clients. As family members, they had family obligations, providing their kin with careers within the church, or revenues from episcopal estates. As individuals in an episcopal succession, they also had responsibilities to the see; and like other clerics were liable to charges of dilapidation.[151] As magnates, and political creatures, they had a position to maintain, with appropriate household expenses and other charges. They were particularly expected to be good lords; and if nobles took that responsibility seriously. Certainly, the involvement of Thomas Savage, Archbishop of York, in the distortion of legal processes on behalf of a client in 1498–9 provides an instructive instance of this, the dispute being a legal feud extending from the mid-fifteenth to the early sixteenth century.[152]

Episcopal careers thus illustrate and illuminate tensions which affected all levels of the secular clergy. Although atypical, the bishops' position reveals the general difficulties of an ecclesiastical career. They are the most obvious 180 secular clergy of a total entering the church which may well have exceeded 150,000. Throughout there was weeding-out, at all stages there were responsibilities and intricate calculations. There always had to be a vacancy before it could be filled, with intense competition to determine who filled it.

2.5   THE RELIGIOUS

Whilst most clergy in later medieval England were seculars, the regulars were not insignificant. It is the male members of the religious orders who will be considered here. The female religious orders, given the church's attitude to women, and the impossibility of their attaining holy orders, will be dealt with as an aspect of lay piety and religious life. Consideration of new foundations and new orders will also be deferred.[153]

The number of male religious houses was not static during the years

---

[150] Rosenthal, *Training of an elite*, pp. 12–18; Rogers, *Loci e libro veritatum* [709], pp. 47–8, 52, 194; Davies, 'The episcopate', pp. 57–64.

[151] The Hereford arrangement to cover dilapidations by transmitting 500 marks from bishop to bishop seems an eminently sensible reaction to the problem: HCA, 1463, 2121. See also the quitclaim between successive bishops of Lichfield in CUL, MS Ll.1.18, ff. 95v–96r.

[152] Ives, *Common lawyers*, pp. 122–5.

[153] See 6/2, at nn. 41–5.

between the Black Death and the Dissolution. The main institutional change was the suppression of several of the alien priories, after an uncertain existence during the first phase of the Hundred Years War. Some were naturalized and continued in existence, while others were suppressed and their possessions transferred to educational and secular foundations. Several other small houses, suffered a similar fate during the period.[154] However, it is not the institutions but their members who demand immediate attention. Calculating the numbers in monastic orders throughout the period is perhaps easier than for secular clerics, given the nature of the sources. Apart from the national estimates derived from the poll taxes of the 1370s and 1380s, the Dissolution records, and the less certain recording of the ordination lists, other material is also useful. Visitations of religious houses are more commonly and more fully recorded than those of parishes; while in episcopal registers records of elections of new heads of houses frequently provide lists of inmates. Contrasting with this material for the monks and canons, there is a serious dearth of evidence for the mendicant orders, for whom the only really constant source is the ordination lists. Unfortunately, the mobility of the friars and their exemption from episcopal jurisdiction make this information difficult to use, and probably understates their numbers. The ordination lists may also under-record the religious. In the Coventry and Lichfield evidence, for instance, the recording of monks seems more erratic than that for seculars. Moreover, the religious orders might arrange their own private ordination ceremonies. Despite the source difficulties, it seems that entry to the religious orders remained at a stable level throughout the late middle ages. For most of the period the number of male regulars was around 9,000 (with 2,500–3,000 of them mendicants). This generalization covers some fluctuation. The Black Death had considerable impact on the religious orders, cutting their numbers by more than half to just over 6,500 (about 2,000 mendicants). By 1422 the total was up to about 9,500, increasing to around 10,000 by 1500 (when almost 3,000 were friars). The slight drop which occurred thereafter to 1534 was not particularly significant, whereafter the rapid Dissolutions removed them all.[155]

The general trends doubtless hide diocesan differences. In Lichfield diocese the late fourteenth century was seemingly a period of growing attractiveness for a monastic/mendicant career, although the small numbers involved – rarely more than twenty religious ordained as priests in a year – make any comparative statements of dubious worth. Reasons for

---

[154] Knowles, *Religious orders*, ii, pp. 157–66, iii, pp. 13–14, 157, 161–2.

[155] For numbers of religious, Russell, 'Clerical population', pp. 184–212; Knowles and Hadcock, *Religious houses* [488], pp. 488–94. For examples and comment on sources see also Wright, *Reg. Langton*, nos. 431, 505, 556; Emden, *Survey of Dominicans* [256]; Swanson, *Reg. Scrope*, ii, p. x n. 16; BL, MS Add.14848, ff. 90v–91r; LJRO, B/A/1/7, f. 130r. See also n. 157.

changes are difficult to assess; and Lichfield might be an oddity: comparative figures for Lincoln diocese suggest that there, religious ordinations in
the later fourteenth century were half those of the later thirteenth.[156] The
Lichfield decline may merely be delayed: in the early fifteenth century
ordination totals drop, numerically to the mid- to high teens in each order,
or something like 40 per cent. As a percentage the decline is just as steep
as that experienced by the seculars; but numerically the drop for the
seculars is much higher. Whether this reflects a crisis in the regular life is
questionable. But unlike the seculars the religious do not recover the
position in any meaningful sense later. Rarely thereafter do quinquennial
averages for any order exceed 20 a year. Yet, if there is no marked rise, nor
is there any noticeable collapse in recruitment. Figures remain hovering in
the teens, with no dramatic surges or falls. The general impression is of
stable recruitment, a picture paralleled by other studies of the period.[157]
Nevertheless, there probably were relative changes among the orders,
although these still require detailed study. The growth of the Carthusians,
and the changing popularity of orders, would doubtless have affected the
distribution of recruits.

The careers and quality of regular clergy are only occasionally known.
There is considerable information on some of them, especially those who
fell foul of the authorities at visitations, or rose to prominence in church or
state. We have the depictions of contemporary satirists, especially Chaucer
and Langland, and as far as these can be tested some regulars fell into the
faults they discussed. The source material is again unequal. For the orders
under episcopal oversight – the Augustinian canons and most Benedictines
– there is no shortage of visitation material, clearly revealing faults in
concerns for private property, sexual misdemeanours, and general laxity
in obedience to the rule. For other orders information is less readily
available. Some visitation records exists for the Cistercians, for example
relating to Hailes abbey, which rather repeats the picture given for the
other orders; while other material – like the correspondence between the
English houses and the central administration of the order at Cîteaux –
provides supplementary insights. Evidence for visitation of Premonstra-
tensian houses shows similar faults there between 1480 and 1500.[158] For

---

[156] Storey, 'Recruitment of English clergy', p. 297.

[157] Russell suggests a drop of some 25 per cent between the late fourteenth century and
the Dissolution ('Clerical population', p. 212), but his omissions (including the Carthusians)
would take up some of this slack. Knowles and Hadcock indicate relative stability between
*c.*1422 and 1534 (*Religious houses*, p. 494). For individual houses, see e.g. Dobson, 'Election of
John Ousthorp' [215], pp. 39–40; Greatrex, 'Some statistics' [314]; Dobson, 'Cathedral
chapters and cathedral cities' [219], pp. 23–5.

[158] Knowles, *Religious orders*, ii, pp. 108–14, 204–18, iii, p. 62–86; chapter 1 above, n. 38;
Harper-Bill, 'Cistercian visitation' [349], pp. 104–14; Gasquet, *Collectanea Anglo-Premonstratensia* [293], ii–iii; Talbot, *Letters from English abbots* [808].

the mendicant orders there is almost nothing. Friars sometimes appear among those accused of sexual misdemeanours in court books, but, given their exempt status, they were never actually brought before those courts.[159]

The significance of the decadence revealed by the visitation and other evidence is not clear. Monasticism had faced problems for centuries; the difficulties of apostacy, money, and discipline which are encountered in late medieval visitation records were already well known before 1350.[160] Moreover, although monasticism may have been changing, it remained attractive, and perhaps actually vocational for many. Granted, not all entered religious orders voluntarily – and there were occasional complaints (of uncertain validity) that children were stolen and forced to take vows.[161] The greater danger was probably not the lack of a vocation on entering an order, but its stultification over time, as administrative tasks piled up; as time spent away from the main house at a grange undermined spirituality, which would not be aided by the lack of companions; and as the general pressures of monastic life produced by contemporary social and economic changes took their toll. However much a regular life should have meant abandonment of the world, all too often the world refused to be kept out. Members of the regular orders were therefore as involved as the seculars in the contemporary social and economic system. Their houses were safe-deposits for deeds, and meeting-places to settle disputes. They faced the same economic disputes, and the same jurisdictional and patronal relationships, so that to insist on a rigid distinction between the regulars and the seculars would be impossible.

For some, however, monasticism had not lost all meaning. The Carthusians were renowned for their spirituality during the period; and individual monks might transfer to other houses or orders in the search for a more religious life.[162] Whilst the satirists and the personal failings dominate the picture, the vocational nature of the monastic and regular life cannot be completely overlooked.

Various factors conspired against the spiritual life. The monasteries were involved in a career structure, with prelacies and bishoprics at its head. Within each order there was an administrative structure to be worked through; within each house a hierarchy of offices, with scope for profit, ending with an abbot or prior (by that time frequently little more than an administrator, distant from his brethren, rather than a spiritual

---

[159] E.g. BIHR, DC/AB.1, ff. 175r, 190v (Austin friars); YML, M2(1)f, ff. 33r, 38r (Carmelites).

[160] Cheney, *Episcopal visitation of monasteries* [138]; Knowles, *Religious orders*, ii, pp. 85–112.

[161] Szittya, *Antifraternal tradition* [806], pp. 204–6, esp. p. 205 n. 62.

[162] Rubin, *Charity and community* [718], p. 156; Bod., MS Tanner 165 f. 98r; BL, MS Add. 14848, ff. 164r, 323r; EDR, G/2/3, ff. 36v, 38r (but cf. f. 94r–v); Madox, *Formulare Anglicanum* [570], p. 15.

father). The religious houses perhaps resembled colleges more than monasteries, albeit with a stricter liturgical round.[163]

The deregularization of the monastic orders was exemplified by their increasing involvement in the benefice system. Apart from providing chaplains, both household and parochial, the religious orders also provided full-scale incumbents. This had long been established for the Premonstratensians and Augustinian canons, whose original inspiration had been pastoral. Now, individual houses occasionally received licences to serve benefices by regulars: in 1378, for example, the Cistercians of Stoneleigh (War.) were allowed to appoint a monk for their appropriated vicarage of Radway. Even more insidious, the period provides increasing evidence of monks and friars receiving dispensations to act as vicars and rectors, and receiving such benefices as a result. Sometimes, indeed, admission might have occurred without dispensation. Occasionally, religious appear acting as parochial chaplains, whether long or short term. In 1519 the dispute over Sandbeck chapel (Yorks.) revealed that the abbot of Roche had appointed a canon of his house as chaplain; while the prioress of Arthington had brought in a friar from Tickhill to maintain the cure, who served for some three months. Some attempts by religious to gain benefices involved collusive action: to avoid the prohibition on a patron presenting himself, religious houses alienated the presentation to a third party, but ensured that the house's head received the nomination. A papal dispensation could achieve the same results.[164] The increasing presence of religious among the parochial clergy, essentially a fiscal solution to an economic problem, could only help to undermine the vocations of the incumbents, rendering them even less distinguishable from the seculars. However, against this erosion should be put the considerable numbers of beneficed regulars who sought dispensations to wear their habits under secular garb, which presumably indicates some continued attachment, against the easier solution of simply abandoning monastic clothing.[165]

Among the religious who obtained benefices were many of the suffragan bishops. They were usually friars, but in the fifty years before the Reformation heads of monastic houses also acted.[166] Most were English by

---

[163] Thompson, *English clergy*, pp. 162–3, 175–6.

[164] Sweet, 'Papal privileges' [804], pp. 603–10 (challenged by Heath, *Parish clergy*, pp. 175–8); Hartridge, *History of vicarages* [353], pp. 185–7; Harper-Bill, 'Monastic apostacy' [350], pp. 9–10; Wilson, *Reg. Coventry and Lichfield, book 5*, p. 140; BIHR, CP.G.93; Bowker, *Secular clergy*, p. 77; Fuller, *Papal letters, Alexander VI*, no. 474.

[165] E.g. Fuller, *Papal letters, Alexander VI*, nos. 118, 223, 245, 370, 582, 614, 626, 680, 691, 742, 898.

[166] Compare lists in Knowles, *Religious orders*, ii, 374–5, iii, 494–5. For seculars as suffragans, Thompson, *English clergy*, pp. 49–50.

birth, so presumably someone made representations on their behalf to the papacy. Sometimes diocesans had a say in the matter, seeking the consecration of a named candidate.[167]

Being both bishops and religious, these suffragans are somewhat hybrid characters, and in some ways reflect the tensions of the contemporary religious life. They had their dignity to maintain, and the rules of monastic or mendicant life could be strictly applied to them only with difficulty. Their means of support varied: unlike diocesans, they lacked estates, so alternative provision was needed. William Northburgh, Bishop *Pharensis*, was one of the most active and obvious suffragans of the late fourteenth century. His work in Worcester diocese during the 1394–5 vacancy is reflected in his contract of employment, which allowed him to share the fees. When he moved to York with Archbishop Scrope in 1398 (having acted as his suffragan at Lichfield) he started collecting benefices, by papal licence, being appointed successively to the vicarage of Nafferton and the rectory of Holy Trinity, Goodramgate, York. He probably continued to receive some fees as well.[168] Other suffragans were effectively salaried officials – Hugh, Archbishop of Damascus, received 40 marks a year as suffragan in York in 1352–3 during the vacancy of the see. In the years immediately before the Reformation, arrangements were more secure: the papal appointments of suffragans confer pensions on them, payable by the diocesan until benefices of equivalent value were received.[169]

Northburgh was an extremely mobile bishop. Originally a Dominican of Lancaster, he received his episcopacy from Urban VI. He remained active for over thirty years, in Lichfield (to 1398) and York (to 1411). His commission in Scrope's York register is a recital of lesser episcopal functions, as is the Worcester contract. The mobility of a suffragan is well revealed in the ordination records of Exeter diocese: although the diocesan sometimes undertook the annual traipse through the diocese for ordinations to first tonsure and distribution of chrism, generally these onerous duties were left to the long-suffering suffragan. Northburgh's Worcester contract required him to maintain his own records, and account for his fees with the diocesan officials. Unfortunately, no obviously suffragan registers now survive, unless some of the ordination registers fall into this category.[170]

---

[167] Smith, 'Suffragan bishops' [766], p. 21.

[168] ibid., p. 22; Willis Bund, *Reg. sede vacante* [914], pp. 356–7; Swanson, *Reg. Scrope*,i, nos. 164, 355 (obtained by virtue of a dispensation granted only in 1396, i, no. 354); Purvis, *Mediaeval act book*, p. 51. For other beneficed suffragans, Thompson, *English clergy*, p. 50.

[169] Smith, ' "Sede vacante" register' [764], no. 35; Smith, 'Suffragan bishops', p. 21; see also e.g. LAO, Bps Rentals 1, f. 12r.

[170] Swanson, *Reg. Scrope*, ii. no. 857; Willis Bund, *Reg. sede vacante*, pp. 356–7. See also n. 30 above; LAO, Bps Rentals 1, f. 10r.

The activities of the suffragans, and the problems experienced by the religious in general, are indicative of a period of tension affecting the relationship between men of God and men of the world. The clergy as a whole had to confront the questions raised by such tensions, for their position as servants of too many masters frequently placed them in an invidious position. It was the clergy who had to act as servants and representatives of the higher order represented by Christianity, but they also had to act within a world which they could not avoid, and which often made considerable demands on them.

3

The Church and the Political Order

3.1   THE PROBLEM OF POLITICS

In 1279 King Edward I succinctly stated his view of the relationship between himself as king and the clergy of his realm: 'The *communitas cleri* live under our rule no less than the rest of the people and enjoy our defence and protection of their temporalities, and for the most part of their spiritualities'.[1] The overtones of lordship in this remark indicate the source of the confrontations between church and state throughout the middle ages: problems of dependence and independence, of the distinction between matters temporal and spiritual, and of relative superiority. In this war of attrition Parliament's declaration in 1533 that the Crown of England was an imperial crown, which cleared the way for the break with Rome, initiated the final phase in a conflict which had underlain much of English history since 1066. Henry VIII's declaration, and its implications, fitted into the tradition of clashes between king and clerics: William II and Henry I against Archbishop Anselm; Henry II versus Becket; John confronting Pope Innocent III; Edward I outfacing Archbishop Winchelsey.[2] Henry VIII may have been following a contemporary continental model: the activities of his father-in law, Ferdinand of Aragon, within his kingdom of Sicily have been suggested as his most immediate inspiration.[3] In the end, of course, Henry outdid them all: they sought merely to curtail papal administrative authority, without denying the papal patriarchate. Henry went further, and set himself up as Supreme Head on earth of the Church in England.

[1] Quoted by Denton, 'Clergy and Parliament' [203], p. 102.
[2] Ullmann, 'This realm of England' [860]; Health, *Church and realm* [373] now covers church–state relations up to 1461; Barlow, *English church* [40] pp. 287–302; Cheney, *Innocent III and England* [139], pp. 294–356; below, n. 53.
[3] Ullmann, 'This realm of England', pp. 188–90.

Discussion of the relationship between church and state in the middle ages generally centres on two main themes: the theoretical relationship between the 'two swords', respectively of secular and spiritual authority (although both wielded to what was ultimately the same purpose), and the practical relationship between a secular, increasingly nationalistic, local ruler, and the church within his domains. Put another way: while the universal church struggled to assert its theoretical sovereignty over one of its fragments, in practice the sovereignty-seeking secular local authority asserted dominion through fragmentation and particularization of the church as a universality. Maintaining a balance which gave actual local supremacy to the prince without shattering the theoretical universality of the church was the principal juggling act of the later medieval period, until the Reformation changed all the rules.

In England, local considerations posed their own problems. It might be a convenient hierocratic notion that the secular power was inferior and subject to the spiritual, but reality inevitably inverted the relationship. The English church existed in a kingdom whose monarchy ultimately owned all the land, even that under ecclesiastical control. Clerics as individuals, and the church as a combination of institutions, were subjects, and as such expected to assume a variety of duties and responsibilities. Many of these were practical, but the relationship had its theoretical aspects. Kings of England ruled *Dei Gratia*, by a grace which the church claimed to mediate. In political thought and theory it could be argued that this ecclesiastical spiritualizing function actually legitimized the state, and confirmed the individual monarch's right to rule. Two corollaries of this view had their own dangers: to the state in claims to reverse this process, authorizing and legalizing revolt; and, to the church, in the threat that the legitimized monarch might push his claims beyond the tolerable, particularly by developing an 'imperial' monarchy which would demote the church from being a partner (however unwilling) in the state, to being most emphatically only one among several groups of subjects. The church's dilemma, supporting the ordination of the powers that be while seeking to limit the amount of service to be rendered to Caesar, set the tone for relations between church and state throughout the period.

Tackling the theoretical relationship between church and state in England in purely English terms confronts an immediate obstacle: the almost complete lack of any theoretical discussions by English writers. After John of Salisbury's *Policraticus*, written in the mid-twelfth century, English authors seem to have felt that that was enough. While they did address political problems, usually this was in reaction to specific debates and concrete difficulties – the degree of royal control over ecclesiastical endowments, and suchlike – rather than abstract analysis providing an ideological explanation of the political structure.[4] It is unlikely that such matters were totally ignored; but, for English intellectual writers, there was little real impetus towards such considerations: lacking a concept of sovereignty based on Roman law, there was little room for the theoretical debates over sovereignty which sometimes preoccupied continental imperialists and papalists. Nor, given England's essentially feudal political cohesion, was there any need for the justifications of political autonomy which occupied many Italian writers of the period, seeking to legitimize the political authority exercised by small units against the increasingly artificial claims of an impotent Holy Roman Emperor.[5]

Yet despite the lack of English writing on the subject, England was not divorced from the general European trends in political theorizing. England did share in the general pattern of views, perhaps with its own idiosyncracies, but still having much in common with the continent. The integration into this broader trend is not necessarily revealed by the writings of Englishmen, but by their dependence on foreigners; the acquisition of copies of works by writers like Giles of Rome, whose *De regimine principum* was well known, and in the frequent translation of continental works into English.[6]

The political theorizing of much of the medieval period has rightly been described as political theology rather than political thought.[7] The basic arguments were only rarely secular, in the sense of excluding a religious element, even when defending monarchical authority against papal incursions. Only in the sixteenth century were political structures and their justification divorced from discussions of Christian morality, and no longer based on definitions of that morality. The debates between 'papalists' and 'royalists' in the thirteenth to fifteenth centuries were essentially about the structure of Christendom and the relations between the various fragments (the kingdoms) and its religious head (the pope). The disputes were less about the nature of authority and its origins than about its mediation: essentially, whether a king *Dei gratia* needed the church as an intermediary between himself and God to legitimize his rule, and how far that rule, once legitimized, allowed him to control the church or subjected him to its oversight. A more secular approach was not totally lacking; but such writings concentrated on royal rights and prerogatives rather than the origins of sovereignty. Perhaps the closest any Englishman came to a work

---

[4] The English contribution to medieval political thought is briefly surveyed in Genet, 'Ecclesiastics and political theory' [295].

[5] Canning, 'Ideas of the state' [125]; Ullmann, 'Medieval idea of sovereignty' [851], pp. 18–24.

[6] E.g. Jones, *Policy of Richard II* [448], p. 161 and n. 45; Genet, 'Ecclesiastics and political theory', pp. 32–3.

[7] Genet, 'Ecclesiastics and political theory', pp. 26–7.

of political theory proper in this period was John Wyclif in the 1370s, with his tract on civil lordship, *De civili dominio*. But even this system of lordship was constructed within an essentially Christian framework: the justification for dominion (and by extension, for the state) was to be found in obedience to divine precepts and the dictates of Christian morality.[8]

That the debate over political morality and organization was really an ecclesiological debate needs to be remembered when turning to practical considerations. In terms of English developments, again the signs are few. Even where the translations flourished, it remains difficult to know precisely how to approach them, and their precise relevance to English experience. Except that a translation was considered justified, its value is uncertain. Nevertheless, while the basic definitions of the relationships between church and state have in the background the continental arguments – for the church's supremacy, and its toleration of kingdoms as a practical necessity, but incorporating them within the structure as institutions whose divine infusion of authority was received through ecclesiastical mediation – there were some specifically English strands. Works were produced by Lollards, by supporters of the monarchy, and by others, attempting to establish the relationship between church and state, and the morality of political organization within the realm.[9] These were often poetic, and in due course increasingly composed by laymen. Although frequently dealing with a prince's duty in relation to the church, they rarely considered fundamentals. They were usually moralistic and practical, unworried about the origins and derivation of political authority. This strain of moralizing and Christian exhortation might fit such works into the genre of *Mirror of princes* literature – moral and practical advice on government – although it has been argued that strictly speaking such literature was of little relevance to the English experience. Even if not offering a mirror, most of the writing still offers advice to a Christian king. The anonymous *Tractatus de regimine principum ad regem Henricum sextum* thus ranges round all the duties and obligations of the monarch, to both God and his subjects, even detailing the daily round of spiritual exercises to be followed. It is aimed specifically at the king, only towards the end discussing the obligations of the rest of society. In contrast, Edmund Dudley's *Tree of Commonwealth*, composed in 1509, offers advice not just to the new king Henry VIII, but as a sort of mirror for society demands wholesale moral reform of all ranks. Nevertheless, this reformation should occur within the context of a specifically Christian polity, one directed by a Christian king as overseer.[10]

[8] Farr, *Wyclif as reformer* [267], pp. 70–7; Wilks, 'Predestination, property, and power' [904], pp. 222–36; Daly, *Political thought of Wyclif* [186], pp. 65–80.

[9] Genet, *Four English tracts* [294], pp. 5–19, 31–9, 53–168, illustrates the variety.

[10] Genet, 'Ecclesiastics and political theory', p. 32; Scattergood, *Politics and poetry* [749],

Throughout the period the notion of a Christian monarchy is repeatedly emphasized, with insistence on the prince's duty as *rex Christianissimus*,[11] and on his obligations towards the church. The concern is mainly with the superficialities of politics, with practicalities. Having purely practical aims, the most important political theorizing was propounded for a very specific end: effective royal control over Parliament. From the last years of Edward III, Parliament could no longer be treated simply as a rubber stamp for royal proposals. Kings (or their ministers) had to argue and cajole, a process which encouraged the development of the so-called 'Parliamentary sermon', linking immediate practical political concerns with a homiletic statement about the proper relationship between the king and his subjects. When Parliament first assembled at the start of each session, it was usual to declare the reasons for the summons. During the later fourteenth century and for much of the fifteenth, when the Chancellor was usually a cleric – and only when the Chancellor was a cleric – this practical statement was normally preceded by a sort of sermon, based on an apposite biblical text. The biblical verses provided a peg for a statement of royal rights and duties, although all too often only the gist of the oration is recorded. On occasion the exegesis was highly royalist, emphasizing the king's exalted state. This was especially true at Richard II's subservient Parliament of 1397. Even more extreme was the speech to Edward III's Jubilee Parliament of 1376, at which the young Prince Richard was presented as heir apparent. Then the Chancellor (the Bishop of St David's) incorporated two rather extreme analogies into his general eulogy. In both, the future king was likened to the infant Christ: his presence at the proceedings was equivalent to the Presentation in the Temple – with Parliament playing the role of Simeon, and Edward III both as another Christ, and also as God the (grand)father. The occasion was also a re-enactment of the Adoration of the Magi, with Parliament offering its allegorical gifts (although possibly even the bishop felt that this was a bit much: he deliberately refrained from allowing the assembly to offer the frankincense, with its overtones of sanctity).[12]

Such extreme royalism was uncommon. Kings called Parliament because they had to – they needed the grants of money – so the 'Parliamentary sermon' usually had to be more supplicatory, frequently invoking the idea

pp. 274–97; Genet, *Four English tracts*, pp. xiii–xix, 57–168 (esp. 112–18, 146–67); Brodie, *The Tree of Commonwealth* [95], esp. 30–1, 42, 101–4.

[11] See e.g. *Tractatus . . . ad Henricum sextum*: Genet, *Four English tracts*, pp. 67, 103, 105, 107, 109, 112, 117, 121, 131, 143, 146, 150, 167–8 (also p. 71: 'christianorum christianissime Rex').

[12] For texts used 1398–1485, see Chrimes, *English constitutional ideas* [142], pp. 165–6; for examples cited (and others), *Rotuli Parliamentorum* [717], ii, pp. 361–2, iii, pp. 98, 347, 608; v, p. 345 (text only); vi, pp. 3 (text omitted), 45. Incomplete drafts survive of sermons prepared in 1483: Chrimes, *English constitutional ideas*, pp. 168–91.

of government's responsibilities, and mutual participation in decision-making. The traditional analogy of the state as a human body appeared on several occasions. Yet the king's supremacy was never in doubt. The drafts of the speeches prepared by Bishop Russell in 1483 refer to the king's obligations to the estates of the realm, and to the body politic, but his centrality is never questioned. The king rules; the subjects obey. The king (and his government) provide the stomach of the kingdom, without whose distribution of nourishment the other parts of the body wither; he is the head beneath which all the other members have their places. Moreover, when it comes to law-making, he is the God of Sinai, whom the lords (Moses) see face to face, while the people (the Commons) stand far off.[13]

Parliament was not the only place where 'political' sermons might be delivered. Meetings of Convocation faced with demands for subsidies doubtless needed reminding of their duties to the king and his role within the realm. Subjects were presumably reminded in sermons accompanying nationalistic prayers and processions of the 'right' relationship between crown and people.

The intellectual impact of this political theorizing remains uncertain. Many of the works by Englishmen survive in few, if not unique, manuscripts, so that the spread of their ideas cannot have been extensive.[14] Moreover, theorizing remains fairly ambiguous: texts could be abstracted for contrary arguments, and the European tradition within which English political thought existed was based on a combination of polarities each of which (if the basic premisses were accepted) was perfectly justifiable. Essentially, the justification for Christian rulership rested on a few biblical verses – primarily Romans 13:1–6. Here, the basic statement that 'The powers that be are ordained of God' (v.1) allowed little room for argument; although interpretation produced dissension, the dispute centred on the nature and implications of the divine ordination. Even so, these verses categorically defined the subjects' obligations, and probably provided the crucial interpretation of rulership which the populace was expected to accept. Certainly it was these few verses which attracted the comments of the author of *Dives and pauper* (written about 1410) when he considered rulership. His discussion was significantly placed within his treatment of the Fourth Commandment: Honour thy father and thy mother.[15] Possibly one of the shocks administered by Wycliffite political thought was its implicit inversion of the accepted view of subjection: the passivity induced

[13] *Rotuli Parliamentorum*, iii, pp. 337, 415, 522, 567; iv, p. 316; Chrimes, *English constitutional ideas*, pp. 159–78, esp. 173, 175, 187.

[14] Only four MSS survive of Dudley's *The Tree of Commonwealth*, only one may be 'contemporary': Brodie, pp. 11–13.

[15] Barnum, *Dives and pauper* [41], i, pp. 332–9.

by the view that God gave people the sort of government their sins deserved was to be replaced by a judgement by the people on the validity of their government based on the sins of the rulers.

The divine ordination of government was not expressed merely as an intellectual exercise. In England it had a practical reality, established through coronation. Perhaps, in the reigns after 1350, coronation was less vital than previously: from 1307 the new king had been deemed to possess regal power from the day after his precursor's death; and from 1483 it became accepted that the crown never dies.[16] Nevertheless, coronation retained an emotional significance, and the ceremony was usually arranged as early as possible in the reign. Even if accession transferred political power, coronation legitimized the transfer – and, in a very real sense, linked king and subjects in the contract of the coronation oath.

By the 1350s the church had effectively lost any claim to determine the succession to the crown. Coronation was now seen as the necessary sequel to accession. Even so, the theory expressed in the iconography of the ceremony remained very much the same; and the coronation oath implicitly defined political relationships and the parameters of governance. The whole ceremony proclaimed the divine sanction and approbation of the ruler, but with the king accepting responsibilities and duties towards his subjects for which he would himself be answerable to God. Yet coronation was not a sacrament – so the church had decided by the thirteenth century. The monarch was thus denied the sacral character which other ordinations could impart, although English monarchs still insisted on a quasi-sacramental aspect of coronation: it was as anointed rulers that they claimed authority over the church, and when he abdicated Richard II, while renouncing his claims to political power, felt unable to relinquish the spiritual character conferred on him by his anointing.[17] The dichotomy between the extreme clerical view of coronation, as establishing a functional ministry on behalf of the church, and the contrary laical interpretation as investing the king with superiority and sovereignty over all within the confines of the kingdom, remained coronation's chief legacy.

As it progressed, the coronation ceremony proclaimed the almost symbiotic relationship between king and church. It was the church which presented the king-elect to the people for acclamation. It was the church which administered the oath, with the obligations towards that institution being often emphasized in its clauses. In the oath, the monarch established

---

[16] Legg, *English coronation records* [505], pp. 81–112; Ullmann, *Liber regie capelle* [855], pp. 74–103; Fryde et al., *Handbook of British chronology* [286], pp. 30–1.

[17] Ullmann, *Liber regie capelle*, pp. 31–3; Ullmann, *Principles of government and politics* [854], pp. 140–1; Chrimes, *English constitutional ideas*, p. 7.

his relationship with his subjects: a compact of good governance, based on justice and law, and a rejection of the arbitrary. Thereafter the ruler was invested – again by the church – with his authority: anointed with holy oil, he was given the regalia, each act of investiture accompanied by an invocation of divine aid and an injunction to good rulership. Thus, when being girt with the sword, the quintessential emblem of secular authority, the notion of ecclesiastical delegation was emphasized with the injunction to receive it

from the hands of the bishops, though unworthy, yet consecrated on behalf of and by authority of the holy apostles, regally placed on you and by our blessing ordained for the defence of the holy church of God,

with the list of protective duties associated with it. Similarly, the ring was granted as a sign of the Christian faith, so that its wearer should be

a founder and protector of Christianity and the Christian faith, so that being faithful in works and steadfast in faith you shall glory with the king of kings.[18]

The ceremony was essentially religious – after all, it was inserted into the Mass – but it also produced a fervent political statement, summarizing the theoretical relations between king and God, king and church, king and people. In some sense the ceremony remade the monarch: in the baptismal symbolism of the peculiarly English anointing ceremony there was clearly the creation of a *novus homo*, a rebirth or transformation of the person. The king was granted authority by God – whether mediately or immediately was debated – and thereafter, by the grace of God, took charge of the realm as a Christian monarch, bound by the Christian code, for the defence of the church and the benefit of the people.[19]

Despite this, English kings were not theocratic rulers. Personal sanctification did not produce theocracy. Nevertheless, he who in the fifteenth century claimed to be anointed with oil delivered to the exiled Becket by the Virgin herself, and who because of his strange divinity could cure both the King's Evil and epilepsy, was clearly set apart from his subjects. While England saw nothing like the sacred princely blood cult which developed in France, indications of increasing theocratic claims appear in changes made to the coronation ritual for Henry VI.[20] By 1500 the king

[18] Legg, *English coronation records*, pp. 95, 97.

[19] See generally Chrimes, *English constitutional ideas*, ch. 1.

[20] McKenna, 'Coronation oil' [560]; Ullmann, 'Becket's miraculous oil' [853]; Sandquist, 'The holy oil' [735]; Bloch, *The royal touch* [70], pp. 53–60, 64–7, 92–5, 100–7 (see also Chrimes, *English constitutional ideas*, pp. 7–8); Ullmann, *Liber regie capelle*, pp. 24–8, 36–41; Wolffe, *Henry VI* [918], p. 50.

constituted a separate 'estate', supported on his eminence by the power of the church as the transmitter of divine approval.

What happened after coronation might be another matter. Occasional changes made to the coronation oath, and especially Henry VIII's attempt to rewrite the whole compact in highly royalist terms, show that there was scope for debate about the ceremony's implications.[21] But once crowned, what was to be the relationship between the king and the church? While there is no formal declaration of a secular definition of political authority, the importance of coronation was diminishing – what increasingly mattered was accession, and in the fifteenth century legitimism. The most dramatic reflection of this came with Edward IV's coup in 1461. His assumption of government was the most secular ceremony of the period. His reign was dated from his taking possession of the kingdom, enacted when he seated himself on the throne of King's Bench in Westminster Hall: placing himself on the seat of supreme (lay) justice in a lay building, and there entering into a form of contract with the kingdom. That done, he moved to Westminster abbey to receive homage from the nobility in a ceremony which was almost a crownless coronation – the real event being delayed some months. This procedure was copied by Richard III at his accession in 1483.[22] Alongside such secularist developments, if the implications read into them were actually there, has to be placed the developing 'imperialism' of the English monarchy. This became especially noticeable under Richard II, with his aspirations to be Holy Roman Emperor, and his view of royal authority which seemingly owed much to the ethos of Roman law. The increased use of an arched crown instead of the open circular diadem, and its developing 'imperial' connotations under the Tudors carried the iconography of monarchy another step along the road to 1533. But the case can be overstated: there are also suggestions of 'divine right' monarchy, again under Richard II, and coronation was not deprived of significance: Richard III appealed to it as well as his right of inheritance to legitimize his accession.[23]

The twin influences of coronation and imperialism, with their implications, potentially threatened the clergy's position within the kingdom. How far the clerics appreciated them is doubtful, until they became blatant in the reign of Henry VIII. Clerics themselves – Wyclif is the most obvious example – provided the core arguments for nationalistic anti-papalism in this period and such arguments could easily be diverted

[21] Legg, *English coronation records*, pp. 240–1; Ullmann, 'This realm of England', p. 183.

[22] Armstrong, *England, France, and Burgundy* [9], pp. 80–90.

[23] Harvey, 'Richard II and York' [359], pp. 213–14, and plates at pp. 206–7; *Rotuli Parliamentorum*, vi, p. 242; Chrimes, *English constitutional ideas*, p. 125. Ullmann, 'This realm of England', pp. 177, 184 n. 33; Grierson, 'Origins of English sovereign' [318], pp. 127–34.

against the English church. In the process the crown's status was correspondingly enhanced. Those involved in more mundane governmental activities also helped to integrate the church within the structure of the kingdom, and thereby effectively contribute towards its subjection. Few, however, seem to have offered theoretical assistance to the monarchy in such terms. Even so, in the fourteenth century the programme for a royally directed disendowment of the church seems to have been originated by the friars, although taken over and made very much his own by Wyclif. In 1515 one of the major pre-Reformation furores occurred when a friar, Henry Standish, supported lay jurisdiction over the clergy, and challenged benefit of clergy. Rounded on by fellow clerics, he appealed to the king for support, his detractors being rapidly brought to heel by threats of the penalties of Praemunire.[24]

If the church did 'make' the king at coronation, could he be 'unmade'? Although not sacramental, was the change in the king's character effected by coronation nevertheless indelible? If the church, acting as God's mediator, had given the king his powers could that church, by the same authority, remove them? If, as extremists claimed, the church conceded rulership to the king conditionally, then logically the ruler could also lose divine support, and the commission be rescinded. The coronation oath, however the precise relationships it created were defined, could be construed as a contract, a 'job specification', even a contract of employment. It established the broad limits within which the monarch had a free hand, and set the pattern which he should follow. By 1300, the canonists had fairly strictly defined the bounds and the models for action if these limits were exceeded, or if the king did not meet his obligations. If the former, he was clearly a tyrant, if the latter, a *rex inutilis* – literally, a 'useless king'. In either case, he forfeited his kingship, and could be removed.[25]

   Such forfeiture and removal were justified not in terms of 'democratic principles', or of subjects' 'rights' to participate in government, but in ecclesiastical terms. During the thirteenth century, the papacy had developed its own deposition theory for lay rulers, closely linked to the theoretical status of several secular monarchs as papal vassals. England meshed into that pattern, because of King John's voluntary subjection to Innocent III – although this vassal, tributary status had few practical results, and was actually repudiated in 1366.[26] England experienced the effect of these

---

[24] Farr, *Wyclif as reformer*, pp. 91–4; Daly, *Political thought of Wyclif*, esp. ch. 4–5; Aston, ' "Caim's castles" ' [16], pp. 50–1; Elton, *Reform and Reformation* [251], pp. 53–6. For benefit of clergy, see 4/2, at nn. 20–9.
[25] Peters, *The shadow king* [654].
[26] Lunt, *Financial relations* [534], pp. 66–70.

deposition theories in 1327, with the rather ramshackle removal of Edward II. But that year's events also showed some of the difficulties of the theory: although the king could be declared to have forfeited his throne, how would he actually lose it? The *rex inutilis* had to be adjudged worthless, but by whom? According to the church's theory, by ecclesiastics; but if they failed to carry the people with them (or, even worse, if the people got carried away, regardless of what the clerics thought), what then? Moreover, the notionally 'contractual' feudalism of the English monarchy could generate a theory for removal without recourse to the church. Canonical processes could be invoked in both accusation and removal of a king, as was suggested with the committee established to organize the removal of Richard II in 1399. Formal implementation of these processes was difficult, and if actually carried through would have raised major questions about the locus of political authority. These could only be avoided by allowing abdication, and only after the renunciation proclaiming deposition. As a result, the development of any proper English deposition theory was still-born: effectively the only way to deprive a monarch was to 'allow' him to deprive himself, as with Edward II and Richard II; or else totally to deny the ex-king's right to rule while accepting his practical status, as was done with Henry VI, Edward V, and Richard III.[27]

The religious sanction to the political order was highly ambiguous in theory and in practice. Religion, or the church, intervened not merely figuratively or theoretically, but to practical effect. Religious associations could glorify the crown, or justify a rebellion; loyalty or opposition could make a saint; 'the church in danger' could rally support for or against the ruler.

The political usefulness of saints had been recognized for centuries, especially when they joined victorious Christian armies in battles. But exploitation could be more subtle. The increasing invocation of specifically English saints in the reign of Henry V has been linked to the growing nationalism in his reign: the Anglo-Saxons could again come into their own because England was rising, and the developing cult of St George as national patron similarly assisted the growth of an English identity.[28] More sinister was the exploitation of saints to justify particular political stances within the kingdom. Most of the English 'political saints' of the later middle ages fit this model: they were usually unlikely, even unfitting, candidates for canonization. But their deaths, seen as political martyrdoms, could serve political ends, especially to justify and augment rulership (particularly if they fell to the opposing view in a political upheaval).

[27] Wilkinson, 'Deposition of Richard II' [903], pp. 337–43; Caspary, 'Deposition of Richard II' [128]; Pollard, 'Tudor gleanings, I' [664], pp. 1–3.
[28] Catto, 'Religious change' [130], pp. 107–8.

Therefore Richard II supported the most unlikely candidate of the period, Edward II, in reaction against the use of precedents from that unfortunate reign to justify rebellion and opposition to himself. This paralleled the contemporary revival of the cult of Edward II's main rival, Thomas of Lancaster, which achieved its political apotheosis in the accession of the Lancastrian dynasty in 1399. In the fifteenth century Richard III and the Tudors in turn exploited the cult of Henry VI, seeking to link themselves with a legitimizing heavenly intercessor, and thereby detract from their rivals. The third main political saint of the period, Richard Scrope, Archbishop of York, bridges the gap between the supporters and opponents of a regime. Executed in 1405 for involvement in rebellion against Henry IV, his death was immediately seen as martyrdom. He was both a successor to Thomas Becket for the northern province (his death resulting from actions 'in defence of the church'), and also a political martyr in opposition to Henry IV. His cult soon spread, being adopted by Henry V in a rather bizarre reaction against his father, and later receiving strong support from the Yorkists who sought to link him to their cause and thus justify their own hostility to the Lancastrians. Although Scrope, like many other 'saints' of the period, was never formally canonized, his cult was relatively widespread, and long-lasting: he was depicted in stained glass in several places, and fifteenth-century chroniclers almost invariably called him a saint. Although the last evidence for discussion of canonization dates from the 1460s, the cult persisted much later.[29]

The 'manifesto' associated with Scrope and the 1405 rebellion provides the only true example of the exploitation of popular sainthood to justify rebellion in the years 1350 to 1540. With its references to ecclesiastical reform, and the need for divine judgement on a usurper, the manifesto legitimizes action against an unlawful and tyrannical ruler.[30] The other two notable English medieval examples of such 'sanctification' of rebellion date from earlier times: the cult of Simon de Montfort, which arose after his defeat and death at the hands of royalists in 1265; and that of Thomas of Lancaster, executed in 1322 for his opposition to Edward II – opposition which provided precedents of both political activity and religious observance to provide the perfect antithesis to Richard II and his claims. The deaths of Simon and Thomas defending what were later regarded as semi-populist and anti-absolutist policies gave valuable legitimization to opposition to the crown. A further royal opponent who was a candidate

[29] Bray, 'Concepts of sainthood' [86], pp. 60–2; McKisack, Fourteenth century [563], p. 467; McKenna, 'Popular canonization' [561], pp. 610–22; Lovat, 'John Blacman revisited' [531], pp. 182–3, 190; McNiven, 'Betrayal of Scrope' [565], pp. 173–213.

[30] See McNiven, 'Betrayal of Scrope', p. 180, and against (amongst others), McKenna, 'Popular canonization', p. 620; see also Wright, 'Provenance and manuscript tradition' [930], pp. 98–9, 101.

for canonization, and who might be considered a political saint, was
Archbishop Robert Winchelsey of Canterbury, the leader of the clergy in
their opposition to Edward I. But the evidence for his cult is small, and
support for his canonization was probably more to be found among the
clergy than among the laity.[31]

Action against a government could also be justified by claims to be
acting for the protection of religion. Archbishop Scrope's involvement in
the 1405 revolt shows how the church might become embroiled in real
political revolt. Such active participation was, however, rare. More serious
was the occasional linkage between ecclesiastical sentiments and political
and social revolt. Here the two key episodes were the Peasants' Revolt of
1381, and the revolts of 1536. However, although clerics overtly participated in the rising of 1381 and in the events of 1536, these cannot really be
considered 'religious revolts'. The Peasants' Revolt was primarily directed
against the exercise of lordship, but did have some hints of Christian
millenarianism and anti-clerical aspirations. Contemporary chroniclers
also sought to associate it with the ideas of John Wyclif, possibly misunderstanding his views on dominion and grace. Wyclif had used the idea
that legitimate lordship was dependent on being in a state of grace to
undermine ecclesiastical lordship; the chroniclers extended it to imply
the undermining of secular lordship as well, although this was clearly
contrary to Wyclif's own thoughts. Conclusive evidence linking Wycliffism
and the revolt has not been found, but that it could be imagined suggests
the force of religious ideas at the time. The social and ecclesiastical
reforms advocated by the rebels – whether in actuality, or merely in the
fictions of their reporters – although traditional in their emphasis on the
rights of the poor, nevertheless could have undermined the social status
quo. If they did actually link with Wyclif's ideas of justification for civil
lordship to reject lordship where the lord was not fulfilling his Christian
duty, then the threat was even greater. There are clear premonitions of
'No bishop, no king' in the response to this intellectual and practical
challenge.[32]

Although Lollardy was not a serious immediate threat, its associated
concept of the elect, and the exclusiveness which allowed something as
hare-brained as the attempted coup of Sir John Oldcastle to occur in 1414,
showed that religious sentiments could threaten political stability. Oldcastle's revolt may have effectively ended the Lollard political threat,
scaring off those among the ruling strata otherwise tempted to tinker with

---

[31] Bray, 'Concepts of sainthood', pp. 46–58, 63–5, 67–8.
[32] Kenny, *Wyclif* [465], pp. 45–7, 49–52, 92; Wilks, 'Predestination, property, and power';
Leff, *Heresy* [503], ii, pp. 546–9; Aston, *Lollards and reformers* [15], pp. 2–7, 11–13; Hilton,
Bondmen made free [393], pp. 207–11, 222–3, 227–9; Heath, *Church and realm*, pp. 191–2.

it, but there are occasional later suggestions of a continuing Lollard political stance.[33]

Not until the Reformation did the exploitation of the church to justify or encourage rebellion again come to the fore. Here, however, there is probably very little sign of a 'theological' concern, save perhaps on the part of the clerical participants. (The same might also be said of the revolt of 1381: the anticlericalism of that year was probably more pragmatic than intellectual, involving attacks on the seignorial and exploitative authority of the church, rather than on its concept of the road to salvation.) In 1536 the use of the church and the Old Religion as a rallying cry possibly depended less on theology and faith than on the church's institutional integration into the framework of parochial self-esteem and local economic activity. Nevertheless, there are some signs of 'Counter-Reformation' tendencies, in occasionally vocal opposition to the Royal Supremacy, and in the defence of monasticism as a vocation. But monasteries as institutions had other local importance. From the first suppressions, the threat which Dissolution posed to the local economies was evidently well appreciated. In 1525 there was a riot at Bayham abbey (Sussex) against dissolution, reaction against the economic dislocation which would result locally being one of several possible motivations.[34] Other areas would have appreciated the social implications, the communal impact, of the sudden removal of a considerable employer and spender. Besides the economic impact, those seeking to encourage revolt could also exploit the proprietary feelings of parishioners for their own churches. Crucifixes, chalices, and vestments all belonged to the local church, but they also belonged to the parishioners whose ancestors (if not they themselves) had given them: ancestral links made them 'theirs'; they also reflected communal pride and self-awareness. Yet what, according to the clergy who incited the rebels of 1536, were Henry VIII's intentions? He was going to expropriate those communities, steal 'their' church ornaments and leave them with fairly base bare necessities. Would they allow 'their' churches to be despoiled to fill the pockets of a rapacious monarch who despised the true faith? Such persuasive arguments appealed to various levels of self-interest to justify action against the crown and its ministers. The problem with the Pilgrimage of Grace, as with other revolts, is to disentangle the plethora of motivations which produced the explosion, and to determine relative importance. In the Peasants' Revolt, for instance, it appears clear that the religious element was of relatively little importance, but the position with the events of 1536–7 is much more complex, betraying a good deal of regional and personal divergence.[35]

[33] Aston, *Lollards and reformers*, p. 36; Thomson, 'A Lollard rising' [827], pp. 101–2.
[34] Goring, 'Riot at Bayham abbey' [307], pp. 2–7.
[35] Davies, 'Pilgrimage of Grace' [187], pp. 62–74; Bowker, 'Lincolnshire 1536' [79],

From making the ruler at coronation, to threatening his government with rebellion, at all levels the church and religious sentiments could be involved in political action. The precise degree of involvement, the importance of such factors balanced against others, is of course debatable, and constantly changed. Throughout, there are contradictions and paradoxes. Doubtless, contemporaries were aware of them, but theories were there to be contradicted: hedging bets was not an unwise proposition. Yet much of the church's formal involvement in the theory of government, in developing constitutional ideas, in justifying or opposing governmental actions, remained on the level of speculation. It was also declining. As political ideas in the fifteenth century concerned themselves less with monarchy than with the abstract entity of the state and considerations of the practicality of government, so the nature of political thinking also changed. Lay involvement increased, speculation became more practical and pragmatic, and increasingly derived from legal thinking rather than theology – it is no coincidence that the century's leading English 'political' writer was a layman, Sir John Fortescue, one-time Chief Justice of England. Even though this pragmatic approach retained 'religious' overtones, such as the interpretation of the Parliament as a Trinity, with its proceedings representing a Mass, advanced in 1401, such views were becoming no more than analogies.[36]

Moreover, practical church influence on the structure of politics was limited. If the king had to be dethroned, as Richard II was, it would have been pointless for the church to try to obstruct the accession of Henry IV. The Bishop of Carlisle did, and for his pains lost his see.[37] Whatever its theoretical stance, in reality the church had to follow leads, and submit to control. That this control was formalized and exploitative is shown by its actual relationship with, and integration into, the governance of the realm.

3.2 THE CHURCH IN THE STATE

Given its wealth, its international connections, and its virtual monopoly of learning until the fifteenth century, it was only natural that the church and its personnel should be firmly integrated into the political structure.

---

pp. 195–212; Dickens, 'Motivations in the Pilgrimage of Grace' [211], esp. pp. 50–64; Davies, 'Popular religion' [188], pp. 58–88.

[36] Chrimes, *English constitutional ideas*, pp. 68–9, 300–32 (the use of the yearbooks elsewhere in the volume admirably indicates these developments); Genet, 'Ecclesiastics and political theory', p. 35; *Rotuli Parliamentorum*, iii, p. 456.

[37] Salter, Pantin, and Richardson, *Formularies* [732], i, p. 182.

It provided bureaucrats, politicians (for want of a better word), finance, and a useful back-up structure to serve the needs of the crown. All of these are important, although their relative status is often difficult to determine, and fluctuated with specific circumstances. Times, and relationships, changed: by 1540, the church's role in administration was much less significant than in 1350; whereas its financial contributions to the state had grown considerably under the rapacious early Tudors.

The political structure was perhaps most dependent on the church to provide basic administrative personnel: the bureaucrats whose pen-pushing was so vital to government record-keeping. This clerical involvement operated at several levels, producing paradoxical results: the period of perhaps greatest clerical influence in policy – Wolsey's time – reveals the supreme governmental influence of an individual churchman just when the clerical influence or participation at the lowest levels of the structure had been virtually eliminated by the laicization of the 'civil service'. The relationship affecting clerics in state service was blatantly symbiotic: individuals were as dependent on the crown for securing their careers within the church as the crown was dependent on the church for providing through those careers sufficient finance and motivation for continued service. In some ways the involvement of the crown's administrative personnel in the clerical career structure was a mutual exploitation of the church for personal gain, in which the institution was the victim.

But the system was not static: changes occurred, although at varying rates. The early fifteenth century witnessed a major change, with the rise of the lay bureaucrat, the gentleman administrator, not committed to a clerical career, and therefore outside the process of ecclesiastical exploitation. The increasing laicization of the royal administration throughout the fifteenth century changed the pressures on the church, forcing the crown to new expedients to ensure payment for its servants.[38]

The role of clerics within the state needs consideration from the lowest levels upwards. Even in the fourteenth century clerks – those who could write – would probably be clerics, even if only in minor orders. The crown's patronage of benefices, whatever their precise status, gave those in orders and royal employment a relatively strong position for securing their future careers. In particular, from the early fourteenth century at the latest, the crown had claimed (and enforced) for its beneficed clerks the priceless privilege of not being bound by the rules of residence. They may also have evaded the obligations to proceed to higher orders on appointment to a benefice. The king's clerks could therefore remain acolytes and non-resident rectors throughout their careers. At some point they would either commit themselves to higher orders if they sought an extended

[38] Storey, 'Gentlemen-bureaucrats' [787], pp. 97–107, 110–22.

church career, or else, having milked their benefices, could assert their lay status, marry, and settle down. There are, indeed, instances of king's clerks who were declared to have vacated their benefices precisely on account of marriage.[39]

The process whereby minor clerks could rise to pre-eminence in royal service, and in the end acquire major clerical positions, remains relatively obscure. As ever, patronage and self-promotion combined to work their charms. Connections with magnates, or dependence on those higher up the administrative ladder, doubtless eased some promotions. Lower down, there are occasionally suggestions of corruption, with officials in charge of the appropriate seals abusing their position to write out their own presentations to benefices. Higher up, self-advertisement was probably necessary: it was said of John Prophet, one of the leading lights of the Privy Seal office under Henry IV, that he did not gain a bishopric for the straightforward reason that he refused to beg for one.[40]

Although not all royal servants obtained benefices there was nevertheless a close correlation between royal service and ecclesiastical promotion. One outcome of this was that among the ecclesiastics were most of the leading government figures. This was largely a matter of exploitation: the prebends and other major benefices provided the incomes which saved money for the crown, and were the potential rewards which tied loyalty to it. Throughout the period, even if there was laicization at the lower levels, the leading state officials (apart from the Treasurers) were almost invariably clerics, from the Lord Chancellors to Chancellors of the Exchequer. The Privy Seal remained in clerical hands throughout, as did other offices. The Masters of the Rolls were with few exceptions clerics, some of them en route to bishoprics.[41] Lesser diplomatic functionaries also tended to be churchmen. During the fifteenth century, much of the diplomatic negotiation was entrusted to clerics, despite the strong leaven of secular aristocrats which such missions necessarily contained. Thus, the envoys to Prussia and the Hanseatic League in 1421–61 included two bishops, a prior of the Order of St John, and various Oxford graduates. Several of these people participated in other missions: the prior of St John, Robert Botyll, was involved in negotiations with France, Aragon, Burgundy, and the papacy.

---

[39] Jones, 'Patronage and administration' [451], pp. 15–23; Wright, *Church and crown* [929], pp. 164–6; Storey, 'Clergy and common law' [786], p. 351; Storey, 'Gentlemen-bureaucrats', pp. 101–2. The problems of orders and non-residence are touched on in the *Articuli cleri* of 1316: the latter is resolved for the king, but orders are ignored (*Statutes* [776], i/2, p. 172).

[40] Storey, 'Clergy and common law', p. 351; Jones, 'Patronage and administration', pp. 21–2.

[41] E.g. Fryde et al., *Handbook of British chronology*, pp. 80–1, 86–8, 94–6, 105–7; see also 4/7, at n. 97. For fifteenth-century royal servants becoming bishops, see Rosenthal, *Training of an elite* [711], pp. 36–41.

Obviously, it was in dealing with the papacy and the frequent general councils of the church in this period that the clerical envoys really came into their own; but even here the laity could participate, so that entrusting such work to clerics did reflect a deliberate governmental choice.[42]

Clerical participation in the upper echelons of government unavoidably meant embroilment in political machinations. Insofar as ecclesiastical promotion resulted from political actions, or connections, this was a logical link. But a cleric's political activity also reflected his general social position: in political matters it may be difficult to differentiate between an individual as a bishop, and that same person as a member of a particular kin-group or affinity. It may have been as bureaucrats that Simon Sudbury (the Archbishop of Canterbury) and Robert Hales (prior of the Order of St John) were murdered in the Peasants' Revolt of 1381; but it was because of their too-obvious alignment with the Duke of Suffolk that Adam Moleyns, Bishop of Chichester, and William Ayscough, Bishop of Salisbury, met their deaths in 1450.[43] Their landed power and spiritual obligations imposed a political role on the clergy, one which they were often determined to play to the full.

To the extent that the higher ecclesiastics, as the crown's leading officials, were the king's own appointees, it was only natural that they should act politically. The hub of national political and administrative activity was at the king's council; not at the occasional Great Councils, which met on important occasions and to some extent corresponded to a reduced House of Lords, but the continual council, which managed much of the state's day-to-day organization.[44] Usually clerics – normally bishops – provided the core of the conciliar structure. Although often a minority among the nominal councillors, the clerical members (who naturally included the chancellor and other great officers) nevertheless constituted the majority in the small group of workhorses who ensured the continuity of government. Thus, in 1392–3, although bishops were only nine of the twenty-four known councillors, they provided five of the seven most regular attenders. This pattern of clerical involvement holds true for much of the period, although there are signs of decreasing influence towards the end, probably due to the laicization of the bureaucracy. Several clerics (possibly because of their administrative responsibilities) outrode the political fluc-

---

[42] Heath, *Church and realm*, pp. 317–30; Ferguson, *English diplomacy* [270], pp. 179, 188, 199, 206–8, 214–18; Rosenthal, *Training of an elite*, pp. 41–5.

[43] Thomson, *Transformation of England* [831], pp. 26–8, 35.

[44] The only overall survey of the council is Baldwin, *King's council* [35], now out of date. A brief survey of the fifteenth century is Brown, 'King's councillors' [99]; see also Thomson, *Transformation of England*, pp. 284–91; Lander, 'Council, administration, and councillors' [493], pp. 166–80; Virgoe, 'King's council, 1437–61' [878], pp. 142, 157–60; Kirby, 'Councils and councillors' [478], pp. 61–5.

tuations of the fifteenth century: Peter Taster, Dean of St Severin's at Bordeaux, first appears on the council in the early 1450s, remaining a member through to the 1470s; and many other clerics successfully crossed the watersheds of dynastic change without any apparent difficulty. While it is rarely possible to go beyond the record of participation in conciliar business to any assessment of active politicking by the clerical councillors, nevertheless council membership was clearly important, occasionally crucial. It was via the council that Henry Beaufort, for one, acquired and maintained his dominant position in Lancastrian politics.[45]

Much of the activity of these clerical politicians remains obscure: the historiography tends to concentrate on the leaders of supposed factions among the lay magnates rather than on their ecclesiastical adherents. However, episcopal involvement in factional activity is occasionally obvious, especially from c.1380 to 1490. Under Richard II, for example, Thomas Arundel, originally bishop of Ely but later promoted via York to Canterbury, was notable for his association with the party of the Appellants – those opposed to the group which had built up around the king in the early 1380s. Given his close family connections with four of the five Appellants, and weaker links with the fifth, his activity is not especially surprising. However, his precise motives for involvement in the palace revolution of 1387–8 remain uncertain. He experienced the king's revenge in 1397, being packed off from Canterbury to the bishopric of St Andrews (effectively *in partibus infidelium*, being held by adherents of the antipope) in the king's counter-coup. But he returned to Canterbury with Henry Bolingbroke, playing a considerable part in the events of the usurpation. Arundel remained a strong political force throughout the reign of Henry IV. He fell victim to factional disputes during the temporary ascendancy of the Prince of Wales from 1409 onwards, when he lost, but later recovered, his position as chancellor.[46]

The reigns of Richard II and Henry IV were merely the foretaste of later episcopal involvement in fifteenth-century factions, when almost every major family had its bishop. The need for monarchs or their controllers to stabilize their parties almost required that bishoprics be used to that end. The factional rivalries of the reigns of Henry VI and Edward IV are reflected in the appearance of associated names on the bishops' bench. This resulted in a spate of episcopal involvement in rebellions, with several bishops losing their temporalities, fleeing to sanctuary, being imprisoned, or going into exile.[47]

It is one thing to view the political activities of clerics in such terms; it is

[45] Virgoe, 'King's council, 1437–61', p. 142.
[46] Thomson, *Transformation of England*, pp. 154, 162–3, 171.
[47] Knecht, 'Wars of the Roses' [481], pp. 110–28.

another to confront the issue of just how far this political activity was specifically 'clerical', or identifiable with 'ecclesiastical' interests. Certainly the church appreciated the value of its support for the political structure, and may have considered that support a saleable commodity. The Canterbury Convocation of 1399, summoned in the immediate aftermath of Henry IV's revolution, and well and truly dominated by the restored Archbishop Arundel, did much to stabilize and legitimize the new regime. But if the church was to gain from the relationship, conditions had to be exactly right. When Henry IV lacked money conditions could be attached to grants of clerical taxes: a reduction in interference by secular justices in ecclesiastical libeties was the price of York's grant in 1404; while at the same time in Canterbury, Arundel was exploiting the king's financial embarrassments to get redress for clerical grievances. Similarly, in 1462, both Convocations delayed their grants until Edward IV had issued a charter of liberties for the church – although in the end that proved relatively worthless. At times, political opposition may have been motivated by truly ecclesiastical considerations: Archbishop Scrope's participation in the 1405 Percy rebellion may have been naive, but his involvement did perhaps reflect a genuine concern to defend ecclesiastical liberties against an increasingly tyrannical monarch who had ignored the promises made at his accession.[48]

Political involvement did not need to be a succession of crises. The clergy also had a continuous political role through their representation in Parliament. The clergy's presence in Parliament usually provided the only forum at which the church of the whole kingdom could claim to be represented – otherwise there were only the two independent provincial convocations. Indeed, it was only the clerical membership which made Parliament itself a truly national gathering, providing the only representatives for the palatine counties of Durham and Cheshire. The rise of Convocation during the fourteenth century, and its continued importance through to the Reformation, overshadows the presence of clerical proctors in the House of Commons and of some abbots and all the diocesan bishops in the Lords. Even if the separate clerical representation in Parliament (other than the abbots and bishops) did atrophy during the later middle ages, it was not completely abolished even by 1536.[49]

In the Lords the bishops were the chief clerical representatives; but they were not alone. Keepers of spiritualities were sometimes summoned, and the heads of several religious houses also attended until the Dissolution.

---

[48] Storey, 'Episcopal king-makers' [788], pp. 85–6, 88–9, 91–3; Swanson, *Reg. Scrope* [796], ii, p. 19; McNiven, 'Betrayal of Scrope', pp. 180–5; see also 4/7 at n. 89.
[49] Kemp, *Counsel and consent* [464], pp. 106–57; Weske, *Convocation* [892]; McHardy, 'Lower clergy in Parliament' [552], p. 107.

By 1400 the number of abbots summoned had stabilized at twenty-seven, at which it remained until Henry VIII made some additions. The summoned abbots represented most of the major abbeys, among them Peterborough, Westminster, Waltham, St Albans, and Battle. The prior of the Order of St John in England also attended: although of a religious order he was technically a layman, and enjoyed the status of a lay peer. Just why particular houses were represented is unclear, but tradition maintained their right to be summoned, even if it could not enforce their presence. There were thus created a number of 'ecclesiastical baronies by writ'. Nominally the clerical membership of the Upper House comprised over half those entitled to a summons – a proportion increased by fluctuations in the numbers of lay peers, and by occasional chimeras like Thomas, Lord La Warre, summoned as a lay baron to Parliaments under Henry IV, V, and VI, but in fact a cleric. Nominal membership did not mean active participation: many ecclesiastical 'lords' obtained royal licences excusing their attendance at Parliament completely, or allowing their representation by proxy; while an even greater number – particularly among the abbots – simply ignored the summonses and did not attend.[50] However, the ecclesiastical lords had not totally renounced their responsibilities to the church. In the Parliamentary debates of the period it was the Lords (especially the bishops rather than the regulars, with their lackadaisical attendance) who provided the main opposition to anticlerical moves.

The clergy also had their official representatives in the lower house, at their most active in the earlier part of the period. Again, the precise basis of their presence is not clear: whether they were considered as representing a distinct 'estate' or just as part of the tax-paying population, whose consent was needed before they could be taxed. The original intention seems to have been to integrate the clergy into Parliament as a unified body representing the whole kingdom; but this idea had collapsed by the 1350s. By 1400, the representation of the lower clergy in Parliament was decreasing, although it had not fizzled out completely. This was partly due to the parallel growth of the Convocations – gatherings of clergy representatives for each of the provinces – which were clearly separate from Parliament after 1340: as an alternative forum for debate and (from the royal viewpoint) of consent to taxation, they gradually replaced Parliament as the main arena for the expression of clerical views. The

---

[50] Denton, 'Clergy and Parliament', pp. 89–91; Roskell, 'Attendance of the lords' [714], pp. 156–60, 168–98, 202–4 (for La Warre, ibid., pp. 173, 203, *Complete Peerage*, iv [160], pp. 150–1); Parliamentary abbots from 1400 listed in Reich, 'Parliamentary abbots to 1470' [692], pp. 349–50, and ibid., pp. 357–9 for the prior of St John (see also Lehmberg, *The Reformation Parliament* [507], pp. 39, 41–5; Lehmberg, *Later Parliaments* [508], pp. 11–13, 52–3).

decline in Parliamentary activity probably also owed something to the clergy's attitude: while accepting the right to be represented, they rejected any idea of obligatory attendance, which therefore tended to be sporadic. The decline may also have owed something to the essential disunity of the English church, especially the division and occasional rivalry between York and Canterbury and reluctance to attend gatherings in the other province.[51]

Even so, the clergy retained a nominal representation in the lower house which is all too easily overlooked. Their full tally would run to ten cathedral priors, thirteen cathedral deans, sixty archdeacons, twenty-three proctors of cathedral churches, and forty-two proctors of parish clergy within the dioceses. However, it was most unlikely that these would all attend at once. Several would simply not appear; others would be represented by proxy – and there are numerous instances of one individual acting on behalf of several other groups in the early fourteenth century. Known proctors before 1340 were all clerics, but later in the century laymen were sometimes appointed. When Richard II's 'counter-coup' was under way in 1397, the clergy as a whole had Sir Thomas Percy foisted on them as a lay proctor so that they could be 'represented' in the political events of the time. The later proctors may have hidden their activities on behalf of the clergy behind their more effective representation of another constituency.[52] Nevertheless, their presence allowed the crown to claim that Parliament did represent the whole kingdom, and that its decisions bound all. This was important fiscally, for the clergy, besides paying taxes as clerics, had further sources of revenue which were subject to temporal exactions; for statutory purposes it might also prevent real rivalry between Convocations and Parliament as the clerics could be deemed to have assented to the new laws along with the rest of the kingdom.

Despite the declining significance of clerical representation in Parliament during the period, the church retained its voice, and continued to present petitions and requests for legal changes. It was in Parliament that the most violent contests between 'church' and 'state' were fought out, providing the venue for clerical (principally episcopal) attempts to quash lay attempts to subject the church to their restrictions.

For the crown, one of Parliament's main functions was to assent to taxation. As a massive landowner, the church could hardly expect to be

---

[51] Denton, 'Clergy and Parliament', pp. 95–7, 100–1, 106–7; Denton and Dooley, *Representation of lower clergy* [205], esp. pp. 49–52.

[52] Denton, 'Clergy and Parliament', pp. 91–2, 105; on proctors see also McHardy, 'Lower clergy in Parliament', pp. 100–7. For known proxies before 1340, see Denton and Dooley, *Representation of lower clergy*, p. 103–21.

untouched by the crown's fiscal demands. Nevertheless, until the late thirteenth century it claimed a basic exemption from taxation by the secular power: spiritual matters could only be taxed by papal authority, and with the clergy's consent (although the clerics' personal property was taxed with the laity's). The 1290s had forcefully rebuffed the clerical stance, in the conflict between Edward I and Archbishop Winchelsey in 1296 which arose from the publication of the papal bull *Clericis laicos*. Edward I needed money; the church, with papal support, resisted his demands. Edward then argued that if the clergy would not be subjects, he would not be their lord – and promptly outlawed them all, leaving them prey to all anticlerical forces with no royal protection. Within months this clerical rebellion collapsed, the penitents paying fines equivalent to the proposed tax to recover crown protection, with the papacy in due course similarly backing down.[53] Henceforth, the church would pay taxes to the crown in times of 'national emergency'; but the king would determine when that was. Thereafter, with monotonous regularity, monarchs issued stereotyped pleas which asserted this necessity, and the church (not always meekly) coughed up.[54]

The procedures of ecclesiastical taxation were complex. The ideally rigid distinction between 'spiritualities' and 'temporalities' was never formally established. The great starting-point, and yardstick for later taxation, was the assessment ordered by Pope Nicholas IV in 1291: despite its disadvantages, and subject to some revisions, it remained in force until the 1520s. It established a notional sum of the church's tax liability, assessing both the spiritualities and the 'temporalities annexed to spiritualities' – the lands then in the church's possession. But ecclesiastical or clerical possession was not static; property constantly drifted into the possession of individuals or institutions. For these post-1291 acquisitions and the properties thereon, the clerics and ecclesiastical corporations were taxed with the laity. Normally, discussions of 'clerical taxation' only consider the levies made in accordance with the 1291 assessment and its subsequent modifications; but they were not the full sum of the taxation extracted from the church: it also contributed to 'lay' tenths and fifteenths, and other types of taxes, for its unassessed possessions.[55]

Evidence for ecclesiastical contributions to such 'lay' taxation is admittedly scarce. That the clergy should pay is clear from the Parliamentary grants; occasionally under Richard II these specifically levied taxes on lands acquired in mortmain since 1291. But hard evidence of payment is

---

[53] Now detailed in Denton, *Robert Winchelsey* [202], pp. 85–135.

[54] For fourteenth-century grants after 1350 see Weske, *Convocation*, pp. 253–70, 285–95; for fifteenth-century grants McHardy, 'Clerical taxation' [556], pp. 179–89 (subject to additions: compare Swanson, *Reg. Scrope*, ii, pp. ii–iii).

[55] Willard, 'English church and lay taxes' [907].

limited. The ossified assessments for the tenths and fifteenths (based on the distribution of taxation in 1332) had made lists of taxpayers unnecessary for central records (although they do survive for Kent, for reasons not immediately apparent, with the names of clerical taxpayers appearing alongside those of the laity). Occasional signs of clerical contribution to lay subsidies are found among other records. Scattered assessment lists survive among borough archives (as at Leicester and Shrewsbury), and other hints in clerical taxation lists (as in Lincoln diocese).[56] The clergy and ecclesiastical institutions also contributed to some of the innovatory taxes of the period. The land tax of 1412, a payment of 6s. 8d. for every £20-worth of land held, was according to the grant to affect both lay and clerical properties 'except lands and tenements purchased in mortmain before . . . [1291] . . . and except lands and tenements in the hands of spiritual lords and religious purchased in free alms since . . . [1291] . . . and for which they pay tenths with the clergy'. The returns to this tax list several religious houses, with a few bishops and individual clerics.[57] A new assessment was also ordered for the subsidy of 1450, a tax on incomes, which extended to clerics for non-spiritualities and lands acquired in mortmain since 1291. York's assessment lists several chaplains (presumably stipendiaries) who were to contribute.[58] However, a problem with these payments to essentially lay taxes lies in determining how much was actually 'church property': while several of the houses listed in 1412 were recently founded institutions – Oxford colleges, and suchlike – some of the property may have been only temporarily in clerical hands. This particularly applies to some of the individual clerics, whose hereditary lands might be being assessed; while other tenures were only short term, as feoffees, or as guardians during a minority.[59]

Until the 1520s the normal form of clerical taxation, on spiritualities, was levied via the two Convocations, with the granting of tenths levied on 'spiritualities and temporalities annexed to spiritualities' according to the assessment of 1291 and subsequent amendments. The king issued the appropriate writ to the archbishops, declaring his urgent need for money for defence of church and realm, and requiring the summons of a Convocation to make a grant. The assembly would be held, and usually granted the tax without too much opposition – although probably rarely with

---

[56] *Rotuli Parliamentorum*, iii, pp. 74, 134; Hanley and Chalkin, 'The Kent lay subsidy' [343], pp. 59–61 (for lists, e.g. PRO E179/124/66, E179/237/57a); Hobbs, 'Shrewsbury subsidy' [404], p. 74; Bateson, *Records of Leicester* [49], ii, pp. 332–4, 351–3; LAO, Sub2/5, ff. 2r, 3r, 4r; Subs.1/7a/1 ff. iv, 3v; Subs.1/7a/2 f. 4r. See also provisions in e.g. HCA, 2065; Salter, *Cartulary of St John* [730], ii, pp. 440–1.

[57] *Rotuli Parliamentorum*, iii, pp. 648–9; *Feudal aids*, vi [433], pp. 395–545, *passim*.

[58] *Statutes*, ii, pp. 172–4; PRO, E179/217/56 (I owe this reference to Dr H.C. Swanson).

[59] *Feudal aids*, vi, pp. 409, 421, 465, 488, 518, 521.

none. Local collectors were nominated (usually heads of religious houses), with responsibility for rendering accounts at the royal exchequer at the appropriate date. The normal levy was a tenth, frequently in two parts. Thus, taking an instance from the province of York, the Convocation of June 1401 granted a full tenth to Henry IV. The demand obviously met vocal opposition, as the meeting continued until late July; but the grant was made. The tenth was due in two halves, one payable at the following Easter, the other in the subsequent February. Collectors were then appointed. The Bishops of Carlisle and Durham presumably made their own diocesan arrangements, but within the bishopric of York itself, collectors – all of them monastic houses – were nominated for each archdeaconry and its peculiar jurisdictions. In due course these collectors (who may have appointed sub-collectors to do much of the work) would account to the royal treasury and, they hoped, be acquitted.[60]

Being based on an outmoded assessment, the system of taxation by tenths was effectively fossilized. The crown could, therefore, estimate fairly precisely the outcome of a clerical grant – but not with total reliability. There was a steady downward drift in the receipts: at the end of the fourteenth century, Canterbury province was assessed at *c*.£16,500, probably actually raising about £13,500. At York the province's small size and poverty put the assessment at only £1,800, but calculation of receipts is more haphazard. Yet the sums involved were not negligible, and could be enough to keep government ticking over in time of need. Kings certainly found it easier to tax the clergy than the laity, both for administrative ease, and for lack of opposition to specific spending. Under Henry IV, for example, clerical taxation was fairly important to the crown's fiscal arrangements: a usurping king dared not demand too much of his lay subjects, especially when reduced taxation had been part of his 'manifesto'.[61]

The unsatisfactory nature of a system based on the taxation of 1291 was generally recognized, even when adjusted (as it had been in York province) following the Scottish raids of the early fourteenth century. The assessment was palpably out-dated, and grants of taxation frequently included exemptions for particular groups – in the north, for instance, the nunneries usually had blanket exemption. Individual houses might also escape, because of natural disasters (such as flooding of the Meaux abbey [Yorks.] estates), general debilitation as a result of over-taxation, or further Scottish raids (which were frequently cited for Holm Cultram [Cumb.]). Normally

---

[60] Swanson, *Reg. Scrope*, ii, nos. 720, 724 (the date for Easter in no. 720 should be 26 March 1402). On the collection machinery, Lunt, 'Collection of clerical subsidies' [533]; McHardy, 'Clerical taxation', pp. 170–3. For the collection in 1401, Abbott, 'Taxation of personal property' [1], pp. 481–92.

[61] Rogers, 'Clerical taxation' [707], pp. 126, 138–9, 141–2; Abbott, 'Taxation of personal property', pp. 492–3, 497–8.

there was a lower limit for liability to taxation, the 10-mark threshold, although this might occasionally be waived.

Exemption was not something conceded only by fellow clerics: kings occasionally granted relief of their own free will – although such exemptions might be challenged. Thus, in 1359, Edward III conceded to the recently founded religious house at Edington (Wilts.) that it should be exempt from taxes levied in Convocation, and from Parliamentary subsidies. The charter was confirmed by Henry IV, and was apparently unchallenged until 1441–2. Then it came under major attack in the royal courts.[62] These exemptions obviously reduced the amount of tax which could be levied; although occasional extensions of the grant – often related to the clergy's attempts to gain additional royal concessions – could provide some compensation for such losses.

Although the collecting arrangements seemed simple, delays were inevitable. An archiepiscopal death could be extremely disruptive: it took some time after the death of Archbishop Waldby of York in January 1398 for the crown to find out whether a grant had actually been made during his brief pontificate. His successor protested ignorance because the register was not available to be checked, and the grant was still being collected in 1401. The possibilities of confusion and disruption were considerable – even before the status of the 1398 grant had been clarified, the deposition of Richard II disrupted the collection of a subsequent levy; while on another occasion the king required a convocation to be summoned for 1 September – but the archbishop did not receive the mandate until 31 August. Individual clerics might also disturb the pattern by challenging their liability to taxation. Moreover the onerous, sometimes costly, task of collection was resented by the religious houses, many of whom purchased royal licences exempting them from such duties.[63]

Nevertheless, the basic system of tenths operated throughout the later middle ages, and was regularly exploited by the crown. But some crucial problems remained. For one thing, until the reassessments of the 1520s, only the benefices listed in 1291 were taxed, at their then valuation (unless modified), but much had changed in intervening years. The chantry movement had created numerous extra benefices, as yet untaxed; while the deficiencies of the original survey omitted several other institutions. Some of these were religious houses, others colleges, rectories, and vicarages. Some benefices had also changed status – most obviously those appropri-

[62] Swanson, *Reg. Scrope*, ii, p. iv, and nos. 708, 720, 773, 861; McHardy, 'Clerical taxation', pp. 176–7; *Cal. charter rolls, 1341–1417* [113], pp. 162–3, 406; *La premiere part Henry le VI* [495], 19 Henry VI, pp. 62–5.
[63] Swanson, *Reg. Scrope*, ii, pp. ii–iii and no. 702; Abbot, 'Taxation of personal property', p. 480; McHardy, 'Clerical taxation', pp. 177–8; Kemp, *Counsel and consent*, pp. 122–34, 140–2.

ated to religious houses. The second major difficulty was that the system effectively ignored the unbeneficed, the numerous hired chaplains. Both problems demanded attention, and received it: when the king needed money, such obvious loopholes were unlikely to be left open for long.

Bringing the unassessed benefices into the system was fairly straight-forward. Although there are few signs of such a move in the northern province, fifteenth-century Canterbury grants regularly included them among the payers. In 1404, therefore, besides the normal tenth on assessed benefices, the grant included a levy of 2 shillings in the pound from un-assessed benefices worth more than £5 p.a.; and from 1449–50 the unassessed benefices were invariably brought under the tenth's umbrella. Being taxed on actual income, the unassessed benefices probably paid a greater proportion of the income in taxes than did assessed benefices, but this is impossible to determine. The first attempt to bring the unassessed into the framework was a novel tax voted in 1371, to parallel the lay experiment in parish-based taxation made that year. Although successful in its results, the tax was not repeated. Instead, poll taxes were instituted, again paralleling the lay experiments of 1377–81. Whereas the lay poll tax died with the Peasants' Revolt of 1381, modified clerical poll taxes became almost normal in the fifteenth century. The modification usually involved the inclusion of a property tax, for pure poll taxes were shown to produce considerably less than the normal tenth. In the diocese of Salisbury, for example, the prototype poll tax of 1377 produced a mere £70, against normal receipts from a tenth of over £1,400. None of the later poll taxes of that experimental period produced even as much as a quarter-tenth – although the combined property and poll tax voted in the Canterbury Convocation of 1379 was more lucrative. This prelude to the later taxes produced slightly more than a tenth within the diocese of Salisbury; a pattern presumably repeated elsewhere. Usually the poll tax element was restricted to unassessed benefices, and to stipendiaries not included in the payments of tenths. This occasionally caused problems, as in 1404 when an extension to stipendiaries was refused by the clergy, possibly on the grounds that as they were not actually represented in the assembly their assent to the grant could not be assumed. Nevertheless, both provinces voted a subsidy of 6s. 8d. from every secular chaplain in 1406, with Canterbury extending liability to unassessed benefices, and to mendicants acting as chaplains. Similar taxes on the clergy of unassessed benefices were levied in subsequent Canterbury Convocations: in 1419, those worth over £10 p.a. were made liable to the normal half-tenth, while unbeneficed clerics and chantry chaplains with incomes over 7 marks a year (or over 40s. with board) were to pay 6s. 8d. each. Rather more complex graduated grants were made in 1429 and 1435. Sometimes grants sought to counter opposition to collecting: those formally exempt from the task of collecting might be expected to pay for the privilege. Between 1449 and 1453 Canterbury Convocation made three grants in which those pleading exemption paid an extra 25 per cent – boosted to 50 per cent in a tax of 1472. An alternative approach to the problem of exemption from collection was simply to ignore the royal patent, appoint the exempt head as collector, and leave the king to battle out the issue with the reluctant abbot through the courts. This occurred at least three times during the fifteenth century: with the prior of Leeds (1441), and the abbots of Waltham (1481) and Shrewsbury (1484).[64]

The sums produced by these extensions of liability still need investigation. However, in 1406, the extensions in both provinces – the poll tax paid by stipendiary chaplains – produced just over £4,150 from an assessment of slightly more than £4,500. Taxes on unassessed benefices were less lucrative: in 1406 the York assessment for this was only £35, Canterbury's in 1404 being £880; actual yields were respectively £25 and c.£635. However, such expedients clearly allowed for an increase in effective clerical taxation of about a quarter, depending on the specific terms of the individual grants.[65] A further major change – as yet unquantified – came in 1522 when Wolsey secured a complete revaluation of English benefices and an assessment of stipendiaries. This may have been subjected to regular updating in subsequent years, while the scheme would certainly have increased the liability to taxation.[66]

On paper, the crown fared well from clerical taxation. In the fifteenth century the grants are roughly estimated to have produced a sum approaching (if not exceeding) £700,000; while the grants of 1486 to 1534 have been estimated at the equivalent of c.£9,000 p.a. But assessments were not receipts. The fluctuations in amounts actually collected, for whatever reason, make generalizations about the crown's cash receipts very difficult, and to some extent pointless. The real impact of the grants on central state finance is also hard to assess: all too often they were pre-empted by other expedients, often to reimburse loans made to the king. In 1401, for example, such assignments accounted for 54 per cent of the Canterbury subsidy, and a massive 81 per cent of York's. Even so, these clerical grants did provide a relatively reliable flow of revenue, which could be levied with relative ease and regularity. It is also unlikely – despite complaints to the contrary – that these levies produced a serious erosion of clerical incomes, at least until the 1520s. While the regularity of

[64] Ormrod, 'Experiment in taxation' [622], pp. 64–8; McHardy, 'Clerical taxation', pp. 174–6, 183–6; Kirby, 'Clerical poll-taxes' [477], pp. 157–60; Hemmant, *Cases in the Exchequer Chamber* [380], pp. 84–95; *Reports Edward le Quart* [512], 21 Edward IV, pp. 44–9; *Reports Edward V* [511], Michaelmas, 2 Richard III, p. 4.

[65] Rogers, 'Clerical taxation', pp. 139–40.

[66] Goring, 'General proscription' [306], pp. 700–1.

the imposts may have been resented, and some individual clerics undoubtedly did suffer, the church escaped the full weight of state fiscal exactions
until the 1530s and 1540s. Then the amount extracted soared dramatically
following the further reassessment of clerical incomes incorporated in the
Valor ecclesiasticus of 1535, and the addition of new general levies, such as
first fruits.[67]

Yet the clerics may have had a point. They were not paying taxes only
to the king, and the totality of exactions – by crown, bishops, and papacy
– may have caused problems. Moreover, the crown's share of clerical
wealth was not restricted to pure tenths. There were the incidental payments for restitutions of temporalities and other fees, which have been
estimated at about £3,500 a year under the first Tudors; and the king's
ability to siphon off some of the papal levies further added to royal
revenues. Some of these expedients were traditional revenues; others were
ad hoc attempts to fleece the church. Fines for temporalities and suchlike
were based on the crown's traditional regalian rights, which allowed the
king (or in Chester, the earl) the income from the temporalities of vacant
bishoprics or religious houses (or, sometimes, during their confiscation).
Although such income was probably declining, with generally shorter
vacancies, and alienations, it could produce useful sums. They also provided an additional source against which assignments could be made to
royal creditors. The same applies to the alien priories, which repeatedly
fell into crown control until their abolition in the fifteenth century. Other
possibilities for reasonably continuous exploitation were provided by the
fees for licences to alienate lands in mortmain. As there was no fixed tariff
for these, they could vary in accordance with the crown's financial needs.
The total amount received for such fines is uncertain, but they contributed
something; and from *c*.1470 were perhaps more burdensome (making
mortmain less attractive) than before. More sinister were expedients like
Henry VII's attempts to divert the revenues of the see of Durham to the
expenses of the Scottish march: Pope Julius II agreed that this could be
done for a time, rather than have Durham kept vacant for a long time.
The feelings of Durham's bishop-elect about the arrangement are not
recorded. The papacy also had to be complaisant about its own revenues,
especially the papal tenths. When they were levied, a good part of the
proceeds were usually diverted to the royal coffers. Even payments for
indulgences could go that way – Henry VII, for example, received a
quarter of the donations for the rebuilding of St Peter's in Rome. Finally,

---

[67] McHardy, 'Clerical taxation', pp. 169–70; Abbott, 'Taxation of personal property',
p. 496; Steel, *Receipt of the Exchequer* [777], pp. 43, 47, 49–55, 59, 78, 176, 273–5, 293, 309–11,
320; Scarisbrick, 'Clerical taxation' [746], pp. 49–54. (The contrast lessens if the changes of
the 1520s are taken into consideration.)

the church could be used to keep the crown afloat by lending money. Much of this was the responsibility of individual ecclesiastics, who provided only part of the crown's borrowings, but even so clerics were major royal creditors during the fifteenth century at least.[68]

Concentration on the tenths levied by the Convocations (and their variants) ignores the grey area of those church possessions which were subject to lay taxation. Here it is difficult to assess the church's contribution with any accuracy; although the impression is that it was fairly small. However, when such subsidies coincided with clerical tenths there was room for administrative confusion, and some double-taxation;[69] while the combination of subsidies and clerical tenths perhaps meant both that some clerics were being taxed more regularly than the laity, and that they were paying proportionately more in taxes.

Besides these crucial contributions to political life in later medieval England, many other less formal relationships allowed the state to exploit the ecclesiastical structure. Practically, perhaps the most significant was the use of the church to spread information, or propaganda. For its own purposes, the church's pyramidical structure provided the main channel for conveying information from the top downwards, and for the spread of information within the locality. The church as a place for proclamations would have been familiar to all, whether for announcing banns of marriage, pronouncing excommunications, or issuing general injunctions on disciplinary matters. It was only natural that the state should appropriate this structure for its own purposes. Through the announcement of special prayers and processions – whether of intercession or thanksgiving – the nation was informed about the king's health, the rampages of the Scots, and (perhaps most frequently) the progress of the French wars. Indeed, during the Hundred Years War the pulpit became a major agent for publicizing victories, actual or claimed, with the distribution of what were virtually official newsletters throughout the dioceses, to be incorporated into the church notices.[70]

Apart from this propagandistic connection with the French wars, the church had more direct links with military matters. There was some ecclesiastical activity within the main armies, whose contingents all needed

---

[68] Scarisbrick, 'Clerical taxation', pp. 49–50; *Cal. Pat. Rolls, 1494–1509* [119], p. 255; Steel, *Receipt of the Exchequer* (*passim* for loans, for assignments see pp. 90, 95, 210); Stewart-Brown, *Accounts of the chamberlains of Chester* [778], pp.251, 268; Legge, *Anglo-Norman letters* [506], pp. 393–4; Kreider, *English chantries* [489], pp. 80–3; Wilkie, *Cardinal protectors* [901], p. 78; see also 5/4 at n. 68.

[69] Wilkins, *Concilia* [902], iii, p. 335.

[70] Jones, 'Church and propaganda' [453], pp. 20–30; McHardy, 'Liturgy and propaganda' [554].

their chaplains and confessors, and their clerical staff. Clerics also engaged in actual fighting; the most spectacular incident of this during the period being the 'crusade' led by Bishop Despencer of Norwich to the Low Countries in the early 1380s, which incurred the virulent condemnation of John Wyclif for being against fellow Christians, and equally virulent attack from the authorities in England for being a total failure. However, the main activity was not foreign adventure, but home defence. By 1350 the military levy due from ecclesiastical tenants-in-chief was quite anachronistic, and appears only in the summons of 1385. Ecclesiastics were more often involved in military administration than active defence of the realm. However, their exercise of local lordship did involve them in the military structure of the kingdom, with powers of muster over their tenants which would involve them in the provision of men and materials for military expeditions. Towards the end the power of muster was a feature exploited by laymen wishing to develop their local authority at the expense of the religious institutions: the attraction of sinecure appointments as stewards of religious estates perhaps lay partly in the authority that provided for the addition of the local estate militia to the steward's own retinue. However, the church did not completely abdicate its involvement in the muster, which could be used for other purposes, as when the abbot of Holm Cultram (Cumb.) mustered his tenants to participate in the Pilgrimage of Grace.[71]

In terms of direct ecclesiastical contribution to defence, the clerical musters were perhaps of greater significance. These, possibly panic measures, took place most frequently between 1369 and 1419, with the clergy being arrayed (sometimes on a national basis) to defend the kingdom against threatened or feared French and Scottish invasions. But the arrays were not confined to those fifty years: there are hints of earlier activity, and summonses are recorded from the reign of Edward IV. Much remains uncertain about these clerical arrays, but there seems (initially) to have been some analogy to crusade, with the prelates in 1369 giving their assent to the idea, and even enforcing clerical attendance by canonical censure. However, the clergy themselves were perhaps not so complaisant: there are occasional signs of ineffective opposition, voiced through Convocation. Yet the arrays were held – and the clergy appear to have attended, in person rather than by lay substitutes, and in arms which varied with the value of their benefice. Clerics sometimes became involved in subsequent

---

[71] McHardy, 'Clergy and the Hundred Years War' [555], p. 175 and refs.; Housley, 'Bishop of Norwich's crusade' [416]; Aston, 'Impeachment of bishop Despencer' [14]; Buddenseig, *Wiclif's polemical works* [103], ii, pp. 588–632; Lewis, 'Last medieval summons' [513], esp. pp. 2, 13–15, 25–6; Kelly, 'Noble steward' [462], p. 137; Davies, 'Popular religion', p. 65.

LUTTRELL PSALTER   The church, royal service, and propaganda: Archbishop Thomas Arundel of Canterbury (1396–7, 1399–1414) reads from the pulpit to a lay audience. The shape and colour of the seal suggest that this is some form of royal proclamation or ordinance.

(The British Library, Ms Harley 1319, f. 12)

fighting, but their array seems originally to have been conceived as some sort of medieval home guard. These arrays raise the problem of the illegality of clerical fighting – even though in defence of the church in England, as well as the realm – brought out by occasional papal dispensations for those who had participated in the wars. The arrays appear to have been organized completely by the clergy and ecclesiastical officials, as purely ecclesiastical concerns, distinct from any secular organization. Thus, in two recorded summonses issued by Archbishop Scrope of York, presumably to meet a threatened Scottish invasion, the arrangements for assembling the clergy were left to archidiaconal officials and others among his ecclesiastical rather than baronial administration.[72]

The links between the church and the political structure in later medieval England were many-faceted. The relationship between clerics and the political system appears symbiotic, but that between 'the church' and 'the state' was perhaps less close. On the one hand there is a clear link between clerical career aspirations and the role of crown service to achieve their fulfilment, and the state's use of ecclesiastical resources to fund its bureaucracy. Conversely, in matters of political theory, and in practicalities such as taxation, the relationship was perhaps more one of some state dependence on the church – in name alone. For while successive kings required the church to legitimize their rule, their own power was the greatest real guarantee of their security: they required the church to make them kings *de jure* (and, in so doing, to decry the usurpation and tyranny of others); but it was their own power which made them kings *de facto*. Similar considerations applied in other areas: ideally, the church controlled events in granting taxes, offering prayers, and so on; but failure to comply with the royal will brought its own perils. The clerical outlawry of 1296 had set an awesome precedent which no one wanted to test again, especially in an atmosphere frequently tinged with strident complaints against the church and its ministers.

But the position was not static. Over time the relationship between the church and the political structure changed markedly. Generally the church was in withdrawal, largely as other forces initiated and hastened that retreat. The slow development towards a lay – but not secular – view of the state, with the emphasis on royal power proceeding directly from God rather than being mediated through the church, challenged, and then shattered, the church's hold on the succession, and on the legitimization of regimes. In terms of personnel, the clerical stranglehold was gradually

---

[72] McNab, 'Obligations of the church' [564]; McHardy, 'Clergy and the Hundred Years War', p. 174; Raine, *Priory of Hexham* [687], i, pp. c, cvii–cviii; BL, MS Cotton Vit.E.xvi, ff. 128r, 130v–131r.

relaxed, in a process which apparently started from the bottom. By 1400 the laicization of the lower echelons was already well advanced, and had been almost completed by 1500. Laicization of the upper ranks was only more slowly achieved, being delayed until the later year s of Henry VIII's reign. Even so, opposition to the idea of clerical ministers had been voiced earlier (as in the government crisis of 1371), while lay treasurers were relatively common in the fifteenth century.[73] The church was perhaps seeking to withdraw from political involvement – or was being pushed out. This seems odd given the glaring inconsistency of Wolsey, but he was the exception to almost any generalization. Although the church was reducing its political role, it was not completely dissolving its integration into the political structure. Particularly under the Tudors, its subject status was being emphasized in matters of taxation, with increasing amounts being demanded in the Reformation period. Ultimately, the position was that insisted on in 1296: the church was a part of the state, a member of the body politic of the realm, a subject institution. It had to live with that position; only the way in which it lived with it might vary.

3.3   THE LOCALITIES: ROYAL AGENTS AND LOCAL RULERS

Although necessarily focusing on the state – the kingdom, the king, and central administration – medieval politics were not confined to that level. The localities had their own political structures, which require separate consideration, alongside their participation in the national order. Towns, lordships, may have been part of a macrocosmic kingdom, but they were also themselves miniature political entities.

As this applies regardless of ecclesiastical involvement, the identification of an 'ecclesiastical' influence on local jurisdiction and administration as an 'ecclesiastical' phenomenon is virtually impossible. The ecclesiastical element is largely accidental; the essential aspect was lordship, which could be exercised by laity or clergy, by secular or religious corporations. Local politics essentially reflected patronage webs, in which religious individuals and institutions were as enmeshed as any others, although perhaps more open to exploitation by the laity than by clerics. They could thus be used to construct local areas of dominance by aspirant regional rulers, who would need to be able to offer rewards and offices to people active at the centre of political life in order to maintain some influence there, even if at a distance.[74] Again, this did not necessarily differentiate

---

[73] Ormrod, 'Experiment in taxation', p. 60; Fryde et al., *Handbook of British chronology*, pp. 102–3.
[74] Kelly, 'Noble steward', pp. 135, 141–2.

'the church' from the problems encountered by local laity. Consequently, although attention is here concentrated on ecclesiastical activities, the comments are often equally applicable to lay experience.

As local instruments of central authority, ecclesiastics were used as tax-collectors, and on the commission of the peace. More significant than such *ad hoc* activities is the ecclesiatical (and, of course, lay) possession of various franchises, which fragmented and effectively alienated elements of royal jurisdiction. Here the 'ecclesiastical' involvement becomes most blurred, creating an artificial distinction between church and laity: the possession of franchises merges into manorial jurisdiction, producing considerable overlap with general considerations of contemporary landlordism. Stressing the ecclesiastical holding of franchises whilst ignoring those in lay possession distorts the picture: there was no real difference between them, and the existence of secular franchises must always be assumed. Beyond the franchises, the role of ecclesiastical institutions in local government also needs attention. The church could act as an irritant, with its institutions disrupting the claims of boroughs to self-government; alternatively it could be a cohesive force. It also united groups divided by jurisdictional boundaries, or provided a focus for identity against a lord, through membership of religious guilds. These especially provided a focus for urban loyalties and the activities of the local patriciate, occasionally overcoming a town's jurisdictional fragmentation to give a form of unity even if the town was technically unincorporate.[75]

The crown naturally sought to use every available resource to enforce its authority in the localities. Its main concerns were with tax collection and the implementation of justice. Clerics participated in both, even if not particularly actively.

In tax collection, the church's role was in decline throughout the period, except for the clerical subsidies. Until the early fourteenth century the interconnections of the monastic houses had made them useful agents for collecting and holding cash: they could be temporal as well as spiritual treasure houses. This role was not extinguished, but had diminishing significance. Even where clerics appear on taxation commissions, this was probably only honorific: the real tasks would be left to their lay colleagues. While the king's clerks were closely involved in tax administration, the developing laicization of the civil service again reduced the ecclesiastical element in such activity.

Ecclesiastical influence perhaps lingered longest in the administration of justice – in its widest sense – and may even have increased. The main feature here is the rise of the justices of the peace in the fourteenth and

[75] See 5/2 at nn. 39–40; 6/3 at nn. 72–3.

fifteenth centuries. In the early stages the JPs were mostly laity.[76] Ecclesiastics were only rarely nominated to the commission, although they were sometimes appointed as commissioners in individual cases, or to special commissions such as those named in 1382 after the Peasants' Revolt.[77] This changed under Henry VI. From 1424 ecclesiastical participation in such commissions became a regular feature. The diocesan bishops were normally included for the counties within their dioceses. Abbots of major houses – Malmesbury, Abingdon, Cirencester, and others – were also named, but not so regularly.[78] Clerical membership of these commissions was not automatic, some counties having lengthy periods with no such involvement, like Hertfordshire and the Cumbrian counties between 1457 and 1461.[79] However, membership in individual counties could be impressive. The Gloucestershire commissions of 1494–1508, for example, included (not necessarily in every instance) both archbishops, the Bishops of Lichfield, Worcester, Hereford, Lincoln, Bath, Bangor, and Salisbury, the Abbots of Cirencester, Winchcombe, Tewkesbury, St Peter's at Gloucester, and Pershore, and the Prior of Llanthony by Gloucester, as well as a few others described simply as clerks. Clerics sometimes appeared on non-county commissions, especially those for the university towns, where the chancellor was invariably nominated, along with a few other members. The Provost of King's College regularly joined the later Cambridge commissions.[80]

The paucity of records for the activities of the justices leaves the degree of clerical involvement in the peace-keeping process unclear. One thing is certain: the clerical members were canonically banned from involvement with 'matters of blood', cases which might result in execution. Accordingly, from 1424, the terms of the peace commission were revised: the clerical members were exempted from participation in dealing with felonies, counterfeiting, and the pursuit of heretics (i.e. their treatment after delivery to the secular arm from the ecclesiastical courts). Such restrictions must have limited their involvement as active justices, although they are revealed as dealing with other matters.[81]

---

[76] For justices of the peace see Putnam, 'Transformation of the keepers' [679]; Putnam, *Proceedings before the justices* [680], pp. xxxvi–lvi.

[77] Ecclesiastics are almost totally absent from normal peace commissions in the early 1380s: *Cal. pat. rolls, 1381–1385* [116], pp. 84–6, 251–5, 346–50, 501–3; they appear in several counties on the special commissions of March and December 1382, ibid., pp. 138–42, 244–9. For an oyer and terminer commission, ibid., p. 500.

[78] Putnam, *Proceedings before the justices*, pp. lxxxi–ii; names of commissioners from 1399 onwards are collected in the appendices to successive volumes of the *Calendar of patent rolls*. For the abbots of Abingdon and Malmesbury see *Cal. pat. rolls, 1494–1509*, pp. 630, 664.

[79] *Cal. pat. rolls, 1452–1461* [118], pp. 663, 667, 680.

[80] *Cal. pat. rolls, 1494–1509*, pp. 640–1; *Cal. pat. rolls, 1452–1461*, pp. 662, 675.

[81] Putnam, *Proceedings before the justices*, p. xxvii (and a commission printed at pp. 257–62); ECL, MS 3533, ff. 69v, 70v; BL, MS Harley 2179, f. 154v; LAO, FOR.3, f. 68v.

Perhaps more significant than ecclesiastics' activity on behalf of the crown in the localities was their role as local rulers in their own right. Although England's kings theoretically ruled the whole realm, in actuality their authority was fragmented, thereby greatly complicating the administrative geography of the kingdom. Royal prerogatives had been alienated over the centuries, and it took further centuries for their recovery. The existence of franchises or liberties contributed to, and reflected, the fragmentation of royal prerogatives and their alienation to local rulers. These rulers might be lay or ecclesiastical individuals, or corporate bodies. The crucial point was that they exercised some fraction of royal authority within territory which was thereby retracted from the normal administrative hierarchy of local government, and to some extent therefore withdrawn from royal oversight.[82]

Technically, each alienation of each individual aspect of royal authority constituted a separate franchise; the areas where accumulations of such franchises impeded the full exercise of royal authority constituting liberties or immunities. The importance of such franchises varied: some were fairly insignificant, others were not. The liberties and franchises were long recognized as detracting from royal power. Under Edward I, a succession of inquisitions on writs of *Quo warranto* investigated franchise holding, and resulted in a closer definition of franchises which emphasized that they were royal concessions. Henceforth, the franchise of return of writs, excluding the sheriff from the liberty in an official capacity (itself defined very much as a reaction to attacks on liberties) became a crucial element in the identification of a major liberty. The *Quo warranto* processes had also insisted that the liberties existed within the kingdom; that their holders were royal ministers rather than independent rulers. Even the Bishop of Durham, with his semi-independent regality, was forcefully reminded of his subject status. Franchises, like other royal privileges, were now liable to withdrawal if not exercised properly (whether by abuse or non-use): they brought responsibilities as well as prestige.[83]

Franchises normally had only local or regional importance: geographical units with fairly strictly defined jurisdictional authority. But one particular franchise had national significance: coining money was a royal perquisite, although England's kings had allowed favoured individuals to maintain their own mints. Many of those so favoured had been ecclesiastics; but by

---

[82] Ault, *Private jurisdiction* [23], pp. 3–7; Sutherland, *Quo warranto proceedings* [792], pp. 1–15, esp. 2–6; Cam, *Liberties and communities* [122], pp. 153–4.

[83] Ault, *Private jurisdiction*, pp. 5–6; Sutherland, *Quo warranto proceedings*; Clanchy, 'Return of writs' [145], pp. 59–79; Fraser, 'Edward I and Durham' [284], pp. 337–42; Cam, *Liberties and communities*, pp. xiii, 183–4, 204.

1300 this privilege had usually been revoked or had fallen into disuse. From 1350 only three non-royal mints remained in England, held by the Archbishops of Canterbury and York, and the Bishop of Durham. Canterbury's minting was intermittent; it had stopped before 1350, and did not resume until 1464. York and Durham, however, were in virtually continuous production. The archiepiscopal mints seemingly had to suspend production whenever the local royal mint was operating, presumably in recognition of their inferior status to the king's mint.[84]

These mints were profitable to the bishops, although the little evidence available (mainly for Durham) suggests that revenues were not high. Under Bishop Thomas Langley (1406–37) the highest sum delivered by the minter in coinage dues, at 5d. per pound of minted bullion, was 76s. 3d., while under the early Tudors the most received (as a rent rather than a direct share of the profits) was £10, and usually much less.[85] For the bishops, the main feature of the mints may have been the prestige they conferred rather than financial gain; but the evidence of the Durham receipts seems to understate the importance of the mints to the country as a whole. Although restricted in the coins they could issue (usually pennies and halfpence, although in later years the archiepiscopal mints also produced half-groats), they may have minted considerable amounts. Indeed, the ecclesiastical mints may have been the major suppliers of pennies for the country in general, the royal mints apparently producing less than their combined total, and possibly concentrating on the higher denominations which produced greater profits. Paradoxically, the prestige attached to minting perhaps contributed to the decline of the ecclesiastical mints. Wolsey certainly seems to have exceeded his powers, producing illicit groats at York which prominently displayed his cardinal's hat. A direct link between Wolsey's fall and the end of minting is unlikely: his successors at Durham and York certainly struck coins. Precisely when minting ended is not clear; the old accepted date of 1534 no longer stands. It may have lasted for another decade, perhaps not coincidentally ending with the Debasement of 1543. Thereafter the crown resumed responsibility for all coinage.[86]

Most franchises were essentially local delegations of jurisdiction. Here the precise definition of franchisal authority tends to blur, as less significant franchises merge into landlordism and manorial jurisdiction. As the royal

---

[84] Blunt, 'Ecclesiastical coinage' [71], esp. pp. xiv–xviii. On the mints see also Challis, 'Ecclesiastical mints' [132].

[85] Challis, 'Ecclesiastical mints', p. 101; Storey, *Langley and Durham* [782], p. 72.

[86] Blunt, 'Ecclesiastical coinage', pp. xiv, xviii (but see Challis, 'Ecclesiastical mints', p. 88); Whitton, 'Coinages of Henry VIII and of Edward VI' [900], pp. 58, 197–206, 209–12; Challis, 'Ecclesiastical mints', pp. 96–8.

courts developed their authority in the later middle ages, this diminution and blurring became more general. But the basic distinction remains: that franchisal authority was a delegated responsibility from the crown, without any necessary connection with proprietorial powers. Domainal jurisdiction, however, clearly reflected property rights, and relations between landlord and tenant.[87]

The level at which most significant franchises operated was the hundred, the main sub-division of the county. In the 1270s, the great inquest into the possession of hundreds identified slightly over 600 in the counties for which returns were made (thus excluding the palatinates of Chester and Durham, the Lake District counties, and Northumberland). Over half of these were in private hands, approximately 100 being held by ecclesiastics or religious corporations. These ecclesiastical hundreds lay mainly south of a rough line from the Wash to the Severn estuary. To the north, significant concentrations of ecclesiastical hundreds existed only in Gloucestershire and Worcestershire. In the other northern counties making returns, there were scattered ecclesiastical holdings in Herefordshire, Warwickshire, Lincolnshire, Nottinghamshire, and Yorkshire, but none in Lancashire, Derbyshire, Staffordshire, Shropshire, or Leicestershire. South of the Wash–Severn line, ecclesiastical hundreds were reported in every county except Bedfordshire and Cornwall, with particularly notable blocks in Kent, Somerset, Hampshire, Suffolk, and Cambridgeshire.

This was not the full picture. The omitted counties contained significant ecclesiastical holdings. Durham was wholly a franchise, while Northumberland contained areas like the Archbishop of York's regality of Hexham. In Cheshire, also, there were ecclesiastical holdings, such as those of Vale Royal abbey. Even for the counties providing returns, the extent of ecclesiastical franchises is probably understated. In Lancashire, for instance, some franchises were held in sub-tenantry, as baronies of the honour of Lancaster.[88]

The distribution of authority reflected in 1274 did not remain static. The essence of hundredal jurisdiction became identified with holding the view of frankpledge, one of the most widely distributed franchises. In the fourteenth and fifteenth centuries, the hundredal map changed as individual landowners with frankpledge rights amalgamated manors (and even hundreds) in a process of jurisdictional rationalization. This sometimes merged scattered manors into one nominal hundred, or amalgamated neighbouring hundreds, a process clearly visible in Wiltshire, where there was a significant reduction in the number of hundreds within the county.

---

[87] Ault, *Private jurisdiction*, pp. 3–8.

[88] Cam, *Hundred and the hundred rolls* [121], map after p. 296, pp. 137–45, 260–85; Ault, *Private jurisdiction*, pp. 242–52, 259–60, 265–6, 302–4.

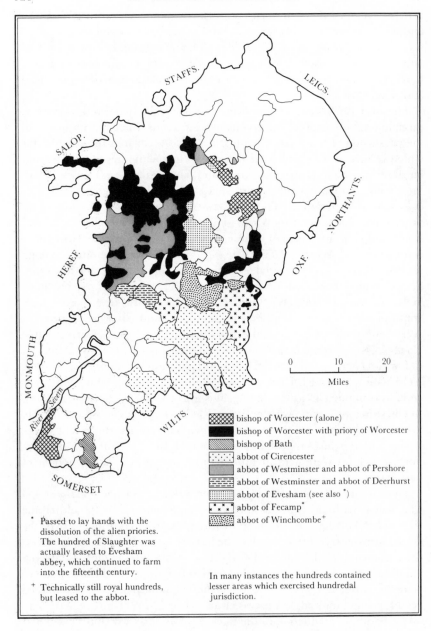

STAFFS.

LEICS.

SALOP.

NORTHANTS.

HEREF.

OXF.

MONMOUTH

River Severn

WILTS.

SOMERSET

0   10   20

Miles

▨ bishop of Worcester (alone)
■ bishop of Worcester with priory of Worcester
▧ bishop of Bath
░ abbot of Cirencester
▒ abbot of Westminster and abbot of Pershore
▤ abbot of Westminster and abbot of Deerhurst
▥ abbot of Evesham (see also *)
✕ abbot of Fecamp*
▨ abbot of Winchcombe+

* Passed to lay hands with the
dissolution of the alien priories.
The hundred of Slaughter was
actually leased to Evesham
abbey, which continued to farm
into the fifteenth century.

+ Technically still royal hundreds,
but leased to the abbot.

In many instances the hundreds contained
lesser areas which exercised hundredal
jurisdiction.

MAP III: Hundreds in the West Midlands held by ecclesiastics, 1274.

The tenurial pattern for the holding of hundreds had its own complexities, especially noticeable in Kent where, according to the 1274 survey, ecclesiastics regularly shared ownership with other authorities or individuals.[89]

Dealing with franchises via the hundreds presents a more straightforward picture than actually existed. For beyond the view of frankpledge, and its effective removal of the area from the control of the county sheriff (although occasionally the view had to be held in the presence of royal bailiffs),[90] many other franchises might be claimed, of more effective jurisdictional importance. Several were primarily economic in concern, such as the right to receive the goods of felons convicted in the royal courts, or amercements for breach of the assizes of bread and ale; more significant were the franchises which, beyond their financial rewards, gave their holders judicial competence. Without diminishing the purely financial rewards of franchises – rights to wreck could provide significant sums, as the Bishop of Worcester clearly hoped when he claimed the cargo of a sunken vessel in 1361[91] – the judicial and jurisdictional exclusion of royal officials carried much more prestige.

The sheer variety of these judicial and jurisdictional franchises prevents general consideration. The franchise of return of writs was widely distributed, preventing the sheriff from entering the liberty to execute writs. That had to be done by the officials of the franchise-holder (unless, for some reason, they failed in their duties, in which case a directional writ to the sheriff *Ne omittas* overrode the liberty).[92] Some ecclesiastical authorities had their own prisons for secular criminals, a privilege frequently confirmed and even extended in the fourteenth and fifteenth centuries. The right to appoint a coroner was also relatively widely scattered among the major religious institutions, sometimes for specific liberties, sometimes for general possession of lands. As late as the mid-fifteenth century, King's College in Cambridge was allowed to appoint a coroner for its lands, while Peterborough abbey received a similar privilege for its liberty in 1493. In the sixteenth century, when franchises were under attack, the right of ecclesiastical institutions to appoint a coroner was the franchise which seems to have attracted most attention.[93]

Additionally, several liberties held delegated powers which removed them from the normal structure of justice. Several held the privilege that their subjects would not be answerable outside the liberty boundaries,

---

[89] *VCH, Wiltshire*, v [875], pp. 51–2; Cam, *Hundred and the hundred rolls*, pp. 141, 270–2 (see also e.g. Ault, *Private jurisdiction*, p. 101).

[90] E.g. Ault, *Private jurisdiction*, pp. 45–6, 107.

[91] Dyer, *Lords and peasants* [243], p. 78.

[92] Cam, *Liberties and communities*, pp. 191–3.

[93] Pugh, *Imprisonment* [674], pp. 95–6; *VCH, Cambridge*, iii [866], p. 384; *VCH, Northampton*, ii [870], p. 423; Garrett-Goodyear, 'Quo warranto' [292], pp. 274–88.

except by way of appeal against judgement. When cases involving their subjects were brought, either locally or at Westminster, the matter would be claimed for decision within the franchise. These franchisal courts generally used royal justices as judges; but the point was their recognition of the geographical distinction between the franchise and the rest of the county or kingdom. Thus, when royal justices visited York, there had to be special sessions for the liberties within the city, highlighting their jurisdictional separateness. Perhaps the highest franchise was that which not only recognized the geographical frontiers, but also allowed the franchise-holder to nominate his own justices. These were few, and apart from the palatinates of Lancashire and Chester, and the liberty of Tynedale, were exclusively held by ecclesiastics. The Bishop of Durham within his palatinate created a whole array of courts and justices nominated and organized according to his own wishes. Within his regality of Hexhamshire, the Archbishop of York had full possession of crown pleas, and appointed justices. The Bishop of Ely's quasi-palatinate within the isle of Ely also had its own court system, which claimed to exclude all royal justices (even the royal household court of the Marshalsea was denied jurisdiction when the king visited the isle), and made the justices' powers dependent on episcopal commission. Other ecclesiastical authorities enjoyed only slightly lesser powers: within the extraordinary *banleuca* (areas of especial liberty round some of the major monasteries, such as Ramsey and Battle) the abbots claimed almost full jurisdiction, and the same applied to the twelve hide liberty of the abbots of Glastonbury. Within the city of Salisbury, the bishop exercised the powers of a justice. Gaol delivery was also claimed by various religious institutions which had their own prisons – although there seem to have been gradations in this franchise, with some claims to gaol delivery being restricted to lesser offences, leaving major felonies for visiting royal justices. These judicial franchises may have developed alongside the system of royal justices, at least in some instances. Thus, in the late fourteenth century, the Archbishop of York was appointing justices of the peace and justices to enforce the Statute of Labourers, although these were relatively new posts within the royal system.[94]

The precise significance of many of the franchises is elusive. Clearly, they were maintained, and jealously guarded. But they did not impose massive

    [94] CUL, MS Add.2951, ff. 30r–36r; *VCH, City of York* [877], p. 38; *VCH, Cambridge*, iv [867], pp. 9, 12–14; Lapsley, *Durham* [496]; Storey, *Langley and Durham*, pp. 52–67, 72–3, 88–9, 98–105 (see also Scammell, 'Liberty of Durham' [744], esp. 470–3); Lobel, 'Ecclesiastical banleuca' [524]; Ault, *Private jurisdiction*, pp. 108–25; Searle, *Lordship and community* [752], pp. 197–246, 387–91, 400–31; *VCH, Wiltshire*, v, pp. 60–1; Pugh, *Imprisonment*, pp. 297–301 (prison costs sometimes appear in liberty accounts, e.g. YML, F3/3, F3/4); *History of Northumberland*, iii [403], pp. 30, 42.

DURHAM SEAL   The church and local political authority: the Chancery Great Seal of Bishop Thomas Hatfield of Durham (1345–81), modelled on that used for royal documents, and used for sealing important documents in the Palatinate. On one side Hatfield is depicted on his episcopal throne; on the other he appears mounted on a warhorse, his shield and horse trappings bearing his coat of arms, and his helmet bearing a mitre surrounded by a coronet to indicate his combination of spiritual and temporal authority.

(Reproduced by kind permission of The Dean and Chapter of Durham)

restrictions on the effectiveness of royal justice in the later middle ages. Contemporary developments in legal organization were generally bringing greater unity to the kingdom, a process in which the survival of franchises was not particularly obstructive. The most common franchise, the view of frankpledge, changed in character and lost its earlier jurisdictional importance; while the legal frontiers which franchises created (and epitomized in the franchise of return of writs) were being eroded by developments in the machinery of royal justice. The franchises were already in retreat by 1300, as hundredal courts declined in significance. Their later survival was largely a matter of prestige, and to some extent profit. Jurisdiction was reduced to relatively trivial matters: although still a collection of delegated royal powers, hundredal authority covered essentially minor trespasses and matters of local public order, with no oversight of felonies. The mainstay of earlier hundredal jurisdiction, the view of frankpledge, became almost anachronistic. Its transformation in the late fourteenth and fifteenth centuries, with the collapse of the tithing system and virtual abolition of its public peace functions, made the later 'view of frankpledge' worthless as a jurisdictional reality. Perhaps the main value of the regular hundredal courts to franchise-holders lay in providing income from amercements for non-attendance levied on supposedly liable vills. Other financial benefits also remained, including claims to amercements in royal courts, and to felons' chattels.[95]

Clerical involvement in the whole system varied: holders of several hundreds in fact farmed their jurisdictions to the bailiffs, as did Bury St Edmunds in both the thirteenth and fifteenth centuries. Farmers obviously expected profits, and as profitability declined, so did rents. Some hundreds (for instance the Bishop of Worcester's Oswaldlow hundred) produced virtually nothing, and found no takers. On the other hand, clerics also farmed hundreds from others: Winchcombe abbey held several at lease from the king, while Evesham abbey leased the hundred of Slaughter from Fécamp abbey and its successors. The importance of profit in the persistence of lesser private jurisdictions is indicated in the decay of the Bishop of London's soke jurisdiction in London: by 1400 it was no more than the title of a list of rents of property, partly because the receipts of jurisdiction had all been grasped by the city authorities, leaving no such profits for the bishop. But it would be wrong to deny all importance to such lesser jurisdictions by the sixteenth century: the Tudor *Quo warranto* proceedings

---

[95] Dyer, *Lords and peasants*, p. 265; Crowley, 'The later history of frankpledge' [180], esp. 12–15. Enforcing jurisdiction was often difficult, producing an accumulation of arrears: see e.g. Cam, *Liberties and communities*, p. 197. Details of amercements appear in jurisdictional accounts, e.g. EDC, D/6/2/26. Amercements of courts within the palatinate of Chester were also returned to liberty-holders: Stewart-Brown, *Accounts of the chamberlains of Chester*, pp. 137, 175; Brownbill, *Ledger book of Vale Royal* [102], pp. 153, 155–7.

were occasionally directed precisely against ecclesiastical claims to exercise the view of frankpledge.[96]

As royal justice developed, the crown sought oversight of the liberties and judgement of criminal cases in them. Until about 1350 royal intervention in the government and jurisdictional independence of the liberties was limited. Proceedings by writs of *Quo warranto* could test claims to specific franchises, but after the major inquest under Edward I, such inquiries were rare. Nevertheless, the Archbishop of York's rights in Hexhamshire were investigated in 1359, and within the palatinate of Chester such inquests may have continued later. A county-wide inquiry was held in Cheshire in 1499, almost the last on that model. Apart from an attempt to deal generally with the Middlesex franchises in 1519, and those of Bishop's Lynn in 1521, later *Quo warranto* procedures were rather different.[97]

While *Quo warranto* investigated the validity of claims to franchises, it did not explicitly check their operation. For such purposes and implementation of royal justice, the system of general eyres was used. These were originally country-wide investigations to clear up outstanding judicial matters; but they, too, were decaying in the fourteenth century. Until 1381, occasional summonses were issued – perhaps significantly, in connection with the major ecclesiastical franchises of Durham and Canterbury, during vacancies of the sees – but all were bought off, without any inquests actually taking place. These were the last flickers of the system: effectively the eyres were extinguished by 1350.[98] New methods were needed to integrate the liberties into the judicial and jurisdictional framework of the realm. The assize justices and justices of the peace provided the answer, their powers usually applying within the liberties as well as without.[99] This expansion of royal rights, as the justices assumed responsibility for dealing with felonies, and the sheriff's judicial functions declined, again curtailed the judicial powers of franchise-holders, unless they could appoint their own justices. In such cases, their franchises became even more important.

Attitudes towards franchises, and their impact on local administration, remain difficult to assess: even the crown's stance was ambivalent until

---

[96] Cam, *Liberties and communities*, p. 196; Cam, *Hundred and hundred rolls*, pp. 142–3; Dyer, *Lords and peasants*, p. 175; EDR, G/2/3, ff. 79v–80v; BL, MS Add. 14848, ff. 53r–54v; Hilton, *Medieval society* [395], pp. 220, 223; BL, MS Cotton Titus C.ix., ff. 35v–36r; Taylor, 'Bishop of London's soke' [815]; Garrett-Goodyear, 'Quo warranto', pp. 274–5, 277–8, 280–3, 285–8, 291–2.

[97] *History of Northumberland*, iii, p. 25 n. 3; Ault, *Private jurisdiction*, p. 242; Stewart-Brown, 'Cheshire writs' [779]; Garrett-Goodyear, 'Quo warranto', pp. 238–40; below, at nn. 112–14.

[98] Crook, 'The later eyres' [172], esp. pp. 263–6.   [99] Above, n. 76.

the early sixteenth century. The problem is partly due to the paucity of detailed information about the operation of franchises. For some a fairly detailed picture can be developed of office-holding and court structure – for example in the liberty of Bury St Edmund's – but normally very little survives. Most detailed information derives from the thirteenth century, and it is this which fleshes out the franchise of (say) Ramsey abbey. For later centuries, just how effectively the franchises were being maintained is problematic. The abbot of Dunstable's claim to appoint his own coroner was certainly upheld in the thirteenth and fourteenth centuries, but the list of known appointees peters out early in the fifteenth century. Yet the franchise had not expired, for the abbey faced *Quo warranto* proceedings about the coronership in 1528, successfully defending its claims. That particular franchises might revert to the crown for non-use or abuse also caused upsets: both St Albans and Crowland abbeys lost their prison rights in the fifteenth century (the former apparently only temporarily). The terms of the original grant of the franchise could be decisive. The Provost and Fellows of King's College, Cambridge, had a coronership over their lands which, as the college was active in the land market, had only temporary significance in some places, providing the novelty of a movable liberty. Individual places might therefore be under its jurisdiction for only short periods: between 1446 and 1475, for instance, the college held the manor of Grovebury in Leighton Buzzard (Beds.), and apparently appointed a coroner for the manor during those few decades.[100]

Franchises might die out or otherwise cease to operate; but they re-mained marks of prestige. A gallows might not be used, but the notional franchise of *infangtheof* which it represented (the power to execute a thief caught red-handed) was still confirmed, and the gallows accordingly main-tained, into the sixteenth century. Moreover, franchise-holders frequently fought hard to maintain their jurisdictions against interlopers, not always simply because court profits were affected. In the early fifteenth century, for example, the Bishop of Ely claimed return of writs for his lands within the liberty of Bury St Edmund's abbey, apparently with the connivance of the local sheriff and support from the local nobility. The Bury monks, concerned to maintain their status, naturally opposed the intrusion, start-ing a quarrel which lasted decades, with all the panoply of contemporary legal proceedings and attempts at arbitration.[101]

---

[100] Cam, *Liberties and communities*, pp. 184, 188–204; Ault, *Private jurisdiction*, pp. 83–108; Hunnisett, *Bedfordshire coroners' rolls* [428], pp. xix–xxi, xliv; Garrett-Goodyear, 'Quo warranto', p. 278 no. 43; Pugh, *Imprisonment*, p. 97.

[101] Dyer, *Lords and peasants*, pp. 264–5; Arnold, *St Edmund's abbey* [11], iii, pp. 188–211 (an incomplete record of the case). See also EDR, G7/29, m.10r.

Perhaps the most violent franchise disputes involving ecclesiastics were more than conflicts over mere status. Occasionally the church was a victim rather than aggressor. This was particularly so in towns, especially as the burghal county developed after 1350. The charters converting individual boroughs into counties were usually sufficiently ambiguous to generate future chaos, especially when a larger ecclesiastical corporation tried to maintain its earlier charters against the novelty. In several towns, especially those with a large abbey or cathedral, conflict between civic and ecclesiastical authorities was almost commonplace in the later middle ages. The franchise issue is, however, distinct from the violent conflicts over lordship which were also fairly common: franchisal disputes reflect clashes between two legally distinct parties over jurisdiction; the conflicts between 'monastic boroughs' and their inhabitants are between lords and tenants about subjection, and quite different in character.[102] Jurisdictional disputes usually erupted when the urban authorities sought to impose their authority on the ecclesiastical territory, or the ecclesiastics sought to evade responsibilities (usually fiscal) within the town. Typical were the conflicts in Norwich and Exeter. Both towns had been converted into counties, but both were affected by antecedent royal grants to the cathedral authorities confirming their privileges. When the civic officials – generally either the sheriff or coroner – tried to act within the ecclesiastical precincts, a dispute erupted, turning on whether the cathedral enclosures were included within the county of the city, or the county of the shire; whether, therefore, the cathedral territories were subject to urban or royal jurisdiction. These disputes occupied much time and money, focusing on prestige. The Norwich case began in the late fourteenth century, dragging on until the early sixteenth. Exeter's dispute was equally long-term, coming to a head in 1447–8, and graphically recorded in the partisan correspondence of the city's mayor, John Shillingford. Similar jurisdictional disputes occurred at Bishop's Lynn, between the urban authorities and the bishops of Norwich, and at Salisbury.[103] Within towns, perhaps the most important aspect of franchises was their economic freedom. They would be exempt from the urban guild system, and ordinances for economic regulation promulgated by the urban authorities could be ignored. Possibly this accounts for the deep hatred between the city of London and the royal free chapel of St Martin le Grand, the city seeking to curtail an island of economic free enterprise which undercut the system of civic economic regulation.[104]

[102] See 5/2 at nn. 38–41.

[103] Tanner, *Church in Norwich* [810], pp. 144–54 (esp. p. 150); Green, *Town life* [315], ii, pp. 340–82, esp. 351–62.

[104] Thornley, 'The destruction of sanctuary' [836], pp. 193–5; the conflict merges into the attack on sanctuary rights, ibid., pp. 188–93.

Despite the conflict between London and St Martin's, that liberty in fact served a purpose: in a complex manner it allowed the city's own franchises to be respected yet, by providing a seat for royal justices in (but not of) the city, integrated the city into the overall royal judicial system. Similar ambiguities arise in considering the impact of franchises on England's administrative geography. The fragmentation of jurisdiction was clearly serious, and could cause problems. At least one case had to be methodically transferred from the Durham courts to Westminster because of problems caused by the jurisdictional frontier between the palatinate and the county of Northumberland. Such rigid frontiers, especially as they affected the return of writs, greatly facilitated the flight from justice: boundary-hopping was an effective means of avoiding capture, since it complicated the administrative processes of arrest. Moreover, when franchise-holders were arguing about precisely who had authority in a particular case, further delays occurred, and the system of justice creaked even more than usual. If the liberty was ill-administered, it could actually block the administration of justice: the liberty of Hexhamshire had a reputation for lawlessness which was discussed in Parliament in 1414.[105]

Although the patchwork impact of the franchises could obstruct good government, they had their beneficial side. Within the liberties, paradoxically, justice might work more smoothly than outside. A local coroner was more accessible, allowing business to be despatched faster and more effectively. Locally tried court cases (especially in civil matters) would be less troublesome than if they had to be trundled off to Westminster – and would probably be less expensive for those involved.[106] As long as royal officials retained some oversight of the liberties, somehow, then the risks of bad government would be diminished, while the good points would be maintained.

In all this, the crown's attitude towards the franchises was crucial. Usually, however, it is obscure, although with no hint of any real opposition to their existence for much of the period. New franchises were granted fairly regularly, and complaints against misgovernment seem to have produced little response. Early fifteenth-century Parliamentary attempts to curb the liberty of Hexamshire were deftly side-stepped.[107] Even the development of the justices of assize and of the peace did not completely undermine the liberties: the rights of certain franchise-holders to appoint justices were respected, and occasionally even where the holder did not appoint the liberty was respected by the issue of commissions additional

[105] Cam, *Law-finders and law-makers* [123], pp. 92–3; Williams, *Year books, 1 Henry VI* [909], pp. 54–8; *History of Northumberland*, iii, pp. 40–1.
[106] Cam, *Liberties and communities*, pp. 187, 217–18.
[107] *History of Northumberland*, iii, pp. 40–1.

to the county commissions. Such are known, for example, for the Durham liberties of Howdenshire and Allertonshire in Yorkshire, and for the liberties of the Archbishop of York in Ripon and Beverley.[108] Possibly the kings were more tolerant of the ecclesiastical franchise-holders than their lay equivalents: it has been suggested that the private prisons lasted longer in ecclesiastical liberties than in those in lay hands. This might, however, be an instance of the ecclesiastical authorities being behind the times, and maintaining franchises for prestige purposes which others were prepared to drop. While kings did intervene in liberties, they may have acted reluctantly. There is an apologetic tone in a letter from Henry VII to an archbishop of York concerning the arrest of traitors in Hexhamshire, stressing that their crime was high rather than petty treason.[109]

Despite this letter and Henry VII's continued granting of franchises,[110] attitudes towards the franchises changed under him and his son. In the liberty of Ely, for instance, the previous episcopal freedom in appointing justices was restricted: the bishops still made the formal appointment, but were now apparently acting in response to royal initiatives, and effectively duplicating a royal commission.[111] These two reigns (especially Henry VIII's) also rediscovered *Quo warranto*, leading to a generalized attack on franchises which culminated in the virtual abolition of the franchisal sanctuaries, and of the independent judiciary rights of the franchise-holders. These Tudor *Quo warranto* proceedings, apart from those in Cheshire in 1499 and Middlesex in 1519, were on a new model. The franchise-holders no longer entered a general defence of their claims, in a wide-ranging inquisition. Now the cases were tackled in the Westminster courts, and were formal defences of rights against specific charges of arrogation of royal prerogatives in named places.[112] This, therefore, was no general assault on franchises, but a piecemeal war of attrition. The abbot of Burton on Trent thus faced three cases in 1517, 1526, and 1537, each relating to a different place. All three involved his right to appoint a coroner, with the last (concerning Burton on Trent itself) also challenging other franchises. The six cases faced by the bishop of Ely all related exclusively to the nomination of coroners – a remarkable limitation, considering the extent of his powers within the isle – ranging in date from 1527 to 1544. Again these were not generalized attacks, but were limited

---

[108] Kimball, *Warwickshire and Coventry sessions* [471], pp. xxiii n. 2, lxxxiv, lxxxvii (nothing similar has been noted for the fifteenth century, so these may be early appointments prior to the recognition of the rights of the franchise-holders to nominate their own justices).

[109] Pugh, *Imprisonment*, p. 95; *History of Northumberland*, iii, p. 41.

[110] E.g. the coronership granted to Peterborough abbey in 1493: *VCH, Northampton*, ii, p. 423.

[111] *VCH, Cambridge*, iv, p. 22 (but see heading to EDR, E1/4/1, m. 1r).

[112] Garrett-Goodyear, 'Quo warranto', pp. 241–2.

to particular locations like Impington (Cambs.), Mitford (Norfolk), and the soke of Somersham (Hunts. – twice challenged).[113] No grand design hides behind these attacks and challenges: this was no concerted attack on the franchises organized and led by arch-royalists at the centre. While individuals like Chief Justice Fineux might elaborate a theory for royal reduction of franchisal authority, the proceedings themselves suggest lesser motives. The generalized challenge to coronerships, for instance, may reflect a determination to ensure proper accounting for the fiscal fruits of justice; while the contemporaneity of challenges to ecclesiastical franchises in 1532 with other attempts to bully the clergy is probably more than coincidental. Non-royal interests also joined in attacks on franchisal juris-diction: several towns exploited the *Quo warranto* procedure in their strug-gles for liberation, whether from total oversight (as in the case of Newcastle upon Tyne [Northumb.] against Tynemouth priory), or from the effect of jurisdictional islands which excluded municipal authority (as in London's assault on the liberty of St Martin le Grand).[114]

The Tudor attack on the fragmentation of royal authority reflected in the franchises can rarely be seen as directed specifically against their possession by ecclesiastics. Franchises could expose their holders to press-ure for particular purposes (especially a problem for clerical franchise-holders in the circumstances of Henry VIII's reign); but for the crown the nature of the franchise, rather than the holder, was what mattered. The Tudor concept of the state, of the imperial kingdom, especially influenced the idea of royal justice and its elaboration throughout the realm. Indeed, it is the elaboration of justice which explains the challenges to many aspects of franchisal authority, insofar as a policy can be detected. This links the reduction of sanctuary (which in many instances was a franchise) with the integration of the major liberties into the realm by the Statute, 27 Henry VIII, c. 24, the *Act for recontinuing of certain liberties and franchises heretofore taken from the crown*. The key feature of this Act was not the wholesale abolition of franchises – which did not happen – but its insistence that henceforth all justices within the kingdom should act in the king's name, and all writs be issued in his name. Henceforth there would be nowhere where the king's writ would not run; and the powers hitherto enjoyed by certain franchise-holders to nominate justices were eliminated. But this did not abolish the geography of franchises, or those not involving the administration of justice. Indeed, the Act's immediate effect was largely restricted to the great palatinates, including the Isle of Ely, Dur-ham, and Hexhamshire.[115]

---

[113] ibid., pp. 274, 277–8, 284–5, 287–8, 292.

[114] ibid., pp. 246–9, 256–9, 264–5.

[115] *Statutes*, iii, pp. 555–8; Cam, *Liberties and communities*, pp. 217–18; Garrett-Goodyear, 'Quo warranto', pp. 269–70. On sanctuary, see 4/3 at nn. 30–9.

The ecclesiastical franchises were not completely abolished; not even the destruction of the religious orders secured that. Franchises remained, liberties continued to fragment the administrative structure.[116] The Dissolution transferred some of the franchises to lay hands; but this merely changed ownership, not quality. The transfers also reveal the difficulty in assessing the church's place in local administration before the Dissolution, emphasizing that franchises were not spiritualities but temporalities, and only accidentally held by ecclesiastical bodies. That the church was so involved in local administration in the later middle ages, and that it enjoyed widespread franchisal jurisdiction was important; but had little to do with its properly ecclesiastical functions.

[116] For East Anglia, Cam, *Liberties and communities*, pp. 186–7.

4

Two Laws, One Kingdom

4.1 CONFLICT DEFINED

In 1072, by a writ whose precise meaning remains uncertain, King William I initiated a major change in the English legal system: henceforth, God's business was to be separated from Caesar's, with the appropriate renders being made in different courts.[1] The writ is usually taken to mark the inception of a distinct ecclesiastical legal jurisdiction in England, initiating a separation which still lingers (although in a greatly diminished form) in the Church of England.

To proclaim the separation of the courts was easy; actually demarcating the jurisdictions was quite another matter. Only in the twelfth and thirteenth centuries was their scope effectively defined, with developments on both the royal and ecclesiastical sides. The crown consistently sought to curb claims to clerical independence, and to bring clerics within the sphere of royal justice. The major common law tracts of the thirteenth century showed that the crown already had considerable practical control over areas of jurisdiction which, on first sight, were logically within the church's purview. Pragmatic political considerations in later years only added justification to the attempts to establish royal authority over the church within the kingdom.[2]

Meanwhile, almost mirroring these developments, the church had formulated its own jurisdictional claims. The creation of the canon law was principally a reflection of developing papal power; but that rise of papal authority and papal legislative activities helped to define the areas over which the church claimed jurisdiction. The integration of kings and other

---

[1] Barlow, *English church* [40], pp. 150–2.
[2] For developments to 1350, Jones, 'Two jurisdictions' [452]; and generally on later developments, Jones, 'Two laws in England' [450].

secular authorities into a theoretical structure which made their positions dependent on the papacy, and the ever-expanding claim to oversight of issues by reason of the sin inherent in the actions (jurisdiction *'ratione peccati'*) which developed during the pontificates of Innocent III (1198–1216) and his successors left little scope for secular jurisdictional autonomy. Summaries of ecclesiastical jurisdiction, produced by canonists such as Hostiensis, or the great lawyer-pope Innocent IV (1243–54) himself, made few concessions to the aspirations of secular authorities, and thereby made conflict virtually inevitable.[3]

These two strands of development created two separate legal systems, which were necessarily competitive. The royalist theory stressed the kingdom and subjection to the crown; the papalist view stressed the universality of the church and the special status of clerics and ecclesiastical issues, which were beyond the competence of mere laymen, and emphasized the superiority of the canonical system over the secular. The resulting competitive stance, the rivalry of jurisdictional claims – ultimately, the clash of definitions of sovereignty – provides an underlying and undying current in the relationships between the secular and ecclesiastical jurisdictions in England through to the Reformation. Yet this inherently contentious duality produced few major clashes. The nominal rivals usually maintained a *modus vivendi*: while the jurisdictions did clash, the most extreme conflicts were usually between England and Rome on specific issues – international rather than internal. Within England there was fairly constant attrition on ecclesiastical jurisdiction, but few major upheavals until the sixteenth century. For, alongside the rivalry, there was also mutuality: an interrelationship of mutual respect, mutual support. These tensions, of the distinction and interrelation of jurisdictions, the drawing of frontiers between areas of competence, provide the bases for the present discussion.

In tracing these developments, 1350 provides a reasonably valid starting-point. The most bitter conflicts over jurisdiction were by then over, and the demarcation line had been drawn fairly firmly, notably by the quasi-statutes of *Circumspecte Agatis* (1286) and the *Articuli cleri* of 1316.[4] The position established was one from which the ecclesiastical authorities would be able only to retreat: between 1350 and the Reformation the process of attrition continued, but without its former intensity. This makes it feasible to attempt a summary of the relationship between the jurisdictions. This requires, first, consideration of the areas of apparently

---

[3] Ullmann, *Medieval papalism* [852]; Watt, *Theory of papal monarchy* [887].
[4] *Statutes* [776], 1/ii, pp. 101–2, 171–4; for *Circumspecte agatis* (with a better edition) Graves, 'Circumspecte agatis' [310], esp. pp. 9–20; for the *Articuli*, Denton, '*Articuli cleri*' [204]. Their continued influence is shown by discussion of both in Lyndwood, *Provinciale* [539], pp. 96–7, 268.

ecclesiastical business which had fallen under secular control; second, attention to ecclesiastical obstacles which limited the full implementation of secular justice; third, discussion of the activities of the church courts, and the enforcement of their decisions (sometimes with assistance from the secular authorities); and, finally, an assessment of the changing balance of forces, as the church's claims were slowly but effectively undercut, until its final humiliation in the early days of the Henrician Reformation.

4.2   SECULAR INCURSIONS

One of the prime obligations of a medieval English king was to maintain peace. This was imposed in the coronation oath, and its implementation required the exercise of jurisdiction over a wide range of activities. These can, effectively, be summarized in two blocks: crime and property. In either case, the element of peace was strong: crime had to be curtailed to prevent harm to the subjects; property had to be protected and rights upheld to save the subjects from loss. However, this jurisdiction operated only in the temporal sphere: there was a recognized distinction between temporal and spiritual matters, although lawyers' casuistry constantly sought to push back the frontier, and reduce the competence of the spiritual courts. (Spiritual jurisdiction may at this stage be very simplistically summarized as matters of ecclesiastical discipline – for clergy and laity, church rights – especially financial exactions, and oversight of morality – which included marriage cases, sexual misbehaviour, slander, wills, and all manner of oaths.) The royal courts' enforcement of secular jurisdiction reflects two differing definitions of their responsibilities: in dealing with crime the intention was to punish, to exact revenge for the disturbance of the peace; with property issues the court provided a venue for resolving differences, where an injured party could receive compensation. In the first instance the driving force in jurisdictional matters was likely to be the crown, represented through its officials; in the second, although the crown doubtless had an interest, the impetus for jurisdictional developments would probably be provided by the interested parties (or their lawyers) as they sought the implementation of their own definition of justice in the most convenient and enforceable form then available.

In matters of property, the state most effectively challenged the rights claimed by the church when dealing with benefices. The church saw benefices as subject solely to ecclesiastical jurisdiction – a stand maintained by the papacy, usually ineffectually, throughout the period. The state, however, eroded these claims and the benefice and its appurtenances were almost totally subjected to secular law during the later middle ages. While the crown accepted that it could not determine an individual's canonical suitability to hold a benefice, and did not seek to usurp the episcopal, and therefore spiritual, aspects of his formal admission to the office, nevertheless the royal courts claimed, and exercised, oversight of disputes relating to the machinery of candidature (patronage), the real property, and much of the income.

Royal claims to jurisdiction over patronage derived from the distinction made between two different pieces of property: the benefice itself, which clearly could not be possessed by a layman, and remained ecclesiastical; and the advowson, the right to present a candidate to occupy the benefice. Advowsons were treated just like any other property, being part of an inheritance, and as such marketable, and even partible (in that patronage could be exercised by turns). Royal jurisdiction over advowsons had been extended and consolidated during the thirteenth century: by 1350 few English clerics would have openly challenged the crown's oversight of such matters, although disputes about the actual possession of benefices (if they could avoid mentioning the patronage issue) were still treated in the church courts.[5] Change in the secular attitude towards patronage cases had been largely conditioned by a concern for royal interests, especially the extension of royal patronage by regalian right, which had been a feature of court actions in the early fourteenth century.[6] Making patronage a matter for the lay courts – and, by extension, thereby generally making disputes about possession of benefices subject to common law – very much threw the bishops on the defensive, for they were named among the defendants in such disputes. The onslaught on ecclesiastical jurisdiction was formalized with the development of the two writs, *Quare impedit* and *Quare non admisit*, each demanding an explanation from the bishop for his failure to admit the nominee of the claimant patron. A *Quare impedit* was not unanswerable, but there soon developed a considerable and complex body of opinion about its validity in differing circumstances; complexities which must have made such disputes even more subject to common law determination.[7]

Naturally, royal claims to patronage cases could only operate within the kingdom. Local ecclesiastical authorities were too frightened to use the canonical procedures for such matters, but others were less callow. In the fourteenth century, the papacy still claimed jurisdiction over disputed successions to benefices – and various other types of cases. It is against this background of rivalry that the Statutes of Praemunire of 1353 and

---

[5] Jones, 'Two jurisdictions', pp. 102–12; for York, Donahue, 'Roman canon law' [225], pp. 661–2.

[6] See 2/4 at n. 124.

[7] Jones, 'Two jurisdictions', pp. 109–12, 119–23.

1393 (especially the former) must be set: as the culmination of attempts to enforce against papal prerogatives the jurisdictional rights over matters 'ecclesiastical' which were already claimed by the crown – here by threatening the party taking the matter to Rome with effective outlawry.[8]

In benefice matters, the royal courts claimed more than just oversight of patronage. The common law's flexibility, which could apparently transmute a case from one issue to another without any great difficulty, allowed legal quibbles to reduce other areas of ecclesiastical liberty. The old notion of frankalmoign, whereby lands were conveyed to the church free of secular services, had initially meant that disputes affecting such property were taken before the spiritual courts. However, once the common lawyers set to work, the definition of frankalmoign property became very tight. Eventually the area left to the competence of the church courts was reduced to the church itself, and its consecrated ground. Even here, ecclesiastical liberties might not be completely respected: in early fifteenth-century London the city authorities took action against the rector of St Michael ad Quern to maintain a public right of way through the church which had been obstructed when the rector blocked a doorway.[9]

The claims of the secular authorities also extended to matters affecting the benefice's income, particularly tithes. The common lawyers' sleight of hand again proved irresistible. Tithes were obviously spiritual issues – and tithe cases to enforce payment consistently appear in the records of the spiritual courts. But tithes might also be considered chattels, or to affect the value of the benefice and thereby link to patronage issues. Casuistry here assisted the transformation: tithes were of course spiritualities – but their sale or lease made them temporalities, and indistinguishable from any other property subject to secular jurisdiction. Only in the late fourteenth century was it decided that tithes as appurtenances of patronage matters were not subject to secular oversight unless they represented over a quarter of the benefice's income – although this left considerable scope for illicit extension of secular interference in practice.[10]

Secular jurisdiction was extended to various aspects of a benefice's outgoings as well as its income. By 1540 many churches and religious institutions were burdened with pensions. Some were permanent, usually those paid to religious corporations or bishops. Many, however, were temporary, either being paid to buy out the rival claimant to a benefice, or to provide an income for a precursor in the benefice after resignation, or an income for a clerk until promoted to a benefice. By extending to these

[8] ibid., pp. 126, 129–30; Helmholz, *Canon law* [379], p. 95 n. 90; Graves, 'Statute of Praemunire' [311].

[9] Jones, 'Two jurisdictions', pp. 132–8; Riley, *Memorials of London* [699], pp. 417–18.

[10] Wunderli, *London church courts* [931], pp. 110–13; Jones, 'Two jurisdictions', pp. 112–15, 157–64 (but c.f. Donahue, 'Roman canon law', pp. 662–3).

pensions arguments like those affecting tithes in general, pension issues also became matters determinable before secular justices. The common law of debt could also be invoked, especially for pensions until the recipient obtained a benefice, or perpetually payable to religious corporations. The dean and chapter of Lichfield acted on this basis to secure payment of a pension due from Winwick church (Lancs.) in the reign of Richard II, and again under Edward IV. Pensions chargeable until a benefice was gained also caused disputes, either because the value of the offered benefice was less than that of the pension, or because the pensioner was canonically disqualified from accepting the benefice to which he had been nominated. The latter problem arose in a case involving Bridlington priory under Henry VI. The claimant argued that as he was under twenty-four he could not hold the offered benefice, a vicarage with cure of souls. As the offer of the benefice, not its acceptance, was legally held to terminate the annuity, there were clear opportunities for sharp practice. For the defendants in such cases, the issues were probably particularly irksome: the original pensions may have been granted unwillingly at the behest of the local diocesan, or even the king.[11]

While the common law thus limited the church's ability to deal with its own property, it still left a considerable amount of property jurisdiction to the church in fact, if not in theory – in areas such as petty debt, and the execution of wills. These were slowly encroached on by the secular courts, although with varying degrees of success. Often, common law was slow in developing its challenge to the church: not until the sixteenth century did the royal courts provide an effective forum for matters of petty debt. In earlier centuries debt cases frequently came before manorial or borough courts, but many – possibly the majority – fell under ecclesiastical jurisdiction.[12] In testamentary matters, similarly, the secular courts were slow to accommodate changing patterns: in intestacy, for instance, the secular courts did not grant any legal personality to the administrator of the estate until 1357; earlier the bishop was held individually responsible for settling the intestate's affairs. The common law's deficiencies also imposed practical limitations on attempts to sue executors for a deceased's debts, again until the sixteenth century. Even where the state did claim testamentary debt cases, such claims might not be enforced: the existence of parallel secular and ecclesiastical jurisdictions could cause problems in this respect, but also presented litigants with a choice of forum for their case.[13]

---

[11] Jones, 'Two jurisdictions', pp. 161–2; *Le premiere part Henry le VI* [495], 19 Henry VI, f. 54, plea 16; Pike, *Year book of Edward the Third* [659], p. 406; Thornley, *Year books, 11 Richard II* [837], pp. 149–52; Hemmant, *Cases in the Exchequer Chamber* [380], ii, pp. 43–55.

[12] Jones, 'Two jurisdictions', pp. 165–7; see also below, 4/7, at nn. 98–9.

[13] Jones, 'Two jurisdictions', pp. 167–78; Helmholz, *Canon law*, pp. 307–10, 314.

The church also retained prerogatives in other areas affecting the transmission of property rights. These applied most often to the determination
of legal rights resulting from kinship. Heirs claimed by descent; widows
and widowers by custom; but all such claims clearly depended on the
validity of a preceding marriage. Yet marriage, and with it the legitimacy
of offspring, were undeniably matters of an essentially spiritual character,
regardless of their side-effects. Despite the implications for inheritances
the common lawyers rarely sought to intervene in determining such matters. They did occasionally put matrimonial matters to a jury, and developed an inquest to decide whether a child was born before or after its
parents' marriage, but such issues were normally left for ecclesiastical
decision. Here, parallel jurisdictions usually worked in association rather
than opposition.

Normally, if a property claim in the royal courts was challenged by
allegations of an invalid marriage, proceedings were halted and a writ sent
to the appropriate diocesan requesting a judgement of the charge. The
resulting certificate decided whether the case continued in the secular
court. Thus, in 1370, when Katherine Hildyard's dower claims were
denied in Common Pleas (her husband's son by a previous marriage
asserting that she had not been legally married to his father) the writ was
sent to the Archbishop of York, and a full-scale investigation followed.
The couple were found to be consanguinous; their marriage could not be
upheld without a dispensation. Although they had gone through a marriage
ceremony (in exceptionally dubious circumstances), this availed nothing:
they had received no dispensation before the husband's death, and the
marriage was accordingly declared null. The certificate having been returned to the royal judges, the claim for dower presumably failed also.[14]

A broadly comparable procedure applied with allegations of bastardy.
This, however, presented a problem. Throughout the middle ages in
England the two laws clashed on the precise definition of a bastard. By
common law, any child born before wedlock was illegitimate, and could
not inherit by right of descent. By canon law, a valid marriage legitimated
the offspring, regardless of date of birth. Yet common law generally
refused to bastardize the offspring of adulterous liaisons, even where the
church would; and where a marriage was annulled common law was
initially more generous in allowing inheritance rights to the issue of
marriages dissolved for affinity or consanguinity, although annulment on
grounds of pre-contract did bastardize. Over time, however, the stance
changed: by the end of the period any nullity of marriage automatically
meant bastardy.

The common law emphasis on the date of marriage to decide the

[14] Jones, 'Two jurisdictions', p. 140; BIHR, CP.E.108.

legitimacy of offspring was a peculiarly English standpoint, but it clearly faced difficulties if the church determined bastardy issues on its own terms. When bastardy was raised at common law, therefore, two different procedures might be adopted. Where specific bastardy was alleged, the matter went to a lay jury, to return whether the child had been born before or after espousals – thus completely avoiding ecclesiastical jurisdiction. A lay jury might also be asked the precise reasons for the nullity of a marriage, but without being asked to determine whether it was actually valid or not. When a more generalized charge of bastardy was raised then, paradoxically, the matter was left for episcopal determination: the writ would issue, the inquest be held, and the certificate returned. Which procedure was most used is impossible to say: episcopal registers contain many returns on writs for bastardy, but the alternative procedure was probably used equally regularly. Unfortunately, despite apparent strictness, the common law principle was easily confounded: by the Reformation, the different interpretations of bastardy at common and canon law were hopelessly contradictory, producing considerable uncertainty as to individual status. However, the common lawyers were anxious to retain control over bastardy pleas, and sought to ensure that the ecclesiastical authorities were only invoked in cases involving pre-emptive declarations of legitimacy (including certain actions for defamation) at their behest.[15]

A final aspect of property cases which needs attention is the secular power's use of the church to enforce financial penalties in disputes which clerics lost. Damages would usually be enforced by a writ requiring the sheriff to levy the due sum from the possessions of the defeated defendant. However, if that defendant was a cleric or religious corporation, a different method was used if the sheriff returned that there were no temporalities to be distrained. The return would note the lack of temporalities, and the defendant's ecclesiastical status. Another writ would then issue, to the ordinary (usually the bishop), who would be required to make the distraint instead.[16] Perhaps this epitomizes the full extent of the church's submission to the secular authority in property matters: the bishop being placed on a par with the sheriff as a royal official obeying orders to enforce the decisions of a secular court against fellow clerics.

Unlike property matters, the secular exercise of criminal jurisdiction left little scope for conflict between the two authorities over spheres of competence. Crime, violence, was almost without exception considered the

---

[15] Helmholz, *Canon law*, pp. 188–94, 196–209; Jones, 'Two jurisdictions', pp. 139–41; see also Plucknett, *Year books, 13 Richard II* [660], pp. 144–8; Barton, 'Nullity of marriage' [46], pp. 30–47.

[16] Jones, 'Two jurisdictions', pp. 203–4; e.g. LJRO, B/A1/6, f. 124v.

responsibility of the lay power; and although clerics might be involved in such cases as individuals, there was no canonistic foundation for a general challenge to the competence of the lay courts. Even so, some border areas remained where the church apparently claimed – or was allowed – some say. Assaults on clerics seemingly remained within its jurisdiction, as did the pollution of consecrated ground by bloodshed. Theft of ecclesiastical property may also have fallen under ecclesiastical jurisdiction, although this is less clear-cut: thefts from churches were certainly treated in the secular forum throughout. The church courts seemingly also dealt with matters raised in defamation cases, if no previous decision on the facts had been made in the secular courts.[17] The spiritual courts also filled gaps in the secular structure. The state was normally concerned only with manifest crimes, those which had actually taken place; it had no procedure to deal with attempted or intended crimes (apart from treason against the monarch's person). That area seems to have been left to the church, although precisely why is a mystery. The church also occasionally assumed oversight of crimes which the state refused to deal with: infanticide, for instance, seems to have slipped through the net of royal justice, and into the lap of the spiritual courts.[18]

Generally, however, the secular courts retained responsibility for criminal justice. While there were apparent anomalies in clerics possessing rights of justice in such matters, these powers were not held by them as clerics, but as holders of secular franchises, and thus fell into the scope of the church's activities in local government. Perhaps harder to explain are the occasional cases in the church courts where individuals responded to overtly secular accusations for murder, theft, and suchlike. These were probably not ecclesiastical infringements of a secular monopoly, but collusive actions by the defendants with the clerical judge in an attempt to clear the defendants of suspicion of such crimes. They perhaps represented a response to common rumour and insufficient evidence, a variant of an action for defamation in which no individual slanderer could be identified.[19]

Even though there were no major conflicts between church and state over competence in criminal matters, the church had by 1350 created two major obstacles to the full rigours of that jurisdiction. These related to the sanctity of ecclesiastical persons, and to the sanctity of ecclesiastical places. Together and individually they could seriously undermine the effectiveness of the justice system; their impact therefore requires some

---

[17] Helmholz, *Canon law*, pp. 125–6, esp. n. 25; Whittick, 'The criminal appeal' [899], pp. 60–1; Baker, *Notebook* [34], p. 39.

[18] Helmholz, *Canon law*, pp. 129–30, 157–67 (but c.f. Bowker, *Episcopal court book* [76], pp. xx–xxi, 53–4); Dyer, *Lords and peasants* [243], p. 233.

[19] See 3/3; Helmholz, *Canon law*, pp. 138–42.

attention in any general assessment of the church's relationship with the secular power.

4.3 ECCLESIASTICAL OBSTRUCTIONS

From the twelfth century, the church claimed that clerics, because of their status, should be exempt from the rigours of secular justice, and be tried only by ecclesiastical judges. This privilege – 'benefit of clergy' – plagued the common law through to the Reformation and beyond. So too did the law of sanctuary, by which parish churches and a number of other ecclesiastical institutions were islands within the mesh of royal justice, usually temporary, but sometimes permanent. Sanctuaries and the threat which they offered to the maintenance of peace especially vexed the lay authorities in the half-century before the Reformation; but their justification was much debated long before then.[20]

Benefit of clergy was perhaps the more serious challenge to royal jurisdiction, chiefly because it became easily exploitable. As it exemplifies the problems of the parallelism of the two laws, fairly detailed consideration is justified. Canon law claimed that all clerics were, quite bluntly, not subject to secular justice. Recognition of that position had been bought with Becket's blood, and the saint's name was regularly associated with the claim. For the canonists benefit of clergy was a right, but the common lawyers disagreed: for them, that a certain category of the king's subjects was beyond the reach of royal justice was a privilege, and in the contrast between privilege and right lay the seeds of discord.[21] Nevertheless, although there was conflict, the idea of benefit of clergy faced few serious challenges until the reigns of the first Tudors.

For present purposes, the starting-point is the 1352 Statute *Pro clero*, which proclaimed the basis of the system: that

all manner of clerks, seculars as well as regulars, who shall henceforth be convicted before secular justices for whatsoever felonies or treasons, concerning persons other than the king himself or his royal majesty, shall henceforth have and freely enjoy the privilege of holy church, and shall without any hindrance or delay be handed over to the ordinaries who shall demand them.[22]

---

[20] For benefit and sanctuary, Jones, 'Two jurisdictions', pp. 178–94; Baker, *Reports of Spelman* [33], ii, pp. *327–46*. On benefit alone, Gabel, *Benefit of clergy* [290]; Bellamy, *Criminal law and society* [54], ch. 6. On sanctuary Trenholme, *Right of sanctuary* [845], and for an anecdotal (and out-dated) survey, Cox, *Sanctuaries and sanctuary seekers* [170].

[21] Gabel, *Benefit of clergy*, pp. 1, 25–8; for reference to Becket under Henry VIII, Baker, *Reports of Spelman*, ii, p. *344*.

[22] 25 Edward III, s.6, c.3; *Statutes*, i, p. 325.

The concession seems fairly wide, and in time proved even wider. The key word is 'convicted': before 1350 alternative methods had been used (and might be rarely thereafter), but from Edward III's reign benefit was usually claimed only after the jury had pronounced its verdict – but before the judge pronounced sentence. As clergy need not be claimed when found not guilty, this was perfectly reasonable; but it also arose from the general stance of the secular judges, that regardless of the possibility of a claim of clergy, the jury should determine the facts. From the mid-fifteenth century it was actually a requirement in the secular courts not to admit a claim of clergy before such a determination was made.[23]

The crimes for which benefit might be claimed were manifold, as the statute of 1352 implied; but they had to be felonies. Lesser crimes, trespasses (which included common assault), did not carry the privilege. Other minor misdemeanours such as poaching (usually dealt with in manorial or borough courts) were also excluded. For some decades after 1352 there was uncertainty about indictments which described defendants as *insidiatores viarum et depopulatores agrorum* or *combustatores domorum*, although they would seem to have been covered by the spirit of the Act. Nevertheless such highwaymen, brigands, and arsonists were in practice denied clergy until the reign of Henry IV. Greater limitation of benefit in treason cases occurred under Henry VII, with the disallowance of petty treason – although the mutability of the definition of treason in the middle ages tended to bring crimes in and out of its scope. In treason cases another practical distinction seems to have been maintained, with benefit being permitted in private accusations but not when the issue was brought by the crown. Other legislation reduced the use of benefit under Henry VIII in cases of murder and theft from churches. As with trespasses, 'civil' suits did not allow claims of benefit, although Edward III conceded that clerics should not be imprisoned for debt. The clergy were thus not fully relieved of their accountability in the royal courts, and so might still be made outlaws, usually for not appearing to answer either a charge or a plaintiff.[24]

Once found guilty by a jury, the claimant would need to prove his clergy. For this purpose, and for taking him (if successful) into ecclesiastical custody, the local ordinaries appointed representatives to attend the courts and demand the clerks. Initially these representatives probably administered the tests to determine clergy themselves, but their powers were gradually hedged with restrictions by the secular authorities. While in the 1360s there are signs of commissions for formal examination, by the

---

[23] Gabel, *Benefit of clergy*, pp. 30–51.

[24] BL, MS Hargrave 87, f. 303v; Gabel, *Benefit of clergy*, pp. 58–9; Pugh, 'English outlaws' [675], pp. 324–5 (see also e.g. *Cal. pat. rolls, 1429–1436* [117], pp. 207–9); Firth, 'Benefit of clergy' [274], pp. 176–7; Baker, *Reports of Spelman*, ii, p. 333; *Statutes*, iii, p. 49.

end of the middle ages the ordinary was little more than a court officer. Initially, the test of clerkship appears to have been possession of at least the first tonsure, a physical sign of ordination. By 1400 this had been all but superseded by a test of reading ability, on the supposition that literacy indicated clerical status. As this test developed, the roles of the ordinary and his representative in the proceedings declined: reading provided a reasonably clear-cut test, and also allowed the justices some say in its assessment. By 1480 they alone decided the issue, the reading being generally from a Latin psalter. There are sometimes suggestions of a set piece – the so-called 'neck verse' – which could be learnt by heart, but the judges apparently retained discretion in the choice of book. Nevertheless, reading could not decide all cases: proof of ordination apparently remained a possible option; whilst the common lawyers also sought ways to cover a variety of contingencies – the mute clerk (who should therefore write), the blind clerk (who should speak Latin – but only be allowed his clergy if he spoke it from education rather than like an Italian), and the clerk who found difficulty with the handwriting because he was a foreigner (and should accordingly be provided with a book from his native land). They were almost stumped by the clerk blinded since ordination and not fluent in Latin, but even that was not entirely beyond their ingenuity: his status should be determined by the local jury.[25]

The change from a basic reading test for clergy to a reading test regardless of orders made benefit of clergy available to unordained male laity, although the reasoning behind the change is elusive. Passing the test required education: the numbers doing so provide striking testimony to the contemporary growth in educational opportunities. However, it need not have been a hard test: enough could be learnt during the remand in gaol – just as tonsures had previously been acquired there – although in such cases the gaoler was held negligent for allowing his prisoner to acquire such knowledge. Whether reading actually made benefit of clergy available to greater numbers is uncertain. For the late middle ages evidence of the numbers receiving first tonsure is scarce, although they considerable outnumbered those receiving major orders. The notion that people were routinely tonsured as protection against secular justice probably has little substance: the order could be conferred on mere boys, and whilst parents perhaps foresaw their sons turning into criminals, the boys themselves probably had no such plans that early. Yet one of the justifications for the papal bull of 1516 depriving those in minor orders of 'clerical' status was precisely that people were exploiting the position – perhaps at that stage by receiving the tonsure in adulthood. The lack of records of first tonsure makes it uncertain whether any machinery existed

<hr>

[25] Gabel, *Benefit of clergy*, pp. 51–8, 64–74; Baker, *Reports of Spelman*, ii, pp. *328–31*.

for its certification to the secular justices. Equally, despite its opportunities, lack of evidence makes it impossible to assess accurately the numbers actually claiming benefit of clergy; although the insubstantial statistics which have been compiled suggest that the numbers increased between the early fourteenth and late sixteenth centuries.[26]

Having proved his clergy to the justices' satisfaction, the convicted clerk would be handed over to the ordinary for imprisonment to await canonical trial. Only rarely could the transfer be rejected and the judicial decision on status be denied. By the time Thomas Kebell lectured on benefit to the Inns of Court *c.*1472, the unfortunate ordinary could be fined for claiming someone whom the justices decided was not a clerk, for refusing someone they said was, or for changing his mind. He could not refuse a clerk for sacrilege, false tonsure, or false clerical clothing. Whilst conviction for heresy did deny the right to benefit, an accusation as yet unproven did not. Indeed, among all the possible objections to a clerk, the only one which withstood the insistence of the common lawyers that he be accepted was bigamy, that the accused had either married twice, or married a widow. This single objection seems rather perverse, and would itself doubtless have crumbled had it not been founded on statute as well as canon law.[27]

After committal to the ordinary's prison, the convicted clerk would await his canonical trial – to the canonists, his real trial. The usual method revealed in episcopal registers is trial by purgation, but this was actually part of a lengthier process, and not a re-trial for the crimes for which benefit had been claimed. The trial on those charges preceded purgation, in an inquest held under ecclesiastical auspices. If that found the allegations true, or the clerk confessed, then he was degraded from orders, reduced to lay status, and suffered penance immediately – including the possibility of lengthy prison confinement. If the inquest found the accusations unproven, the nature of the case changed. The clerk would be admitted to purgation not on the original indictment, but as a victim of defamation. Not all clerks reached this stage: often when the clerk was handed over the lay courts ordered that purgation should not be allowed, or be granted only by royal licence; it was definitely not permitted in cases of outlawry (until remitted), or return following abjuration of the realm.[28]

Purgation itself involved the accused taking an oath of innocence,

---

[26] Baker, *Reports of Spelman*, ii, pp. *329–30*; Gabel, *Benefit of clergy*, pp. 74–8 (although using inaccurate figures for first tonsures); Bellamy, *Criminal law and society*, pp. 138, 156–7.

[27] BL, MS. Hargrave 87, ff. 304r–v (for date and manuscript see Ives, *Common lawyers* [435], pp. 48–9, 54–5); Gabel, *Benefit of clergy*, pp. 87–90; Jones, 'Two jurisdictions', pp. 189–90; Baker, *Reports of Spelman*, ii, pp. *327–8, 331*.

[28] Gabel, *Benefit of clergy*, pp. 92, 94–111 (the commission printed at p. 96 suggests the change to a defamation charge); Baker, *Reports of Spelman*, i, p. 50.

supported by the oaths of others that they believed him – not assertions that he was innocent, but that the compurgators believed his protestation of innocence. Passing the test thus negated the guilty verdict of the secular courts. Compurgation obviously had potential faults, some of which the clerical authorities sought to counter by summoning objectors against the purgation from the region where the crimes had occurred. It is impossible to draw any real conclusions about this system: the ecclesiastical evidence is insufficient. The documents entered in episcopal registers are usually notifications of successful purgation; but the register would be most un-likely to record failures, or earlier stages of the process at which the convicted clerk had failed to pass the inquest. It remains a valid objection that benefit of clergy did allow individuals to commit crimes with some-thing approaching impunity, once they reached compurgation. Whether the horror stories of contemporaries about the scale of repeated criminality hold any truth is largely unascertainable, with clear evidence of repeated purgation being scarce; but that such complaints were made indicates feelings about possible exploitation of the privilege. The developing re-strictions on clergyable crimes in the fifteenth century mark an attempt to limit this activity; so does the major change effected in 1489, by which benefit of clergy was to be allowed only once to everyone if proved by reading. This would be the only opportunity for laymen to claim benefit: murderers were on delivery to the ordinary to be branded with an 'M', other felons – generally thieves – with a 'T'. The brand was not to be considered proof of recidivism in future cases, but would warn the court to search the records for the earlier conviction. Real clerks could evade these stipulations by production of their letters of orders – which suggests that this exemption was restricted.[29] The application of benefit of clergy to particular crimes continued to be whittled away thereafter, but the privilege itself lingered on well after the Reformation.

The second major ecclesiastical obstacle to the implementation of royal justice was the notion of sanctuary. At common law this had a dual origin. First, there was the sanctity accorded to every parish church (and some other consecrated places) within the realm, whereby a criminal could demand short-term sanctuary in each location. Secondly, there were the areas of greater immunity, whose origins were basically franchisal: there the privilege was based on a combination of royal and papal grants – with the precise terms of the royal grant in time becoming increasingly important. In the ordinary sanctuaries the criminal who had committed a felony could take refuge for up to forty days, during which he was not to be

---

[29] Helmholz, *Canon Law*, p. 131; Bates, 'Edward Leche' [48]; Gabel, *Benefit of clergy*, pp. 123–4; Baker, *Reports of Spelman*, ii, p. 332.

molested. In that time he could request the attendance of the local coroner, who would anyway arrive when the time elapsed. The refugee then faced a choice: confess guilt and abjure the realm, or surrender. (There was a third option, to stay put, but after the initial forty days all assistance was withdrawn and it became a criminal offence to supply food and drink, so that some refugees actually starved to death in the churches.) If abjuration was chosen, the criminal had to confess – the grounds for abjuration had to be public knowledge – and had to admit a felony. Thereafter, having taken the required oath, the exile had to quit the kingdom, often by an assigned route, and theoretically (although perhaps not in practice) would be guided along the journey by the local constables. While travelling to the assigned departure point (usually a port, but exiles to Scotland might go by land) the banished individual remained under royal protection. By the end of the middle ages the restrictions on the traveller were perhaps slightly less rigid than earlier – deviation was permitted to find food and so on, but the route had to be resumed as soon as possible – and on reaching the frontier the exile had to leave the realm at the earliest opportunity.[30]

How many of those formally abjuring the realm actually left England is unknown – perhaps only a minority, given the opportunities to escape en route. Nevertheless, abjuration was intended as a final step; anyone returning without royal pardon, unless capable of claiming benefit of clergy, was liable to summary justice – and some who took the risk paid the price. Even so, enforcement of abjuration was undoubtedly difficult, and in 1529 branding was introduced for those exiled, to ensure their compliance with the sentence.[31]

Abjuration was not imposed within the greater sanctuaries, which conferred perpetual immunity within the precincts unless the privilege was forfeited by sacrilege. Abjuration could also be delayed by flitting between lesser sanctuaries. Refugees were meant to be kept under close watch to prevent escapes, but such watchfulness was hard to maintain. Within parishes, the individual township was responsible for containing refugees in local churches, chapels, and hospitals, and an escape produced a fine on the township. Regulating such fines again attracted the attention of the common lawyers: c.1472 Thomas Kebell listed in considerable detail the circumstances under which a fine would or would not be levied. Despite the possibility of a fine, escapes must have been relatively common.[32]

---

[30] Baker, *Reports of Spelman*, ii, pp. *334–8*; Hunnisett, *The medieval coroner* [429], pp. 41–50 (see also *Sanctuarium Dunelmense* [734], pp. 30–1; Sayles, *Select cases in King's Bench* [742], p. 3).
[31] Baker, *Reports of Spelman*, ii, pp. *337–9*; Sayles, *Select cases in King's Bench*, pp. 2–4.
[32] BL, MS. Hargrave, 87, ff. 305v–306r; generally Baker, *Reports of Spelman*, ii, p. *336*.

A major problem with the sanctuaries lies in assessing how and why they were actually used. Only the great immunities maintained records of sanctuary-seekers, and the printed lists from two of the leading northern sanctuaries – Beverley (Yorks.) and Durham – raise several questions, and suggest caution. In many cases the culprit was clearly fleeing from a fairly recent crime, sometimes in ignorance of its outcome, but in others the journey to sanctuary involved considerable distances, for crimes committed long before. Had the Yorkshireman seeking sanctuary at Beverley in 1488 for a crime committed in Derbyshire in 1483 only just been accused? Had someone who killed at Dartmouth (Devon) fled north and only recently been recognized? Or had both spent the intervening months and miles sanctuary-hopping (and, if so, in the Dartmouth case why hop to Beverley, rather than one of the more accessible southern sanctuaries)? Cases represented include flights for debt, sheer accident, and gang warfare. But one important aspect of sanctuary – perhaps too easily denigrated – lies in its providing time for reflection after an incident. Not everyone who sought sanctuary had actually, or wilfully, committed a crime. They might have fled to avoid the repercussions of unjustified suspicion; or indeed be totally innocent, but still fear others. It was political disorder and suspicion which caused Queen Elizabeth Woodville to take all her children (except Edward V) with her into sanctuary at Westminster in 1483; while when John Ward sought sanctuary at Bishop's Lynn (Norfolk) in 1413 it was discovered that his motive was not to evade punishment for any felony but because he feared for his life. Indeed, flight to sanctuary may have been a reflex response to serious accidents. In about 1409 the inadvertent wounder of a child at Laverstock (Wilts.) had sought sanctuary fearing the child's death, but later testified to her miraculous recovery in the canonization proceedings of St Osmund.[33]

The major attack on sanctuary, when it came, was principally directed against the great immunities: those islands of exemption from royal justice where hardened criminals could remain in freedom, occasionally sallying forth to wreak havoc in the neighbourhood, if the propaganda against them can be believed.[34] This role of the immunities as boltholes attracted crown attention in the late fifteenth century, especially when they were exploited by traitors. Until then matters had proceeded rather intermittently. Occasional major crises aroused by individual conflicts, usually involving a breach of sanctuary (sometimes by royal officials) provoked

[33] *Sanctuarium Dunelmense*, esp. pp. 151, 153, 155; Owen, 'Asshebourne's book' [628], no. 134; Ross, *Richard III* [715], pp. 73, 86–7, 100–1; Malden, *Canonization of Osmund* [572], pp. 64–5.

[34] Baker, *Reports of Spelman*, ii, pp. *339–40*. For the attack, see Thornley, 'The destruction of sanctuary' [836] (but occasionally distorting by assuming that a sanctuary was just like any other liberty or franchise).

immediate response, both on the royal and clerical sides. In 1378 a breach of sanctuary at Westminster abbey, arising from a seizure for debt, left a dead body in the church and provoked a major row which reverberated through the proceedings of the Parliament at Gloucester. That crisis produced a change in the law relating to debt and sanctuary: henceforth perpetual sanctuary would not be allowed for fraudulent debtors who managed their affairs to ensure their own income before debunking on their creditors, but would only be granted to allow time to make restitution. The 1378 crisis also resulted in a major tract on sanctuary, the *Objectiones et argumenta contra et pro privilegiis sanctuarii Westmonasterii*, a massive summary of current opinion on both sides of the question. Although apparently of little immediate effect, its arguments were dusted off and reused later. In due course, Westminster proved to be one of the most resilient of all sanctuaries, retaining its privileges beyond the Reformation because it had the archives to circumvent the increasingly restrictive definition of the privilege.[35]

As the fifteenth century progressed, so the determination to limit the abuse of the great sanctuaries as boltholes increased, by emphasizing their 'imprisonment' aspect. Although an attempt to place royal guards at the exits (and, by definition, entrances) to the sanctuary of St Martin le Grand in London in the 1450s provoked complaints from the local clerical authorities, later Pope Innocent VIII did allow Henry VII to take precisely that action in general terms. However, perhaps greater emphasis was placed on passing responsibility for the safeguarding to the clerical authorities. The threats to ecclesiastical liberty posed by the compact between Innocent VIII and Henry VII may have stimulated the church to greater care in keeping the sanctuaries.[36]

Breach of sanctuary was probably more common than the surviving records suggest. The church took such cases seriously, as did those seized. Infraction was punished with automatic excommunication of the perpetrators. In 1411, for instance, one Robert Jordan was murdered in breach of sanctuary at Grittleton (Wilts.), and in due course his killers were brought to penance. A similar course of action was probably anticipated for the Hungerford (Berks.) parishioners reported at visitation in 1405 for ejecting robbers from the churchyard, although some cleared themselves of the charge. Physical force was necessary to effect the breach – trickery which beguiled a fugitive into voluntary exit from the church did not lead to restitution. Breach of sanctuary also had a remedy at common law, with the abducted individual demanding restoration on the

---

[35] Kaufman, 'Henry VII and sanctuary' [457], pp. 471–2, 475–6; Perroy, 'Gras profits' [652], pp. 577–9; Harvey, *Solutions to the schism* [360], pp. 10–12.
[36] Kaufman, 'Henry VII and sanctuary', pp. 473–5.

grounds of illegal seizure. The resulting cases could range from the banal to the extremely important. One detained refugee claimed that he had been wrongly taken because he had only nipped out of his sanctuary to go to the public privy. The demand for restoration was taken seriously – to the extent of a jury investigation of whether he could have relieved himself elsewhere without running the risk of capture. The jury found against him. More significant were two major cases which led directly to drastic reductions in the scope of sanctuaries, especially the immunities: Stafford's case in 1486, and the case of John Savage V in 1516–19.[37]

Stafford's case produced a major redefinition of the availability of sanctuary for treason, and increasing restrictions on the immunities. Humphrey Stafford, Duke of Buckingham, had been attainted after Henry VII's victory. Originally a refugee at Colchester (Essex), he emerged to raise rebellion, and then fled to Culham (Oxon.). He was there seized and dragged from sanctuary. He demanded restoration, but his plea failed: sanctuary was not pleadable in cases of treason, and the Culham sanctuary was invalid – it was traditionally one of the greater immunities, but had no precise documentary support, and such merely prescriptive rights could not run against the king. Henceforth royal charter evidence was needed to support the claims for a sanctuary. Papal grants of immunity were held insufficient, so that the sanctuaries associated with the houses of exempt religious orders were thereby demolished at one blow.[38]

The case of 1516–19 developed this assault on the sanctuary system, doing much to undermine it. The detailed attack on the foundations continued, stressing the need for documentary evidence not merely for the origins of the immunity, but for its continuous recognition. Most seriously, the judges largely overthrew the concept of the perpetual sanctuary: only forty days were permitted, as in any other parish church. This immediately undermined the immunities, unless they could prove usage pre-dating 1189. But some survived, and were if anything reinforced by an Act of 1530 which required those abjuring the realm not to go abroad but to concentrate in certain specified sanctuary areas, as they were considered too dangerous as potential soldiers to be sent to join enemy forces abroad.[39]

Part of the attack on the sanctuaries was probably connected with contemporary concern for religious reform; part reflected concern about the

---

[37] Timmins, *Reg. Chandler* [841], p. 43; Horn, *Reg. Hallum* [411], nos. 1004–5; Sayles, *Select cases in King's Bench*, pp. 120–1; LJRO, B/A/1/11, ff. 78v–80r; Hemmant, *Cases in the Exchequer Chamber*, ii, pp. 115–24; Kaufman, 'Henry VII and sanctuary', pp. 469–70; Baker, *Reports of Spelman*, ii, pp. *341–5* (see also Baker, *Notebook*, pp. 31–2); Ives, 'Crime, sanctuary, and royal authority' [434], pp. 297–303.

[38] Baker, *Notebook*, pp. 37–41.

[39] Baker, *Reports of Spelman*, ii, p. *339*

scandals they permitted; part derived from Henry VIII's own views on royal authority; part from Thomas Cromwell's antipathy to any obstacles to centralization, equating the sanctuaries with other franchisal liberties. But it was not so much the notion of sanctuary which was attacked as its abuse – Thomas More, whilst arguing for change, nevertheless wanted the basic system maintained.[40] But both benefit of clergy and sanctuary did disrupt the performance of royal justice, although in different ways. The attack on benefit was perhaps unfairly directed against the church, considering that it was the common lawyers who had foisted their definition of its lawful recipients on the ordinaries, and crushed any resistance. Sanctuary, however, was a different matter, and there the ecclesiastical authorities had greater responsibilities. Both obstacles impeded royal justice on a more fundamental level than the occasional upsets which occurred in property matters. This was due to the parallelism of the jurisdictional systems established independently by church and state. Before surveying the overall relationship between the two jurisdictions, and the process of attrition, the full system of ecclesiastical jurisdiction requires attention, and the way in which it in turn was inhibited or assisted by the powers of the crown.

4.4　THE COURTS CHRISTIAN

As with the secular courts, the structure of the ecclesiastical courts was largely a product of the twelfth and thirteenth centuries. It arose contemporaneously with the territorial spiritual jurisdictions, and with the rise of canon law as a universal system for the church which was ultimately validated by papal approval or promulgation.

The nineteenth century saw some controversy about the nature of the canon law of medieval England, especially over whether it had formally to be 'accepted' locally before it could be implemented. Yet although parts of the law were inoperative in fact, they remained theoretically valid – and medieval clerics might well assert the theoretical position against the actual, sometimes with unfortunate results for themselves.[41] England's basic canon law was identical to that applied elsewhere within the church: Gratian's *Decretum* of the 1140s, the *Liber extra* promulgated by Gregory IX in 1234, and additions made by Boniface VIII, Clement V, and John XXII. Canon law also included other papal decretals not in the *Corpus iuris canonici*, but made effective by developments in canonistic jurispru-

---

[40] ibid., ii, pp. 345–6.
[41] Gray, 'Canon law in England' [312]; Donahue, 'Roman canon law', pp. 647–708, esp. pp. 647–56.

dence. In addition, the local law incorporated provincial legislation – although that usually reinforced declarations made at a higher level, and sought to eliminate inconsistent English customs. Even so, custom and local practice were vital components of the operative law, producing a flexible structure which, for instance, allowed the bishops in late medieval England to retain considerable control over mendicant preaching by twisting the meaning of the decretal *Super cathedram*, even if they did not completely subvert it.[42]

The law's application in England was also within the mainstream of the experience of the whole western church. In consequence, the English canonistic tradition cannot be rigidly separated from the traditions of the rest of the church. Discussions of local legislation provide two of the greatest monuments to medieval England canonistics – John Acton's commentaries (of *c.*1334) on the thirteenth-century legatine constitutions of Otto and Ottobono, and the better-known *Provinciale* produced by William Lyndwood in the 1420s – but they do not stand alone. The *Oculus sacerdotis*, written by William de Pagula in the 1320s, and the derivative *Pupilla oculi*, produced by Johannes de Burgo *c.*1384, also stand out. All these drew extensively on continental writers, such as Hostiensis (d.1271). Both the *Provinciale* and the *Pupilla oculi* were eventually printed, continental versions perhaps again indicating the integration of English practice into the universal tradition.

Canon law, moreover, was not an arcane study. It permeated much of contemporary theology, and of course administrative practice. Indeed, the works of Lyndwood and de Burgo were essentially administrative and legal handbooks, while the *Oculus sacerdotis* was considered so instructive that later in the fourteenth century John Mirk turned it into his versified English *Instructions for parish priests*. At one end of the scale are such handbooks, at the other the records of the law's practitioners, like the notebook produced by John Lydford at the turn of the fourteenth and fifteenth centuries, or the occasional citations of canonistic authorities in surviving records of the spiritual courts. Continuity in practice is well illustrated by a mid-thirteenth-century English manuscript of Gratian's *Decretum*, which was still being used and annotated by a Gloucestershire notary public two centuries later. The integration of canon law into semi-theological studies is shown in John Baconthorpe's commentary on the *Sentences*. Whilst these works were certainly by Englishmen, and although English practice sometimes raised eyebrows in Rome, these books were

---

[42] Richter and Friedberg, *Corpus iuris canonici* [697]; Ullmann, *Law and politics* [857], pp. 139–46, 165–70; Donahue, 'Roman canon law', pp. 677–99; Kedar, 'Canon law and local practice' [458], pp. 17–25; Helmholz, *Select cases* [378], pp. xvii–xxvi; Helmholz, *Canon law*, pp. 145–55.

primarily the works of churchmen – which probably explains why Bacon-thorpe dealt so extensively with the nature of papal power within the church as a whole.[43]

A complex amalgamation of traditions contributed to the practised canon law. Consequently, that law cannot be seen as a rigid structure. The incorporation of custom, the considerable emphasis placed on interpretation, created a system neither static nor monolithic. It was a law mutable with circumstances, not tied by precedent – the spirit of justice and charity theoretically overrode the dead letter, the concern for the salvation of souls superseded the precision of words.

The courts which applied this law formed a complex hierarchy, but one which could be entered at almost any level. The system rose from ruridecanal chapters or the archdeacon's courts (or courts of peculiar jurisdictions with archidiaconal authority) to the episcopal courts, of which there might be several within a diocese – consistory, exchequer, audience, or commissary. Above the diocesan were the provincial courts (in Canterbury, the Court of Arches) and even higher, overseeing the whole structure, the papacy and the *Curia Romana*. The peculiar jurisdictions naturally fragmented the structure, and might themselves contain suggestions of another hierarchy, as shown by the attempts of the chapter of York Minster to supervise the prebendal courts of individual canons. Duplication within the system, especially at the diocesan level with the several episcopal courts, also causes some problems. For a decade after 1518 a national unity was imposed on England by Wolsey's legatine court, interposed between the provinces and Rome. Unfortunately, evidence of its activities is almost wholly lost, although it certainly heard appeals, and could call up cases from lesser jurisdictions.[44]

The hierarchy was mainly to cope with appeals, but plaintiffs retained some choice of court. In particular, proceedings could be initiated at Rome without working through the structure: the pope, as 'universal ordinary', claimed cognizance of all ecclesiastical causes at first instance. But the church courts cannot be seen as top-heavy, or permanently clogged by appeals. The evidence is imperfect, but appeals occurred only in small minority of cases, and the lower courts (as is shown by the surviving court records of the bishop of London's commissary in

---

[43] Boyle, 'The *Summa summarum*' [82]; Boyle, 'The *Oculus sacerdotis*' [83]; Ullmann, 'John Baconthorpe' [858]; Owen, *John Lydford's book* [626]; CUL, MS Ee.5.4; Donahue, 'Roman canon law', pp. 683–94; Owen, 'The practising canonist' [627]; Pollard and Redgrave, *Short-title catalogue* [665], i, p. 181, ii, p. 127; Kristensson, *Mirk's instructions for parish priests* [490].

[44] Wunderli, *London church courts*, pp. 7–19; Brown, *Courts of York Minster peculiar* [100], p. 16; Woodcock, *Medieval ecclesiastical courts* [919], p. 13; PRO C270/28/25; LJRO, B/A/20/1, f. 22v; HCA, Baylis, i, pp. 239–40.

the fifteenth and sixteenth centuries) transacted much of their business summarily.[45] Nevertheless, appeals to Rome remained possible, English procedure incorporating the oddity of simultaneous appeal to the archbishop's court. Technically, this appeal was for 'tuition' – for protection of the appellant during the appeal to Rome. The archdiocesan officials could, on such appeal, inhibit proceedings in lower courts, and thereby facilitate the transfer of the case to Rome.[46]

The cohesion of the system varied: the geographical frontiers between jurisdictions were very real, and actions in one court involving cross-border issues were not always matched by corresponding cases in the neighbouring jurisdiction. The duplication of diocesan courts also produced competition for business within the same area, a position complicated even more by active archidiaconal courts. While the multiplication of courts for the same authority was not necessarily a problem, the existence of multiple authorities for the same area was. Occasionally this could be remedied by fudging: one man would act as both archdeacon's official and bishop's commissary within an archdeaconry, combining offices and courts. This happened in the archdeaconry of Buckingham between 1480 and 1525. In Chichester diocese, a similar approach was adopted in the 1520s to integrate the peculiar jurisdictions. One area where the hierarchical system was particularly lax was probate. In York province, the archbishops only established a prerogative probate jurisdiction in the sixteenth century, making probates granted by their courts valid in all subsidiary jurisdictions. Hitherto probate had had to be obtained in each jurisdiction where the will would be executed. The southern province was more advanced, the prerogative jurisdiction appearing in the fourteenth century. But it faced challenges: in the 1490s Archbishop Morton encountered opposition from Bishop Hill of London, and in the 1510s the greater contest between Archbishop Warham and several of his suffragans became something of a *cause celèbre*, with its own political ramifications.[47]

Lower down, jurisdictional clashes could be equally violent, as officials sought to extend their authority beyond the formal frontiers, or to exercise overlapping jurisdictions. Years of conflict over the delineation of the respective authorities of the bishop and archdeacon of Ely were finally resolved only in 1401. Elsewhere, particular incidents provoked comment.

[45] For London commissary, Wunderli, *London church courts*, pp. 10–11; on appeals, Woodcock, *Medieval ecclesiastical courts*, p. 63.

[46] Woodcock, *Medieval ecclesiastical courts*, pp. 65–7; Donahue, 'Roman canon law', pp. 671–4.

[47] Brown, *Courts of York Minster peculiar*, p. 16; Marchant, *Church under the law* [574], pp. 103–7; Elvey, *Courts of Buckingham* [254], pp. xvi, xviii–xix; Lander, 'Church courts' [494], pp. 219, 221–3; Harper-Bill, 'Bishop Hill and Canterbury' [347], pp. 7–12; Churchill, *Canterbury administration* [144], i, pp. 380–412; Kitching, 'Court of Canterbury' [479], pp. 193–5.

In 1405, for instance, the visitation of the deanery peculiar of Salisbury revealed that the apparitor of Sherborne (Dorset) had been undermining the prebendary of Axford's jurisdiction by citing the latter's subjects to his courts. Some such attempts to extend jurisdiction were little more than personal vendettas, as when the subdean of Salisbury harried Robert Crome on a charge of adultery in 1414. Usually the hierarchical system of jurisdictions resolved these difficulties eventually; while the procedural complexities caused by the existence of overlapping jurisdictions, or a multiplicity of courts with equal competence, could also be resolved by compromise.[48]

Although most cases in the church courts received summary treatment, full or plenary proceedings did occur, and could be extremely complex. While there are suggestions of some informality, the decreed procedures had to be precisely followed. The English court system had generally to conform to that operating elsewhere within the church: procedurally it therefore owed more to Roman law, as adopted by the papal legal institutions, than to the English common law. In particular, plenary proceedings in the ecclesiastical courts consumed massive amounts of parchment. These extended cases generated a convoluted and comprehensive series of documents: libels (outlines of the case), interrogatories, responses, statements of witnesses, and so on, culminating in a written definitive sentence. These provide much of the information about the court machinery, and, if they had all survived, would be invaluable to the social historian. Unfortunately, little does survive apart from the court books themselves – and those, frequently only for relatively late in the period, and only for some of the many courts which might be operating within any one diocese. Even the books are of limited use, usually giving little more than a skeletal outline of proceedings, and often no indication of the outcome. However, additional documents do occasionally survive. At York, where the series of consistory court books begins only in 1417, with massive gaps later in the century (1430–84, 1489–97), the cause papers, containing individual documents as issued or produced, extend back to the thirteenth century and forward beyond the Reformation, filling a number of gaps. The records of the dean and chapter provide seemingly greater continuity in the late fourteenth and fifteenth centuries, while records of processes occur intermittently from 1316 throughout the fourteenth century; but the survival of cause papers has been much less consistent. Unfortunately, York's is the only large collection of such material for the later middle ages. Elsewhere, witnesses' depositions were recorded in volumes, like the early sixteenth-century survivors for Norwich's consistory court. Country-wide,

---

[48] Feltoe and Minns, *Vetus liber* [269], pp. 180–96; Horn, *Reg. Hallum*, no. 1024; Timmins, *Reg. Chandler*, no. 46 (see also no. 193); Woodcock, *Medieval ecclesiastical courts*, pp. 26–7.

the survival of court material is extremely patchy. For the diocese of Lichfield scarcely any evidence remains: a few episcopal court books from the fifteenth and sixteenth centuries, and for the jurisdiction of the dean and chapter occasional records of cases in chapter act books and other sources, but virtually nothing else.[49]

The procedures which brought cases before the church courts fall essentially into two groups. First, there were the so-called 'office' cases, initiated by the church's own actions (often following local investigations and denunciations), and brought by the holder of the jurisdiction *ex officio*. These might, in an oversimplistic generalization, be considered equivalent to criminal prosecutions. Secondly, and again oversimplifying, there was the 'instance' business, the equivalent of civil cases: cases with a defendant who was accused by (*'ad instanciam'*) a plaintiff. But the distinction between office and instance business cannot be rigidly maintained: the same type of case could occur under either head, depending on the preliminary process. There were also distinctions within the office procedure, between cases brought by the ecclesiastical authorities on their own volition (*'ex officio mero'*), and those in which the authorities acted on behalf of a third party (*'ex officio promoto'*), which procedurally were often scarcely distinguishable from instance cases. The structure of the ecclesiastical system perhaps also permitted collusive actions, with individuals conniving at their own prosecution in an ostensibly office case, in self-defence against common rumours and without having to identify a specific defendant.[50]

Two main channels might result in office cases. The normal functions of the holders of major ecclesiastical jurisdictions – archdeacons and their equivalents, upwards – included visitation. This involved travelling throughout the jurisdiction, and holding inquests to reveal the state of the parishes. The best secular parallel would be the general eyre, rather than the assizes (which perhaps have their equivalent in the peripatetic archdeaconry and diocesan courts). Formally, archidiaconal visitation was an annual round; bishops should visit their dioceses triennially; and archbishops should hold a provincial visitation once during their pontificates (and also visit individual dioceses when vacant). Surviving evidence does not permit any

---

[49] Woodcock, *Medieval ecclesiastical courts*, pp. 50–9, 68–71; Helmholz, *Marriage litigation* [377], pp. 7–22, 124–35; Woodcock, *Medieval ecclesiastical courts*, pp. 139–42; Smith, *Guide to the archive collections* [763], p. 53; Brown, *Courts of York Minster peculiar*, pp. 4–5 (with additional material for 1316–33 scattered through YML, M2/1a); Donahue, 'Roman canon law', pp. 657–9; Longley, *Cause papers: dean and chapter* [529], pp. 1–11, 149–51; Stone and Cozens-Hardy, *Norwich depositions* [780]; LJRO, B/C/1/1–2 (1464–79), B/C/2/1–3 (1524–35), B/C/13 (heresy), D.30/II, ff. 30v–33v, 35r–43v, 58r–59r, 62v, 65v–68v, 72v.

[50] Wunderli, *London church courts*, pp. 32–3.

firm conclusions about how frequently or assiduously visitations were performed. Of archidiaconal visitations almost no evidence survives: by the fifteenth century many archdeacons treated the task solely as a source of revenue from the fees payable by the places visited, and acquired papal licences to collect the money without doing the work. In such circumstances, meaningful visitation would be irregular, most visitations being no more than perfunctory. Episcopal visitations leave more evidence, but still not much. There are indications of fairly frequent visitations before 1350, thereafter evidence declines. Reasonably full returns survive for a visitation of Hereford diocese in 1397, as an isolated example. A visitation itinerary can sometimes be reconstructed from episcopal registers – such as Archbishop Bowet's visitation of York in 1409–10, or the archiepiscopal visitation of the vacant diocese of Durham in 1438 – and smatterings of presentments occasionally survive from diocesan visitations, like those for parts of the archdeaconry of Richmond in 1428. But only in the sixteenth century do detailed regular records of defects discovered during diocesan visitations reappear. Evidence for episcopal visitation of religious houses is relatively abundant, but that is rather different in nature from parochial visitation. Lack of evidence for parish visitations need not mean that they did not occur: the sources rather than the bishops might be at fault. The evidence for fairly regular visitation in Lichfield diocese, for example, derives only from references to the receipts in accounts of spirituality revenues. Even where the episcopal itinerary does not indicate personal visitation by the bishop, it could have been done by commission. However, it seems likely that the triennial requirement was not being generally fulfilled. Although general visitations thus declined, there was scope for a multitude of minor visitations by commission of individual areas which aroused concern – although that would also mean incomplete surveillance of the diocese. Thomas Langley, Bishop of Durham (1406–37), thus held only one full visitation of his diocese, but arranged for *ad hoc* visitation of individual parishes and colleges. As for archiepiscopal visitations, the northern province provides scarcely any sign throughout the period other than vacancy visitations, as at Durham in 1438. Greater evidence survives for Canterbury province, but it is not very informative. What visitations occurred were intermittent, rarely covering the entire province. Some of the most consistent evidence for visitations comes from the peculiar jurisdictions, especially those of deans overseeing capitular and prebendal jurisdictions. At Salisbury the registers of Deans John Chandler (1404–17) and John Davyson (1473–85) contain fairly full details of their visitations, the former having visited his jurisdiction in 1405, 1408–9, and again in 1412. In York, fairly detailed records of visitations of the dean and chapter jurisdiction survive from the fourteenth century onwards. For the diocese of Lichfield a fragment survives from the 1460s indicating that decanal visitations there were equally intensive, with Dean Heywood in 1466 describing his projected visitation as triennial. Returns also survive from 1458 for the parishes annexed to St Paul's, London.[51]

The visitation procedure involved searching enquiry: examining the local clergy, disclosing local moral offences, and anything else the visitor chose to ask about. Although there were objections to the use of lay juries to make presentments under oath at visitation, juries were apparently the norm – possibly in ordinary courts of presentment as well as at visitations. Such jurors regularly incurred the hostility of those whose peccadilloes were revealed. Following the presentments, whether by full juries, or (as the early sixteenth-century evidence increasingly suggests) by church-wardens alone, appropriate orders would be issued for defects capable of immediate rectification (like rebuilding churchard walls) while matters requiring court decisions were set down for hearing in due course.[52]

Outside visitations, other means produced office cases. Visitation alone could not account for all the office cases entered in the court books – especially if visitations were intermittent. Current rumour perhaps stimulated some proceedings when the offence was considered so notorious that action was unavoidable: notoriety was a critical factor in the proceedings in the church courts, with witnesses being required to testify in their depositions to the notoriety of their facts. The parish clergy may also have reported some cases, while the minor curial officials could have provided channels for reports to percolate back to the authorities who actually issued the citations. Chaucer's Summoner of *The Friar's Tale* may not be totally fictional, and summoners certainly attracted considerable hostility. In the early sixteenth century, there are indications of summoners increasingly issuing frivolous citations, which may have been exploited to increase

---

[51] Woodcock, *Medieval ecclesiastical courts*, pp. 33–6, 68–9; Elvey, *Courts of Buckingham*; Thompson, *English clergy* [824], pp. 43, 61–2; Woodruff, 'An archidiaconal visitation' [924]; Swanson, 'Episcopal spiritualities: Lichfield' [803], at nn. 20–1; Bannister, 'Visitation returns of Hereford' [38]; Wood-Legh, *Kentish visitations* [922]; Thompson, 'Documents relating to visitations' [818], esp. pp. 152–93, 201–38; Storey, *Langley and Durham* [782], pp. 182–4; Churchill, *Canterbury administration*, i, pp. 288–347 (esp. pp. 314ff.); ii, pp. 142–57; Timmins, *Reg. Chandler*, pp. xv, 1–50, 72–129; YML, L2(3)a, ff. 1r–46v, L2(3)c, ff. 1r–222v (extracts printed in Raine, *Fabric rolls* [686], pp. 242–74, see also Brown, 'Peculiar jurisdiction of York Minster' [940], pp. 250–76); LJRO, D.30/XVIII; Simpson, *Visitations of churches* [761], pp. 65–114.

[52] The churchwardens' increasing role appears in Thompson, *Visitations of Lincoln* [822], compare vol. 1 (for 1517–18) with vol. 2, pp. 1–70 (for 1530); see also Wood-Legh, *Kentish visitations* (perhaps the best printed representation of the aftermath of visitations). For the variety of business, see Timmins, *Reg. Chandler*, index, under offences (pp. 233–5). Jones, 'Two jurisdictions', pp. 199–200 (suggesting that jurors were abnormal); Timmins, *Reg. Chandler*, p. xvii (for hostility to jurors see PRO, C270/34/17; EDR, F5/32, f. 28v; and perhaps Leadam, *Court of requests* [502], p. 16).

their fee income, and thereby contributed to the growing disaffection from the ecclesiastical courts.[53]

Although office cases were significant, it was instance business which provided most of the cases in the church courts, matters of debt, defamation of character, and matrimonial issues clearly dominating. Here the parties would simply bring the case before the courts, employ lawyers, and let things run their course. The role of the church courts in instance cases may have been chiefly as a forum, and a place for arbitration, backed up by penance and punishment. Office cases were similarly aimed at imposing penance on the guilty. But some apparently office cases may reflect collusive action. With secular charges, as already mentioned, the defendant might be seeking to clear his name against malicious rumours. Similar arguments could well apply in office cases for other crimes, such as fornication. In such collusive actions, the concern was not to prove guilt and impose punishment, but to find the accused party innocent. Collusion probably did not occur very often, but the possibility remains open.[54]

4.5 SPIRITUAL JURISDICTION

Organizationally the church courts covered the whole of the kingdom. But a structure alone was insufficient: it needed to be used. Moreover, to be maintained it had to serve a purpose – and not just the church's disciplinary purpose. It needed to function effectively for petitioners in order to be validated, although there might well be conflict between disciplinary and popular functions.

The extant archives of the church courts give an impression of an overriding concern for the more salacious aspects of human existence. The surviving fifteenth-century records of the dean and chapter of York, and those of the London commissary court from 1470 to *c*.1520, are fairly typical: in the latter, sexual matters regularly accounted for 80–90 per cent of all cases heard. The initial impression is reinforced by the visitation material, which often reports allegations of sexual improprieties (although they are notably absent from Warham's Kentish visitations in 1511–12). The concern for sexual activity was more than a prurient voyeurism. The church's duty to maintain moral standards required it to investigate rumours – frequently no more than rumours – which were brought to its attention in office matters. When such accusations involved clerics (as

---

[53] Woodcock, *Medieval ecclesiastical courts*, pp. 48–9, 79; Wunderli, *London church courts*, pp. 33–40; Wunderli, 'Pre-Reformation London summoners' [932], pp. 210–15.

[54] Above, at n. 19.

they did in York with depressing regularity) the disciplinary incentive was even more urgent. On the instance side, matrimonial matters were highly important to the parties involved; while sexual slander was treated as particularly damaging – reputations were important, and needed to be defended.[55] The moral standards asserted were not just those imposed by the church, but those of society in general (or, at least, of the social group which organized that society). The church's involvement in moral cases was often reactive rather than positive, with similar moral concerns some-times finding expression in records of manorial courts.[56]

The statistical dominance of sexual crimes largely reflects action taken by the courts themselves. When office cases are subtracted, the spread of business usually changes. Focusing on what concerned individuals privately (rather than as upholders of communal morality) reveals a change in emphasis. During the later fifteenth century it seems that most cases – in the extant records of some courts, certainly over half – concerned breach of agreements ('*fidei laesio*') usually connected with monetary or commercial debt. Most remaining instance cases dealt with defamation, or matrimonial issues between the parties.[57] Any of these could, however, be brought as office matters, either promoted, or *ex officio mero*.

Three main classes of business thus appeared before the spiritual courts – breach of faith, defamation, and sexual/matrimonial matters. Breach of faith, despite its all-encompassing definition, was founded on a relatively simple principle: that oaths should be obeyed. Thus anything established under oath, any form of contract, was determinable by the church courts, by virtue of the oath's binding force. However, lack of a formal oath or promise to fulfil the agreement undercut the jurisdiction, so that individuals might acknowledge their involvement in a transaction, but deny any promise for its completion. Without proof or acknowledgement of the promise the whole case fell. Nevertheless, the ecclesiastical courts tried to ensure that such promises were recorded, as in the successive 'Registers of condemnations' among the dean and chapter archives at York. Such agreements covered a wide variety of transactions, from a simple debt contract to the equivalent of deferred payment for goods (or deferred delivery after payment) and apprentices' indentures. Indeed, the church's probate jurisdiction was partially founded on the concept of *fidei laesio*: binding the executors to perform the will, or the administrators to admin-ister the estate. Considerable testamentary business would be found among

---

[55] Woodcock, *Medieval ecclesiastical courts*, p. 79; Wunderli, *London church courts*, pp. 81–102, esp. p. 81; Purvis, *Mediaeval act book* [676], p. 4.

[56] E.g. McIntosh, *Autonomy and community* [559], pp. 258–9 (this may be an incipient court for a peculiar jurisdiction: see ibid., pp. 71–2).

[57] Helmholz, 'Canonical defamation' [376], p. 256; Helmholz, *Canon law*, pp. 264, 283–4; Woodcock, *Medieval ecclesiastical courts*, pp. 87–9.

the *fidei laesio* actions in the church courts, for only there could the executors effectively be sued for the debts of the deceased; executors also exploited the courts' jurisdiction to enforce debts due to the deceased.

Fidei laesio cases were probably the bread-and-butter of the spiritual courts for much of the later middle ages. However, in the early sixteenth century they virtually disappear from the records, for reasons to be discussed later. By 1540 *fidei laesio* was no more, despite continued ecclesiastical claims to such jurisdiction, except as the basis of testamentary actions.[58]

Defamation was the second main category of routine business for the church courts, to which it was confined by the end of the fourteenth century. It was obviously taken seriously by those slandered, although many cases probably reflected words uttered thoughtlessly in argument, rather than deliberate assault on a reputation. Until the fifteenth century the slander usually carried imputations of a crime, but by 1500 wider, more generally slanderous statements were being included in the actions. The secular authorities were content for the spiritual courts to tackle most of the cases, but things changed after 1500, when defamation based on accusations of criminality passed to the jurisdiction of the secular courts. Throughout the period a loophole in the whole system, which might allow a defendant before the secular courts to bring defamation charges against his accusers, or even against a jury finding him guilty, posed something of a problem. However, the state here intervened, and successfully blocked such actions.[59]

The most complex area of activity for the spiritual courts dealt with human sexuality. Some cases were fairly straightforward, as when ordained clerks were convicted of fornication. Here, where one party was meant to be chaste, complications were few. However, dealings with the laity could bring difficulties. With charges such as prostitution, or keeping a disorderly house, it was merely a matter of fact. But where the church did get hopelessly entangled was in its handling of matrimonial issues.

The church's acquisition of jurisdiction over marriages, and the creation of marriage law, had been slow processes extending over centuries, involving the imposition of an ecclesiastical definition of marriage on a more popular attitude.[60] The conflict between the rigid canonical definition and the more fluid vulgar approach to marriage is the essential tension affecting matrimonial jurisdiction in England in the later middle ages, rather than any clash of competence between church and state. The ecclesiastical view

---

[58] Helmholz, *Canon law*, pp. 267–8, 272–3, 276–7, 283–5, 309–25; YML, M2/1a, M2/4f (these seem to fit the context established in Vodola, *Excommunication* [879], pp. 36–9).

[59] Helmholz, 'Canonical defamation', pp. 256–68; Wunderli, *London church courts*, pp. 63–80; Woodcock, *Medieval ecclesiastical courts*, pp. 88–9, 134–5; Helmholz, *Select cases*, pp. xiv–xlvi, lviii–lxiv, 3–24.

[60] Helmholz, *Marriage litigation*, p. 5.

rested essentially on a theory of contract, but one with peculiar spiritual significance. This contract was, therefore, to be strictly enforced, regardless of the consequences. They, at times, were chaotic; for while the circumstances allowing voidance of the contract were few, those in which it might be made were manifold. Marriage was contracted with incredible ease, by a simple declaration. It was no two-stage process, of engagement and later ceremony: the engagement, the plighting of troth, made the contract; and in theory ecclesiastical involvement was unnecessary. Solemnization in church might occur to regularize an otherwise clandestine union, but was not mandatory. It was encouraged by the church, but only became a general requirement in the sixteenth century.[61] The contractual element at its heart also meant that marriage could be celebrated in the future tense, making it conditional on a future contingency, whether long or short term. Future parental consent might thus be invoked, while the ecclesiastical authorities also exploited such future conditionality in disciplinary proceedings against sexual misbehaviour. Usually sex after a promise of marriage consummated the contract; where couples were found guilty of 'living in sin', but had no intention of regularizing the arrangement, the spiritual authorities often imposed a marriage which was conditional in nature, so that any subsequent sexual relations would bind them in a legally married state. Conditional marriages naturally produced complications: in 1415, for instance, Thomas Dobynson sought to enforce a marriage before the Durham church courts, alleging that he had offered marriage to Isabella Lane with the gift of gloves and a belt. The acceptance of the present on those terms would have made the marriage, but she, although acknowledging receipt, denied any condition in the gift.[62]

The very informality of marrying, the almost accidental way in which contracts might be made (even in childhood) rendered medieval marriage law potentially (and often actually) a layman's nightmare. Marriages were either void or valid, with no middle path. Modern divorce, recognizing the validity of previous dissolved marriages, was unknown. There was merely a version of judicial separation, difficult to obtain, and in which the contract nevertheless remained binding.[63] Litigation therefore sought to either substantiate or annul a contract (the latter often seeking to validate another marriage in the process). By contrast, despite varied grounds on which nullity might be alleged, such litigation was less common than might be expected. Nevertheless, all cases proved complex if not

---

[61] Sheehan, 'Formation and stability of marriage' [758], pp. 239–40; Helmholz, *Marriage litigation*, pp. 26–30, and comments at p. 167.

[62] Sheehan, 'Formation and stability of marriage', pp. 246–7, 253–5; Helmholz, *Marriage litigation*, pp. 47–57, 172–81; *Depositions and ecclesiastical proceedings* [206], p. 29.

[63] Helmholz, *Marriage litigation*, pp. 100–7.

settled summarily. Moreover, that actions might be brought *ex officio*, or by third parties asserting a prior claim to one of a couple as their own spouse, further added to the complexities. On the other hand, the private nature of the marriage-making process, and the difficulty of dissolution, could work to the advantage of the couple against external pressure. The classic case of this is Margery Paston, whose marriage to Richard Calle, the family's land agent, horrified her family when it was revealed. Attempts to break the marriage foundered on their determination to remain wedded.[64]

The contractual element accounted for much of the marriage litigation, and usually sought to prove a marriage. This often involved invalidating another contract by asserting claims of pre-contract, that one or both of the parties to the challenged contract had previously contracted with someone else. Any such earlier arrangement immediately nullified a subsequent marriage. Such cases might be brought by one of the parties, by someone claiming to be married to one of them, or even occasionally by someone else. The most dramatic English invocation of this concept occurred in 1483 with Richard III's allegation that Edward IV's marriage to Elizabeth Woodville was invalidated by the late king's pre-contract with Lady Elizabeth Butler. Having thus bastardized Edward V, and with legal impediments to the succession of intervening Plantagenets, Richard himself took the throne. Pre-contract probably provided the most conflict between the canonistic and popular views of marriage: common opinion apparently viewed the church's 'binding contract' as only a preliminary stage – an engagement rather than a formal union. Conflict might ensue if the spiritual authorities, aware of the existence of the earlier 'marriage', sought its enforcement. Equally, individuals could manipulate the canonical rules to their own advantage. The idea of pre-contract rendered marriage an extremely fragile institution, all too subject to the possibilities of collusion or malice to secure an annulment, or deliberate forgetfulness to ensure that a later marriage remained in force.[65]

If pre-contract provided the most potent challenge to existing marriages, consanguinity and affinity were the biggest obstacles to making a legal marriage in the first place. It is indeed difficult to see how so many people could legally have been married in medieval England. Consanguinity regulations meant that, counting from a common ancestor, it was illicit to marry anyone closer in blood than a third cousin unless a dispensation was obtained from the papacy or its agents. As the requirements applied to all the descendants of each of the sixteen great-great-grandparents, this

[64] Richmond, 'Pastons revisited' [696], pp. 31–3.

[65] Sheehan, 'Formation and stability of marriage', pp. 251–3, 257–63; Helmholz, *Marriage litigation*, pp. 25–6, 31, 33–66, 76–7; Ross, *Richard III*, pp. 89–91.

must have often severely limited local choice. The rules of affinity further restricted the possibilities for legal union. Affinity encompassed spiritual relationships, banning marriage between those united by godparenthood or godchildhood: in 1402, for instance, Alice de Manston and Laurence atte More needed a dispensation to legitimize their marriage because she had acted as godmother to his children. Affinity also covered relationships between in-laws, and even applied generally to sexual relationships. It was therefore illegal to marry anyone within the fourth degree of consanguinity with someone with whom either party had had sexual relations. A papal dispensation was thus needed to marry the third cousin of a previous spouse, or any previous sexual partner.[66]

Such complexities meant that many marriages were formulated in ignorance – feigned or otherwise – of their invalidity. Episcopal registers contain scores of dispensations sought by individuals, either to permit or confirm marriages, which might otherwise be illegitimate. The few included in the Lichfield episcopal register for 1415–19 provide a reasonable cross-section, although still incomplete. Most involve invalidity because of the relationships between the parties. Thus, Thomas de Assheton and Elizabeth Borun sought a dispensation because Thomas, when aged eleven, had contracted to marry Elizabeth's sister – although she had died aged eight, and at an age when the marriage could not have been legally enforced. Ralph de Radeclif and his prospective wife Cecilia similarly faced a problem of previous relationships, Ralph being kinsman to Cecilia's first husband, Hugh de Venables. John Hatton and Margaret Hycheson presented a more complex difficulty. Before his marriage John had had carnal relations with one Alice, related to Margaret in the fourth degree of consanguinity. The emphasis on covering possible loopholes by dispensation is highlighted by the marriage between Ralph de Langtre and Isabella Leverlerd, which required two dispensations: in applying for the first, they had miscounted their generations, declaring a relationship in the fourth degree on both sides. In fact the relationships were in the third and fourth degrees. They therefore procured a second dispensation to ratify the first.[67]

Precisely when individuals thought of procuring a dispensation is not always clear. Many were obviously obtained before marriage; but, equally, many couples delayed the application, perhaps hoping to present the church with a *fait accompli* and then get the dispensation, or even that the impediment would pass unnoticed. In such circumstances, the ease of marriage-making probably worked in their favour: as banns had to be called for marriages solemnized in church, such unions were perhaps

---

[66] Helmholz, *Marriage litigation*, pp. 77–87; Swanson, *Reg. Scrope* [796], ii, no. 725.
[67] LJRO, B/A/1/8, ff. 24r, 25r–26r, 28v–29v.

more likely to incur objections than the more informal clandestine arrangements. Nevertheless, many illegalities were unearthed, and not all could be remedied. Couples might seek dispensations but not obtain them: the proctor acting for John and Katherine Hildyard at Avignon in the 1360s claimed he had been told that one could not be granted even if he offered £1,000 for it. Separation was obviously seen as the initial response to illicit marriages, but in many cases the bishops possibly took the first steps to arrange annulments, in line with their moral and spiritual responsibilities. In Lichfield diocese the consanguinous marriage of Thurstan de Pemberton and Emmota de Wynstanley came to the attention of the authorities only some years after it occurred, suggesting that it had been generally accepted in the locality; but then they sought a dispensation, granted in 1417.[68]

Other grounds for annulment were few. Impotence might be alleged, but proof was difficult; and if the man later became a father all sorts of difficulties resulted, annulling the annulment and all subsequent contracts by either party. More common were pleas for nullity for lack of consent, either because the parties had been under age when the marriage was contracted (child marriages requiring affirmation in adulthood, but precisely how the reaffirmation was made remained a grey area), or because of some degree of intimidation. As consent was a crucial component of the contract, its absence provided a valid reason for annulment, but again proof presented difficulties.[69]

The possibility of annulling a marriage some years after its occurrence – even after the death of one of the parties – obviously threatened inheritances. Where there were offspring to challenge the annulment of their parents' marriage, matters could become hopelessly complicated, especially given the differing attitudes of the ecclesiastical and secular authorities to the offspring of annulled marriages. In 1411 the Archbishop of York received a papal commission to investigate a particularly intricate case. Sir Gilbert Kikely was the second husband of a certain Margaret, whose first marriage (to Sir Robert Worswick) had been annulled, Sir Robert also remarrying. But the daughters of the annulled union, concerned about their own status, had tested the nullity of their parents' marriage in the archdeacon of Richmond's court – and had won. They were therefore declared legitimate, and Kikely's marriage to Margaret was necessarily invalidated. He, not unnaturally, objected to this, and had petitioned the papacy for a remedy. Pope John XXIII passed the buck, and the unfortunate arch-

---

[68] Sheehan, 'Formation and stability of marriage', pp. 236, 238; Helmholz, *Marriage litigation*, pp. 86–7, esp. n. 40; BIHR, CP.E.108; YML, L2(3)c, f. 55r; LJRO, B/A/1/8, ff. 27v–28v.

[69] Sheehan, 'Formation and stability of marriage', p. 261; Helmholz, *Marriage litigation*, pp. 87–100 (see also Fuller, *Papal letters, Alexander VI* [287], nos. 185, 283).

bishop (or, more likely, his commissary) was left to sort out the mess, supposedly without the possibility of further appeal. What the actual outcome was remains unknown.[70] While breach of faith, defamation, and sexual and matrimonial matters provided much of the business of the ecclesiastical courts, they do not encompass all of it. Several miscellaneous areas also fell to the church courts, some of them also claimed by the secular authorities. Thus, tithe cases not infrequently appear among the records, usually seeking to enforce payment rather than disputing possession. What appear to be patronage cases are sometimes also found. The church's concern with matrimonial matters gave it an interest in the enforcement of conjugal rights,the spiritual courts reacting to allegations of domestic disharmony and mal-treatment of a spouse to provide a solution – a charitable, rather than legalistic, exercise of spiritual jurisdiction. Nor is it surprising that the bishop regularly sought to ensure respect for the sanctity of holy days: workers and traders were frequently hauled up for working on Sundays and festivals, or for trading when they should have been at church. Cases of sorcery and allegations of witchcraft, heresy matters, and attempts to ensure the enforcement of monetary dues to the church, all make their appearance in the records with varying degrees of regularity. A relatively rare variant of *fidei laesio* action was for perjury in the secular courts. This was, apparently, conceded to the ecclesiastical authorities as being pri-marily a spiritual offence, although not without a certain erosion as the state dealt with it by statute.

One category which was strictly left for spiritual judgement was heresy, although royal assistance was occasionally invoked in the process. The increasing concern for heresy derives from two possible explanations, which will require more detailed treatment elsewhere: either a real increase in the incidence of heresy (a legacy of Wycliffism and foretaste of the Reformation), or a growing concern about opposition to the unreformed church which may have caused a stretching of the definition of heresy to include actions (such as the withdrawal or refusal of church dues) which earlier would have been decided under a lesser heading.[71]

A final area of jurisdiction concerned wills and probate. By 1300 the church had sufficiently secured its hold over probate jurisdiction to say that wills were thereafter generally a matter for the spiritual authorities. But the jurisdiction applied only to bequests of moveables: land could not

---

[70] Swanson, 'Papal letters' [794], no. 46. For a post-mortem annulment, Helmholz, *Canon law*, p. 199; and for a case seeking to bastardize a claimant's *father*, BIHR, CP.G.46.

[71] For the variety, Woodcock, *Medieval ecclesiastical courts*, pp. 80–1, 86–7; Wunderli, *London church courts*, pp. 108–13, 122–8, 130–1; Donahue, 'Roman canon law', pp. 662–3; Jones, 'Two jurisdictions', p. 200; Guy, *The cardinal's court* [322], pp. 20–1; see also 7/3 at nn. 103–6.

usually be bequeathed by will, and even where it could (as in London and other corporate towns) the competence of the church authorities was limited by the existence of local lay courts to oversee such transfers. Wills might also be proved ordinarily before borough or manorial courts. *In toto* the probate jurisdiction has left perhaps the most extensive evidence among surviving ecclesiastical archives – the great runs of registers of the Prerogative Court of Canterbury, for example, or the will registers and probate act books in the archives of the archbishopric of York. Perhaps, overall, probate jurisdiction constituted the main area of business for the spiritual courts. The chapters held by the archdeacons of Buckingham between 1483 and 1523, for instance, were mainly concerned with proving wills and granting administrations. The preponderance of probate activity would have been emphasized in the sixteenth century as other types of business declined. But, although important, probate activity perhaps falls into a category distinct from most of the other business so far considered. Probate jurisdiction *per se* was not so much disciplinary as bureaucratic and administrative; disciplinary issues would arise only when there were doubts regarding the validity of a will, or where executors had difficulties in fulfilling their obligations, or refused to carry them out. It is in such contexts that probate activity comes under consideration of court business proper, particularly as it generated other concerns in oversight of testamentary debt (creating a sort of pre-Reformation law of bankruptcy), and even the enforcement of enfeoffments to uses (the creation of trusts) for which the secular authorities did not provide appropriate machinery.[72]

Wide-ranging in content, the spiritual jurisdiction of the medieval English church would have touched almost every inhabitant of the kingdom at some point. Its pervasiveness made it a potent force; but the degree to which it was actually effective is another matter entirely.

4.6   THE EFFECTIVENESS OF THE ECCLESIASTICAL SYSTEM

The effectiveness of the church courts would have depended on the nature of the procedures, the quality and efficacy of the sentences, and partly on the nature of the business itself. Clearly the courts were meeting needs beyond the imposed disciplinary concerns of the spiritual authorities; why else was there so much instance business? However, although they provided justice of a sort, it may not have been the justice that was sought: that the forms of redress provided by the church courts were considered inadequate

---

[72] Sheehan, *The will in medieval England* [757], pp. 164–76, 196–205, 211–30; Wunderli, *London church courts*, pp. 115–17; Houlbrooke, *Church courts* [415], pp. 90–108; Elvey, *Courts of Buckingham*, pp. xxi–xxvii, 1–214, *passim*; Helmholz, *Canon law*, pp. 291–305.

is suggested by their rapid loss of effective jurisdiction in the majority of debt and certain defamation actions in the early sixteenth century, once the secular courts circumvented their own conventions to provide the right type of justice.[73] Moreover, the courts' processes provided many opportunities for corruption, and for abuse of the system. The partisan nature of the proceedings encouraged evasiveness, if not perjury, especially in matrimonial cases. Collusive actions could easily 'discover' a pre-contract, whether desired by one, both, or neither of the parties to the disputed marriage. Evidence, despite being offered under oath, could still be suspect: in the Hildyard marriage case of 1370, for example, the testimony advanced on behalf of the defendant, Katherine – denying knowledge of any consanguinity – is vague and unconvincing, especially as one of the opposition witnesses had actually attended the marriage ceremony; whereas the evidence offered to negate the marriage rings true. Nevertheless, matrimonial cases covered issues where the courts' authority probably was respected: it was usually in the parties' interests to clarify their status, so there would probably be little real obstruction. Most marriage cases were concluded reasonably quickly, either summarily or within a few months. Real obstruction might be offered when a case was brought *ex officio*, with the court on its own authority interfering in people's private lives; while a determined attempt to enforce a marriage might force the case to Rome and back again, a time-consuming business.[74]

While litigants exploited the courts in their own interests, the courts' attitude towards offenders was also important. The concern was often only for the specific geographical jurisdiction rather than the general principle of correction. There are several instances where the flight of an accused terminated the case – having quit the jurisdiction he was no longer that particular court's problem. While there are occasional signs of follow-up, and the process of caption for excommunicates would increase these, they probably applied more to instance than office cases. Indeed, courts sometimes encouraged offenders to leave their jurisdiction, to get rid of the responsibility. On the other hand, the existence of the frontiers could prevent cases being brought, as an anonymous would-be husband complained when his alleged wife flitted between the dioceses of London and Ely to avoid being brought to court.[75]

Assuming that cases were actually followed through, a major obstacle to acceptance of the church courts as effective tribunals (applicable in

---

[73] Below, at nn. 98–9.

[74] BIHR, CP.E.108; Woodcock, *Medieval ecclesiastical courts*, p. 83; Helmholz, *Marriage litigation*, pp. 113–18, 155–9, 162–3.

[75] Below, at nn. 84–6; Sayers, 'Monastic archdeacons' [741], p. 194 n. 88; Bowker, *Episcopal court book*, p. xiii; Purvis, *Mediaeval act book*, p. 28; Legge, *Anglo-Norman letters* [506], p. 40.

cases of benefit of clergy and much of the summary business) is the large number of acquittals through compurgation. But concentration on compurgation conceals another important aspect of the church courts: the numerous cases where no action was taken at all, or which dropped en route. In late medieval London the cases in which no citation was actually issued, added to those which drop from the records, regularly equalled or exceeded the number of cases ended by purgation. If only completed cases are treated in statistical considerations of compurgation, then it does appear to end an overwhelming percentage of cases; but it cannot be discussed in such isolation.[76]

At first sight, compurgation seems a peculiar method of proceeding. The notion that an accused should swear to his innocence and produce others (the number specified by the judge in the individual case) to swear that they believed that he would not have perjured himself by denying guilt left clear opportunities to abuse and corruption, ranging from bringing along friends to support the oath, to the existence of professional compurgators. Moreover, it is questionable how seriously the ecclesiastical judges themselves expected the system to work: often the required type of purgation was not actually performed, yet the individual concerned was considered to have demonstrated innocence. In some adultery issues the case was suspended, compurgation being deferred for fear of causing greater scandal if the news reached the other party in the marriage. At times, moreover, the judges appear to have been unconvinced by compurgation: in 1466 William Benesleve, vicar choral of York Minster, successfully purged an accusation of fornication, but because he was an habitual offender the judge still held him 'suspect'.[77]

The whole basis of compurgation has been heavily attacked for the way in which it was used in the London courts for summary business. There, it is argued, it could not be expected to work: compurgation might be effective among a small, static, village population, but not among the teeming masses of the capital. Yet it is perhaps too easy to denigrate the system, and mistake its purpose. For one thing, it was possible to fail in purgation by not producing the required assistance – and despite the borderline cases where the rules were twisted, several people did fail. Moreover the opposing party – or anyone else – could challenge the compurgators. The validity of the process is certainly undermined by cases like that of John Shaw at York in 1475: there the seven 'honest' vicars choral who were his compurgators included six who had appeared on similar fornication charges, two being especially notorious offenders. However, two other York cases rehabilitate the process. In 1459 M.

---

[76] See statistical tables in Wunderli, *London church courts*, pp. 142–7.
[77] Purvis, *Mediaeval act book*, pp. 24–5, 28, 32.

William Byspham protested against the purgation of Robert Walker; and in 1460 the purgation of Emmota Bygan was apparently rejected because the chosen compurgators were felt not to know her well enough. A striking objection to purgation followed the visitation of the decanal jurisdiction of Salisbury in 1405. John Frye was charged with not paying towards a lamp in Bere Regis church (Dorset), and after denying liability was assigned a date for purgation. On the date a strong objection was launched against the compurgators: one was excommunicate, three were household servants of the defendant, and in all probability suborned, and the fifth was considered the 'instigator and supporter' of the matter, and the defendant's heir. The objections were accepted, and a lengthy court case ensued.[78]

Although compurgation can be considered suspect, it cannot be dismissed outright. Theoretically it worked, and had safeguards intended to prevent abuse. The compurgators were almost invariably neighbours of the accused, and for clergy were usually clerics themselves. They should, thus, have known both the individual and his likely activities. In cases of compurgation terminating appeals of benefit of clergy, the preliminary stages to assess accusations against felonious clerks may actually mean that compurgation was real proof of innocence. Failed purgation might produce immediate punishment, or offer the chance of a second attempt later – which raises questions about the purpose contemporaries assigned to it. That compurgation was so often successful has been seen as a weakness in the ecclesiastical system, but that view may distort medieval approaches to justice. Possibly simply bringing a case was considered sufficient punishment: mud, once thrown, would stick. This particularly applies in instances which might be considered 'criminal' – the obvious areas being sexual misbehaviour, and actions against defamers. Attitudes to justice in ecclesiastical courts cannot be divorced from attitudes to justice elsewhere, and precisely the same pattern of acquittals (which is what successful purgation represented) appears in proceedings of the major secular courts: juries seem very reluctant to pronounce a guilty verdict. Maybe secular judges were also reluctant to implement guilty verdicts, using the possibilities of granting benefit of clergy as a means of exercising leniency. In both secular and spiritual courts, criminal cases generally ended in acquittals (if they actually reached the trial stage), and civil cases terminated with no decision, because the aim was not to gain a victory in court but force a settlement outside. In secular matters this applied especially to disputes over title to land; in the spiritual sphere, it probably applies most in cases of *fidei laesio*. But it could affect other matters. In 1460, for instance, a defamation case before the consistory

---

[78] Wunderli, *London church courts*, pp. 48–9; see also Brown, *Courts of York Minster peculiar*, pp. 24–5; Purvis, *Mediaeval act book*, pp. 24–7; Timmins, *Reg. Chandler*, no. 10.

court of Lichfield was stopped immediately before sentence and withdrawn for arbitration – supplied by the bishop before whose court the case was being heard. Such out-of-court settlements should have been impossible in matrimonial matters, but even these provide occasional indications of private arrangements being made.[79]

When sentences were actually pronounced in the church courts, the nature of the punishment was dictated by the essentially spiritual character of jurisdiction. Some matters provided their own solutions: matrimonial cases made or broke a marriage; proof of *fidei laesio* upheld the original contract. Even in these cases additional penalties might be imposed; while other areas lacked any automatic outcome. The key concept was penance. Ideally the aim was not to impose punishment, but to incite remorse. Nevertheless, many penances do appear punitive in effect, and often degrading. For the laity of around 1350 penance regularly involved public floggings, usually around the churchyard or the local market square. The clergy might suffer similar discipline; but other remedies included public demotion in processional orders, or standing during services reciting a psalter, clad in penitential clothes, and then making an offering at the altar. The laity could also be required to make offerings. In the fourteenth century monetary fines also became common, sometimes as commutation of penances. Commutation probably first applied to the clergy, but also met popular demand as an alternative to the public degradation of flogging. By Chaucer's time, however, 'Purse is the archdeacon's hell' – and quite possibly the bishop's too. The overall balance between monetary and physical penalties cannot be assessed. Fines may have been imposed where penance had proved insufficient – as a failed deterrent, or to encourage attendance at courts. Certainly not everyone was fined; fifteenth-century episcopal accounts from Carlisle diocese suggest that in some years no one paid in the decanal courts, because everyone chose penance instead. Other punishments were also available: pilgrimages appear not infrequently; while some form of public confession might also be required, especially when the imputed crime threatened to undermine ecclesiastical discipline among the parishioners, or had blackened a reputation. As the church became increasingly concerned with heresy, imprisonment and public recantation of heretical beliefs were added to the range. Heresy could also carry the ultimate penalty of death – but this, officially, was imposed by the secular power rather than the ecclesiastical courts.[80]

[79] Helmholz, *Canon law*, pp. 131–6, 139–40 and refs.; Neville, 'Gaol delivery' [604], pp. 56–7, 59; Whittick, 'The criminal appeal', pp. 63–4; CUL, MS Ll.1.18, ff. 89v–90r; Helmholz, *Marriage litigation*, pp. 135–8. Compare McIntosh, *Autonomy and community*, pp. 195–9.
[80] Timmins, *Reg. Chandler*, pp. xxix–xxx and refs.; Purvis, *Mediaeval act book*, pp. 48–9; Jones, 'Two jurisdictions', pp. 197–8; Woodcock, *Medieval ecclesiastical courts*, pp. 98–9;

The penalty most commonly incurred was excommunication. Where a whole community was being disciplined (usually preliminary to accepting ecclesiastical jurisdiction) an interdict was sometimes imposed: a ban on services of all sorts. Excommunication took two forms: lesser merely excluded the individual from church services; greater theoretically imposed social death. The penalty was rarely meant to punish following a court decision, but to enforce obedience to the court's orders, and acceptance of the church's jurisdiction. In that sense, it paralleled outlawry for non-appearance at the royal courts. The penalty frequently worked as a social control. The Great Curse, repeated four times a year in every parish church, recited a sonorous roll-call of offences which incurred automatic excommunication. Contracts registered before ecclesiastical authorities also commonly made failure to fulfil the terms result in automatic excommunication for the defaulter. The long list of excommunicable offences meant that some people might incur the penalty unwittingly; but from the church's standpoint the ability to excommunicate persons unknown probably compensated for that difficulty.[81]

The efficacy of excommunication is another matter. It imposed no physical constraints, and could backfire – an obstinate excommunicate could disrupt church services for his neighbours, and cause considerable trouble within the parish. Nevertheless, excommunication did have side-effects, most importantly perhaps in depriving excommunicates of rights to sue at common law. This could have been more of a deterrent against disregarding the spiritual sword than the sentence's spiritual implications. The common lawyers upheld certificates of excommunication presented in the royal courts, and thus contributed to the secular exclusion (although as usual they hedged their acceptance with restrictions). Even the mere suggestion of excommunication might halt proceedings, the plaintiff against whom it was alleged having to produce proof that he was not excommunicate. Given the implications of excommunication, it was probably more effective against some social groups rather than others: against merchants and tradesmen, whose livelihood required the fulfilment of contracts, and against landholders who if excommunicate would be unable to prosecute claims to titles to land.[82]

Realistically, the church was virtually impotent to enforce its jurisdic-

---

Wunderli, *London church courts*, pp. 51–3; CCCO, B/14/2/3/7; CRO, DRC 2/8, 2/20 (although the registrar's statement includes £14 12s. 8d. for 'correcciones maiores'); Helmholz, *Select cases*, pp. xl, 24–5; Swanson, *Reg. Scrope*, i, pp. 105–6; 7/4 at n. 81.

[81] Vodola, *Excommunication*, esp. pp. 36–7; Logan, *Excommunication* [526], pp. 13–15; YML, M2/1a; Kristensson, *Mirk's instructions for parish priests*, pp. 104–7.

[82] Hemmant, *Cases in the Exchequer Chamber*, ii, pp. 11–12; Baildon, *Select cases in Chancery* [28], pp. 23–5; Vodola, *Excommunication*, pp. 180–90; see also Woodcock, *Medieval ecclesiastical courts*, pp. 101–2.

tion, either over its claimed subjects, or against the claims of a rival power. Against recidivists, against persistent law-breakers, against those ignoring its judgements, it could do little. Excommunication and interdict were its only forms of compulsion, but their effectiveness depended on the submissiveness of the punished. Lacking powers of physical coercion, the church had to seek secular assistance. In England the ecclesiastical and secular authorities were clearly collaborating from the twelfth century onwards, with the state aiding the church to enforce excommunication by constraining the recalcitrant. The evidence is there, but unquantifiable in any meaningful terms. Those unconsciously incurring excommunication cannot be numbered; nor can we know how many were officially proclaimed excommunicate and rapidly submitted. The contracts recorded in the early fourteenth-century York 'Registers of Condemnations' all invoke excommunication as the penalty for non-fulfilment; but provide no indication of how many contracts went unfulfilled. For the years 1316–1333, only two cases have been noticed where someone is described as excommunicate for non-payment, and in both the debt was apparently rescheduled.[83]

Undoubtedly the church recognized the dangers of the devaluation of its penalties. It therefore turned to the crown for support. But the relationship between the powers in this procedure was ambivalent. The clerics considered royal support obligatory, but the secular authorities saw their involvement in upholding excommunication as an act of grace.[84] The latter stance (not unexpectedly) eventually carried the day.

By 1350, the procedures whereby the state helped to enforce excommunication were well established. Following failure to obey an ecclesiastical court, the offender would be proclaimed excommunicate, being allowed forty days in which to submit. If he then remained contumacious, a writ of caption would be sought from the crown. This signification of excommunication requested the offender's capture and imprisonment until he submitted. The power to signify rested primarily with the diocesan bishops, but lesser authorities might receive the privilege from the crown on a permanent or temporary basis. Amongst those found issuing significations are the deans of royal free chapels, and abbots of exempt monastic jurisdictions (like Westminster, St Albans, and Bury St Edmunds). That the power of signification was a royal concession is shown by letters issued by Richard II in 1391 revoking all concessions save those to diocesans, the abbot of Westminster, and the chancellor of Oxford University. Until the late fifteenth century papal officials could not signify; but at that point papal judges delegate appear issuing such documents in increasing num-

---

[83] Logan, *Excommunication*, pp. 20–3; YML, M2/1a, ff. 27r (from 1319), 38r (from 1332 – that he was excommunicate is perhaps less certain in this case).

[84] Jones, 'Two jurisdictions', p. 144.

bers, and Thomas Wolsey also issued them to support his legatine juris-diction.

Following signification, the writ would issue to the sheriff, for imprison-ment if captured. The 'if' is important: writs might need to be sent to several sheriffs, but still could not guarantee arrest. When captured, the offender was imprisoned until prepared to receive absolution by submitting, provided that the whole process was not nullified by an appeal against the original sentence and consequent release. If the procedure ran its full course, the confessed and absolved excommunicate would eventually be freed, after the bishop notified the king of the absolution, requesting another writ to the sheriff to authorize the release.[85]

The effectiveness of this elaborate and time-consuming process is in-determinable. The crown would not make caption automatic, and restricted the issue of writs against its own officials. The initial forty-day period for submission provided ample opportunities for flight, thereby making the miscreant untraceable when the writ actually issued. Precise numbers of significations and subsequent writs are unknown, but surviving evidence must understate the total. Moreover, signification was not used against every excommunicate, even those exceeding the forty-day limit, so that the effectiveness of caption is no guide to the usefulness of the penalty as a punishment in itself. The restricted channels for obtaining the writ of caption probably worked against efficiency, as did the generally over-burdened state of the church's bureaucracy. Significations were probably issued only when third parties requested action by the bishops – although several do appear to result from office cases, perhaps reflecting the activi-ties of particularly scrupulous administrators. Others would presumably be left in their excommunicate state, to face the threat to their souls at their peril. There is certainly evidence of people (including clerics) being excommunicate for years on end, apparently without action being taken against them or their taking steps to have the penalty lifted.[86]

That no such need was felt offers a graphic comment on general attitudes towards the ecclesiastical courts during this period. But it would be wrong to proceed from this to a general denigration of the whole system of spiritual justice. While the coercive aspects of the courts might have been resented, and resisted, the multiplicity of instance cases indicate some sort of popularity, and that the system was satisfying a need. In due course, however, the ability to meet those requirements changed as the relationship

---

[85] For procedure, Logan, *Excommunication*, pp. 72–150, *passim* (pp. 30–3, 176–83 for papal officials and non-diocesans). For chancellors of Oxford signifying excommunicates, see Salter, *Snappe's formulary* [731], pp. 22–39.

[86] ibid., pp. 29–39; Logan, *Excommunication*, pp. 43–50, 66–8.

between the spiritual and secular authorities altered, in a process of attrition between church and state over jurisdictional matters which continued throughout the late medieval centuries.

4.7 ATTRITION AND EROSION

In 1300 an increasingly confident monarchy, with its own definition of sovereign competence in temporal matters, confronted a decreasingly self-confident but still tenacious canonical definition of the papacy's universal jurisdictional competence. Between the two definitions of sovereignty were the people of England, clerics and laity, as objects of the jurisdictional rivalry and as actors in their own right, capable of balancing the two protagonists to their own advantage. The opposition of royal and papal definitions of sovereignty and jurisdictional competence moulded the relationship between church and state in England throughout the later medieval period, not just in matters of legal jurisdiction. Ultimately, the crown was bound to win: it was present, it could enforce its claims and decisions, and its claims to sovereignty were accepted and supported by its subjects. During the Reformation, the declaration of the imperial capabilities of the English crown formalized those claims to supreme government within the English church, epitomized in schemes to revise canon law and validate it by royal promulgation.[87]

Before the Reformation, however, there was little hint of any major conflict between the two definitions of jurisdictional competence, certainly not in the sense of 'church versus state'. The temporal was accepted as the crown's concern, the spiritual as the responsibility of the church. Where disputes occurred – rarely instigated by the kings themselves – was at the shared frontiers, as in the cases of sanctuary and benefit of clergy. In this area of debate, canon lawyers would sometimes be asked to advise their common law equivalents. But the common lawyers themselves frequently had some canonistic knowledge, and felt quite competent to debate matters amongst themselves. Discussions of matters ecclesiastical therefore appeared in their readings at the Inns of Court, especially on issues which overlapped with the other jurisdiction, as in the case of writs of *Quare impedit*. Discussions also occurred during cases. The year-books for the reign of Henry VII report one particularly complex case. It originated in a defamation case before the church courts, in which a woman had been judged guilty, and the plaintiff awarded 'un certein some pur ses costages et pur le diffamation'. Before paying the money the woman married, made a will, and died, leaving her husband as executor. The original plaintiff

---

[87] Ullmann, 'This realm of England' [860]; Baker, *Reports of Spelman*, ii, p. 70.

then procured a citation against the widower, as executor, to secure payment. The response was a writ of prohibition, transferring the case to the secular court. The lawyers' debates were supposedly about whether the issue should be sent back to the spiritual court, but in the process they ranged widely over several issues. At what point, for instance, did the frontier between the two jurisdictions lie: did a monetary payment awarded in a suit in a spiritual court become a temporality when it was in turn disputed? The validity of the husband's appointment as executor was also questioned, in view of the incompatibility of secular and canon law on the matter.

Despite appearances of moderation, hints of the conflict's ultimate resolution appear throughout the period. The decisions of the common law courts regularly opposed ecclesiastical – especially papal – claims to jurisdiction. Papal excommunications were not accepted as valid, and papal grants of privileges could not be pleaded in secular courts – a doctrine used most effectively in the attack on the greater sanctuaries. When canon law was raised against common, it would be argued that the latter took precedence. In about 1472 Thomas Kebell noted that the bishops in making a provincial constitution for the church could not alter the law of the realm; and papal decretals were considered ineffective against the common law – how could an external authority change a system which had operated from time out of mind? The conflicting parallelism of the two structures is evidenced in a case of 1483 over a pension due from Edington rectory (Wilts.) to the free chapel of Wanborough (Wilts.), by then united to Magdalen College, Oxford. As the case progressed, it increasingly concentrated on the union of the chapel and college. In the process, the separation of the two legal traditions became obvious: although the institutions were united by canon law, this could not be recognized by the royal courts because it did not meet the requirements for validity at common law.[88]

The process of attrition on explicitly jurisdictional terms thus operated at the border, and not at the heart of the issue. Arguments could flow both ways, as they did with benefit of clergy. There, the church consistently reacted against lay attempts to limit the privilege; and as the church frequently had to be wooed by the crown, its complaints might prove temporarily effective. The changes under Henry IV probably owed something to his need for money, and the financial offerings of the Convocations; while at the start of Edward IV's reign the clergy exploited their position

---

[88] Ives, 'Crime, sanctuary, and royal authority', p. 299; Hemmant, *Cases in the Exchequer Chamber*, i, pp. 108–10; Thorne, *Readings and moots* [835], pp. 110–18, 125–8; Baker, *Reports of Spelman*, i, p. 65; *Reports . . . Edward V* [510], Trinity, 12 Henry VII, pp. 22–4, plea 2; Ives, *Common lawyers*, pp. 175–8.

as a potential support to extract considerable concessions from the new ruler. Edward IV granted the clergy a charter of privileges which included an almost total retreat on the limitations on the exercise of benefit of clergy – henceforth clerics should be triable only in ecclesiastical courts, without any preliminary hearing before a secular tribunal. Unfortunately for the clergy, although the charter was confirmed by Richard III, it proved worthless.[89] Nevertheless, the occasional rows which erupted about benefit and sanctuary indicated that the frontiers of jurisdiction were contested, and that major conflict was not unimaginable.

The potential for conflict is also shown in the gradual encroachment of statute law on spiritual jurisdiction, and the accompanying debates in Convocation which occasionally resulted in lists of *gravamina* – petitions for redress of grievances which themselves sought statutory remedy for ecclesiastical complaints against lay encroachment. The debates, and statutes, reflect the changing balance between the jurisdictions. In 1352 the clergy made some gains with the Statute *Pro clero*, but thereafter Parliamentary enactments frequently limited the church's claims. Sometimes this was achieved by limiting contacts with Rome, which restricted avenues for the enforcement of jurisdictional claims. The Statutes of Provisors and Praemunire both did this, curtailing papal interference in proprietorial patronage rights in England by preventing papal appointments to benefices, and by effectively preventing appeals on such matters to Rome. By imposing the equivalent of outlawry for breach of the regulations the king effectively discouraged such intervention, but retained powers to dispense with the regulations at will. Other changes were perhaps motivated more by the aspirations of the Commons than the crown. Changes in the definition of certain crimes, particularly treason, altered the availability of benefit of clergy; and when benefit and sanctuary were affected by statutes, it is difficult to determine whether this represented royal policy or the force of 'public opinion'.[90] The influence of statutes over the church's claims was ultimately revealed at the Reformation: the changes were implemented by Parliamentary Acts, not provincial constitutions.

Even more insidious before the Reformation than the passage of Acts to limit spiritual jurisdiction was the restrictive interpretation of some statutes. This particularly applies with the Statute of Praemunire of 1393 which, with its innocent *alibi* reference (subjecting those taking cases 'elsewhere' than the royal courts to its penalties) set a time-bomb ticking

---

[89] Storey, 'Episcopal king-makers' [788], pp. 92–3; Gabel, *Benefit of clergy*, pp. 122–3; Firth, 'Benefit of clergy', pp. 179–80, 189; Bellamy, *Criminal law and society*, pp. 126–8.

[90] Jones, 'Bishops, politics and the law' [449], pp. 231–8; Waugh, 'Great Statute' [888], pp. 189–91, 193–4; Donahue, 'Roman canon law', p. 668.

under the whole edifice of the spiritual courts. In the early fifteenth century, despite complaints in Convocation, there are indications that '*alibi*' was being applied not merely to foreign (that is, papal) courts, but also to non-royal courts within the kingdom, principally those of the church. This was definitely so by 1465. However, this did not reflect deliberate royal policy, but lawyers' ingenuity. Generally, the cases concerned were between parties: only under Henry VIII was Praemunire systematically exploited by the crown against the church. In private issues, the likely loser in the church courts exploited the statute to have the case stopped. Sometimes, as when testamentary executors sought to enforce debts due to the deceased, such actions had an obvious immediate advantage. Extending the statute's penalties to laity as well as clerics by this means also considerably increased its scope. The reasons for the increased application may perhaps only partly lie in the nature of the penalties involved; a tit-for-tat mentality may have operated as well. The church had concurrently developed a relatively effective counter to the other main block to action in the church courts, the writ of prohibition (to be considered later); this new use of Praemunire might have been a response to that circumvention.

Under Henry VIII the statute became a major weapon for cowing the clergy in the prelude to the Reformation. In 1515 the judges declared that proceedings in the spiritual forum against a cleric favoured by the crown rendered all participants liable to the penalties of the statute. Wolsey's fall in 1529 also reflected use of the statute. Increased use of Praemunire paved the way for the general submission of the clergy in 1531, and the creation of an effective royal supremacy in the English church.[91]

Normally conflict was avoided. This owed much to the reality of royal superiority. The king, ultimately, had coercive authority: when clerics proved too obstreperous, they could be quelled by threats. Outlawry had produced disarray and submission in the 1290s; the threat of deprivation of temporalities was a potent weapon throughout the period; and in the sixteenth century use of Praemunire swiftly quelled opposition. But the absence of conflict on jurisdictional matters also depended on the duality of the secular and ecclesiastical structures, so that neither side had formally to deny the other's competence in a whole batch of cases. Rather, remedial procedures were offered in both spheres, and the litigants (in cases between parties) were left to choose their forum. The relationship between secular and spiritual courts was actually determined not by the supreme authorities in either field, but by those who sought justice: where it was available,

---

[91] Storey, 'Episcopal king-makers', pp. 89–90; Waugh, 'Great Statute', pp. 197–200; Helmholz, *Canon law*, pp. 75, 315–17; Baker, *Reports of Spelman*, ii, pp. *66*, *68–9*; Storey, *Diocesan administration* [784], pp. 30–2; Guy, 'Henry VIII and *Praemunire*' [323]; Helmholz, *Select cases*, pp. xliii–xliv, lxvii.

they would take it – and they would accept whichever type of justice met their requirements. The ebb and flow of court cases from one jurisdiction to another thus does not represent a deliberate conflict between rival authorities, but procedural change which allowed litigants thereafter to obtain more appropriate remedies in one court (usually the secular) than had previously been available. It was a delicate balancing act which gradually (and after 1500 dramatically) tilted in favour of the royal courts.

Remedy was only one aspect of the issue. 'Justice' was a rather amorphous concept. Obstructing a process was as much part of the search for justice as was promoting it. Here also the parallelism between the secular and ecclesiastical jurisdictional claims could be exploited. The church's defamation jurisdiction could be used to impede criminal actions in the secular courts.[92] Judicious exploitation of uncertain frontiers allowed cases to be very neatly obstructed: a dispute about a York inheritance in 1386 produced law suits in both secular and ecclesiastical courts, during which John de Emelay found himself excommunicated by the church courts, unable to take further action in the secular courts (where he had initiated the original action) as a result, and threatened with imprisonment by writ of caption.[93]

Serious as such cases were for individuals, for the church a greater threat was the use of writs of prohibition to prevent actions in the spiritual courts, on the basis that their subject-matter was really determinable at common law. These writs had developed in the thirteenth century. As ever, the crown had provided a possible remedy, and then sought customers. It was the litigant who, facing an action before the church courts, applied for the writ. On receipt, this immediately stayed all further ecclesiastical proceedings, and transferred the case to the secular forum. In theory the church (or the promoter in the ecclesiastical case) could seek to annul the prohibition, but how often this occurred is unknown. The church clearly resented such intrusions, and was quite liable to take action against the procurer of the prohibition – a situation which provided scope for further litigation.[94]

The thirteenth and fourteenth centuries were the heyday of the writ of prohibition. By the fifteenth century only a few were actually produced in the spiritual courts. However, they were highly effective: when produced, the action did cease. Possibly prohibitions were used to pre-empt cases in the spiritual courts completely: in 1399 the clerical *gravamina* protested that prohibitions were being sought even before an action started in the church courts, whether in office or instance cases. By the fifteenth century

---

[92] Above, at n. 59.

[93] PRO, C270/28/7.

[94] Helmholz, *Canon law*, pp. 78–93, 96–9. For a case returned to the church courts after a writ of consultation, Windsor, XV.55.19.

the ecclesiastical authorities could rarely act against the procurers of the writ: the crown had successfully prevented clerical reprisals by introducing writs supposedly following a general complaint (*'ex relatu plurium'*), leaving the actual complainant anonymous. Even so, the church did not let matters slip, and may even have recovered ground. Fifteenth-century ecclesiastical lawyers successfully evaded many prohibitions, largely through the laxity of Chancery. That (once its court had become established) was where the writs were normally debated, deciding the validity of the prohibition on the basis of the original libel or accusation produced in the spiritual court. Given the ambiguity of approaches to many actions, which depending on standpoint might fall to either ecclesiastical or secular courts, the canon lawyers constructed their statements of the case to eliminate any indication of possible secular jurisdiction, and thereby negated the prohibition. This greater ease in defending ecclesiastical jurisdiction perhaps had a negative aspect, with the avoidance of prohibition leading to greater use of Praemunire as a more certain barrier to actions in the church courts.[95]

While the crown provided the writ of prohibition to remove cases to its courts, a major weakness in the church's claims to spiritual jurisdiction was the absence of any machinery to enforce a reverse migration – although attempts to that end were sometimes made.[96] The business allowed to the church courts was, therefore, very much a matter of gap-filling: in spiritual matters, because that jurisdiction was readily conceded, and in practical terms because 'appropriate' remedies were not always obtainable from the secular tribunals. However, where the secular courts could provide remedies, then the litigants turned to them, regardless of their own status.

Clerics were just as litigious as their lay compatriots, if not more so. They sought remedies against each other, and against laymen. If the state offered such remedies, they would happily use its machinery. Clerics therefore appear as plaintiffs in many actions before the secular courts which, if the church's claims were enforced, would have gone to its courts. They thus brought patronage matters, tithe cases, and other issues before the royal courts, possibly to the chagrin of the Roman curia. When new types of litigation became available at common law, clerics eagerly exploited them: ecclesiastical disputes were regularly dealt with in Chancery and the developing prerogative courts of equity – for whose rise clerics were largely responsible. Chancery and Star Chamber were, after all, overseen by the Chancellor, who was normally an ecclesiastic; while the smaller Court of Requests originated in the royal chapel. Even in the

---

[95] Helmholz, *Canon law*, pp. 71–5, 81–2 nn. 20–7 (finding only 52 references to receipt of prohibitions among surviving records for 1293–1501), see also pp. 84–6; Jones, 'Bishops, politics, and the law', p. 257; Baker, *Reports of Spelman*, ii, pp. 66–8.

[96] Helmholz, *Canon law*, pp. 93–5.

common law courts, clerics were active, hiring attorneys, exploiting quibbles, and overseeing the process. The Master of the Rolls was always a cleric, sometimes en route to a bishopric. Although ecclesiastics were excluded from judging felonies by this time, they could still deal with lesser crimes. Although clerics did not become assize judges, they were still involved in the judicial system, most notably as justices of the peace.[97]

The litigiousness of clerics probably meant that they ignored the claims of the church courts if they did not offer the desired remedy. Moreover, the adaptability of the secular system meant that the spiritual courts would lose business, without being formally deprived of jurisdiction, when changes occurred. This happened dramatically under the first Tudors, when defamation for criminal actions and a good deal of *fidei laesio* business suddenly transferred from the spiritual to the secular courts.

In both instances the crucial period was *c.*1500–10, although the reasons were slightly different. Defamation involving imputation of a crime had been savagely curtailed in the spiritual courts since about 1485 by use of Praemunire actions, but the state had not provided any alternative remedy, leaving those defamed unable to take action. In any event, the best that the defamed could hope for from the church courts (other than an out-of-court settlement) was penance for the slanderer, and the formal restoration of his own reputation. With *fidei laesio* cases the situation was slightly more complex. The crown courts had always claimed cognizance of debt, especially when based on a written contract. Usually the sums involved exceeded 40 shillings (debts for lesser sums often being dealt with in manorial and borough courts). But the scope of secular jurisdiction was limited by procedures: while the royal courts could deal with cases where contracts had been incompletely met, they would not accept those where the conditions had been simply ignored: nonfeasance was not malfeasance, and the latter alone was triable. Furthermore, particular types of debt, such as those due to a creditor from an executor, were not determinable there either. In all such instances, the spiritual courts could act to secure enforcement through their *fidei laesio* jurisdiction. The church courts might also have financial attractions for debt cases: their costs would be lower than before the secular judges.[98]

[97] Guy, *Cardinal's court*, pp. 23–50, 109; Storey, 'Ecclesiastical causes' [783], pp. 239–58; Storey, 'Clergy and common law' [786], pp. 346–52 (and editions of cases elsewhere in the article); Ullmann, 'Decision of the Rota Romana' [856], pp. 468–78; Ives, *Common lawyers*, pp. 131–2, 135, 139, 288, 300–1, 397, 399–400; Fryde et al., *Handbook of British chronology* [286], pp. 86–8; Mitchell and Morse, *Chronicle of English judges* [583], pp. 25, 28, 31, 34, 36, 40, 43–5, 47.

[98] Baker, *Reports of Spelman*, ii, pp. 236–7, 244–5; Helmholz, *Select cases*, p. lxvii; Beckermann, 'Forty-shilling jurisdictional limit' [52], pp. 111–13.

This changed in the early sixteenth century. From about 1508, defamation cases based on accusations of felony moved almost exclusively to the secular courts. There was no formal denial of jurisdiction to the church courts, it was simply the outcome of lawyers' enterprise to get round the problem of Praemunire. Additionally, by stretching analogies to trespass to bring such cases under secular law, the plaintiffs could now claim and receive monetary damages, arguing that the words had caused financial loss which could be recouped through the courts. A similar change occurred with *fidei laesio*. In 1499 nonfeasance was defined as an extreme form of malfeasance, and increasingly thereafter this view was adopted. This brought contract within the range of *'assumpsit'* actions, which again provided monetary damages for breach of the agreement. The massive increase in *assumpsit* actions coincides with the decline and virtual extinction of *fidei laesio* actions in the spiritual courts. The royal courts were not the only beneficiaries: at the same time borough courts also increased their share of such cases.[99]

The church could not counter this movement, even if it had wanted to – and there is no real evidence that it did. Yet the drastic changes had been effected in an essentially informal manner. The church courts suddenly lost business, because they no longer provided appropriate or adequate remedies for litigants, whereas the secular courts did. This says much about the vexed question of the 'popularity' of the spiritual courts. There is a basic contrast between the amount of business they transacted and the frequent evidence of their unpopularity, which requires some comment.

Several issues are here raised together, and loaded words must be avoided. To call the church courts 'popular' or 'unpopular' implies a great deal. Clearly, they were busy – but were they actually 'popular'? They were available, and for a time provided remedies for particular problems which could not be resolved elsewhere. 'Unpopularity' must be dealt with similarly. likewise 'opposition'. Court processes were frequently obstructed. A cleric might fear a local landowner, and therefore fail to serve an order, as happened with the parochial chaplain at Hemingbrough (Yorks.) in a tithe case of 1399. Officials might be abused, orders left unexecuted, and citations ignored. But does such wilful obstruction indicate unpopularity, or that those responsible expected to lose their cases anyway? All too often the insults offered to court officials read like immediate reaction to receiving a citation or losing a case: the individuals concerned would doubtless prosecute actions before the church courts readily enough if necessary.[100]

---

[99] Wunderli, *London church courts*, pp. 67–8, 105; Baker, *Reports of Spelman*, ii, pp. *237–44, 255–86, 292–8*; Helmholz, *Select cases*, pp. lxvi–lxxxv (see also pp. 42–51); Helmholz, *Canon law*, pp. 270–87 (esp. 283–5), 320.

[100] Swanson, *Reg. Scrope*, i, no. 670; Timmins, *Reg. Chandler*, nos. 2, 13, 256, 315, 583; Woodcock, *Medieval ecclesiastical courts*, pp. 48–9, 111.

Occasionally there are signs of a deeper opposition. Some may have felt the spiritual courts were exploitative, and a focus of corrupt practices. Certainly, there were complaints against their financial exactions, which passed into the satirical literature of the period. Moreover, some court officials did deserve their poor reputations: the crown claimed to oversee the activities of ecclesiastical officials who abused their powers, and extortionate archidiaconal and ruridecanal officials were occasionally reported to the secular courts. Much of the evidence for unpopularity centres on the financial exactions of the courts – complaints being usually about fees, about administrative practice rather than the actual exercise of jurisdiction. Towards the sixteenth century, more serious undertones are suggested. Just before the Reformation, the church's increasing concern with heresy apparently stimulated court activity, and heresy charges had serious implications. Attacks on the spiritual courts at that point may reflect real fear, a reaction against their effectiveness, and the result of a particular combination of circumstances.[101]

The norm, however, was relatively peaceful co-existence. The two jurisdictions could assist each other where necessary, overlapping in mutual reinforcement. Occasionally they clashed, but often that was due to the availability of a choice of forum. Writs of prohibition, threats of Praemunire, and so on, reflect a choice of court by one party, and the exploitation of the availability of a choice by the defendants. On one side there is the apparent opposition to the church courts displayed by John Frye in 1405: having been defeated in the ecclesiastical courts, he sought revenge in King's Bench. To counter that, there is the action by John Bull against William Flawne in the archdeacon of Canterbury's court in 1517, suing for defamation with the support of the under-sheriff of Kent, following a malicious action against him for theft before the secular authorities. In the middle stand the churchwardens of St Andrew's, Canterbury, who in 1490 prepared for actions to recover chantry revenues in both spiritual and secular courts, before deciding to press the case before ecclesiastical judges.[102]

In the end, the problem of the relationship between the lay and ecclesiastical courts resolved itself. The litigants were still there, but the remedies available to them had changed. The suitors voted with their feet, and in the search for 'justice' took their business from the church's courts to the king's. The changes of the early sixteenth century, even of the Reformation, did not extinguish ecclesiastical jurisdiction: the church courts, despite the turmoil of the Reformation years, were to recover and remain a force for some time, serving social purposes which they continued to fulfil.

---

[101] Bowker, 'Some archdeacons' court books' [78], esp. pp. 310–12. For a one-sided emphasis on the courts' corruption, Hahn and Kaeuper, 'Text and context' [328], esp. pp. 83–4 and refs. for action against extortionate officials.

[102] Timmins, *Reg. Chandler*, p. 7 n. 1; Woodcock, *Medieval ecclesiastical courts*, pp. 88–9, 107, 134–5; see also Donahue, 'Roman canon law', p. 700 n. 248.

5

The Church and Economic Activity

5.1 THE CHRISTIAN ECONOMY

England's late medieval economy stands between two watersheds. In 1348–9 the Black Death reduced the population by between a third and a half, with extensive repercussions. The 1530s and 1540s saw the major transfer of lands from ecclesiastical to lay possession on the Dissolution of the monasteries and the chantries, the Tudor inflation, and a major debasement of the coinage in 1543. The state of the English economy in the intervening period is disputed, with debates about the level of population, the state of the towns, and whether the period was one of growth or stagnation.[1]

The church's economic activities must be set against this background. But talking bluntly of 'the church' oversimplifies matters; a distinction must be drawn between the institution and its message. Christianity as a moral force must be separated from the reality of ecclesiastical participation in economic actions. Further sub-divisions are also needed, for economic activity includes both the direct involvement of church institutions, and lay participation in spiritual activities (whether individually or in groups) which had economic effects. Even this makes the distinction too precise: how is a chantry created as a formally endowed benefice to be differentiated from one based on feoffment to uses – controlled by trustees – employing a stipendiary priest? Nevertheless, distinctions can be drawn between morality and reality, and between various aspects of that reality, even if precise boundaries cannot always be established.

---

[1] For England's economy to 1500, see generally Bolton, *Medieval English economy* [74], pp. 207–86; Outhwaite, *Inflation* [623], pp. 11–16; Coleman, *Economy of England* [155], pp. 21–4.

For Christians, the reconciliation of other-worldly aspirations with this-worldly existence has always posed problems. The difficulty of implementing the injunctions of the Beatitudes in a world apparently organized on completely different principles generates tensions which become especially acute when tackling wealth. Scattered contradictory references in the New Testament have to provide (or try to provide) a coherent statement about the relationships between rich and poor, and the morality of economic activity. While inherently favouring the have nots, Christianity has to recognize the haves, not just dismiss them. Institutionally, the church also has to ensure its own continuity and maintain its functions, a stance which usually places it among the possessors rather than the dispossessed.

The problems of the medieval church's wealth were, generally, submerged in wider issues of the relationship between rich and poor; although it did occasionally become an issue in its own right. The most significant conflict arose within the Franciscan order in the thirteenth century, with one group (the Spirituals) producing a total denial of any right to possessions, and complete dependence on charity. This dispute forced a major reassessment of the status of ecclesiastical wealth, resulting eventually in the legitimization by papal decrees of ecclesiastical ownership of property.[2] Nevertheless, the way in which possessions were used provided a toe-hold for continued opposition to church wealth. English Austin friars argued for dispossession in the 1370s; and after them Wyclif and the Lollards strongly condemned the wealth of the religious orders, urging an end to ecclesiastical property-owning in order to re-establish the pristine church. Further disputes erupted in London in the 1460s, when the Carmelites condemned the wealth of the secular clergy (although they may have been hoping to divert some of it to themselves). Not only mendicants appreciated the problem of church wealth. Richard Caistor, a Norwich (Norfolk) vicar, showed his concern in his will of 1420, leaving most of his possessions to the poor because 'according to the canons, the church's possessions are the goods of the poor'. Ecclesiastics seem rarely to have responded argumentatively to the attacks, with the notable exception of Bishop Reginald Pecock's lengthy justification of ecclesiastical temporalities against attacks by the Lollards.[3]

The dispute over ecclesiastical wealth was to some extent an internal matter for the church. However, the visible contrast between Christian precept and clerical practice was unavoidable, and affected the relationship between the church and its encompassing society. Awareness of the

---

[2] Leff, *Heresy* [503], i, pp. 51–166, *passim*.

[3] Aston, '"Caim's castles"' [16], pp. 49–57, 63–4; du Boulay, 'Carmelite friars and the secular clergy' [232]; Tanner, *Church in Norwich* [810], p. 232; Foss, 'Overmuch blaming' [279].

lay spectators perhaps also exacerbated the internal conflicts. But it is difficult to determine how far lay opposition to clerical wealth was principled, and how far motivated by jealousy and greed, a desire to replace one set of landowners by another.[4] A more fundamental social problem arose in the reaction to the basic division between rich and poor, when Christianity's tenets rather favoured the latter. Again, how far poverty was in itself a laudable estate was disputed. Advocacy of poverty was balanced by an acceptance of social divisions and mutual obligations, adopting the morality of the parable of Dives and Lazarus, and exemplified in contemporary English writings by the economic considerations in the tract *Dives and pauper*. The poor existed, and had a right to charity. The rich existed, and had an obligation to offer charity: their possessions, as testators sometimes put it, had only been lent by God. Wealth existed primarily for charitable uses – although the rich should not beggar themselves (except to attain the holy state of apostolic poverty), they were to share their wealth with the less fortunate. The relationship between rich and poor was essentially symbiotic, although perhaps placing greater emphasis on the obligations of the rich, to avoid the sin of 'spiritual homicide'.[5]

The problem with this social construct was that poverty could be as exploitative as wealth. Poverty might be a natural state, requiring alleviation by charity, or a holy estate, adopted in order to know God; but it could also be adopted by the lazy or wanton to avoid their social duties. Various forms of poverty were therefore distinguished: the commendable poverty of those abandoning the world for the love of God; the acceptable poverty of the unfortunate who did not complain, and therefore merited charity; and the condemned poverty of the wilful and indolent, who had brought their state of themselves, did not deserve charity, and whose complaints about their situation earned further criticism. Actually distinguishing between the groups was difficult; it was all too easy to view all the poor as scroungers. Moreover, attitudes differed: the Lollards challenged mendicant begging with the assertion that the friars were sturdy enough to work for their livelihoods.[6]

The attempt to assuage poverty by charity chiefly reflected individual spiritual concerns; but it also links with economic morality. When applied to a whole society, Christian economic morality had to reconcile apparently

---

[4] Thomson, 'Tithe disputes' [826], pp. 4, 11; Aston, ' "Caim's castles" ', p. 56; see also McNiven, *Heresy and politics* [566], p. 7.

[5] Gilchrist, *Church and economic activity* [299], pp. 77–82, 118–19, also (in the context of the doctrine of charity) Rubin, *Charity and community* [718], pp. 58–74, 82–98; Barnum, *Dives and pauper* [41], esp. i, pp. 63–5, ii, pp. 136–7; Thrupp, *Merchant class* [838], p. 174; Shaw, 'Canonical and episcopal reform' [756], p. 56.

[6] Aston, ' "Caim's castles" ', pp. 57–60, 62–3; Barnum, *Dives and pauper*, i, pp. 57–8, ii, pp. 286–7.

contradictory biblical texts. This had largely been done by 1300, as theology and canon law developed together, producing a Christian code of economic practice which remained largely unaltered throughout succeeding centuries. Essentially based on the fraternal requirements of Christianity, it aimed to prevent exploitation, and imposed moral rather than jurisdictional constraints. The aim was fairness, but achieving it was more difficult.[7]

To ensure fairness, market dealings were placed on a moral plane. Immediate commercial contracts were dealt with by the concept of the 'just price'. Although by the fourteenth century this was effectively identical to the prevailing market price, Christian precepts had not been renounced. Even if governed by market forces, appropriate authorities could still intervene to keep prices down for the benefit of the poor; while a stronger religious imperative perhaps was offered by specific injunctions against exploitation. The just price was the price determined without trickery – without using false measures, or artificially cornering the market, for instance. Moreover, although a seller did not have to reveal information which might reduce prices, it was strongly suggested that such compassionate considerations should apply. Morality was itself a market force.[8]

The idea of fairness also applied to credit transactions, although here the church never fully caught up with the developing economy, or reconciled itself to the mechanics of the money market, so that its theory became divorced from reality. From the eleventh century, canonists and theologians opposed the concept of lending at interest, finding the notion of charging for time unacceptable. However, whilst maintaining a blanket opposition to crude usury, the theologians did admit some element of compensation for the lender, and several such compromises had emerged by 1300. At this point the world and the church to some extent parted company. Lending at interest was a normal part of economic life, and credit an indispensable element of economic activity, with even ecclesiastics involved. But the world's morality and the church's had not totally diverged: in a sense, the morality of the just price affected the credit market also. Lending at interest became acceptable, provided it was not exploitative. Usurers brought before the authorities were generally accused not simply of taking interest, but of taking above the going rate.[9]

Whilst the church thus encouraged a Christian economic morality, its enforcement was another matter. 'Real life' had an unfortunate habit of

---

[7] Gilchrist, *Church and economic activity*, pp. 48–82; Bolton, *Medieval English economy*, pp. 331–8.

[8] Gilchrist, *Church and economic activity*, pp. 55–6, 58–62, 116; Barnum, *Dives and pauper*, ii, pp. 153–5.

[9] Gilchrist, *Church and economic activity*, pp. 62–70, 108, 114–15 (see also Barnum, *Dives and pauper*, ii, pp. 197–205); Helmholz, *Canon law* [379], pp. 333 n. 50, 337.

not conforming to Christian precepts. Concepts of fairness had to stand against the practicalities of contemporary social and economic life which, especially in the aftermath of the Black Death, threatened to overwhelm the morality of mutual obligations.[10] Yet, in some spheres, the church did claim jurisdiction (although not without challenges). It laid claim to usury matters, and usurers were sometimes presented at visitations – although those tackled were usually relatively small fry. Emphasizing the oath element in formal contracts, and the concept of *fidei laesio*, it claimed oversight of enforcement of debts and contracts. Its exhortatory influence spread to develop charitable activities and care for the poor. When institutionalized these were almost inextricably tied into contemporary spirituality, being linked to the doctrine of purgatory and reciprocal prayers for souls.[11]

The church also intervened in economic life because of explicitly religious concerns. Its worship affected the calendar, making some days more important than others. Sundays, the major feasts associated with Christ's life, and a plethora of other dates, were set aside for purely religious purposes, with economic activity being banned (although canonistic refinements produced an extensive grey area). Sundays and nationally celebrated feasts should have caused few difficulties, but local celebrations of individual saints often did: dates varied with locality, and possibly even from parish to parish. The effect of these irregular holidays was considerable, and contradictory, for in many places – such as Ely – local celebrations were the occasions to encourage economic activity with a fair, and Sunday markets were also relatively common. Holidays cut considerably into the working year: with Sundays, something like a hundred days could be affected (with Saturday afternoons often added as well). Technically, activity should then have stopped, although local agreements might not mean loss of pay for all of these days. The church might tolerate labour on less significant feasts, as Archbishop Islip of Canterbury allowed in a constitution of 1362. The irrationality of holidays in terms of natural calendars, the growing number of holidays as new feasts were promulgated, and the idiosyncracies of local differences merely compounded the problems. From the fourteenth century, reformers throughout Europe criticized the increase in holidays, and even sought to reduce their number, although with negligible success in England before the Reformation. Yet life's practicalities, and individual need or greed, frequently meant that days of supposed rest were not treated as such, the prohibitions were ignored, and the church courts were kept busy with cases of illicit working or trading.[12]

---

[10] Aers, *Chaucer, Langland* [3], ch. 1.

[11] Helmholz, *Canon law*, pp. 326–37; for money-lending by clerics, see below, at nn. 119–21; see also 4/5 (at nn. 57–8, 98–9), 6/4.

[12] Rodgers, *Discussion of holidays* [706], pp. 33–45, 93, 97–8, 101–20; Harvey, 'Work and

This was all well and good when the church was the only enforcement agency. However, other authorities were erecting parallel systems of economic regulation in later medieval England. When the mayor and corporation of London assumed jurisdiction over usury within their city, or the lawhundred of Colchester acted against craftsmen working on Sundays and feasts, did this reflect the influence of the church and religion in economic life, or purely economic interests? What, precisely, is to be made of Parliamentary enactments banning fairs and markets on Sundays and feast days, such as that concocted in 1449?[13] When does religiously motivated concern for the poor fade into charitable activity as a social obligation and reflection of social status? The driving forces might still be moral, but the morality different. Whilst purgatory still loomed, charitable activity perhaps retained some religious imperative, but it is difficult to see more than vestigial remnants in the other areas where ecclesiastical jurisdiction was being replaced by secular action.

5.2   LANDHOLDING

In tackling the church's involvement in the economy, the direct participation of the church and its officers, as landowners, purchasers, and sellers, must be separated from the 'knock-on' effect of 'ecclesiastical' activity in processes of capital formation and cash circulation. Some distinction is also needed between the activities of ecclesiastics as clerics, and their non-clerical dealings with family or other wealth – although enforcing such differentiation is practically impossible.[14]

The institutional wealth of the medieval English church is undeniable, although not precisely quantifiable. The wealth derived mainly from land, with one estimate holding that ecclesiastical institutions controlled between a fifth and a quarter of agricultural England in the later middle ages. Contemporary statements reveal perceptions rather than reality: one early fifteenth-century estimate made at Selby abbey gave the church 28,015 of the 60,000 knights' fees in England, with a tithe of church goods as £208,021 18s. 10d. Simon Fish c.1529 (and probably exaggerating for effect) said that the church owned a third of the country. By 1350, the main rush

---

festa ferienda' [356] (esp. pp. 303–4, 306–8); Harvey, *Mediaeval craftsmen* [358], pp. 60–1 (with a list of holidays observed at the Tower of London in 1337 at pp. 196–7); for presentments for trading on Sundays and feast days, Wood-Legh, *Kentish visitations* [922], pp. 73–4, 118–19, 147–8, 267, 269; Bannister, 'Visitation returns of Hereford' [38], vol. 44, pp. 445–6, 448, vol. 45, pp. 92, 100, 446, 448, 452, 454, 462.

[13] Britnell, *Colchester* [93], pp. 242–4; Thrupp, *Merchant class*, p. 175; *Statutes* [776], ii, pp. 351–2.

[14] For inherited and other wealth, Pound, 'Clerical poverty' [669], pp. 392–6.

of landed donations had dried up: the great monastic and episcopal estates had been created, and the landed holdings of the major institutions remained broadly static thereafter.[15] Thirteenth-century concern about the effect of apparently unceasing donations of land for pious purposes and the activity of the religious in the land market had in 1279 produced the Statute of Mortmain, whereafter transfers of land to religious control required a royal licence. The ban was not totally effective, and various expedients allowed the institutions to evade the restrictions. In 1391 another statute blocked one of the main loopholes, enfeoffment to uses (which transferred the land to trustees), and thereafter, whilst there was probably continued small-scale evasion, the religious houses showed little interest in land acquisition except, perhaps, through a juggling of ecclesiastical possessions. However, non-perpetual chantries and other institutions remained active: the guilds and fraternities were controlled by the Act of 1391, and the chantries were restricted by the final Act of 1532. Guilds as well as houses were denied enfeoffment to uses in 1391, although previously they had used it extensively to build up their endowments, and possibly continued clandestinely afterwards. After 1300 land grants for ecclesiastical and religious purposes tended to be small in size if not number, and for less prestigious foundations (with the exception of certain royal establishments). New chantries did not need massive endowment, the scale being very different from the accumulated manors of bishops and religious houses.[16]

Ownership was not the sole means for exploiting land. Although debarred from unlicensed acquisitions, the religious houses and others could still take land on lease, and frequently did. Only in 1529 were statutory limitations placed on the land-farming activities of clerics, individually or institutionally.[17]

While constantly acquiring other lands – licitly or otherwise – the church's possessions were not always secure. Dispossession was not impossible, although canon law technically prevented voluntary alienations, as did the Statute of Westminster of 1285. The constant process of attrition and erosion took its toll, but the main disendowment during this period (leaving aside seizure of lands acquired contrary to the Statute of Mortmain) occurred with the dissolution of the alien priories – those outposts of French monasticism which originated with the Normans and early

---

[15] Cooper, 'Social distribution of land' [166], pp. 420–1; BL, MS Cotton Vit.E.xvi, f. 158v (cf. McNiven, *Heresy and politics*, pp. 192–3); Furnivall and Cowper, *Four supplications* [289], pp. 1–2; Heal, *Of prelates and princes* [365], pp. 20–1.

[16] Generally, Raban, *Mortmain legislation* [681], esp. pp. 12–28, 38–71, 91–2, 95–100, 117–19, 127–9,. 142–4, 151–2, 157–8, 167–70, 172–4, 177–86, 189; Blair, 'Religious gilds as landowners' [61], pp. 37–44.

[17] Raban, *Mortmain legislation*, pp. 107, 113–14.

Plantagenets. Those which were still considered foreign possessions were suppressed in the first decades of the fifteenth century. Other dissolutions of relatively small houses occurred throughout the period. Most of the lands stayed in ecclesiastical hands: the estates and properties usually went to other houses, or to new secular colleges and university foundations. Occasionally laymen gained control, as happened with the main manor of Leighton Buzzard (Beds.) after the dissolution of the alien priory there (a cell of Fontevrault). In 1480 it passed to St George's chapel, Windsor, but doubts remained about the legality of the transfer.[18]

The problem of erosion, small-scale decay which reduced endowments, was perhaps a more serious threat than large-scale alienation. It operated at two levels: first, patrons retained common law rights through the process of *cessavit* – if the religious functions funded by the endowment were not being maintained, it could be retracted. Secondly, there were straightforward problems of retaining control over property, and preventing its decay. Tenant-held land might 'accidentally' be lost, because the tenant surreptitiously converted it to freehold, or another landlord usurped possession.[19] Unrepaired property collapsed, and once ruined would be difficult to restore. The problem of decay perhaps applied especially to chantries: other foundations seemingly kept a reasonably tight hold on their possessions or, being funded by rural holdings, possibly found enforcement of dilapidation regulations rather easier. Despite being supposedly perpetual, it is likely that many chantries disappeared within a few generations of their establishment. The evidence still awaits proper evaluation; but it is clear that several remained in existence only by intermittent augmentation and amalgamation.[20] Other benefices suffered similar erosion, again producing amalgamations; but further forces such as depopulation also took their toll.

Given the extent of their landholding, it was primarily as landlords that ecclesiastics impinged directly on economic life in late medieval England. Their properties were scattered, in both town and country, yielding differing produce and profits. Consideration of ecclesiastical landlordship needs to focus on manorialism – the general theme common to the period of relations between lords and peasants; on the problem of rents for non-manorial holdings – usually glebe lands of rectories and vicarages, or chantry endowments; and on the church's urban properties – a somewhat

---

[18] Raban, *Mortmain legislation*, pp. 2–3, 35–7; Jones, 'Bedfordshire' [447], pp. 224–5; Morgan, 'Alien priories' [597], pp. 206–12; Morgan, *Lands of Bec* [598], pp. 124–6, 131–5; Knowles, *Religious orders* [484], iii, pp. 157–8, 161–3.

[19] Farr, *Wyclif as reformer* [267], pp. 104–7; Bod., DD.Bertie.c.16, 21, 34.

[20] Hill, ' "Chaunterie for souls" ' [391], pp. 244, 249–50, 252; Dobson, 'Foundation of perpetual chantries' [214], pp. 31–2; Tanner, *Church in Norwich*, pp. 92–3, 96.

artificial distinction as many towns were under the manorial jurisdiction of ecclesiastical institutions.

The church's manorial holdings, like all ecclesiastical landholdings, varied in size. The magnates stand out, individual clerics like the Archbishop of Canterbury, or major monastic houses like Westminster. But the great estates were the exceptions, and not the sole instances of manorial jurisdiction. Some individual rectories had sufficient endowment to qualify as manors, as did Prescot (Lancs.). Even a lowly chantry might have manorial authority: the manor courts of the Guild of St Christopher at Thame (Oxon.) were sometimes held by the chantry priest, sometimes by the lay wardens.[21]

Relations between ecclesiastics as landholders – as manorial lords – and their tenants obviously varied with the types of revenue received or demanded. Income did not derive solely from rents of agricultural lands. Towns under ecclesiastical lordship generated rental income, as did mills and industrial buildings. Various ecclesiastics also profited from mineral rights. The Bishops of Durham and Lichfield, for example, both leased out coal mines, although the available evidence does not indicate ruthless exploitation. Once lead-mining revived in Weardale (Dur.) in the 1370s, the Bishops of Durham became closely involved in that industry, especially when leasing gave way to active smelting after the 1420s. Again, however, this was not truly exploitative; and until Wolsey's time was often downright uneconomic. Other extractive industries where ecclesiastics were active included iron, with Durham priory and several Yorkshire houses owning mines; and salt, exemplified in the Bishop of Worcester's involvement at Droitwich (Worcs.). These mines and workings were usually leased out, the Droitwich works at a relatively low rent (frequently unpaid), or even as a favour with no rent demanded. However, the two chantry priests whose proposed endowment in 1347 included a Droitwich salthouse with six boiling pans were probably less altruistic, and would presumably seek a proper return.[22]

Nevertheless manorialism does mainly concern the rural agricultural economy. Here, the church's experience generally matched that of con-

---

[21] Harvey, *Westminster abbey* [357]; du Boulay, *Lordship of Canterbury* [236]; Dyer, *Lords and peasants* [243]; Heath, *Clerical accounts* [367], p. 16 (but is manorial status due to appropriation by King's College, and therewith incorporation into a franchise?); Bod., DD.Bertie.c.16, 21–34.

[22] Blake, 'The medieval coal trade' [63], p. 22; Heal, *Of prelates and princes*, p. 34; Dobson, *Durham priory* [216], pp. 278–9; Blanchard, 'Seigneurial entrepreneurship' [67]; Blanchard, 'Commercial crisis and change' [66], pp. 77–9, 81–4; Finberg, *Tavistock abbey* [271], pp. 153–4, 190–1, 194–6; Simpson, 'Coal mining' [759], pp. 576–90, 595–7; BRL, 435125, m.2d; SRO, D1734/3/2/3, m.50d; *Cal. pat. rolls, 1345–1348* [115], p. 336.

temporary lay landlords, although with some differences in the development of trends.

The precise state of England's economy in the early fourteenth century
remains rather obscure: the trends were contradictory, and still need
reconciliation. Population decline became a rapid fall in 1348–50, when
the Black Death emphasized the changing equations, producing a sudden
increase in labour costs (and attempts to regulate them by legislation),
but less obvious immediate signs of major disruption (other than tenurial)
in agriculture. Population levels were apparently recovering in the immediate post-plague years, until plague returned in the 1360s, became
endemic, and with additional sicknesses and lower birth rates effectively
blocked population recovery until the late fifteenth century. This long-
term population stagnation had more severe effects than the first plague
attacks, effects which were more difficult to overcome. Lay landlords
apparently recognized the changes, so that by the mid-1380s the 'feudal
reaction' which had been the instinctive response to the problems was in
retreat, as demesnes were leased out, serfdom eroded, and a new economic
order slowly established.[23]

The church was slower to adjust to the changes, and remained hopeful
of a return to previous 'normality'. Such aspirations are reflected in many
of the new tenurial arrangements on Westminster abbey estates in the
later fourteenth century, and elsewhere in leases of incomplete holdings
'until a tenant will take up the whole'.[24] The uncertain economic position,
with continuing hopes of a return to profitable demesne farming, are
indicated in the intermittent leasing of some estates alternating with
periods of direct management, as occurred with Westminster's estates of
Feering and Kelvedon (Essex) in the late fourteenth century, continuing
elsewhere into the fifteenth.[25] But direct cultivation was increasingly
uneconomic, given the low returns and high labour costs, so that a policy
of leasing was generally adopted. This often continued and expanded
trends evident before 1350. Initially, the demesnes might be leased in
small parcels, and there are suggestions of considerable competition to
acquire such holdings in some areas in the first post-plague generations.
Later the demesnes were generally leased in large blocks, or complete
estates and manors, a pattern established by the 1430s. But there were
regional variations. On the Wiltshire chalklands, and in the West Country,
the final victory of leasing was delayed for half a century and more.

[23] Bolton, *Medieval English economy*, pp. 180–218; Hatcher, *Plague, population* [364].

[24] Harvey, *Westminster abbey*, pp. 244–5, 247, 250, 255–6; Faith, 'Berkshire' [262], pp. 124–
5; Hilton, *Class conflict* [396], p. 29.

[25] Britnell, *Colchester*, p. 146; Harvey, *Westminster abbey*, p. 150; Hare, 'Monks as landlords'
[345], pp. 83–4, 87–9, 91.

Conversely, after 1500, direct management reappeared on some estates. The reasons for the late change to leasing are unlikely to be found in the economic equations drawn from the later fourteenth century, and alternative explanations are needed.[26]

The process of change was not confined to the demesne. Landlordly authority was also being challenged on tenant holdings, as customary tenure replaced the post-plague ad-hocery. Even if the wording of the leases suggested precarious tenure, with some manors emphasizing tenure at the lord's will well into the fifteenth century, the formulae ossified and were ineffective against a totally different agrarian regime. Throughout most of the fifteenth century, there was a glut of land. Tenants could pick and choose, and had to be cajoled to take on holdings. Entry fines were usually reduced or abandoned, and landlords increasingly subsidized prospective tenants by writing off rent arrears and contributing to buildings and other capital projects. Again there were local variations and exceptions: at Dedham (Essex) in the 1430s and 1440s, a localized land-hunger allowed the prioress of Campsey Ash to charge increased entry fines for customary lands, and higher rents for demesne leases. London, too, distorted the general pattern, as shown by the history of rents charged by Westminster abbey.[27] Nevertheless, the general pattern of leasehold held throughout the rest of the pre-Reformation period. Indeed, such was the ossification that the landowners (especially the bishops) failed to take economic opportunities when they came. The early sixteenth century saw a gradual shift in favour of direct farmers, linked to the effects of contemporary inflation. Ecclesiastical institutions seem not to have exploited this situation: leases remained the norm, being if anything made for longer periods, at static rents. The farmer therefore gained the increased profits, while the lessor received a rent of declining value – unless unrecorded profits were being made from increased entry fines. The general picture appears to reflect missed opportunities, although there were occasional attempts at economic reform, such as Wolsey's over-ambitious enterprise at Durham in the late 1520s.[28]

If the transfer from direct farming to leasehold is one outcome of the population history of the period, another was the gradual decline (but not

[26] Halcrow, 'Decline of demesne farming' [339], pp. 349–50; Dyer, *Lords and peasants*, p. 123; Hare, 'Monks as landlords', pp. 84–8, 93; Youings, 'The church' [933], p. 312.

[27] Harvey, *Westminster abbey*, pp. 158, 276–7, 279–85; Faith, 'Berkshire', pp. 116–17, 156–7; Lomas, 'South-east Durham' [528], pp. 306–7 (but note contrast with episcopal lands at p. 307); Britnell, *Colchester*, p. 252.

[28] Heal, *Of prelates and princes*, pp. 31, 47; Harvey, *Westminster abbey*, pp. 54, 150–1, 154–5, 161–3; Youings, 'The church', pp. 318–20; Dyer, *Lords and peasants*, pp. 190–2.

total abolition) of serfdom.[29] Here again, ecclesiastics faced the same forces as their lay counterparts, but were seemingly less willing to give way. This may reflect a different perception of their duties: an ecclesiastical landlord was but the temporary custodian of the properties for his successors, and was duty bound not to diminish his see, house, or whatever. Possibly, also, some of the ecclesiastical landlords suffered from constraints on their freedom of manoeuvre. Unless an individual managed to dominate matters, the supposedly shared government of religious houses meant that there were checks on alienation without consent. Similarly, bishops faced checks, with manumissions, leases, and grants of offices needing the assent of cathedral authorities, whether secular or monastic.[30] Ensuring the recognition and maintenance of lordship was thus an obligation, but one which entailed conflict. In the mid-thirteenth century the peasants of Halesowen (Worcs.) began a lengthy struggle against their lord, the abbey, which was seeking to extend and enforce its authority over them. At that point the peasants successfully resisted. After the Black Death, the abbey began another offensive, demanding all its ancient rights and more. Again there was resistance, culminating in a revolt in 1386, and again the abbey gave way. Halesowen abbey's reluctance to accept the changed situation with regard to lordship after 1349 appears fairly typical of religious institutions. Canterbury cathedral priory shows a similar pattern of exploitation, reversing the commutation processes begun before the plague, so that compulsory labour services on its estates in 1390 exceeded those of 1314. Not unnaturally these increased pressures generated opposition and revolts.[31] Even if religious institutions did not actively exploit their powers, they kept them in reserve, seemingly delaying concessions for as long as possible. Consequently, it was not until well into the fifteenth century that Durham priory stopped drawing up lists of serfs; and some houses perhaps continued to identify them into the sixteenth. When the estates of the prebends of Salisbury cathedral were visited in 1405, the numbers of serfs on some of them were carefully recorded (although there were not many). Concern with possession of serfs is also shown in attempts to recapture fugitives at Ely, Bury St Edmunds, and Peterborough later that century. Even in the 1440s, Bury was enforcing some rights over its serfs, granting licences to live outside the lordship in

29 For Westminster abbey, Harvey, *Westminster abbey*, pp. 269–75; generally Hilton, *Decline of serfdom* [392].

30 Many documents in Greatrex, *Common seal* [313] are ratifications of episcopal acts by the prior and convent of Winchester. The bishop of Coventry and Lichfield needed ratification from both the secular chapter at Lichfield and the monks of Coventry: BRL, 435125, mm.2d, 3r.

31 Razi, 'Abbots of Halesowen and their tenants' [689], pp. 154–66; Smith, *Canterbury cathedral priory* [768], pp. 119–27, esp. 127; see also Hilton, *English peasantry* [394], pp. 60–4.

return for annual payment of 12d.; and a decade later the Bishop of Ely tried to charge for the marriage of serfs' daughters.[32] Where anything as total as manumission was allowed it was mainly individual, the piecemeal issue of the grants suggesting a reluctance to permit full-scale and widespread liberation.[33] Apart from possessory considerations, in such cases the lords also had to consider their own economies: given increased labour costs in a free market, manumissions and commutations could mean an overall loss of revenue, with the sale of works not compensating for the costs of replacement labour. Moreover, despite the immediate opportunities for rent revisions after the Black Death, customary rents (if they could be enforced) were perhaps more profitable *c.*1400 than the negotiated market rents of leased properties. Therefore, when liberation occurred, it had to be bought. Although general economic pressures militated against enforcement of servile dues, nevertheless the desire for liberation gave the lords a lever over their peasants. Thus, the commutation of labour services agreed between the abbot of Bury St Edmund's and his tenants at Rickinghall (Suffolk) in 1438 recorded a complex range of equivalents – for each quarter of barley due, he received 2s. 4d.; for each winter and summer work, 1d., with autumn works at 3½d. each; for each horse-work (i.e., carrying service) he received 1½d., with 1d. for each foot-work; and finally a general rent increase of ¼d. per acre, to exonerate the tenants from providing a reeve and a messor. Other reductions in feudal dues similarly had their price, although the case of Broomfleet (Yorks.) suggests that liberation cannot always be taken at face value. The serfs there belonged to St Leonard's hospital, York, which in the 1390s was being steadily mulcted by its master, William Botheby. He saw manumission as a source of profit – for himself, not the house – and sold perpetual liberation to the Broomfleet serfs for £13. 6s. 8d. The sale was included in the complaints against Botheby in a royal inquiry into his mismanagement in 1399, being cited as a weakening of the house, rather than improvement.[34]

Overall, regardless of terminology, the ecclesiastical lords' control over their serfs was in decline. Although the vocabulary remained – references to servile payments appear, for example, in an account of the bishopric of Lichfield in 1502–3, and Westminster abbey demesne leases continued to grant the lessees the customary labour services from the serfs – in fact

---

[32] Faith, 'Women's marriage' [261], pp. 147–8 (but see Searle, 'A rejoinder' [753], p. 158); Lomas, 'South-east Durham', p. 282; Timmins, *Reg. Chandler* [841], nos. 11–12, 14, 17–18, 61; BL, MS Add. 14848, ff. 143r, 340r, 350v, MS Add. 25288, f. 120r; EDR, E1/16: Saturday after St Etheldreda, 30 Henry VI, and Saturday before St Martin, 30 Henry VI.

[33] For individual grants see Greatrex, *Common seal*, indexed under 'manumission' (at pp. 235–6).

[34] Harvey, *Westminster abbey*, pp. 245, 257–63; BL, MS Add. 14848, ff. 333r–v (see also Finberg, *Tavistrock abbey*, pp. 254–5); PRO, C270/20/2, 5.

things had changed. Enforcement of servile dues, especially labour services like those demanded at Hurdwick (Devon) from Tavistock abbey's tenants in 1497, seemed increasingly anachronistic.[35] Moreover, even when services had been commuted for money, the tenantry might reduce the additional charge through resistance, as the nuns of Syon conceded at Cheltenham (Glos.) in 1451. Tenants were not powerless against their lords, and a dual system of rents depending on the status of the land (customary tenure or freehold) seemed increasingly irrelevant. Tenants acted against their lords with lethargic performance of labour dues, denials of court fines, refusal to pay traditional dues, and outright retraction of rents, all used against fifteenth-century bishops of Worcester. Even if ecclesiastical lords could support their authority with quasi-ecclesiastical sanctions, such as Archbishop Courtenay's enforcement of carrying services at Wingham (Kent) in 1390 by a process rather like public penance, their power was not utterly unshakeable.[36]

Serfs on ecclesiastical lands had one weapon not available to those subject to lay lords. The Statute of Mortmain had sought to curb the acquisition of lands by religious houses, except by royal licence. But one attribute of lordship was that the lord could rightfully expropriate his serfs of any freehold land they acquired (although the land at issue might be leased back by the lord). This introduced an anomaly: was an ecclesiastical lord to be denied the enforcement of his rights because of conflict with statute law? The response was ambivalent. A couple of late fourteenth-century Bedfordshire cases show royal escheators stepping in when Ramsey abbey expropriated serfs in such circumstances, with the intervention being sought (possibly collusively) by the serfs themselves. In one case, care of the disputed lands was granted to another serf, possibly connected to the dispossessed holder. However, this expedient was perhaps available only for lands acquired outside the lordship: other evidence shows that ecclesiastical lords could resume tenements on their manors acquired by serfs, especially if inheriting from a marriage between a servile father and free heiress mother.[37]

Whilst rural lordship was being eroded, the most violent conflicts between ecclesiastical lords and their subjects seem to have occurred in towns.

[35] Harvey, *Westminster abbey*, p. 271; BRL, 435125, m. 2r–d; Finberg, *Tavistrock abbey*, pp. 258–9.

[36] Hilton, *English peasantry*, pp. 67–9 (the status of some of the tenants in question may have been of some importance); Dyer, 'Redistribution of incomes' [242], pp. 200–7, 212–13; du Boulay, *Lordship of Canterbury*, p. 189.

[37] Jones, 'Bedfordshire', pp. 213–15; Raban, *Mortmain legislation*, pp. 31–3; Finberg, *Tavistock abbey*, pp. 79–80; Baildon, *Religious houses of Yorkshire* [27], i, p. 202 (compare also the use of the statute in the Coventry dispute in 1334: Gooder and Gooder, 'Coventry' [304], p. 17).

Relationships between ecclesiastical lords of towns and their urban subjects varied in proportion to the degree of control, and the lord's proximity.
Where lords shared control, the existence of rival jurisdictions would have
an erosive effect, with the townspeople exploiting the rivalry for their own
benefit. Thus, in Coventry (War.), which after 1250 seemed to be developing into a unified borough controlled by the cathedral priory, the intrusion
of Queen Isabella as lady of half the town in the 1330s permitted collusion
between her and the townsmen which eventually constricted the area of
abbey jurisdiction, and produced effective reunification of the town outside
monastic control in the 1350s. Although the abbey retained jurisdiction
over its own precincts, its hold elsewhere was virtually eliminated.[38]
Developments were less spectacular in Warwick, where the various lords
included the priory of St Sepulchre and the college of St Mary. This
fragmentation of authority was countered by the development of urban
unity through the creation of a fraternity or guild, which to some extent
superseded the authority of the manorial officials. Guild replacement of
lordly authority also happened at Stratford on Avon (War.), wholly
subject to the Bishop of Worcester. The bishop's distant authority permitted the evolution of a form of urban autonomy through the Holy Cross
guild, which continued to recognize episcopal lordship, but effectively
governed by itself, and resisted strongly if the bishop's officials intervened
too actively.[39] On the other hand, a strong immediate presence could
crush guild aspirations. At Cirencester (Glos.) the Trinity guild rose to
challenge the abbey's lordship in the late fourteenth century, acquiring a
royal charter from Henry IV. However, the abbey fought back, and in
1418 the charter was cancelled and the town's independent spirit crushed.
This contrasts with developments in Evesham (Worcs.) where, from the
1480s, a good degree of self-government was obtained, despite the presence
of the abbey.[40]

Towns controlled by local monasteries were especially prone to conflict.
Like other towns, the monastic boroughs sought self-government and
incorporation; aspirations which were impeded when, as at Bury St Edmunds (Suffolk), monastic officials had control and treated the borough as
just another source of revenue. Perhaps, as with manumissions, the ecclesiastical lords were more reluctant than others to grant incorporation to
their boroughs, continuing to exploit the profitability of urban lordship
and resources. Almost inevitably, a clash of interests resulted, with the
lords anxious to prevent emancipation, and the townspeople seeking it. A

[38] Gooder and Gooder, 'Coventry', pp. 12–24, 26–7.
[39] *VCH, Warwick*, viii [874], pp. 476–9; *VCH, Warwick*, iii [873], p. 247; Dyer, *Lords and peasants*, p. 280; Hilton, *English peasantry*, p. 93.
[40] Trenholme, *Monastic boroughs* [846], pp. 68–70; Tittler, 'End of the middle ages' [843], p. 482.

constant undercurrent of conflict thus persisted, occasionally surfacing in major upheavals. Two great waves of opposition to lordship, in the 1320s and 1381, were at their most forceful in monastic boroughs such as Abingdon (Berks.), Bury St Edmunds, and St Albans (Herts.). Lordship was not the only reason for conflict – the outbreak in 1381 at Bury was compounded by a disputed succession to the abbacy, which exacerbated local rivalries – but the general coincidence is notable. Yet, while conflict was inherent, most authorities could compromise: the clashes of 1327 and 1381 are exceptions, rather than typical. Taking Bury again as the example, in practice there was almost a condominium between the monastic ministers and the burgesses under their own alderman.[41]

Lordship was not the only manifestation of ecclesiastical landholding. Many institutions had lands without lordship; for every benefice was a piece of landed property. All rural parishes had their landed endowments, their glebe, as well as assorted buildings. The extent and value of the glebe varied considerably, but might be highly important to the incumbent, who could either lease it out or exploit it directly. Unfortunately, not enough is known about either the organization or the exploitation of glebe in the later middle ages. Most runs of terriers – statements of a church's property – begin only in the seventeenth century, and while possibly reflecting earlier property-holding, are unlikely to be exactly the same. The extent of the glebe would be a major consideration in appropriations of rectories to other institutions, but how the appropriator treated it varied. Glebe held by Tavistock abbey at '*Thele*' from 1190 was effectively treated as just further peasant freeholding; but post-plague appropriations may have led to a more market-oriented system of farming. Most surviving parochial accounts concern appropriated benefices, with the glebe being farmed out, and give an incomplete picture of the situation. For Riston (Yorks.) a statement of glebe production in 1487–8 does survive: 17 quarters, 1 bushel of wheat, valued at £4 6s. 3d.; 27 quarters of barley, worth £3 0s. 8d.; 2 quarters of rye (8s.); 13 quarters of peas (29s. 3d.); and 5 quarters of oats (worth 6s. 8d.). Given the general dietary standards of the period this should have sufficed to feed the incumbent and his household – and although the glebe acreage is not stated, contrasts markedly with the rental values declared in valuations of benefices. In 1470 a claimant in the royal courts valued the grain – wheat, oats, and beans – produced by 18 acres of glebe at Trent (Som.) at £6; even allowing for exaggeration, this still would have exceeded rental receipts, although working costs would have to be deducted and might substantially reduce

---

41 Lobel, *Bury St Edmund's* [525], pp. 31–59, 72–95, 120–67; Trenholme, *Monastic boroughs*, pp. 19–94.

the profits. The management of the glebe was not trouble-free. If the incumbent rector (vicars usually had much less, if any, glebe allowance) did work the land personally, or hired labour to do it, he would also be affected by changing economic relations. Rising agricultural wages after the Black Death might force him to lease the glebe at whatever rent it would bring – quite possibly reducing his standard of living. Later, as the Tudor inflation set in, his position would deteriorate further, unless the method of exploitation changed, or rents could be increased. The possession of glebe also laid the incumbent open to the various pressures and conflict associated with tenure, involving him in disputes with neighbours, or dilapidations problems at the end of an incumbency. The incumbent's concern to exploit his glebe might also cause friction within the parish, sometimes provoking complaints from parishioners that clerics were allowing their pigs the run of the churchyard, or drying their grain in it.[42]

With the glebe land, and sometimes equally important, went the rectorial buildings. For the lessees of appropriated rectories, the buildings might well be more attractive than the lands. Thus, the valuation of Harlow (Essex) made in 1398 lists the glebe (15 acres of arable) as worth 20s. a year; but the rectorial manse and outbuildings, covering 4 acres, were valued at 24s. a year: the vicar, when appointed, was to have another house worth only 2s. a year.[43]

Urban parishes had little if any glebe (some patches might be scattered around the outer fringes of a town), and the incumbent's position was correspondingly weaker. But churches and other religious institutions did gain revenue from urban properties. Indeed, most late medieval foundations – chantries, hospitals, fraternities, and so on – probably derived most of their income from rented property, whether urban or rural, rather than manorial acquisitions. In consequence many town-dwellers inhabited buildings which were rented from ecclesiastical foundations, or which had rent charges imposed on them which went to such establishments.[44]

How the economic changes of the later middle ages affected these endowments remains rather obscure, although the broad trend is clear. Like other rents, those for glebe and urban properties declined after the Black Death. The glebe of Pattiswick (Essex) was leased for £9 before the

---

[42] Finberg, *Tavistock abbey*, p. 240; Heath, *Clerical accounts*, pp. 16–17, 52 (see also pp. 40–1); Dyer, 'English diet' [244], pp. 197–212 (esp. p. 203 n. 28); Neilson, *Year books, A.D. 1470* [603], pp. 6–9; Zell, 'Economic problems' [937], p. 37; Heath, *Parish clergy* [369], pp. 158–9; Fisher, Richardson, and Fisher, *Anthology* [276], no. 166; Bannister, 'Visitation returns of Hereford', vol. 45, p. 96.

[43] CUL, MS Add. 6847, f. 78v.

[44] For ecclesiastical rental income in London in 1392, see McHardy, *Church in London* [553], pp. 39–77. For urban rentals see e.g. Littlehales, *London city church* [518], pp. 74–6, 124–6; Templeman, *Records of the guild of Coventry* [816], ii, pp. 48–139. Mendicant houses also received rents from property: Purvis, 'Four antiquarian notes' [677], pp. 52–3.

plague, but had slowly dropped by 1406/7 to under £4. Appropriated rectories were as problematic for their owners as other lands, with the need to cajole takers. In the fifteenth century, a Bishop of Lichfield leased out his appropriated rectory of Wybunbury (Ches.) for £30 a year, but received barely half the rent, as the arrears grew to over £180. Farmers were in a good position, and could exploit it, although in this particular case the rectory seems to have reverted to some form of direct management in the early sixteenth century.[45]

Urban rents pose rather different problems, complicated by the variable status of the ecclesiastical institutions as owners or lessees. Urban rents received by religious institutions were of two distinct sorts. First, the basic ground rents which were an acknowledgement of lordship – the original burgage rents which by 1350 were usually small fixed charges, which could be increased only if the individual buildings reverted to the ground-owner. Secondly, the economic market rents, reflected both in increments where burgages had been bought up, and in ecclesiastical involvement in semi-speculative leasing, where an institution holding a burgage tenement sub-let it for an economic rent. The system is illustrated at Gloucester in 1455, where St Bartholomew's priory leased a tenement and bakery from the urban authorities at the customary fixed rent of 1s. 2d. This was sublet to Llanthony priory, for 18s. a year, and they leased it to a baker for 40s. a year. Similarly at Warwick, in 1421, St Mary's college was receiving several fixed burgage rents, bringing in small sums, plus a number of 'economic' rents, which considerably augmented its income.[46]

For the urban ecclesiastical property-holders, the difficulty with 'economic' rents was their speculative character, dependent on a constant demand for tenancies. Many English towns suffered a period of contraction in the fifteenth century, reflected in declining rents, increased arrears, and the decay of buildings. Altered rent levels and methods of leasing often reflect these changes, providing measures of the fortunes of individual towns. At Winchester (Hants.), the bad years after 1350 are revealed in leases for terms of years, replaced in the early fifteenth century (when the position seems to have improved) by tenancies at will. As Winchester slowly decayed thereafter, tenancies for years reappeared. Changes in rent income for the vicars choral of York Minster similarly reflect the changes in that city's prosperity between 1350 and 1525. Their rents dropped to a mere £56 a year in 1352, increasing to c.£160 a year in the first quarter of the fifteenth century. By 1521 rents had slipped back to £64.[47]

---

[45] Britnell, *Colchester*, pp. 144 (and n. 27), 151, 153 (see also p. 254); SRO, D1734/3/2/4, m.8; WSL, MS 335/i, m.24r–d; PRO, SC6/Henry VIII/7154, m.5 r–d.

[46] Hilton, *Class conflict*, pp. 169–71.

[47] Keene, *Medieval Winchester* [461], i, p. 192; Bartlett, 'Expansion and decline of York'

But to use the drop in rents as a precise mirror of a town's decline runs the risk of over-simplification. The rents of St John's hospital, Winchester, show a more complex picture, with much depending on the type of property being leased, and its location. In declining towns, major religious institutions could perhaps stave off some of the worst effects of the economic changes. Again at Winchester, the contrasting stability and decline of different parts of the town in the fifteenth and sixteenth centuries has been linked to their proximity to the major religious establishments (notably the cathedral and Hyde abbey) as employers and consumers. Equally, the non-speculative rents derived from urban properties might be less subject to fluctuation: at Winchester, episcopal income from burgage rents was hardly affected, and the same applied at Tavistock (Devon). Burgage rents would be affected only if there was a wholesale retreat of population, with large sections of the town (in ecclesiastical lordship) being left unoccupied, or with the buildings left ruinous.[48] Perhaps institutions with scattered holdings suffered most from these fluctuations, since new investment in a declining town would not be worthwhile.

As landowners, then, the varied ecclesiastical institutions were being squeezed by economic changes. All would have suffered a reduction in income, with serious consequences given that they lacked many of the opportunities available to secular lords to recoup their fortunes – and were themselves open to exploitation by those secular lords. With its economic foundations eroded, the church's status would have been seriously impaired, forcing concentration on other expedients, or on structural changes which might have worked against the church's spiritual character.

5.3 THE SPIRITUAL ECONOMY

While the church's endowments produced considerable revenues, its ecclesiastical functions also generated substantial sums. This happened most obviously at the parochial level: there the clergy had immediate contact with those who supported them; whilst for their part the parishioners had to assume responsibility for a share of parochial concerns, appointing churchwardens and receiving their accounts, which created a localized spiritual economy providing for other parochial needs. Beyond the parish there were other levels to the spiritual economy. The considerable (and increasing) number of parishes appropriated to religious institutions meant that parish revenues were often concentrated at locations remote from

[45], pp. 24–6, 28, 30, 32. See also Butcher, 'Rent and the urban economy' [111], pp. 18–43; Blair, 'Religious gilds as landowners', pp. 45–6.

[48] Keene, *Medieval Winchester*, i, pp. 144, 146, 196–7, 243–8; Butcher, 'Rent and the urban economy', pp. 40, 43; Finberg, *Tavistock abbey*, p. 203.

their source. The parish's spiritual revenues were also only one layer in the system of payments which were generated throughout the ecclesiastical administrative structure, for the most part affecting the benefice and its incumbent, but in certain instances (especially court fees and probate charges) also affecting the laity. Additional to such involuntary payments – to incumbent, archdeacon, bishop, archbishop, and pope – there were a multiplicity of voluntary contributions made for religious purposes, which also need consideration. They usually represent aspects of contemporary spirituality: payments for indulgences, offerings at shrines, and guild membership fees. Their immediate importance is as part of the process of moving money around the country, and contributing to general economic change.

The parish was the chief point of contact between the people of late medieval England and the church, affecting their pockets on a regular annual basis which was effectively one of taxation. The church claimed for itself that tenth part of produce dedicated to divine service in the Old Testament, and in most parishes tithes provided the incumbent's basic

ASHLEWORTH RECTORY   The church in the local community: the importance of the idea of the benefice appears in the complex of buildings of Ashleworth rectory (Glos.), with (left to right) the rectory manse, the church, and the tithe barn. (B. T. Batsford Ltd. photograph: Royal Commission on the Historical Monuments of England)

income. Almost everything fell within the range of tithing, although local customs sometimes altered details. Technically, the tenth was a payment of the annual increase, an ecclesiastical VAT, affecting everything which could be grown or give birth, or was naturally produced, and was charged on overall production, not just sales. Minerals were generally exempted, but not always: the bishops of Exeter received an annual composition of £16 13s. 4d. from the Duchy of Cornwall for tithes of tin (the payment having no relation to actual production), and the dean and chapter of Lichfield profited reasonably handsomely from the tithes of lead production in Derbyshire. Durham priory also received some income from tithes of coal.[49] The church also claimed to tithe profits and individual wages (minus expenses), as a form of lay income tax. Such personal tithes, and levies on rents (where made) could be especially significant in towns, where many of the products tithable in the country were clearly not available. However, such personal tithes were perhaps the easiest to avoid by deceit.[50]

Precisely what was tithed, and how, depended on local custom. At Scarborough (Yorks.), the fish tithes were a tenth of only part of the catch, with some species being tithed at only a twentieth or fortieth, all after deducting expenses, and all commuted to payment in cash rather than kind. Some towns, like Torksey (Lincs.), incorporated a recital of tithing practice into their statements of borough customs. There, many animal tithes had been commuted to monetary levies, with formal restrictions also on the levy of personal tithes. The possibilities for commutation were clearly appreciated by both incumbents and parishioners. Often, as at Ramsbury (Wilts), the precise number of lambs born dictated whether tithes were in cash or kind. At Durham, by contrast, the prior and convent tried to profit regardless of the situation: in years of good harvest (and low market prices) they were sometimes content to take grain tithes in money; but in the reverse position they insisted on receiving the grain.[51]

The difficulty with tithes was their variability, and sometimes uncertainty about liability. Many religious orders and their lands were exempt from their collection by papal decree; while the movement of animals across parish boundaries when pasturing provoked disputes between incumbents about receipt. These uncertainties are reflected in tithe cases between ecclesiastics, as rivals claimed tithes from the same lands or animals. Com-

---

[49] Swanson, 'Episcopal income: Exeter' [802], esp. at n. 33; Blanchard, 'Derbyshire lead production' [65], p. 134; Fowler, *Account rolls of Durham* [281], ii, pp. 285, 295.

[50] Little, 'Personal tithes' [515]; Bridgen, 'Tithe controversy' [91], p. 287 n. 8.

[51] Heath, 'North Sea fishing' [368], p. 56 (but see n. 15); Bateson, *Borough customs* [50], ii, pp. 212–13; Timmins, *Reg. Chandler*, no. 69 (see also Brownbill, *Ledger book of Vale Royal* [102], pp. 157–9; Wood-Legh, *Kentish visitations*, p. 177); Lomas, 'South-east Durham', p. 319.

pacts specifying the precise arrangements for settling conflicting claims are not uncommon, whether between neighbouring rectors (as in 1364 between the incumbents of Clifton Campville [Staffs.] and Newton Regis [War.]), between religious houses (as with the arrangements for the tithes of Over [Ches.] in 1475), or between parts of the same corporation, such as the division made between the dean and chapter of Hereford in 1453.[52] Other disputes hinged on tithing of specific products: in general it seems that opposition was not to the principle of tithing, but to individual practice. When there were principled objections, they usually concerned the use to which tithes were put; Lollards, for example, arguing that they should not be paid to unworthy priests, and should be used for charitable purposes. One of the great disputes of the mid-fourteenth century involved the definition of types of wood classifiable as *silva cedua*, and therefore tithable: the controversy even engaged Parliament, with an Act of 1376 seeking to settle the matter, although with incomplete success.[53]

Clashes between incumbents and tithe-payers were fairly common. The clergy's dependence on their parishioners for so much of their income placed them in an invidious position: if they tried to collect their dues with too much enthusiasm, they could be accused of un-Christian behaviour. They (or their farmers) had few means of enforcing payment, other than excommunication and going to court, unless they exploited the suscepti-bilities of their parishioners by refusing the sacraments until settlement was made – a sanction which could result in complaints to higher auth-orities. In the event, there was no shortage of tithe business for the church courts (or, in certain cases, the secular courts as well). In London (where normal rural tithing practice was clearly inapplicable) there were years of dispute in a search for a system of tithing which commuted all dues to money payments, in a manner acceptable to both clergy and laity. In its various phases the conflict continued through much of the fifteenth century, and well into the sixteenth.[54]

The variety of tithable products, and their relative importance to a benefice, is illustrated in occasional detailed valuations (especially those

---

[52] Brownbill, *Ledger book of Vale Royal*, pp. 150–3; Wilson, *Reg. Coventry and Lichfield, book 4* [917], pp. 34–5; HCA, 244.

[53] Tanner, *Church in Norwich*, pp. 5–7; Aston, ' "Caim's castles" ', pp. 60–1; Brigden, 'Tithe controversy', pp. 290–1; *Statutes*, i, p. 393; Jones, 'Two jurisdictions' [452], pp. 163–4 (for later disputes over tithe woods see Wood-Legh, *Kentish visitations*, p. 177; Plucknett and Barton, *Doctor and student* [661], pp. lxiv–lv, 300–14, and for a case bandied between courts, Windsor, XV.55.19).

[54] Bannister, 'Visitation returns of Hereford', vol. 44, p. 286, vol. 45, p. 447; Jones, 'Two jurisdictions', pp. 113–15; Thomson, 'Tithe disputes', pp. 2–17; Brigden, 'Tithe controversy', pp. 290, 293–301. For a particularly dramatic imbroglio at Hayes in 1530, where a tithe dispute involving a farmer mixed a variety of other offences and ended up in Star Chamber, see Elton, *Star chamber stories* [250], pp. 174–217.

made prior to an appropriation), and in surviving parish accounts. The valuation of Harlow (Essex) taken in 1398 was dominated by the tithes of sheaves and grain, worth £20. Hay tithes were valued at 26s. 8d., less than receipts from wool and lambs (at 33s. 4d. each). Thereafter, in order of importance, came tithes of calves and piglets (13s. 4d. each), geese (10s.), personal tithes (6s. 8d.), tithes of pears, apples, and other tree-borne fruit (5s.), hemp and flax (3s. 4d.), coppice wood at 2s., and finally honey and the Harlow mill, at 1s. each. In many ways this is probably a typical account, but local differences would change the emphases. At Holme-next-the-sea (Norfolk), for instance, many of the entries reappear, but the figures are generally lower (although grain tithes remain at £20). However, there were compensations: eggs were tithed, at 2s. 4d. (at Harlow, although these were untithed, there is mention of 'egg rent' at 2s.); while the seaside location is reflected in sea fishing tithes (30s.), and tithes called 'Ebbe se' worth 3s. 4d. However, no personal tithes were entered. The sea was also important at Scarborough, where the surviving benefice accounts give a catalogue of payments from the fishing fleet. There, personal tithes were also significant, although they declined over the years.[55]

Valuations cannot accurately reflect the volume of goods diverted to ecclesiastical uses by the tithing system. In some instances quantities are available, with prices. At Hornsea (Yorks.) a tithe lamb was worth 8d. in 1484–5, with 39½ being accounted for (the half obviously by commutation, the rest possibly), and an additional 28d. being offered for odd fragments otherwise untithable. Wool was offered in fleeces, with some cash again for odd amounts, producing 55½ fleeces and 12½d. The fleeces totalled 8 stones of wool, sold at 2s. 9d. a stone (3s. in other years). Tithes of piglets show variations, with 29 being accounted for that year, at individual prices ranging from 3d. to 10d., but bringing in a total of 10s. 8d. Eggs (800 of them) were also accounted for, at 4d. a hundred. Geese were reckoned at 2½d. each, totalling 2s. 6d. Poultry – hens, cockerels, and doves – were disposed of at 9d. the dozen, for five dozen. Other products also appear in the accounts, including hemp, pears, honey, and wax; although priced, no quantities are indicated.[56]

As Hornsea was a vicarage the accounts omit the grain tithes; but quantities are available elsewhere. At Ely, for example, the sacrist's accounts usually contain details of tithe and demesne production. In 1478–9 wheat tithes amounted to 26 quarters, peas to 20 quarters, and barley to 190 quarters. Much of the produce was apparently used in the house, and is

[55] CUL, MS Add. 6847, f. 78v; Bod., Shropshire charter 27B (the return for Holme vicarage in 1535 shows some changes from the appropriation valuation, including 23s. 4d. for privy tithes: *Valor* [120], vi, p. ii); PRO, E101/514/31–2 (on the MSS see Heath, 'North Sea fishing', pp. 54–5, income from fish and personal tithes tabulated at pp. 67–70).

[56] Heath, *Clerical accounts*, pp. 43–6, 48 (1 stone = 14 lbs.)

therefore unpriced. Tithes of wheat in this case produced as much as the demesne, with tithes of peas and barley both exceeding demesne yields.[57] Such yield comparisons provide some indication of the relative importance of tithes. Only rarely, however, can their significance in terms of estate sizes be deduced. At Havering (Essex) such comparison is possible: there the tithe receipts exceeded the income produced by the 1,900 acres held by the appropriators (New College, Oxford) within the parish – by a considerable amount if the tithes due from that estate are also taken into the reckoning.[58]

A major problem with tithes was the fluctuation in annual production, and their subjection to natural forces and disasters like the floods which ruined the hay at Reedness and Swinefleet (Yorks.) in 1421.[59] Moreover, if not consumed by the incumbent or by the appropriating house, or distributed in poor relief, they had value only in terms of the market. This often put the tithe-seller in an unenviable position: dependent on the parishioners for the tithes themselves, he would be competing with them in the market. For the incumbent, tithes meant that, unless he cultivated his glebe effectively, his economic position was parasitical and unstable. Much depended on continuity of production, both in quantity and in types of produce, if livings were to retain their value. This was a major concern when tithes were divided between rector and vicar, as usually happened with appropriated benefices: there the appropriator generally retained the great tithes, the grain, whilst the vicar received the smaller tithes, including hay, wool, and lambs. The changing economy of the later middle ages produced something of a revolution in the tithing system. The retreat of cultivation to the better lands, alongside the decline in population, meant a drop in overall grain production, which rectors immediately felt in reduced tithe receipts.[60] Whilst production declined, there was no compensatory price rise: with generally higher living standards, because of the smaller population, the pressure of demand also dropped. Grain prices did rise somewhat, but probably not enough to counter the drop in production in cash terms, or to cancel out the increased labour costs which may have crept into other areas of benefice administration. Furthermore, not only were grain receipts declining, but the distribution of produce was also changing. A general decline in production may have substantially reduced the income of some vicars, thereby forcing reconsideration of ordinations, and possibly encouraging the trend towards stipendiary vicarages. But the most dramatic change would have been the

---

[57] EDC, 5/10/36d.

[58] McIntosh, *Autonomy and community* [559] pp. 75, 147.

[59] Holt, 'Two rolls' [410], p. 44.

[60] E.g. Britnell, *Colchester*, pp. 150–1, 155 (although Feering seems to have been staggeringly productive in 1382).

shift in emphasis to livestock, with concomitant changes in population distribution as villages were abandoned and in due course converted to pasture. This increased tithes of lamb and wool, with possibly a further deliberate reduction in grain production. The main beneficiaries of this change would be the incumbents receiving such tithes – in appropriated benefices, the vicars; this might lead to a paradoxical inversion of the tithe position compared to the original appropriation, with vicarial tithes now exceeding those of the rectory.[61] Of course, it was not just the shift to wool which changed tithe income. The decline of the Scarborough fishing industry is mirrored in the drop in tithe income in the benefice accounts. Changes in the local market for tithe produce would also affect receipts from personal tithes. Whilst some of these doubtless reflect the population shifts in the period – the effect of the plague on Scarborough has been blamed for the collapse of personal tithe payments there in the 1430s – alterations in trade which affected local mercantile families would also be significant, especially if they paid *pro rata* rather than *per capita*. The Scarborough evidence on personal tithes may therefore reflect the decline of the fishing industry just as effectively as do the changes in payments of tithes for fish.[62]

Important as tithes were, they were not the only source of benefice income. Others were more precisely linked to the spiritual functions of the priest, and of the parish. Thus, the valuation of Holme-next-the-sea lists among the receipts the oblations at funerals and obits, gifts made on the main feast days, and offerings at the purifications of women after child-bearing. The income from spiritual actions totalled 30s., although whether it fairly reflected actual receipts cannot be checked. Like many other elements in parochial revenues, these spiritualities were extremely variable, especially reflecting influences on population – the proctor of Selby abbey at Whitgift (Yorks.) in 1420–1 remarked on the increase in funeral receipts after the pestilence there that year. At Hornsea, purifications were normally charged at 1½d. each, with marriages at 4d. and funerals at 6d. (with another 6d. for the commemoration on the octave). Charges for anniversaries were less regular. The position at Scarborough appears more fluid, with payments varying, and burials usually including additional payments for wax.[63] The implied compulsion of some of these payments was sometimes resented, as, perhaps, was the uncertainty of the level of demands which might be made by the clergy. Occasionally, as at Torksey,

---

[61] For an earlier switch, du Boulay, *Lordship of Canterbury*, p. 141.

[62] Heath, 'North Sea fishing', pp. 62–8 (the 'pincer' effect of the decline in fishing producing a reduction in mercantile activity is suggested by the disproportionate decline in personal tithes compared to those for fishing).

[63] Bod., Shropshire charter 27B; Holt, 'Two rolls', p. 43; Heath, *Clerical accounts*, pp. 28–30, 35–6, 42–3; PRO, E101/514/31–2.

the levels were fixed by borough custom. Later Lollard opposition to such payments paralleled an old-established resentment of excessive demands made by the clergy, reflected in occasional conflicts between incumbents and parishioners.[64]

Particularly resented among such levies were mortuaries, which with tithes provided the commonest reason for conflict between cleric and parishioner: the celebrated case of Richard Hunne began with the demand for a mortuary on the death of his infant in 1514.[65] Officially, the mortuary was a payment to the church due at death, technically for tithes forgotten, although having more of the connotations of a heriot – the payment due on a tenant's death to his manorial lord – as a recognition of spiritual lordship. By the fifteenth century the payment was largely treated as a traditional perquisite of the incumbent, regularly appearing in wills. But it was occasionally resented, and sometimes evaded. In rural areas a beast was usually handed over; in towns the position varied, but the best robe or gown seems to have been the standard payment.[66] However, some mortuary recipients were more demanding: at Doncaster (Yorks.) in the 1350s, St Mary's abbey at York was claiming mortuaries which (according to the complainants) included anvils, small boats, lead brewing vessels, and other goods with an economic significance considerably out-stripping that of an old coat. Precisely who was liable to pay mortuary is not clear – the dispute in Hunne's case seems to have been about the demand applying to a child rather than the general idea; and at Torksey (again) the clause regarding mortuaries in the borough customs specifically excluded children from liability. Wives were also often exempt. These payments are also confused by the division of spoils of appropriated benefices, or local farming arrangements: for example a lease of chapelries by Selby abbey at the end of the fourteenth century did not allow the lessee to receive mortuaries. The absence of mortuaries from benefice accounts may not reflect their non-payment, but a failure to sell them, or the loss of the series of accounts in which their receipt was entered. The picture is generally too obscure to allow real conclusions from runs such as the Scarborough accounts, which note some mortuaries, but significantly fewer than the recorded funerals. It is unlikely that the difference can be made up by wives or children not liable to the payment.[67]

[64] Bateson, *Borough customs*, ii, pp. 210–14, esp. 210–11 (see also the London ordinance of 1382 discussed in Thomson, 'Tithe disputes', p. 3); Swanson, *Reg. Scrope* [796], i, p. 105; Drew, *Early parochial organisation* [230], pp. 15–16.

[65] Ogle, *Lollards' tower* [615], pp. 52, 54–6.

[66] Hartridge, *History of vicarages* [353], pp. 228–9; Moorman, *Church life* [591], pp. 130–1.

[67] Baildon, *Religious houses of Yorkshire*, ii, pp. 66–7; Bateson, *Borough customs*, ii, pp. 211–12, esp. 212 (mortuaries paid to the dean and chapter of Lichfield were almost all for adults, although there are occasional references to [mature?] children, e.g. LJRO, D.30/E26, E27;

Where the mortuary was merely a piece of clothing its loss, whilst a capital loss for the bereaved family, was probably not too serious in the long run. However, where an animal or something like an anvil was involved, the effects could be more significant: a piece of productive equipment had been alienated, which would probably need to be replaced, and whose loss might well be resented. Moreover, if several mortuaries were levied on the same family the cumulative burden could be considerable. Accounts of the dean and chapter of Lichfield reveal such multiple mortuaries: in 1400–1, two bullocks were received from one farm, following the deaths of husband and wife, being valued at 23s. In the same year another family lost a horse and two cows, worth 42s., after the deaths of a couple and their son. If these accounts are representative, many of the live mortuaries were repurchased by the deceased's family: husbands, widows, and sometimes sons appear buying back animals surrendered to the dean and chapter.[68] Some, however, would have been consumed by the receiving bodies, or added to flocks and herds, or sold to third parties.

Besides being a benefice, the parish was also a community of parishioners, with their own religious responsibilities. These are best reflected in the shared liability for the structure of the church, the rector being responsible for the chancel, and the parishioners for the rest, with the churchyard enclosure. By the 1350s, the effective headship of most parishes was being taken by the churchwardens, whose accounts thereafter provide most of the information about lay parochial administration. They are also evident at visitations, seeking to enforce their church's rights against those unwilling to play their part. Primarily the churchwardens' duty was to maintain the fabric of the church (or that part for which the parishioners were responsible); to that end, they administered the parochial funds and property. They usually assumed responsibility for goods bequeathed to the church – money, movables to be sold for specific building or charitable purposes, lands for chantry purposes, and (mostly in country areas) animals left to provide a long-term source of revenue. The hives of bees and odd sheep or cattle left in wills would be hired out by the churchwardens, the hirer receiving the basic produce, whilst the wardens received the rent and usually any animals bred during the lease. The wardens were

for a child's mortuary in London [but, perhaps significantly, after the Hunne case], see Brigden, 'Tithe controversy', p. 286); BL, MS Cotton Vit.E.xvi, f. 146r–v; Heath, *Parish clergy*, p. 154; PRO, E101/514/31–2 (the accounts of the proctor of Selby abbey at Whitgift in 1420–1 distinguish between cash receipts and stock receipts, showing that not all mortuaries [or tithes] were sold. Accounts which are solely cash records could misrepresent the reality: Holt, 'Two rolls', pp. 43–4, 50); Bannister, 'Visitation returns of Hereford', vol. 44, p. 284.
[68] LJRO, D.30/E26, E27, F8.

also responsible for collecting the rents of parish properties, and other rent charges due in cash or kind.[69]

Much of this administration was rather *ad hoc*, and additional to the wardens' basic duties of fund-raising for the church. Considerable income was produced by parish celebrations – the frequent church-ales, plays, and other entertainments recorded in accounts.[70] But there was more to it than that. In early sixteenth-century Westminster, rebuilding work on St Margaret's church was funded by a variety of activities, the final bell of the new peal being cast from metal collected by what can only be called a salvage drive. At Prescot (Lancs.) in 1524, the parish organized its own levy to pay for hanging the bells. Such activity suggests considerable administrative sophistication. Certainly, there are indications that church rates were being levied for parochial purposes by the late fifteenth century – and being avoided – although it is unclear how widespread such practices were.[71]

The churchwardens were often trustees of lesser religious foundations within the parish: chantries, or votive lights. By 1500 they commonly supervised the administration of endowments for such purposes, even if they did not have direct control. This oversight sometimes extended, in the case of chantries, to actually paying the priests.[72]

The financial needs of rural parishes are also reflected in other sources. In the fifteenth century, court fines in several manors were used to bolster church funds, perhaps especially for buildings, with the fines being divided between the lord and the church. The parishioners' concern for 'their' church is evident in many respects. Sometimes the incumbent became little more than a salaried official. At Ludlow, for instance, disputes over the rebuilding of the church, with the rector unwilling to spend his money on the chancel when the parishioners wanted the nave improved, were resolved by the expedient of the parish farming the benefice, and allowing the rector a stipend.[73] Additionally, there was a strong sense of cohesion,

---

[69] For flocks and rents: Wood-Legh, *Kentish visitations*, pp. 56–8, 62–3, 66, 68–9, 87–95, 103, 108–9, 122–3, 127–8, 141, 145, 147–8, 155, 166, 170–1, 175, 180–1, 184–5, 192–4, 216–17, 219–20, 229–32, 236, 239–41, 252–3, 256–7, 263–5, 275, 277, 279, 286–90; Littlehales, *London city church, passim*. For a general survey of churchwardens' accounts and their contents, Cox, *Churchwardens' accounts* [171]. For the early development of the office, Drew, *Early parochial organisation*.

[70] For the variety of receipts, Johnston, 'Parish entertainments' [445], pp. 335–7. For one parish's revenues from such sources, to 1539, Northeast, *Boxford churchwardens' accounts* [608], pp. xiii, 1, 3–4, 6, 10, 13, 16, 18–20, 22–3, 25–6, 30–2.

[71] Rosser, 'Vill of Westminster' [716], p. 103; BIHR, CP.F.150; Bailey, *Churchwardens' accounts of Prescot* [30], p. 2 (with other pre-1540 levies at pp. 12, 19, 20).

[72] E.g. Littlehales, *London city church*, pp. 82–91, the first of several such accounts in that volume.

[73] Ault, 'Manor court and parish church' [24], pp. 53–64, 67 (the system seemingly

with the parish as a unit taking legal action against those who were not making their proper contribution. It was this sense which doubtless motivated many of the presentments at visitation, trying to force parishioners to accept their financial responsibilities. Some cases involved the liability of particular lands for church rates – especially complex when the lands were held by a neighbouring incumbent, claiming that they were actually a detached portion of his own parish.[74] Other disputes reflected clashes between communities, involving contributions to the mother church by dependent chapelries. Mother churches could rarely afford the secession of their chapelries, although such attempts were common. In the late fourteenth century the parishioners of Snaith (Yorks.) acted against the inhabitants of Carlton who had purchased papal bulls to create their own chapelry which would have diverted revenues from Snaith. Those embroiled in the conflict eventually included the abbot of Selby and the future Henry IV, Carlton being in time forced to surrender. Opposition to such attempts at independence might be lessened if some form of continued financial contribution was arranged. In the 1380s the chapel of Bardfield Saling thus agreed to offer oblations at the mother church of Great Bardfield (Essex) and contribute towards its upkeep, on pain of interdict.[75]

The churchwardens' income also included a variety of fees, notably for burial in the nave and churchyard (here paralleling receipts by collegiate bodies such as the chapter of Beverley [Yorks.] for similar burials within their churches). They could also be integrated into the hierarchical structure of ecclesiastical organization, with responsibility for the collection of Peter's Pence.[76]

Above the basic parochial unit the church acted as an extracting force mainly through its jurisdictional and administrative structure. Despite the complexities of that system, there were generally two main levels of extraction: the archdeaconry and the diocese, deriving incomes from both clergy and laity. Only by distinguishing between demands made on these

operated when manor and parish were coterminous, or when a complete parish was included within a single manor); Bannister, *Reg. Spofford* [36], pp. 150–2.

[74] Wood-Legh, *Kentish visitations* (many cases were resolved shortly after presentment, the threat of action apparently forcing a solution); BIHR, CP.F.150.

[75] Timmins, *Reg. Chandler*, no. 263; Bannister, 'Visitation returns of Hereford', vol. 44, p. 446, vol. 45, pp. 448, 451–5; BL, MS Cotton.Cleo.D.iii, ff. 199r–202r (for the bulls, perhaps less destructive than Snaith's inhabitants claimed, see Bliss and Twemlow, *Calendar of papal letters, 1362–1404* [69], pp. 392, 394); McHardy, *Church in London*, no. 644.

[76] Wood-Legh, *Kentish visitations*, pp. 59, 68, 71, 124, 143–4, 151, 158, 175–6, 183, 203, 233, 236–8, 243–4, 273–5, 277–8, 286; Littlehales, *London city church*, pp. 78–366; for burials at Beverley see HCRO, DD.BC/III/33, m.3, DD.BC/III/34, pp. 25–6; Lunt, *Financial relations* [534], pp. 31–2.

groups can the system be properly explained, although the separate levels in the hierarchy also require individual consideration.

From the laity, jurisdictional intervention provided the main source of revenue. Court fees and fines brought profits, although the precise amount is generally uncertain. Few accounts give much detail, although in Wiltshire archdeaconry in the first years of the sixteenth century there are records of payments for convictions, as well as fines for contumacy during proceedings.[77] Probably contumacy fines were the more lucrative for the archdeacon, although the commutation of penances for money (and perhaps fines for recidivism not allocated to fabric and other funds) would have increased the total. But if the archdeacons profited little from precise court cases, their officials (and officials of other courts) clearly did: the frequent hostility to the ecclesiastical courts was perhaps mainly directed against the administrative rather than punitive costs, which could be quite heavy.[78] The same applied to the other main area of extraction from the laity, probate fees, with basic administrative costs going to the officials concerned. However, probate fees themselves aroused considerable resentment. There may have been something of a special interest among the wealthy operating here; for although archdeacons and bishops did charge for probate, sometimes heavily, against this there are many instances of gratuitous probate grants, or grants in return for pious acts, such as prayers for the ecclesiastical officers. Moreover – although this would be little consolation to the payer – the charges might well be diverted to pious uses, as in London, where many of the probate fees levied in the commissary court were allocated to the St Paul's fabric fund. It was probably the absence of any properly enforced scale which provoked the opposition, and the feeling that the church was creaming off wealth which should be kept within the family. Parliamentary action under Edward III and Henry V had attempted regulation, but failed or was not enforced; while the limitations imposed in provincial constitutions seem to have lapsed. Only in 1529 was the system of probate fees reformed, drastically. Henceforth, the maximum fee was set at 5s., producing a considerable drop in receipts. Previously, probate had been a major component of the incomes of ecclesiastical hierarchs – over half the income in the Wiltshire archdeaconry accounts, while payments for probate to the bishops of Lichfield were usually between £20 and £50 in the surviving accounts.[79] Other

77 PRO, E135/8/31–2.

78 For court costs, Wunderli, *London church courts* [931], pp. 54–5.

79 ibid., pp. 114–15; Elvey, *Courts of Buckingham* [254], pp. 307, 312–14; Timmins, *Reg. Chandler*, no. 71 (at p. 36); *Statutes*, i, p. 350, ii, pp. 195–6 (Henry V, suggesting 5s. maximum), iii, pp. 285–8, esp. p. 286 (Chichele's probate constitution of 1416 had also set a 5s. limit: Jacob, *Reg. Chichele* [438], iii, pp. 16–18); Bowker, *Henrician Reformation* [80], pp. 51–3; Swanson, 'Episcopal spiritualities: Lichfield' [803], p. 5; PRO, E135/8/31–2.

demands on the laity were apparently few, their main contribution being at the parish level; but fees could be levied from them for licences to hold services in private chapels, for processing dispensations, for veiling widows, and other things. There were also levies of odd shillings and pence for suffragans for consecrations of altars and dedication of church furnishings, although the evidence is meagre.[80]

The arrangements for the collection of Peter's Pence best illustrate the way in which each level of the church operated as an extracting force. England's annual payment to the papacy was fixed at slightly under £200, but at the parish level considerably more was collected. The local collectors – rural deans and churchwardens – took their cut, as above them did most archdeacons, who were primarily responsible for the levy. Where the arch-deacons passed their receipts to the bishops, they too often (but not necessarily) took a share of the proceeds.[81]

With the clergy, the evidence is stronger overall, and the signs of extortion greater. Here, the diocese was the main unit, in charges for connections between bishops and priests. Archdeacons also profited from their fellow clerics, receiving annual procurations for visitation (which were quite useful sums), payments for inductions (often 6s. 8d. a time, which might have to be split with the Official if he actually performed the ceremony), and a share (generally a third) of the synodals.[82] Some archdeacons had specific privileges, especially the semi-autonomous arch-deaconries of Chester and Richmond. In the former, much of the episcopal jurisdiction was delegated in exchange for a pension; in Richmond the archdeacon's near-episcopal authority produced an appropriate income, being supplemented by receipts of first-fruits from new incumbents within the archdeaconry – that is, the equivalent to the whole of the first year's income, according to the official taxation list.[83]

Episcopal receipts from their clerics could be extensive. Unfortunately, surviving evidence on these is scattered and incomplete. With no full study of episcopal incomes available, the profits of spiritualities are diffi-cult to assess. Virtually every stage of a cleric's career involved fees: for ordination, for institution, for licences of various sorts (non-residence, letters dimissory, licences to farm, agreements about pensions on resignation, etc.), for probate and mortuary. From the benefice, rather than individual incumbents, various sums would also be extracted. Annual synodals

[80] ECL, MS 3690, f. 16v; Bailey, *Churchwardens' accounts of Prescot*, pp. 2–3; Littlehales, *London city church*, pp. 198, 277; Cox, *Churchwardens' accounts*, pp. 92, 124–7; CRO, DRC/2/16; LAO, Bps Rentals 1, f. 11v, Bps Accts.7, ff. 10v–11r.
[81] Lunt, *Financial relations*, pp. 1–5, 27–38, 717; Swanson, 'Episcopal spiritualities: Lich-field', pp. 3–4.
[82] ibid., at n. 13; CRO, DRC/2/7.
[83] Heath, 'Archdeaconry and bishopric' [370], pp. 245–50; *Statutes*, iii, p. 495.

would be due, forming the basis of regular repetitive income from the clergy. There would also be income from visitation procurations, providing major windfalls every three years. The least regular extraction was of subsidies, which in the dioceses were probably mainly intended to cover the bishop's costs on promotion to his see; but when levied on the province, for archiepiscopal benefit, could be put to other uses.[84]

Beyond these sums, the bishop's position allowed him to intervene in lower jurisdictions. Visitation interrupted the archdeacon's powers, which temporarily lapsed to the bishop. Archidiaconal authority, and revenues, also reverted ot the bishop during a vacancy of the archdeaconry: Barnstaple thus provided a bonus of £32 to the bishop of Exeter in 1531–2.[85] Devolution also applied to parochial vacancies, the diocesan having nominal responsibility for the cure between incumbents (usually being represented in the locality by sequestrators). Usually these parochial vacancies brought in little, if anything, although much depended on their length and timing. If a prolonged vacancy occurred, allowing the bishop to receive grain tithes, it could produce a considerable profit.[86] A bishop's spiritual income also included the annual pensions received from certain appropriated churches – which formed one of the mainstays of regular income – and receipts from the bishop's own appropriated rectories, most bishops having one or two of these.[87]

Because the episcopal financial administrative systems are obscure, and surviving accounts so incomplete, it is extremely difficult to assess the bishops' receipts from spiritualities with any certainty. The *Valor ecclesiasticus* of 1535 provides the only raw figures, of doubtful value. The figure given for spirituality profits at Exeter appears roughly correct, insofar as it can be compared with diocesan material; but similar analysis of the recorded sum for the bishopric of Lichfield suggests that it is quite untrustworthy – receipts were probably averaging around £300 a year rather than the £180-odd stated by the *Valor*. As ever, actual receipts depended on individual circumstances and local peculiarities, such as Exeter's supplement for tin tithes from the Duchy of Cornwall. One of the richest dioceses in terms of spiritualities must have been Norwich, whose bishop

[84] Harper-Bill, 'Archbishop Morton and Canterbury' [348], p. 15 n. 77; LAO, Bps Accts.5, Bps Accts.6, ff. 6r–v, 8r, 9r–v, Bps Accts.7, ff. 5v–8r, 9r, 10v–11r, 14r–15v, 19r–20r, 21v–22r, 23r–v, 25r–26r, 28r–v, 29v–30r, 31v, Bps Rentals 1, ff. 6v–8v, 9v, REV. L/1/3, ff. 19r, 24r, 25r–v; Swanson, 'Episcopal spiritualities: Lichfield', pp. 5–6, 14; Swanson, 'Episcopal income: Exeter', pp. 523–6; du Boulay, 'Charitable subsidies' [231], pp. 147–64; Lunt, *Financial relations*, pp. 282–92.

[85] PRO, E135/8/32, f. 3r; Swanson, 'Episcopal income: Exeter', p. 526; see also LAO, FOR.2, f. 40r–v.

[86] Swanson, 'Episcopal income: Exeter', p. 526; Swanson, 'Episcopal spiritualities: Lichfield', p. 14.

[87] *Valor*, ii, p. 289 (Exeter), iii, pp. 128–9 (Coventry and Lichfield); v, p. 273 (Carlisle).

was the only English diocesan to receive first-fruits from incumbents. Bonds for payment of these dues are meticulously recorded, but evidence for payment is scarce. What there is suggests that this source alone provided about £200 a year. Other individual idiosyncracies made their own, generally insignificant, contributions, such as the few shillings provided annually for the Bishop of Worcester from the division of the proceeds of the shrines of SS Wulfstan and Oswald in Worcester cathedral.[88]

Income from spiritualities was also received above the diocesan level, with the archbishops receiving the proceeds of vacant bishoprics, and of inhibited diocesan and lesser jurisdictions (which might include the peculiars) during visitation. Little evidence survives for the proceeds of simple provincial visitation; but vacancy jurisdiction was a useful supplement to the revenues of both archbishoprics. From the mid-fifteenth century the Canterbury archbishops exercised such vacancy rights assiduously, receiving both procurations and other profits of jurisdiction. Archbishop Morton acquired some £1,500 from this source during his pontificate, and Warham was equally assertive. Canterbury's archbishops also profited from the development of their prerogative probate jurisdiction, although this was strongly contested through to the sixteenth century. Just how much these wills provided is not clear, but vacancy visitations occasionally differentiate between the wills theoretically subject to diocesan or archiepiscopal jurisdiction, and the latter almost inevitably provide the largest fees.[89]

The papacy also benefited from the exploitation of English spiritualities. The activities of the papal collector during the fourteenth century resulted in considerable sums passing to Rome, largely through the profits of provisions. The effective abolition of such charges in the fourteenth century meant that the main payments directly extracted from the church in later years were the fees for promotions of bishops and certain heads of monastic houses. Profits of actual taxation were limited: despite papal claims to impose taxes, and attempts to levy them, none were in fact taken from the English church after the Black Death. The popes received occasional grants of subsidies, intended to compensate for the refused taxes, but these were few and far between. The papacy also received other money from England, including court fees paid in Rome, and the charges for dispensations, but these cannot be quantified. Purely voluntary spiritual pay-

---

[88] Swanson, 'Episcopal income: Exeter'; Swanson, 'Episcopal spiritualities: Lichfield'; NRO, SUN/1(a), Reg. 9–10, DCN/5/1–4; HWCRO, e.g. 009:1 BA 2636 172 92422, 92430, 92431, 92436 – although in some years nothing was received.
[89] LJRO, D.30/F8. Harper-Bill, 'Archbishop Morton and Canterbury', pp. 14–15. LPL, Reg. Warham, i, ff. 198v–9v, 209r–212v; ii, ff. 220v–221v, 231v, 235r–v, 237r, 243r–45r, 250r–251v, 253v, 254v, 268v–269r, 270r–v, 271v–272r, 275r–v, 279v–281r, 282v–283r, 285v–285ar, 289v–291v, 294r–v, 302r–307r, 310r–v, Reg. Morton, ff. 156v–157r.

ments – as for indulgences – could also produce profits for the curia (whether in fees for processing the grant, or in division of spoils with local authorities, or indeed with all the profits intended for papal projects). Again, however, the patchy nature of the evidence prevents proper quantification. No actual totals of such sums extracted by the papacy from the English church can be produced, although in the last half-century of England's acceptance of papal authority, payments destined for Rome may have reached something like £4,800 p.a., if the sums nominally due were actually paid.[90]

Before turning to purely voluntary payments, there remain some involuntary charges which went outside the generally hierarchical structure of the church. Sometimes these were payments by benefices, sometimes by parishioners, recognizing a different series of relationships from that enshrined in the diocesan structure. Payments between benefices, or to religious houses, recognized former subjection or compensated for lost rights. At Holme-next-the-sea, for instance, the rector of Hunstanton owed an annual pension of 10s., although precisely what for is not stated. Patronal rights could be bought out by grants of such pensions, the nuns of Syon being forced to accept an annual payment of 20s. from Eccleston (Lancs.) when Sir John Stanley usurped their patronage rights in the fifteenth century. Pensions were numerous, and scattered throughout the country; when concentrated in the hands of recipients, they could reach fairly high sums. When cathedrals were involved, the payments frequently reflected the appropriation of a church by a religious house, as happened with pensions assigned to bishops for similar reasons.[91]

Other recognitions of subjection were made by the parishioners to the cathedral church, as small annual payments. These – usually called Pentecostals because of their timing – were collected in most dioceses, although precise arrangements and local nomenclature varied. Originally levied on each household within the diocese, they had become fixed sums payable by the parish (via the churchwardens). Collecting arrangements varied, as did the destination of the receipts. In Worcester diocese, the archdeaconry of Gloucester apparently paid a fixed sum of £5 10s. 8d. (which went to the bishop), although the amount actually collected was larger, as the archdeacon received a share. The archdeaconry of Worcester paid £6, which went to the cathedral sacrist. At Lichfield the 'Chad farthings' were farmed out by the dean and chapter on a regular basis.

[90] Lunt and Graves, *Accounts* [535]; Lunt, *Financial relations*, pp. 57–9, 95–305, 379–80, 411–12, 415, 431–3, 436–9, 444, 457–9, 471–2, 481–4, 506–11, 517, 521, 568–72, 581–2, 584, 589–90, 598, 600, 608, 619–20, 720–840; Scarisbrick, 'Clerical taxation' [746], pp. 42–9, esp. 49.

[91] Bod., Shropshire charter 27B; Hosker, 'Stanleys of Lathom' [414], 218–19; Swanson, *Reg. Scrope*, i, no. 144.

Overall, the amounts extracted by such charges were probably not large: Ely farthings were generally £6–£9 a year, declining as time passed. Hereford accounts mention receipts of £4 3s. 3d. in Pentecostals, which were added to the sums available for division between the canons. Equivalent payments may also have been made by the benefices: the valuation of Holme-next-the-sea includes among the annual expenses a payment of 2d. to Norwich cathedral 'for the annual procession',[92] but nothing similar has been noticed in other parish accounts.

Paralleling these essentially obligatory payments was a substantial spiritual economy based on voluntary donations. By its nature this evades proper analysis. Potentially, it was an extremely wide-ranging area of activity, including donations to religious objects, charitable action during life, membership of guilds and fraternities, and pious bequests at death. If taken at its widest extent, it must have been a major economic force, involving massive amounts of cash.

Direct offerings to churches comprised the most obvious form of voluntary spiritual payment – oblations made at the great feasts, and for particular purposes, as well as bequests. Besides cash, such donations included wax and other goods, among them jewels, and are always difficult to value. In parish churches, the oblations were sometimes included in formal valuations: at Harlow, for instance, oblations in the church and at the image of St Petronilla were assessed at £5 13s. 4d. – but are impossible to check. The Scarborough accounts record the annual flow, with offerings at special masses, at lesser chapels, and on specific dates. Bequests were erratic, but the channelling of small amounts could produce a useful total. Gifts and legacies to the fabric fund of Lincoln cathedral, in cash or kind (usually jewels which were apparently sold) provided useful contributions towards expenses. In the 1520s and 1530s the totals varied between £16 and £45 a year, generally from gifts of a shilling and under.[93]

As well as contributions towards the church fabric, there was also a flow of gifts resulting from pilgrimages, revealed in accounts of shrine-keepers. Their interpretation is problematic. Many shrines suggest a decline in offerings, as at St Cuthbert at Durham, St Hugh at Lincoln, St Edward at Westminster, and St Thomas at Canterbury.[94] How far that decline was

---

[92] Owen, *Church and society* [624], pp. 41–2, 107; *VCH, Stafford*, iii [872], pp. 150, 158–9; Salter, *Eynsham cartulary* [728], i, pp. 424–8; EDC, 5/10/*passim*; HCA, 2450; HWCRO, 009:1 BA 2636/10 43699, 009:1 BA 2636/9 43696, ff. 159v, 160v. (see also Major, 'Finances of Lincoln' [571], p. 153; *Valor*, iii, pp. 217, 226); Bod., Shropshire charter 27B.

[93] CUL, MS Add. 6847, f. 78v; PRO, E101/514/31–2; LAO, Bj1/4, Bj5/19; see also, e.g., EDC, 5/11/6–7 Henry VII (½ oz jet sold for 6d.); HCRO, DD.BC/III/33 m.3 (1½ oz broken silver, sold for 2s. 6d., and other bits of metal unsold). HCA, R585, f. 22r (bequeathed bullock sold).

[94] Harvey, *Westminster abbey*, pp. 44–5; Venables, 'Shrine of St Hugh' [864], pp. 142–50;

real is uncertain. Surviving shrine accounts are few, and generally exclude offerings in kind, for which evidence is limited. Two Durham lists of such donations from the turn of the fourteenth and fifteenth centuries show that their value could be considerable: one list totals £689 12s. 5d., spread over about four years, and including a golden statue of the Virgin with the arms of Durham, given by Sir William de Scrope, and valued at £500. Some of these gifts may have been sold, or used within the church for other purposes. In 1438–9 the Durham shrine-keeper received 50s. 10d. from the sale of belts and beads, presumably gifts to the shrine.[95] Changes in recorded totals of cash gifts may also reflect changes in accounting practice. If the Westminster figures reflect reality, then the shrine of Edward the Confessor at the start of the sixteenth century received absolutely no offerings at all in some years, which is unbelievable. Perhaps the administration had suffered some of the vicissitudes experienced by St Thomas Cantilupe's shrine at Hereford. The accounts in which that shrine's revenue 'should' have been entered show a total evaporation of the flow of donations by the 1450s. But this is a mirage: the funds had been transferred to different accounts, and the shrine continued to produce healthy sums through to the Reformation. Indeed, the first figures suggest that the stated income in the late fourteenth century is an under-assessment. Only after 1512 is there much suggestion of a real decline in donations to Cantilupe.[96] Ely evidence for gifts to St Etheldreda supports the Hereford suggestion that, in fact, there was little overall decline in donations. The extant shrine accounts regularly record amounts received, sometimes permitting assessment of cash flow during the year. In such cases, donations were made at the major feasts of the saint, especially at the fair held during the period of indulgence in summer, the approach to which showed an increase in donations. But these accounts may not reflect the full picture; for obscure sums entered in the sacrists' accounts suggest that the shrine produced further income. Sums over £80 are mentioned before 1420, with later years recording transfers of £30–£40 from the shrine-keeper, but without any detailed attribution.[97]

Raine, *St Cuthbert* [685], pp. 115–20; Fowler, *Account rolls of Durham*, ii, pp. 420–5, 440–83; Woodruff, 'Cult of St Thomas of Canterbury' [923], pp. 20–5.

[95] Fowler, *Account rolls of Durham*, ii, pp. 444–5, 450–4 (my total for gifts deducts £3,335 13s. 4d. for the great emerald and five rings previously held by the shrine-keeper and placed on the shrine during these years), 470; Dobson, *Durham priory*, pp. 29–30; Raine, *St Cuthbert*, pp. 149–50, 157, appendix p. 10; Woodruff, 'Cult of St Thomas of Canterbury' p. 21 n. 2.

[96] WAM, 19768, 19776; Morgan, 'St Thomas Cantilupe' [599], p. 152; HCA, R369, R585, ff. 1r, 5r, 8v, 11r, 14r, 22r, R586.

[97] EDC, 5/11/*passim* (the accounts vary in format, and sometimes appear not to include the receipts for the period of indulgence in the summer), 5/10/*passim* (the largest sums noted are in 5/10/20, 26, 30).

It was not just saints' shrines which produced gifts. The Ely sacrists' accounts well illustrate the multiplicity of offerings which flowed into their hands. In 1477–8, for example, receipts from the feretrum of St Etheldreda amounted to £39 9s. 4d. Ely farthings (Pentecostals) totalled £6 10s. Offerings at the cross in Holy Trinity church came to £12 19s. 8d., with a further £8 4s. 7d. from offerings at the altar of the cross in St Mary's church. Lesser sources of oblations were the Black Cross and image of the Saviour (12s.), the chapel of the bishop and prior (with small tithes, worth 16s. 8d.), oblations on Good Friday (4d.), oblations at Chettisham chapel (Cambs.) (26s. 8d.), and offerings at the image of St Mary at the door of St Mary's church (2d.). Adding wax sold at the feast of the Purification (32s.) gives a sum of £71 11s. 5d., out of the year's total income of £272 17s. 7d. Of course, donations could change. In the sixteenth century, gifts appear for Bishop Alcock's chapel – 118s. 1d. being mentioned in 1509–10, and £4 7s. 2½d. in 1516–17 – with odd shillings from the oblations of local guilds. At the same time, some sources of income declined: offerings at the Black Cross and image of the Saviour in those years were respectively 2s. 5d. and 16d., while income from Chettisham was only 10s. 7d. in 1509–10, and 7s. 9½d. in 1516–17.[98]

Beyond payments 'to the church', there were many other areas of contribution. Some of these were to 'lay' organizations, such as guilds and fraternities, although the precise degree of spirituality in such payments is sometimes questionable. But insofar as they produced spiritual benefits, they can be considered part of the spiritual economy, even more so when they offered indulgences. This would have applied to many enrolled in guilds such as that of Knowle (Warw.); few can have been active members, but all received the benefits.[99] Other indulgences and sharing in prayers had a financial aspect. Many of the letters of indulgence and confraternity which survive from the period, and which were obviously mass-produced even before the spread of printing, must have been sold; although at what price is generally unknown. The surviving documents often concern mendicant orders, with others for specific institutions such as Wybunbury hospital (Ches.), or ventures like the anti-Turkish crusades; but none of these leave any accounts. There are, nevertheless, some hints of the price of indulgences. That for Compostela in 1498 was seemingly available for less than 3d. a time; with others apparently dispensed according to a sliding-scale of charges varying with the wealth of the purchaser. Besides all these, there were contributions to the maintenance of English churches, towards the relief of individuals suffering from misfortune, or contributions towards public works; but again there is insufficient evidence of receipts to permit analysis. Where the collection of indulgences was farmed out, as

[98] EDC, 5/10/35, 43–4.
[99] See chapter 6/3 below, at nn. 69–77.

happened with contributions towards the fabric of Beverley Minster, then the reality of donations is completely hidden.[100] Much would have depended on loyalty and immediacy: the collections for the relief of Constantinople in 1399 seem to have struck a chord, with recorded receipts from Lincoln diocese totalling £315 11s. 10d., deposited in chests in various towns in the diocese.[101] The considerable scale of the indulgence trade is shown by the experience of St Anthony's hospital, London. That house had an annual income approaching £550. Of this over £500 was provided by sums paid by farmers of the questorships of the house throughout the country – the equivalent of some 30,000 offerings a year if the rate was 4d. per donation (and without allowing for costs and the questors' profits).[102]

The final category of these spiritual payments includes all the voluntary donations made at death. These are too individual to summarize, and too massive to quantify. With their donations to religious orders, arrangements for chantries, contributions towards almshouses and parish churches, and all the other bequests which had a spiritual aim by requiring the recipients to pray for the donor's soul, they involved a massive and constant redistribution of wealth, if they were actually implemented.

The extent to which the church's spiritual functions and jurisdictional structure made it a wealth-generating institution is too easily overlooked. But it would probably not be far wrong to put the value of the spiritual economy as almost equivalent to the church's landed wealth. However, the spiritual economy was not wholly a 'church' economy: it expanded into areas controlled by the laity, and was dependent as much on voluntary donations as formal extraction. So much money, so regular a redistribution of wealth (especially as a result of testamentary dispositions) would have far-reaching consequences for the economy as a whole. The extent of the spiritual economy may be hard to elucidate, but its existence and impact cannot be ignored.

5.4   THE CHURCH IN THE MARKET

As landowner, as purchaser, as employer and consumer, the church was closely involved in commercial activity. Whatever it wished its relation-

---

[100] Bod., Cheshire charter 11; PRO, C270/32/4, 10, 12–18, 32; SRO, D593/A/1/32/9, 13, D593/A/1/33/2–3; Lunt, *Financial relations*, pp. 494, 502, 586, 602–4; Cox, *Churchwardens' accounts*, pp. 19, 30–1; HCRO, DD.BC/III/33, m.3.

[101] Lunt, *Financial relations*, pp. 556–7.

[102] Windsor, XV.37.4, 15, 25 f. 2v, 27 f. 1r–v, 29–30, 33 f. 2v, 39. For payments for licences, etc., see e.g. CRO, DRC.2/11/1, 2/12, 2/13; 4d. is the usual payment to pardoners and questors in the Willoughby family account books of the early sixteenth century: *Manuscripts of Lord Middleton* [402], pp. 327, 338, 342 (8d.), 348, 354, 359, 365–9, 385.

ship with the world to be, entanglement was unavoidable. Yet to illustrate ecclesiastical involvement in the market beyond a mere listing of activities presents difficulties. Gradations of scale also intervene, forcing qualification of generalizations – the economic impact of a major institution like Westminster abbey would differ from that of the small and shadowy hospital of St Thomas at Birmingham (War.), or an individual chantry priest. Discussion of ecclesiastical economic activity normally focuses on relatively large institutions as producers, although all institutions and individuals require consideration as consumers. As a consumer the church made specific demands for its specific functions, besides requiring basic provisions for its officials. The impact of ecclesiastics in the market-place also raises the question of clerical money-lending; while there is finally the vexing issue of the importance of leasing and sale of tithes in commerce, especially as they affected the laity.

The church's commercial impact as producer remains largely uncharted. The main impetus was clearly rural – it is hard to envisage urban clerics as having much importance. Urban clerics cannot be dismissed as mere drones, for they doubtless had numerous petty occupations, some making them scarcely distinguishable from their lay neighbours; but they were rarely specifically producers, or perhaps more explicitly, sellers, unless they had rural resources. Rural clerics with their glebe and tithes, and major landed institutions, could sell. They could dispose of their own produce – their only viable option if the estates were scattered and distant from the centre – and they would also have their concentrated tithe collections available for the market. However, their clerical status did militate against too active a marketing role. Commercial activity might be necessary, but profiteering was discouraged. The Hereford visitation returns of 1397 include odd complaints against clerics acting as dealers, buying and selling for profit. Similarly, *c.*1502, the merchants of York protested to the abbot of Fountains about his 'beying and sellyng lede and other marchandise as a fre marchaunt, contrary to Goddes lawis and mans', threatening to complain to the Archbishop of York. On occasion bishops also acted against over-enthusiastic marketing of tithes.[103]

The overall scale of marketing by religious institutions cannot be assessed. Nor is it clear whether, and to what extent, there was conscious exploitation of opportunities for specialization. Marketing seems, essentially, to reflect sales of surpluses. Most landed establishments seemingly aimed at some degree of self-sufficiency, so that regardless of changes on distant estates, for those closer to the centre only the surplus would be sold. Ely

---

[103] Bannister, 'Visitation returns of Hereford', vol. 44, p. 446, vol. 45, pp. 99, 447, 452; Sellars, *York mercers* [754], pp. 110–11; CUL, MS Add. 7802, f. 19r.

was probably typical: there, much of the tithe and demesne produce received by the sacrist was consumed within the priory. If an appropriated rectory was close to the possessing house, its glebe could presumably also be used in a similar way.[104] Bishops also continued to draw on stocks if possible, although such opportunities were reduced by their relatively peripatetic existence, and more of their estates were used for other purposes. Still, Henry Wakefield of Worcester used manorial produce during his diocesan travels, and the household book of John Hales, Bishop of Lichfield, in 1461 records the consumption of animals raised on the estates, even if most other supplies were bought in. A successor even had fish sent to him at London from his Lichfield ponds.[105]

The desire for continued self-sufficiency might persist even after estates were leased out. Westminster abbey thus retained some payments in kind throughout the fifteenth century, which may have increased in the sixteenth as prices began to rise. Such far-sightedness was not confined to the capital: several other houses insisted on some payments in kind throughout the period. The practice extended beyond the monasteries; occasional leases by the dean and chapter of Hereford cathedral show them letting estates for grain rents. A rather more complex relationship appears in a lease of Farnborough rectory by Lilleshall abbey in the reign of Henry VI. A cash rent was payable to the abbey; but the farmer had to supply grain of various types to the vicar, as part of his stipend.[106]

When selling was an option, there was no lack of opportunities. Tithe income incurred no production costs for the recipient, although collection might be expensive. Concurrently, tithe permitted economies of scale. Large accumulations would be sold, whose bulk would be attractive to a purchaser looking for one major transaction rather than several lesser deals. Even if amounts of tithe grain dropped after the Black Death, an abundance of other produce was available. Scale is illustrated by one year in the 1480s, when the dean and chapter of Lichfield received 3,565 tithe fleeces from their jurisdiction in the Peak District, although their destination is unknown.[107] Demesne production may also have offered cost advantages for clerics in the first decades after 1349, although the impact could go the other way: if they needed hired labour, its absence could bring ruin, as the Bishop of Lichfield acknowledged when visiting

---

[104] EDC, 5/10/passim; Harvey, Westminster abbey, pp. 136–7, 139–40, 146–7; Hare, 'Monks as landlords', pp. 86–7; PRO, E101/517/27, ff. 1r, 2v, 3v, 4r, 5r, 6r–v, 10r.

[105] Dyer, Lords and peasants, pp. 133–4, 146–7; BRL, 435125, m.1d; SRO, D.1734/3/3/264; Heal, Of prelates and princes, p. 32.

[106] Harvey, Westminster abbey, pp. 156–7, 160; Hare, 'Monks as landlords', p. 89; Finberg, Tavistock abbey, p. 241; Youings, 'The church', pp. 321–2; HCA, 1882, 2512, 2513, 3167; SRO, D593/A/1/9/15.

[107] LJRO, D.30/II, ff. 46r–51v, 54r–55v.

Shrewsbury abbey in 1354 – the decayed state of buildings was not the monks' fault, but due to the 'bad state of the times and shortage of labourers'.[108] However, enforcement of feudal obligations could reduce production costs, if inefficiency was checked.

Even when the leasing of estates excluded demesne production from the equations, the religious institutions could still engage in profitable agricultural activity: they might lease their arable, but retain the pasture, maintaining extensive interests in sheep-farming, and thus in wool production. Such practices tended to have a regional character, the main phase of direct interest ending in the mid-fifteenth century as the flocks were also leased out. Such generalization has to allow exceptions, and some institutions (Battle abbey for one) were developing an innovative and efficient agricultural interest during the period, using techniques of 'convertible husbandry'.[109]

Economies of scale generally gave the larger houses and producers an edge over their competitors. With their own farm production and tithe receipts, they would not need to sell surpluses immediately, but could store them to exploit the market. Occasionally, monastic houses even tried to corner the market – Durham priory claimed right of first purchase of its tenants' harvest surpluses, which would further have strengthened its market position.[110]

Sales were not limited to grain and tithe produce. Mortuaries might also be sold, while various industrial raw materials were by-products of domestic consumption, again providing economies of scale for the purchasers. Thus, the kitchener of Selby abbey in 1416–17 sold all his hides to one tanner (ninety-four pieces), all the wool-fells, pells, and lambskins to another individual, all the tallow to one chandler, and all the intestines to someone else – presumably to make sausage skins.[111]

Beyond production, the church had an obvious impact as consumer. All clerics and their households needed food, their dietary requirements matching those of the laity of similar social standing. Bishops would equate to magnates, while the chantry household at Bridport (Dorset) was equivalent to a 'middle-class' fmaily, although possibly distorted by the priests' frequent hospitality.[112] In several areas the church's specific demands also had an effect. The maintenance of the fabric, and the continuation of the services, provided their own imperatives. In parish accounts, the incumbent appears purchasing bread and wine for the services, and the oil

---

[108] LJRO, B/A/1/3, f. 135r.

[109] Hare, 'Monks as landlords', pp. 85–6, 90; Bolton, *Medieval English economy*, pp. 243–5.

[110] Dyer, *Lords and peasants*, pp. 133–4; Halcrow, 'Decline of demesne farming', p. 352; Lomas, 'South-east Durham', pp. 320–1; LJRO, D.30/E26, E27.

[111] Haslop, 'Selby kitchener's roll' [363], p. 124; see also PRO, E101/517/27, f. 10v.

[112] Dyer, 'English diet', pp. 191–5; Wood-Legh, *A small household* [920].

needed for liturgical use. More significant were the constant, and extensive, building works, whether on cathedrals such as York Minster, on parish churches like Lavenham (the monument to cloth-making prosperity in East Anglia), or on chantries like the Beauchamp chapel at Warwick. On these their designers and supporters lavished money and materials – the luxurious Beauchamp chapel cost over £3,000 in building alone. Important as new building was, the constant struggle to repair extant buildings was probably more significant, both in the quantity of work done, and the amount of employment generated. It was the small works, like the repair of Wybunbury chancel in 1484–5 for a mere £9, and the other repairs frequently enjoined (even if not always implemented) in visitation records, which would have kept the building craftsmen of the period in business. Those craftsmen would also be needed to maintain parsonage houses and associated outbuildings, and the properties with which chantries and other foundations were endowed, which might be the responsibility of trustees, churchwardens, chaplains, or guilds.[113]

Nor was it simply a matter of keeping the walls and timbers in repair. Other craftsmen would help to maintain and beautify the church. Metal-workers would lead the roofs, make bells, and provide a wide range of ornaments, as well as mundane keys and other utensils. Glass would be required for the windows, often donated by parishioners, and frequently stained. Other ornamentation included sculpture and painting – including the 'Nottingham' alabasters which were a major industry in the period, serving the English ecclesiastical and funerary market, being sold to satisfy the demands of lay piety, and enjoying a strong export market.[114] For the services themselves books, vestments and ornaments would be needed, all potentially costly. A well-bound service book could cost over £10 (although prices dropped dramatically with the invention of printing), and plate had an obvious intrinsic value. Vestments could also be expensive – with what they lacked in quality being compensated for in quantity: the Holme chantry in St Mary Castlegate, York, possessed twenty sets of vestments in 1428, worth over £27.[115]

[113] Hicks, 'Beauchamp trust' [383], p. 140; PRO, SC6/Henry VII/1846, m.13d; Wood-Legh, *Kentish visitations*, pp. 56–292; Wood-Legh, *A small household*, pp. 14–15, 18–21, 29–32, 36–41, 44–5, 51–5, 62–5, 72–8, 80; Littlehales, *London city church*, 61–338.

[114] Cheetham, *English medieval alabasters* [136]; Gardner, *Alabaster tombs* [291]. The funerary business included work in other materials, see Blair, 'Henry Lakenham' [62] and refs. Yarmouth customs accounts indicate a country-wide trade in gravestones, recording various payments, usually for individual stones but rising to the 23 imported by John Berde and Peter Prevet of Corfe (a suggestive origin) in 1452/3 (NRO, 159/12/11; see also 152/30/16, 153/29/10, 153/34/10, 154/24/12, 155/10/2, 159/5/18, 159/13/7, 159/14/14, 162/25/18, 163/16/14 – I owe these references to Mr Terry Adams).

[115] Swanson, 'Thomas Holme' [797], pp. 5–6; Cox, *Churchwardens' accounts*, pp. 106–11, 128–33, 138–42.

YORK MINSTER WINDOW   Piety and the spiritual economy: hoping for (or acknowledging) a miracle, a pilgrim offers a wax model of a leg as a votive at the shrine of St William of York. Similar wax models – perhaps mass produced in York itself for sale to pilgrims – hang before the shrine.
(Reproduced by kind permission of the Dean and Chapter of York)

One consistent demand was for wax, used in abundance. Clerics bought it principally for candles, as did the laity when offering at funerals, marriages, and suchlike. It was also used for votive purposes at shrines, usually as candles or tapers, but also as representations of afflicted parts of the body, or other models. The laity could bring their own wax; but might well buy it at the church, as evidenced by the Ely accounts. Indeed, those accounts suggest that wax was regularly recycled: the shrine-keeper's accounts include entries for '*relucro cirici*' which suggest that old offerings were regularly removed for melting and resale within the church, or disposed of in some other way. Westminster abbey also reveals recycling, with partially consumed candles being melted down and reformed. The scale of the demand for wax within one church is shown by one statement for Westminster: if it can be believed some 4,500 lb of wax were consumed within one year, for only some of the services.[116] While most wax was presumably obtained locally, some had to be bought further afield. Ely accounts mention purchases from London, and wax from Lubeck and (probably) Danzig which was presumably purchased locally from the importers. Canterbury accounts similarly refer to imported wax, purchased via London. Candle-making for the church could provide profitable employment: one female chandler at Westminster apparently maintained a fairly lucrative business supplying the abbey in the early sixteenth century.[117]

To quantify the scale of ecclesiastical involvement in the market economy is clearly impossible; but it must have been considerable. The church and its activities were an ever-present part of economic life, rarely in the foreground, but never absent. In two particular areas ecclesiastical involvement was perhaps highly significant. The church's structure channelled considerable sums of money into the hands of ecclesiastics, which was not immediately spent. These accumulated funds would include specifically ecclesiastical revenues, and surpluses available for investment from a variety of other sources. That cash was often used in the credit system. The second area of influence derived from estate administration. Its extensive lands necessarily involved the church in the property market, not selling, but leasing. The impact of the leasing of ecclesiastical lands and tithes on the general economy was potentially revolutionary.

The credit economy in medieval England still requires detailed investigation. It is clear that, by at least the early fourteenth century, a well-developed credit system was in operation, reflected in royal provisions for bonds by statute (such as the Statute of Acton Burnell of 1283), and in debt litigation in manorial and other courts.[118] The church's theoretical attitude was clear-cut; lending was quite legitimate, provided it was done charitably rather than for profit. Reality may have been different, although proving it is difficult. There is plentiful evidence of clerics advancing credit in the later middle ages. In early fourteenth-century York, clerics from incumbents to proctors in church courts acted in numerous credit transactions. Later, clerks in the royal administration appear as moneylenders (although how far they were 'churchmen' may be questionable); and in the early sixteenth century the dean and chapter of Exeter were

---

[116] EDC, 5/10/*passim*, 5/11/*passim* (see also Wilson, *Accounts of Worcester* [915], p. 37; the sacrist in 1521–2 accounted for £49 9s. 11d. as profits of wax offered at the image of St Mary; against cash oblations of £11 7s. 2d.); Finucane, *Miracles and pilgrims* [273], pp. 95–7; Malden, *Canonization of Osmund* [572], p. 78; Radford, 'Wax images' [683], pp. 164, 166–7 and plates; WAM, 19819.

[117] EDC, 5/10/18, 35, 44; Cant., Accounts of the priory feretrarius; WAM, 23001.

[118] Postan, 'Credit' [668]. For local debt jurisdiction, e.g. Clark, 'Debt litigation' [146].

advancing loans from their fabric fund. Bishops were perhaps the greatest lenders of all, with evidence of activity in all centuries: William Melton at York and Walter Langton at Lichfield in the fourteenth; Henry Beaufort of Winchester in the fifteenth; and Hugh Oldham at Exeter in the sixteenth, to name but a few instances. Religious houses were also involved in the credit system – even mendicants participated, as is shown by a case involving a Dartford house in 1363. Such lending may have been justified at times by some moral imperative, as a lender of last resort out of charity, or as part of the responsibility for parishioners of appropriated parishes, but this would not account for every case by any means.[119]

These individuals and institutions were clearly lending surplus wealth; but the precise purpose and terms are often obscure. The money could be for investment in business enterprises, with profit in mind, as well as pure loans. The dean and chapter of Hereford made at least one loan specifically for trading purposes, with provisions to account for any profits. However, nothing is recorded of the reasons for or terms of the loans made by Hugh Oldham. Some loans were clearly made at interest: Robert de Ripplingham, Chancellor of York, expected a profit of 50 per cent over three years from a loan to Bolton priory in 1317 (although he does not appear to have received it); and several other loans made by him probably carried similar terms. The hostility incurred by Walter Langton a few years earlier owed something to his ruthless exploitation of money-lending to extend his lands. Later bishops also gained from their loans in various ways, like the rents and corrody received in the 1440s and 1450s by John Delabere of St David's in return for loans to Peterborough abbey. There are also instances of clerics being charged with usury.[120]

One aspect of the credit economy, loans to central government, poses particular problems. These may not have been at interest, being offered out of loyalty (or compulsion). Perhaps profit came as political favours, but actual payment of interest appears scarce. Thus, Henry Beaufort, Bishop of Winchester, made numerous large loans to the Lancastrian government, which made him one of its major supporters. That he received no interest seems incredible, but there is no evidence for it, and some

[119] YML, M2/1a; ECL, MS 3551, ff. 34v–35r, 44v, 50v, 61r, 94v; Pugh, 'Mediaeval moneylenders' [673], pp. 274–83, 288–9; Butler, 'Archbishop Melton' [112], pp. 55–63; Beardwood, *Trial of Walter Langton* [51], pp. 26–31; Heal, *Of prelates and princes*, pp. 69–70; Raban, *Mortmain legislation*, p. 117 n. 43 (see also p. 119); Bod., MS Tanner 165, f. 101r (for Beaufort's government loans, below, n. 121); for Oldham, see n. 120; Postan, 'Credit', p. 79; Madox, *Formulare Anglicanum* [570], p. 362; Rubin, *Charity and community*, pp. 223–5.

[120] HCA, 2623; ECL, MS 3690, ff. 44r, 45v–46r, 50r (see also Heal, *Of prelates and princes*, pp. 69–70); Kershaw, *Bolton priory* [468], pp. 174–5, 191–2; Beardwood, *Trial of Walter Langton*, pp. 14–17, 29–31; Thompson, 'Corrody from Leicester abbey' [820], pp. 122–5; Bannister, 'Visitation returns of Hereford', vol. 44, p. 285; vol. 45, p. 447; see also Butler, 'Archbishop Melton', pp. 57–62.

indicating that he did not. For him, the political advantages may have outweighed possible financial losses.[121]

The clerical contribution to the credit economy, even if not at interest, was considerable; easing the circulation of wealth in a society where money, although not actually scarce, was not abundant. The great hand-overs of cash at the quarter- and term-days of the year must have seen the rapid settlement of a whole series of transactions at one go, with relatively little bullion. The role of clerics in this cannot be measured precisely, but the role itself cannot be overlooked.

Mirroring their lending, clerics were also borrowers, or users of credit. None were more inveterate debtors than the religious houses, although much of this debt was short term, and usually manageable: debts might mount, but could usually be cleared fairly rapidly.[122] As borrowers the ecclesiastics could receive from laity as well as clergy, and might pay interest to either. Frequently, but not exclusively, clerics borrowed from each other.[123] Besides living on credit many religious houses gambled with it by playing the system of corrodies – annuities in kind (usually bread, ale, and robes, sometimes with accommodation). There is here some over-lap with monastic charity, and also scope for confusion, as corrodies were also granted to officers and servants. But ignoring the purely charitable or service nature of such grants, and the corrodies granted at royal nomination which were no more than imposed pensions, others were intended to serve the immediate financial needs of the house. Sometimes they reciprocated donations, such as that granted in 1397 in return for a gift of property to St Oswald's priory, Gloucester. Often they were expedients, attempts to keep the house afloat, as perhaps applied to the grant made by Peter-borough abbey to the Bishop of St David's in 1456, which could have been a mortgage for a loan. How general this abuse was is hard to judge, although episcopal visitation injunctions repeatedly sought to prevent sales of corrodies which imposed intolerable burdens on monastic finances. The corrodies granted at the Carmelite friary at Bishop's Lynn (Norfolk), recorded between 1367 and 1407, may well have drained resources; while at Selby so many were said to have been sold under Abbot John Sherburn that the finances were completely undermined. The impact (and attrac-tion) of corrodies is perhaps best illustrated by the experience of St Leonard's hospital, York, in the 1390s. During the 1380s, the house's debts had slowly been brought under control by the combined efforts of the master and a lay warden. But then a new master, William de Botheby, was appointed, with rather different economic ideas. He removed the lay

---

[121] Harriss, 'Cardinal Beaufort' [352], pp. 129–48.

[122] E.g. Smith, *Canterbury cathedral priory*, pp. 194–7.

[123] Pugh, 'Mediaeval moneylenders', pp. 283–6; Butler, 'Archbishop Melton', pp. 56, 59, 62–3.

overseer, and embarked on a programme of blatant expediency aimed at reducing the immediate debt and raising cash for himself. Within a few years he had sold some forty corrodies, of various types, bringing in about £2,000. The capital cleared the immediate debts, but the resulting annuities imposed a long-term burden. Annuities were worth while if their recipient died quickly, letting the house profit; but a long-lived annuitant was expensive. When royal commissioners investigated the finances of St Leonard's in 1399, the corrodies which were meant to solve the problem had merely compounded it: the hospital's official inmates were being starved to pay the allowances, which had in fact increased the overall debt, and considerably worsened the annual budget.[124]

The use of corrodies for credit persisted throughout the middle ages. Religious houses, whatever their determination, were constantly in debt. Stringency could rapidly improve the finances (and when Ixworth priory used much of the profit from Downham church to buy further treasures, there was clearly scope for economies in some houses),[125] but the general approach was on the whole incompetent, so that however soon cleared, debts would almost inevitably reappear.

If corrodies reflect exploitation of resources for immediate ends, so too do many of the leases entered into by ecclesiastical bodies and individuals. Here, three different classes of property are involved: manors, tithes, and appropriated rectories wich involved both land and incidental revenues – glebe and tithes. All might be leased out, in parcels or as a block. With the general drift from demesne farming, the leasing of manors was obviously advantageous, especially for distant estates. Even close to, the administrative complexities of direct management sometimes meant that corporations customarily leased their estates – several of the secular cathedral chapters by 1349 allowed the residentiaries first refusal of leases of capitular estates. How far they actively farmed them, or in turn sublet (on presumably precarious leases, dependent on the life of the prebendary) is unknown. The Black Death, however, significantly affected leasing practices at all levels. At Lincoln, for example, its immediate effect was a reluctance by the residentiaries to take on farms at the old rates, and new rentals had to be prepared.[126] Elsewhere declining values – of manorial rents, or tithe

---

[124] Thompson, 'Corrody from Leicester abbey', pp. 116–25; Williams, 'Tudor Cistercian life' [911], pp. 77–91, 285–94, 301–9; Swanson, *Reg. Scrope*, i, no. 652; Thompson, *Visitations of religious houses* [817], ii, index (at p. 490) under 'corrodies, injunctions regarding'; Little, 'Corrodies at Lynn' [517], pp. 9–14, 17–26; Haslop, 'Selby kitchener's roll', p. 120 n. 3; PRO, C270/20.

[125] PRO, E101/517/27, ff. 1r–4r: the end of each account gives the profit, and then what it was spent on – vestments, plate, etc.

[126] Major, 'Finances of Lincoln', p. 160.

income – would have affected the policies of individual institutions. Indeed, the general reduction in tithes would have significantly reduced the value of many benefices, especially if outgoings remained static. Holme-next-the-sea, for example, had been valued at £40 in 1291. By 1401 it was worth only £26 10s., with outgoings to maintain the services and various fees totalling roughly £5 10s. Further deductions for royal tenths and first-fruits of a new incumbency would reduce the true value to the incumbent even more. After the appropriation to Lilleshall abbey, the value continued to fall: in 1535 the vicarage was assessed at £7 2s. 11½d., while the rectory's farm (obviously not the full value of its product) was only £8 a year. Deductions had hardly changed, apart possibly from the payments to the crown. Holme's story is mirrored elsewhere, with tithe revenues declining in response to the Black Death; and little sign of any recovery before the Reformation.[127]

The clergy had an important role as farmers, especially of benefices, until their activity was savagely curtailed by law in 1529. Prebendaries sometimes leased their prebends to residentiaries, and lower down, instances of parish clergy leasing demesnes and tithes (thereby sometimes augmenting their stipends or vicarages) are not uncommon. It was perhaps normal for a vicar or parish chaplain to act as farmer for the religious house which had appropriated his church, or for a temporarily absent incumbent. Like the laity the clergy undertook such farms for profit, some of them farming several benefices concurrently. That considerable profits were possible is suggested by the case of a cleric who actually paid his rent two years in advance. Theoretically, such leasing out of benefices required episcopal licence, but this was not always obtained.[128]

Clerical farming activities were not confined to church property. As elsewhere, the clergy as a class and the church as an institution cannot be rigidly distinguished from their surroundings. Just as clerics owned non-ecclesiastical lands, so they might also lease lay properties, acting like other lessees on the make. If the identification is correct, a fifteenth-century rector of Rushall (Wilts.) built up a considerable leasehold estate centred on his rectory, consisting mainly of Duchy of Lancaster demesnes in whose administration he had earlier been involved.[129]

The relationship between the ecclesiastical landlords and their lessees was always complex, but no more than any similar contemporary relation-

---

[127] *Taxatio* [813], p. 89; Bod., Shropshire charter, 27B; *Valor*, iii, pp. 197, 375; Dyer, *Lords and peasants*, p. 250; Dobson, *Durham priory*, p. 271.

[128] Harvey, *Westminster abbey*, p. 153 and nn. 1, 3; LJREO, D.30/E33, E34; ECL, MS 3551, ff. 1v–2v, 4r, 31v, 68v; BL, MS Harley 2179, f. 105r; Wood-Legh, *Kentish visitations*, pp. 103, 146, 154; Bannister, 'Visitation returns of Hereford', vol. 44, pp. 287–8, vol. 45, pp. 94, 98, 449, 461; SRO, D593/A/1/12/15–18.

[129] Hare, 'Demesne lessees' [344], pp. 8–9.

ship. The only specifically 'ecclesiastical' element in the equations might be the concept of mortmain, which could have given greater stability to the arrangements. The relationships were both social and economic – the leasing policy might be adopted for economic reasons, but the choice of tenants could reflect other considerations. On episcopal estates, family patronage played a part, nepotistic concern to establish a territorial base, as with the kin-grouping around Archbishop Warham at Canterbury. On monastic estates, similar considerations might also apply. Reward for loyal service could also be involved; indeed then the lease might provide recognition of some sort of dependence by the lessor on the lessee. The continuity of local administration and receipts from non-demesne properties were intertwined with continuity among the demesne lessees. Some lay administrators (especially in the fifteenth century when gentry families perhaps became more conspicious) sought to exploit their position by obtaining leases at cut rates or for extended terms, to establish a local power base which could be virtually independent of the central estate administration.[130]

Not all lessees aimed to plant themselves and their families in perpetuity. Church land could also be integrated into the normal ebb and flow of peasant landholding, the size of holding reflecting the tenant's life cycle: small beginnings, expansion in middle age, and then retraction towards death. Thus, in the 1470s, Walter Bate's holding at Kempsey (Worcs.) reached its greatest extent when he took on part of the demesne (held from the Bishop of Worcester) and the farm of the rectorial glebe. By his death in 1500, his holding had reverted to a 6-acre customary holding.[131]

Farmers did not enjoy complete freedom on their holdings. Landlords were anxious to keep control, and tried to restrict their tenants by limiting sub-letting and (until the late fifteenth century) making most leases for under ten years.[132] Leasing was a gamble for both sides, and sometimes the farmers lost. Most demesne farmers appear to have been reasonably conscientious: there is little sign of 'asset-stripping', and the continuity of family holdings is often impressive. The continued oversight of the estates by the lessors, and frequent visits by their officials for rent-collecting and other purposes (where the lease was held of a major landlord) may well have restrained over-exploitation. Perhaps the least conscientious lessees were the short-term farmers of benefices and glebe, where a non-resident incumbent without a local agent could not maintain effective supervision.

---

[130] ibid., pp. 1–15; du Boulay, 'Who were farming?' [234]; Harvey, 'Abbot of Westminster's demesnes' [355]; Dyer, *Lords and peasants*, pp. 159–62, 211–17; Smith, *Canterbury cathedral priory*, pp. 193–4.

[131] Dyer, *Lords and peasants*, p. 307.

[132] SRO, D593/A/1/12/18; Harvey, 'Abbot of Westminster's demesnes', p. 26; du Boulay, 'Who were farming?', pp. 447–8.

Here there are signs of real exploitation. The farmer of the prebend of Ogbourne (Wilts.), presented at the Salisbury deanery visitation in 1405, had not only allowed buildings to decay, but reportedly even stripped the lead from a chancel roof. Similar complaints elsewhere originated in either greed or incompetence. One instance – the parties are unidentifiable – presents a catalogue of carelessness by the farmer which had caused considerable dilapidation. The lease appears to have been a short-term farm, presumably to cover temporary non-residence. The incumbent's surviving complaints claim damages amounting to £45, with trees having been cut without authority, rent for stock remaining unpaid, sheep so badly shorn that the wool fetched a low price, the sheepfold requiring a new roof, and so on. A Hereford case of 1450–1 shows further consequences of incompetence by a benefice-farmer. The lessee was behind with his rent (for which the dean and chapter began legal action), and had also ignored orders to pay an amercement of 33s. 4d. to the bailiff of Wormelow hundred. The bailiff had therefore distrained on grain worth £7 3s. 8½d., much to the chapter's chagrin.[133]

This case was not alone in revealing the major difficulty confronting lessors, of actually collecting their rents. The calculations involved before taking action were again complex. Deliberate arrears seem to have been scarce, unless the parties were in dispute on the terms. Landlords sometimes carried large arrears before going to the extreme of dispossession, perhaps a comment on the contemporary land market. Thus, the bishopric of Lichfield accounts suggest that a late fifteenth-century farmer of Wybunbury rectory (Ches.) paid virtually nothing for eleven years, at which point he was at last ejected. That the tenant was making a loss seems unlikely; although his successor's equal reluctance to pay may suggest it. Status and distance could also affect the assiduity of payment. Towards the close of the period, the gentry appear to have resisted payment, and it was sometimes difficult for the ecclesiastics to act against them. This problem, however, was not confined to land rents – it also occurred with amercements and feudal dues. Distance was probably particularly important when the landlord had scattered estates and insufficient administration.[134]

The leasing of properties, especially demesnes, had considerable social implications. If the lessees were generally the long-established leaders of

[133] Faith, 'Berkshire', pp. 166–7; Harvey, 'Abbot of Westminster's demesnes', p. 25; Halcrow, 'Decline of demesne farming', pp. 353–4; Timmins, *Reg. Chandler*, p. 37; PRO, E135/24/46; HCA, R488.

[134] Dyer, *Lords and peasants*, pp. 179–82, 185–6; Harvey, 'Abbot of Westminster's demesnes', pp. 21–3; du Boulay, 'Who were farming?', p. 449; Swanson, 'Episcopal spiritualities: Lichfield', p. 18; Finberg, *Tavistock abbey*, p. 217. See also e.g. SRO D(W)1734/3/2/2, m.41r; NRO, DCN.8/4.

the local peasantry, this access of additional land can only have contributed to the greater social stratification of that class, some with aspirations to even higher status. The rise of the yeomanry, and the gentrification of some of them, owed much to the availability of land from leased demesnes, whether lay or ecclesiastical. Leasehold also provided opportunities for landholding to some of the landless, although obviously requiring some initial capital. A rectory was not just land, but a functioning economic enterprise; the stock would be leased with the glebe and other perquisites, thereby saving the immediate capital expenditure involved in taking on unstocked land. Further wealth would then be generated, providing a basis on which a family might construct its fortunes.[135]

In due course, leasing became the general practice, for manors and appropriated rectories. The farmers obviously profited, although exactly how much is not clear. When demesnes and glebe were leased, the lessor's receipts perhaps showed little reduction (or even an increase); but with the more variable tithes, greater discrepancy is likely. The farm of grain tithes at Holme-next-the-sea was set at £14 15s. od. in 1400, but the valuation completed in 1401 assessed them at £20.[136] That farmers struck a hard bargain is suggested by a scrap of evidence from sixteenth-century Yorkshire. There, the tithes held by Lewes priory around Halifax were farmed to John Waterhouse. He sublet, allowing one subtenant to commute his tithes for £4 a year. Presumably this was worthwhile for both parties, representing more than Waterhouse's own commutation for the same tithes in his annual rent. Unfortunately, the full extent of sub-letting cannot be gauged, although at least one lease issued by Lilleshall abbey stipulated that none should occur without licence.[137]

Their potential profitability perhaps made tithes especially liable to speculation and exploitation. If there is a connection between investment and economic return in the middle ages, then one area ripe for lay involvement was tithe-farming. Consortia of laymen appear in the early fourteenth century buying tithes from clerics, a practice which continued later. The parcels of tithes leased out by the dean and chapter of Lichfield later that century were frequently held by partnerships when the annual return exceeded £3 – unless they were held by knights. For gentry, too,

---

[135] Bolton, *Medieval English economy*, pp. 238–9; Timmins, *Reg. Chandler*, pp. 76–7; Windsor, XI.G.69; du Boulay, 'Who were farming?', p. 451.

[136] Hare, 'Monks as landlords', pp. 88–9; SRO, D593/A/1/12/5; Bod., Shropshire charter 27B; Dyer, *Lords and peasants*, pp. 145–6. Canterbury cathedral priory income reached an all-time peak in 1411, after the farming transition was completed: Smith, *Canterbury cathedral priory*, p. 194.

[137] BIHR, CP.G.3378 (see also Bailey, *Prescot records* [29], pp. 4–7, 25); SRO, D593/A/1/12/15 (similar concern to keep control may be reflected in stipulations that death terminated a lease, preventing alienation to another party, e.g. SRO, D593/A/1/9/15).

regularly leased such revenues. Sir Hugh de Stredley thus held the tithes of four townships for £7 5s. od. a year, while Sir Thomas de Wennesley held the tithes of three for slightly less.[138] Indeed, such leases were a springboard for local authority, with individuals farming collections of neighbouring benefices to enhance their local standing. The development of the 'kulak' group among the later medieval peasantry is well established, but usually approached in terms of the dispossession of lesser peasantry. However, if seeking opportunities for short-term exploitation with quick returns, then possible peasant (or yeoman) involvement in benefice farming must also be considered, both glebe (which would increase landholding) and tithes (which would increase produce available for marketing). The 'capitalist' implications of such farming are shown by the appearance of non-rural investors during the fifteenth century, especially noticeable around the major towns, or in the joint lease of the rectory of Denford (Northants.) by a London merchant and a Northamptonshire esquire in the 1450s.[139]

Like other forms of farming, the leasing of ecclesiastical lands and revenues provided opportunities for individual economic gain, and contributed to social change. Church lands and the profits from tithes were valuable: their availability for lay (and clerical) exploitation was doubtless appreciated. That exploitation perhaps also whetted appetites for the wholesale transfer of both lands and tithes to lay ownership, which was one side-effect of the Reformation. As a whole, the church was an effective and important force within the economy, whose contribution to the mechanics of economic change in late medieval England has so far received rather less attention than it merits.

5.5   ECONOMIC SIDE EFFECTS OF ECCLESIASTICAL ACTIVITY

In addition to the immediate local impact of the institutional church's economic activities, spiritual and religious action produced several other economic results. The effects of this ecclesiastical activity might be felt some distance from the original contact with the market, and have ramifications which affected the whole of society.

The church's market dealings in its own produce had major consequences. Apart from the impact in terms of scale of production and supplying raw materials for local industrialists, there may have been

---

[138] YML, M2/1a, ff. 45v, 48v; LJRO, D.30/E26, E27.
[139] Harvey, *Westminster abbey*, p. 152; Timmins, *Reg. Chandler*, pp. 16–17, 81; LJRO, B/A/1/11, f. 68r–v.

indirect effects. Thus, with mortuaries, the quality of the beasts demanded could have had a knock-on effect for individual farmers. If mortuaries were retained by individual houses or rectors, or normally sold to one purchaser to provide breeding-stock, the quality of that particular herd would have been boosted, creating an unofficial 'pedigree' concentration.

More important would be the long-term impact of the farming of tithes and rectories. Although this could produce disasters, it might be beneficial. The profitability of such enterprises would assist capital formation, as would the farming of other revenues, such as indulgences and letters of confraternity. The indulgence for the fabric of Beverley Minster was generally farmed at £10 a year, but occasionally less. The farmers presumably expected a decent profit – in one year they claimed a rebate because they had been prevented from collecting in Durham diocese – and with little need for capital equipment, costs were presumably low (although the farmers would pay fees for episcopal licences to collect, and to incumbents of parishes where they sold their wares, plus production costs of the documents). Farms of other collections, such as the papal collector's procurations (at about two-thirds of anticipated receipts), would similarly bring profits, which could be diverted to other projects. It is perhaps no accident that the status of 'questor' or 'pardoner' was considered a proper trading qualification in fifteenth-century York, and presumably elsewhere, when acquiring the freedom of the city – although the precise economic standing of such people remains uninvestigated. The farming of the questorships of St Anthony's hospital, London, was certainly 'big business', but few of those taking out leases are specifically identified by occupation in the surviving documents.[140]

The ramifications of ecclesiastical activity were varied. No precise assessment of the impact of churchwardens and voluntary associations is possible; yet their contacts would have economic results, especially the fraternities which doubled as trade or other associations. More significant would be the movements of cash generated by the church's economic activities, especially landholding and manorialism. The profits of the scattered estates and appropriated benefices were frequently siphoned off for the benefit of a third party (even farming would do this, although less obviously than direct management). Cash would be extracted at one end,

---

[140] HCRO, DD.BC/III/33, m.3r–d, DD.BC/III/34, p. 25; Madox, *Formulare Anglicanum*, pp. 149–51; CRO, DRC.2/12, 2/16; LAO, Bps Rentals 1, f. 10v, Bps Accts. 7, ff. 9v–10r; ECL, MS 3551, f. 31v; Windsor, XI.F.31 (the farmer identified as a Winchester clothier), XV.37.12–14, 16–20, 34 (questors presumably sublet – this is the only conceivable way in which these leases could operate, see also e.g. YML, M2/1a, f. 43r); Heath, *Clerical accounts*, pp. 28–30, 35–6, 42–3; Lunt, *Financial relations*, pp. 702–4; Collins, *Freemen of York* [158], i, pp. 69, 85, 99, 102, 129, 141, 145, 151, 154, 158, 166–7, 178, 180, 183, 194–5, 199, 200, 207, 210, 221, 225, 229, 232–3, 236 (see also EDR, E1/4/1, m.2r).

and concentrated at the other, at the static religious house, or in a bishop's (or abbot's) more peripatetic household. It would then be released into a different local economy, although admittedly with some diversion en route – for legal fees in London, and other expenses. However, much would be concentrated, and disbursed around the residence of the main recipient. The economy around the estate or the appropriated benefice might thus be depressed, but be kept buoyant around the receiving house. The effect of such concentrations perhaps accounts for some of the local opposition to the dissolution of religious houses under Henry VIII: but for their disbursements, as consumers and employers, the local economy would go into depression.[141]

The mechanics of cash concentration are generally elusive; and some leakage would have been unavoidable. Much must have been directly delivered to the recipients, either at a central point, or during their travels. Hugh Oldham's accounts as Bishop of Exeter (1504–19) record his receipt of money at various places within his diocese, as well as at London. Intermediaries often had to be used, perhaps especially with transfers of rent to religious houses. Lilleshall abbey's dealings with the rectory of Holme-next-the-sea (Norfolk) are instructive: some of the extant rectory leases specify payment at the Shropshire abbey, as the farmer's responsibility, but others show the use of agents. Two leases require payment at London in a lump sum: one stipulates payment at St Dunstan's in the west, precisely between 1.0 and 2.0 p.m. on the appointed day; the other requires delivery to the prior of St Bartholomew's, Smithfield, 'or elsewhere where the said abbot [of Lilleshall] or his successors may happen to assign in London', indicating that agents sometimes changed. Bishops could use a similar system, with leases of Denford rectory (Northants.) by the Bishop of Lichfield in 1455 and 1460 again demanding payment at London.[142]

The cash which resulted from ecclesiastical or religious activity had many destinations. At the provincial level the archbishops had their own claims, especially of vacancy income, or of provincial subsidies. Within the realm as a whole there was a drift towards the royal coffers, from taxation, from custody of estates during vacancies and seizures, and various other charges. These included occasional usurpations of spirituality income, although the only instance of this so far noticed occurred with the vacancy of Lichfield diocese in 1532.[143]

---

[141] See 3/1 at nn. 34–5.

[142] ECL, MS 3690, ff. 15r, 16v–17v, 18v, 47v; SRO, D593/A/1/12/15, 17, 18; LJRO, B/A/1/11, f. 68r–v, B/A/1/12, f. 126r.

[143] PRO, SC6/Henry VIII/7156, ff. 2r–3r; for other royal receipts from the church, see 3/2 at nn. 54–69.

Some money was also exported as a result of ecclesiastical activity. Obvious instances were payments to the papacy and ancillary costs of maintaining proctors at Rome. The straightforward costs for arranging curial business in person would also need to be added to the reckoning. Payments for some indulgences (often connected with crusading) also went overseas, as did the money spent on pilgrimages. Some religious houses, as members of great international organizations, would also make Payments for some indulgences (often connected with crusading) also compensatory bullion imports, largely from pilgrimages, but this was probably fairly minor in scale.

Spiritual activity had particularly important effects on the circulation of wealth. Some of this derived from the church's jurisdictional claims. Its virtually undisputed control of probate allowed it to supervise the execution of wills, and thus oversee the distribution of considerable sums. Admittedly, non-execution of wills was frequently reported at visitations, but such reports probably led to a general enquiry into the administration of the estate.[144] While the church supervised the payment of specific bequests, most of which involved cash transfers, the traditional arrangements whereby 'the residue' was left for unspecified pious purposes meant that further unspecified sums were also involved. Those dying intestate also needed provision for their estates, which the church supervised. It also had – or assumed – jurisdiction in cases where debts exceeded the estate, creating a sort of post-mortem bankruptcy process with the creditors being paid off with only part of the debt.[145] The concern for deceased debtors was probably mainly moral in origin, as was ecclesiastical involvement in the distribution of wealth within families which derived from a concern for the proper maintenance of children. The church occasionally supported a child's claim to share in an inheritance, although by 1400 it was normally accepted that fathers could disinherit, and the automatic claims of children had effectively gone. Arrangements were also made for the maintenance of illegitimate children by their putative fathers (or other relatives). Orders were issued to provide dowries for women who had had children fathered on them, and might thereby forfeit claims to parental support. Although these orders were backed up by ecclesiastical censure, their effectiveness cannot be tested, nor their generality. Moreover, the sums involved would be fairly small.[146]

Apart from money transfers, pious and charitable concerns had other effects. Their practical impact lay especially in the area of 'public works'.

---

[144] For probate, see 4/5 at n. 72. For visitation reports, Wood-Legh, *Kentish visitations*, pp. 65–270, *passim*.
[145] Helmholz, *Canon law*, pp. 292–302.
[146] ibid., pp. 171–84.

Individual incumbents were sometimes responsible for maintenance of particular bridges, as was the vicar of Harlow (Essex), but generally the upkeep of roads and bridges was counted as a charitable activity – benefactions would earn prayers. Many wills therefore made bequests to such enterprises (and the hermits who often maintained them), while others could earn indulgences by their contributions.[147] Such indulgences presumably reflect the appointment of collectors, rather than a requirement to visit the place concerned.

Testamentary dispositions could also have long-term effects on family wealth, not just in alienation of goods, but in temporary transfer of lands to trustees to perform the will. The trust which came into operation on the death of Richard Beauchamp, Earl of Warwick, in 1439, had immediate and reversionary control over fifteen manors to perform the pious deeds decreed in his will. The main tasks were not completed until the mid-1460s, with others incomplete as late as 1482; in the meantime only the surplus profits from the lands (if any) had been available for Beauchamp's heirs.[148]

Not so precisely spiritual, but still having direct economic consequences, were the jurisdictional franchises linked to the greater sanctuaries. These artificial concentrations of economic forces were threatened by the attack on sanctuaries, with Beaulieu for one seeking to retain its sanctuary status even after the abolition of the monasteries. Apart from the great territorial sanctuaries, many urban ecclesiastical liberties provided islands of exemption from the economic policies practised by the town or its oligarchs, and from urban taxation. Within the liberties, whether places like St Martin le Grand in London, or the precincts of the mendicant friaries, it was therefore possible to carry on a trade without the restrictions of quality and working practices imposed by urban craft guilds (or their civic masters). This possibly contributed to the hostility shown by some towns to the ecclesiastical liberties in their midst, most obviously in the lengthy conflict between London and St Martin le Grand; but also in sporadic outbreaks like the attacks on the Dominican and Franciscan friaries and St Leonard's hospital in York in 1381.[149]

A major stimulus was offered to the economy by religion's encouragement of travelling, and therewith service industries, including a form of tourism. The church's jurisdictional structure itself stimulated movement. The fixed locations of major ecclesiastical courts, the arrangements for visitations,

---

[147] BL, MS Add. 14848, f. 173r; EDR, F5/32, f. 35v.

[148] Hicks, 'Beauchamp trust', pp. 139–48.

[149] Kaufman, 'Henry VII and sanctuary' [457], p. 467; Thornley, 'The destruction of sanctuary' [836], pp. 193–6; Dobson, 'York, Beverley, and Scarborough' [220], pp. 121, 124 (see also p. 118 and n. 15).

usually forced people to travel to perform their duties or protect their interests. The fixed courts would have more impact than the short-term influx occasioned by a visitation; and the cathedral cities and centres of leading peculiar jurisdictions would have to provide accommodation and supplies for the visitors. The costs of such journeys often appear in records of court cases, or in clerical accounts for attendance at synods and similar gatherings.[150]

Pilgrimage provided another incentive to travel and associated economic development, which must have outstripped court activity in significance, and had more widespread effects. Not only was the local economy stimulated by the pilgrims' basic outlay on travel and accommodation; but the visit's very function generated exchanges. Offerings of alms would provide considerable cash. This was clearly a major element in any pilgrimage, and frequently one encouraged by indulgences: those who contributed when visiting the specified church or shrine on stated days would earn the indulgence. Additionally, pilgrims stimulated the economy by their demand for votive offerings – especially wax. Pilgrim demand in fact stimulated competition among suppliers in the towns affected, and occasional disorder on the approach roads. In mid-fifteenth-century York the chandlers were ordered not to sell images in Stonegate (the main approach to the Minster) because they clogged the road; but several were fined for just that.[151]

Beyond accommodating the pilgrims and providing their offerings, pilgrim centres also benefited from the rise of a souvenir industry. Many pilgrims wanted mementoes of their visit to a shrine, usually in the form of cap-badges. For shrines like Canterbury or King Henry VI at Windsor these must have made significant contributions to their manufacturers' pockets. Pilgrims seeking indulgences, or certificates of completion of pilgrimage (especially if imposed as penance) would also have maintained the writing, and, later, printing, industries – although the latter was also encouraged outside pilgrimage sites by the production of various certificates, pious woodcuts, and the advertising material which accompanied the sale of indulgences and letters of confraternity.[152]

Spiritual or disciplinary concerns might also allow other forms of economic activity to flourish without ecclesiastical approval. The later medieval centuries witnessed the rise of what can only be termed an ecclesiastical black economy (leaving aside theft from churches, which also contributed).

[150] Heath, *Clerical accounts*, pp. 34, 39, 46, 49, 54–6.
[151] Lunt, *Financial relations*, pp. 473–6, 487–505; Dobson, *York chamberlains' rolls* [218], p. 145.
[152] Spencer, 'Medieval pilgrim badges' [772]; Spencer, 'King Henry of Windsor' [773]; Mitchiner, *Medieval badges* [587]; Pollard and Redgrave, *Short-title catalogue* [665], ii, pp. 2–9; Needham, *Printer and pardoner* [602], pp. 44–5; Windsor, XV.59.1, m.10d; Dodgson, 'English devotional woodcuts' [223].

Throughout the period the religious susceptibilities of the faithful, and the administrative needs of some clerics, were exploited by the unscrupulous. At Rippingale (Lincs.) about 1386 a rural cross became an unauthorized shrine, attracting pilgrims and offerings. This, the evidence suggests, was a clear attempt to rook visitors and increase the revenues of the parish church, the contributions being put to unstated purposes. Episcopal attempts to stop the practice proved unsuccessful, a petition being submitted for a papal licence for the chapel which by-passed the bishop, and presented a somewhat fraudulent history of the site. Other forms of fraud and exploitation saw pseudo-mendicants exploiting religious sentiments and false summoners relying on fear of the church's jurisdictional claims to extort money. Further opportunities were presented by attitudes towards indulgences and purgatory. The portrayal of Chaucer's Pardoner, despite the overdrawing, is close to some known cases. Indulgences were difficult to regulate – bishops did license questors, but the system was not efficient. There were clearly many false collectors, selling false indulgences either because the project was itself fictitious, or because they lacked proper authorization. Thus, in 1411, Bishop Hallum of Salisbury warned against admitting any pardoners to his diocese without his licence, whilst Canterbury Convocation in 1424 legislated to curb what was considered a plague of false questors throughout the province. In the archdiocese of York, the chapter of Beverley Minster at one point complained of false pardoners claiming to collect on their behalf, authorizing the true questor to arrest the imposters 'with all their false relics and muniments whatsoever'. Yet such was the demand for indulgences that one fiction even ended up in print, presumably for sale. It was not just false pardoners who profited illicitly from indulgences. Duly authorized collections could still be misappropriated, as was reported at the Herefordshire visitation of 1397, where a licensed collector for bridge repairs had kept 20s. for his own use.[153]

False relics might be manufactured from a variety of sources. False documents were another matter. Although obscured, there was clearly a market in forged ecclesiastical documents – especially papal bulls – throughout the later middle ages. Detailed evidence is (unsurprisingly) scarce, although some cases were revealed before the London authorities in the late fourteenth and early fifteenth centuries. Such forgery was presumably profitable (one papal bull was sold for 10 marks), and worth while to the purchaser, saving travel costs and the uncertainty of curial proceedings.

[153] Owen, 'Bacon and eggs' [625], p. 141; Riley, *Memorials of London* [699], pp. 320–1, 584, 586–7; Jacob, *Reg. Chichele*, iv, p. 256; Horn, *Reg. Hallum* [411], no. 871; Owst, *Preaching* [631], pp. 99–110; EDR, F5/32, f. 34v; Jackson, 'Three printed indulgences' [437], p. 230; Bannister, 'Visitation returns of Hereford', vol. 45, p. 48.

Ecclesiastics themselves appear as forgers of various documents, including wills and letters.[154]

Quantifying the impact of these miscellaneous side-effects of ecclesiastical activity on the total economy is impossible. Forgery's impact, for instance, was probably minimal; but pilgrimage and the attendant tourist industry would be highly important in some places (varying with popularity, while the increasing number of shrines in the fifteenth century probably changed the distribution). What is clear is that the impact of church life, direct or indirect, was substantial. The economy was stimulated by the church's active involvement, and by its attempts at regulation. There was also a reciprocal effect, on the church as an institution and as a spiritual entity.

Considering the impact on the church requires a change of emphasis, less economic, and more social and spiritual. At a basic level, the effect on the church was, it appears, somewhat deadening. The church was increasingly aware of itself as an economic machine, as a structure whose functioning included the collection and distribution of cash. It had not lost its spiritual function – this clearly remained – and emphasizing the economic side need not denigrate the spiritual, or indicate decay. However, it does suggest that the church was becoming, in self-perception, materialist and fiscal as well as spiritual. This probably reflected the times: if a curate could not subsist on 8 marks a year, perhaps he was justified in threatening to quit unless his stipend was increased.[155] If tithes provided the bulk of an incumbent's income, perhaps he had no alternative but to chase reluctant payers through the courts. But there is a feeling (possibly false) that in the last decades before the Reformation the priesthood was considered a job rather than a vocation; another form of paid employment. The commutation of penances for money, the charges for probate, assiduous collection of mortuaries, all, if taken at face value, suggest an increasing concern for the fiscal side of ecclesiastical life. Similarly, the increasing materialism of monastic life, the payment of salaries to monks, the receipt of benefices, the frequent small gifts, the greater relaxation within the larger houses and virtual abandonment of communal life, again suggest decay and a perception of the church as providing a life of economic ease.

Within the church, this situation produced tensions, awareness of which is revealed by men like John Colet, who in 1512 condemned the decadence which resulted from the church's over-indulgence in secular concerns, among them the hunt for wealth.[156] More serious than these internal

---

[154] Riley, *Memorials of London*, pp. 583–4, 587–9; BIHR, DC/AB.2, f. 22v; Bannister, 'Visitation returns of Hereford', vol. 44, p. 449, vol. 45, p. 92.

[155] Wood-Legh, *Kentish visitations*, p. 107.

[156] Lupton, *Life of Colet* [536], pp. 300–2.

tensions was the lay hostility which could result in anticlericalism. If the clergy were perceived as exploiters, or as individually undeserving of ecclesiastical revenues, opposition could result. Clearly there were such perceptions – reflected in the pseudo-Donatism of the Lollards, and the notion that tithes should not be paid to 'bad priests'. But such perceptions need not produce heresy. If a priest felt he had to act against his parishioners for his tithes, they might conversely consider him an extortionist. If, as occasionally occurred, a cleric demanded more than the proper rates, again antipathy would develop, possibly leading to real anticlericalism rather than personal animosity (the difference is important).[157] Perhaps this did occur in the early sixteenth century, being reflected in the hostility to probate and other fees which merged into the early stages of the Reformation.[158]

But if this antipathy between clergy and laity developed because of the church's economic activity, it must be set in proper perspective. Whilst the clergy did take money from the laity, so did other laymen – indeed, the churchwardens possibly had more responsibility for financial affairs than is usually appreciated. They probably had more frequent contacts with their fellow parishioners in 'church-centred' economic activity than the clergy. Yet there is little evidence of any hostility developing towards the office of churchwarden, or any concerted attempt to change the financial system within which they operated. To see financial disputes between clergy and laity as reflecting serious anticlericalism may overstate the case.

The activities of churchwardens, and lay control over much church wealth (chantry foundations and suchlike) would foster ideas of lay control over the church in a wider sense. If this seemed increasingly 'natural', then attempts to extend it would not face strong lay opposition. As the churchwardens and others were responsible for many spiritualities, it was perhaps not unreasonable for the king to seek similar control over the church as a whole. The change in mental perspectives may be one of the most important reasons for the lack of effective opposition to Henry VIII's Reformation, when it came.

The overall contribution made by ecclesiastical and religious concerns to the late medieval English economy was probably beneficial. Although it had some detrimental aspects, it is perhaps too easy to emphasize the church as an extracting force whose activities removed goods and land from circulation. The deadness of mortmain, and the freezing of assets in shrines, clearly did drain the economy; but probably not as much as is

---

[157] Wood-Legh, *Kentish visitations*, pp. 97, 177.
[158] See 7/2 at n. 51.

sometimes implied. Moreover, much of the cash and produce extracted by the church – whether by compulsion or voluntary donation – in due course returned to circulation. Indeed, because of its moral and financial demands, and its fostering of the credit economy, the church may well have encouraged circulation when the natural tendency was in the opposite direction. The church's institutional needs also contributed towards industrial and commercial activity, again probably generally beneficial. To create a divide between 'Church' and 'Economy' is, as usual, to make a false separation within the society. The church's role was very much as a social service, an integral part of the infrastructure, with investment in it stimulating employment, trade, and commerce. The medieval church also produced additional dividends for its investors: if they were lucky it earned them Heaven, and that, rather than purely mercenary economic concerns, was probably the main consideration. To emphasize the economic impact alone misinterprets the aims and aspirations of the society within which the church operated, highlighting side-effects rather than the main concern.

6

Windows on Men's Souls:
Orthodox Spirituality

6.1   RELIGIOUS ATTITUDES

Investigating how far the people of late medieval England believed in and acted on the demands of Christianity encounters major obstacles. Contradictions and contrasts abound, now stressing belief in the church and its creeds, and manifesting orthodox piety; now suggesting ignorance, anticlericalism and impiety. Against the intense religious experience of Julian of Norwich stand the somewhat crude outpourings of Margery Kempe; the cult of the Name of Jesus contrasts with that of the devil-conjuring John Schorn; devotion to the Eucharist exists alongside the belief that excommunication could be transferred from men to plants and make brambles wither.[1] Concentration on Christianity also ignores the existence of other patterns of belief, an underground flow which rarely surfaces. Contemporary comments reveal the disparities in practices: the author of *Dives and pauper* deplored popular irreligion, and a mid-fifteenth-century cleric wrote that people

come to matins no more than three times a year . . . they chatter, they lark about, they kiss women, and hear no word of the service but mock the priest, saying that he dawdles over his mass and keeps them from their breakfast.

An Italian visitor only decades later was rather more impressed:

Although they all attend mass every day, and say many Paternosters in public (the women carrying long rosaries in their hands, and any who can read taking the office of Our Lady with them, and with some companion reciting it in church verse by verse in a low voice, after the manner of the religious) they always hear mass on Sundays in their parish church, and give good alms . . . nor do they omit any

---

[1] Elton, *Star chamber stories* [250], p. 206.

indication of being a good Christian; there are however many with various opinions concerning religion.[2]

Such contradictions enliven and obscure analysis of English spirituality between 1350 and 1540. Yet the years between the Black Death and the Reformation provide the first valid indications of the nature of popular spirituality, rather than individual or group experiences. The evidence and the artefacts – the written records and the extant churches – make the people visible to an unprecedented extent. But the evidence, in bulk and in particulars, remains ambiguous, leaving doubts about how satisfactorily it reflects thoughts and deeds.

Numerous influences regulated the modes of spiritual expression, and the laity's mental relationship with the church. Spiritual commitment could be revealed in several ways, through dedication to a religious life – the collegiate commitment in monastic orders, the friars, and the nuns, or individual statements made by anchorites, hermits, and other recluses, as well as commitment shown solely by a vow of chastity. This individual dedication might ultimately lead to mysticism, and the fourteenth and fifteenth centuries were notably the age of the English mystics. Few could attain their levels of dedication. Most remained attached to the world, expressing their piety within it. The question of piety – how religious were the English people, and in what ways? – is massive, all-embracing, but unavoidable. In the prelude to the Reformation, it is vitally important to consider whether the English were actively religious, weighed down with religiosity, or immersed in superstition, and indeed whether such distinctions are valid. In assessing the level of piety, but as an independent element in it, the practical side-effects need some thought: what, when expressing their piety through their pockets, did people spend their money on? Such expenditure both reflected the influences which made up contemporary piety, and also gave practical expression of the precepts of Christianity.

At first sight the sheer bulk of surviving evidence suggests that a proper analysis of spirituality is a real possibility. In fact, however, the evidence complicates the task. The picture presented often remains insubstantial, the manifold variations make generalizations dubious. The reasons for this derive partly from the chronological limitations of the period under consideration. At one end the Black Death is an obvious break, although its precise cultural significance requires further analysis. At the other extreme stands the start of the Reformation, the inflow of Protestant thought, and the apparently easy demolition of the old religious order.

---

[2] Barnum, *Dives and pauper* [41], i, p. 189; Hodgson, 'Ignorantia sacerdotum' [405], p. 11; Sneyd, *Relation of England* [771], p. 23.

Particularly significant in contrasting the two termini is the Reformation's total demolition of the medieval cult of death.[3] The plague's impact is more difficult to assess: while the demographic decline is undeniable, the mortality may merely have heightened a pre-existing concern with death. For death was a major Christian rite of passage, given that the religion was posited on a terrestrial pilgrimage, with a posthumous Final Judgement of that earthly existence. The concept of the transitory life as a pilgrimage was strong, reflected in vernacular literature, and emphasizing the need to prepare for death. A cult of death is highly visible throughout the pre-Reformation centuries, in literary genres such as the Dance of Death, in funerary monuments with their skeletal representations, in the production of instruction manuals in the *ars moriendi* – the art of dying. Contemporary religious observances also emphasized death and the post-mortem life. Prayers for the souls of the departed rose perennially in every parish church and religious establishment; individuals made bequests specifically to gain the prayers of others – and the longer the better. New foundations satisfied this concern, and every benefaction made a contract between donor and recipient, in a currency of psalters, prayers, and masses. The correct interpretation of this material, however, remains uncertain. Did the cult of death express hope, or fear? Were some of its manifestations (as has been suggested for some of the *memento mori* monuments) a matter merely of fashion and social grouping?[4] While death loomed everywhere, it is difficult to penetrate the evidence to see what individuals actually felt about the after-life. There are occasional suggestions of panic, with demands for masses to be said as quickly as possible, and in extraordinary numbers, but there is also the suggestion of playing safe: that trust in Christ was the only guarantee, but the post-mortem benefactions might just help somewhere along the way. At heart, the concern for death devolves into the doctrinal debate about justification, through faith or works, but most people probably did not think deeply about it. It is easy to see the period as too concerned with works; but faith had a place somewhere, which in the nature of things can only rarely be revealed.

Yet the question persists, faith in what? The piety of the time shows many strands, with new feasts and many modes of expression; but rarely

---

[3] See Kreider, *English chantries* [489], pp. 92–153.

[4] Siraisi, 'Introduction' [762], pp. 12–13, 16–17 (and works referred to there, esp. Wenzel, 'Pestilence and literature' [889], pp. 148–52); Sumption, *Pilgrimage* [791], pp. 290, 310 (some of the English works are translations, e.g. Henry, *Pilgrimage of the manhode* [381], which is one of several translations of Guillaume de Deguileville's *Le pèlerinage de la vie humaine*); O'Connor, *Art of dying well* [611]; Chené-Williams, 'Vivre sa mort' [137]; Collins, 'Little known "Art of dying"' [159], pp. 181–90; Hicks, 'Piety of Lady Hungerford' [385], pp. 27–9; King, 'English cadaver tomb' [473], pp. 45–57.

reveals the heart of religious observances. The late middle ages raise major questions about the depth of religious feeling, which the evidence only partly resolves. The contrasting statements of the English clerics and the Venetian envoy reveal the problem; but it goes deeper than that. The period 1350 to 1540 also presents the contrasts between religion and religiosity, and between faith and credulity. Certainly, there is evidence of greater ritual during this period – revisions to the Sarum ordinal, for instance, suggest a virtually complete remodelling of the celebrations in the mid-fourteenth century, into a more elaborate performance than before. There is a greater concern for the 'beauty of holiness', with (for instance) the spread of polyphonic music.[5] But was this merely superficial? There is also evidence of gullibility, of something like superstition in some of the new cults, in the concern for indulgences, and in the magical elements of the faith. The cult of the Eucharist ran such risks – and was duly condemned by Wyclif. Other beliefs seem more magical, like the use of manuscript prayer rolls, supposedly as long as Christ's body, as girdles to secure safe childbirth; and the preservative properties attributed to certain religious observances. There was an amuletic quality to the mass *pro mortalitate evitanda*, which prevented sudden death, just as the Mass of the Name of Jesus (at least according to one dubious indulgence associated with it) guaranteed that the celebrant or purchaser would not die without communion and proper ritual, and would be admitted to eternal joy within thirty days of death.[6]

The conflicts and contrasts can only be resolved by considering the nature of the evidence, and trying to determine what it actually means. But that evidence itself almost prevents proper assessment. Much of it is, necessarily, written, but ambiguous. The literature of the time can be interpreted in many ways; the wills, which survive in relative abundance, give insights into individual dispositions but still have to be treated cautiously. Other sources – court material, sermons, and so on – also have possibilities, and dangers. But before the sources receive further consideration, one element needs initial treatment: the effect of lay control over the church on lay perceptions of religion.

The later middle ages have been portrayed as a period when lay control over the church was at its height. The Reformation further entrenched lay dominance over the ecclesiastical establishments; but its wholesale abolition of many of the sub-parochial institutions – guilds, chantries, and votive lights especially – also demolished many of the opportunities for the laity to engage in control.[7] Certainly, the degree of lay control would affect how individuals viewed their church, and responded to it as a religious institution.

To stress 'lay control' is, however, to overstate the case. The laity had always had some control; only its form changed with time. Visitations had always provided opportunities for parishioners to complain about their clergy – for how else would a bishop or archdeacon know that observances were being maintained, and the priests doing their duties? This role of the laity as guarantors of priestly performance was acceptable; but more emphatic proprietorial control was resented. The post-Conquest replacement of outright lay possession of churches by rights of patronage over them had been part of the struggle. In England, the patron's rights remained extensive, and could perhaps still be considered to amount to 'control'.[8] The development of royal authority over the church, in all its manifestations, similarly reflected 'lay control'.

But patronal and royal control was not 'popular control'. The power of the populace in exerting authority or influence over the church developed slowly, but was fairly important by 1500. It was certainly no novelty in 1350; but the period from 1350 to 1540 provided greater opportunities for people to show their views about the church.

The old rights of overseeing the priests' activities continued. Visitation reports often show churchwardens commenting on clerical activities, including complaints about the non-provision of services. This sometimes suggests feelings about the services themselves: it was a real grievance when children died unbaptized, or priests refused to give the sacraments to the dying, or abandoned their parish unserved. There is here a feeling that the services did matter, and people missed them.[9] A similar concern to ensure the continuity of services appears in conflicts between priests and parishioners about the maintenance of chapels for outlying hamlets. Usually the parishioners took the lead, demanding that the incumbent maintain arrangements established (as they claimed) by his predecessors.[10] This, and the process of visitation, did not so much reflect lay control over the clergy, as lay insistence that the bishop exercise control, and maintain discipline in religious matters.

Actual control arose when the laity assumed responsibility for ensuring

---

[7] Scarisbrick, *Reformation* [748], pp. 165–7.

[8] Barnum, *Dives and pauper*, i, pp. 351–3.

[9] Wood-Legh, *Kentish visitations* [922], pp. 62, 64, 101, 105, 115, 117, 119–20, 129, 132, 140, 162, 184, 226–7, 236, 250, 263, 282 – some of these may have been unjustified complaints; several were quickly resolved (see also Bridgen, 'Religion and social obligation' [90], p. 75; Windsor, XI.K.6).

[10] E.g. BIHR, CP.F.260; Swanson, *Reg. Scrope* [796], i, pp. 86–7; Bowker, *Episcopal court book* [76], pp. 37–40.

the services. Within the parish, this might involve the nomination of a parish (or hamlet) chaplain – in some instances a non-resident, or the incumbent of a large parish, allowed the inhabitants to choose the parish curte although retaining responsibility for paying the wages.[11] More stringent oversight developed from a concern for celebrations and the multiplicity of religious endowments. When establishing chantries, founders often retained the patronage for themselves and their heirs, and foundation charters frequently included provisions for disciplining the clergy and continued oversight of the establishments. Guilds and fraternities employed their own priests, often on an annual stipendiary basis, and had extensive authority over them. So extensive, in fact, that the laity might even challenge the normal ecclesiastical authorities. Thus, when the dean and chapter of Lichfield sought to prevent a clash of services by prohibiting celebrations by the guild chaplains of St Mary in the town church, a chaplain passed the inhibition to a guildsman who promptly threw the chapter's messenger out, threatening to make him eat the inhibition if he tried to prevent the guildsman having 'his' mass.[12]

That the laity employed many priests, whether for long- or short-term duties (including household chaplaincies) was only one aspect of the total position. The clergy's endowments were often under lay regulation, making the clerics little more than hirelings, answerable to their employers. Church-wardens overseeing chantries were in that category; but they controlled much of the church's economy as well, and could thereby gain influence over the incumbent. Certainly, their concern for the provision of services by their own foundations would affect their attitude to the parish clergy. In some respects, the laity were almost constructing their own ecclesiastical organization. Within towns, their responsibility for chantries could virtually create a peculiar jurisdiction: admission procedures sometimes parallel those adopted by ecclesiastical ordinaries, with formal letters of presentation to the York corporation for admission to chantries, and the Beverley town governors claiming that their installations to chantries involved both institution and induction. Moreover, the disciplinary activities of such bodies, and their regular examination of accounts, are tantamount to the creation of something like an extra-ecclesiastical archdeaconry, quite beyond the oversight of the church authorities.[13]

Assessing religious mentalities is further complicated by uncertainty about lay reaction to the church as a holy place. As a building the church had a social function, as did ecclesiastical events, and the interplay between

---

[11] LAO, FOR.3, ff. 107r–108r; Wood-Legh, *Kentish visitations*, p. 71.

[12] Wood-Legh, *Perpetual chantries* [921], pp. 74–90, 170–1; Barron, 'Parish fraternities' [43], pp. 33–4; LJRO, D.30/XVIII, f. 2v (see also Kettle, 'Lichfield before the Reformation' [469], pp. 163–4).

[13] HCRO, DD/BC.II/7/1, f. 89r; Wood-Legh, *Perpetual chantries*, pp. 165–6.

social and religious activities was often intricate. Plays were held in churches; a certain amount of marketing was done there – or in the churchyard; rents were paid at specified tombs as fixed points, or in church porches; and all sorts of other business could be conducted. Sunday services were perhaps the one common fixed point in individual weekly timetables, and could be exploited accordingly. The multiple uses for the church account for a rather secular approach to the buildings: local magnates could gather there to settle disputes; a priest might be celebrating at one altar whilst a near-riot erupted elsewhere. Other activities, like teaching, or lawyers and prostitutes touting for business (as at St Paul's cathedral, London) would also disturb the services.[14] The noise and bustle of the church as a centre of local life contrasts with its 'sacred' character; but the contrast was perhaps ignored by contemporaries. It was, after all, perfectly normal.

So, also, was the exploitation of 'religion' for social purposes; whether mere status display, or for more ethereal reasons. Patrons and benefactors exploited the building for self-proclamation, decorating it with their coats of arm and other devices, declaring their social rank on tombs and memorials. Vestments and other furniture similarly proclaimed the donor, with embroidered heraldic devices, or engraved shields on plate, or portraits and inscriptions in stained glass.[15] Less tangible was the social status proclaimed by precedence. The spreading provision of seating in churches in the fifteenth century allowed those with claims to social rank to gain a territorial foothold, by either the rental or purchase of pews. Institutional precedence was also established with pews being reserved for local officials, especially the mayors and corporations of towns. But even before pewing became general, social status could be created and recognized through membership of patronage committees or similar bodies, the member thereby being identified as one of the parish worthies; and also by precedence in processions or other ecclesiastical rituals. Occasionally, disputes over processional precedence provoked violence: skirmishes occurred between parishes about their placing in Pentecostal processions, and rival guilds jostled for position in Corpus Christi celebrations. Individuals also valued such public recognition, and Chaucer's Wife of Bath was not unique in resenting challenges to her position.[16] The integration of the

---

[14] Elton, *Star chamber stories*, pp. 195–6; Bennett, *Community, class, and careerism* [57], pp. 22, 47–8; Moran, *English schooling* [595], p. 86; Davies, *Secular use of church buildings* [189], ch. 2, 3.

[15] Vale, *Piety, charity, and literacy* [862], pp. 9–10; Bennett, *Community, class, and careerism*, pp. 82–3; Fleming, 'Charity, faith, and the gentry' [277], p. 51; Dahmus, *William Courtenay* [183], pp. 272–3; CUL, MS Mm.I.48, pp. 8–9; Owst, *Preaching* [631], pp. 162–4.

[16] Cox, *Churchwardens' accounts* [171], pp. 186–7, 190, 193; Owen, *Church and society* [624], p. 107; Robinson, *Works of Chaucer* [703], p. 21 (see also Brigden, 'Religion and social obligation', p. 78; Owst, *Preaching*, pp. 170–2, 216–17).

church and its routines into a wider social milieu could almost submerge the ecclesiastical purpose of some actions. The cult of Corpus Christi manifested devotion to the Body of Christ in the Host, and was intended to evoke the brotherhood of the church itself, that mystical body of the faithful which was itself Corpus Christi. But the enmeshing rituals which surrounded the feast in many towns rather overshadowed the religious features. The feast remained an ecclesiastical celebration in rural areas and towns like Exeter, but elsewhere (as at York, Chester, and Coventry) the elaboration of processions and plays allowed the occasion to be hijacked by the urban elite for other purposes: the declaration of the unity and hierarchy of the urban authorities, and the glorification of the town itself. Similar qualifications apply to other celebrations: the processions at Bristol on the feast of St Katherine, for instance, have been interpreted as evocations of the town's essential unity, transcending the jurisdictional frontiers created by the existence of intramural franchises.[17]

Even without jurisdictional frontiers, the church and parish reflected local loyalty. The claims of chapelries to independence, which led to frequent court cases, provide one indication of this. The rivalry between parishes in beautifying their churches is also important. Perhaps the greatest reflection of local loyalties came when there was uncertainty about which building was actually the parish church. Such clashes seem impossible now, and were probably rare then. Nevertheless, some did occur, as in the conflict between the townships of Withernsea and Hollym (Yorks.) which began in the 1440s and lasted until the early sixteenth century. Coastal erosion had forced the abandonment of the original church at Withernsea whose inhabitants, following archiepiscopal inquest, had constructed a new church elsewhere. Meanwhile Hollym's inhabitants (who already had their own chapel) had concurrently procured an archiepiscopal mandate giving their chapel the functions of the parish church, a move in turn resisted by Withernsea. In the end, Withernsea won; but the rivalry between both townships seems to have been quite intense.[18]

The influences which integrated the church into the social world would have been reflected in the developing relationship between clergy and people. There was obviously scope for the development of anticlericalism; but despite ample evidence of individual hostility, with violence on clerics, presentments at visitation, resentment of payments, and the complaints in some of the reformist literature, there seems to be remarkably little evidence for real anticlericalism. Even contemporary literature, with its brutal comments on clerical failings, does not specifically call for the total rejection of the clergy. Most people probably accepted the clergy as they

[17] James, 'Ritual, drama, and social body' [441], pp. 3–29; Sacks, 'The demise of the martyrs' [725], pp. 150–3.
[18] BIHR, CP.G.209.

were, and thought little of theoretical quesitons. In a religion where the quality of the celebrant was irrelevant to the efficacy of his actions, especially his sacramental actions, then anticlericalism could have only shallow foundations. Certainly, there are no signs of wholesale rejection of the mass, and there are positive indications of acceptance of clerical authority, including excommunication. Indeed, that acceptance of clerical authority may have been increasing; for while the clergy were more subject to lay oversight, the spiritual changes which emphasized the presence of Christ in the Host would elevate the importance of the only people capable of performing the necessary consecration. The laity may have had the power of the purse, but the clergy had the power of their orders, and the power of the keys.[19]

Discussion of lay control cannot settle the question of the nature of spirituality; other indicators need investigation. One major source is clearly contemporary literature. The late medieval centuries saw an efflorescence of writing in English (with some in French and Latin for lay reception). Attempts to categorize this literature all face major obstacles, even a distinction between 'secular' and 'religious' works being hard to maintain with any rigidity. The intentions of the vernacular literature vary considerably; but implicitly or explicitly much of it involves spiritual guidance. As well as the prose there is a good deal of religious poetry, with varying purposes.[20] However, these literary works are not easy to treat. While the writer's intentions are important, the audience's reaction is more significant – an the audience is every reader, then and now. For modern commentators, in particular, the dangers seem considerable. This is shown in the varying responses to the religious sentiments in Chaucer's works, seeing him as anything from a traditional critic nevertheless loyal to the church, to an almost post-religious opponent of the church as a social encumbrance. With literature, more than elsewhere, there is a very real danger of opinions and interpretation being imposed on the material, rather than drawn out of it.[21] Medieval reactions demand more attention,

---

[19] Thomson, *Transformation of England* [831], pp. 345–6; Scarisbrick, *Reformation*, pp. 41–2; the problem of priestly status is as yet unstudied for England, but for the possible tensions Zika, 'Hosts, processions, and pilgrimages' [938], esp. pp. 26–7, 59–61, 63–4.

[20] Prose works 'for spiritual guidance' are listed in Joliffe, *Middle English spiritual guidance* [446] (see esp. pp. 15–20, 25–32 for types of work which he excludes); see also Muir, 'Translations and paraphrases' [600], D'Evelyn and Foster, 'Saints' legends' [208], Utley, 'Dialogues, debates, and catechisms' [861], Raymo, 'Religious and philosophical instruction' [688]; also discussion in Russell, 'Vernacular instruction of the laity' [720], Sargent, 'Minor devotional writings' [737], Barratt, 'Works of religious instruction' [42], Coleman, *English literature in history* [156], pp. 69–71.

[21] Aers, *Chaucer* [4], esp. pp. 37–61, seems to me open to this charge. For other assessments of Chaucer, Wagenknecht, *The personality of Chaucer* [880], pp. 119–38; Gerould, *Chaucerian essays* [296], pp. 3–6.

whatever the writer's purpose, for each response is individually valid. The translations of the period (which include much of the spiritual writing) indicate the problems. Several vernacular versions of St Augustine's works have been linked with the Lollards, and could have been used by them. But their users need not have been exclusively Lollards, and the works could easily pass into the mainstream of vernacular spirituality. Similarly, although the English Bible is traditionally associated with the Lollards, its readers were not all heretics. For many, access to the scriptures in English aided comprehension of the Latin, and it was presumably for this purpose that it was used by (say) the nuns of Syon, who also possessed English translations of their religious offices to aid comprehension of their services.[22]

The modern critical tradition surrounding literary productions with ecclesiastical implications is dominated by the 'English literature' of writers like Chaucer and Langland, who criticize the church in their depiction of some of its ministers – notably the mendicants, but also Chaucer's Pardoner – and in suggesting the rarity of good clerics, exemplified by the Poor Parson. They also suggest that the laity were not much better, as with the aspiritual description of the Wife of Bath's religious activities. Certainly, all these elements could be found in contemporary life; but the authors were not necesarily presenting valid generalizations about the church and attitudes towards it. Both Chaucer and Langland were to some extent dealing in stereotypes, and the 'estates' model which both adopted repeats common complaints of uncertain validity. The attacks on the friars, for instance, fit into a tradition of anti-mendicant writing dating back to the 1250s, much of it produced by other ecclesiastics. Concentrating on the individuals as portrayed also runs the risk of ignoring the possible purpose of these works. Langland, for instance, seems to be writing to reverse the picture he presents, a reformist stance which has its own spirituality. Chaucer may be more ambiguous, possibly refusing at times (such as in the Prologue) to adopt a moral stance. But the positioning of the *Parson's Tale* at the end of the *Canterbury Tales* (if Chaucer intended it to go there) cannot be ignored. That strongly sermonizing prose admonition against the Seven Deadly Sins terminates the work harshly, dramatically recalling the original purpose of the pilgrimage, emphasizing the religious aim. By responding to the stances taken in preceding tales it also stresses the need for personal and societal *renovatio* to create an earthly Jerusalem, yet strongly suggesting that Canterbury was not the only goal of pilgrimage in a life whose journey continued after death.[23]

---

[22] Joliffe, *Middle English spiritual guidance*, p. 27; Blunt, *The myrroure of Oure Ladye* [72], pp. 70–1.

[23] Knight, 'Chaucer's religious Canterbury Tales' [483]; Mann, *Chaucer and estates satire* [573] (esp. pp. 189–201); Robinson, *Works of Chaucer*, pp. 21, 81; Szittya, *Antifraternal tradition*

The traditional constituents of some of this literature, such as the anti-mendicant attacks, suggest that some of these assaults may lack substance. Post-medieval interpretation of the great literary works has generated a whole industry of commentary and glossing, some of it contradictory, and in bulk impossible to synthesize. But such synthesis is not needed here, for in approaching general spirituality what matters is not an author's individual standpoint, but the medieval readers' recognition that the works mirrored their own spirituality.

Unfortunately, the spiritual concerns of the readers of such 'literary' works are usually totally obscure. The only guide to reception and comprehension is citation and possession, but mere possession is no sure evidence of understanding, or indeed of reading. Possession may reflect interest, but this can be only imperfectly analysed: perhaps a general sympathy for affective piety in the writings of the mystics, or an appreciation of satire on the church in the readers of Chaucer and Langland, with some concern for improvement in institutional and private morality; but little more can be assumed.

The more explicitly 'religious' writing of the period ranges from intensely personal records like the 'autobiography' of Margery Kempe and the *Livre des seints medecins* of Henry of Lancaster,[24] to anonymous short pieces providing impersonal translations and expositions of the Creed and other devotional instruction. They reflect an almost insatiable hunger for spiritual guidance. Many of the writings survive in unique copies, although there were 'best-sellers' like Nicholas Love's *Myrrour of the blessed lyf of Jesu Christ*, or Richard Rolle's *Emendatio Vite* (both in its original Latin version, and in the English translation made by Richard Misyn in 1434, as *The Emendation of Lyf*).[25] Much of the writing consists of 'modules' which can be considered individually and subjected to different purposes; while the distribution of works within individual manuscripts may also hint at differing uses reflected in the overall character of the compilations. The wide appeal of such writings was obviously appreciated by those seeking to influence opinions, with the Lollards interpolating otherwise orthodox

[806]; Bennett, *Middle English literature* [55], pp. 437–55; Aers, *Chaucer, Langland* [3], ch. 2 (he seems to accept the push for reform but to want to deny the spirituality, an aim only partly achieved – see pp. 5–79, *passim*); Patterson, 'The "Parson's Tale"' [645]; Jordan, *Chaucer and creation* [454], pp. 227–41; Olson, *Canterbury Tales and good society* [616], pp. 276–93. (For an assertion that the *Parson's Tale* is 'not literature', see Pearsall, *The Canterbury Tales* [649], pp. 289–93.)

[24] Arnould, *Le livre des seints medecins* [13] (see also Arnould, 'Henry of Lancaster' [12], pp. 364–86); Meech and Allen, *Margery Kempe* [579].

[25] For MSS and printed versins of Love's work, Salter, *Nicholas Love's "Myrrour"* [726], pp. 2–10, 18–19; also Salter, 'Manuscripts of Love's *Myrrour*' [727], pp. 123–6; Doyle, 'Some MSS. of Love's Myrrour' [229]. For MSS and printed versions of Rolle, Allen, *Writings ascribed to Rolle* [5], pp. 230–45.

works to propagate their own views among possibly unwary readers.[26] The instruction given is generally straightforward, but some works reveal a deeper spirituality. The 'mystical' writers, such as Richard Rolle, Walter Hilton, and Julian of Norwich, grappled with the problem of expressing a tradition of Latin spirituality in English, and had to stretch the language considerably (although in less mystical treatises the writers worked largely within the extant vocabulary). The problem of using human language to describe divinity had been long appreciated, and was recognized by some of the 'mystics'; but others (especially the more individual and less 'theological' writers) perhaps experienced such difficulties without acknowledging them – or may not have appreciated the intricacies of the language from which they derived some of their ideas. Modern reactions to a work like Margery Kempe's *Book* may thus be affected by its author's inability to communicate effectively her feelings about God, making her spirituality seem cruder than it really was.[27]

The period's spiritual writing firmly integrated English spirituality into a wider tradition. Medieval England is sometimes considered a land of conservative spiritual leanings, largely unaffected by contemporary continental movements, notably the Flemish pietistic strand known as the *devotio moderna*. This is only partially true. England's integration into the western Christian tradition meant that it shared the continental theological heritage, evidenced in the linguistic treatment of mysticism, for instance. The cross-currents which allowed Wycliffism to influence the development of Bohemian Hussitism are mirrored in the influence of continental movements in England. Given the problems of dissemination, these influences were naturally small-scale; but it is too easy viewing the continent from England to magnify some of the continental movements and assume that individual outbreaks of particular forms of spirituality had immediate continent-wide applications. The Flemish *devotio moderna* differed from the spirituality of Catherine of Siena and Brigit of Sweden; yet England was receptive to both. The Flemish movement was perhaps the more easily imported, and is reflected in vernacular translations of several devotional works. The latter movements had less direct links. Brigittine influence was more royal and aristocratic in origin, but still resulted in some distribution of vernacular versions of Brigittine writings. The influence of St Catherine is less obvious, but is shown in an English

---

[26] Barratt, 'Works of religious instruction', pp. 427–8; Martin, 'Middle English manuals' [576]; Hudson, *Lollards and their books* [420], p. 203 and refs.

[27] Riehle, *The Middle English mystics* [698], esp. pp. 8–9; Salter, *Nicholas Love's "Myrrour"*, pp. 222, 226–7, 237, 239–40, 243, 256; Evans, 'Borrowed meaning' [259], pp. 165–75. The problem of developing a vernacular theological language also faced reformist writers, with 'Lollardy' being responsible for many neologisms in this period: Aston, 'Wyclif and vernacular' [17], pp. 303–4.

version of her *Dialogus*, translated as the *Orcherd of Syon*. Margery Kempe herself reflects continental influences. Her book has considerable affinities with Middle English translations of works of continental beguines, and her experiences parallel those of other continental female *dévotes*. Moreover, a notable feature of her life is her extensive contacts with Germans.[28]

There were also other continental imports, of cults and works. English spirituality shows little extensive contact with these movements until the late fifteenth century; but influence would not need direct contact. The consistent tradition of western theology here becomes important, as does the close parallel between fifteenth-century theological developments and those of the twelfth. As continental writers rediscovered and reinterpreted the major twelfth-century theologians, late medieval English spirituality reveals similar trends in its search for God. These links are perhaps most explicitly indicated by a fifteenth-century vernacular translation of Latin sermons by the twelfth-century Parisian master William de Montibus. Other translations indicate similar dependence.[29]

The translation movement was important. Available evidence suggests that continental spiritual works were available in English in only limited numbers until the middle or late fifteenth century, so that their full impact must perhaps be sought in the early sixteenth century. The mechanics of dissemination effectively precluded widespread distribution until the advent of printing. Additionally, much of the spiritual writing of the major continental movements was in their vernaculars – Dutch or Italian. Their importation generally involved a process of double translation: first into Latin, and thence into English. Typical instances were the translations of some of the works of Ruysbroek (one of the luminaries of the *devotio moderna*) and the writings of Catherine of Siena. English itself caused problems, requiring 'translations' even from Northern to Southern English.[30] Despite difficulties of dissemination, texts were transmitted in England, especially via the Carthusians. They apparently sought deliberately to make spiritual writings available within their order both nationally and internationally, even preparing Latin versions of English writings for

[28] Heath, 'Urban piety' [372], p. 228; Lovat, '*Imitation of Christ*' [530], p. 117; Riehle, *The Middle English mystics*, esp. pp. 24–33 (on the presence of the *devotio moderna*, ibid. pp. 22–3); Kaminsky, *Hussite revolution* [456], pp. 23–55; Hodgson and Leigey, *The Orcherd of Syon* [407]; Atkinson, *Mystic and pilgrim* [21], p. 168; Stargardt, 'Beguines, Dominican nuns, and Margery Kempe' [775] (more successful in placing Margery in her spiritual context than the more usual comparisons with female continentals; cf. Atkinson, *Mystic and pilgrim*, ch. 6).

[29] Spencer, 'Fifteenth-century translation' [774]. On general links see Constable, 'Twelfth-century spiritual writers' [161]; Constable, 'Twelfth century spirituality' [162].

[30] Lovat, '*Imitation of Christ*', p. 111 and n. 4; de Soer, 'Relationship of the Latin version' [207]; Denise, 'Introduction' [199], pp. 290–1 (see also Hodgson, '*The Orcherd* and the mystical tradition' [406], pp. 230–2); Salter, *Nicholas Love's "Myrrour"*, pp. 11, 12 n. 44 (at p. 13).

continental circulation – further evidence of England's integration into a wider world. The Carthusians' role seems to have been preservative rather than distributive, with the notable exception of Nicholas Love's *Myrrour of the blessed lyf of Jesu Christ*, which does seem to have been deliberately widespread to counter Lollardy. The Carthusians also helped to spread the works of some of the English mystics, notably Richard Rolle and Walter Hilton.[31]

Printing substantially increased the availability of spiritual works. Even so, the translations which were prepared were probably intended for religious orders, or small coteries of intellectuals (for example that surrounding Lady Margaret Beaufort, which sponsored the first printed English version of the *Imitatio Christi*). But once printed, such works became increasingly available, allowing these new strands of religious experience to be assimilated into general lay spirituality.[32]

The writings themselves do not allow an assessment of the overall acceptance of these spiritual trends among the English people, although individual works testify to their presence. The Bible-centred views of Sir John Clanvowe (if he was the author) reflected in *The Two Ways* to the exclusion of all other authorities, thus suggest his attitude to the focus of authority for the Christian life; while Margery Kempe's references to hearing the books of other writers for spiritual guidance indicate her spiritual aspirations, even if her text cannot attain the spiritual heights of her mentors. 'Fictional' writers cause rather different problems. The miscellaneous nature of Chaucer's canon almost prevents the extraction of any coherent spirituality, forcing emphasis on specific aspects of his possible beliefs which may or may not be significant. With Langland, the position is even less clear. Although his work clearly has a spiritual intention, the density of its construction, and the changing emphases in the successive recensions of the text, render its precise message obscure (whether by text or subsequent commentary) except at a very general level.[33]

As literary works can indicate only uncertain generalizations, or individual stances, more comprehensive assessments of spirituality must be sought elsewhere. Any quantitative approach to spirituality and religion requires material capable of such analysis. For late medieval England, the main such corpus is provided by the wills, thousands of which survive – although many thousands more have perished. The small fragment of the population

---

[31] Lovat, '*Imitation of Christ*', pp. 107–12; Sargent, 'Transmission by Carthusians' [736] (see also Sargent, 'Minor devotional writings', pp. 149–57, 161).

[32] Lovat, '*Imitation of Christ*', pp. 97–100.

[33] Scattergood, *Works of Clanvowe* [750], pp. 19–21, 57–80, 86–9; Meech and Allen, *Margery Kempe*, p. 39 (see also below, n. 91); Colledge and Evans, 'Piers Plowman' [157], p. 121.

actually leaving wills, and their limited social range (usually omitting the labouring classes and the peasantry), necessarily limit the conclusions which can be drawn. Moreover, wills were not complete dispositions of property: they were usually death-bed statements, and frequently ignore pre-mortem gifts and donations. Except in towns enjoying the privilege of disposal of real property by bequest, wills also generally ignore lands and estates, and therewith a large part of an individual's wealth. The will's main significance lies in its being made at a specific point, in fear or expectation of death, thus reflecting aspirations and preparations for the after-life. But the degree of individuality reflected in each will, and the voluntary nature of the donations, are questionable. At the point of death the testator would be prey to numerous pressures; where illiterate, and thus probably dependent on a cleric to write the will, many of those pressures would be religious and spiritual, tending to produce a formulaic response. Individual bequests may therefore be skewed by fear for the after-life and the machinations of the scribe, while the wording of some sections may also give a distorted picture of individual spiritual concerns.[34]

This is of particular importance in the more abstract areas of the will. Saints are usually invoked, and pious statements made, but the reality of that piety is uncertain. Will prologues, the hopeful statements about the soul's future, have been identified as a convenient means of assessing changing religious sentiments, especially during the Reformation period. Whilst this may well apply to those years, as Catholic formulae gradually declined in the prologues, it probably cannot be used extensively earlier. The role of the amanuensis could have been quite significant: for the period 1540 to 1640 it has been suggested that the scribe might impose his own prejudices on the religious sentiments expressed in the will, or follow the precedents in formularies. That such practices applied earlier is hinted at by a group of early fifteenth-century Salisbury wills.[35]

Furthermore, the 'spiritual' elements in wills were essentially literary constructions, and thus may reveal little of their producers. Hints of individuality may emerge, but those which reveal a testator's soul are in a very small minority. Judgements that a group of wills reflect a particularly 'shallow' type of spirituality have to be made with caution: the wills may not reveal much, but can conceal much.[36] Nor, when individuality is

---

[34] For extant wills, see Gibson, *Wills and where to find them* [297] or (slightly better) Camp, *Wills and their whereabouts* [124]; on property and will-making Sheehan, *The Will in medieval England* [757], pp. 266–81; Owst, *Literature and pulpit* [632], pp. 164–5.

[35] Cross, 'Wills as evidence of popular piety' [177]; Timmins, *Reg. Chandler* [841], p. xxxv and n. 124, nos. 403, 499, 505 (see also references to God as Creator ibid., nos. 472, 482, 501, 527, 556, 603).

[36] For this reason, Heath's assessment of the Hull wills ('Urban piety', p. 229) strikes me as being far too subjective. For 'revealing wills' see Vale, *Piety, charity and literacy*, pp. 14–15.

indicated, can the idiosyncracies necessarily be linked with identifiable trends. The existence of 'Lollard wills' has been suggested between 1380 and 1420; but their formulae, disregarding worldly pomp and ignoring funeral trappings, need not be heretical: such wills crop up throughout the period, reflecting something of a minor fashion. They may be no more than a particularly developed expression of that 'self-denigrating, contemptuous, penitential' piety which was shared by many among the upper classes, and doubtless aped by their inferiors. The apparent concentration around 1400 may be mere archival accident, or reflect a particularly energetic period in such will-making (sufficiently common for such parsimonious practices to be condemned in *Dives and pauper*), embracing an archbishop of Canterbury as well as some knights linked to areas where Lollardy was relatively strong.[37]

A will's omissions may be as important as its contents – absence of provision for spiritual bequests may show either a lack of spirituality, or forward planning with arrangements already made. The amount of charitable activity during life is a very obscure area of late medieval spirituality; it is unquantifiable, but cannot be ignored. Nor, really, can wills be subjected to dependable statistical analysis. There is always the problem of the disposition of the residue of the estate, usually for pious purposes which are rarely revealed. The sums involved, and the discretion allowed to executors, makes merely counting the value of bequests a fairly worthless exercise. Where inventories survive, they can indicate the disparity between the amount bequeathed and the sum actually available. The leeway left to executors is shown by the will of one Thomas Fyneham. In 1518 he left his executors the task of distributing an outstanding debt as it was gradually repaid. The sum of 415 marks was to be

disposed in works of mercy and deeds of charity by the discretion of my executors, that is to say to priests to sing for my soul, in repair and construction of highways, in distribution to poor folk where need requires, to prisoners in prison, and in ornaments and jewels to be given to churches, and for the exhibition of poor scholar students.

But how much was actually spent would depend on how much was collected; while its disbursement in this case (but perhaps not others) would reflect the priorities of the executors rather than the testator.[38]

---

[37] Vale, *Piety, charity and literacy*, pp. 2–3, 11–14, 17–20; Barnum, *Dives and pauper*, i, pp. 213–17; Dobson, 'Residentiary canons of York' [217], p. 169; McFarlane, *Lancastrian kings* [548], pp. 207–20; Weaver, *Somerset medieval wills* [889], p. 41.

[38] Dobson, 'Residentiary canons of York', p. 168; Moorman, *Friars in Cambridge* [592], p. 251; see also Weaver, *Somerset medieval wills*, pp. 148–9. For the general problem of the reliability of wills, Burgess, ' "By quick and by dead" ' [106], pp. 840–5, 854–6.

Changing patterns of formalized bequests may also reveal little about levels of spirituality. Change in numerical patterns probably cannot be taken to indicate changing beliefs in practice: it may be merely a matter of changing customs, which need to be elucidated from other sources.[39]

Perhaps the greatest difficulty with wills is that despite their detail they are only statements of aspirations, produced in the hope that they would be implemented. In some cases the money did not exist, and alternative arrangements had to be made. Execution itself could take time – even years – especially when large amounts of cash were involved and complex legal transactions might be needed (always assuming that the will was not challenged, producing further legal action). Sometimes executors refused to act; for the formal assumption of the execution incurred the obligation to fulfil the bequests even if the estate was insufficient, thereby leaving the executor out of pocket as well. Once assumed, the obligations of execution were also transmitted to the executor's heirs, and such inheritance carried with it increased risks of non-execution. Occasionally duties were assumed but not completed; sometimes obstruction prevented execution. Visitation returns contain frequent complaints against non-execution, often failures to perform bequests for the testator's soul which would have benefited the local church. But not all non-execution was deliberate. An executor dying with his own affairs in confusion might mean that the original testator's affairs were left in chaos, and bequests could not be paid.[40]

Despite the dangers in basing assessments of religious attitudes and spirituality on such varied, incomplete, and possibly misleading material, the attempt has to be made. Even if proper qualitative or quantitative analysis is impossible, an impression is gained of how far individuals committed themselves to a religious life, of how they expressed their piety, and of the concern for their fellows revealed by charitable activities.

6.2   RELIGIOUS LIFE

Christianity as a religious vocation provided many roads to spiritual satisfaction in late medieval England. The degree of commitment demanded by that vocation varied, as did its institutional format. In particular,

---

[39] See comment of Chiffoleau, 'Les testaments provençaux' [141], p. 143.

[40] Heath, 'Urban piety', pp. 212–13 (even archbishops made provision for the insufficiency of their estates: Dahmus, *William Courtenay*, p. 276); Moorman, *Friars in Cambridge*, p. 251; Burson, '". . . for the sake of my soul"' [110], pp. 132–6; Weaver, *Somerset medieval wills*, pp. 148–9; Hicks, 'Beauchamp trust' [383], pp. 139–41; Wood-Legh, *Kentish visitations*, pp. 65–289 (esp. pp. 160, 162, 170–1, 238, 288); Richmond, 'Religion and the English gentleman' [695], pp. 195–6; Barnum, *Dives and pauper*, ii, pp. 268–9, 278–80.

the late middle ages reveal modes of life for which earlier evidence is scarce – notably increasing lay activity and a mystical strand in devotion. Commitment was also expressed through the religious orders, monastic, mendicant, and military.

With the male religious orders the concern is not with their continuing appeal numerically, but with the rise of new orders which reflected changes in spirituality and declining appreciation of the older system. This was a European phenomenon, in which England appears somewhat laggardly, with the old monastic and mendicant orders facing few real challenges. The only notable change occurred with the increase in Carthusian foundations, rising from three houses in 1350 to eight by 1420. While the number of inmates was not large (there were never more than 200 Carthusians in English houses at any one time), nevertheless the new houses do suggest the integration of a new strand of spirituality, with the Carthusian ethic of retreat from the world merging into the mystical strand of contemporary devotion. It is perhaps significant that some Carthusians chose their life rather late in their careers, having begun as secular clerics, sometimes with fairly high office, as with the 'ex-Lollard' Nicholas Hereford, whose career as Chancellor of Hereford ended with him entering the Charterhouse at Coventry. Although few in number, England's late medieval Carthusians were not insignificant, providing a model for much lay devotion, and a channel for the transmission and preservation of many of the major devotional and mystical writings of the time.

Other new religious orders developed on the continent, but had little impact in England. The only projected house of Celestines – planned for Henry V's collection of religious houses at Sheen – foundered at its inception. The Observant Franciscans were the only reformed group among the mendicants to be introduced, but found little support. The order arrived late, again under royal auspices, and only a few houses were established. The known Observants in England were mainly foreigners, suggesting a lack of English enthusiasm (although odd English Observants are known in continental houses).[41] However, England may not have needed an Observant movement: there are signs of a strand among the English Franciscans which was throughout fairly rigid in its approach to the rule. There was certainly a continuing popular commitment to the friars in their 'unreformed' state, which will need consideration elsewhere.[42]

Female regulars perhaps provided the main non-clerical element of late medieval conventual life. Women were incapable of becoming priests; but

---

[41] Knowles, *Religious orders* [484], ii, pp. 129–38, 181–2; Lovat, '*Imitation of Christ*', p. 113 (also citing a late recruit among the Brigittines); Emden, *Oxford* [255], ii, pp. 914–15; Little, 'Observant Friars' [513], pp. 455–71. On numbers of male religious, 2/5 at nn. 155–7.

[42] Whitfield, 'Conflicts of personality and principle' [897], pp. 325, 340–2; below, at nn. 116–17.

holy virgins had long been praised, and nunneries and female religious orders were old-established. English nunneries were relatively numerous, but usually poor (with Shaftesbury and Amesbury being notable exceptions to that generalization). The number of nuns had been halved by the Black Death, to *c.*1,500. They had recovered to about 2,300 by 1420, thereafter again dropping slowly and slightly, to around 2,100 in 1500, and 2,000 at the start of the Reformation.[43] Female religious life in the later middle ages suffers from even greater evidential problems than encountered in dealing with male houses. Their lay status leaves scant material revealing the appeal of the life to women; and the possibility that nunneries were 'dumping-grounds' for unwanted daughters prevents assessment of religious commitment from the scant evidence of numbers. Nevertheless, the nunneries existed. Like male houses, they sometimes appear in a poor light – the visitation reports are often bad for both sexes. But the visitation reports are an insecure guide to vocations: they reveal the bad, but the good can only be inferred. Yet services may often have been neglected, or little understood. The general inability to read Latin (or even, despite Chaucer's Prioress, French) cannot have aided understanding of their devotions, possibly giving them a purely rote character. Lack of comprehension cannot have added to the sincerity of their main oratorical task, the repetition of psalters for specific intentions. There were attempts to remedy such defects, such as Richard Rolle's English Psalter, providing a sort of parallel text to assist understanding, English Bibles, and works like the *Myrroure of Oure Ladye* (a vernacular rendition of the services maintained at Syon, to aid the nuns). Nunneries probably owned other English devotional works, but the surviving indications of their book-ownership are sparse.[44] Ultimately, despite what is known about the nunneries, surprisingly little is revealed about individual vocations or the attitude of non-errant nuns towards their devotional life. The only place providing much evidence is Syon, an anomaly as the only house of the new double Brigittine order in England. Its proximity to Sheen Charterhouse is reflected in its sharing in Carthusian spirituality and the semi-mystical tradition of the period; but this again only stresses the house's extraordinary character.[45]

---

[43] On nunneries in general, Power, *English nunneries* [671]. For numbers of inmates, Russell, 'Clerical population' [721], pp. 181–4; Knowles and Hadcock, *Religious houses* [488], pp. 493–4.

[44] Power, *English nunneries*, pp. 246–55, 494–8; Blunt, *Myrroure of Oure Ladye*, pp. 72–332; Ker, *Medieval libraries* [467], pp. 3–4, 6, 28, 50, 87, 93, 95, 104, 106–7, 123, 128–9, 140, 177, 182, 184, 187, 197–8, 201–2; Watson, *Medieval libraries; supplement* [884], pp. 1–2, 13–15, 56, 62, 64–5.

[45] Knowles, *Religious orders*, ii, pp. 175–81.

Many opportunities existed outside the regular life of the orders for individuals to find spiritual fulfilment, or declare their spirituality, through commitment to a specific way of life. Sometimes this supplemented a formal regular existence; sometimes it was outside such constraints. Just how widespread this desire for a regulated spiritual life actually was is indeterminable. The author of *The abbey of the holy ghost* suggests that

> many wolde ben in religioun but they mowe nowt for poverte or for awe or for drede of her kyn or for bond of maryage. Therfore I make here a book of relygyon of the herte . . . that tho that mow nout been in bodylyche relygyon mow been in gostly.[46]

Occasionally, signs of this wider appeal break through, but only occasionally.

Several distinct types of formal commitment to a spiritual life were available outside the orders. Perhaps the most regular was the connection with a hospital, often staffed by lay brethren and sisters as well as their clerical members. They were quasi-regular in organization, usually having a regime based on the Augustinian rule. The lay brethren and sisters took on spiritual duties within the houses, which included recitations of Paternosters and Aves, although precise evidence for numbers involved is relatively scarce.[47]

The other available modes of living were more individual. Both sexes might take vows of chastity, which appear especially ritualized for widows. For them, the ceremony included taking a veil and being invested with a ring – but without making the individual fully a nun. Many such vows are recorded in episcopal registers. There are hints that they approached a concept of order, with the women being examined in a process paralleling the examination of clerical ordinands. Married women (and sometimes their husbands) also took oaths of chastity: Margery Kempe eventually persuaded her husband to share her determination to be chaste, both taking their oaths before the Bishop of Lincoln, while the vow of chastity taken by Lady Margaret Beaufort, mother to Henry VII, apparently originated while she was married to the Earl of Derby. Sometimes a vow of perpetual chastity followed the supercession of a marriage – when a husband wished to become a priest or an anchorite.[48]

Men also took an oath of perpetual chastity when they adopted the life of a hermit. Numbers entering this life before the fifteenth century are

---

[46] Blake, *Religious prose* [64], p. 89.

[47] The only general treatment of English hospitals remains Clay, *Mediaeval hospitals* [150], although rather anecdotal. For the brethren, Rubin, *Charity and community* [718], p. 179.

[48] Swanson, *Reg. Scrope*, i, pp. 19–21, 42, 93; Smith, 'A reconstruction' [766], p. 40; LAO, FOR.3, f. 94r–v; BL, MS Add. 14848, f. 79v (see below, n. 56); Cooper, *Memorial* [165], pp. 97–8; see also Clay, *Mediaeval hospitals*, p. 147.

unrecorded, as the acquisition of hermit status seems to have been quite unregulated. But the fifteenth century suggests a greater definition of the hermit life, most adopting the way of living codified in the so-called Rule of St Paul the First Hermit. The lay hermits remained laity, with modest religious obligations which for the unlettered were little more than repetitions of the Paternoster and Ave at the canonical hours. They were usually under the jurisdiction of the local clergy (although sometimes having their own chapels or oratories), and were frequently associated with public works, especially the maintenance of roads and bridges. They presumably lived from their own labours, or from charitable donations – and there may be a link between the increasing evidence for hermits in the fifteenth century, and bequests for roads and bridges at that time. Some would also have benefited from the receipts for indulgences. Spiritually, they also gained from the prayers for such works and workers which were sometimes offered with the mass.[49]

The organizational framework for these hermits remained weak. Whatever their obligations, many were clearly not bound to a particular location. Several were wanderers, although still called hermits; whether they were actually 'holy tramps' or 'medieval hippies' is open to question. Their wanderings may indeed have been encouraged: some received bequests to perform vicarious pilgrimages, perhaps forming a pool of semi-professional pilgrims living off such benefactions.[50] Some hermits were secular or regular clergy, but their primarily lay and unregulated status perhaps allowed the life to be assumed without any formal commitment. Richard Rolle's impromptu assumption of hermit clothing lacked formal ecclesiastical sanction, his life involved considerable instability, and it is doubtful whether he ever attained any official standing within the ecclesiastical system.[51] Several of the 'early Lollards' of the late fourteenth century may have been in a similar situation. The group outside Leicester led by William Swinderby apparently consisted mainly of laymen, with William being considered a hermit. His activities (like Rolle's enhabiting) contain reminiscences of a primitive Franciscanism – with the Leicester chapel substituting for the Assisi Portiuncula.[52]

---

[49] Davis, 'Rule of St Paul' [198], pp. 204–13 (compare the profession at p. 206 with the vows of perpetual widowhood in Jacob, *Reg. Chichele* [438], iv, p. 221); Wilson, *Reg. Coventry and Lichfield, book 5* [916], pp. 24, 28, 37–8; Clay, *Hermits and anchorites* [151], chs 1–6, *passim*, and pp. 85–90, 101–3, 105–6, 108–9; Madox, *Formulare Anglicanum* [570], p. 321; Simmons, *Lay folks' mass book* [760], p. 65.

[50] Tanner, *Church in Norwich* [810], p. 62; see also Pearsall, *Piers Plowman* [647], p. 30; Hamilton, *Religion* [342], p. 186.

[51] Woolley, *Officium and miracula* [925], pp. 5–6, 23–4; see also Marzac, *Richard Rolle* [577], pp. 25–33. See also citation of Langland in Davis, 'Rule of St Paul', p. 205.

[52] McFarlane, *Wycliffe and non-conformity* [547], pp. 90–1, 107–10.

In this unregulated state, individual vocations are generally untestable. Rolle's obviously persisted; but others may have lapsed. Langland thought many contemporary hermits were frauds, assuming the life as a cloak of holiness to evade work – a charge possibly reflected in legislation requiring hermits to have formal testimonial letters from their bishops. The writer of *Dives and pauper* was equally uncomplimentary, suggesting that many abandoned the life after a while, having taken it on for the wrong reasons. Interestingly, he regarded women as having more fixed vocations than men (although here referring especially to the final category of ordered life available to the laity, that of anchorite or recluse).[53]

An anchorite's life represented perhaps the ultimate in commitment, for it involved being walled up in a small cell, usually attached to a church, in a life supposedly devoted to God.[54] Although this was a drastic step, it was not totally anti-social: such recluses were normally dependent on charity for sustenance, so their cells were usually where charity could be offered. Towns therefore had more than their fair share. But recluses might be religious as well as laity; so they were relatively widespread. There are several instances of anchorite nuns, and monks, to parallel the lay experience. As with hermits and veiled widows, there are suggestions of a concept of order, with those anchorages which were formally endowed virtually constituting benefices, and subject to all the patronage and other tensions of that status.[55]

Given the scantiness of the evidence, it is difficult to reach many conclusions about the anchorites of medieval England. Again, their commitment is untestable – but, given the rigours, the vocation required some investigation before being conceded, and bishops were anxious to ensure that postulants did not take it on lightly. Individuals sometimes wavered from their single-minded devotion to God, but on the other hand their intensity did sometimes affect the outside world. Julian of Norwich was consulted by Margery Kempe, and her influential *Book of Showings* was aimed at a wider public. The Westminster recluse was consulted by Richard II and Henry V; while Richard Methley was inspired by an anchorite to make his own commitment to the Carthusian life. Some made the choice late in life, like William Cheney, a London merchant who embraced an anchorite's life while still married.[56] Some of the period's

---

[53] Pearsall, *Piers Plowman*, p. 30; Davis, 'Rule of St Paul', p. 206; Barnum, *Dives and pauper*, ii, pp. 92–3.

[54] Clay, *Hermits and anchorites*, pp. 73–84, 90–100, 103–15, 128–45; Warren, *Anchorites and their patrons* [883], pp. 7–124, 286–9.

[55] Warren, *Anchorites and their patrons*, pp. 37–51, 65–71, 74–5, 127–286; Power, *English nunneries*, pp. 365–6.

[56] Peers and Taylor, 'Some recent discoveries' [650], pp. 156–9; Hogg, 'Mount Grace Charterhouse' [408], p. 28; Clay, *Hermits and anchorites*, pp. 153–5; Meech and Allen, *Margery*

spiritual writings were addressed to anchorites to strengthen their devotion, such as the meditation written by the Cistercian William Rymyngton, originally addressed to a reclusive monk, but acquiring a wider audience. The potential intensity of the anchorite's spirituality is shown in Julian of Norwich's work, one of the most powerful vernacular theological works of the period. Other solitaries reached similar heights: in the 1360s Durham's cell at Farne held a recluse – probably John Whiterig – whose meditations strongly reflect his personal devotions.[57]

Other forms of lay religious life may have been available in England, but leave virtually no evidence. In the thirteenth century, continental lay spirituality had developed two significant strands: the beguinage, and the tertiaries of the main mendicant orders. Beguinages held groups of laity (mainly women) living a communal life, lacking formal religious commitment, but accepting some sort of rule. Initially distrusted, they were later accepted as a valid expression of spirituality, and incorporated into the ecclesiastical structure. They were especially evident in the Low Countries and the Rhineland. It is possible that similar groups were established in England; but evidence is decidedly scanty. The hospital or chapel of Stow near Quy (Cambs.) sheltered a community of women which seems to have disappeared *c.*1350; while 'communities resembling beguinages' have been identified in fifteenth-century Norwich. Like anchorages, they would usually be ignored by official records, so could have existed undetected; but the totality of the silence is significant. Perhaps such groups are to be identified among the lay sisters who ran hospitals, but for which usually only the male clergy are identified.[58]

The tertiaries of the mendicant orders developed on the continent as lay branches of the orders, assuming some of their religious activities, and often responsibility for administering the order's property. They rather paralleled the fraternities, and assumed charitable activities. However, there is no English evidence for their existence; perhaps the fraternities took on all the work, and met all the religious needs. Possibly association with the mendicants by confraternity replaced the need for formal membership of a lay order like the tertiaries. Links between mendicant houses and individual fraternities (such as the guild of St Francis at Lynn

---

Kempe, pp. 42–3; Warren, *Anchorites and their patrons*, pp. 182–3; BL, MS Add. 14848, f. 79v (for a later reference, Clay, *Hermits and anchorites*, p. 92).

[57] McNulty, 'William of Rymyngton' [567], MSS listed at pp. 243–5; for editions of Julian, von Nolcken, 'Julian of Norwich' [606], pp. 97–108; Lagorio and Bradley, *Fourteenth century English mystics* [491], pp. 105–26; for the Farne meditations Farmer, 'The meditations' [264], pp. 141–245 (translation in Farmer, *The monk of Farne* [265], authorship discussed at pp. 2–6), see also Farmer, 'The monk of Farne' [266], Pantin, 'The monk-solitary of Farne' [636].

[58] McDonnell, *Beguines and beghards* [546]; Tanner, *Church in Norwich*, pp. 64–6; Rubin, *Charity and community*, pp. 135–6; Clay, *Mediaeval hospitals*, pp. 152–5.

[Norfolk], which met in the Franciscan house) might suggest the existence of 'unofficial' tertiaries; but the evidence is again inconclusive.[59]

Finally there were the military orders, whose members (if involved in fighting) were definitely lay. They adopted many of the obligations of a monastic life – services, chastity, obedience – and can be considered regulars. But as knights they remained laymen. The Order of St John (the Hospitallers) had an English branch – the English *langue* (which incuded the Scots, Welsh, and Irish) – whose existence was continuous throughout the period, and with retained links with the main order despite the vicissitudes of the Great Schism. Then the leadership supported the Avignon pope, while the English branch probably adhered to the Roman line, like the rest of England.[60] The precise number of English knight-brothers is hard to determine. The English contingent at the main fortress at Rhodes remained a steady twenty-eight, but there were doubtless others in England. However many there were, their life provided another means of expressing commitment to a religious and spiritual existence.[61]

Although so much regulation existed, in the end only a small minority of the English people made the formal commitment which regulation entailed. Most lived outside any sort of ordering, but were still members of the church. Their more popular piety needs as much consideration as the regulated – especially as the religious observances of the orders were a part of the general spiritual climate.

6.3 PIETY

Piety in late medieval England rested on acceptance of the catholic faith, and its reflection in devotional practices. For present purposes such practices will be treated as essentially spiritual, although not all 'good works' can be left out: actions like the establishment of chantries and prayers for the soul must be included. One false trail is the tradition of treating 'popular' piety as something distinct from the piety of the upper classes or the clergy; the differentiation lacks any real justification, and will not be maintained here.

Before assessing acceptance of the faith, it is worth considering what people were expected to believe, and where they obtained that knowledge.

[59] Moorman, *Franciscan order* [593], pp. 40–5, 216–25, 417–28, 560–8; Whitfield, 'Third order of St Francis' [895]; Owen, *Lynn* [630], p. 324.

[60] Loyalty to Avignon is argued by Tipton, 'English hospitallers' [842], pp. 91–124; but King, *Grand priory* [472], pp. 47–50, has them remaining loyal to Rome. See comment in Swanson, 'Obedience and disobedients' [798], p. 381 and n. 20.

[61] King, *Grand priory*, p. 34 for establishment, and for other totals pp. 38–9, 66–8, 72–4, 88–9.

The faith's formal content is readily accessible, in the instructional works produced during the period. Some of these were directed to the laity themselves, others to the clergy. Lay people were usually expected to know the Creed, Paternoster, and Ave Maria, and be able to identify the sacraments, the seven deadly sins, the works of charity, the acts of mercy, and the seven virtues. Generally there appears to have been little exposition – the impression is of knowledge which was little more than recitation; acceptance, acquiescence, and belief, rather than understanding, although the recitations presuppose a wider definition and knowledge of the meanings of the words.[62] A lay person was also required to confess and receive the Eucharist at least once a year, as established by the Fourth Lateran Council in 1215. Generally, the theological appreciation of the main church service, the mass, may have been unsound. The mass certainly attracted a strong devotion, but this seems to have emphasized the magical grace-imbuing properties of the celebration, concentrating on transubstantiation. There developed a veritable cult of the consecrated elements, especially the Host, most vividly expressed in the concept of Corpus Christi. The cultic element of the devotion to the Host – in which actual communion seemed almost irrelevant – was perhaps the strongest aspect of lay piety of the time. It linked in with the strongly Christocentric . approach to Christianity, with the creation of new Jesus feasts, the proliferation of pilgrimage crosses (and fragments of the True Cross), and an emphatically Christ-centred strand in devotional and meditative writing. These emphases threatened to trivialize the central elements of the faith and reduce their intellectual content. The emphasis on the consecrated elements at the expense of other aspects of Christian life produced the situation of which William Thorpe complained in 1407, recalling the virtual stampede from his sermon when a sacring bell rang elsewhere in the church and the audience dashed off to witness the elevation. It was against such virtual idolatry (as they saw it) that Wyclif and contemporary continental reformers reacted by seeking a change in emphasis in the 1380s and later, although with little success in England.[63]

Such devotion to the mass highlighted the sacrificial element in the celebration, and the priest's peculiar status as celebrant. His role, per-

[62] Meech, 'John Drury' [578], pp. 76–9; Russell, 'Vernacular instruction of the laity', pp. 114–17 (although for instances of greater exposition in individual cases, ibid., pp. 105–6, 111, 113–14); Aston, 'Wyclif and the vernacular', pp. 301–2.

[63] Richter and Friedberg, *Corpus iuris canonici* [697], ii, col. 887–8; Salter, *Nicholas Love's "Myrrour"*, pp. 126–78; Bossy, 'The mass as a social institution' [75] (some of his comments, esp. at pp. 48–52, seem questionable: the communion of the Holy Loaf as a replacement for the communion of the consecrated elements in producing social integration requires further attention); Aston, *Lollards and reformers* [15], pp. 130–1; Catto, 'Wyclif and the Eucharist', pp. 275–86.

forming an essentially private rite in the chancel, rather excluded the laity from much involvement in the central core of the services. Yet the laity obviously attended masses, in considerable numbers. In some churches, if there were sufficient priests, a timetable staggered masses to accommodate those who wished to attend. Yet, although the laity attended, the surviving texts produced for their use suggest that they were actually participating in a different service. Their main role was as spectators. The service they recited was one of their own, in which the choreographical directions and verbal cues were provided by the chancel rite, but the script was different. They were encouraged to a series of recitals of Creeds, Aves, and Paternosters, at identified points in the service, together with a litany of prayers for benefactors and others. The lay celebration was a counterpoint to the priest's, a syncopation placing lay 'participation' in a somewhat different perspective.[64]

As deep doctrinal awareness was not expected of the laity, the required knowledge was probably acquired early. John Drury, the schoolmaster of Beccles (Suffolk), was perhaps typical in including religious education in his curriculum, and producing an instructional tract (admittedly, fairly elementary). Lower education was directed mainly at boys, and it is unclear how much religious instruction girls obtained. Probably most people received no formal religious education. Modern notions of confirmation (and confirmation classes) as a necessary prerequisite to communion have few parallels in medieval England. Whilst advocated, confirmation was not considered absolutely necessary, and if administered was often conferred in childhood (even seven years being considered rather old), with little evidence of any programme of instruction. Most people probably did not bother to receive a sacrament which added little, if anything, to the effect of baptism. It is equally unlikely that any detailed knowledge of the faith was needed to claim confirmation. The instructions given by one priest to godparents deal mainly with keeping the child alive and avoiding dangers; the religious obligations being limited to inculcating the Paternoster, Creed, and Ave. These three elements apparently formed the total religious knowledge demanded of the unlettered, although some would also know other liturgical elements, such as the psalm *De profundis* (Psalm 130).[65]

Such minimal requirements were hardly great hurdles, and most people

[64] Kreider, *English chantries*, pp. 52–3; Aston, *Lollards and reformers*, pp. 122–4; Simmons, *Lay folks' mass book*, pp. 2–60 (see also Legg, *Tracts on the mass* [504], pp. 19–29, Pantin, 'Instructions' [639], pp. 399, 404–5).

[65] Meech, 'John Drury', p. 79 (see also Lupton, *Life of Colet* [536], pp. 286–90, and for attempts to prevent schoolmasters *mis*teaching on the sacraments, Wilkins, *Concilia* [902], iii, p. 317); Moran, *English schooling*, pp. 31–3, 53, 69–70; Fisher, *Christian initiation* [275], pp. 120–36; Littlehales, *English fragments* [518], p. 5.

DODDISCOMBSLEIGH CHURCH WINDOW   The church and spiritual life: Christ in majesty surrounded by representations of the Seven Sacraments. On the left the Eucharist (top), marriage, and confirmation; penance in the centre; on the right ordination (top), baptism, and extreme unction.
(Royal Commission on the Historical Monuments of England)

duly became communicants. The precise age of first communion is unclear: confirmation, if received, would offer a logical introduction, but
fourteen is another possibility.[66] Instruction in, or acquisition of, elements
of the faith would continue later, from many sources. Pictures and their
explanations served part of the process (but difficulties in iconographical
interpretation could have proved an obstacle as much as an aid). Literary
works would assist those who could read (and their hearers); but for most
the main authoritative source was probably sermons intended to impart
the knowledge summarized by John Drury. Sermons pose problems, for it
is impossible to tell how far surviving 'sermon literature' actually reflects
the practice of preaching. Many extant 'sermons' are of doubtful theological worth, being based mainly on *exempla* and encouraging repentance
rather than explaining the faith. But Margery Kempe's attachment to
them is obvious, and she would not have been unique. The increasing
availability of manuscript – even printed – versions of some sermon cycles
further indicates their popularity. Mystery and morality plays also provided some instruction, even if conveying anachronistic impressions, and
somewhat dubious illustrations of their meaning. Indeed, the interplay
between the many possible sources of religious instruction – sermons,
drama, literature, pictures, songs, and so forth – is a notable feature of the
period; their combination could only contribute towards the creation of a
pervasive but perhaps unconscious spiritual ethos. Finally, there were
discussions among the laity. Although doctrinal discussion was frowned on
when it occurred among the Lollards, the orthodox indulged in something
similar. Margery Kempe's table-talk provides one illustration, such discussions also being advocated in some of the rules for Christian domestic
life.[67]

However the faith was acquired, it was generally accepted. Too few
were ever questioned about their beliefs to justify the declaration that
England was doctrinally a truly catholic country; but it behaved like one
in its rituals and outward practices. Confusions could still exist, like those
expressed by George Carter in a visitation of Lincoln diocese in 1525.
Something of a visionary, he tried to explain his understanding of transubstantiation to his examiners. He was clearly not totally orthodox (and
in fact based his view on private revelation against ecclesiastical authority),

---

[66] Simmons, *Lay folks' mass book*, p. 121.

[67] Aston, *Lollards and reformers*, pp. 116–19, 127–9; Hamilton, *Religion*, pp. 72–3, 106;
Wenzel, *Preachers, poets, and lyric* [891], p. 7; Owst, *Preaching* (see esp. p. 193 and n. 4); Owst,
Literature and pulpit; Blench, *Preaching in England* [68], pp. 1–31, 71–86, 113–41, 209–15, 228–
52, 257–63, 321–34; Heffernan, 'Sermon literature' [375], pp. 177–9, 182–6; Nolan, 'Nicholas
Love' [605], pp. 92–3 and refs.; Robinson, 'Late medieval cult of Jesus' [704]; Dunn,
'Popular devotion' [238]; Cawley, 'Medieval drama' [131]; Meech and Allen, *Margery Kempe*,
p. 61; Pantin, 'Instructions', pp. 399–401, 407–8.

but was nevertheless trying to comprehend an extremely complex matter. Others may similarly have sought understanding through their own efforts, but left no trace unless accused of heresy. The clergy and orthodox intelligentsia did fear that, by meddling with theology and its intricacies, the populace might be led into error and heresy. This fear (regardless of any other overtones) is clear in concern about the spread of Lollardy and theology in English: misunderstanding was a greater danger than understanding. Similar concern appears in Thomas More's anxiety to encourage piety and devotion while fearful that people were tempted to delve into matters too deep for them.[68]

Piety found many outlets in the later middle ages. Some were collective – processions and fraternities which served collective civic purposes as well as private devotional ones. Others were individual: contrasting with collectivity there is a strong sense of retreat, of a search for private communion with God, explicit in some of the instructional literature and mystical writings.

The collective activities are the most visible aspect of late medieval piety. The main collectivity was the parish, with its organization of churchwardens, its taxation, and its shared services and entertainments. In many senses the parish was itself a fraternity, a point perhaps not usually given the emphasis it deserves. Communality manifested itself in activities like the distribution of the Holy Loaf, a blessed (but not consecrated) loaf divided among the parishioners after the Sunday mass in a lay version of the Eucharist. The parish's fraternal element is not immediately obvious in surviving records, but surfaces forcefully at Keele (Staffs.), whose extra-parochial status as a possession of the Order of St John stimulated the development of a system for lay administration of the services and hiring of priests under the auspices of a parish guild containing all the households.[69]

The guilds and fraternities achieved greater significance as purely voluntary associations. Their ubiquity, and the shared membership of both sexes, made them a major means of expressing religious sentiments; but equally rather obscures the nature of their spirituality.[70] Their great

---

[68] Peacock, 'Lincoln visitations' [646], pp. 252–3 (see also Bowker, *Henrician Reformation* [80], p. 63); Aston, 'Wyclif and the vernacular', esp. pp. 301–5; Lovat, '*Imitation of Christ*', p. 97.

[69] Owen, *Church and society*, pp. 102–3; Cox, *Churchwardens' accounts*, pp. 96–7 (failure to provide the loaf was sometimes presented as an offence at visitation: Timmins, *Reg. Chandler*, pp. xxiv, 4–6, 17, 37–8, 73, 81, 99–100, 108, 111). See also Owen, 'Bacon and eggs' [625], pp. 141–2; Studd, 'A Templar colony' [790], pp. 8–9.

[70] For a general European consideration (mostly for an earlier period) see Reynolds, *Kingdoms and communities* [693], pp. 68–78. The main work on English guilds is Westlake,

variety in aims and continuity partly explains this, ranging from miniscule groups maintaining a single altar light, to the massive urban guilds which achieved almost national importance – Corpus Christi at York, the Trinity Guild at Coventry (War.), and others. Some of these national institutions took on characteristics of what has been seen as a distinct form of grouping, the confraternity, which is usually treated as formal association with religious houses and hospitals. Guilds like that of Boston (Lincs.) similarly approached that status. Some guilds remain obscure: Knowle's (War.) had a massive membership, but precisely why remains unknown. Large guilds, with private chapels and hired priests, were clearly different in scale from their smaller counterparts, and perhaps also in intention.[71] Differences in size also produced differences in function. Many guilds, whilst maintaining religious associations, sought to serve two masters. Social and political functions were absorbed when specific guilds were identified with an urban elite. In some towns, like Coventry, the guild structure was enmeshed in the progression through the ranks of urban office. Elsewhere guild membership was virtually a pre-requisite for admission to the town's government, as with the Holy Cross guild at Stratford-on-Avon (War.) or the fraternity of St George at Norwich (Norfolk) after 1452.[72] A parish fraternity's subjection to its churchwardens stood in marked contrast to Coventry's subjection to the wardens of the Trinity guild. The guilds also assumed an economic function, being associated with particular crafts and trades. The medieval craft guilds were frequently (and often initially) religious associations; only the exploitation of the fraternity structure for other purposes emphasized their craft element. Possibly this misrepresented the members' priorities: craft guilds have significance because of craft regulations imposed by urban authorities – but those authorities would be uninterested in regulating their religious activities. The tilers' guild established in Bishop's Lynn (Norfolk) in 1329 began as a guild honouring the Purification of the Virgin. The tilers' wives were eligible for membership, sharing in the spiritual benefits. The craft's internal regulations reflected the links between religious and economic functions, with fines for breaches of the statutes being paid in wax to

Parish guilds [893]; see also Baron, 'Parish fraternities', pp. 13–37; Scrisbrick, *Reformation* pp. 19–39; Brigden, 'Religion and social obligation', pp. 94–101; Owen, *Church and society*, pp. 127–31; Rubin, *Charity and community*, pp. 253–8; McCree, 'Religious gilds and regulation' [569]; White, *St Christopher guild* [894]. Various ordinances and returns to the 1389 inquest are printed in Smith, Smith, and Brentano, *English gilds* [769].

[71] Barron, 'Parish fraternities', pp. 17–18 (but see also p. 18 n. 21); for typical registers see Bickley, *Register of the guild of Knowle* [60], Scaife, *Guild of Corpus Christi in York* [743], pp. 10–249.

[72] Phythian-Adams, *Desolation of a city* [658], pp. 118–22; Tanner, *Church in Norwich*, p. 81; Brigden, 'Religion and social obligation', p. 100; Owen, *Church and society*, p. 131.

maintain the guild's light. But in terms of surviving evidence the civic function of craft guilds could end up totally overwhelming the spiritual, as happened, for example, at Coventry. The civic function of guilds also meant that a new fraternity might be viewed as a threat by the urban authorities, as primarily a political and economic association. There were therefore occasional attempts to clamp down on the formation of new guilds, especially among the lower orders. Such gatherings, although ostensibly for spiritual purposes, might actually serve other ends, as foci of opposition to the established order which had to be crushed. Guilds could also be bases for opposition among the political elite, shown at York in 1537 by the conflict between the corporation and the guild of St Christopher.[73]

The guilds which have left extensive documentation are exceptions. Many remain nebulous in character: as associations of individuals they needed no endowments, and might flourish briefly before withering away. The guild of St James at Bishop's Lynn apparently experienced several incarnations; its response to the great royal survey of guilds in 1389 seemingly reflects a time of decay following the ravages of the Black Death,

in which . . . the greater part of the brothers and sisters died, and afterwards few entered . . . For a long time they had received neither brothers or sisters, because none cared for that fraternity because they were few and have little in goods.

By that date, the guild was reduced to no more than a spiritual association:

They hold no gatherings except at the time of the principal feasts, and in exequies of the dead. The other observances . . . are not used.[74]

With the great fraternities, the large membership raises problems. How realistic was individual involvement? Certainly, when the dead enrolled, their participation can only have been nominal. Nor can the most notable members of several guilds – royalty, major nobility, and bishops – actually have attended meetings. For them the prayers gained by membership were probably more important. Presumably many guilds depended on a small core of active members who attended the meetings and feasts, with

---

[73] Reynolds, *Kingdoms and communities*, pp. 70–2; Barron, 'Parish fraternities', pp. 14–17; Owen, *Lynn*, pp. 319–21; Phythian-Adams, *Desolation of a city*, gives virtually no consideration to the spiritual concerns of the guilds despite the extensive consideration of craft activities (ibid., pp. 99, 118 n. 2, 137–8, 160 n. 9); Swanson, 'Illusion of economic structure' [793]; Riley, *Memorials of London* [699], pp. 495, 542–4; White, *St Christopher guild*, pp. 6, 17–18. For a decidedly criminal fraternity, Hilton, *English peasantry* [394], pp. 92–3.

[74] Owen, *Lynn*, p. 322; see also Barron, 'Parish fraternities', p. 35.

other purely nominal members who hoped to benefit from the prayers. Collecting scattered subscriptions was a complex business. The Palmers' guild of Ludlow (Shrops.) had stewards who toured the country collecting money, often in instalments until the full amount was paid. Other guilds similarly sent out collectors, although it is not always clear whether they were really collecting subscriptions or selling confraternity and other privileges. Presumably the scattered evidence for farming of receipts reflects the latter practice – confraternity, the sharing of spiritual rewards, for a one-off payment, perhaps providing the second rank of 'less active' members. This would place some of the guilds on a par with institutions like the Trinitarian house of Thelsford (War.), which farmed out the collection of confraternity receipts on condition that the names of the purchasers were recorded and returned to the house's registry. Multiple membership of scattered fraternities, such as the Londoner John Thurston's links with the guilds of St Audrey at Bishop's Lynn, Our Lady of Boston, and Jesus in St Paul's, would similarly undermine the reality of membership. A major factor in the popularity of some guilds may have been an indulgence for members. Knowle possessed only a minor indulgence, but the Boston guild offered much more. In the early sixteenth century its officials invested over £3,000 in enlarging their indulgence, and presumably expected to recoup the money from membership fees.[75]

However real or unreal the members' involvement in guild activities, such associations were an expression of some sort of spirituality. The frequent close links with parish churches and religious houses emphasize the reality of their spiritual concerns. The stress was on fraternity, and the guilds sought to establish and maintain charity between their members. They provided mechanisms to resolve conflicts without going to law. They were also active charitable bodies, frequently involved in maintaining almshouses and educational provision. This was partly a matter of mutual assistance: the guild members would be required to bail out their less fortunate colleagues, although the economics of these 'insurance' arrangements are sometimes questionable. 'Social obligation' might also arise with the more organized charitable foundations, perhaps an attempt to resolve the problem of the guilt associated with wealth.[76]

[75] *VCH, Shropshire*, ii [871], pp. 137–8; Westlake, *Parish gilds*, pp. 77–8, 96–7; for Thelsford, Madox, *Formulare Anglicanum*, p. 149; Brigden, 'Religion and social obligation', p. 100 (he also listed membership of the 'gildes' of Hounslow, Burton Lazars, and Our Lady in the Sea – but these would reflect confraternity or indulgences from the Trinitarians of Hounslow, Burton Lazars hospital, and, probably, the chapel of St Mary at Newton [Cambs.]. Their appearance alongside the guilds is suggestive – perhaps guild membership was seen in the same light as a collection of confraternity letters, for which see below, at n. 103); Bickley, *Register of the guild of Knowle*, pp. xl–xlii, 2–3; Lunt, *Financial relations* [534], pp. 509–12.

[76] Owen, *Lynn*, p. 322; Barron, 'Parish fraternities', pp. 25–7; Brigden, 'Religion and social obligation', pp. 96–9; Rubin, *Charity and community*, pp. 254–6.

For the guild members, the shared spirituality during life was important, providing a major reason for joining. The guilds were insurance groups, friendly societies. The main aim of many was provision of post-mortem benefits, both physical and spiritual. A good funeral was guaranteed, often with the membership being obliged to attend funerals of deceased fellow members on pain of fine, and with a guild hearse or other accoutrements being provided to ensure appropriate solemnity. The guild's assumption of financial responsibility for the funeral would also relieve the deceased and the heirs of some worries. Equally important, the guild provided prayers for the repose of souls, and thereby eased the way from Purgatory. In a small group, this might be merely an annual mass-commemoration, after the initial obsequies (which might well involve a trental or series of masses). The larger guilds, with their own chaplains, would provide daily masses, again for the whole membership, living and dead. A low-cost funeral, with guaranteed post-mortem masses and prayers, preferably in perpetuity, was doubtless the guild's supreme function for most members, although there may have been a slight change in attitudes towards the end of the period.[77]

While collective activity was an important outlet for religious sensitivities, it should not be allowed to obscure individual actions. Even when religious activities were shared, as in processions and pilgrimages, they still involved personal associations with God and Christ. Between 1350 and 1540 there were many new expressions of private spirituality, and many new expressions of spirituality which, while becoming shared, were also individual.

By definition, the scale of private devotion in late medieval England cannot be assessed. Privacy need not mean withdrawal, and private devotions might well occur publicly. Indeed, given the laity's spectator status at mass, most devotion must have been private: the lay involvement being through their own prayers, recitations, and meditations, although the authorities were anxious to channel these private devotions through spiritual direction and confession.

This 'public privacy' accompanied a movement for greater secluded privacy in religion. How far this penetrated society is uncertain. The gentry have been seen as increasingly withdrawn from the parish church; but that may be a social rather than religious phenomenon, revealing little about the nature of spirituality (and contrasting with greater gentry concern to claim church space and fabric for their own glorification).[78]

---

[77] Barron, 'Parish fraternities', pp. 23–5, 27–8; Scarisbrick, *Reformation*, pp. 19–21.

[78] Richmond, 'Religion and the English gentleman', pp. 198–203, stresses the gentry's alienation from 'popular' religion, using the evidence of the Paston letters. Some of his arguments evoke sympathy, but I feel that the generalization rests too much on a personal response to the gaps in the letters, and ignores the fact that much of the activity – personal

The surviving literary evidence suggests more private contemplation than hitherto visible: instructional literature arranging life outside the church to incorporate religious experience; the directions requiring those seeking contemplation to withdraw into a private retreat; woodcuts depicting the Passion, Resurrection, or Pieta, whether loose or in printed service books, for private contemplation which could occur without or within church; the contemplation of statues and images; and so on. Once more there is no absolute contrast between 'private' and 'public' devotion – the retreat might be from the church nave into a small side chapel, or within the nave away from 'open-plan' worship into the privacy of a pew.[79]

Getting beyond the superficialities is almost impossible. Lists of books, references to rosaries, provide scant hints of the welter of spirituality; but no proper indication of its reality. Only rarely is the curtain lifted, as in the depictions of the daily round maintained by such as Cecily, Duchess of York, and Lady Margaret Beaufort, both of them necessarily extra-ordinary. Nevertheless, the provision of daily routines in the instructional literature suggests that they were meant to be followed, and possibly were.[80]

At its most intense, private devotion could become mysticism. The fourteenth and fifteenth centuries reveal the expansion and development of a mystical tradition in England, represented by individuals like Richard Rolle, Julian of Norwich, and the unknown author of the *Cloud of unknowing*. Most evidence of this mysticism is literary, and the mystical movement is generally studied as a literary genre. But the mystics were people, members of the church, and require consideration as such.[81]

Clearly, there was no 'normal' mystic: all were unusual individuals, their modes of life varying from the hermitages of Richard Rolle and the monk of Farne to the anchorage of Julian of Norwich and the active life of Margery Kempe. Her *Book* seems to fall outside the norms of the mystical tradition, so that her mysticism is sometimes questioned; but she was evidently not unique, and fits well into the pattern of female devotion and mysticism which is known from continental examples.[82]

books of hours, private chapels and chaplain – was fairly widespread even in the fourteenth century. See also the riposte in Carpenter, 'Religion of the gentry' [127].

[79] Pantin, 'Instructions', pp. 398–413; Richmond, 'Religion and the English gentleman', pp. 198–9; Hirsh, 'Prayer and meditation' [400], p. 57; Aston, *Lollards and reformers*, pp. 119–21. See also below, at n. 101.

[80] Pantin, 'Instructions', pp. 398–400, 403–9, 411–13 (for Cicely, also Armstrong, *England, France, and Burgundy* [9], pp. 140–56); Mertes, 'Household as religious community' [581].

[81] The chief representatives of the group are treated in Knowles, *The English mystical tradition* [486]. The mystics are now an industry in their own right, with a rapidly expanding bibliography: for publications to 1981 see Lagorio and Bradley, *Fourteenth century English mystics*.

[82] For this context, Atkinson, *Mystic and pilgrim*, pp. 153–94.

Mysticism, by its very intensity, was individualistic. Its spiritual ambitions made it necessarily an extremely Christocentric devotion. As mediation on Christ was a traditional part of the contemplative scheme, however, it was not automatically divorced from the general patterns of devotion. Many mystics saw their role as extending beyond their own experience, attempting to communicate it through their works. This concern to share experience is perhaps the keypoint of the mystical writings. But the very intensity of mysticism carried dangers; it could rarely be communicated without approaching the limits of theological orthodoxy. Some of the statements of the monk of Farne approach heresy; while the translation of the *Mirror for simple souls* into English made available a text which, while encouraging devotion, was suspect because of its association with the heresy of the Free Spirit, stressing an individualism which could challenge the church. The translator sought therefore to reduce the chances of such misconstruction by glossing the questionable passages. Such active individualism was the second main danger of mysticism. If it was contained by a regulated life, all well and good; but Margery Kempe's case clearly reveals the threat. Personal contact with God, negating the need for ecclesiastical mediation, was dangerous not just to priestly power, but to society as a whole, perhaps especially if the claim to independence was made by a woman so dominant in the relationship with God that he 'at times resembles a hen-pecked husband'. Margery's active unorthodoxy in dress, her gift of tears, her fearless condemnation of the great, her flitting between confesors to find one in accord with her whims (and the dictates of Christ, of course), and her tedious self-proclamation, hardly endeared her to contemporaries. Yet a surprising aspect of her life is that she was tolerated by the ecclesiastical hierarchy (with a few notable exceptions), while feared by the laity.[83]

As well as these general devotional developments there were more specific movements which affected contemporary piety. In the two centuries before the Reformation the church made several additions to the feasts it celebrated, most of which penetrated into England. For some the adoption was slow, and perhaps incomplete by 1540. The new observances often commemorated Christ or the Virgin, in the former case emphasizing ethereal elements of devotion like the Sacred Heart and the Holy Name. Manuscripts

---

[83] Salter, *Nicholas Love's "Myrrour"*, pp. 126–78; Farmer, 'Monk of Farne', p. 155 (see also Pantin, 'The monk-solitary', pp. 176–7, for comment on the monk's warning against over-devotion to the saints, especially poignant given his misdating of the work to *c.*1350 – he has misidentified the chapters, which are actually chs. 27–8 in the edition); Doiron, 'Middle English translation' [224], pp. 133–4, 141–6; Atkinson, *Mystic and pilgrim*, pp. 39–56, 105–28; Beckwith, 'Very material mysticism' [53] (emphasizing Margery as a feminist threat); Stargardt, 'Beguines, Dominican nuns, and Margery Kempe', p. 304.

reveal their incorporation into service books; but more general adoption is less easily traced. Specific individuals were associated with certain cults and their extension. Edmund Lacy thus encouraged the feast of St Raphael within his Exeter diocese, while the feast of the Visitation of the Blessed Virgin was supposedly introduced at St Albans by William Wyntreshulle, a monk there.[84] Children's names may also indicate devotion, although the limited range of names usually given to English children, and our ignorance of their naming practices, make this uncertain. But not all parents used the usual names, and deliberate breaches in naming habits may show devotion to particular saints. In the fifteenth century recent canonizations and greater devotion to the Anglo-Saxon saints sometimes affected the naming of offspring. This especially applies to the Yorkist royal family, Cecily, Duchess of York and her descendants. Her own name is unusual, and presumably indicates devotion to St Cecilia among the Neville family. Two of her grand-daughters were significantly named Ursula and Bridget – both novel but expanding cults of the time. George for the Duke of Clarence may be less important, being already a Neville name, but there are other signs of a real Yorkist allegiance to that cult, certainly with Edward IV's son, George of Windsor.[85] It may also be important that the fifteenth century shows signs of an expansion in the range of names in general use; but links between this and changing devotional patterns still require investigation.

Other evidence for devotion to saints is equally dangerous. Given the generally formulaic nature of testamentary clauses concerning the soul – commending it usually to God, the Virgin, and All Saints – mention of other saints might indicate personal allegiance. This certainly seems the case in some individualistic Hull wills, and with bequests made to particular lights or altars (assuming that there are no alternative explanations); but often the commendation to a saint merely reflects the dedication of the testator's parish church, and can carry little weight.[86]

Most of the new devotions of the later middle ages were continental imports, with little sign of any English initiative in the processes. But that England made so few contributions to the official calendar does not mean a lack of native cults. A major key to spirituality in any age is its definition of sainthood, reflected both in the characters of those promoted, and the construction of their commemorative offices. Between 1300 and 1540 there

---

[84] Pfaff, *New liturgical feasts* (esp. pp. 46–7); Orme, 'Two saint-bishops' [620], pp. 413–15 and refs.

[85] Tanner, *Church in Norwich*, pp. 82–3, 211; *Cal. i.p. m. Edward III* [114], p. 90 (the choice of names for the two sons of Henry III – Edward and Edmund – is also significant in this regard); Armstrong, *England, France, and Burgundy*, pp. 138 (and n. 7), 151.

[86] Heath, 'Urban piety', pp. 214–15 (see also Vale, *Piety, charity, and literacy*, p. 16); Tanner, *Church in Norwich*, pp. 83–4.

were only three new English saints: Thomas Cantilupe of Hereford (in 1320); John of Bridlington (died 1379, canonized in 1401); and the Anglo-Norman Osmund of Salisbury (canonized in 1456). Cantilupe represented an idealized bishop; Bridlington was an obscure prior linked to prophecies; while Osmund's process had begun centuries earlier. By 1350 the requirements of canonization were well specified at Rome, the process lengthy, expensive, and uncertain. It took over two centuries to secure Osmund's canonization, at enormous cost. Records of expenses for the 1450s show that in the last few years of the process over £700 was spent; taking into account earlier stages of the negotiations the real cost must have been much higher. But there was a wide gap between those whom the Roman church considered saints, and those whom the localities venerated. Late medieval England supported numerous unofficial cults, evidenced by records of offices, miracle stories, bequests, pilgrimages, and other forms of commemoration. It was clearly hoped that some of these cults would end in formal canonization: the extant office for Richard Rolle maintains the distinction between private prayers before canonization, and the formal office which could be publicly recited only after official recognition. The case of Thomas de la Hale, a monk of Dover murdered by French raiders in 1295, reached the stage of formal investigation in the 1380s, but got no further.[87]

Of the unofficial saints of later medieval England, several were promoted for purely political reasons. The cults of Thomas of Lancaster and Richard Scrope clearly originated in the legitimization of political opposition, like the earlier 'sainthood' of Simon de Montfort. Scrope could also be invoked under the Yorkists (and possibly even under Henry V) to emphasize political legitimacy – his see of York and opposition to the 'usurping' Henry IV made him an obvious candidate for association with Edward IV and the notion of restored rights, just as the toleration of his cult by Henry V indicated a break with Henry IV. The few signs of veneration of Richard II would also fit into a legitimist tradition, while the cult of Henry VI was encouraged by Henry VII to bolster his own position, his 'martyrdom' having earlier been used against the Yorkists to justify political opposition.[88]

Henry VI's cult was perhaps the only truly national cult to develop during these centuries. Devotion was not restricted to his successive shrines at Chertsey (Surrey) and Windsor (Bucks.), but leaves widespread

---

[87] Bray, 'Concepts of sainthood' [86], pp. 75–7; Page, 'Office for St Thomas of Lancaster' [633], pp. 134–43; Kemp, *Canonization and authority* [463], pp. 123–4, 138–40, 176; Malden, *Canonization of Osmund* [572] (details of the expenses in the 1450s at pp. 187–215); Vauchez, *La sainteté* [863], esp. pp. 479–88, 626–9; Woolley, *Officium and miracula*, p. 12.

[88] McKenna, 'Popular canonization' [561], pp. 618–22; for 'political saints' see 3/1, at nn. 29–31.

evidence; while the miracles associated with him occurred throughout southern England. Despite initial popularity, the cult fizzled out: Hereford's commemorations were probably extinct by about 1512.[89] Other saints had more local appeal, numerous commemorations developing and then subsiding. Several bishops attracted devotees. Apart from Scrope (the persistence of whose cult is important), John Dalderby of Lincoln was thus promoted, and Robert Winchelsey at Canterbury, while there was long-lasting devotion to Edmund Lacy at Exeter. Richard Rolle's cult was mainly confined to the north-east, but persisted into the sixteenth century. As for other 'saints', Pope Boniface IX attempted to quash the unauthorized cult of Thomas Grethan, abbot of Thornton (died 1393) which that house was encouraging; minor cults are evident among the accounts of Durham cathedral priory, revealing little beyond the names of the venerated; while the devil-conjuring John Schorn drew pilgrims to his North Marston (Bucks.) tomb from about 1314 to c.1480, when his remains and the focus of devotion were removed to Windsor.[90]

Pre-Reformation England thus had no lack of would-be saints. Indeed, some individuals perhaps viewed themselves as potential saints: Margery Kempe's life story has been interpreted along such lines, and there are perhaps similar signs in the writings of the late fifteenth-century Carthusian Richard Methley of Mount Grace (Yorks.).[91] No matter how strong the cult, none of these prospective saints secured the accolade of papal approval, and therewith inclusion in the universal calendar.

The later middle ages also witnessed a proliferation of Marian and Christ-centred devotions. The period's developing mystical concern was reflected in increased pilgrimage to what were essentially man-made shrines. The numerous statues, images, and rural crosses which attracted devotees – the Holy House of Walsingham (Norfolk), the rood of Boxley (Kent), and others – were integrated into the spiritual concerns of contemporaries; and perhaps in some respects were more significant than the human saints. Attitudes towards these cults are indeterminable: some of the statues were mere mechanical contraptions, such as the rood of Boxley, much castigated by sixteenth-century reformers. They could be treated more as tourist attractions than encouragements to piety. These

---

[89] Grosjean, *Henrici VI miracula* [320] (locations of miracles tabulated at pp. 76*–95*); HCA, R585, ff. 1r, 5r, 8v, 11r, 22r (no offerings are recorded for 1511–12, f. 14r); Spencer, 'King Henry of Windsor' [773], pp. 235–57; Wolffe, *Henry VI* [918], pp. 351–8; McKenna, 'Piety and propaganda' [562].

[90] Bray, 'Concepts of sainthood', pp. 46–51; Orme, 'Two saint-bishops'; Allen, *Writings ascribed to Rolle*, pp. 522–3; Boyle, *Survey of the Vatican archives* [84], pp. 143–4; Fowler, *Account rolls of Durham* [281], ii, pp. 476–83, iii, p. xxi; Spencer, 'King Henry of Windsor', pp. 239–40, 248–9, 257–8; Tanner, *Church in Norwich*, pp. 89–90.

[91] Bray, 'Concepts of sainthood', pp. 72–5; Hogg, 'Mount Grace Charterhouse', p. 37.

devotions and pilgrimages resulted in considerable transfers of cash: among the shrines with details of offerings recorded in the *Valor ecclesiasticus* of 1535, there is none to match the receipts of Walsingham, at £260 a year.[92]

While shrines and pilgrimages were linked to non-human devotions, a key element in the veneration of saints was their humanity and their physical existence. The power of their sanctity was closely linked to their physical reality, and to objects associated with them which were somehow felt to trap their spiritual force. Hence the valuing of relics, the attempts to control the power of the saint or the holy force through possession of fragments of the body or associated souvenirs. The force of relics remained strong in later medieval England. Institutions like Durham cathedral had massive collections; while thousands more were scattered among parish churches. Thus Lyme Regis (Dorset) had a little bone from St Blaise's arm, and one of St Petroc; Durnford (Wilts.) had bones of SS Andrew and Blaise; while at Sonning (Berks.) the collection included bits of Mount Calvary, the Holy Sepulchre, and Mary's tomb, with relics of the prophet Daniel and the youths of the fiery furnace. There was obvious room for fraud, and the false stock-in-trade of Chaucer's Pardoner would have had a ready market. The relics at Heytesbury (Wilts.) included ten bones from unknown saints, but they were still relics; other bits of the collection were only said to have belonged to St Edmund.

Possession of relics was not confined within the church. The laity also collected them, from kings downwards. Richard II thus acquired two of the Holy Innocents massacred by Herod (in exchange for exemption from customs duties for the seller!), while wills occasionally mention relics lower down the social scale, with fragments of the True Cross being divided and sub-divided as their possession proliferated.[93]

The shrines and cults reflect one aspect of popular devotion and desires. But they did not exist in isolation: saints had to earn veneration. In the long term, their intercessions and prayers helped people through Purgatory; in the short term, they could procure miracles. The acceptance of the miraculous is an important element in late medieval religion, whose ubiquity and underpinning of spirituality are too easily overlooked. In a sense, in the mass and transubstantiation, the miraculous was an everyday occurrence – although technically transubstantiation was not a miracle. In any sense it was special, but not rare. It was (and long had been) something of a literary cliché that miracles were less common than hitherto

---

[92] Sumption, *Pilgrimage*, pp. 56, 262, 270, 279–80; Finucane, *Miracles and pilgrims* [273], pp. 195–202, 205; *Valor* [120], iii, p. 388.

[93] Fowler, *Account rolls of Durham*, ii, pp. 425–40; Timmins, *Reg. Chandler*, pp. 56, 61, 67, 70; Robinson, *Works of Chaucer*, pp. 23–4; Legge, *Anglo-Norman letters* [506], pp. 67–8; Fleming, 'Charity, faith, and the gentry', p. 43.

(either because they were less needed, or less merited), but *miracula* were not infrequent. Collections of miracles in preparation for canonization proceedings survive relating to Richard Rolle, Osmund of Salisbury, and Henry VI. Miracles continued after canonization, like those from the 1370s ascribed to St Edmund. Miracles were also linked to the Virgin, and to other holy objects. A miracle of Our Lady of Ipswich in 1516 gained considerable publicity, and reveals the heightening of spiritual fervour which could occur; while Hailes abbey may have sponsored the printing up by Robert Pynson of the miracles associated with its Holy Blood as publicity for the shrine. Other scattered references indicate that miracles were accepted as a part of life, such as those linked to Margery Kempe, or the case from Lichfield of a child who was submerged in a stream for half-an-hour but (presumably) lived, which was probably attributed to St Chad.[94]

From this evidence, the miraculous might be quite mundane. Not surprisingly, most miracles concerned healing: the insane restored, the blind and deaf recovering their faculties, the resuscitation of people presumed dead (especially children). But there were others. Animals were also healed, and lost possessions recovered – including stolen church goods which were found in a churchyard. Henry VI also miraculously reloaded a cartload of wood which had been dislodged, and extinguished a fire in a field. In a singularly un-Henrician action, he took revenge on someone who had insulted him. As a defender of the faith, he intervened in the sickness of a man who had condemned pilgrimages as worthless, changing his opinions to heal him both in body and mind.[95]

Miracles not only reveal a cult's spread, they may also show the level of intensity, and the manner of its encouragement. Thus, Richard Rolle's cult was rather fortuitously stimulated at Leicester in 1383 when his invocation by a wanderer from outside the town led to the miraculous recovery of an apparently drowned child. Three of Henry VI's miracles related to one household, Thomas Symon's at Portsmouth. The king's intervention had saved them from plague, healed two horses, and recovered three stolen pigs.[96]

If miracles were both reflections of the power of saints (sometimes of rivalry between them) and intended to encourage piety (a task which they

---

[94] Finucane, *Miracles and pilgrims*, p. 54; Woolley, *Officium and miracula*, pp. 82–93; Grosjean, *Henrici VI miracula*, pp. 1–305; Malden, *Canonization of Osmund*, pp. 57–83, 142–3; Barnum, *Dives and pauper*, i, pp. 209–10; Horstmann, *Nova legenda Anglie* [413], ii, pp. 677–88; McCulloch, *Suffolk* [545], pp. 143–5; CUL, MS Mm.I.48, p. 6; Oates, 'Pynson and Hayles' [610]; see also Grosjean, 'S. Iohanne Bridlingtoniensis' [319], pp. 121–5, 127.

[95] Woolley, *Officium and miracula*; Grosjean, *Henrici VI miracula* (for the cited instances, ibid., nos. 6, 7, 92, 144 [animals], 9, 59 [treasure and church possessions], 76, 96 [reloaded cart, fire], 53 [revenge], 131 [heretic]).

[96] Woolley, *Officium and miracula*, pp. 85–6; Grosjean, *Henrici VI miracula*, nos. 5–7.

especially assumed when reinforcing doctrinal orthodoxy, as with tales of Eucharistic miracles used against the Lollards),[97] piety was further encouraged by the proliferation of indulgences after 1350. Getting to the heart of approaches to indulgences is almost impossible, a somewhat mercenary interpretation of the practice being virtually unavoidable. The basic theory of the indulgence – the power to relax penance, even grant plenary indulgences from the penalty and guilt of sin – is fairly readily comprehensible. The pope or his agents claimed the power to control or abate Purgatory, the indulgence reducing or even obliterating its pains. They were not intended (however perceived) to be a mechanistic trading-off of sins: to be effective the sinner had to be sincerely contrite as well.[98] The association of indulgences with specific objectives like the relief of Constantinople, assistance in building churches, or the relief from poverty of named individuals, is again readily comprehensible, to encourage charity and aid the church on earth. Indulgences permeated the medieval church, sometimes (especially with bridge repairs) aiding public works, at others (as with support for almshouses, or collections for the ransoming of prisoners) working as voluntary collecting charities. They might be focused on individuals as well, with bishops issuing numerous letters to relieve people who had accidentally fallen into penury. Indulgences also encouraged devotional practices, like the celebration of specific masses or reading certain books.[99]

Initially indulgences were restrained. Episcopal grants were always limited to a maximum of forty days per enterprise per bishop, with gradations for higher authorities. Papal generosity was greater, extending to the plenary indulgence issued to those participating in crusades (although hedged around with conditions). For other purposes, such as encouraging contributions for the maintenance of decayed or newly established churches, odd years would be granted. Like other papal prerogatives, the power to indulge could be delegated – although perhaps rarely. Wolsey, however, did have such authority, issuing indulgences for the hundred days permitted to him as cardinal, and larger remissions by virtue of the delegation. Even kings were involved in the indulgence machinery. Under Henry VIII at least, royal encouragement was given

---

[97] Haines, ' "Wilde wittes and wilfulnes" ' [335], p. 149; Aston, 'Wyclif and the vernacular', pp. 296–7.

[98] For the complexity of the theory of indulgences, and their developments (concentrating on papal grants, and mainly continental examples), Lea, *Auricular confession* [499], iii, pp. 9–124, 145–214, 224–8, 234–45, 277–95, 336–56.

[99] Rubin, *Charity and community*, pp. 265–8 (I disagree with her comments at n. 176, although the religious institutions probably had a more efficient collecting machinery); Lunt, *Financial relations*, pp. 447–611, *passim*; Sargent, 'Transmission by Carthusians', pp. 232–3 (although it poses problems by having apparently been transferred – illicitly? – between books).

by letters patent or other approbation of collections, especially for charitable purposes like the support of chapels or contributions to aid individuals – an involvement which developed into the post-Reformation 'church briefs'.[100]

Shortly after 1350, a dramatic change occurred. The basic small-scale grants continued, with a more frenetic activity developing alongside as the amount of indulgence offered multiplied outrageously, debasing the idea in the process. Plenary indulgences became more easily available; while massive amounts of pardon were associated with simple and relatively trivial acts. By the sixteenth century the circuit of the stations of Rome on specified days was said to bring up to 150,000 years of remission from Purgatory, and a plenary indulgence. Various English groups, including guilds, secured equivalent indulgences, one group in 1521 being required to visit local churches and altars on the named dates. The cult of the Holy Name may have been spread by the indulgence associated with its mass, with 3,000 years' remission supposedly being granted to those who celebrated it, or paid for its celebration for thirty days. Even less was demanded for indulgences associated with the Image of Pity, which was incorporated into some printed service books. By simply reciting five Paternosters, five Aves, and a Creed whilst contemplating the depiction, between 26,000 and 33,000 years were docked off Purgatory. Moreover, this post-mortem deposit account increased by that amount with each repetition of the prayers. Admittedly, the prayers were to be said 'devoutly', but it remains difficult to make the necessary mental leap to appreciate indulgences as the normality which they were then. That most of these excessive indulgences were highly spurious must be overlooked: in popular eyes their repetition gave them validity.[101]

Indulgences clearly were appreciated. Perpetual grants were treated (perhaps invalidly) as cumulative, and were good publicity material. The circular issued by a bishop of Lichfield to encourage membership of the fraternity of St Chad at Lichfield recited the full benefits linked with membership: papal and episcopal indulgences, and the multiple repetition of masses and psalters in the monasteries and nunneries of the diocese.

---

[100] Lunt, *Financial relations*, pp. 472–6; Capes, *Reg. Trefnant* [126], pp. 192–3; Parry, *Reg. Mascall* [644], pp. 190–1; Bannister, *Reg. Bothe* [37], p. 360 (the list of 'licences to collect alms', ibid., pp. 354–60, includes some explicit grants of episcopal indulgences as well, others were possibly but not obviously conceded); Housley, *Avignon papacy* [417], pp. 128–43; Jackson, 'Three printed indulgences' [437], pp. 229–30; Rogers, 'Friends of North Newington' [708], pp. 253–4; Pollard and Redgrave, *Short-title catalogue*, ii, nos. 14077c.131, 14077c.133; CUL, MS Add. 6969, ff. 84v, 95v.

[101] Lunt, *Financial relations*, p. 452 (other holders of such indulgences at p. 509); Cooke, *Ordinale Sarum* [164], ii, pp. 46–58; Pfaff, *New liturgical feasts*, pp. 63–5; Sumption, *Pilgrimage*, pp. 242–4 (see also pp. 290–5).

The indulgence offered by the Boston guild, one of the most extensive in the country, would similarly attract members. The anxiety to obtain indulgences is shown in 1480–1, when the crowding of the calendar with new feasts, many having indulgences, required papal action to sort out one confusion. Several feasts fell within the octave of the recently decreed Feast of the Visitation of the Blessed Virgin Mary, disrupting the observances necessary to obtain its indulgence. The pope ordered that the full celebrations should be observed, allowing those who said the office of the Visitation privately on the intruded dates to receive the full indulgence.[102] Equally indicative of popular attitudes is the apparently indiscriminate collecting of letters of indulgence and confraternity. Whilst the two were technically distinct, the frequent combination of indulgence with confraternity doubtless encouraged their popular synonymity. Thousands of such letters must have been sold by the proctors of the issuing bodies. Whole collections were built up, like that accumulated by Henry and Katherine Langley in the late fifteenth century containing indulgences and confraternity letters for the defence of Rhodes, support of the English hospital in Rome, membership of the Boston guild, support for the chapel of St Mary at Newton (Cambs.), and links with the Trinitarian and Dominican orders.[103] Indulgences might even be 'privatized' to secure releases from Purgatory with reciprocal benefits. In 1508 Robert Gardener of Norwich directed in his will that an indulgence should be bought at Rome (if costing under £5) of 300 days' pardon for those praying for him and his two wives. More ambitious, and subtle, is the brass for Robert and Elizabeth Legh in Macclesfield church (Ches.), which depicts the Mass of St Gregory and promises pardon of 26,000 years and 26 days for five Paternosters, one Ave, and a Creed – and also asks for prayers for their souls.[104]

Many indulgences would have been purchased from travelling questors, but others could be obtained only by visiting the churches or shrines concerned. Pilgrimage is a well-attested aspect of medieval piety, and underlies many other contemporary reflections of it. Chaucer's pilgrims are legendary, and in many respects faithfully portray the attitudes of real people. Pilgrimage was a jaunt, albeit one with a serious purpose. The journey was to be enjoyed, no matter how solemn the arrival.

---

[102] Haines, 'A confraternity document' [336], esp. pp. 131–2; BL, MS Harley 2179, f. 118–v; Smith, 'Reconstruction', p. 34 (some of the allowances seem odd here); Lunt, *Financial relations*, pp. 480–1, 495–8; Pfaff, *New liturgical feasts*, pp. 47–8.

[103] PRO, C270/32/12–18. On letters of confraternity, see Clark-Maxwell, 'Some letters' [148]; Clark-Maxwell, 'Further letters' [149].

[104] Tanner, *Church in Norwich*, p. 102; Glynne, *Churches of Cheshire* [301], pp. 90–1.

When Margery Kempe proved too serious, she was shunned by her companions.[105]

Just how many people went on pilgrimage, and why, are unanswerable questions. Some pilgrimages were clearly associated with healing, to seek or give thanks for a miracle. Some were imposed for ecclesiastical crimes. Some were fitted into business trips, or were themselves the business, as with Frederick Winter's visit to Peterborough abbey from Switzerland in 1481, acting as envoy of the incumbent of Zug to procure relics of St Oswald for the church being built there in his honour.[106] Many pilgrims also acted out of true devotion. Margery Kempe's travels indicate the range of possibilities, with lengthy tours of England (taking in York and the shrine of St John of Bridlington), a visit to Rome and the Holy Land, a journey to Wilsnack (the Precious Blood), and to Compostela (St James). Visits to Compostela and Rome were relatively common, and the former must have been devotional journeys. For Rome, curial business would provide an opportunity for a journey, while the indulgences associated with the periodic Jubilees or Holy Years provided both encouragement and pretext. The Holy Land was perhaps the ultimate goal, with a steady trickle of pilgrims going there throughout the period. England itself contained a multitude of shrines and other places offering indulgences to visitors. This was a two-way traffic: continentals came to England, to venerate both old and new saints.[107]

One of the rarest of pre-mortem acts of piety, but perhaps less rare than might be supposed, was participation in crusades. There are scattered references to English involvement on all fronts of the late medieval crusading movement, in Spain, north-east Europe, and the eastern Mediter-

---

[105] For pilgrimage narratives and guide-books, see Zacher, 'Travel and geographical writings' [935], pp. 2236–53, 2452, 2457–60, 2462–4. The main general survey of pilgrimage is Sumption, *Pilgrimage*; see also Owen, *Church and society*, pp. 125–7.

[106] Finucane, *Miracles and pilgrims*, pp. 41–7; Swanson, *Reg. Scrope*, i, p. 51; GL, MS 25165; EDR, F5/32, f. 45v; Baker, 'St Oswald' [32], pp. 109–11, 122–3. For healing miracles and pilgrimages see the miracle collections cited in n. 94. The search for a miracle could involve several pilgrimages: a Biggleswade (Essex) man visited both Thomas at Canterbury and William at York before gaining satisfaction from Osmund at Salisbury (Malden, *Canonization of Osmund*, pp. 142–3).

[107] Atkinson, *Pilgrim and mystic*, pp. 53–7; Tanner, *Church in Norwich*, pp. 85–90; Fleming, 'Charity, faith, and the gentry', p. 44; Lunt, *Financial relations*, pp. 459–66; Cordero Carrete, 'Embarque de peregrinos' [168], pp. 348–57; Storrs and Cordero Carrete, 'Peregrinos ingleses' [789], pp. 211–22; parks, *English traveler* [640], pp. 352–82; Mitchener, *Medieval badges* [587], esp. pp. 261–73; Dobson, *Durham priory* [216], p. 28; Grosjean, 'S. Iohanne Bridlingtoniensis', pp. 123–5; Baker, 'St Oswald', pp. 109–11, 122–3. There is no catalogue of English pilgrimage sites during this period. Misunderstanding of the organization of indulgences perhaps meant that few pilgrims were actually entitled to claim the remissions: Sumption, *Pilgrimage*, pp. 143–4.

ranean. Whilst some of the participants were doubtless seeking financial gain, the inclusion of an indulgence among the attractions probably played some part. It may be no accident that known English crusaders included two of the leading lay devotional writers of the late fourteenth century, Henry of Lancaster, who fought in Spain, and Sir John Clanvowe, who in 1391 joined the Duke of Bourbon's crusade against Tunis, and died at Constantinople the following year, possibly on pilgrimage. Nor, though less praiseworthy, can English participation in the partisan pseudo-crusades of the period be ignored, notably Bishop Despencer's campaign against Flanders in the 1380s, and John of Gaunt's Castillian adventure, both enterprises which exploited the papal rivalries of the Great Schism.[108]

There remains perhaps the most important and ubiquitous reflection of late medieval piety: the provision of post-mortem prayers and masses by bequests and chantries. Such foundations were not the only pious acts provided for after death, but they were the most important. Bequests to shrines, lights, and images, and vicarious pilgrimages (whereby the recipient of a bequest – often anonymous in the will – undertook a pilgrimage on behalf of the deceased) are also not unusual.[109] Support for building work in churches also counts, although sometimes verging into ostentatious memorialism. However, the main immediate concern is with the prayers rather than associated charitable acts, important though those were.

The habit of funding prayers and chantries reflects both religious concern and social status. Insofar as prayers and chantries established a memorial, they might establish social status as much (or even more than) a religious observance. A chantry was a concrete benefaction by an identifiable individual, a declaration of social position – and when associated with charitable activities a proclamation of wealth demanding the reciprocal service of prayers even after death.[110]

The blurring of functions is evident even at the funeral. This was very much a social event, as well as a religious commital. As an event it received considerable attention in wills, with provisions regarding attendance and payment which proclaimed the testator's munificence as much as his or her piety. There was a strand of piety throughout the period which abhorred such display; but that in turn had its detractors. Testa-

---

[108] Housley, *Avignon papacy*, pp. 100, 236–8; Keen, 'Chaucer's knight' [459]; Scattergood, *Works of Clanvowe*, p. 27; Goodman, 'Henry VII' [305], p. 118; Perroy, *L'Angleterre* [653], pp. 175–209, 223, 227–8, 235–6, 243, 259; Housley, 'Bishop of Norwich's crusade' [416]; Riley, *Registra abbatum* [700], ii, pp. 191–2.

[109] Vale, *Piety, charity, and literacy*, pp. 16–17; Tanner, *Church in Norwich*, pp. 85–7; Owen, *Lynn*, p. 252 (a will requiring six such pilgrimages). Vicarious pilgrimages could also collect indulgences: Lea, *Auricular confession*, iii, pp. 116–17; Blench, *Preaching in England*, pp. 236–7.

[110] Fleming, 'Charity, faith, and the gentry', pp. 39–40.

mentary funeral arrangements therefore encouraged clerical attendance with payments; sought the presence of the poor by mingling charitable activity with snobbery in stipulations that a certain number should receive clothing or payment, or carry tapers. There were frequently provisions for burning torches or candles around the corpse, these lights being then donated to the church for ceremonial purposes. The funeral's social element is less evident in the wills, but appears at the wake, with social stratification being emphasized in the menus offered to the differing ranks attending the funeral feast.[111]

Piety is pre-eminent in the provisions for prayers and post-mortem masses. Arrangements for establishing perpetual chantries would normally be made before death, to ensure their fulfilment. Successful creation of a chantry after death was an uncertain business, dependent on completing all the legal business (including a mortmain licence where needed), on actual funding and endowment, and on the executors completing their task satisfactorily. The increasing difficulty of such matters, and perhaps the impetus to avoid the mortmain legislation by establishing concealed chantries, apparently reduced the number of such perpetual foundations in the period 1350 to 1540. However, wills provide plentiful evidence of a continued provision for prayers, usually as short-term chantries, hiring priests for stated periods. Most testators were content with (or unable to afford more than) a payment for six months, a year, or anything up to five years; periods over ten years are relatively scarce. As hiring a priest could cost 10 marks a year (£6 13s. 4d.) lengthy arrangements were obviously expensive. These foundations were not just meant to provide the mass, but to secure additional prayers. Provision of a mass was itself a public benefaction, with an audience as well as a celebrant. The will of John Norys, vicar of South Lynn (Norfolk), acknowledges this, his regulations for the augmentation of the chantry of the Trinity guild in that church requiring the celebrant to urge his congregation to say a Paternoster and Ave for Norys's soul.[112]

Besides hiring priests for set periods, bequests were also made for other commemorative celebrations. The wealthy would arrange obits and anniversaries, special commemorations (sometimes in addition to chantries) which would ease the soul through Purgatory. (For the less wealthy these would be paralleled by the annual commemoration services of the fraternities.)[113] Prayers and masses were purchased in abundance.

---

[111] Tanner, *Church in Norwich*, pp. 99–100; Vale, *Piety, charity, and literacy*, p. 24; Kingsford, *Stonor letters* [475], i, pp. 143–4 (see also Gottfried, *Bury St Edmunds* [308], p. 184).

[112] Tanner, *Church in Norwich*, pp. 92–8, 100–2, 106; Hicks, 'Chantries, obits, and almshouses' [384], pp. 126–41; Wood-Legh, *Perpetual chantries*, pp. 30–64; Owen, *Lynn*, p. 252.

[113] Owen, *Church and society*, pp. 92–3; Burgess, ' "By quick and by dead" ', pp. 847–9; Burgess, 'Service for the dead' [107].

Technically, of course, they were not bought, for that would be simony; but there was clearly a recognized rate per mass, and probably some sort of bargaining over the payments involved. Sometimes the 'purchase' is explicit, with money being provided for a stated number of masses – and attitudes towards Purgatory being hinted at with requests for them to be completed as soon as possible. The quantity of prayers demanded is sometimes staggering: Archbishop Courtenay of Canterbury, for instance, provided in his will for 15,000 masses (with stipulated forms) and 2,000 matins of All Saints. Laymen might be equally insistent: one Richard Weyvyle in 1417 somewhat optimistically demanded that 3,000 masses be celebrated for him within three days of his death, at the miserly rate of 1d. per mass.[114] Whether such bequests reflect a real fear of Purgatory, or a slightly cynical hope of getting through it swiftly, is uncertain. By 1400 prayers were also available for purchase in set blocks, especially the trental, a succession of thirty masses on consecutive days, or the more elaborate Trental of St Gregory, which required a whole year for its celebration, and was consequently more expensive.[115] Bequests were frequently made to religious houses and individual religious to encourage such celebrations, trentals especially being favoured. Many bequests to religious houses were to friaries and nunneries, with the older male orders seemingly being less popular. The bequests to mendicants reveal their continuing popularity, despite contemporary satires.[116] Friaries were still chosen as burial places; although perhaps less often than before the Black Death. Less than 10 per cent of Norwich testators between 1370 and 1532 sought such burial; while only one possible case of burial at the Carmelite house at Scarborough (Yorks.) appears in that parish's surviving accounts. The option of mendicant burial was obviously limited by the distribution of houses; but there are other signs of devotion. The orders were successfully disposing of letters of confraternity throughout the period. Many lay purchases would have been included in general collections of such privileges; but for some confraternity was clearly significant. Sir John de Meaux, for one, sought burial in the Franciscan habit in 1377 as a lay brother of the order. The spirit of confraternity also surmounted the academic and intellectual animosity between the friars and the secular clergy: even while some seculars were lambasting the pretensions of the mendicants in the mid-1370s, others were entering confraternity with the orders, and seculars

---

[114] Barnum, *Dives and pauper*, ii, pp. 184–92; Fleming, 'Charity, faith, and the gentry', pp. 38–9; Dahmus, *William Courtenay*, p. 267 (see also Furnivall, *Fifty English wills* [288], p. 23; Weaver, *Somerset medieval wills*, p. 80).

[115] Pfaff, 'St Gregory's Trental' [656].

[116] But I doubt that gifts to them 'were so commonplace in medieval wills as to imply a social pressure close to obligation' (Warren, *Anchorites and their patrons*, p. 235).

continued to make bequests to them and seek burial in their churches.[117]

All masses assisted the souls of the departed: every mass for the dead commemorated all the faithful departed, even if spotlighting named individuals. It was not therefore absolutely necessary to establish prayers to gain salvation – and perhaps most people were ultimately incapable of doing so, banking on the effectiveness of their inclusion among the rest in the specific foundations. Nevertheless, those leaving wills certainly seemed concerned not to be overlooked in the rush on St Peter's gates. Such individualistic concern appears typical of the piety of the period, whether in terms of the life on earth, or the life after death.

6.4 CHARITY

The key feature of medieval wills is that almost every bequest was somehow intended to assist the testator's progress to Heaven. Charitable activities gained givers a reputation as benefactors, who merited prayers from those whom they aided: again there is the mingling of piety, charity, and social status. However, as charitable benefactions differ in kind if not intention from acts of piety, they reflect different priorities which must be treated in their own terms.

In the second of its Great Commandments, Christianity enjoined a love of neighbours which could only find expression through charity. The demands of charity, of *caritas*, were both mental and physical. Its absence justified the refusal of communion to those not at peace with their neighbours, forcing individuals to assess their righteousness before taking the sacrament. Its presence obliged them to care for their neighbours, defend widows and orphans, comfort the bereaved, help the sick, visit the imprisoned, and so on. The obligations of generalized *caritas* merged into the specific moral and financial obligations of those with money to assist those without: charity was a moral imperative on the wealthy. The Seven Corporal Acts of Mercy were a guiding force throughout life – so much so that one unknown benefactor to a York church had himself depicted in a stained-glass window fulfilling the six which derived directly from the

---

[117] Moorman, *Friars in Cambridge*, pp. 246–58; Tanner, *Church in Norwich*, pp. 119–20, 189; Fleming, 'Charity, faith, and the gentry', pp. 48–9; Vale, *Piety, charity, and literacy*, pp. 13, 20–22; PRO, E101/514/32, f. 14v (burials in mendicant houses and the division of the proceeds still produced disputes and local arrangements: Owen, *Lynn*, pp. 116–17; Williams, 'Mendicant friars and secular clergy' [908], pp. 63–73; Legge, *Anglo-Norman letters*, pp. 35–6); Little, 'Franciscan letters' [516]; Whitfield, 'An early letter of confraternity' [896] (for less up-to-date listing, for all the mendicant orders, Clark-Maxwell, 'Some letters', pp. 52–7; Clark-Maxwell, 'Some further letters', pp. 209–13).

ALL SAINTS, NORTH ST, YORK Social obligation and Christian responsibility: a benefactor performs the Corporal Acts of Mercy enjoined by Christ for those seeking eternal salvation (Matthew 26: 34–46). On the left feeding the hungry (top) and clothing the naked; in the centre giving drink to the thirsty (top) and visiting the sick; on the right entertaining the stranger (top) and relieving the imprisoned.
(Royal Commission on the Historical Monuments of England)

words of Christ (the seventh, burial of the dead, was taken from the apocryphal Book of Tobit, where it appears in chapters 2 and 11).[118]

Late medieval charitable activity defies adequate assessment. Wills provide most of the direct evidence, and can be subjected (albeit with questionable validity) to some degree of statistical analysis.[119] But charity was not exclusively offered after death, and some contemporaries considered post-mortem benefactions as an evasion of duties: better a gift during life than after death.[120] Technically, the church was responsible for charitable distribution of some of its own income; but despite canonical requirements the system seems to have been moribund in later medieval England. Just how effectively the church (whether seen as the benefice, or the lay community represented in its parochial organization) fulfilled the requirements of charity is untestable.[121] It is also usually impossible to test the status of the recipients and whether it changed as the debate about provision for the 'undeserving poor' gradually led to more discriminatory distribution.

As things stand, only post-mortem charity can be properly discussed. Only the concerns and aspirations of testators can be analysed, not the reality of distribution: without executors' accounts, we can rarely tell whether wills were actually fulfilled – visitation material suggests frequent laxity in this field.[122]

Testamentary charity was mainly directed to securing prayers. It therefore had to be widespread, and economical, ensuring that prayers would continue for as long as possible. The distribution of charitable bequests falls into four main categories: chantries and their attendant charitable institutions; gifts to religious orders; bequests for educational purposes (which overlap slightly with chantry bequests); and generic 'public works' – the upkeep of roads and bridges, and donations for the maintenance and building of churches.[123]

---

[118] Clay, *Mediaeval hospitals*, pp. 88, 90; Brigden, 'Religion and social obligation', esp. pp. 67–8, 73–4, 79; Owst, *Literature and pulpit*, p. 154. For the moral implications of wealth, see 5/1, at n. 5.

[119] The chief advocate of a statistical approach is W.K. Jordan, whose several works on English philanthropy between 1480 and 1660 are extensively based on wills. For his methodology see *Philanthropy in England 1480–1660* [455], pp. 22–40, although it seems fundamentally flawed for the pre-Reformation period. More recent approaches (e.g. Fleming, 'Charity, faith, and the gentry') assess percentages of testators making bequests for specific purposes, which at least reveals the interests and concerns, if not the precise extent, of donations.

[120] Barnum, *Dives and pauper*, ii, pp. 277–8.

[121] For parochial poor relief in late medieval England, Tierney, *Medieval poor law* [839], pp. 128–31.

[122] See n. 40.

[123] This is by no means the total range. See the injunctions for charity prescribed by Langland for the wealthy in Pearsall, *Piers Plowman*, p. 162.

Chantry bequests were principally concerned with securing prayers, but many foundations had additional obligations. Several were linked to hospitals and almshouses, the priests being responsible for caring for the inmates. Such were the hospital of the Annunciation established at Newark (Notts.) by John de Plumptre in 1400, and the almshouses founded by Sir Robert Knolles and his wife at Pontefract (Yorks.). Other chantries had specifically educational purposes, providing a local school. Archbishop Rotherham's foundation of Jesus College at Rotherham (Yorks.) was fairly typical, with its links between prayers and benefaction. (Many chantry priests may well have provided some sort of teaching on an informal basis as well – but this does not fall under the same heading.) A number of chantries were linked to public works like the maintenance of bridges (as at Wakefield [Yorks.]); others were established to assist with parochial work. The latter could serve as privately funded chapels-of-ease, thereby saving treks to the more distant parish church. The symbiosis of chantry and chapelry is perfectly expressed in the scheme for re-establishing a chantry at Leverington (Cambs.) in 1459; a decayed chantry was to be transferred from the manor of Fitton Hall to the chapel of Parson Drove. While the chantry funds provided insufficient endowment, the priest was to act as the local chaplain, receiving the necessary supplement to his income from the inhabitants. Where the chantry priests did not have additional formal responsibilities, they would be expected to assist the parish priest and be under his supervision. Even if it lacked defined ancillary functions, a chantry could still serve a charitable function through the distribution of doles. William Wakebridge's chantry at Crich (Derby.) was burdened with the annual distribution of 10s. in farthings, and the monition delivered prior to the distribution reminded the recipients to pray for the benefactor. The prayer element was crucial, and in most cases the chantry element probably took priority over the supplementary functions: if funds were insufficient to continue the charity with the chantry, then the charity might well be discarded.[124]

Even if the chantry was only funded in the short term, the other charitable bequests were still meant to secure prayers. Thus, bequests to relieve prisoners, to hospitals, to provide dowries for poor girls, all secured the suffrages of the recipients. Distributions to 'the poor' at funerals encouraged attendance and again purchased prayers, although few can have been as ambitious as John Hosier of London, who in 1518 planned for the presence of no fewer than 4,800 paupers at his funeral. Such

---

[124] Swanson, *Reg. Scrope*, i, pp. 44–6, 76–9; Moran, *English schooling*, pp. 80–1, 85 (for Rotherham statutes Leach, *Early Yorkshire schools* [501], ii, pp. 109–30, esp. 120–2); Kreider, *English chantries*, pp. 55–7; EDR, G/2/3, f. 3r–v; Saltman, *Wakebridge chantries* [733], p. 185; Hicks, 'Chantries, obits, and almshouses', pp. 129–30.

provision might be made annual by generously funded obits. The numbers benefiting from these could be surprisingly high, in reality as well as anticipation: in 1429 the obit for Thomas Hungerford (died 1398) attracted 93 priests and 363 paupers, and 43 priests and 572 paupers in 1430.[125] Scattered and haphazard as most bequests for charitable purposes were, they provided the only real system of social assistance in medieval England outside the fraternities and whatever remained of the parochial system – and many of the charitable institutions linked to chantries were in any case associated with fraternities. As 'Puritan' attitudes towards the poor developed in the fifteenth century, decrying those considered unworthy or undeserving of charity, indiscriminate distribution was perhaps replaced by more directed local handouts, reflecting a variety of forces which may have included a concern for local status.[126] But it would be dangerous to push this argument too far: the beneficiaries of much of the 'indiscriminate' charity were probably local inhabitants anyway, except in some of the larger towns.

Bequests to the religious orders, to the holy poor, merit separate consideration. Here the distinction between donations during life and after death becomes especially important, for the post-mortem gifts are intimately associated with prayers for souls rather than charity itself. For the monastic orders and nunneries, post-mortem donations may have been the chief form of such gifts; but other considerations apply with the mendicants. The friars supposedly lived solely from begging, just the sort of activity to leave little concrete evidence. Mendicants acted as confessors, and received preaching and penitentiary licences. Their activities were much debated throughout the period, most notably by Wyclif and Reginald Pecock, and discussed in vernacular literature by Chaucer and Langland and in the poems of 'Jack Upland'.[127] But definite evidence of mendicant receipts from the living is all but untraceable, unsurprisingly as most records of mendicant finances have been lost. Even what survives is opaque. Most evidence relates to post-mortem donations, or purchases of prayers, usually expended in pittances to the friars. However, there are occasional indications of collections, such as the odd 40d. apparently given to the Franciscans of Cambridge by the burgesses of Bishop's Lynn in 1366 – odd because that town was not in Cambridge's official collecting area.[128] Just

[125] Vale, *Piety, charity, and literacy*, pp. 23–8; Fleming, 'Charity, faith, and the gentry', pp. 44–5; Gottfried, *Bury St Edmunds*, p. 177; Hicks, 'Chantries, obits, and almshouses', p. 127 n. 8; Brigden, 'Religion and social obligation', p. 107; Burgess, 'Service for the dead', pp. 189–90.

[126] Fleming, 'Charity, faith, and the gentry', pp. 45–6; McIntosh, *Autonomy and community* [558], pp. 238–40.

[127] Generally Szittya, *Antifraternal tradition*, chs 3–7.

[128] Moorman, *Friars in Cambridge*, pp. 70–4, 242–5.

how much the mendicants might expect to collect within their allocated districts is unknowable, as are the precise motives of the donors. Piety and charity presumably commingled, in varying proportions depending on the donor's concerns. Perhaps devotion was slackening slightly as the middle ages ended; but what evidence there is is scattered and inconclusive.

The third main area of charitable benefaction was education.[129] Gifts for this purpose varied enormously in form and size, from donations of books through to foundation of schools and university colleges; from support for individual students in the household or elsewhere to contributions towards the building funds of functioning institutions. For some donors the charitable motive may have been replaced by a sense of duty, with the universities demanding benefactions, especially from their alumni. The desire to be visibly a patron must also be taken into account. The precise imperatives towards benefaction cannot usually be adequately disentangled, but the possibilities themselves demand recognition. Generally, medieval English educational provision still leaves plenty of scope for study, and revision. The various levels at which it operated may well have produced different reactions from potential donors. Again, however, charity was often linked to a demand for prayers, which cannot be ignored.[130]

Basic education was provided within the parish, with elementary reading and singing schools, and some grammar, all closely linked to training for participation in the church services. While there were numerous schools, few seem to have been properly endowed before the sixteenth century. However, the grammar-school movement, which burgeoned in the fifteenth century, saw a greater spread of endowed schools. Godshouse, Cambridge, was partly established to remedy the shortage of masters for such schools, its alumni being instructed to take posts within schools founded since *c*.1400. The foundation of grammar schools was a common charitable action. Many guilds, like that of Holy Cross at Stratford-on-Avon (War.), set up their own schools; but charitable as these were, they probably need to be differentiated from those founded by individuals. These, such as Henry Chichele's establishment at Higham Ferrers (Northants.), or Hugh Oldham's at Manchester (Lancs.), were intended to provide free education for local children, who in return would suitably commemorate their benefactors. The receipt of a Latin education would supposedly provide a sound basis for future life, where they would receive honours which would redound to the glory of their deceased patrons. How many schools offered free education is not clear; but charity was not confined to their establishment. Individuals might also be assisted, with many wills leaving money

---

[129] Generally Moran, *English schooling*; Orme, *English schools* [618].

[130] Jewell, 'Bishops as educational benefactors [443], pp. 152–61; Rosenthal, 'Lancastrian bishops' [712], pp. 201–7; Moran, *English schooling*, pp. 7–17.

to see people through the schools. Here two different forms of support are reflected: gifts to named individuals, which can be seen as post-mortem continuation of earlier patronage to a friend or relative; and more abstract bequests granting a sum of money to a specified number of scholars, which were more acts of charity than an exercise of patronage, and more concerned with receiving the rewards of being a benefactor. Such bequests were made to people attending local schools, and also to university students. Indeed, as there were very few places available through established colleges, such individual provision at universities was highly important. Edmund Dudley fully appreciated the position in 1509, urging the wealthy to continue supporting scholars, arguing that 'a better chantry shall you never find'.[131]

The ultimate in educational benefaction was, presumably, the creation of a university college, and several were founded during this period. Their purpose was both the general expansion of learning, and sometimes provision for specific studies: Bishop Richard Fleming set up Lincoln College, Oxford, in the 1420s especially to encourage theology (the course for which was particularly lengthy and expensive) in order to combat Lollardy and heresy. Again, many aims combined in these foundations: provision of education on its own, patronage, and the rewards of being a benefactor. Some colleges added other features, seeking to limit those qualified for admission. These restrictions were usually geographical or based on connections with particular schools, like the linkage between Winchester College (Hants.) and New College, Oxford, or Eton (Bucks.) and King's at Cambridge. Sometimes the limits were genealogical, the system of 'founder's kin' giving the founder's relatives first call on the available places.[132]

Provision was also needed for the educated. University colleges were partly founded to permit the continuation of higher studies, removing some of the problems of patronage and finance which graduates might otherwise encounter. Other individual benefactions invoked the chantry element, ordering that only graduates should receive particular posts. Some gifts to support preaching fit into this context: bequests to engage graduates on preaching tours revealed a concern to defend and improve the church, while announcing the benefactor's name would augment the prayers for his soul.[133]

[131] Moran, *English schooling*, pp. 46–8; Rackham, *Early statutes* [682], pp. 2–3, 24–7; Swanson, 'Universities, graduates and benefices' [799], pp. 55–6 and n. 120; Brodie, *The Tree of Commonwealth* [95], p. 63.

[132] Green, *Lincoln college* [316], p. 6; Swanson, 'Universities, graduates, and benefices', p. 59 n. 137.

[133] ibid., pp. 53–4; Weaver, *Somerset medieval wills*, p. 182; McIntosh, *Autonomy and community*, p. 237; Thrupp, *Merchant class* [838], p. 188; Orme, 'Medieval clergy' [619], p. 96 and n. 119.

The arrangements to support preaching merge into the category of public works. As the church was an integral part of the social infrastructure, bequests for many ecclesiastical purposes were by extension public benefactions. Those assisting rebuilding and similar works thus aided employment, and generally contributed to economic activity. However, such bequests are not of the sort which would now be considered as public works; they would probably concentrate on the establishment of almshouses and bequests to maintain roads and bridges.

Almshouses and similar foundations have yet to receive the scholarly attention they deserve. The later middle ages clearly recognized a growing problem of poverty, with provision for the elderly and indigent becoming of increasing concern. Frequently repeated demands that churches make due provision from parochial income were largely ineffective. Even the monastic orders, whose duties included charitable distributions, were seemingly making little effective contribution. Their annual alms-giving is generally assessed at around (and often under) 3 per cent of income. (This has to be put in perspective: Thomas Cromwell's injunctions of 1536 required non-resident clerics 'which may dispend yearly twenty pounds or above' to distribute only 2.5 per cent of their benefice revenues to the poor; while a slightly earlier proposal of Christopher St German suggested 5 per cent.)[134] Social provision was largely a matter for individual donations, for whatever specific purposes. Almshouses fall under the same umbrella, their foundation spreading considerably in the fifteenth century. Some had a formally regulated chantry aspect; others were the less regulated *Maisons Dieu*. Not being benefices, and thus lacking formal connection with the ecclesiastical structure, these *Maisons Dieu* leave few traces; although administratively and organizationally they were probably similar to the hospitals. With the hospitals they made some positive contribution towards poor relief, although information about their inmates is scarce. St Mary Roncevalles at Westminster certainly served as a hostel for the destitute; but elsewhere the position is less clear-cut. The inmates at St Leonard's, York, in 1399 were clearly not all paupers, having paid anything up to £54 13s. 4d. for their places; nor were all the inhabitants of Ewelme hospital (Oxon.), one of whom left goods worth over £10 in his room at his death. Other hospitals changed their functions over time. That at Royston (Cambs.) declined into little more than a free chantry, while in Cambridge the main hospital of St John gradually extinguished its involvement with the local poor, so that its eventual transformation

---

[134] Snape, *English monastic finances* [770], pp. 110–18 (but see Tierney, *Medieval poor law*, pp. 79–82); Williams, *English historical documents, 1485–1558* [910], p. 808; Guy, *St German* [324], pp. 27, 130.

into St John's College was merely the completion of a process long under way.[135]

While such foundations cared for the destitute and the sick, the gifts for bridges and road repair eased travel, trade, and communications. Frequently a testator paid only for the upkeep of a designated stretch of road, but that the roads were maintained at all is the real point. Again, there was probably a chantry element in such donations, with part of the money perhaps going to support hermits. Some, also, may have been used to provide a form of outdoor relief, especially if oversight of the bequest was left to the churchwardens.[136]

The varied expressions of orthodox spirituality available in late medieval England make adequate synthesis of the trends difficult. There was clearly considerable vitality, and considerable development over time. The importation of new feasts, linked with the spread of new shrines (especially crosses and shrines of the Virgin) correlate with the expanding cult of Corpus Christi and the Christocentric emphasis of private devotions, whether quasi-mystical or not. It appears that in terms of piety, and despite occasional indications to the contrary, England was fully in line with the rest of Christendom. Catholic spirituality was well entrenched, and (despite the Lollards) faced no major challenges.

The main problem remains evidential: to be assessed spirituality must be expressed. While the available evidence allows some generalized deductions, there is no guarantee that that evidence does reflect the feelings of the mass of the populace. Almost all the evidence is in some way elitist: the great unheard may have felt quite differently, but remain unheard.

The connections between spirituality and piety are matched by the connections between spirituality and charity; but again there are dangers. The available evidence is skewed towards testamentary gifts, whose representative nature cannot be tested. The wills provide plenty of evidence for charitable concerns, although admittedly with a self-seeking motivation. The question of the implementation of those concerns is another matter – the numerous complaints about false executors are a useful counter to mere bequest-counting. For although people worried about their own

---

[135] Rosser, 'Vill of Westminster' [716], pp. 108–9; *VCH, City of York* [877], pp. 365, 423, 485; Burgess, ' "By quick and by dead" ', pp. 845–7; Rubin, *Charity and community*, pp. 140–2; PRO, C270/20/4 (St Leonard's: Beatrice de Selby paid £54 13s. 4d.; among others William de Feriby paid £45 and Katherine Andrew £46 13s. 4d. Alice Fynde paid £40 to become a sister of the hospital, and Alice de Westcogh £33 6s. 8d.); Bod., DD.Ewelme.a.6.A35B(14) (other references to goods of deceased inmates are scattered throughout these accounts, always producing smaller sums, e.g. A35B(23); A35B(26)).

[136] Fleming, 'Charity, faith, and the gentry', pp. 46–7; Wood-Legh, *Kentish visitations*, pp. 219–20.

souls, their non-fulfilment of wills showed little concern for the souls of others. To go beyond a mere quantitative statement to a qualitative evaluation of the types of charity offered is impossible. While individual testamentary practices may have altered the emphases revealed within wills, it is doubtful if evidence of such changes in pre-Reformation England can lead to any valid arguments about the 'preferred' destination of charitable bequests during the period. It may be that the destination of the residues was also changing, with assumptions about that destination being built into wills and needing no specification. In the end all that can be said is that charitable bequests were extremely numerous, covering the whole range of potential activities. They were not immediately concerned with charity for itself: the charity was subordinate to a highly self-centred concern to ensure release from Purgatory by investing in other people's prayers.

7

Nonconformity and Dislocation

7.1   CONTEXTS

The church's close involvement with its society almost inevitably caused tensions – especially if that church is considered in human rather than institutional terms. It had to face the challenges of its changing social position, and changing demands. The English situation was part of a European phenomenon: enmeshed in the social and political structure and entangled in economic life as both producer and consumer the church pervaded all of contemporary society. Its personnel were influential at all levels. Its spiritual obligations, and spiritual control, gave it considerable supervisory authority over popular mentalities. However, individual conflicts were endemic, and general clashes between church and governments commonplace. The contradictions between what the church preached, and what it did, were glaringly obvious. The post-plague years saw successive demands for varied forms of reformation – Wyclif and his followers, the Hussites in Bohemia, Bernardino of Siena and numerous others in Italy (including the revolution of Savonarola in Florence) – in due course leading to The Reformation itself.[1]

Within England, although some aspects of orthodoxy approached the frontiers of unorthodoxy at times, few actually crossed over into heresy. That was virtually unknown in the English church until the late fourteenth century, although there are occasional notices of individual heretics, or small groups, from the twelfth century onwards. These usually relate to academic heretics: individual thinkers carried away by their ideas. Perhaps typical was the writer Uthred of Boldon (died 1397): ideas associated with him were condemned in the 1370s. Some references seemingly prefigure

---

[1] For the similarities between these movements (from a different perspective), see Mullett, *Popular culture* [601], ch. 4. For Wyclif, below, and 7/2.

later Lollardy; while other mentions are tantalizingly vague and cannot be followed up.[2] After 1380, however, the definition and defence of orthodoxy became critical issues, as the church authorities confronted the challenge presented by John Wyclif and his successors, the Lollards. In responding they also faced other tensions which created their own crises, as in the accusations levelled against Reginald Pecock in the 1440s.

The apparent absence of popular heresy from England before 1380 could have several explanations. The most obvious would be deficiency in the sources: heresy existed, but is not revealed. As so few church court records survive before 1450, there might be something to the argument. Alternatively, there may have been no heresy. Its apparent absence can be explained not as acceptance of the rigid official definition of the faith, but by the laxity of that definition.[3] The image of a church anxious to quell all debate about itself and its beliefs until the Reformation opened the flood-gates is totally false. There ws a fluidity about much of what the church professed which often allowed for a plurality of opinions, condemned only when they became jurisdictionally subversive or sometimes – but rarely – in a panic. Fierce debates could be conducted on a variety of subjects, such as the Immaculate Conception and papal infallibility, without in-curring formal condemnation. Social interpretations of Christianity were also fluid: what the church demanded was basic acceptance of the defini-tions which it eventually did produce, principally on the components of the Creeds (and also on aspects of intercession, transubstantiation, and suchlike) after they had been thoroughly argued through. Mistakes could be tolerated, provided that they were corrected. Where the mistake seemed insignificant, it could be ignored. People were not generally required to explain their beliefs; but they were expected to accept the definitions provided for them by the church.

This relatively lax definition of orthodoxy meant that the church was accustomed to confronting heresy: although apparently monolithic, its doctrinal machine simply could not be maintained without facing an occasional threat. Theologically that threat was greatest when the search for doctrinal definition degenerated (as the church saw it) into a rejection of orthodoxy, and urged the unacceptable. Heresy, however, was not a straightforward matter of discipline, but of faith and its interpretation. Thus, using the definitions advanced by some Cambridge doctors in the 1390s:

Heresy is false dogma, contrary to the catholic faith and the determination of the church, which is pertinaciously defended. . . . A heretic is so named who discovers

---

[2] Several references collected in Bacher, *Prosecution of heretics* [26], chs 2, 4 (including Irish evidence) – see esp. pp. 16–17; Knowles, 'Censured opinions' [485].

[3] For the weakness of the church, McGrath, *Intellectual origins* [549], pp. 16–28.

a new opinion or doctrine contrary to the faith or determination of the universal church, or to a proper understanding of the holy scriptures, or who follows such discoveries of others and pertinaciously defends them.

Thus, and critically, heresy was not seen in every theological novelty, but only in a persistent refusal to accept that the ideas advanced were wrong if the church so decreed: it was a failure to admit mistakes when they were determined to be such. Such mistakes would not be mere matters of organization, but more serious undermining of doctrinal purity: an intellectual as well as pragmatic challenge.[4]

To stress doctrinal purity imposes an illusory rigidity on the systems of belief operating within the late medieval church. Heretics were sought out in concern for the faith and its defence; but the definition of the faith was rarely so narrow as to allow only one interpretation. Generally speaking, provided that an article of faith was not formally denied (or, perhaps, so nuanced as to appear to be denied), then regardless of the way in which it was accepted or made intelligible, that was usually sufficient.

Moreover, not everything was covered by formal pronouncements. Doctrine was malleable, as was tradition, capable of development, and if need be compromise, to ensure the continuity of the total structure. The most notable compromise of all occurred in 1436 with the compacts between the Bohemians and the Council of Basle, establishing an admittedly uneasy regime which allowed the moderate Hussites to receive communion in both kinds and thereby reintegrated Bohemia into the catholic framework after the upheavals of the religious wars.[5]

The problem of heresy also needs to be set against the other tensions confronting the late medieval church, principally the call for reform, which provides a constant undercurrent in the period both in England and on the continent. Reform had been a problem for the church for centuries. Indeed, the church had never been unaware of the need to adjust to changing circumstances, which could amount to a type of Reformation. But the call for reform, locally and internationally, grew ever more strident after 1350. The universal church then entered an era of prolonged crisis, bringing the demand for reform 'in head and members'. Such institutional disciplinary reform would have changed the relationship between the papacy and the localities, raised the level of parochial care, and revitalized Christian spirituality. In some of its manifestations it attacked contemporary practices by exerting greater control over popular cults and greater care over the canonization of saints – indeed, a reduction in the generally crowded calendar was occasionally demanded. Europe

---

[4] Leff, *Heresy* [503], pp. 1–3; for the quotation see Parry, *Reg. Trillek* [643] p. 393.
[5] For the compacts and their ambiguity, Heymann, *George of Bohemia* [382], pp. 6–12.

then witnessed reform movements like that in Bohemia in the late fourteenth century, before it spawned Hussitism, and the attempts of the Councils of Pisa, Constance, and Basle to produce Reformation – unsuccessfully.

Many of the reforms demanded were traditional, complaining about clerical abuses, trying to ensure residence and the educational standards of the clergy, and so on, most of them virtually sermon commonplaces.[6] Yet the ferment of reform, particularly as channelled in the 1530s, produced Reformation. The challenge to the church, the process of change, demand consideration. On the one hand there were the reform movements which operated very much within the church; on the other were the forces seeking more dramatic change, although not consciously outside the church, exemplified by Lollardy from about 1380 onwards, and under Henry VIII by the breach with papal authority.

7.2   THE PROBLEM OF REFORM

England's Reformation was unique. The sudden change in the headship of the church preceded the longer-term transformation which brought reform of the doctrines and discipline of the institution, and the dissolution of many of the religious forms which had integrated the medieval church into its society. It was a slow process, rather than an event, and certainly not completed until well after the mid-sixteenth century.

From a medieval viewpoint, the Reformation is highly problematic. Not only does its course require explanation, but the fact of its occurrence is also surprising. The crucial changes occurred suddenly and unexpectedly, and cannot be explained by a simplistic contrast between degenerate medieval Catholicism and vigorous modern Protestantism. The Reformation was at times very tentative; precisely when England ceased to be a 'catholic' country being impossible to say. Yet, although its inception causes problems, the Reformation's overall development presents different difficulties; for, once started, there was something inexorable – but not irreversible – about the progression. That, however, was perhaps more a reflection of the circumstances in which it occurred than a comment on the state of England's pre-Reformation church.[7]

The pre-history of England's Reformation makes the actual outcome rather surprising: it can plausibly be argued that there were three distinct but overlapping reform movements operating in late medieval England,

---

[6] Owst, *Literature and pulpit* [632], pp. 242–86.
[7] For the problem of the speed and success of the Reformation, Haigh, 'Recent historiography' [332].

whose competition became increasingly intense after 1500. First, there was a catholic movement, essentially disciplinary, a constant trend intensified by the impact of Christian humanism on the institutions of the medieval church, seeking to re-edify established religion through changes which would maintain the essence of the establishment while making it more suitable for its times. Second, there was a doctrinal movement which would in due course develop into Protestantism, challenging many of the tenets of catholicism, and aiming to build a church whose disciplinary traditions would bring a break with medieval religion by establishing a more primitive and responsive institution. Finally, there was the 'laicizing' movement, perhaps itself needing separation into two strands, one reflecting the aims of (part of) the laity, the other specifically reflecting the king's desires, his personal concern with royal authority and individual satisfaction. Generally, this movement lacked any clear doctrinal or disciplinary aims other than a reduction of ecclesiastical involvement in lay society. Separating the strands is an artificial process, imposing from hindsight categories which contemporaries would not have recognized or accepted; but the distinctions do seem sustainable, and worthy of consideration individually and jointly, for it was their interaction which produced the Lollard movement of the fourteenth and fifteenth centuries, and then set the pace for the progress of the English Reformation.

Most discussion of reform in pre-Reformation England was unconcerned with abstruse matters of theology. The emphasis was on concrete issues of ecclesiastical organization and function, matters which were essentially disciplinary: questions such as the scope of ecclesiastical authority, the duties and qualities of priests, the church's involvement in worldiy activities, and the nature of popular piety and instruction, sometimes providing the ammunition for vitriolic attacks on the church like Simon Fish's *Supplication of the Beggars* of c.1529.[8] The concern was with practical, remediable, issues and the role of the church within society. These matters could (and eventually did) merge into the question of supremacy within the church, transforming into a debate centring on the nature of royal power over the ecclesiastical structure. But that did not become a major issue until specific circumstances drove Henry VIII to his break with Rome.

In Europe disciplinary concern generated the Observant branches of some of the mendicant orders, and stimulated actions like attacks on the cult of the Holy Blood of Wilsnack.[9] England shared in these trends from

---

[8] Furnivall and Cowper, *Four supplications* [289], pp. 1–15.
[9] Oakley, *Western church* [609] (p. 240 for Cusa and Wilsnack); Kaminsky, *Hussite revolution* [456], pp. 7–23.

the 1350s. Wyclif, before his rejection, was advocating much that was not unusual, sharing some programmes (such as ecclesiastical disendowment) with some of the friars. His ideas have to be set against a general background of academically inspired reform, his proposals having similarities with those of Richard Ullerston (in the early fifteenth century) and Thomas Gascoigne (in the mid-fifteenth). The University of Oxford proposed a lengthy reform programme to the Council of Pisa, reiterated at Constance; and also sought provincial action in 1414. Even York shared in this movement, with the reissue of older legislation by Archbishop Neville at a provincial synod in 1466, and by Thomas Wolsey's major compilation of the York *Provinciale*.[10]

The main aim was to reform the clergy; few gave much thought to the extension of disciplinary reform to the laity. John Colet was perhaps typical in the early sixteenth century, arguing that lay reform would follow logically from clerical reform. Over half a century earlier Reginald Pecock had demonstrated concern for the laity; his proposals to make the church more 'relevant' to its flock have much in common with early sixteenth-century schemes, to produce a church responsive to lay aspirations but within the catholic tradition. After the 1460s, the vociferous reform movement rather subsided in England, other than in sermons, although there are continued signs of disciplinary concern. Diocesan visitations reflect continued attention to the quality of local services – and the church's continued inability to enforce discipline consistently. There may have been greater success with some of the monastic orders, with the archbishops of Canterbury gaining visitatorial control over some of the exempt houses and orders, and thereby seeking to instil disciplinary reform.[11] Additionally, there are some signs of concern with changing lay perceptions, and worries about the nature of popular beliefs. Here the ecclesiastical authorities were seemingly fighting a losing battle against the proliferation of mechanical shrines and other places of pilgrimage, and the growing interest in indulgences and similar benefits – an attitude in part shared by Lollardy, itself demanding the purification of the institutional structure, and less 'abuse' in popular practices such as pilgrimage and devotion to images.[12]

In the sixteenth century the call for reform became more vocal, and more insistent. The church's leaders show a greater concern for their responsibilities. Laymen shared elements of this concern: in 1509 Edmund Dudley's *Tree of Commonwealth* included proposals for ecclesiastical discip-

[10] *Northern Convocation* [690], pp. 183–202; Woolley, *The York Provinciale* [926]; Wilkins, *Concilia* [902], iii, pp. 662–81. For earlier Oxford proposals, *Concilia*, iii, pp. 360–5.
[11] Knowles, *Religious orders* [484], ii, p. 161; Churchill, *Canterbury administration* [144], i, p. 504; Lupton, *Life of Colet* [536], p. 302.
[12] See 7/3 at n. 56.

linary action, especially when dealing with education and the acquisition of benefices.[13] But the initiative was retained by the clerics, some influenced by continental ideals of Christian humanism and working for a revitalization and rebirth of the church through a return not to the organization and practices of the early church, but to its original moral and doctrinal principles. William Melton, in his sermon to ordinands of *c.*1510, spelt out in considerable detail how the clergy should approach their task; and his views were clearly shared by John Colet, who gave the sermon his imprimatur. The humanist message of renewal and reform, and a return to basic principles within the catholic structure, received considerable support. John Colet for one clearly shared in the Italian Christian humanist tradition, and sought to implement its ideas in England. Addressing the Canterbury Convocation in 1512 (a sermon later printed in English) he pleaded forcefully for a reformation of the church which would involve its withdrawal from the world and rediscovery of its true form. It was, he claimed, largely a personal and moral reformation – it needed no new legislation, merely obedience to existing canons. The sermon was intended to initiate a total reform, given his assumption that clerical reformation would automatically bring lay reformation with it. The language of reformation simultaneously involved a strong affirmation of the church's status, perhaps typical of the time. Colet repeated the hierocratic notion of the lowest cleric being superior to the prince, demanding that the church should not be tainted by worldly concerns.[14]

However, in trying to implement such a Catholic Reformation the church faced a major dilemma: its spirituality was largely a reflection of popular demand. Moreover, the degree of lay control over clerical careers, and the pressures and connections of patronage, meant that clerical enforcement of reform would be difficult, forcing confrontation with vested interests. The laity might complain in the Reformation Parliament about ecclesiastical abuses, but many of them were their responsibility, the outcome of their exploitation of the church for other purposes. Nevertheless, there is evidence of local concern with reform, even if not countrywide. Individual bishops like John Longland in Lincoln tried to improve their diocesan systems, and resolve some of the tensions which otherwise hindered effective action. There is even evidence of a reformist streak in the Canterbury Convocation which paralleled the Reformation Parliament: proposals were discussed, although whether any action was taken, or worked, is not clear. In any event, clerical vested interests could also

[13] Brodie, *The Tree of Commonwealth* [95], pp. 24–6, 42–4, 56–7, 62–6, 99–101.

[14] Porter, 'The gloomy dean' [667], pp. 18–33; Rupp, 'Battle of the books' [719], pp. 5–9; Lupton, *Life of Colet*, pp. 293–304; see also Hunt, *Dean Colet* [430], pp. 18–72; Clebsch, 'John Colet' [152].

obstruct reform: John Colet's attempted revision of the statutes of St Paul's cathedral, London, foundered on vigorous opposition from the chapter and lower clergy, and not even the invocation of Wolsey's authority could produce their submission.[15] This process of rationalization (which was, in part, what the catholic reform movement involved) was largely overtaken by the changes of the Henrician Reformation.

The monasteries were one area where reform had been in progress for some time. The relevance of monasticism was a constant problem, but there is no evidence of a widespread desire to undermine it completely. The monastic vocation was still felt to be a real one; the problem was generally considered in terms of over-provision of monasteries for that demand. The solution to decadence was, therefore, piecemeal dissolution. Thus, the alien priories had been diverted to educational or collegiate purposes during the later stages of the French wars, and other dependent churches transferred to English ownership. This rationalization continued in the sixteenth century, again with the aim of converting the property to other beneficial (usually educational) purposes. The processes of 1536 and (perhaps) 1539, the final dissolutions, followed logically from these precedents. Yet although the Dissolution of the monasteries became the most memorable element of England's Reformation, it was not a necessary element in it: monasteries did survive for some years under the Henrician system, after all.[16]

Other rationalization schemes were put forward under Henry VIII. Wolsey is not usually seen as a reformer, but he has some claims to that status, his schemes being pre-empted by events and opposition. He 'had none of the spiritual qualities of a reformer' and 'lacked entirely the ardour of a reformer', but he nevertheless was one.[17] His standing as legate *a latere* had considerable significance within England. For once the two provinces were united in subjection to one local head, an efficient and unified administration could be created. Whether it was constructed remains largely unknown, as most records of Wolsey's legatine activities have been lost; but his courts and dispensations would have instilled more uniformity and efficiency into the whole system.

Even before acquiring his legation *a latere*, Wolsey revised the provincial laws of York, making them more like those of Canterbury. His attempts at other reforms faced obstruction, notably from the lesser clergy who saw their activities and prospects curtailed by greater efficiency and selectivity.

[15] Hunt, *Dean Colet*, pp. 51–6; Lehmberg, *The Reformation Parliament* [507], pp. 116–17, 142–3; Bowker, *Henrician Reformation* [80], pp. 4–64.
[16] See 2/5 n. 154; Youings, *Dissolution* [934], pp. 1–2.
[17] Quotations from Knowles, *Religious orders*, iii, pp. 158, 160; see also e.g. Oakley, *Western church*, p. 239 n. 30. The only concerted defence of Wolsey as a reformer is the totally uncritical Taunton, *Wolsey* [812], esp. chs 4–8.

To some extent, the reassessment of clerical incomes which Wolsey instituted in the 1520s also fits into the pattern of disciplinary reform – for the
first time since 1291 the valuation of the English church was completely
reassessed, allowing the establishment of a more realistic taxation system.[18]

In other areas, Wolsey sought to abolish minor orders, which had long
caused headaches – the evidence suggests that their recording was patchy,
and their rationale was questionable – but achieved only partial (and
temporary) success. He also advocated reform in the religious orders,
proposing visitations and seeking to amend statutes. Some of his proposals
aroused protests because of their harshness, forcing him to back down. He
also sought rationalization among the religious houses; his dissolutions
were not solely intended to fund his collegiate foundations at Oxford and
Ipswich, but also amalgamated houses with few inhabitants – a precedent
for the official policy proclaimed in 1536. The Oxford and Ipswich foundations also showed Wolsey's concern for educational reform, part of a
grandiose scheme which doubtless (like all such schemes) was meant to
redound to the glory of its promoter, but would also have made a significant contribution to a long-term programme of wider reform.[19]

Finally, and potentially of most impact, Wolsey urged geographical
rationalizaton. Just what his scheme for redrawing diocesan boundaries
entailed is not clear – although Henry VIII's later proposals were doubtless predicated on a version of it. More dioceses would have reduced some
of the excessively large bishoprics, thereby making the church more accessible to the people, reducing the problems of access to church courts
and administrative remoteness. If implemented, the scheme would also
have affected the distribution of ecclesiastical endowments – many of the
new bishoprics were to replace older monastic or collegiate foundations,
whose revenues would need corresponding reorganization. Possibly extant
episcopal estates would also be redistributed, although how this would
have worked is not known.[20]

So far, the clerical leadership of the disciplinary reform movement has
been emphasized; but lay involvement was increasingly evident in the late
1520s and early 1530s, coinciding precisely with the first phase of the
Reformation. This lay involvement overlaps with the laicizing movement,
from which it cannot be totally divorced. As it represents a distinct type of
disciplinary reform – being essentially an attempt to expel the clerics and
the ecclesiastical structure from involvement in lay life – it really merits
consideration later.[21]

---

[18] Salter, *Subsidy collected in Lincoln* [729], pp. iv–v; Goring, 'General proscription' [306].
[19] Pollard, *Wolsey* [663], p. 54; Bellamy, *Criminal law and society* [54], p. 138; Knowles,
Religious orders, iii, pp. 159–64; Dowling, *Humanism* [228], pp. 77–80, 119–22.
[20] See 1/1 n. 2.
[21] Below, at nn. 45–50.

However, one element of the disciplinary reform, while affecting the laity, does need consideration here. The early sixteenth century is notable for the church's reassertion of its prerogatives, especially in the Hunne case and defence of ecclesiastical liberties, or the later possibility that Archbishop Warham was preparing to take a Becket-like stand against the royalist subjection of the church in the 1530s.[22] This appears highly anachronistic; but fits in well with the attitudes of reformist clerics. There was a strong movement for the separation of church and world – in some senses an antithesis of the laicizing reform movement – which had developed alongside Christian humanism. The church had thus sought to end lay involvement in its sphere not be renouncing any of its claims, but by a rigid distinction leading to clerical withdrawal from the world and lay retreat from spiritual matters. In the circumstances this could be no more than wishful thinking, but it provided one element in schemes for ecclesiastical regeneration, and cannot be dismissed as a mere historical oddity.

The second main reform current in the late medieval church concerned doctrine. Yet, given the scope for interpretation built into the definitions of the faith, a context which almost allowed spiritual individualism, to talk of 'doctrinal reform' may seem improper. Rather, perhaps what needs consideration is not conscious reform, but the search for doctrinal development: that this search eventually split the church was an unfortunate side-effect, a deformation rather than a reformation.

Signs of the search within England are scarce between 1350 and 1530, except for Wyclif and the Lollards. But the concern was not absent; English religion was not uninspired and catatonic, even if doctrinal development seemingly aroused only limited interest. The general trend was towards a contemplative appreciation of Christ and the church in contemporary devotional movements, alongside increasing veneration of the Virgin. In short, development along 'traditionally catholic' lines, rather than towards 'Protestantism'. Against this there are contrary suggestions, essentially responses by intellectuals to the challenges facing the church, although of differing significance.

The main contribution to pre-Reformation doctrinal reform in England was provided by John Wyclif and his followers – if they were followers. The 'if' is important: how far Wyclif's ideas, or Wycliffism, actually inspired Lollardy is debated. Recently it has become something of a tradition to contrast the intellectual Wyclif with the debasement of his ideas in Lollardy, although one with its opponents.[23] Yet there is a great difference between saying that Lollard ideas can be identified in Wyclif's

[22] Elton, *Reform and Reformation* [251], pp. 54–8, 152–3.
[23] Hudson, *Lollards and their books* [420], pp. ix–x.

writings, and that those ideas actually derived from him. The difficulty may be, and probably is, irresolvable. Moreover, Wycliffism as a heresy (or combination of heresies) has to be separated from Wyclif the heretic – for while he lived he never was a heretic. Until his death he remained a beneficed and officiating priest, despite the condemnation of arguments extracted from his works in 1382. Only in 1415 at the Council of Constance (when that assembly was trying to legitimize its own position, and also face the Hussite threat) were formal moves made against the man rather than his works. His condemnation in a posthumous investigation then produced an order for his exhumation, not actually implemented until 1427.[24]

A Yorkshireman, probably ordained priest in 1356, Wyclif's career involved a characteristic combination of academic concern and government service. Despite his reformist protestations, Wyclif was very much a career cleric, with many of the failings which he readily castigated in others. A collector of benefices, he accepted the revenues without maintaining residence or (in the case of his prebend at Westbury college [Glos.]) providing a vicar as substitute. Despite his attacks on papal provisions he sought his own advancement with a provision (ineffective) to a canonry of Lincoln. In 1374 his governmental links were shown by his nomination to the rectory of Lutterworth (Leics.) and involvement in negotiations with the papacy at Bruges concerning taxation and appointments to benefices.[25] Meanwhile he was active in academic circles. Having completed the basic arts course, and made his mark as a philosopher, he started on theology. Applying scholastic linguistic logic to doctrine, he rapidly developed an individualistic approach to the church which effectively subverted the accepted system, whilst bolstering the claims of the crown. Initially dealing with church property, he developed his novel theory of lordship or dominion, which effectively denied many basic papal jurisdictional and administrative prerogatives. Later, application of this linguistic logic to other church teachings produced a denial of transubstantiation, and a view of the Eucharist based on remanence: that the bread and wine did not change materially at consecration, even if symbolically altered.[26] Wyclif also challenged contemporary ideas of free will and predestination, and the efficacy of the priesthood. When the friars turned against his view on the Eucharist, and eventually against all his teaching (having earlier been among his main adherents) he turned against them,

[24] Dahmus, *Prosecution of Wyclyf* [184], pp. 153–4; Tatnall, 'Condemnation of Wyclif' [811].

[25] Dahmus, *Prosecution of Wyclyf*, pp. 3–4; for his possible ordination, Dobson, 'Mendicant ideal and practice' [222], p. 119.

[26] Wilks, 'Predestination, property, and power' [904]; Catto, 'Wyclif and the Eucharist' [129].

with a bitterness which rings out from his anti-mendicant tracts. As his ideas developed, being expressed in a prolific literary output,[27] he not surprisingly aroused opposition, which became prosecution. The first action was taken by the authorities of Canterbury – possibly directed by Bishop Courtenay of London – in 1377. The charges are unknown, but probably concerned his developing theory of dominion and ecclesiastical property. The trial was abortive, but months later the dominion theory was definitely behind papal action against him, which was delegated to the English authorities for determination. These moves were again inconclusive, although they possibly stimulated the crown to silence all those involved in the debate. By 1381 Wyclif's Eucharistic ideas were the centre of attention, being condemned at Oxford that year. All these moves culminated in 1382 in the Blackfriars Council, which condemned several propositions taken from Wyclif's works, although without naming him: the condemnation was supposedly an abstract determination on unattributed ideas. Precisely why and how Wyclif escaped personal condemnation remains uncertain (although the precedent of the treatment of Uthred of Boldon comes to mind – he too had ideas condemned without being attacked in person). Unlike his adherents at Oxford Wyclif was not harried, although there are hints of further papal action against him in 1383 or 1384.[28] From autumn 1381 Wyclif had withdrawn from Oxford, and virtually from all notice, to Lutterworth. There he died in 1384, still a beneficed priest, and still producing works attacking the evils of the institution which had turned against him.

That Wyclif left Oxford in 1381, and that his supporters were driven out in 1382, are both important. The attacks were on a body of thought as yet uncodified, indeed still to some extent incomplete. The Oxford purge of 1382, dramatic as it was, was not the end of a phase, but merely a halfway point.[29] Equally, the Blackfriars Council did not end attacks on Wyclif's works. Another Oxford commission in 1410 extracted further heretical propositions from them, with more condemnations at London in 1411, and at the Councils of Rome and Constance in 1412 and 1415.[30] It is also important that most evidence for attack on Wyclif's thought derives from an academic setting. Although much is known of these events, much is obscure. Many of the attacks on Wycliffism seem directed not against what Wyclif said, or thought he meant, but at what others thought he had

---

[27] Thomson, *Latin writings of Wyclyf* [834] lists a total of 435 tracts. 246 are individual sermons (ibid., nos. 54–299), but the bulk remains impressive. Whether Wyclif actually produced any works in English is undecided. Most of the anti-mendicant works are edited in Buddenseig, *Wiclif's polemical works* [103].

[28] Dahmus, *Prosecution of Wyclyf*, pp. 19–33, 38–52, 59–61, 66–72, 89–98, 129–32, 139–47.

[29] ibid., pp. 104–27.

[30] Below, at n. 54.

said, or understood him to mean. The Oxford purge may therefore be given an undeserved importance, particularly as it affected the careers of some of Wyclif's major supporters. The pursuit of individuals like Nicholas Hereford and Philip Repingdon, and their subsequent reincorporation into the ecclesiastical hierarchy (Hereford as Treasurer of Wells, and Repingdon successively Abbot of Leicester and Bishop of Lincoln) can be too conveniently interpreted as Lollards seeing the errors of their ways, masking the need to consider them as individual thinkers. The events at Oxford in 1382, although focusing on Wyclif's ideas, were also an internal university matter, part of the age-old conflict between reason and faith, linked to another outburst of the recurrent rivalry between the mendicants and the secular clergy. Few individuals are known to have been expelled from Oxford for supporting Wyclif's views, and most of them apparently recanted fairly quickly. In a sense, the Oxford events are as much a clash between old and new ways of thought, between rival philosophical systems, as between old and new theologies.

Furthermore, Wycliffism was within a general current of academic church reform which did not depend on Wyclif as an individual, and was not extinguished when he and his adherents left. That this reformist tradition cohabited with a lingering strand of Wycliffism appears in later years. Until about 1420 individuals were occasionally expelled for their adherence to banned ideas, and the possible forceful resurgence of Wycliffism was a constant concern, reflected in further investigations and the establishment of a committee of experts at the university (with a parallel committee at Cambridge) to examine individuals suspected of heresy and expurgate Wycliffite writings. This concern, and odd scraps of Lollard works which testify to a continued Wycliffite influence at Oxford, suggest that even in the fifteenth century the university was a centre from which explicitly Wycliffite ideas might spread, besides being the centre for a more orthodox reform movement reflected in the proposals of, say, Richard Ullerston. If this was so, that role had probably been lost by the 1420s.[31] Thereafter, for a century, both universities were apparently unaffected by heresy, even if energetic in their attacks on ecclesiastical corruption. In his attacks of abuses in the 1450s, the Oxford Chancellor Thomas Gascoigne shared many of the concerns of Wyclif and his supporters, the church's failings worrying him more than the threat of heresy.[32]

Because of their gradual development it is hard to say precisely when Wyclif's ideas moved from tolerable criticism into intolerable deviance.

---

[31] Hudson, *Lollards and their books*, pp. 20–3, 77–9; Hudson, 'A Wycliffite scholar' [423], pp. 301–3, 314–15; Hudson, 'Wycliffism in Oxford' [421], pp. 75–84; Keen, 'Influence of Wyclif' [460], pp. 134–6. For Ullerston, Harvey, 'English suggestions on reform' [941]; Hudson, *Lollards and their books*, pp. 71–6.

[32] Pronger, 'Thomas Gascoigne' [672], pp. 29–32.

His idea of dominion was certainly suspect in 1377, when the pope suggested that he had resurrected the errors of Marsilius of Padua and John of
Jandun, condemned only decades before by John XXII. His views on
apostolic poverty also exposed him to accusations of heresy, being almost
as extreme as those of the Spiritual Franciscans, similarly condemned by
John XXII after considerable discord within the church. But it is more
likely that the 1377 charges raised disciplinary rather than doctrinal
issues, reflecting Wyclif's lack of respect for the papacy as an institution
rather than challenge to an article of faith. His continued attacks on
an unworthy priesthood opened Wyclif to further accusations by their
similarity to one of the oldest heresies, Donatism. The rejection of the
efficacy of sacraments performed by unfit priests, asserting that their
effectiveness derived not from their performance alone, but from the
quality of the performer, had been condemned by no less an authority
than St Augustine, and not even Wyclif could be allowed to contradict
him. An appropriate article therefore appeared in the condemned propositions of 1382.[33] Wyclif's attitude to predestination, effectively denying free
will and works as means to salvation, was also suspect; but where he certainly went too far was in his Eucharistic doctrine, reviving a controversy
supposedly settled at the Fourth Lateran Council of 1215 by challenging
transubstantiation. By rejecting substantial change of the consecrated
elements into the Body and Blood of Christ while they remained in all
visible and tangible respects bread and wine, and arguing that they stayed
precisely what they appeared, Wyclif seemed to be repeating views propounded by Berengar of Tours in the mid-eleventh century. Although his
real views were probably more novel and advanced than his contemporaries
allowed, it was the appearance which mattered.[34]

The rejection of transubstantiation overtly denied the received view of
the mass, and explicitly contravened one of the church's major tenets
(although not one contained in the Creeds). Such a challenge could not be
ignored, and left little room for compromise. For many of Wyclif's adherents this venture into theological dissidence was too much, and he
immediately forfeited their support. This abandonment was probably not
due solely to the 'theological' nature of his ideas, but also to the associated
attacks on the developing cult of the consecrated Host, now one of the
most potent elements of popular Christianity.[35] The challenge to transubstantiation also brought some of his other ideas into disrepute. They also

---

[33] Dahmus, *Prosecution of Wyclyf*, pp. 38–9, 41–2, 46, 48 (the fourth of the propositions
condemned in 1382 suggests Donatism: ibid., pp. 94–6); Leff, *Heresy*, ii, pp. 527–9.

[34] Lucas, *Capgrave's Abbreuiacion* [532], p. 185; Hudson, *Lollards and their books*, pp. 214–15;
Catto, 'Wyclif and the Eucharist', pp. 270–5. For the original controversy, Gibson, *Lanfranc of
Bec* [298], pp. 63–97.

[35] Catto, 'Wyclif and the Eucharist', pp. 274–5, 281–2.

were tainted, and would be included among the tenets of Wycliffism; but the sheer variety of these ill-matched opinions is evidence of the artificiality of 'Wycliffism' as a construct.

For this Wycliffism (or Lollardy) remained an agglomeration of opinions rather than a creed. It was a combination of ideas, few in themselves heretical, which together appeared symptomatic of heresy. Many of its views, including much of its anticlerical and anti-papal stance, fitted a traditional pattern of opposition to exploitation by the church, disciplinary rather than theological offences, which are found elsewhere being treated simply as disciplinary issues. However, Lollardy was explicitly heretical in its Eucharistic teachings, which usually provided the key identification. It could have variations – sometimes including hints of the heresy of the Free Spirit, or (in one manuscript) limiting the hostility to the religious orders while retaining the Eucharistic views,[36] but these were merely variations on a theme.

If Wyclif provides the wellspring for one form of doctrinal reform, another was offered by one of his later opponents, although with little real impact. Reginald Pecock was the only pre-Reformation English bishop to lose his see as a heretic. His career incorporates many of the major strands of fifteenth-century ecclesiastical life.[37] Probably born in 1392 or 1393, his Oxford education coincided with the dying embers of academic Wycliffism, which probably gave him his respect for the application of logical linguistic reasoning to the demands of faith. After a fellowship at Oriel College came a beneficed career between 1424 and 1444, when he composed many of his works. In 1444 he became Bishop of St Asaph, and in 1450 was translated to Chichester. He was a prolific writer, and essentially academic by inclination; he was not a political bishop, or particularly effective as a diocesan if the criticism of Thomas Gascoigne and the gap in the Chichester episcopal registers mean anything. Against the spirit of the times he was not particularly concerned with reform, to the chagrin of the Oxford academics – and his defence of his views (especially his defence of non-preaching bishops) caused the first of several furores in the late 1440s. However, the real attack was delayed until 1457 when, in an extraordinary process carried out principally before the royal council, his works were combed for heretical statements and, once these were found, condemned. As a loyal churchman – a stance which dominated his writings throughout – Pecock abjured his discovered errors, and possibly amended his works as well. But thereafter he was kept under house arrest, and in 1458 was deprived of his see not by the ecclesiastical authorities, but by political

---

[36] Swanson, *Reg. Scrope* [796], i, pp. 105–6; Hudson, *Lollards and their books*, pp. 113–14, 202–14.
[37] Jacob, *Later medieval history* [440], pp. 1–34; Brockwell, *Reginald Pecock* [94].

manoeuvrings which exploited the procedures of the Statute of Provisors against him for seeking papal reinstatement. A heretic was not to be allowed to recant and evade the consequences.[38]

Pecock's many writings, of which only some survive, were courageous attempts to tackle theology in English, in an imprecise language which required lengthy circumlocutions to ensure that the right meaning was conveyed – 'he had . . . the courage to be tedious'.[39] Moreover, he tried to redirect the logical battle against the Lollards: if they could apply reason to faith so could he, to defend the church rather than subvert it. Although the Pecock episode is odd, it indicates some aspects of the background of the continuity of heresy – or rationalism, if that is a better word – at this point. Pecock wrote principally as an academic rather than a pastor. He recognized the seriousness, perhaps also the mechanical validity, of the Wycliffite challenge to the church. In turn, he perhaps shows that Wyclif's ideas had not been completely expunged from the university milieu, but absorbed into general academic thinking.

Pecock's schemes for church reform included a programme of doctrinal purification to eliminate some of the accretions which had encrusted the church over the centuries. Following a traditional idea of returning the church to its pristine state – but recognizing the historic changes which realistically could not be undone – he worked to create a more responsive church. His application of historical methodology places him alongside contemporary humanists (as in his refutation of the Donation of Constantine – although he thought that a minor matter, insignificant for the church's position in society), and also makes him a precursor of the Reformation seekers for doctrinal purity (as in his analysis of the Apostles' Creed, urging the excision of the reference to Christ's descent into Hell as a late and unwarranted interpolation). But Pecock risked the perversion and miscomprehension of his ideas, and it was miscomprehension (possibly wilful) which caused his downfall. His literary style also posed dangers. Simply by writing in English he exposed himself to challenges, for theology in English was dangerous in itself – as he realized, and sought to avoid. His philosophical approach to the problems of the faith, turning from mysticism and seeking a reconciliation between philosophy and theology, placed him between two by then irreconcilable disciplines. And by approaching theology in rational terms, by seemingly putting reason before faith and logic before the Bible, he again ran the risk of misunderstanding: by using reason in response to Wycliffism, rather than literal approaches to the dictates of the church and the Fathers, he was descending to the level of the heretics. When the assault came he was forced to publicly

---

[38] Brockwell, *Reginald Pecock* (esp. pp. 156–67); Jacob, *Later medieval history*, pp. 5–22.
[39] Jacob, *Later medieval history*, p. 16.

recant the misreadings of his works, which were consigned to bonfires in both London and Oxford.[40] He stands alone, ultimately insignificant. nevertheless, he demonstrates possibilities, and although there is no sign of others with similar ideas, their existence cannot be completely ruled out.

The final force advocating doctrinal reform before 1500 was provided by the friars. From their foundation they had advocated doctrinal development, most urgently on the questions of poverty and ecclesiastical property. Possibly they had also been arguing for reform in other areas – Wyclif in his *De apostasia* appealed to them to continue to support him; but by then he had overstepped the mark by challenging the Eucharist. In the fifteenth century, similarly, they continued to urge changes; although the evidence is limited. There are not infrequent references to clashes with the secular clergy, which suggest continued concern with poverty and related matters. The author of *Dives and pauper*, if as suggested a friar, was similarly reformist, maintaining doctrinal orthodoxy alongside criticism of ecclesiastical practices. The prosecution of the friar Thomas Richmond at York in 1426 laid charges about his doctrine of the priesthood which parallel some elements of Lollardy. The anti-secular and anti-sacerdotal contents of some mendicant preaching continued during the fifteenth and into the sixteenth centuries, mainly concerned with disciplinary reform, but verging towards the doctrinal, as with Robert Barnes' castigation of the church at Cambridge in 1525 in which (according to his report, after his explicit defection to the reformers) he attacked the secular clergy with considerable violence.[41]

The trend represented by fifteenth-century mendicants continued later: members of the religious orders were notable among the English (and continental) reformers. While the dissolution of the English monasteries and the occasional resistance of some individuals – the executions of Carthusians and some abbots – attract attention,[42] the reformist religious also deserve notice. A significant number of the most vocal advocates of Reformation were originally regulars, especially friars. Generally well educated, and often theologians, they were apparently pushing hard for change. They appear especially vocal in the 1530s, writing and preaching

---

[40] Jacob, *Later medieval history*, pp. 8–9, 24–32; Haines, 'Reginald Pecock' [337], pp. 129–34.

[41] Gwynn, *English Austin friars* [325], pp. 266–7; Barnum, *Dives and pauper* [41], 1/i, p. x (see also Hudson, *Lollards and their books*, pp. 211–12); *Northern convocation*, pp. 146–72 (the conclusions summarized at pp. 170–1); Lusardi, 'Robert Barnes [537], pp. 1372–83 (some commentators treat the sermon as a Lutheran effusion, but Barnes denied that it was, and at least one major conservative contemporary seems to have considered it within the normal latitude allowed to friars but for one element: ibid., pp. 1374, 1382–3).

[42] Knowles, *Religious orders*, iii, part 3; Youings, *Dissolution*.

in support of Henry VIII and his policies, and arguing forcibly against transubstantiation and other doctrines.[43]

The immediate pre-Reformation tendency to doctrinal reform appears most forcefully in the case of Thomas Bilney. His career perhaps reveals the problems of doctrinal change in the period. A Cambridge don, his speculations led him to a reformist stance categorized as Evangelism, placing him in a current evident elsewhere in Europe. His trials for heresy in 1527 and 1531 – especially the first – revealed an attitude towards the faith which was in some respects the culmination of traditional spirituality, although involving some doctrinal differences with strict orthodoxy. His highly Christocentric fideism emphasizing justification through Christ's passion led to the derogation of invocation of saints; but not a rejection of the church. At his burning, in 1531, he apparently preached a conservative sermon, and the extent to which he was actually a heretic (rather than merely erroneous) is questionable. He was not alone in his ideas; odd cases of the period reveal similar views, although with little sign of any contacts between those accused. These ideas showed some sympathies with the Lollards in the rejection of saints, and perhaps Bilney's preaching stimulated a ruder opposition to images and works than he intended. Certainly, his death was followed by a spate of iconoclasm in East Anglia, the scene of his most significant preaching tours.[44]

The third major reformist force affecting the pre-Reformation English church aimed to reduce clerical influence over lay society. Its precise formulation poses problems: for most people, it probably reflected a desire to lessen their accountability of the clergy, and to reduce the church's extractive powers – which could amount to a policy of disendowment founded on jealousy. In some formats, notably the opposition to mortuaries revealed in Hunne's case, and the attacks on heresy jurisdiction, this might be classified as anticlericalism; although it is not really a rejection of the clergy as·clergy.[45] Another element – in the event perhaps more significant politically – involved the continuation and culmination of the struggle for supremacy between the two laws, canon and common.

Both aspects of the laicizing reform movement had long histories. Resentment of ecclesiastical extraction had been one of the mainstays of Lollardy (although not confined to Lollards), and recurred repeatedly after 1350. The laity resented charges for spiritual benefits, objected to some aspects of the tithe system, and disliked having clerics as landlords.

---

[43] Knowles, *Religious orders*, iii, pp. 55–60; see also Peacock, 'Lincoln visitations' [646], pp. 264–6.

[44] Davis, 'Thomas Bylney' [195]; MacCulloch, *Suffolk* [545], pp. 154–5.

[45] Haigh, 'Anticlericalism' [333], pp. 65–74; Davies, 'Popular religion' [188], pp. 80–1, 83. I find the riposte to Haigh in Dickens, 'Shape of anticlericalism' [213] unconvincing.

Clerical involvement in the market was probably also resented as unfair competition. Such antipathy generated plans for disendowment, the most elaborate being invented by Lollards between 1380 and 1415. The cry for disendowment was not confined to the Lollards, occasionally finding Parliamentary expression, as in 1404.[46]

In the legal sphere, the war of attrition between the two systems reached a head under Henry VIII, with ecclesiastical legislative independence being challenged and overthrown by the Acts of the Reformation Parliament, subjecting ecclesiastical discipline to statutory control. The leading exponent of this aspect of reform, which essentially involved a redefinition of the 'temporal' and 'spiritual' spheres, was Christopher St German. In a series of works extending from 1528 (possibly 1523) to the mid-1530s, he emphasized the legislative supremacy of a Parliament which, as he put it in 1535, 'representeth the whole catholyke churche of Englande' much more than the Convocations.[47] This movement to assert Parliamentary supremacy developed alongside – and sometimes in conflict with – a more specific trend to expand royal control over the ecclesiastical institutions. This move for the royalist nationalization of the church was to be a decisive factor in the progress of England's Reformation. Its main thrust was to reduce papal jurisdictional control over the English church, increasing its subjection to the crown. This was not a whole-heartedly anti-papal policy – the pope's spiritual supremacy was not denied, nor his role in many aspects of ecclesiastical administration, from provision of bishops and archbishops to granting dispensations and resolution of court cases. However, what was sought by England's monarchs (and by other secular governments) was limitation on papal freedom of administrative action within the realm.[48] Popes might issue bulls, but the crown controlled their admission to the country; popes were needed to make provisions, but the king nominated the providees, or licensed them to petition Rome. The developing restrictions on papal freedom to act, and on the freedom of clerical contacts with Rome, were considerable. Statutes like those of Provisors and Praemunire threatened links with the papacy and its benefice administration, while enforcing royal claims to jurisdictional competence in areas where the church had traditionally been involved as well. The church was also subjected to further control through secular taxation, and limitations on the export of money to Rome.

This increasing royal encroachment meant that effective headship of the church was *de facto* transferred to the kings. It has been claimed that

---

[46] Aston, ' "Caim's castles" ' [16], pp. 49–65; McNiven, *Heresy and politics* [566], pp. 7, 49, 169–71, 190–7.

[47] Guy, *St German* [324], pp. 19–21, 24, 26–8, 40–4.

[48] Thomson, *Popes and princes* [830], pp. 145–200.

the 'effective seizure of ecclesiastical sovereignty by Edward III' meant that there 'was hardly any need for the English king to claim to be *caput Ecclesiae*'; while 'In all but name, more than a century before the title could be used, Henry V had begun to act as the Supreme Governor of the Church of England'.[49]

In reality, then, the nationalization of the English church had been accomplished well before 1530. However, the crown initially had nothing like the theological status which was to be claimed for it in the Reformation. The stance adopted was common to several countries, and cannot of itself explain the creation of a schismatic church in the 1530s. For that it was necessary to incorporate Lutheran ideas of headship, first imported with William Tyndale's *Obedience of a Christian man*, and rapidly developed in the 1530s.[50] That, like the development of laicizing reform, took the church rather further along the road to change, but still had some way to go in 1529.

The crucial point for the *Ecclesia Anglicana* came in the 1520s. Various interest groups were converging in their aim to reduce clerical freedom and involvement in lay society – and to pick the bones of the emaciated church which would be left. The coalition came to the fore in the years 1529–34, in the Reformation Parliament, when lay complainants were allowed their heads, passing a series of measures which settled long-term grievances, and imposed some disciplinary reforms on the church. But the correct interpretation of these moves is uncertain. Traditionally, the legislative attacks on probate fees, mortuaries, spiritual jurisdiction, and clerical abuses are taken to indicate generalized 'anticlericalism'. This can be challenged, many of the new laws perhaps reflecting the special interests of London groups rather than general sentiments. Certainly, if they did reflect national concerns, some explanation is needed for the delay until 1534 of legislation on the custom of the archdeaconry of Richmond whereby local incumbents received between a ninth and a third of the goods of deceased parishioners; and for the numerous loopholes inserted into the Act against pluralism and non-residence. That Act, however, had potentially massive consequences for the clergy by banning their taking leases for terms of years and forcing their withdrawal from marketing activities. This provision would have completed the effective transfer of the exploitation of most ecclesiastical estates from clerics to laymen, perhaps providing a staging-post on the way to full-scale lay ownership of the lands.

Equally significantly, when Parliament turned to reform the church courts in 1532, the Act against malicious citations was directed not against

---

[49] Wilks, 'Royal priesthood' [906], p. 68; Catto, 'Religious change' [130], p. 115; see also Dahmus, 'Henry IV of England' [185], pp. 45–6.

[50] Haas, 'Luther's "Divine Right" kingship' [326], pp. 317–25.

spiritual jurisdiction as a whole but against exploitation of the church courts in inter-party suits: not office but instance cases (specifically tithes and defamation). The provisions that people could not be cited outside their diocese or peculiar jurisdiction applied only in such cases; the Act specifically retained citation in spiritual causes (unlimited), heresy, and the prerogative probate jurisdiction of the two archbishops, as well as cases going up the hierarchy on appeal.

However, the changes in the heresy laws in 1533 did place heresy processes under greater lay (and royal) control – perhaps reflecting group interests of the common lawyers rather than general sentiments, although this remains questionable. Such reduction in clerical autonomy would be important in limiting the clergy's freedom to act in defence of orthodoxy during the latter years of the reign of Henry VIII.[51]

In this maelstrom of conflicting tensions demanding changes in the church two key features stand out. The first is the specifically English experience of Lollardy, a threat from 1380 to the Reformation. The second is the Reformation itself which provides, if not a terminus, at least, in its Henrician phase, a chronological break in the development of the English church.

7.3 LOLLARDS AND LOLLARDY

The sudden eruption of apparently widely distributed heresy in late fourteenth-century England contrasts markedly with the quiescence suggested by the sources for the centuries before 1380. Bishops' registers show frequent attempts to curtail the spread of religious dissent, in proclamations, restrictions on preaching, and records of actual heresy trials. Some court books dedicated specifically to recording such trials also survive, detailing action in Norwich diocese in the 1420s, and in Coventry and Lichfield diocese in 1511–12. After the Reformation Protestant martyrologists, notably Foxe in his *Book of martyrs* and background papers, also mention cases for which contemporary evidence is now lost. Sometimes the evidence for heresy is extremely scanty – as with before 1380, an unsubstantiated mention of the charge in a writ of caption for an excommunicate, for instance. Clearly, what survives understates the prevalence of heresy in later medieval England; but there is equally a risk of overstatement: an accusation in a writ of caption may actually be for sorcery or witchcraft, treated as heresy during the period.[52] Despite the evidential problems it

---

[51] Haigh, 'Anticlericalism', pp. 60–2; Davis, *Heresy and Reformation* [196], pp. 12–19; *Statutes* [776], iii, pp. 292–6, 377–8, 454–5, 510–11.

[52] Tanner, *Heresy trials* [809], Fines, 'Heresy trials' [272] (see also Hudson, *Lollards and their books*, p. 59 and n. 77); Thomson, 'John Foxe' [828]; Richardson, 'Heresy and the lay

appears incontrovertible that from about 1380 to the Reformation there was a seemingly continuous thread of heresy in England, even if occasionally geographically and chronologically disjointed. Contemporary perceptions and historiographical tradition dictate that the dissenters be called Lollards, and be associated with John Wyclif.

As a movement, Lollardy does fit into some sort of general pattern, especially of nationalism and developing national churches: it is, archetypically, the 'English' heresy. Yet the scale of the challenge faced by the English church once Wyclif's thought escaped the confines of Oxford, and the nature of the reaction, perhaps exaggerate the significance of Lollardy. It was not particularly novel: many of its comments on the church had been made before.

One difficulty is the time taken to identify and define Lollardy. It cannot be assumed to have appeared at the condemnation of heresies and errors in 1382. The definition of Wyclif's heresy took time, lasting from 1377 until the attack at Constance. Of the original twenty-four propositions denounced in 1382 only some (principally concerning the mass and transubstantiation) were declared heretical; the others were only considered erroneous – that is, as defined by the Cambridge doctors in the 1390s, 'against the truth or the general determination of the learned'.[53] The distinction between heresy and error may seem semantic, but as error did not involve an article of faith, suggests differing levels of gravity. These erroneous opinions covered issues like the validity of excommunication and dominion: perhaps they were felt to be more tolerably debatable than the views on the mass. In any event, the condemnations of 1382 meant that the Wycliffite heresy was then defined (if heresy and error are conflated) precisely, and only, in terms of Eucharistic doctrine, church possessions (including receipt of money for prayers), and the use and validity of canonical powers of correction. The many other features of 'typical Lollardy' (general anticlericalism, opposition to pilgrimage, denial of saints, and so on) could only be included by generous extension. But that extension was made, producing the first serious confrontation with popular heresy yet in England.

Even as the attack on Wyclif's writings was being further refined, these 'typically Lollard' beliefs were rarely explicitly mentioned. Most of the official refinements dated from 1410 to 1415 (although a late source suggests a precise attack in 1386, which seems doubtful). The 267 propositions extracted from Wyclif's works by Oxford masters c.1412 cover the range of condemned ideas, repeating earlier denunciations and providing new

power' [694], p. 16; Dickens, *Lollards and protestants* [212], p. 16; for significations of heretics, Logan, *Excommunication* [526], pp. 189–93.

[53] Wilkins, *Concilia*, iii, pp. 157–8; Parry, *Reg. Trillek*, p. 394.

lists of rejected arguments for later use. These gave more refinement and precision on transubstantiation and the mass, on the attacks on papacy and clergy, on the theory of dominion. Additionally (perhaps to enforce the theological statements) there are condemnations of some of Wyclif's philosophical ideas, going beyond the issues considered in 1382 to include articles on specific sacraments, such as baptism and marriage.[54]

The attack on Wycliffism thus became more precise over the years; but the problem of extending that attack to the generality of Lollardy remains. The questions for the examination of Lollards in Bishop Thomas Polton's register at Worcester seem to exceed the limits of the condemnations of Wyclif, bringing in questions on the validity of oaths, and even on the marriage of priests. The articles acknowledged by those accused in the Norwich trials of the 1420s appear to follow a similar questionnaire, similarly extending the net. William Bate's confession thus admits his denial of transubstantiation and the sacramental powers of clerics, but also denies offerings to the church, asserts that only consent is needed for a marriage (without formal contract or solemnization in church), argues for priestly marriage, denies oaths, pilgrimages, and the validity of court processes and warfare, even denies the legality of the crafts of painting and sculpture (presumably for making images).[55] This is a far cry from the intricacies of Wyclif's thought, or of the academic replies to it.

Some of the obscurity about the links between Wyclif and the Lollards may be due to the telescoping of views. William Bate's pacifism, for instance, recalls the charges of opposition to crusading (linked specifically to Flanders and warfare between Christians) preferred against John Corringham in 1384, probably via the anti-war argument in the tenth of the twelve conclusions supposedly posted by Lollards at St Paul's in 1395. Indeed, those conclusions may provide the Lollards' own definition of their ideas, which the church then appropriated for its own use. Among other things they attack priestly celibacy and female vows of chastity, repudiate 'unnecessary crafts' in churches, and oppose pilgrimages, intercession of images, the union of secular and ecclesiastical lordship, and prayers for the dead.[56]

Wyclif's challenge clearly struck a chord outside academic circles as, somehow, his theories were integrated into the more popular Lollardy. On the one hand stood the intelligentsia of the fourteenth-century church – Wyclif and his Oxonian adherents – for whom rationalistic logical debate

---

[54] Wilkins, *Concilia*, iii, pp. 339–49; Mitchell, *Epistolae academicae* [586], pp. 285–318 (*n.b.* p. 294 art.45 n. 2); see also Dahmus, *Prosecution of Wyclyf*, pp. 151–3.

[55] Hudson, *Lollards and their books*, p. 134; Tanner, *Heresy trials*, pp. 157–60.

[56] McHardy, 'Buckingham and the Lollards' [551], pp. 132–3; Hudson, *Selections* [418], pp. 24–9.

was part of a genuine intellectual training. On the other stood the laity
and lower clergy who provided many of the Lollards, and whose status
apparently declined as time passed. Creating links between the two
groups is problematic; indeed, actual defining 'Lollardy' is problematic.

It is clear that preaching was highly important for spreading dissent,
especially after the Oxford purge in 1382. But the use of books was
equally, perhaps more, significant. Until recently the mechanics of the
dissemination of Wycliffism seemed fairly straightforward. After leaving
Oxford, Wyclif spent his last years producing a flurry of Latin tracts
which were then translated and supplemented by his faithful amanuensis
and secretary, John Purvey, for distribution to Lollard cells with Purvey's
own prolific writings. This view has now collapsed: Purvey's career is less
clear-cut than had been thought, his role in early Lollardy has been all but
debunked, and the dissemination problem becomes even greater.[57] Many
of Wyclif's works were certainly translated – although not always precisely:
it is sometimes a matter more of dependence than parallel texts – and
achieved some sort of popular circulation. This is most obvious with the
English sermon cycle, which attained almost production-line copying.
Insofar as the use of writings was a deliberate ploy (and the constancy of
writing, plugging gaps created by the activities of the church authorities,
is attested by Lollards themselves), there are hints of a deliberately graded
scheme of production, at least in the first phase of Lollardy. Standardized
versions of the 'official' texts were produced, whose regularity contrasts
with the 'unofficial' pamphleteering of the years after 1414. A fairly strong
academic vein may have persisted in the first decades, evident in works
like the *Opus arduum*, written in Latin in 1390. There was also an apparently
deliberate programme of epitomizing Wyclif's works, producing handbooks for preachers like the *Floretum* or *Rosarium theologie*, initially composed
in Latin but later rendered into English, in formats which may have
changed depending on the capacities of the reader or projected audience.
Just how organized all this was remains obscure. The mechanics of
producing the sermon cycle show some organization, and the various
redactions of the *Rosarium* suggest control over format; while references to
a deliberate tractarian policy in the *Opus arduum* add more to the overall
picture.[58] In the end, nevertheless, it is impossible to demonstrate anything
like a Lollard tractarian factory, or a central structure.

But dependence on the written word probably allowed much Lollard
publicizing to go relatively unnoted. The strong tradition of vernacular
spiritual writing would have stimulated such translations, and permitted
the subversive intrusion of Lollard ideas into otherwise unimpeachable

---

[57] Hudson, *Lollards and their books*, pp. 85–110.
[58] ibid., pp. 14–29 (also nn. 9–10), 44–65, 184–90.

works. It also encouraged the production of Lollard vernacular works through to the Reformation.[59] Contemporary England certainly contained attitudes towards the church which would easily have latched onto Wyclif's ideas: the false connections established by chroniclers between Wyclif and the millenarianism of the Peasants' Revolt are sufficient indication of this. By the mid-1390s, at the latest, groups of heretics were evidently sharing views which in combination reflected ideas ascribed to Wyclif. Typical of these was the Northampton group found in 1393–4, which was already self-perpetuating and probably derived in turn from an earlier Leicester cell.[60] But it remains to illustrate precisely how Wyclif's ideas converged with this underground movement to produce Lollardy – if that phenomenon ever existed.

Some fairly direct links can be established between Wyclif and the heretics, usually via clerics with known Oxonian connections. Thus John Corringham, vicar of Diddington (Oxon.), was arraigned on heresy charges in 1384. He was an Oxford graduate. Although only two of the articles against him match those delivered at Blackfriars in 1382 others, like his views on the schism and on Despencer's crusade, place him in the general Wycliffite tendency. His case may even provide one instance of one method of disseminating Wyclif's views, by exploiting patronage connections centred on Oxford.[61]

However, when going beyond these few individuals to Lollardy in general, the links prove more tenuous. The evidence is usually vague, and there is a danger of unity being imposed after the event on to a considerable variety of opinions. This may have been partly a logical process once Wyclif's views began to circulate: their influence on their readers could help to create a unified view among the religious dissidents. Perhaps there was also a deliberate policy of proselytizing by Wyclif and the 'Poor Priests' which the old hagiography pictured him as directing. If these commissioned adherents did exist, they could have begun their work as early as 1377.[62] More serious, however, are historians' preconceptions and contemporaries' misconceptions. There is a temptation to think automatically of Wyclif's influence, with his ideas radiating from Oxford and the Lollards deriving their theories from him, in no matter how bastardized a fashion. Contemporaries, once Wyclif's ideas had been condemned,

---

[59] ibid., p. 203 and refs., 249–52; Talbert and Thomson, 'Wyclyf and his followers' [807]; Hudson, 'Wycliffite prose' [419].

[60] 3/1 at n. 32; also Dahmus, *Prosecution of Wyclyf*, pp. 82–5 (for Wyclif on the revolt, Wilks, 'Wyclif and Hus' [905], pp. 125–7); McHardy, 'Buckingham and the Lollards', pp. 137–45.

[61] ibid., pp. 131–3, 143; McHardy, 'Dissemination' [557].

[62] For assertion that such preachers existed, Wilks, 'Wyclif and Hus', pp. 119–21; see Hudson, *Lollards and their books*, pp. 13–14.

felt similarly, and applied the names of Wycliffite and Lollard to all and sundry. But another view is possible, with Wyclif's puritanism and reformism themselves reflecting a more general movement, which he further refined with his Eucharistic views and definitions of dominion. Once those ideas had been condemned, and were being spread by his Oxford adherents, they would merge back into the general reformist current. Those seeking out heresy would meanwhile assume an identity between the beliefs of Wyclif and those of the Lollards, creating their own stereotype to be applied as and when necessary.

The events of the Blackfriars Council may confirm this approach. Whilst the condemnation of the Wycliffite propositions commands most attention, the gathering also dealt with other matters, principally the spreading activities of unlicensed preachers (a concern which may reflect fears engendered by John Ball in the recent Peasants' Revolt).[63] Much of the evidence for early Lollardy demonstrates this latter concern rather than a fear of Wycliffism, although the two merged fairly rapidly. Thus the first 'Lollard' trial, of William Swinderby (for which the initial moves were made before the Blackfriars condemnation) ended by finding him guilty of charges quite different from the Blackfriars articles. Although the preliminary list of allegations included denial of the Real Presence, his abjuration listed only charges of Donatism, of advocating leniency with defaulting debtors, and justifying withdrawal of tithes from a lecherous priest. Similarly, the articles against the Northampton Lollards in 1393 ignore the ideas condemned in 1382 – even though they are similar to views expressed in some of Wyclif's works.[64] Perhaps, then, the church authorities faced a double problem: Wyclif and his academic heresy on one side, on the other a movement of puritanical reformist preaching (which may have included a lay element – one charge against Swinderby was that he was only a pretended priest) similar to those which regularly emerged in periods of spiritual crisis within the church, the most obvious parallel being with the twelfth century. It is perhaps significant that one of the few strands of pre-Lollard heresy which does emerge from the evidence centres precisely on hermits and wandering preachers, even if not giving much indication of their teachings.[65] Once the leading Wycliffites were driven from Oxford and joined forces with the popular movement, the two strands merged, refining the views of the popular preachers, increasing dissemination of Wyclif's thought, and tarring popular views with the ideas already officially condemned as heretical. An indication of this

[63] McFarlane, *Wycliffe and non-conformity* [547], p. 93.

[64] ibid., pp. 107–10; McHardy, 'Buckingham and the Lollards', pp. 139–45.

[65] Bolton, *Medieval Reformation* [73], pp. 26–9, 56–7, 63, 65–6, 96–7 – especially noteworthy are similarities between 'Lollardy' and the Waldensians; Clay, *Hermits and anchorites* [151], p. 69.

comes with a monition issued by Bishop Wakefeld of Worcester in the mid-1380s against 'Lollard' preaching, in which identifiable followers of Wyclif, such as Nicholas Hereford, are named alongside popular preachers like William Swinderby (if he is meant: the document gives the name as Robert). All were condemned as unlicensed preachers, especially for their spreading of Wyclif's opinions.[66] How far this reflects one movement is unclear: it may be a portmanteau condemnation, but the merger was occurring. Initially the precise definition of some of the heresies may have been doubtful (Bishop Trefnant of Hereford at least twice sought academic reports on the views of those accused before him)[67] but eventually the identification of Wycliffism with Lollardy was completed. Thereafter there was a full list of suspect views, which defined the stereotype Lollard, so stereotyped that bishops could examine by questionnaires which could easily be integrated into the visitation procedure.

By 1400 the church could hunt heretics according to its checklist of erroneous opinions, avoiding long and detailed inquiries into the nature of individual belief. Use of this questionnaire approach to the problem is shown by the statements of witnesses in real trials, and the survival of lists of questions in episcopal registers. The Lollards themselves recognized the practice: one of their tracts provided equally stereotyped responses to the questions.[68] With this approach, individual idiosyncracies in belief became irrelevant, imposing a false conformity, and thereby creating the 'Lollard' movement. The dangers of misconstruction were especially acute at the frontiers of orthodoxy, as the acceptable merged into the heretical but had to be distinguished. Matters such as the questionable orthodoxy of *Dives and pauper*, which was at the heart of the charges against Master Robert Bert in 1429, were probably not infrequently raised, evoking suspicion by the meagrest of associations.[69] Once again, the Lollard 'movement' may be no more than an historians' construct: medieval questioners may have seen things differently. An awareness of different types of dissent is suggested by Bishop Alnwick of Norwich's commission for the detection of offenders in 1428 at Bury St Edmunds (Suffolk), demanding the indictment of

heretics and their believers, receivers, and supporters and defenders, *as well as* [*vel*] anyone celebrating private conventicles or making conventicles away from the common gathering of the faithful, and on festival days withdrawing themselves

---

[66] Marrett, *Reg. Wakefeld* [575], no. 832.

[67] McFarlane, *Wycliffe and non-conformity*, pp. 119, 122.

[68] Hudson, *Selections*, pp. 19–24; Hudson, *Lollards and their books*, pp. 125–40.

[69] Tanner, *Heresy trials*, pp. 98–102; see also Hudson, *Lollards and their books*, p. 125. The tract's editor considers it 'neither apology for the shortcomings of the clergy nor a plea for a Wyclifian reform of doctrine but something in between the two' (Barnum, *Dives and pauper*, 1/i, p. x).

from churches or the general converse of men, or holding exceptional views on the faith or sacred matters, and possessing or learning from books in our vulgar English tongue, and those who are suspected, known, or reported of the above or any one of them.[70]

Given that problem, early Lollardy (through to 1413) is extremely difficult to quantify.[71] The concrete identification of individuals as Lollards is tricky, except where they proclaimed their links with a wider movement and advocated a Wycliffite programme. The real proof of individual Lollardy requires an individually volunteered statement of belief, rather than third-party identification. Some such declarations do survive, like the articles presented by William Swinderby in 1390 at his second trial, in Hereford diocese.[72] But such spontaneity is rare; usually the church's definitions have to be accepted, and superimposed on the records. Where there is a considerable overlap perhaps the identification as a heretic can be upheld – although a 'typically Lollard' statement on one issue does not provide a complete pigeon-holing of an individual's beliefs. Other objective criteria for the identification of Lollards are scarce. The most extensively applied yardstick in recent years has been the 'Lollard will', which by emphasizing poverty in burial practices and the sinfulness of the testator has been considered indicative of Lollard tendencies.[73] But this is challengeable, probably reflecting a strand of contemporary piety rather than association with a heretical sect. The concept of 'Lollard wills' falls into the same trap as the church authorities did: the frontier between orthodoxy and heresy was very precise, and against the background of late medieval piety historians can force individuals across it just as improperly as contemporaries perhaps did.

For not even contemporaries provide indisputable identification of Lollards. Chroniclers point to a clique of Lollard knights associated with the court of Richard II, but the validity of the identifications is questionable. While some gentry involvement in the protection of Lollardy at this point is undoubted, the identity of the protectors is unclear. The chroniclers' nominations may be correct, but cannot be proved: the evidence is circumstantial, or aasumes guilt by association. Only in one instance is an overtly 'Lollard' action described, an iconoclastic outburst by Sir John Montague reported by Thomas Walsingham. For the others the greatest accumulation of evidence surrounds Sir Thomas Latimer of Braybrooke (Northants.), but even here little that is concrete can be made of a court

---

[70] BL, MS Add. 14848, f. 109v (the version at f. 110r is slightly different).
[71] For a survey, McFarlane, *Wycliffe and non-conformity*, pp. 107–43.
[72] Capes, *Reg. Trefnant* [126], pp. 237–51.
[73] McFarlane, *Lancastrian kings* [548], pp. 209–20; for 'Lollard wills' of different form at Coventry in 1511, Luxton, 'The Lichfield court book' [538], pp. 123–4.

case linked to a local riot when attempts were made to disrupt heretical preaching, a scrappy reference to his possession of heretical books (which neither proves that he owned them, or believed their contents), and his relationship with a priest who while admittedly involved in heretical activities later first gained attention for his actions some three years after Latimer's death.[74] Although a general sympathy for reformism in the late fourteenth century is unquestionable, and in which the gentry were involved (perhaps only as exponents of a vocal anticlericalism), that these knights were individually adherents of Lollardy is less certain. If the works ascribed to one of them – Sir John Clanvowe – were actually written by him, the position is even less clear. For he could compose a romantic lyrical piece, a courtier's frippery, as well as a strongly moralistic tract expressing strong religious convictions but without overt Lollard statements. This piece is unusual, especially in its dependence on the Bible, but it is not noticeably heretical.[75] The only valid approach is to assume orthodoxy, but allow the possibility of heresy. But then, contemporaries uninformed of the determinations made in 1382 evidently did not know what constituted Lollardy either. Leicester, that hotbed of heresy (as we are told), and in 1414 one of the centres of Oldcastle's revolt, was the scene of Margery Kempe's trial as a Lollard in 1417. Whatever her religious beliefs actually were, she was no Lollard; but that her compatriots made that mistake neatly illustrates the problem of the borderline. Henry Knighton, a major source for the identification of the Lollard knights, is equally unreliable: he made mistakes about events purportedly happening under his very nose at Leicester (where he was an Augustinian canon), and so misunderstood Wyclif's Eucharistic doctrines as to incorporate into his chronicle as Wyclif's 'confession' and submission a forthright declaration of the theory of remanence.[76]

Eventually the search for early Lollardy has to abandon any attempt at precise identification, and rely on a more generalized quantitative approach: accepting common report about its spread, acknowledging the results of the heresy-hunts for want of anything better, and taking as valid whatever indications there are of the scope and organization of the movement. There are certainly signs of active Lollard gatherings and conventicles; while the systematic and organized production of Lollard works, especially the English sermon cycle and early Bible translations, is also

[74] McFarlane, *Lancastrian kings*, pp. 148–226, esp. pp. 168, 193–6 (the discussion of Robert Hook at p. 196 rather overstates his heresy: the report of his trial [Jacob, *Reg. Chichele* [438], iii, pp. 105–12] suggests that it was neither as proven or significant as McFarlane makes out).

[75] Scattergood, *Works of Clanvowe* [750], pp. 57–80 (extracts and comment in McFarlane, *Lancastrian kings*, pp. 201–6); see also Hudson, *Lollards and their books*, p. 54.

[76] Meech and Allen, *Margery Kempe* [579], pp. 111–19; McFarlane, *Lancastrian kings*, pp. 141, 149–52; Hudson, *Selections*, pp. 17–18, 141–2.

significant, even if owners can rarely be identified.[77] On such bases Lollardy up to 1413 can probably be accepted as fairly wide-spread, but not large scale. Perhaps the gentry were fairly extensively involved – they would have been able to afford the more expensive books, and were leading the opposition to the clergy in Parliament. But Lollardy also attracted the lower orders, as shown in its frequent expression of social grievances like those expounded in the relatively early tract *Of servants and lords*, cataloguing complaints against lawyers and other exploiters.[78] Inchoate and amorphous, Lollardy was a force to be reckoned with, although the reckoning which came with Oldcastle's revolt in 1414 proved less dramatic than might have been expected.

7.4   THE RESPONSE TO HERESY

The absence of large-scale heresy from England before the appearance of Lollardy meant that there was no need to create a machinery to deal with it. Except for a brief spell under Edward II, the Inquisition was kept out, and thus its structure for discovering and eradicating error was never established. Instead, English procedures left that task to the bishops (as papal agents), working through a combination of visitation and inquest procedures.[79] Bishops in their diocesan visitations leave no records of discoveries – but few records of such visitations survive anyway. The reaction to heresy within the church as a whole can be seen as bureaucratic, carrying the danger that the threat of heresy might be perceived purely in administrative terms, so that any administrative threat to the church could be seen as heretical, or if need be ignored. This approach has produced an argument that, because the response to heresy was purely administrative, England was tacitly allowed to be the most heretical country in late medieval Europe, with the effective rejection of papal authority being consistently ignored by the central authorities so that, although actually heretical, England was allowed to remain nominally orthodox.[80] This, however, must be a misinterpretation, over-stressing the bureaucratic view of papal jurisdiction, and seeing the response to heresy solely as a disciplinary issue.

While the English church theoretically had ways of dealing with heresy before 1380, in practice the only recourse observable was the tedious process of excommunication and caption, at best haphazard, at worst

---

[77] Hudson, *Lollards and their books*, pp. 186–90.

[78] Coleman, *English literature in history* [156], pp. 223–9.

[79] Jones, 'Two jurisdictions' [452], p. 154; Jacob, *Reg. Chichele*, iii, pp. 18–19; see also BL, MS Add. 14848, f. 109r.

[80] Wilks, 'Royal priesthood', p. 69.

useless. After 1382, however, the system changed, with suspected heretics liable to immediate arrest and (from 1388) a greater secular role in their discovery and imprisonment. From about 1397 (although there are some earlier references) pressure increased for the imposition of the death penalty for recidivists, a punishment enacted in 1401 by the Statute *De heretico comburendo*: in certain circumstances heresy became a capital offence.[81] Preaching was also subjected to increasing restrictions, especially after Archbishop Arundel's constitutions of 1409. The dangers of clerics themselves spreading heresy were recognized with the insistence on licences for preachers, and attempts to limit the scope of sermons.[82] Equally important was ecclesiastical action against the use of English, especially in books. In 1409 Arundel decreed a system for the inspection of theological works in English which, while leaving few formal traces, seems to have been maintained in some form through to the 1520s. Vernacular books were by definition suspect, suspicions becoming more entrenched in the fifteenth century. Action against books in English is evident from 1388, and was thereafter a constant element in the fight against Lollardy.[83] The church's overall response at times appears an over-reaction, but this may misinterpret the ecclesiastics' concerns.

It is clear that the immediate ecclesiastical response was of fear. Divided by the Great Schism, the church was unsure of its own foundation; confronted by burgeoning popular piety it appeared to be losing control over the laity; contemporary social and economic changes presented massive difficulties both locally and internationally. In particular, the church faced a growing threat to its status, the result of greater lay participation in religious activity, demands for the enforcement of rigid standards on the clergy (including reduction in their economic power), and the threat to clerical authority at all levels of the hierarchy. Hence the opposition to the 'misuse' of theological knowledge, which it was feared would result from popular acquaintance with vernacular tracts, especially an English Bible; hence too the opposition to disendowment, the reaction against threats to the hierarchy. This could have been stimulated by the perceived links between Lollardy and the Peasants' Revolt, which came close to declarations of 'No bishop, no king'. Another strand may have been provided by Lollard pacifism; especially if that applied to the knights it threatened the whole social structure, for fighting was their social function.

---

[81] Richardson, 'Heresy and the lay power', pp. 5–25.

[82] McHardy, 'Buckingham and the Lollards', pp. 133, 135–7; Wilkins, *Concilia*, iii, pp. 315–16.

[83] Hudson, *Lollards and their books*, pp. 152–8; Wilkins, *Concilia*, iii, p. 317 (see also Salter, *Nicholas Love's "Myrour"* [726], pp. 1–2, 111; Blunt, *The myrroure of Our Ladye* [72], p. 71; perhaps Owst, *Preaching* [631], pp. 292–3). Oxford university complained about the dangers of inept translations: Wilkins, *Concilia*, iii, p. 365.

The church's fear and uncertainty made the persecution of dissent a prominent feature of the later middle ages. The approach to this activity is not at all clear-cut. Certainly, clerical pressure produced the machinery whereby bishops could certify heretics directly to the local sheriff rather than use the cumbersome process of excommunication and caption with all its inbuilt ineffectiveness, and in 1401 similar pressure secured the enactment of the Statute *De heretico comburendo*. Lay reaction was initially unenthusiastic – in 1383, the year after its institution, there was considerable Parliamentary pressure to repeal the system of notification to sheriffs. After the Oldcastle fiasco, however, Lollardy became a statute crime, punishable under Act of Parliament, and with power to deal with Lollards being written into the peace commission.[84]

As far as the evidence goes, the church was not single-mindedly seeking out and destroying all opponents. Neither the procedure of 1382, nor the statute of 1401, produced a massive surge of anti-heretical activity in any obvious extremist form. Burning was very much the last resort, for second offenders who refused to conform, and was quite possibly a reaction to political rather than ecclesiastical pessures, as has been suggested for the burning of John Badby in 1411.[85] The church's real concern was not to destroy but to save – and that included saving the heretics, if only from themselves. Little evidence of the process of persuasion survives among the records, but odd vignettes, like the debate between Archbishop Arundel and William Thorpe mentioned in the latter's trial, do suggest a pattern. Admonitory sermons also fit in, warning the faithful against the deceptions of heresy and the dangers of meddling with matters too great for them. These were usually warnings rather than proofs of error, except where substantiated by miracle stories.[86] Until Reginald Pecock tried to formulate a compelling logical defence of the church against the heretics' charges, in English, the church had little more than its own authority to advance against the threat of heresy. Most accused were not burnt but accepted (how completely is uncertain) the definitions of faith provided for them by the church at their trials. The penalties rarely involved burning, most usually suffering little more than a beating.[87] The process of reconciliation was much more significant, especially when applied to the most effective 'heretics' of the first phase – to Wycliffites rather than Lollards. Among those connected intimately with Oxford and Wyclif, and who suffered for those associations, many were eventually brought back.

---

[84] Tuck, 'Nobles, commons, and 1381' [847], pp. 210–11; *Statutes*, ii, pp. 181–4.

[85] McNiven, *Heresy and politics*, ch. 11.

[86] McFarlane, *Wycliffe and non-conformity*, pp. 138–9, 149; Haines, ' "Wilde wittes and wilfulness" ' [335], pp. 147–53; Aston, 'Wyclif and the vernacular' [17], p. 292.

[87] Fines, 'Heresy trials', p. 170; Tanner, *Heresy trials*, pp. 22–5.

The most notable case was Philip Repingdon, back at Oxford by 1400, Abbot of Leicester, and later Bishop of Lincoln. That generation also contained Nicholas Hereford, who joined the ranks of cathedral clergy and ended his life as a Carthusian monk; while John Corringham, the heretical vicar of Diddington, returned to Oxford and eventually became a canon of Windsor. Less certain is the case of John Purvey, who for a while was beneficed at West Hythe (Kent), but later resigned and may have reverted to Lollardy.[88]

The persecution after the initial late fourteenth-century outburst appears remarkably random. Perhaps this reflects the real problem of defining the heresy, coupled with the uncertainty of the searchers. Eventually this degenerated into simple mistrust of vocal expressions of English pietism, characterized in the fifteenth century by fear of possession of almost anything written in English (incuding, besides the moralistic but orthodox *Dives and pauper*, even the works of Chaucer), and dislike of religious exuberance exemplified in Margery Kempe. The equation between the vernacular and suspicion of heresy was so close in the late fifteenth century that even knowledge of prayers in English could render individuals liable to accusation. Nevertheless, despite the equation, nothing was done to prevent the spread of such works completely, not even the English Bible.[89]

One major weakness of Lollardy as a movement was its lack of any obvious centre. Wyclif had not provided a specific focus to distinguish his followers from the orthodox, nor had he achieved martyrdom to sustain his successors. Lacking academic respectability and continuity, and possibly of decreasing interest to the gentry, Lollardy by 1401 was perhaps already fairly debased. But its debasement concealed a potent threat, that the lower orders with a smattering of literacy would produce their own individualistic theology and social morality. In the fifteenth century this perception of a threat was tempered by something like episcopal incomprehension when faced with the debasement. The ecclesiastical establishment had to tackle a movement deprived of the intellectual stimulus of its original academic thrust, and increasingly identified as a theology of the lower classes. At the same time, before 1414, a vocal political strand existed demanding changes within the church, although these suggested disestablishment rather than a really theological challenge. Having permeated society, heretical ideas proved difficult to eradicate, and perhaps became less consciously heretical. The position from around 1450, if not before, could have been similar to that identified in the following century:

---

[88] McHardy, 'Buckingham and the Lollards', p. 133; Emden, *Oxford* [257], i, p. 494, iii, pp. 913–15; Hudson, *Lollards and their books*, pp. 88–9.
[89] Above, n. 69; Hudson, *Lollards and their books*, pp. 146–62.

Heretical ideas floated freely about the country and were held – with most varying degrees of conviction and piety – by people who did not for a moment claim to be theologians and had no intention of going to the stake.[90]

For such people, once informed of their error, abjuration would follow relatively easily and painlessly; but the ideas would still be floating about. In some ways, the defenders of orthodoxy were to blame for this: their refutations of heresy often included a summary (if not a complete statement) of the views they were challenging, so that from Thomas Netter against the Lollards in the 1420s to Thomas More against Tyndale in the 1520s, the orthodox made unorthodoxy available to others.[91]

The major turning-point in the Lollard movement came in 1414, with Sir John Oldcastle's revolt. It seems undeniable that Oldcastle was an active Lollard sympathiser. Having been imprisoned and awaiting death for his heresy, he escaped and planned a rising whose precise aims are unclear. The scheme involved mass action by his adherents – supposedly all Lollards – and the kidnapping of the royal family. This madcap venture failed abysmally; and just how far it was actually a 'Lollard rising' is obscure. To involve the heresy might be convenient in the search for scapegoats (and with its social implications might also deter further gentry involvement with the movement); but its aftermath, notably the paucity of evidence for the imposition of penalties for heresy, makes the connection uncertain.[92]

Regardless of the nature of the revolt, its outcome is clear: a virtually complete collapse of Lollardy as a force (if it ever had been one). The revolt's end marks the end of gentry participation in the spread of Lollardy – or so it seems: although they kept the books, they seemingly lost interest in the ideas. Thereafter Lollardy was even more of a hidden movement. It occasionally surfaces in records of trials (Norwich diocese in the 1420s, Lichfield in the 1480s, and throughout Canterbury province in investigations of 1511–12, for instance).[93] Although retaining urban links, as at Coventry (War.), generally it appears to have dispersed to smaller towns and rural areas, based on small cells (the Lollard 'schools') in which women were noticeably active, although perhaps not dominant. What organization there was became regional, dependent on fragile links between communities maintained and extended by mobile individuals throughout

[90] Dickens, *Lollards and Protestants*, p. 243.
[91] Hudson, 'Wyclif and English' [422], p. 102 n. 65; Clebsch, *England's earliest Protestants* [153], pp. 287–8.
[92] McFarlane, *Wycliffe and non-conformity*, pp. 144–65; see also Thomson, *The later Lollards* [829], ch. 1.
[93] Tanner, *Heresy trials*; Fines, 'Heresy trials', p. 160; generally Thomson, *The later Lollards*.

the country: in the Cotswolds or East Anglia, or along the road from Coventry to London. The production of Lollard writings declined, with only the merest trickle from the 1430s (although much may have been lost). The movement also lost its initial purity. The opponents of 'Our Lefdy of Falsyngham, the Lefdy of Foulpette, and . . . Thomas of Canker-bury', hostile to relics and saints, acquired their own martyrs who were treated as intercessors in heaven, such as William White, burnt at Norwich in 1428. In some ways Lollards almost merged into the tradition of popular holy men – even beneficed clerics would exploit their ashes for the coffers of their churches.[94]

Given the stereotyping of heresy hunts, determining the continuity of the movement through to the Reformation becomes exceedingly difficult. Much depends on the approach to the sources: do they reveal the tip of a much larger iceberg, or reflect individual sporadic concerns and im-mediate crises which might have different origins for the individuals examined? Given the fluidity and weakness of the movement – despite some indications to the contrary, it was never sufficiently organized to constitute an anti-church[95] – there is either the chance of weak continuity, or the probability of individual persecutions finding groups of unorthodox whose continuity is provided merely in locations and accusations, rather than in belief and affiliation. Certainly many of the 'standard' Lollard tenets, with their rationalistic approach to religion, could have been derived from the application of a little lettered logic (obtained from reading a vernacular Bible) to the church which surrounded them, rather than any direct Wycliffite inheritance. This is particularly important in the debate on the influence of Lollardy on the Reformation.

The Lollardy of the late fifteenth century poses many problems, all connected with the question of survival. Lollardy in this century was a lower-class movement, or so it appears from the extant court records. But other material, notably the splendid volumes of sermons, and the English Bibles, hint at a strand of gentle Lollardy which never came to court.[96] As the owners of the sermon volumes are unknown, this is possible – their quality makes it unlikely that they would be other than family treasures. Possession of an English Bible is less significant: even the nuns of Syon (Surrey) owned them, and they certainly cannot be accused of Lollardy.[97]

---

[94] Tanner, *Heresy trials*, p. 148 (punning on the shrines of Walsingham, Woolpit, and Canterbury); von Nolcken, 'Another kind of saint' [607], pp. 431–2; Fines, 'Heresy trials', pp. 163–4; Thomson, *The later Lollards*, pp. 148–50.

[95] For celebration by a Lollard 'priest', Hudson, *Lollards and their books*, pp. 111–19; for hints of their own ministry in 1511, Fines, 'Heresy trials', p. 166.

[96] The only 'gentle' Lollard appears to be Lady Yonge, widow of a Lord Mayor of London. Her mother was also burnt: Thomson, *The later Lollards*, p. 156.

[97] Power, *English nunneries* [671], pp. 254–5.

Possibly, if arguments about the increasing use of heresy accusations in church courts in the early sixteenth century hold good, there is something to the idea of obscured gentle Lollardy. Something of a double standard might be operative, with the spiritual authorities being particularly anxious to prevent the spread of Wycliffism among the lower orders – whose 'misunderstanding' might produce social unrest – while tolerating a degree of intellectual questioning among the higher social groups provided that it reached the correct conclusions, or kept quiet if it did not. Possibly, also, volumes like the sermons could be tolerated because they were simply anticlerical: they did not challenge matters of faith, only discipline, allowing a distinction between anticlericalism and anti-sacerdotalism. Certainly, although Wycliffism was identified as an 'English heresy', the church did not undertake a wholesale purge of English theological works; in fact the fifteenth century witnessed an efflorescence of vernacular pietistic works.[98]

The problem is epitomized by the anti-Lollard writings of Reginald Pecock: lengthy, but in English. The question immediately arises of the audience to which they were directed. The unique surviving manuscripts argue against wide circulation; even though burnings account for some losses, the tracts' sheer bulk probably means that not many copies were actually produced, or, if produced, read. But they must have been aimed at a readership which would be happy to read them in English and might be in danger of being infected by Lollardy.[99] Presumably these were people who might already own Wycliffite works like the sermon cycle, perhaps among the reasonably well-off and the gentry. Again, this suggests a continuity of heretical leanings among the upper levels of society of which little trace remains in the surviving court material. However, Coventry evidence from the early sixteenth century shows that there at least heresy was established among the town's mercantile elite. Even if no longer attractive to the landed classes, Lollardy perhaps retained an appeal for the monied, the yeomanry, burgesses, and wealthier levels of rural society, in addition to those lower down.[100]

Besides social rank, gender may have been a significant feature among the later Lollards, allowing women to fulfil a religious vocation in a world which prevented them celebrating the sacraments. Certainly there were outstanding women Lollards, such as Hawisia Moon in East Anglia, and women clearly were important in keeping Wycliffite ideas alive within their groups. But whether Lollardy did have a particular appeal to women is uncertain. To stress the role of women in Lollardy is inevitably to

   [98] Fines, 'Heresy trials', pp. 164–5.

   [99] Brockwell, *Reginald Pecock*, pp. 19–22.

   [100] Luxton, 'The Lichfield court book', pp. 122–3; Cross, 'Religious and social protest' [175], p. 74; see also Plumb, 'Rural Lollardy' [662]; Britnell, *Colchester* [93], pp. 231, 258.

underplay their role within the orthodox church. Even if they could not be priests (and there is no real evidence of any Lollard intention to remedy that situation, except by generally proclaiming the priesthood of all believers), they could be active within the church. Indeed, this period is notable for the number of women who gained prominence as mystics and religious leaders – Brigit of Sweden and Catherine of Siena stand out on the continent, in England Margery Kempe and Julian of Norwich.[101]

A final doubt about fifteenth-century Lollardy must focus on reality. Accusations in church courts can rarely be taken at face value; often they are veiled requests for investigation of suspicions rather than statements of fact. A notable feature of many of the actual trials – where the individual does not offer a specific defence – is the readiness to submit. Sometimes people evaded charges by purgation, like Walter Hopere of Yetminster (Dorset), denounced for denying that offerings could be made to statues during the visitation of the dean of Salisbury's jurisdiction in 1405.[102] Many others offered only partial defences, denying some charges but accepting the church's judgement and acknowledging their mistakes in others. In such cases the authorities seem content with abjuration, even if this meant abjuring beliefs not actually held, possibly as a guarantee of future good behaviour. To be suspect was the initial danger, threatening to infect society at large. The accusation was critical, hence the defamation cases brought against those referring to others as heretics. To be reintegrated into the church, either by a substantial denial of the charges, or by abjuration and penance, or by a successful action for defamation, was the aim. Recidivism, whilst not totally unknown, was rare; deaths rarer.

This pattern seems to have been maintained throughout most of the fifteenth century, as far as any continuity is visible. The church was keenly aware of the dangers of heresy, but was not unduly worried about it. Lollardy was a movement which could be contained, and if the infection threatened to spread, cauterized.

As a response to doctrinal challenges, the English reaction to heresy until the arrival of Lutheranism is essentially a response to Lollardy. But there is a possible twist to the tale which also needs to be incorporated. The attack on Lollardy is usually seen as directed at the lower social orders. In the sixteenth century, however, the gentry too may have been facing the threat of heresy accusations, which could provide a reason for the reaction against the church courts in the 1520s and early 1530s.[103] The link is

---

[101] Cross, ' "Great reasoners in scripture" ' [174]; Aston, *Lollards and reformers* [15], pp. 49–70; Atkinson, *Mystic and pilgrim* [21], ch. 6.

[102] Timmins, *Reg. Chandler* [841], no. 31 (at p. 19).

[103] Bowker, 'Some archdeacons' court books' [78], pp. 310–12.

tentative, but suggestive. While increasing activity against heresy may represent a drive against the first signs of the Reformation, the revival of heresy charges in the sixteenth century may also represent clerical action in defence of spiritual jurisdiction over the laity.

The apparent pettiness of some heresy accusations in those years rather bolsters the notion of a church frantically trying to enforce subjection. It certainly appears that heresy accusations were being made more often, but why this was so needs further thought. It can be no accident that the renewed concern almost coincides with the revival of Catholic doctrinal concerns and reformism, manifested in demands made at the Fifth Lateran Council (1512–17).[104] Ecclesiastical regeneration required a purge of evil influences, so that moves against heresy in England can be seen as part of the pre-reform Reformation. Clearly, however, a distinction must be made between those trials in which heresy really was the issue, and cases where the heresy accusation justified other actions by the church.[105]

By 1500 the jurisdictional independence of the spiritual courts had been considerably circumscribed by developments in royal justice, some of which occurred with the connivance if not encouragement of the church authorities. The process of Praemunire frequently removed cases from the spiritual to the secular courts; and even where cases were brought in the church court without initial opposition, the shadow of the statute hung over the proceedings. The church's jurisdiction was unquestionable only in matters of faith; in short, heresy. If the church wished to retain its jurisdictional autonomy it had to bring heresy accusations where previously lesser charges had sufficed – or, mirroring the secular power, retain the possibility of a heresy charge to force acceptance of ecclesiastical jurisdiction. (Possibly heresy accusations were also more effective administratively: the courts had powers of direct arrest rather than having to wait for the process of caption to take effect, or allow escape.) The plaintiffs would have to choose between Praemunire and the penalties for heresy, to choose the lesser of two evils. The notorious case of Richard Hunne offered precisely this choice, but is not unique. In 1495 a tithe case had been dealt with in the church courts as heresy. The accusation was challenged in the royal courts on the basis that tithe issues were normally determinable before royal justices; but the case was remitted to the church courts because, as the common lawyers declared, it was beyond their competence to decide what constituted heresy. Other evidence is scarce, but London church court cases in the 1490s likewise suggest use of heresy jurisdiction to enforce obedience to the ecclesiastical courts.[106] This, if widely used,

[104] See n. 109.
[105] Luxton, 'The Lichfield court book', pp. 122–3.
[106] Wunderli, *London church courts* [931], pp. 124–5; Ives, *Common lawyers* [435], pp. 274–5.

could have allowed the church to reverse the secular encroachments on its jurisdiction; but not without considerable turmoil before a final decision was reached. That decision had not been made by the time of the Reformation, but the turmoil was certainly there.

7.5 DISLOCATION

The church's ability to quell 'Lollardy' temporarily quashed some calls for reform, but could not completely contain the pressures. The situation developed considerably after 1500, with the coalescing of several strands to suggest that some of the reformist calls might be brought to fruition. A fundamental change was the spread of printing. Used extensively to support traditional spirituality, in both full-length books and ephemera ranging from indulgences to devotional woodcuts, it was nevertheless a double-edged invention: if differently directed it could be employed against traditional orthodoxy. Moreover, it may have helped succour a general increase in popular literacy, and with that the confidence to question the established order.[107]

The development of Christian humanism also contributed towards the general pattern. Drawing on a classicist concern with the restoration of the pristine church, and preferring the doctrines of the Patristics to later theologians, this intellectual movement also shared in the general concern for moral reform and some of the ideas of the *devotio moderna*. Internationally, its supreme exponent was Erasmus. Others shared his concerns, and perhaps had a more practical determination to translate thoughts into actions. In England this trend was represented by John Colet, Dean of St Paul's cathedral, London; William Melton, Chancellor of York Minster; and John Fisher, in due course Bishop of Rochester and martyred Cardinal. To them must be added the chief exponent of English lay humanism, Thomas More, perhaps more concerned to maintain the old piety without having the jurisdictional and disciplinary concerns (and duties) of his clerical compatriots – except, as Chancellor, when dealing with heretics.

These people, and others like them, were influential throughout the early sixteenth century, their ideas receiving extensive promulgation. But this Christian humanism cannot be divorced from preceding movements. For all its Christocentricity and laicizing near-mysticism, Christian humanism was firmly linked to earlier spiritual trends. Although railing against

---

[107] Febvre and Martin, *Coming of the book* [268], discusses printing and the (continental) Reformation at pp. 283–318. For a more diffuse discussion of the links between printing and religious changes (from fifteenth to eighteenth centuries) see Eisenstein, *The printing press* [249], i, pp. 303–450.

ecclesiastical abuses, and demanding the restoration of a purified church, it did not negate late medieval spirituality. In many ways, indeed, it seems to represent its logical culmination.[108]

Christian humanism was one part of a wider orthodox reform movement. Concerned bishops were active in several parts of Europe, at least in the first decades of the sixteenth century. This again had its English representatives, especially when the 'humanists' joined the bench. But concern needed action as well. The universal church appreciated the demands, and sought to respond to them. The Fifth Lateran Council, summoned in 1512, was meant to bring reform, to satisfy the complaints being made about the laxity of papal government and general standards in the church. In session until 1517, it proved incapable of its tasks. Nevertheless, its occurrence was significant, even if it provided no remedies. Alongside that reform movement there was also the spreading (if localized and fragmented) reform of several of the religious orders, a continuation of the fifteenth-century movement with a proliferation of novel and stricter orders as the sixteenth century passed.[109]

Concern and attempts at reform were all very well; but a further characteristic of the development of the late medieval western church also needs mention. The fifteenth century had seen the inexorable development of national churches, although remaining nominally under papal headship. This ecclesiastical nationalization proceeded apace in the sixteenth century. Major concordats were agreed between the papacy and several leading realms, notably the Concordat of Bologna of 1516 between Leo X and Francis I of France. In Spain, the rulers of the united kingdoms had gained almost complete control over their churches, even with their own royally managed Inquisition. Under Cardinal Ximenes, the church was ruled very much as a national body, only vaguely subject to papal authority. The same occurred in Naples, where Ferdinand 'the Catholic' brought to a logical conclusion the royalist claims of the *Privilegia Sicula*, whereby the king arrogated to himself the authority of a papal legate within his realm.[110]

England shared in these developments. The decade of Wolsey's domination of the church must have had a considerable impact on the institution, and on perceptions of it. His administration unified the provinces of York and Canterbury, and effectively provided a local curia which would

[108] McConica, *English humanists* [544], esp. pp. 14–43; Dowling, *Humanism*, ch. 2.

[109] Minnich, 'Incipiat iudicium' [582]; Schoeck, 'The Fifth Lateran Council' [751]; Oakley, *Western church*, pp. 231–8 (for sixteenth-century new orders, Evennett, 'The new orders' [260]).

[110] Oakley, *Western church*, pp. 247–51; Ullmann, 'This realm of England' [860], pp. 188–91 (see also pp. 198–9); Knecht, *Francis I* [482], pp. 53–65.

have supplanted most of the normal contacts between Rome and England. This may have encouraged a nationalistic view of the church, available for exploitation in hostility to the foreign interloper when Henry VIII turned against the papacy which refused him his divorce, and converted the *Ecclesia Anglicana* into an Anglican Church.

To cap it all, there were the stirrings of Protestantism. Or, rather, the reopening of old sores which had long troubled the church, and which could now exploit the circumstances of the period to receive more wide-spread discussion and provoke wider reactions. Luther's academic complaints about the church could exploit the potentialities of printing, the aspirations of monarchs, and the intellectuality of the universities attended by humanists who would become parish priests, to spread a message threatening the basic tenets of the catholic faith. These German ideas had their impact in England. The importation cannot be traced precisely, and the influence of the ideas is largely untestable. Nevertheless, books were coming in, printing was making ideas more accessible, and individuals were sharing new views about the church. Some of these views were gaining a foothold among the laity, but to what extent is largely unknown.

Luther's works were the main import, entering the country from *c.*1519. They were mainly influential at the universities, where Lutheranism apparently developed fairly quickly, perhaps replicating the situation of Wycliffism in the 1370s. Numbers affected are unknown, but their significance cannot be underestimated. Because there was scope for interpretation within the doctrines of the church, Lutheran ideas were not necessarily irreconcilable with orthodoxy. They could have been integrated into a general pattern and process of doctrinal development which might apply to the whole church. The universities' significance was largely as centres for the distribution not of doctrines as such, but of people – parish priests who, after completing their studies, would take their newly acquired ideas elsewhere, and assist their spread. Obviously, however, the process of dissemination would only be on a small scale – given the numbers attending the universities, not every parish could have been touched; nor would all the recipients intend to serve as parish priests. But even lay graduates, although unable to spread the ideas publicly via the pulpit, could do so in private. Lutheranism was therefore developing in England, and among those with influence; but its strength should not be overstated. For most of the time Lutheranism was a theology of an elite – there were few English versions of Lutheran (let alone Luther's) works available until the very late 1520s, and by then Lutheranism itself was only one of several strands of reforming ideas being made available in English, and one which en-countered strong opposition from Henry VIII. Moreover, even if a threat, Lutheranism was not considered a major danger. The reaction to it stressed not its novelty, but a sense of *déjà vu*: some of the chief works against it in England treated Luther's ideas as yet another mish-mash of old heresies, including a revival of Wycliffism.[111]

Of the reform tendencies, Pecock was too individual to be important. The friars reflect a more widespread approach, but one only rarely revealed. Lutheranism, the novelty of the 1520s, was consciously intellectual, spreading among the intelligentsia and some influential laity. But as forces for doctrinal change these movements were not particularly significant. They were rather marginalized by the demands of popular piety, and the opposition of the ecclesiastical hierarchy. The ideas could not be completely contained, but they probably posed a lesser threat than 'Lollardy' did. Lollardy cannot be assessed with any accuracy in the pre-Reformation decades. Fairly amorphous, it retained some loyalty in certain areas, especially towns such as London and Coventry. It was clearly a movement for doctrinal change – although to some extent a movement of denial rather than positive advance: denial of transubstantiation, denial of the invocation of saints, denial of the cult of the dead. We know what Lollardy wanted to remove, but not what it intended to establish.[112]

The church appreciated the doctrinal threats presented by the reformist ideas of the 1520s, and that decade was very much the first phase of the struggle between the various forces in the Reformation. The defenders of orthodoxy tried to root out the new ideas and their supporters with a major drive against heresy in 1527–8.[113] Then orthodoxy was relatively unthreatened: heretics had been caught, and burnt, and many of the recalcitrant had been driven overseas, there to vituperate, translate, and publish, hoping that their ideas would reach an English audience somehow. The debates of these years are largely literary, with the humanists being forced to take sides (as Fisher and More most obviously did for orthodoxy).[114] Balancing the books is fraught with dangers, but even allowing for increased challenges to the church derived from the new ideas, and the revivification of Lollardy (although that may have been rather delayed: most Lollard printings date from the 1530s) orthodoxy was probably not seriously threatened at Wolsey's fall. Reformist cells

---

[111] Brigden, 'Youth and the Reformation' [89], pp. 41–2; for the theologies of the various Protestant works available in England between 1525 and 1535, see Clebsch, *England's earliest Protestants*; Hall, 'Rise and decline of Lutheranism' [341], pp. 104–19; Lytle, 'Wyclif, Luther, and Powell' [543], pp. 473–5.

[112] The role of 'Lollardy' in the English Reformation remains debatable. It is forcefully asserted in Davis, *Heresy and Reformation*, but I am not convinced. The problem is essentially one of continuity and definition as a movement: that individuals by their own investigation of scriptures reached conclusions which the authorities (and later historians) might consider typically Lollard does not necessarily Lollardize either the conclusions, or their holders.

[113] Elton, *Reform and Reformation*, pp. 74–7, 95–7.

[114] ibid., p. 77; Elton, 'Persecution and toleration' [253], pp. 164–71.

there were, and dubious books in circulation (despite attempts to keep them out); but with the king and his government still loyal to Rome there was little scope for the changes which would be necessary to alter that position.

The English Reformation began in 1529. Its later progress has been much and well charted,[115] but the ground must be partly recovered, to assess how far the changes affected the relationship between the church and its society, and thus brought in a new order.

The precise format of any English Reformation was unforeseeable in 1529. From the proposals of Wolsey and others it seems incontrovertible that some reform was inevitable, but not necessarily a Protestant reform. The church's social role may have been reduced, but England might well have remained within the overall fold of Catholicism.

The crucial element in the English Reformation was the seizure of the headship of the church by Henry VIII. That was, essentially, a political act, in some ways reflecting the old quarrel between kings and papacy which had simmered since the late eleventh century. The immediate cause of the crisis was almost accidental, in Henry VIII's concern for the succession and desire that his marriage to Catherine of Aragon be annulled to free him to marry Anne Boleyn. The search for an annulment was a long and fairly sordid business, with the king now accepting, now rejecting, papal authority; begging the pope and then bludgeoning; and apparently not recognizing the many inconsistencies of his own position. The case for annulling the marriage was extremely weak, but as it led to jurisdictional conflict produced a major difficulty for both main protagonists: neither side was prepared to back down. But the crisis took time to play out – the search for the annulment started in 1527, but the breach with Rome was delayed until the mid-1530s; and even then the popes hoped that it would be temporary. While in 1531 the clergy were forced to accept Henry VIII as the church's 'chief protector, only and supreme lord, and also, in so far as the law of Christ allows, supreme head', with the papal nuncio identifying this headship as a 'new papacy', the formal statement of supremacy was made only by Act of Parliament in 1534. Even that Act was extremely vague in its wording – short, it makes no mention of the papacy or any transfer of power; nor are the powers of the Supreme Head defined with any precision. It is not completely incompatible with a retained papacy, although its anti-papal intent soon became clear. Certainly, 1534 witnessed England's formal secession from the universalist church, with another Act establishing suffragan sees in several

---

[115] The classic brief exposition is Dickens, *The English Reformation* [210]; see also Hughes, *The Reformation in England* [425].

towns and making provision for the method of appointment of the new bishops, abrogating the old system of employing bishops with titles from sees *in partibus infidelium*. Yet while Henry VIII enjoyed the title of Supreme Head, it is not strikingly evident that he, or his advocates, had any shared notion of just what that entailed.[116]

The machinations to obtain the annulment, with the accompanying political manoeuvrings, allowed reformism to take root in England. In this process, catholic reform lost – rejection of royal headship brought execution for Fisher and More; those who wished to maintain traditional doctrinal orthodoxy within the royal supremacy found themselves trapped by their concessions, with bishops like Longland of Lincoln realizing only too late just what they had unleashed, and being forced on the defensive against the spread of even more radical ideas within their dioceses. Meanwhile Lutheran, Lollard, and other tendencies received wider opportunities through the challenge to papal authority presented by those pushing Henry VIII, and by the king's promotion of the German-infected Cranmer to the archbishopric of Canterbury (even though married, and via papal provision) to implement the marriage with Anne Boleyn. Political expediencies here blur the stances of some of the key individuals. Anne Boleyn, for instance, can be seen as a supporter of the reformers with her patronage of some of the 'evangelicals' of the day. But her modernity may have had limits, and her views been more hybrid: supporting the opponents of papacy and advocates of the English Bible to gain her own ends while remaining loyal to most basic catholic doctrines; but managing to suggest (not least to those she patronized, or opposed) that she supported some sort of Protestantism.[117] The king's determination to be independent of the papacy, and ability to browbeat, also gave the laity in Parliament the opportunity to change the church's disciplinary arrangements – in probate, mortuaries, and suchlike. But this legislation must be separated from the more obviously royalist oppressions, as reflected in the pardon for the clergy in 1531, or their submission in 1532. The former forced the clergy to purchase royal pardon for their Praemunire offence of obedience to papal and legatine jurisdiction. Effectively this somewhat grotesque replay of Edward I's struggle with Boniface VIII was an attempt at conquest of the church, for the main element of the charge was the clergy's acceptance of Wolsey's legatine authority, even though Henry VIII had

---

[116] For the annulment proceedings, Parmiter, *The King's great matter* [641] (see pp. 1 n. 2, 156–8); for the later problem of the supreme headship, Loades, *The Oxford martyrs* [521], pp. 42–69. See also *Statutes*, iii, pp. 492, 509–10.

[117] Parmiter, *The King's great matter*, p. 273; Dowling, 'Ann Boleyn and reform' [227] (the ambiguity of her rejection of a Protestant work cited at p. 44 seems ideally to reflect the ambiguity of her whole religious stance; she merits comparison with St German, Guy, *St German*, pp. 46–54, esp. p. 48).

encouraged its grant to him, and shared in its exploitation. The laity were potentially victims of a similar attack, and offered stouter resistance in Parliament (but still received a pardon).[118] The separation from Rome was complete by 1536. In that year the double deaths of Catherine and Anne Boleyn offered the possibility of drawing an accommodating veil over the whole unfortunate episode, but the king was now totally opposed to papal jurisdiction, an opposition made concrete with the refusal to attend Paul III's Council at Mantua in 1538.[119] Once the English church became the Church of England and not just the Church in England, change proceeded inexorably.

But which reformation was it to be? The changes which occurred under Henry VIII were tentative, and often contradictory. Several tendencies pulled in varying directions, especially among the 'humanists' who were central to the direction of affairs, and with politics often overlying or actually dominating ecclesiastical developments.[120] The church obviously suffered major and dramatic alterations, with the abolition of the cult of saints and pilgrimages, the dissolution of the religious orders, and attacks on chantries which culminated in their suppression in 1547, along with the fraternities and guilds. The basic structure remained intact: there were still bishoprics (in fact, more than previously), archdeacons, rural deans, and parishes. Although English Bibles were made available, as part of the anti-papal weaponry, Henry VIII soon agreed with earlier ecclesiastics about the power of the vernacular to distract from orthodoxy – and in 1543 access to English Bibles was restricted. The canons of the church remained essentially unchanged, proposed revisions not getting beyond a draft stage. The mass remained, in Latin (although some people advocated services in English). Piecemeal liturgical revisions were changing the services and increasing awareness of English forms through new primers for the laity setting out the modified viewpoint more explicitly.[121]

Critical to this Henrician phase of the Reformation was the fact that the annulment proceedings essentially reflected a political movement. Such politics dictated the later doctrinal developments, for the creation of any Anglican settlement would be predicated on the twin pillars of Royal Supremacy and Apostolic Succession, effecting merely a change in head-ship which would not affect the spiritual continuity of the ecclesiastical body. The intention was to ensure continuity of the unitary national

[118] Elton, *Reform and Reformation*, pp. 139–45, 150–5; Parmiter, *The King's great matter*, pp. 158–9.

[119] Elton, *Reform and Reformation*, p. 276.

[120] McConica, *English humanists*, pp. 150–99, 218–34.

[121] Greenslade, 'English Bible' [317], pp. 894–7; Logan, 'The Henrician canons' [527]; for English in the mass before 1547, MacCulloch, *Suffolk*, pp. 159 n. 10, 161, 163 (its use could lead to heresy charges: Davis, *Heresy and Reformation*, p. 90); for liturgical developments under Henry VIII, Cuming, *Anglican liturgy* [182], pp. 49–61.

church; denominational pluralism was not on the agenda, even if there was some suggestion of greater liberalism within the unitary whole. The insistence on a unitary church was initially shown by Thomas Cromwell's appointment as the king's vicegerent in spirituals: the lay pope was to be assisted by a lay legate *a latere regis*, whose authority like Wolsey's united the provinces of York and Canterbury into the one Church of England.[122]

In seeking separation from Rome, Henry VIII had to tolerate anti-papalists – and rediscovered the anti-papalism of earlier centuries. Lollardy seems to have received some sort of quasi-toleration (at least, from 1532 when the denial of papal supremacy was declared not to be heretical), and the state almost connived at the promulgation of some of its views by encouraging the printing of Wycliffite works. But this again was a political rather than spiritual move. Older anti-papal ideas were also being revived, such as those derived from Marsilius of Padua's *Defensor pacis*, made available in English translation.[123] Once the king had achieved his break with Rome, reaction set in against doctrinal impurity – although the purificatory changes of 1537–8 (the attack on the 'idolatrous' aspects of the cult of the saints) can be seen as moves 'towards Lollardy', Lollards were generally considered just as heretical in the 1540s as they had been in the 1510s.[124]

The support for printing was perhaps a significant element in developing the Reformation. In the 1520s, attempts had been made to keep printed Lutheran works out; and much of the printing of reformist English books throughout the period was done on the continent. However, printing in England also developed, in and against royal aims. The mass-production of heretical works, and their distribution, made it difficult to control their spread, no matter what action the authorities took against them. Equally, once printed with official sanction, it was impossible to destroy all copies when doctrines changed, or to prevent smuggling. But printing was not limited to 'heretical' works: there was also a continuous production of traditionally pious works, including translations of Erasmus, which maintained the purified catholicism of the late fifteenth century. The radical reformers, perhaps learning from their Lollard precursors, may have tampered with some of these works for their own ends: Richard Whytford, sometime monk of Syon and a reasonably prolific traditionalist writer, complained of such manipulation of his works in 1541. To some extent,

---

[122] Elton, 'England and the continent' [252], p. 15; Loades, 'English Protestant national-ism' [523], pp. 298–9 (see also Cross, 'Churchmen and supremacy' [173], p. 18; Loades, 'The royal supremacy' [522]); Elton, *Reform and Reformation*, pp. 230–1. The Faculty Office jurisdiction gave another unification, in the machinery to grant dispensations, but this did not provide an institutional unity to match Cromwell's.

[123] Marsilius was also available to the learned in Latin: see Guy, *St German*, pp. 40, 43, 51.

[124] For moves 'towards Lollardy', Davis, *Heresy and Reformation*, p. 15.

also, the orthodox undermined their own efforts, the extensive citation of challenged works in their rebuttals helping to spread heretical ideas.[125]

Also significant for the spread of the Reformation was the use of the old structures to implement changes. The retention of peculiar jurisdictions and the old patronal structure must have been of great local importance. The Archbishop of Canterbury's peculiar of Hadleigh (Suffolk) thus provided a base for the reformers under Cranmer, immune from conservative forces in the surrounding diocese of Norwich. The jurisdictional immunity here was significant but, equally, Cranmer was able to appoint clerics of his sympathies to posts under his control, and lay patrons doubtless followed a like pattern. Reformers could thus exploit the patronage structure in the church to increase their hold in the country; and with the wholesale switch in patronage patterns which accompanied the dissolution of the monasteries, the scope for such exploitation was considerable.[126]

Until 1535 or so the English Reformation was only a schismatic movement. Although subversive elements were abroad, and with Cranmer and Cromwell had inveigled themselves into two of the most important posts in the land, nevertheless their freedom of doctrinal activity was limited. While anti-papal preachers had been tolerated for fear of royal disapproval, other forms of anti-catholicism had not been accepted: heresy trials had continued against Lutherans and others. Only with the breach with Rome, and the need to establish just what sort of church was now to be maintained in England, did the opportunity arise for real doctrinal transformation.

That Cranmer was Archbishop of Canterbury and Cromwell in charge of government in 1536 were crucial elements in the change, greatly assisted by promotions to the episcopal bench since 1529. Whatever Henry VIII actually was, he, was no Protestant. Cromwell was definitely a reformer, while Cranmer was affected by German ideas. The first definition of Anglican doctrine – the Ten Articles of 1536 – exposed the immediate tensions, with Henry VIII seeking a much more orthodox confession than Cranmer could accept. In this instance the archbishop won, and modified Lutheranism became the official basis of religion; paradoxically so, for the Act was supposedly in response to complaints from the clergy which were partly against the growing threat of Lutheranism.[127] However, this initial drift was soon checked. Later statements reflected a gradual return, culminating in 1539 in the Act of Six Articles, whose unitarist intent is

---

[125] Loades, 'The press' [520], pp. 30–4; Reed, 'Regulation of the book trade' [691], pp. 162–72, 178–83; early English Protestant works which had to be smuggled in listed in Hume, 'English books printed abroad' [426]; McConica, *English humanists*, pp. 114–16, 123, 128–9, 131–2, 147, 167–93, 207–8; see also n. 91.

[126] MacCulloch, *Suffolk*, pp. 163–4.

[127] Davis, *Heresy and Reformation*, pp. 13–14 identifies the majority as 'Lollard'.

evident in its title as an Act 'abolishing diversity in opynions'. Transubstantiation was retained in this strongly traditional statement, which
insisted that communion in both kinds (both bread and wine) was not
necessary, that priests might not marry (*pace* Cranmer!), that vows of
chastity remained valid, that private masses were licit, and that auricular
confession was mandatory. The state assumed authority for enforcing this
Act, with rejection of transubstantiation meriting the pains of heresy but
the other articles carrying only the penalties of felony, without benefit of
clergy. Even so, there were notable omissions. Indulgences disappeared
entirely, their only remnant being the church briefs, licences to collect
alms which were issued by the crown and clearly represent a continuation
(or revival) of royal support for charitable collections. The cult of the
saints was also shattered – their status had been changed in 1536, and
royal despoilation had since then removed many of the shrines in the
attack on 'superstition'. Many fraternities collapsed: the demolition of
Purgatory undercut their function, while attacks on the saints perhaps
also questioned their observances. The suppression of many of the institutions in which they operated also contributed to their demise.[128]

 After 1539, the drift back to Caesaro-Catholicism continued, reaching
its peak with the publication of the King's Book in 1543. But although
traditionalism was reasserted, changes had to be acknowledged. The main
victim was masses for the dead – individual intentions were denied, the
argument being that masses could not be directed for the salvation of
particular souls, but had to apply to all. At one stroke, the *raison d'être* of
many of the country's charitable institutions was abrogated; within a few
years the guilds and chantries followed the monasteries into oblivion.[129] The
King's Book marks the high point of the Henrician Counter-Reformation,
establishing a religious authority with combined secular and ecclesiastical
machinery to combat heresy, and renewed controls over the printing and
reading of books as many of the previously tolerated Protestant writers fell
under official ban, ranging from Wyclif to John Bale. However, beneath
the traditionalist exterior, Protestantism was developing around the future
king. The reign of Edward VI revealed the full dangers of the royal
supremacy: for if the king was supreme, change could come by royal
decree, regardless of the concerns of conservatives in doctrinal matters.[130]

 The impact of doctrinal changes was visible in the impact on institutions. The Reformation of the monasteries in 1536 did not necessarily

---

[128] Brigden, 'Popular disturbances' [92], pp. 262–3, 273–4 (see also pp. 263–8); *Statutes*,
iii, 739–43; Phillips, *Reformation of images* [657], pp. 70–6, 78–9 (see also Bowker, *Henrician
Reformation*, pp. 94–5; Finucane, *Miracles and pilgrims* [273], pp. 205–12).

[129] *The King's Book* [474]; Kreider, *English chantries* [489], pp. 150–3.

[130] For resulting problems of conscience under Edward VI (and Mary), Cross, 'Churchmen and supremacy', pp. 19–21.

presage their total destruction; but by 1540 all had gone – and with them a huge number of chantries as well. The suppression of the monasteries (without automatically releasing their inhabitants from their vows) had significant economic implications, and perhaps also contributed to a hiatus in the recruitment of ordinands to the church: the generational gap in priestly recruitment between the 1530s and the reign of Edward VI is perhaps an unconsidered element in the progress of the Reformation. In rural areas the destruction of the monasteries removed local centres and undercut spiritual links with the associated destruction of pilgrimage sites and ties of confraternity. The suppression of monastic and mendicant chantry obligations was also significant.[131]

The destruction of the monastic chantries could be taken as serving notice on all chantries. Governmental intentions were further revealed by the 1539 Act which, besides the monasteries, also threatened to suppress the secular colleges and hospitals – a number of which went before the death-knell was sounded in the 1545 Chantries Act. It is thus not surprising that benefactions for chantry purposes declined after 1535: why present a rapacious king with a sitting target? Equally, if private masses were ineffective, then chantries had lost their point. Therefore, although they continued to be served right through to their dissolution, there was a quickening process of piecemeal suppression, as benefactors and patrons sought to recover the alienated property or convert it to other uses.[132] The collective chantries of the guilds and fraternities also seem to have gone into immediate decline: membership lists start to peter out after 1536, with fewer enrolments. Perhaps, however, this testifies to the earlier popularity of indulgences – once they went, the recorded memberships were restricted to the really active participants.

The peculiarities of the progress of the English Reformation, especially under Henry VIII, cause several problems when attempting to trace its immediate impact. It is especially difficult to determine just how the populace as a whole reacted to these extraordinary events. Those who see the medieval church as a totally decadent and repressive body view the speedy changes as evidence of their whole-hearted acceptance. Against them, recent writers have suggested that popular conversion was much less easily secured, with the fear of royal displeasure being as strong a force for acquiescence as real conviction. Certainly, there is evidence of lingering Catholicism throughout much of the sixteenth century, until eventually *Roman* Catholicism developed under Elizabeth I. Continuities in personnel must have considerably eased the transitions. Whether such

---

[131] Hicks, 'Chantries, obits, and almshouses' [384], p. 142; Kreider, *English chantries*, pp. 128–9; Hutton, 'Local impact' [431], pp. 117–18.

[132] Kreider, *English chantries*, pp. 155–64, 211–13.

individuals deserve to the considered as collaborators or fifth-columnists (whichever religion was dominant) is debatable; but it is undeniable that this continuity did allow gradual development, regardless of which way the state eventually went.[133]

There was, clearly, developing criticism of the church in the 1530s, assisted by the influx of printed Protestant works, by the English Bible, and by the semi-official support for something like Lollardy. Contemporary social and economic developments perhaps also made some doctrines more relevant to contemporaries, and thus more acceptable, by reinforcing prejudices which had been developing in previous decades.[134] The uncertainties of the period were nevertheless outweighed by the structural continuity: as long as the Reformation was promulgated through the accepted machinery of authority, as long as the conflicts involved remained in many ways 'traditional', there would be little active opposition, or real need for repression. It was probably the official nature of the changes which explains the speedy collapse of so many practices: pilgrimages and the cult of the saints seem to have disappeared virtually overnight (or so the Devon evidence suggests), with little opposition, and with complaints only from those whose pockets suffered. Yet the collapse might not reflect willing denial of the old ways, merely (in some cases) a realistic appreciation that overt opposition would profit the crown more than the parish or the church which was visited.[135] Social factors and self-interest must also be taken into account – some of the divisions between traditionalists and innovators reflect economic and social divisions within localities; while the concern to maintain a local social position might force those loyal to the old order to exploit its physical destruction for self-preservation. Similarly, the collapse of the chantries in the 1540s may reflect an alliance which offered liberation from obligations to individual heirs, burdened with responsibilities for the souls of their ancestors, at the expense of corporate endowments which might yet be recovered for local use.[136] There is little sign of active opposition to the changes, but it was there – as the Pilgrimage of Grace reveals. Many of the external changes were resented, while the required internal changes were perhaps only improperly appreciated.

---

[133] See Haigh, 'Recent historiography'; O'Day, *Debate* [612], chs 5–6; the somewhat self-consciously revisionist view is summarized in Haigh, 'Introduction' [331]; Haigh, 'Continuity of Catholicism' [334], pp. 178–80, 185, 191–2, 205–8 (see also McGrath, 'Elizabethan Catholicism' [550], p. 419].

[134] McIntosh, *Autonomy and community* [559], p. 262.

[135] Whiting, 'Abominable idols' [897].

[136] Clark, 'Reformation and radicalism' [147], pp. 118–19, 123–4; Scarisbrick, *Reformation* [748], pp. 71–2; Palliser, 'Popular reactions [635]; Burgess, ' "By quick and by dead" ', p. 857.

Many clerics resented the alterations, and as they were to be the main channels for the imposition of the new orthodoxy, their role was clearly crucial. But cowed by royalist activity, and with their leadership crushed by the king's exploitation of Praemunire in the 1530s and the almost wholesale transformation of the episcopal bench in that decade, the opportunities for active resistance were limited. Passive resistance to doctrinal changes remained a potent force, and conservative clergy had to be reckoned with for decades to come. The undramatic opposition of conservative bishops like Longland at Lincoln and Gardiner at Winchester perhaps did more to prevent the spread of heresy (even if unable to end the schism) than did dramatic martyrdoms.[137]

The extent of popular appreciation of the doctrinal changes is a critical issue. In areas where iconoclasm occurred in parish churches – the smashing of windows and shrines – the changes were obvious, and perhaps resented. But many places experienced few immediate changes; the main onset of such iconoclasm was delayed until the reign of Edward VI. While the services seemed little changed, there is unlikely to have been much immediate impact on the average parishioners (although the services did change, and churchwardens do seem to have carried out the required changes with relative alacrity, sometimes indeed undue haste). Moreover, usually those who would have been taken as leaders conspired in the changes, initially. The royal supremacy and the transfer of papal powers to the Archbishop of Canterbury changed few appearances: people still collected dispensations from a London agent, who replaced the papal representative but to all intents and purposes maintained the old procedures. Some individuals who sought bulls at Rome at the last minute found themselves needing royal pardons and confirmations, but these were granted. Papal authority, although rescinded, was not uprooted: the royal chancery in the first years after 1534 must have been busily issuing confirmations of papal appropriations of churches and other privileges.[138]

The processes for disseminating reform were equally significant. While books were important, sermons (especially in the towns) were probably more influential. The sermon tradition was a strong one, even for orthodoxy's opponents – the Lollards, after all, had been important as wandering preachers, and Thomas Bilney in East Anglia had spread his views

---

[137] Powell, 'Reformation in Gloucestershire' [670], pp. 102–4; Cross, 'Priests into ministers' [176], pp. 211–20; Haigh, 'Monopoly to minority' [329], pp. 130–1.

[138] Phillips, *Reformation of images*, pp. 53–100, *passim* (the images in monasteries and other religious houses were put down: for the fate of some see Blench, *Preaching in England* [68], p. 122); Hutton, 'Local impact', pp. 114–20, 137–8 (see also Haigh, 'Introduction', pp. 12–13, 15); Chambers, *Faculty office registers* [135]; BIHR, YM/D/YOR.6–7 (confirmations of appropriations to St Leonard's hospital); NRO, Will Reg. Coppynger, ff. 70 [j]ʳ–70[k]ᵛ (confirmation [dated 22 January 1536] of a dispensation granted to William Tymperlay on 8 November 1533, he having been 'commune opinione et errore seductus et deceptus').

through sermons. Among the orthodox, sermons were also normal, being delivered by mendicants and the travelling preachers maintained by bequests in the pre-Reformation era. From the 1530s, the reformers apparently exploited sermons effectively, taking over the mendicant tradition of publicly lambasting the corruptions of church and society, and injecting doctrinal elements into their harangues. The upholders of orthodoxy seem not to have appreciated the dangers, their sermons being based on old models and not properly responding to the new challenges. Even so, a charismatic conservative preacher, such as Dr Wattes in Salisbury and London in 1539, could counter the reformers quite well. The key element here was authority: occasionally an unfortunate listener would end up arrested for heresy, for believing someone he took to be an authorized preacher. Equally, as little changed externally, there would be little awareness of things being altered. Yet change was occurring: old ceremonies had new meanings and significances, but their ceremonial retention made the changes in content less obvious and more acceptable. Such subtle dissemination of new patterns of religion, from those considered and accepted as hierarchs and authorities, could not have been other than effective. Other authority also operated: besides the king's central supremacy there were the supremacies of local rulers whose views would affect the reception or rejection of changes, and which may well account for the varying attitudes to reform in different places.[139]

It is perhaps the piecemeal character of the Reformation which reconciles the contrary traditions in approaches to it. The changes seem speedy and effective because, doctrinally, there was at first little 'reformation' under Henry VIII. Rather there was a transfer of authority at the apex of the church, a secession from the universality of Rome, whose implications filtered down through the hierarchy, being followed by individual doctrinal and organizational changes which whilst collectively significant could be individually accommodated with few major qualms of conscience, if they were noticed. Only under Edward VI did a fully state-sponsored Reformation begin, and thereafter the chaos of formal changes in religion.

But England's Reformation was not, in fact, speedy. Its pacific character owes much to the time it took for the ideas to penetrate the country. It also owes much to its being a Reformation which was not 'popular'. It was mainly led from above – by clergy and local rulers – and operated within the accepted social order. It would therefore probably not be as strongly resented as a Reformation locally perceived as foisted on the country by

---

[139] Brigden, 'Youth and the Reformation', pp. 60–1; Brigden, 'Popular disturbances', pp. 260–1; for a charge of heresy for believing an authorized(?) preacher, Powell, 'Reformation in Gloucestershire, p. 100; on orthodox preaching, Blench, *Preaching in England*, pp. 248–52; Clark, 'Reformation and radicalism', pp. 120 n. 57, 125–6.

'outsiders' or inferiors. At first the concern seems to have been for slow reformation, with doctrinal changes being instilled over generations (in part perhaps because no one was quite sure which Reformation was occurring). The Protestantism of the 1530s and 1540s borrowed much from catholic practice in its propagation. Infant baptism and child communion remained, and thus the catechizing of children in a manner to accept without necessarily understanding. A developing catholic concern with education before 1530 was matched by a growing concern to indoctrinate the young in the new ideas after 1536. Uncertainties about just what that religion actually was produced confusion in some of the printed catechisms, but the most significant aspect is the concern to inculcate views which became increasingly Protestant. These subtle educational developments were accompanied by greater access to other printed works, producing generations better educated in religious matters than their elders, and knowing no other arrangements.[140] The concurrent generational and familial dislocations which affected many adolescents meant that, by Mary's accession in 1553, a whole generation had been brought up in many places on the reformed doctrines, or had discovered them for themselves. In such cases a process of veritable reconversion would be needed to re-establish catholic truth among them.[141]

[140] Tudor, 'Religious instruction' [848].

[141] Brigden, 'Youth and the Reformation', esp. pp. 43–67. Much depends on the degree of involvement with the church under the age of 17, and the age at which they were considered of 'spiritual discretion'. Age 14 postulated ibid., pp. 52–3 seems to me too late, but this cannot really be tested. The difficulty confronted by the Marian reaction with children who had never known the papal church is certainly striking: ibid., pp. 65–6.

Conclusion

The Reformation changed the ecclesiastical history of England. It therefore stands at the end of the middle ages, as the terminus of the present work. However, in many respects it is not the end. The changes imposed by Henry VIII and his successors clearly affected the church's structure, and its role in society,[1] but did not obliterate it. Massive and dramatic though many of the changes were, several were insubstantial, or parts of a developing process. Geographically the map changed little apart from the introduction of new dioceses: peculiar jurisdictions remained, even where taken over by laymen; bishops and chapters continued to rule; the parochial map was scarcely altered (except in towns). Church courts continued to claim jurisdiction in a variety of cases, even if those claims were not always recognized. But the courts remained, serving popular purposes in many cases, and perhaps especially significant for their continued probate jurisdiction. The church remained a landowner – although this was an area where it had suffered most, with the suppression of many institutions, and despoilation of the bishops as well. But the strength of ecclesiastical landholding clearly diminished, perhaps most obviously in towns, where the dissolutions produced major changes in the distribution of both wealth and power.[2] Economically, the church remained a force: tithes were still paid (in many instances now to the laity who had succeeded suppressed monastic houses as impropriators of their benefices), and remained a cause of disputes – perhaps more than before. Other fees were also demanded. The voluntary spiritual economy had probably collapsed, although partly replaced by a new economy of charity. Insofar as the Church of England remained the Established Church, the Reformation necessarily altered its social role and its power within society, but it did not negate it. However,

[1] For some consideration, O'Day, *Debate* [612], ch. 7.
[2] Tittler, 'End of the middle ages' [843].

the situation confronting this new *Ecclesia Anglicana* was markedly different in two major respects from that facing the pre-Reformation church. Within a few generations the concept of the unitary church disappeared, no matter how much Anglicanism might declare its devotion to the principle. Whatever the intentions of those responsible for the breach with Rome, the Church of England soon had to accept that it was but one of the churches in England. Denominational pluralism necessarily complicated the relationship between the established church and its society, especially when that church continued to claim powers over people who no longer considered themselves part of it, and when rights of patronage involved non-Anglicans in the career patterns of the Anglican clergy. It was perhaps only in the nineteenth century that the Church of England came to terms with the impact of the Reformation, and the medieval relationship between church and society was finally extinguished. Only then were its administrative order, its jurisdictional competence, and its economic demands redefined, by the abolition of the peculiar jurisdictions, the establishment of civil registration and probate, the reduction in the powers of the church courts, changes in parochial and diocesan structures, the process of tithe commutation, and the institution of the Ecclesiastical Commissioners.

Appendices

Names in [ ] indicate ineffective creations

Name	Creation as cardinal	Death
Simon Langham, OSB	Sept. 1368	July 1376
[William Courtenay]	Sept. 1378	
Adam Easton, OSB	Dec. 1382; deprived 1385; restored Dec. 1389	Aug. 1398
[Philip Repingdon, OSA]	Sept. 1408	
[Thomas Langley]	June 1411	
[Robert Hallum]	June 1411	
Henry Beaufort	May 1426*	Apr. 1447
John Kemp	Dec. 1439	Mar. 1454
Thomas Bourchier	Sept. 1467	Mar. 1486
John Morton	Sept. 1493	Sept. 1500
Christopher Bainbridge	Mar. 1511	July 1514
Thomas Wolsey	Oct. 1515	Nov. 1530
John Fisher	May 1535	June 1535
Reginald Pole	Dec. 1536	Nov. 1558

* An earlier papal attempt to make him a cardinal in 1417 had foundered on the opposition of Henry V.

A2   TENURE OF BENEFICES IN SELECTED DEANERIES IN
YORK DIOCESE

These figures derive from material in Gurney and Clay, *Fasti parochiales: Craven* [311]; Lawrance, *Fasti parochiales: Buckrose* [497]; and Train, *Clergy of central Nottinghamshire* [844], taking the first datable institution after 1 January 1350, through to the last datable institution before 1 January 1540, and counting incumbencies completed between those dates and beginning before 1 January 1540 but ending thereafter. With the figures for the individual deaneries, and for the combined totals, column A records the number of institutions within each category of length, column B that figure as a percentage of the total number of recorded institutions (given at the bottom of the table).

| Length | Buckrose | | Craven | | Nottingham | | Combined | |
(Years)	A	B	A	B	A	B	A	B
0–1	21	8.2	17	7.9	23	8.7	61	8.2
1–2	21	8.2	15	7.0	23	8.7	59	8.0
2–5	36	14.1	28	13.1	43	15.2	107	13.1
5–10	47	18.4	30	14.0	46	16.3	113	15.1
10–20	73	28.7	56	26.1	75	25.6	204	27.5
20+	57	22.3	68	31.8	72	25.5	197	26.6
Total quantified	255	74.8	214	70.6	282	62.8	751	68.7
Total overall*	341		303		449		1.093	

* i.e. the total number of recorded institutions which definitely occurred between the limiting dates, even if the length of the incumbency cannot be determined.

As the main defining characteristic is date of institution, rather than dates of institution and death (although such precision has been used where possible), there is bound to be some slight miscalculation at the boundaries, with a drift lengthening the incumbencies. I do not feel that this is significant in its effects on the interpretation offered of the figures. The length of overall average incumbency of 14.5 years is provided by 81 parishes × 190 years ÷ 1,093 incumbencies – a very rough calculation indeed.

The approach adopted in determining length of incumbencies differs from that adopted in Hair, 'Mobility of parochial clergy' [338], pp. 165–7, where the method is statistically unsatisfactory. Nevertheless, his comments, and the illustrations of particular careers given ibid., pp. 170–3, are very useful.

It must be stressed that these calculations are *not* indicative of the incumbents' overall careers among the beneficed: for many, exchanges and promotions to major sinecures would considerably extend their length.

Glossary

A full-scale glossary would make a long book longer than could be justified. Most uncertain words should be readily accessible through a dictionary. The purpose of the following brief list is mainly to supplement dictionary definitions which may be inadequate, and to deal with the odd technical terms which may not be found there.

apparitor   An official of the ecclesiastical courts, who summoned people to appear before them.

assumpsit   A range of common law actions developed in the early sixteenth century which, essentially, allowed for the recovery of damages for breach of an oral or written agreement.

chrism   A mixture of oil and balm, used for sacramental rituals, and distributed annually among the churches. The receipt of chrism from a particular authority reflected a jurisdictional relationship between the issuer and the recipient church.

corrody   Provision of an annual allowance of food, accommodation, and money (or a combination) to non-members of a religious house or hospital. Usually granted in return for service, or at the nomination of the king, or by purchase.

fidei laesio   Literally 'breach of faith', used to categorize actions in the church courts for breach of contract.

first tonsure   The first stage in the progression through clerical orders, giving clerical status without requiring the abandonment of a lay life (including marriage).

glebe   The landed endowment of a parish church.

in partibus infidelium   Literally 'in the regions of the faithless'. Used to designate episcopal sees to which a succession of bishops was maintained by the western church, but for which the actual territories were no longer actually in Latin Christian hands (if the location of the sees was actually known). Titles of this sort were often given to suffragan bishops.

legate/*legatus*   A papal representative. There were two distinct categories: (1) *legatus natus* (literally 'born legate'), a status accorded to the archbishops of Canterbury and York *ex officio* to reinforce their supremacy within their provinces; (2) *legatus a latere* ('legate from the side'), directly commissioned by the pope, always a cardinal, and with powers which gave him quasi-papal status within the area of his legation.

mortmain   Applied to the way in which undying institutions, especially those connected with the church, held real property, and thereby could not be liable for the exactions which would be due to a lord at the death of an individual.

mortuary   A payment due on death to the parish church (or, from incumbents, to the bishop) in acknowledgement of spiritual subjection. Usually either a beast or a robe, but precise demands and liabilities varied.

penitentiary   The official of the papal court responsible for overseeing the processing of the majority of dispensations.

provisions, papal   The arrangement whereby the papacy claimed authority to nominate and appoint to any benefice within the catholic church, mandating the local ecclesiastical authorities to grant possession of the post. The appropriate mandates were in two different forms: (1) *in forma pauperum*, whereby the recipient was given the right to demand nomination to any benefice in the gift of a named patron (in England almost invariably an ecclesiastical institution); (2) *in forma speciali*, whereby the recipient was nominated to a specified post (used especially for cathedral prebends and bishoprics).

Rota   The main tribunal of the papacy.

royal free chapel   Among peculiar jurisdictions, deaneries not subject to episcopal jurisdictional authority in which the authority of the crown was (or had been until passed to others) paramount.

Chronology

This is not intended to be a fully comprehensive chronology of the late medieval English church, being confined to events which have some significance for the purposes of this book. For the years after 1349 I have also included changes of king, and the successive appointments of the archbishops of Canterbury and York (appointments which were not completed are contained in [ ]).

1215   Fourth Lateran Council: promulgation of doctrine of transubstantiation, and of requirement for annual lay confession and communion

1279   First Statute of Mortmain, regulates gifts of property to religious houses

1286   Writ *Circumspecte Agatis* defines relationship between ecclesiastical and spiritual jurisdictions

1291   Taxation of Pope Nicholas IV

1296   Bull of Boniface VIII, *Clericis laicos*, provokes conflict over royal taxation of the church, won by the crown

1316   *Articuli cleri* define relationship between ecclesiastical and spiritual jurisdictions

1320   Canonization of St Thomas Cantelupe

1327   Edward III, King (d. 1377)

1340   William Zouche, Archbishop of York (d. 1352)

1343   Ordinance on provisors, to curtail papal provisions

1349   Black Death
        Thomas Bradwardine, Archbishop of Canterbury (d. August)
        Simon Islip, Archbishop of Canterbury (d. 1366)

1351   First Statute of Provisors

1352   John Thoresby, Archbishop of York (d. 1373)
        Statute *Pro clero* defines benefit of clergy

1353	First Statute of Praemunire
1363	Second Statute of Praemunire
1366	Repudiation of papal feudal overlordship of England
	Simon Langham, Archbishop of Canterbury (resigned 1368)
	Inquiry into pluralism in Canterbury province
1368	William Whittlesey, Archbishop of Canterbury (d. 1374)
1371	Experimental taxation based on parishes
	Lay resentment leads to removal of clerical ministers
	Calls for ecclesiastical disendowment
1373	Alexander Neville, Archbishop of York (deprived, 1388)
1375	Simon Sudbury, Archbishop of Canterbury (d. 1381)
1377	Richard II, King (deposed 1399)
	First clerical poll tax
	First moves against John Wyclif
1378	Outbreak of the Great Schism in the papacy
	Dispute over sanctuary rights
1379	Second clerical poll tax
1380	Third clerical poll tax voted (collected 1381)
1381	Peasants' Revolt: murders of Archbishop Sudbury (Chancellor) and Sir Robert Hales (Treasurer)
	William Courtenay, Archbishop of Canterbury (d. 1396)
1382	Heresy trial of William Swinderby – the first 'Lollard' trial
	Blackfriars Council – condemnation of Wycliffite heresies and errors
	Purge of supporters of John Wyclif in Oxford University
1383	Crusade of the Bishop of Norwich in Flanders
1384	Death of Wyclif
1388	Alexander Neville deprived of archbishopric of York in political upheaval, appointed bishop of St Andrews and exiled
	Thomas Arundel, Archbishop of York (to Canterbury, 1396)
1389	Royal inquiry into guilds and fraternities
	Second Statute of Provisors
1391	Second Mortmain Act, affects guilds and fraternities
1393	Third Statute of Praemunire
1395	Twelve Conclusions of the Lollards posted in London
1396	Thomas Arundel, Archbishop of Canterbury (deprived 1397)
	Robert Waldby, Archbishop of York (d. 1397/8)
1397	Thomas Arundel deprived of archbishopric of Canterbury in political upheaval, appointed bishop of St Andrews and exiled
	Roger Walden, Archbishop of Canterbury (deprived/resigned, 1399)
1398	Richard Scrope, Archbishop of York (executed, 1405)
1399	Deposition of Richard II, Henry IV becomes King (d. 1413)

Thomas Arundel, restored as Archbishop of Canterbury (d. 1414).

Bishop of Carlisle deprived for adherence to Richard II

1401   William Sawtry burnt for heresy – the first Lollard burning

Statute *De heretico comburendo* establishes death penalty for repeated heresy

Canonization of St John of Bridlington

1404   Parliament at Coventry urges temporary seizure of ecclesiastical temporalities

1405   Percy revolt: execution of Archbishop Scrope

[Thomas Langley, Archbishop of York (quashed 1406)]

1406   [Robert Hallum, Archbishop of York (appointed bishop of Salisbury 1407)]

1407   Henry Bowet, Archbishop of York (d. 1423)

1409   Council of Pisa fails to resolve Great Schism: England transfers allegiance from Gregory XII to Alexander V (and his successor John XXIII)

Publication of Archbishop Arundel's constitutions to limit spread of heresy

1410   Lollard Disendowment Bill

1411   Oxford University extracts further heresies from Wyclif's writings

1413   Henry V, King (d. 1422)

1414   Revolt of Sir John Oldcastle

Act giving justices powers to deal with heresy

Alien priories suppressed by legislation (although implementation took time)

Council of Constance opened, to seek end to Great Schism (continued to 1418)

Henry Chichele, Archbishop of Canterbury (d. 1443)

1415   Condemnation of John Wyclif by the Council of Constance

1422   Henry VI, King (deposed 1461)

1423   [Philip Morgan, Archbishop of York (quashed 1424)]

1424   [Richard Flemyng, Archbishop of York (resigned, 1425)]

1425   John Kemp, Archbishop of York (to Canterbury, 1452)

1427   Exhumation and burning of John Wyclif

1428–31 Heresy trials in Norwich diocese

1443   John Stafford, Archbishop of Canterbury (d. 1452)

1452   John Kemp, Archbishop of Canterbury (d. 1454)

William Booth, Archbishop of York (d. 1464)

1454   Thomas Bourgchier, Archbishop of Canterbury (d. 1486)

1456   Canonization of St Osmund of Salisbury

1457   Condemnation of Reginald Pecock for heresy
1461   Edward IV, King (fled, 1470)
1465   George Neville, Archbishop of York (d. 1476)
1470   Henry VI, restored as King (deposed 1471)
1471   Edward IV, restored as King (d. 1483)
1476   Lawrence Booth, Archbishop of York (d. 1480)
1480   Thomas Rotherham, Archbishop of York (d. 1500)
1482   Introduction of Observant Franciscans with establishment of house at Greenwich
1483   Edward V, King (deposed, June)
         Richard III, King (d. 1485)
1485   Henry VII, King (d. 1509)
1486   John Morton, Archbishop of Canterbury (d. 1500)
         Stafford's case limits idea of sanctuary
1489   Statute limits benefit of clergy
1491   Statute limits benefit of clergy
1501   [Thomas Langton, Archbishop of Canterbury (d. January)]
         Thomas Savage, Archbishop of York (d. 1507)
         Henry Deane, Archbishop of Canterbury (d. 1503)
1503   William Warham, Archbishop of Canterbury (d. 1532)
1507   Christopher Bainbridge, Archbishop of York (d. 1514)
1509   Henry VIII, King (d. 1547)
1511–12   Heresy trials in Kent, Chilterns, and Coventry
1512   John Colet's reformist sermon to Convocation
         Act limiting benefit of clergy in cases of murder
1514   Thomas Wolsey, Archbishop of York (d. 1530)
1514–15   Richard Hunne's case
1515   Standish case, on benefit of clergy
         Wolsey appointed Chancellor
1516–19   Savage case undermines idea of sanctuary
1518   First grant of legation to Wolsey (subsequently extended)
1521   Henry VIII given title of 'Defender of the Faith' ('*Fidei defensor*') by Pope Leo X
1524   Wolsey made legate *a latere* for life
1527   Start of proceedings for annulment of marriage of Henry VIII and Catherine of Aragon
1529   Legatine court fails to annul marriage of Henry VIII
         Wolsey dismissed as Chancellor
         Meeting of Reformation Parliament (continues to 1536)
         Acts limiting rights of sanctuary, mortuaries, non-residence, pluralism, and clerical involvement in leasing
1531   Edward Lee, Archbishop of York (d. 1544)

Act conditionally limiting payment of annates to Rome

Submission of the clergy, with acceptance of royal headship of the church

1532   Declaration that denial of papal headship of the church is not heretical

1533   Thomas Cranmer, Archbishop of Canterbury (deprived 1553)

Annulment in England of marriage of Henry VIII and Catherine of Aragon

Act to restrain appeals to Rome

1534   First Supremacy Act

Acts abolishing payments to Rome

1535   *Valor ecclesiasticus*

1536   Second Supremacy Act: King incorporates title of Supreme Head in royal style

First Dissolution Act initiates dissolution of lesser religious houses

Ten Articles begin definition of Anglican doctrine

Act on franchises abolishes independence of major liberties in matters of justice

1536–7 Lincolnshire Rising and Pilgrimage of Grace

1539   Second Dissolution Act confirms dissolution of all religious houses

Act of Six Articles

1541   New bishoprics established

1543   The King's Book

1545   First Chantry Act, for dissolution of chantries

1547   Edward VI, King (d. 1553)

Second Chantry Act: dissolution of guilds and chantries

Bibliography

MANUSCRIPTS CITED

Beverley: Humberside county record office

DD.BC.II/7/1; DD.BC/III/33; DD.BC/III/34

Birmingham: reference library

435125

Cambridge: university library

Ee.5.4; Ll.1.18; Mm.I.48; Add.2951; Add.6847; Add.6969; Add.7802

Cambridge: university library. Ely dean and chapter archives

D/6/2/26; 5/10/; 5/11/

Cambridge: university library. Ely diocesan records

E1/4/1; E1/16; F5/32; F5/33; F5/35; G/2/3; G7/29

Cambridge: university library, university archives

Collect.Admin.9

Canterbury: cathedral, city, and diocesan record office

Account of priory feretrarius, I

Carlisle: Cumbria county record office

DRC/2/7–8, 11–13, 16, 20

Exeter: cathedral library

3351 (I am grateful to Dr J. A. F. Thomson for the loan of a microfilm of this manuscript); 3533; 3690

Exeter: Devon record office

Reg. Oldham (I am grateful to Dr J. A. F. Thomson for the loan of a microfilm of this manuscript)

Hereford: cathedral archives

244; 1180; 1463; 1580; 1882; 2065; 2121; 2450; 2512; 2513; 2623; 2928; 3167; 3220; R369; R462; R482; R488; R585; R586; Baylis, i [= manuscript transcription by P. G. A. Baylis of Hereford cathedral chapter act book, vol. 1, cited by folio of the original act book which is still extant but in poor condition]

Lichfield: joint record office, Lichfield diocesan archives

B/A/1/1; B/A/1/2; B/A/1/3; B/A/1/6–13; B/A/1/14ii–iii; B/A/17/1; B/A/20/1; B/A/21/123984; B/C/1/1–2; B/C/2/1–3; B/C/13

Lichfield: joint record office, Lichfield dean and chapter archives

(being relisted: the numbers below are those currently in use)
D.30/II; D.30/XVIII; D.30/E26; D.30/E27; D.30/E33; D.30/E34; D.30/F8; D.30/Hh4

Lincoln: Lincolnshire archives office

Bj1/4; Bj5/19; Subs.1/7a/1–2; Sub/2/5; Bps Rentals 1; Bps Accts 5–7; Add Reg. 7; FOR.2–3; REV.L/1/3

London: British library

Add. 14848; Add. 25288; Add.ch.19836; Cotton.ch.v.38; Cotton.ch.xi.75; Cotton. Cleopatra.D.iii; Cotton.Galba.E.x.; Cotton.Titus.C.ix; Cotton.Vit.E.xvi?; Hargrave 87 (I am grateful to Prof. E. W. Ives for lending me a copy of this manuscript)?; Harley 2179

London: Guildhall library

25165

London: Lambeth palace library

Reg. Courtenay; Reg. Kempe; Reg. Morton; Reg. Warham

London: public record office

C270/17/20; C270/20; C270/28/7, 25; C270/32/4, 10, 12–32; C270/34/17; E101/514/31–2; E101/517/27; E135/8/31–2; E135/24/46; E135/25/13/1–2; E179/124/66; E179/217/56 (I am grateful to Dr H. C. Swanson for allowing me to consult her transcript of this document)?; E179/237/57a; SC6/Henry VII/1846; SC6/Henry VIII/7154–6

Norwich: Norfolk and Norwich record office

DCN/5/1–4; DCN/8/4; Reg.9–10; SUN/1(a); Will Reg. Coppynger
I am grateful to Mr T. Adams for providing references to the following documents: 152/30/16; 153/29/10; 153/34/10; 154/24/12; 155/10/2; 159/5/18; 159/12/11; 159/13/7; 159/14/14; 162/25/18; 163/16/14

Oxford: Bodleian library

Ashm.864; Barlow 54; Cheshire charter 11; DD.Bertie.c.16.21–34; DD.Ewelme.a.6.A35B(14); DD.Ewelme.a.6.A35B(26); Shropshire charter 27B; Tanner 165

Oxford: Corpus Christi College

B/14/2/3/7 (I am grateful to Dr C. C. Dyer for allowing me to consult his abstract of this document)

Stafford: Staffordshire county record office

D593/A/1/9/15; D593/A/1/12/5; D593/A/1/12/15; D593/A/1/12/17–18; D593/A/1/32/9; D593/A/1/32/13; D593/A/1/32/19; D593/A/1/33/2–3; D593/A/1/35/2; D(W)1734/3/2/2; D1734/3/2/3; D1734/3/2/4; D1734/3/3/264; D1734/J1948

Stafford: William Salt library

335/i

Westminster: Westminster abbey muniments

19768; 19776; 19819; 23001

Windsor: St George's chapel

XI.F.31; XI.G.69; XI.K.6; XI.41.80; XV.7.10; XV.37.4, 12–20, 25, 27, 29–30, 33–4, 39; XV.55.19; XV.59.1

Worcester: Hereford and Worcester county record office

009:1 BA 2636/9 43696; 009:1 BA 2636/10 43699; 009:1 BA 2636 172 92422, 92430, 92431, 92436; 716:093 BA 2922

York: Borthwick institute of historical research

Cav.Bk.1; CP.E.108; CP.E.143; CP.F.11; CP.F.60; CP.F.66; CP.F.82; CP.F.125; CP.F.150; CP.F.180; CP.F.260; CP.F.288; CP.G.46; CP.G.82; CP.G.93; CP.G.117; CP.G.125; CP.G.137; CP.G.209; CP.G.240; CP.G.870; CP.G.3378; DC/AB.1–2; YM/D/YOR.6–7

York: Minster library

F3/3; F3/4; L2(3)a; L2(3)c; M2/1a; M2(1)f; M2/4f; M2(5)

PRINTED WORKS CITED

In order to save space, the following abbreviations have been used:

Arch.	*Archaeologia*
Arch.	Archaeological
BIHR	*Bulletin of the institute of historical research*
BJRL	*Bulletin of the John Rylands library*
BP	Borthwick papers
BTC	Borthwick texts and calendars
CSMLT	Cambridge studies in medieval life and thought
CYS	Canterbury and York society
EcHR	*Economic history review*
EETS	Early English text society
EHR	*English historical review*
e.s.	extra series
HBS	Henry Bradshaw society
HJ	*Historical journal*
Hist./Hist.	*History*/Historical
J.	*Journal*
JEH	*Journal of ecclesiastical history*
LRS	Lincoln record society
Med.St.	*Mediaeval studies*
NH	*Northern history*
OHS	Oxford historical society
P&P	*Past and present*
PIMS	Pontifical institute of mediaeval studies
PMAA	Publications of the mediaeval academy of America
Proc.B.A.	*Proceedings of the British Academy*
Q.	*Quarterly*

R.   *Review*
RS   Record society
SCH   *Studies in church history*
Sel.   Selden society publications
Spec.   *Speculum*
SS   Surtees society publications
Trad.   *Traditio*
Trans.   *Transactions*
TRHS   *Transactions of the royal historical society*
YAJ   *Yorkshire archaeological journal*
YASRS   Yorkshire archaeological society record series

[1] Abbott, I. A., 'Taxation of personal property and clerical incomes, 1399 to 1402', *Spec.*, 17 (1942), pp. 471–98.

[2] Adams, R. H., *The parish clerks of London: a history of the Worshipful Company of Parish Clerks of London*, London and Chichester, 1971.

[3] Aers, D., *Chaucer, Langland, and the creative imagination*, London, 1980.

[4] Aers, D., *Chaucer*, Brighton, 1986.

[5] Allen, H. E., *Writings ascribed to Richard Rolle, hermit of Hampole, and material for his biography*, Modern Language Association of America, monograph ser. 3, New York and London, 1927.

[6] Allmand, C. T., 'Alan Kirketon, a clerical royal councillor in Normandy during the English occupation in the fifteenth century', *JEH*, 15 (1964), pp. 33–9.

[7] Allmand, C. T., 'Some effects of the last phase of the Hundred Years War upon the maintenance of clergy', *SCH*, 3 (1966), pp. 179–90.

[8] Archer, M., *The register of Bishop Repingdon, 1405–19*, LRS, 57–8, 74 (1963–82).

[9] Armstrong, C. A. J., *England, France, and Burgundy in the fifteenth century*, London, 1983.

[10] Arnold, M. S., et al., *Of the laws and customs of England: essays in honor of S. E. Thorne*, Chapel Hill, NC, 1981.

[11] Arnold, T., *Memorials of St Edmund's abbey*, iii, London, 1896.

[12] Arnould, E. J., 'Henry of Lancaster and his *Livre des seintes medecines*', *BJRL*, 21 (1937), pp. 352–86.

[13] Arnould, E. J., *Le livre des seintes medecines: the unpublished devotional treatise of Henry of Lancaster*, Anglo-Norman texts, 2, Oxford, 1940.

[14] Aston, M., 'The impeachment of bishop Despencer', *BIHR*, 38 (1965), pp. 127–48.

[15] Aston, M., *Lollards and reformers: images and literacy in late medieval England*, London, 1984.

[16] Aston, M., ' "Caim's castles": poverty, politics, and disendowment', in [221], pp. 45–81.

[17] Aston, M., 'Wyclif and the vernacular', in [424], pp. 281–330.

[18] Aston, T. H., 'Oxford's medieval alumni', *P&P*, no. 64 (February, 1977), pp. 3–40.

[19] Aston, T. H., et al., *Social relations and ideas: essays in honour of R. H. Hilton*, Cambridge, 1983.

[20] Aston, T. H., Duncan, G. D., and Evans, T. A. R., 'The medieval alumni of the university of Cambridge', *P&P*, no. 86 (February 1980), pp. 9–86.

[21] Atkinson, C. W., *Mystic and pilgrim: the book and the world of Margery Kempe*, Ithaca and London, 1983.

[22] Atthill, W., *Documents relating to the foundation and antiquities of the collegiate church of Middleham, in the county of York*, Camden soc., 1st ser. 38 (1837).

[23] Ault, W. O., *Private jurisdiction in England*, Yale hist. pubs., miscellany, 10, New Haven and London, 1923.

[24] Ault, W. O., 'Manor court and parish church in fifteenth-century England: a study of village by-laws', *Spec.*, 42 (1967), pp. 53–67.

[25] Axon, E., 'The family of Bothe (Booth) and the church in the 15th and 16th centuries', *Trans. Lancashire and Cheshire antiquarian soc.*, 53 (1938), pp. 32–82.

[26] Bacher, J. R., *The prosecution of heretics in medieval England*, Philadelphia, 1942.

[27] Baildon, W. P., *Notes on the religious and secular houses of Yorkshire*, YASRS, 17, 81 (1895–1931).

[28] Baildon, W. P., *Select cases in Chancery, A.D. 1364 to 1471*, Sel., 10 (1896).

[29] Bailey, F. A., *A selection from the Prescot court leet and other records, 1447–1600*, RS of Lancashire and Cheshire, 89 (1937).

[30] Bailey, F. A., *The churchwardens' accounts of Prescot, Lancashire, 1523–1607*, RS of Lancashire and Cheshire, 104 (1953).

[31] Baker, D., *Reform and reformation: England and the continent, c.1500–c.1750*, SCH, subsidia, 2, Oxford, 1979.

[32] Baker, E. P., 'St Oswald and his church at Zug', *Arch.*, 93 (1949), pp. 103–23.

[33] Baker, J. H., *The reports of Sir John Spelman*, Sel., 93–4 (1976–7).

[34] Baker, J. H., *The notebook of Sir John Port*, Sel., 102 (1986).

[35] Baldwin, J. F., *The king's council in England during the middle ages*, Oxford, 1913.

[36] Bannister, A. T., *The register of Thomas Spofford, bishop of Hereford (1422–1448)*, Hereford, 1917.

[37] Bannister, A. T., *Registrum Caroli Bothe, episcopi Herefordensis, A.D. MDXVI–MDXXXV*, CYS, 28 (1921).

[38] Bannister, A. T., 'Visitation returns of the diocese of Hereford in 1397', *EHR*, 44 (1929), pp. 279–89, 444–53; 45 (1930), pp. 92–101, 444–63.

[39] Barlow, F., *Durham jurisdictional peculiars*, Cambridge, 1950.

[40] Barlow, F., *The English church, 1066–1154*, London, 1979.

[41] Barnum, P. H., *Dives and pauper*, 1/i–ii, EETS, o.s. 275, 280 (1976–80).

[42] Barratt, A., 'Works of religious instruction', in [246], pp. 413–32.

[43] Barron, C. M., 'The parish fraternities of medieval London', in [44], pp. 13–37.

[44] Barron, C. M., and Harper-Bill, C., *The church in pre-Reformation society: essays in honour of F. R. H. du Boulay*, Woodbridge, 1985.

[45] Bartlett, J. N., 'The expansion and decline of York in the later middle ages', *EcHR*, 2nd ser., 12 (1959–60), pp. 17–33.

[46] Barton, J. L., 'Nullity of marriage and illegitimacy in the England of the middle ages', in [442], pp. 28–49.

[47] Bassett, S. R., 'Medieval Lichfield: a topographical review', *Trans. South Staffordshire arch. and hist. soc.*, 22 (1980–1), pp. 93–121.

[48] Bates, J. C., 'Edward Leche – a recidivist criminous "clerk" ', *Nottingham medieval studies*, 30 (1986), pp. 97–100.

[49] Bateson, M., *Records of the borough of Leicester*, ii, London, 1901.

[50] Bateson, M., *Borough customs*, Sel., 18, 21 (1904–6).

[51] Beardwood, A., *The trial of Walter Langton, bishop of Lichfield, 1307–1312*, in *Trans. American Philosophical soc.*, n.s. 54/iii, Philadelphia, Pa., 1964.

[52] Beckermann, J. S., 'The forty-shilling jurisdictional limit in medieval English personal actions', in [442], pp. 110–17.

[53] Beckwith, S., 'A very material mysticism: the medieval mysticism of Margery Kempe', in *Medieval literature: criticism, ideology, and history*, ed. D. Aers, Brighton, 1986, pp. 34–57.

[54] Bellamy, J. G., *Criminal law and society in late medieval and Tudor England*, Gloucester and New York, 1984.

[55] Bennett, J. A. W. (ed. D. Gray), *Middle English literature*, Oxford, 1986.

[56] Bennett, M. J., 'The Lancashire and Cheshire clergy, 1379', *Trans. hist. soc. Lancashire and Cheshire*, 124 (1972), pp. 1–30.

[57] Bennett, M. J., *Community, class, and careerism: Cheshire and Lancashire society in the age of Sir Gawain and the Green Knight*, CSMLT, 3rd ser., 18, Cambridge, 1983.

[58] Bennett, N. H., *The register of Richard Fleming, bishop of Lincoln, 1420–31*, i, CYS, 73 (1984).

[59] Betcherman, L. R., 'The making of bishops in the Lancastrian period', *Spec.*, 41 (1966), pp. 397–419.

[60] Bickley, W. B., *The register of the guild of Knowle in the county of Warwick, 1451–1535*, Walsall, 1894.

[61] Blair, J., 'Religious gilds as landowners in the thirteenth and fourteenth centuries: the example of Chesterfield', in *The medieval town in Britain*, ed. P. Riden, Cardiff papers in local hist., 1, Cardiff, 1980, pp. 35–49.

[62] Blair, J., 'Henry Lakenham, marbler of London, and a tomb contract of 1376', *Antiquaries j.*, 60 (1980), pp. 66–74.

[63] Blake, J. R., 'The medieval coal trade of north east England: some fourteenth-century evidence', *NH*, 2 (1967), pp. 1–26.

[64] Blake, N. F., *Middle English religious prose*, London, 1972.

[65] Blanchard, I. S. W., 'Derbyshire lead production, 1195–1505', *Derbyshire arch. j.*, 91 (1971), pp. 119–40.

[66] Blanchard, I. S. W., 'Commercial crisis and change: trade and the industrial economy of the north-east, 1509–1532', *NH*, 8 (1973), pp. 64–85.

[67] Blanchard, I. S. W., 'Seigneurial entrepreneurship: the bishops of Durham and the Weardale lead industry, 1406–1529', *Business hist.*, 15 (1973), pp. 97–111.

[68] Blench, J. W., *Preaching in England in the late fifteenth and sixteenth centuries: a study of English sermons, 1450–c.1600*, Oxford, 1964.

[69] Bliss, W. H., and Twemlow, J. A., *Calendar of entries in the papal registers relating to Great Britain and Ireland: papal letters, vol. IV: 1362–1404*, London, 1902.

[70] Bloch, M., *The royal touch: sacred monarchy and scrofula in England and France*, London, 1973.

[71] Blunt, C. E., 'Ecclesiastical coinage in England, Part II: after the Norman conquest', *Numismatic chronicle and j. royal numismatic soc.*, 7th ser., 1 (1961), pp. i–xviii.

[72] Blunt, J. H., *The myrroure of Oure Ladye*, EETS, e.s., 19 (1873).

[73] Bolton, B., *The medieval Reformation*, London, 1983.

[74] Bolton, J. H., *The medieval English economy, 1150–1500*, London, 1980.

[75] Bossy, J., 'The mass as a social institution', *P&P*, no. 100 (August, 1983), pp. 29–61.

[76] Bowker, M., *An episcopal court book for the diocese of Lincoln, 1514–1520*, LRS, 61 (1967).

[77] Bowker, M., *The secular clergy in the diocese of Lincoln, 1495–1520*, CSMLT, 2nd ser., 13, Cambridge, 1968.

[78] Bowker, M., 'Some archdeacons' court books and the Commons' Supplication against the Ordinaries of 1532', in [104] pp. 282–316.

[79] Bowker, M., 'Lincolnshire 1536: schism, heresy, or religious discontent?', *SCH*, 9 (1972), pp. 195–212.

[80] Bowker, M., *The Henrician Reformation: the diocese of Lincoln under John Longland, 1521–1547*, Cambridge, 1981.

[81] Boyle, L. E., 'Aspects of clerical education in fourteenth-century England', *Acta: proceedings of the SUNY regional conferences in medieval studies*, 4 (1977), pp. 19–32, reprinted in [85].

[82] Boyle, L. E., 'The *summa summarum* and some other English works of canon law', in [491], pp. 415–48, reprinted in [85].

[83] Boyle, L. E., 'The *Oculus sacerdotis* and some other works of William of Pagula', *TRHS*, 5th ser., 5 (1955), pp. 81–110, reprinted in [85].

[84] Boyle, L. E., *A survey of the Vatican archives and of its mediaeval holdings*, PIMS, subsidia mediaevalia, 1, Toronto, 1972.

[85] Boyle, L. E., *Pastoral care, clerical education, and canon law, 1200–1400*, London, 1981.

[86] Bray, J. R., 'Concepts of sainthood in fourteenth-century England', *Bulletin of the John Rylands University Library of Manchester*, 66 (1984), pp. 40–77.

[87] Brewer, J. S., *Letters and papers foreign and domestic of the reign of Henry VIII, vol. 4*, 3 vols, London, 1870–6.

[88] Brewer, J. S. (ed. R. H. Brodie), *Letters and papers foreign and domestic of the reign of Henry VIII, vol. 1*, 2nd edn, 3 vols, London, 1920.

[89] Brigden, S., 'Youth and the English Reformation', *P&P*, no.95 (May, 1982), pp. 37–67.

[90] Brigden, S., 'Religion and social obligation in early sixteenth-century London', *P&P*, no.103 (May, 1984), pp. 67–112.

[91] Brigden, S., 'Tithe controversy in Reformation London', *JEH*, 32 (1981), pp. 285–301.

[92] Brigden, S., 'Popular disturbances and the fall of Thomas Cromwell and the reformers, 1539–1540', *HJ*, 24 (1981), pp. 257–78.

[93] Brintell, R. H., *Growth and decline in Colchester, 1300–1525*, Cambridge, 1986.

[94] Brockwell, C. W., jr, *Bishop Reginald Pecock and the Lancastrian church: securing the foundations of cultural authority*, Texts and studies in religion, 25, Lewiston, NY, and Queenston, Ont., 1985.

[95] Brodie, D. M., *The Tree of Commonwealth: a treatise written by Edmund Dudley*, Cambridge, 1948.

[96] Brooke, C. N. L., 'The missionary at home: the church in the towns, 1000–1250', *SCH*, 6 (1970), pp. 59–83.

[97] Brooke, C. N. L., et al., *Church and government in the middle ages: essays presented to C. R. Cheney on his 70th birthday*, Cambridge, 1976.

[98] Brooks, P. N., *Reformation principle and practice: essays in honour of Arthur Geoffrey Dickens*, London, 1980.

[99] Brown, A. L., 'The king's councillors in fifteenth century England', *TRHS*, 5th ser., 19 (1969), pp. 95–118.

[100] Brown, S., *The medieval courts of the York Minster peculiar*, BP, 66, York, 1984.

[101] Brown, W., *The register of William Greenfield, lord archbishop of York, 1306–1315, part 1*, SS, 145 (1931).

[102] Brownbill, J., *The ledger book of Vale Royal abbey*, RS of Lancashire and Cheshire, 68 (1914).

[103] Buddensieg, R., *John Wiclif's polemical works in Latin*, 2 vols, London, 1883.

[104] Bullough, D. A., and Storey, R. L., *The study of medieval records: essays in honour of Kathleen Major*, Oxford, 1971.

[105] Burgess, C., ' "For the increase of divine service": chantries in the parish in late-medieval Bristol', *JEH*, 36 (1985), pp. 46–65.

[106] Burgess, C., ' "By quick and by dead": wills and pious provision in late medieval Bristol', *EHR*, 102 (1987), pp. 837–58.

[107] Burgess, C., 'A service for the dead: the form and function of the anniversary in late medieval Bristol', *Trans. Bristol and Gloucestershire arch. soc.*, 105 (1987), pp. 183–211.

[108] Burgo, Johannes de, *Pupilla oculi*, Paris, 1518.

[109] Burns, C., 'Papal gifts and honours for the earlier Tudors', *Miscellanea historiae pontificiae*, 50 (1983), pp. 173–97.

[110] Burson, M. C., ' ". . . for the sake of my soul": the activities of a medieval executor', *Archives*, 13 (1977–8), pp. 131–6.

[111] Butcher, A. F., 'Rent and the urban economy: Oxford and Canterbury in the later middle ages', *Southern hist.*, 1 (1979), pp. 11–43.

[112] Butler, L. H., 'Archbishop Melton, his neighbours, and his kinsmen, 1317–1340', *JEH*, 2 (1951), pp. 54–68.

[113] *Calendar of charter rolls, vol. V: 15 Edward III – 5 Henry V, A.D. 1341–1417*, London, 1916.

[114] *Calendar of inquisitions post mortem . . . vol. VIII: Edward III*, London, 1913.

[115] *Calendar of the patent rolls, Edward III, vol. VII: A.D. 1345–1348*, London, 1903.

[116] *Calendar of the patent rolls, Richard II, A.D. 1381–1385*, London, 1897.

[117] *Calendar of the patent rolls, Henry VI, vol. II, A.D. 1429–1436*, London, 1907.

[118] *Calendar of the patent rolls, Henry VI, vol. VI: A.D. 1452–1461*, London, 1910.

[119] *Calendar of the patent rolls . . . Henry VII, vol. II: A.D. 1494–1509*, London, 1916.

[120] Caley, J., and Hunter, J., *Valor ecclesiasticus*, 6 vols, London, 1810–34.

[121] Cam, H. M., *The hundred and the hundred rolls: an outline of local government in medieval England*, London, 1930.

[122] Cam, H. M., *Liberties and communities in medieval England: collected studies in local administration and topography*, Cambridge, 1944.

[123] Cam, H. M., *Law-finders and law-makers in medieval England: collected studies in legal and constitutional history*, London, 1962.

[124] Camp, A. J., *Wills and their whereabouts*, London, 1963.

[125] Canning, J. P., 'Ideas of the state in the thirteenth and fourteenth-century commentators on the Roman law', *TRHS*, 5th ser., 33 (1983), pp. 1–27.

[126] Capes, W. W., *Registrum Johannis Trefnant, episcopi Herefordensis, A.D. MCCCLXXXIX–MCCCCIV*, CYS, 20 (1916).

[127] Carpenter, C., 'The religion of the gentry of fifteenth-century England', in *England in the fifteenth century: proceedings of the 1986 Harlaxton symposium*, ed. D. Williams, Woodbridge, 1987, pp. 53–74.

[128] Caspary, G. E., 'The deposition of Richard II and the canon law', in [491], pp. 189–201.

[129] Catto, J. I., 'Wyclif and the cult of the Eucharist', in [882], pp. 269–86.

[130] Catto, J. I., 'Religious change under Henry V', in *Henry V: the practice of kingship*, ed. G. L. Harriss, Oxford, 1985, pp. 97–115.

[131] Cawley, A. C., 'Medieval drama and didacticism', in *The drama of medieval Europe: proceedings of the colloquium held at the University of Leeds, 10–13 September 1974*, Leeds medieval studies, 1, Leeds, 1975, pp. 3–12.

[132] Challis, C. E., 'The ecclesiastical mints of the early Tudor period: their organisation and possible date of closure', *NH*, 10 (1975), pp. 88–101.

[133] Chambers, D. S., 'Cardinal Wolsey and the papal tiara', *BIHR*, 38 (1965), pp. 20–30.

[134] Chambers, D. S., *Cardinal Bainbridge in the court of Rome, 1509 to 1514*, Oxford, 1965.

[135] Chambers, D. S., *Faculty office registers, 1534–1539: a calendar of the first two registers of the archbishop of Canterbury's faculty office*, Oxford, 1966.

[136] Cheetham, F., *medieval alabasters, with a catalogue of the collection in the Victoria and Albert Museum*, Oxford, 1984.

[137] Chené-Williams, A., 'Vivre sa mort et mourir sa vie: l'art de mourir au XVème siècle', in *Le sentiment de la mort au moyen âge: études présentées au cinquième colloque de l'Institut d'études médiévales de l'université de Montréal*, ed. C. Sutto, Montreal, Quebec, 1979, pp. 169–82.

[138] Cheney, C. R., *Episcopal visitation of monasteries in the thirteenth century*, Manchester, 1931.

[139] Cheney, C.R., *Pope Innocent III and England*, Päpste und Papsttum, 9, Stuttgart, 1976.

[140] Cheyette, F., 'Kings, courts, cures, and sinecures: the Statute of Provisors and the common law', *Trad.*, 19 (1963), pp. 295–349.

[141] Chiffoleau, J., 'Les testaments provençaux et contadins à la fin du moyen âge: richesse documentaire et problèmes d'exploitation', in *Sources of social history: private acts of the late middle ages*, ed. P. Brezzi and E. Lee, PIMS: papers in mediaeval studies, 5, Toronto, 1984, pp. 131–52.

[142] Chrimes, S. ·B., *English constitutional ideas in the fifteenth century*, Cambridge, 1936.

[143] *The church in a changing society*, Pubs. of the Swedish soc. of church hist., 30, Uppsala, 1978.

[144] Churchill, I. J., *Canterbury administration*, 2 vols, London, 1933.

[145] Clanchy, M. T., 'The franchise of return of writs', *TRHS*, 5th ser., 17 (1967), pp. 59–82.

[146] Clark, E., 'Debt litigation in a late medieval English vill', in [684], pp. 247–79.

[147] Clark, P., 'Reformation and radicalism in Kentish towns, c.1500–1553', in [589], pp. 107–27.

[148] Clark-Maxwell, W. G., 'Some letters of confraternity', *Arch.*, 75 (1924–5), pp. 19–60.

[149] Clark-Maxwell, W. G., 'Some further letters of confraternity', *Arch.*, 79 (1929), pp. 179–216.

[150] Clay, R. M., *The mediaeval hospitals of England*, London, 1909.

[151] Clay, R. M., *The hermits and anchorites of England*, London, 1914.

[152] Clebsch, W. A., 'John Colet and Reformation', *Anglican theological r.*, 37 (1955), pp. 167–77.

[153] Clebsch, W. A., *England's earliest Protestants, 1520–1535*, Yale studies in religion, 11, New Haven and London, 1964.

[154] Clough, C. H., *Profession, vocation, and culture in later medieval England: essays dedicated to the memory of A. R. Myers*, Liverpool, 1982.

[155] Coleman, D. C., *The economy of England, 1450–1750*, Oxford, 1977.

[156] Coleman, J., *English literature in history, 1350–1400: medieval readers and writers*, London, 1981.

[157] Colledge, E., and Evans, W. O., 'Piers Plowman', in [881], pp. 121–31.

[158] Collins, F., *Register of the freemen of the city of York from the city records, vol. I: 1272–1558*, SS, 86 (1897).

[159] Collins, M., 'A little known "Art of Dying" by a Brigittine of Syon: *A daily exercise and experience of death* by Richard Whytford', in [814], pp. 179–93.

[160] *Complete Peerage*, iv, London, 1916.

[161] Constable, G., 'The popularity of the twelfth century spiritual writers on the late middle ages', in *Renaissance studies in honor of Hans Baron*, ed. A. Molho and J. A. Tedeschi, Florence, 1971, pp. 5–28; reprinted in [163].

[162] Constable, G., 'Twelfth century spirituality and the late middle ages', in *Medieval and renaissance studies*, 5, ed. B. B. Hardison, jr, Chapel Hill, NC, 1971, pp. 27–60, reprinted in [163].

[163] Constable, G., *Religious life and thought (11th–12th centuries)*, London, 1979.

[164] Cooke, W. (ed. C. Wordsworth), *Ordinale Sarum, sive directorium sacerdotium*, HBS, 20, 22, London, 1901–2.

[165] Cooper, C. H., *Memorial of Margaret, Countess of Richmond and Derby*, Cambridge, 1874.

[166] Cooper, J. P., 'The social distribution of land and men in England, 1436–1700', *EcHR*, 2nd ser., 20 (1967), pp. 419–40.

[167] Cooper, T. N., 'The papacy and the diocese of Coventry and Lichfield, 1360–1385', *Archivum historiae pontificiae*, 25 (1987), pp. 73–103.

[168] Cordero Carrete, F. R., 'Embarque de peregrinos ingleses a Compostela en los siglos XIV y XV', *Cuadernos de estudios Gallegos*, 17 (1962), pp. 348–57.

[169] Cowan, I. B., and Easson, D. E., *Medieval religious houses, Scotland*, 2nd edn., London, 1976.

[170] Cox, J. C., *The sanctuaries and sanctuary seekers of mediaeval England*, London, 1911.

[171] Cox, J. C., *Churchwardens' accounts from the fourteenth century to the close of the seventeenth century*, London, 1913.

[172] Crook, D., 'The later eyres', *EHR*, 97 (1982), pp. 241–68.

[173] Cross, C., 'Churchmen and the royal supremacy', in [366], pp. 15–34.

[174] Cross, C., ' "Great reasoners in scripture": the activities of women lollards, 1380–1530', in *Medieval women*, ed. D. Baker, SCH, subsidia, 1, Oxford, 1978, pp. 359–80.

[175] Cross, C., 'Religious and social protest among lollards in early Tudor England', in [143], pp. 71–5.

[176] Cross, C., 'Priests into ministers: the establishment of Protestant practices in the city of York, 1530–1630', in [98], pp. 203–25.

[177] Cross, C., 'Wills as evidence of popular piety in the reformation period: Leeds and Hull, 1540–1640', in *The end of strife: death, reconciliation, and expressions of Christian spirituality*, ed. D. M. Loades, Edinburgh, 1984, pp. 44–51.

[178] Crossley, E. W., 'The testamentary documents of Yorkshire peculiars', in *Miscellanea*, ii, YASRS, 74 (1929), pp. 46–86.

[179] Crowder, C. M. D., 'Four English cases determined in the Roman courts during the Council of Constance, 1414–1418', *Annuarium historiae conciliorum*, 12 (1980), pp. 315–411.

[180] Crowley, D. A., 'The later history of frankpledge', *BIHR*, 48 (1975), pp. 1–15.

[181] Cruickshank, C. G., *The English occupation of Tournai, 1513–1519*, Oxford, 1971.

[182] Cuming, G. J., *A history of Anglican liturgy*, London, 1969.

[183] Dahmus, J., *William Courtenay, archbishop of Canterbury, 1381–1396*, University Park, Pa., and London, 1966.

[184] Dahmus, J. H., *The prosecution of John Wyclyf*, New Haven and London, 1952.

[185] Dahmus, J. W., 'Henry IV of England: an example of royal control of the church in the fifteenth century', *J. church and state*, 23 (1981), pp. 35–46.

[186] Daly, L. J., *The political thought of John Wyclif*, Chicago, 1962.

[187] Davies, C. S. L., 'The Pilgrimage of Grace reconsidered', *P&P*, no. 41 (December, 1968), pp. 54–76.

[188] Davies, C. S. L., 'Popular religion and the Pilgrimage of Grace', in *Order and disorder in early modern England*, ed. A. Fletcher and J. Stevenson, Cambridge, 1985, pp. 58–91.

[189] Davies, J. G., *The secular use of church buildings*, London, 1968.

[190] Davies, R. G., 'Richard II and the church in the years of "tyranny" ', *J. medieval hist.*, 1 (1975), pp. 329–62.

[191] Davies, R. G., 'Alexander Neville, archbishop of York, 1374–1388', *YAJ*, 47 (1975), pp. 87–101.

[192] Davies, R. G., 'After the execution of archbishop Scrope: Henry IV,

the papacy, and the English episcopate, 1405–8', *BJRL*, 59 (1976–7), pp. 40–74.

[193] Davies, R. G., 'Martin V and the English episcopate, with particular reference to his campaign for the repeal of the Statute of Provisors', *EHR*, 92 (1977), pp. 309–44.

[194] Davies, R. G., 'The episcopate', in [154], pp. 51–89.

[195] Davis, J. F., 'The trials of Thomas Bylney and the English Reformation', *HJ*, 24 (1981), pp. 775–90.

[196] Davis, J. F., *Heresy and reformation in the south east of England, 1520–1559*, Royal hist. soc., studies in hist. ser., 34, London, 1983.

[197] Davis, N., *Paston letters and papers of the fifteenth century*, 2 vols, Oxford, 1970.

[198] Davis, V., 'The rule of Saint Paul, the first hermit, in late medieval England', *SCH*, 22 (1985), pp. 203–14.

[199] Denise, M., '*The Orcherd of Syon*: an introduction', *Trad.*, 14 (1958), pp. 269–93.

[200] Denton, J. H., *English royal free chapels, 1100–1300: a constitutional study*, Manchester, 1970.

[201] Denton, J. H., 'Royal supremacy in ancient demesne churches', *JEH*, 22 (1971), pp. 289–302.

[202] Denton, J. H., *Robert Winchelsey and the crown, 1294–1313: a study in the defence of ecclesiastical liberty*, CSMLT, 3rd ser., 14, Cambridge, 1980.

[203] Denton, J. H., 'The clergy and Parliament in the thirteenth and fourteenth centuries', in *The English Parliament in the middle ages*, ed. R. G. Davies and J. H. Denton, Manchester, 1981, pp. 88–108.

[204] Denton, J. H., 'The making of the *Articuli cleri* of 1316', *EHR*, 101 (1986), pp. 564–95.

[205] Denton, J. H., and Dooley, J. P., *Representation of the lower clergy in Parliament, 1295–1340*, Royal hist. soc., studies in hist., 50, Woodbridge, 1987.

[206] *Depositions and other ecclesiastical proceedings from the courts of Durham, extending from 1311 to the reign of Elizabeth*, SS, 21 (1845).

[207] de Soer, G. B., 'The relationship of the Latin version of Ruysbroek's "Die geestelike Belocht" to "The chastising of God's children"', *Med.St.*, 21 (1959), pp. 129–46.

[208] D'Evelyn, C., and Foster, F. A., 'Saints' legends', in [755], pp. 410–57, 553–649.

[209] Dewindt, E. D., *The liber gersumarum of Ramsey abbey: a calendar and index of BL Harley MS 445*, PIMS, subsidia mediaevalia, 7, Toronto, 1976.

[210] Dickens, A. G., *The English Reformation*, London, 1964.

[211] Dickens, A. G., 'Secular and religious motivations in the Pilgrimage of Grace', *SCH*, 4 (1967), pp. 39–64.

[212] Dickens, A. G., *Lollards and Protestants in the diocese of York, 1509–1555*, 2nd edn, London, 1982.

[213] Dickens, A. G., 'The shape of anticlericalism and the English Reformation', in *Politics and society in Reformation Europe: essays for Sir Geoffrey Elton on his sixty fifth birthday*, ed. E. I. Kouri and T. Scott, Basingstoke and London, 1987, pp. 379–411.

[214] Dobson, R. B., 'The foundation of perpetual chantries by the citizens of medieval York', *SCH*, 4 (1967), pp. 21–38.

[215] Dobson, R. B., 'The election of John Ousthorp as abbot of Selby in 1436', *YAJ*, 42 (1967–70), pp. 31–40.

[216] Dobson, R. B., *Durham priory, 1400–1450*, CSMLT, 3rd ser., 6, Cambridge, 1973.

[217] Dobson, R. B., 'The residentiary canons of York in the fifteenth century', *JEH*, 30 (1979), pp. 145–74.

[218] Dobson, R. B., *York city chamberlains' account rolls, 1396–1500*, SS, 192 (1980).

[219] Dobson, R. B., 'Cathedral chapters and cathedral cities: York, Durham, and Carlisle in the fifteenth century', *NH*, 19 (1983), pp. 15–44.

[220] Dobson, R. B., 'The risings in York, Beverley, and Scarborough, 1380–1381', in [397], pp. 112–42.

[221] Dobson, R. B., *The church, politics, and patronage in the fifteenth century*, Gloucester, 1984.

[222] Dobson, R. B., 'Mendicant ideal and practice in late medieval York', in *Archaeological papers from York presented to M. W. Barley*, ed. P. V. Addyman and V. E. Black, York, 1984, pp. 109–22.

[223] Dodgson, C., 'English devotional woodcuts of the late fifteenth centrury, with special reference to those in the Bodleian library', *Walpole soc.*, 17 (1928–9), pp. 95–108.

[224] Doiron, M., 'The Middle English translation of 'Le Mirouer des simples ames' ', in *Dr. L. Reypens-Album: Oopstellen aangeboden aan Prof. Dr. L. Ruypens s.j. ter gelegenheid van zijn tachtigste verjeerdag op 25 februari 1964*, ed. A. Ampe, Studien an Tekstuitgraven van Ons Geestelijk Erf, 16, Antwerp, 1964, pp. 131–52.

[225] Donahue, C., jr., 'Roman canon law in the medieval English church: Stubbs vs. Maitland re-examined in the light of some records from the church courts', *Michigan law r.*, 72 (1974), pp. 647–716.

[226] Donaldson, R., 'Sponsors, patrons, and presentations to benefices in the gift of the prior of Durham in the late middle ages', *Arch. Aeliana*, 4th ser., 38 (1960), pp. 169–77.

[227] Dowling, M., 'Anne Boleyn and reform', *JEH*, 35 (1984), pp. 30–46.

[228] Dowling, M., *Humanism in the age of Henry VIII*, London, 1986.

[229] Doyle, A. I., 'Reflections on some MSS of Nicholas Love's "Myrrour of the Blessed Lyf of Jesu Christ" ', *Leeds studies in English*, n.s. 14 (1983), pp. 82–93.

[230] Drew, C., *Early parochial organisation in England: the origins of the office of churchwarden*, St Anthony's Hall pubs., 7, York, 1954.

[231] du Boulay, F. R. H., 'Charitable subsidies granted to the archbishop of Canterbury, 1300–1489', *BIHR*, 23 (1950), pp. 147–64.

[232] du Boulay, F. R. H., 'The quarrel between the Carmelite friars and the secular clergy of London, 1464–1468', *JEH*, 6 (1955), pp. 156–74.

[233] du Boulay, F. R. H., *Registrum Thome Bourgchier, Cantuarensis archiepiscopi, A.D. 1454–1486*, CYS, 54 (1957).

[234] du Boulay, F. R. H., 'Who were farming the English demesnes at the end of the middle ages?', *EcHR*, 2nd ser., 17 (1964–5), pp. 443–55.

[235] du Boulay, F. R. H., 'The fifteenth century', in [497], pp. 197–242.

[236] du Boulay, F. R. H., *The lordship of Canterbury: an essay on medieval society*, London, 1966.

[237] du Boulay, F. R. H., and Barron, C. M., *The reign of Richard II: essays in honour of May McIsack*, London, 1971.

[238] Dunn, E. C., 'Popular devotion in the vernacular drama of medieval England', *Medievalia et humanistica*, n.s. 4 (1973), pp. 55–68.

[239] Dunning, R. W., 'Rural deans in England in the fifteenth century', *BIHR*, 40 (1967), pp. 207–13.

[240] Dunning, R. W., 'Patronage and promotion in the late medieval church', in *Patronage, the crown, and the provinces in later medieval England*, ed. R. A. Griffiths, Gloucester, 1981, pp. 167–80.

[241] Dunstan, G. R., *The register of Edmund Lacy, bishop of Exeter, 1420–1455: registrum commune*, CYS, 60–3, 66 (1963–72).

[242] Dyer, C., 'A redistribution of incomes in fifteenth-century England', in *Peasants, knights, and heretics: studies in medieval English social history*, ed. R. H. Hilton, Cambridge, 1976, pp. 192–215.

[243] Dyer, C., *Lords and peasants in a changing society: the estates of the bishopric of Worcester, 680–1540*, Cambridge, 1980.

[244] Dyer, C., 'English diet in the later middle ages', in [19], pp. 191–216.

[245] 'The East Riding clergy in 1525–6', *YAJ*, 24 (1917), pp. 62–80.

[246] Edwards, A. S. G., *Middle English prose: a critical guide to major authors and genres*, New Brunswick, NJ, 1984.

[247] Edwards, K., *The English secular cathedrals in the middle ages*, 2nd edn, Manchester, 1967.

[248] Eeles, F. C., 'On a fifteenth-century York missal formerly used at Broughton-in-Amunderness', in *Chetham miscellany, vol. VI*, Remains hist. and literary connected with the palatine counties of Lancaster and Chester, 94 (1935).

[249] Eisenstein, E. L., *The printing press as an agent of change: communications and cultural transformations in early modern Europe*, 2 vols, Cambridge, 1979.

[250] Elton, G. R., *Star chamber stories*, London, 1958.

[251] Elton, G. R., *Reform and Reformation: England, 1509–1558*, London, 1977.

[252] Elton, G. R., 'England and the continent in the sixteenth century', in [31], pp. 1–16.

[253] Elton, G. R., 'Persecution and toleration in the English Reformation', *SCH*, 21 (1984), pp. 163–87.

[254] Elvey, E. M., *The courts of the archdeaconry of Buckingham, 1483–1523*, Buckinghamshire RS, 19 (1975).

[255] Emden, A. B., *A biographical register of the University of Oxford to 1500*, 3 vols, Oxford, 1957–9.

[256] Emden, A. B., *A survey of Dominicans in England, based on the ordination lists in episcopal registers (1268 to 1538)*, Rome, 1967.

[257] Erbe, T., *Mirk's Festial: a collection of homilies by Johannes Mirkus (John Mirk)*, EETS, e.s., 96, London, 1905.

[258] Eubel, C. (ed. L. Schmitz-Kallenberg), *Hierarchia catholica medii et recentioris aevi*, iii, 2nd edn, Münster, 1923.

[259] Evans, G. R., 'The borrowed meaning: grammar, logic, and the problem of theological language in twelfth century schools', *Downside r.*, 96 (1978), pp. 165–75.

[260] Evennett, H. O., 'The new orders', in *The new Cambridge modern history, iii: The Reformation, 1520–1559*, ed. G. R. Elton, Cambridge, 1958, pp. 275–300.

[261] Faith, R., 'Debate: seigneurial control of women's marriage, II', *P&P*, no.99 (May 1983), pp. 133–48.

[262] Faith, R., 'Berkshire: fourteenth and fifteenth centuries', in [362], pp. 106–77.

[263] 'The Fallow papers', *YAJ*, 21 (1911), pp. 225–53.

[264] Farmer, D. H., 'The meditations of the monk of Farne', in *Analecta monastica: textes et études sur la vie des moines au moyen âge*, iv (*Studia Anselmiana*, 41), Rome, 1957, pp. 141–245.

[265] Farmer, D. H., *The monk of Farne: the meditations of a fourteenth century monk*, London, 1961.

[266] Farmer, D. H., 'The monk of Farne', in [881], pp. 145–57.

[267] Farr, W., *John Wyclif as legal reformer*, Studies in the hist. of Christian thought, 10, Leiden, 1974.

[268] Febvre, L., and Martin, H.-J., *The coming of the book: the impact of printing, 1450–1800*, London, 1976.

[269] Feltoe, C. L., and Minns, E. H., *Vetus liber archidiaconi Eliensis*, Cambridge antiquarian soc. pubs.: octavo ser., 48, Cambridge, 1917.

[270] Ferguson, J., *English diplomacy, 1422–1461*, Oxford, 1972.

[271] Finberg, H. P. R., *Tavistock abbey: a study in the social and economic history of Devon*, 2nd edn, New York, 1969.

[272] Fines, J., 'Heresy trials in the diocese of Coventry and Lichfield, 1511–12', *JEH*, 14 (1963), pp. 160–74.

[273] Finucane, R. C., *Miracles and pilgrims: popular beliefs in medieval England*, London, 1977.

[274] Firth, C. B., 'Benefit of clergy in the time of Edward IV', *EHR*, 32 (1917), pp. 175–91.

[275] Fisher, J. C. D., *Christian initiation: baptism in the medieval west, a study in the disintegration of the primitive rite of initiation*, Alcuin club collections, 47, London, 1965.

[276] Fisher, J. H., Richardson, M., and Fisher, J. L., *An anthology of Chancery English*, Knoxville, Tenn., 1984.

[277] Fleming, P. W., 'Charity, faith, and the gentry of Kent, 1422–1529', in [666], pp. 36–57.

[278] Fletcher, A. J., 'Unnoticed sermons from John Mirk's *Festial*', *Spec.*, 55 (1980), pp. 514–22.

[279] Foss, D. B., ' "Overmuch blaming of the clergy's wealth": Pecock's exculpation of ecclesiastical endowment', *SCH*, 24 (1987), pp. 155–60.

[280] Foster, J. E., 'The connection of the church of Chesterton with the abbey of Vercelli', *Proc. Cambridge antiquarian soc.*, 13 (n.s. 7) (1908–9), pp. 185–212.

[281] Fowler, J. T., *Extracts from the account rolls of the abbey of Durham, from the original MSS*, ii, SS, 100 (1898).

[282] Fowler, J. T., *The coucher book of Selby*, YASRS, 10, 13 (1891–3).

[283] Fowler, R. C., and Jenkins, C., *Registrum Simonis de Sudburia, diocesis Londoniensis, A.D. 1362–1375*, CYS, 34, 38 (1927–38).

[284] Fraser, C. M., 'Edward I and the regalian franchise of Durham', *Spec.*, 31 (1956), pp. 329–42.

[285] Frere, W. H., *The use of Sarum*, 2 vols, Cambridge, 1895–1901.

[286] Fryde, E. B., *et al.*, *Handbook of British chronology*, Royal hist. soc., guides and handbooks, 2, 3rd edn, London, 1986.

[287] Fuller, A. P., *Calendar of entries in the papal registers relating to Great Britain and Ireland, papal letters, vol. XVI: Alexander VI (1492–1503), Lateran registers, part one: 1492–1498*, Dublin, 1986.

[288] Furnivall, F. J., *The fifty earliest English wills in the court of probate, London*, EETS, o.s. 78 (1882).

[289] Furnivall, F. J., and Cowper, J. M., *Four supplications, 1529–1553 A.D.*, EETS, e.s. 13 (1871).

[290] Gabel, L. C., *Benefit of clergy in England in the later middle ages*, Smith College studies in hist., 14, Northampton, Mass., 1928.

[291] Gardner, A., *Alabaster tombs of the pre-Reformation period in England*, Cambridge, 1940.

[292] Garrett-Goodyear, H., 'The Tudor revival of Quo warranto and local contributions to state building', in [10], pp. 229–95.

[293] Gasquet, F. A., *Collectanea Anglo-Premonstratensia*, Camden soc., 3rd ser., 6, 10, 12 (1904–6).

[294] Genet, J.-P., *Four English political tracts of the later middle ages*, Camden soc., 4th ser., 18 (1977).

[295] Genet, J.-P., 'Ecclesiastics and political theory in late medieval England: the end of a monopoly', in [221], pp. 23–44.

[296] Gerould, G. H., *Chaucerian essays*, Princeton, NJ, 1952.

[297] Gibson, J. S. W., *Wills and where to find them*, Chichester, 1974.

[298] Gibson, M., *Lafranc of Bec*, Oxford, 1978.

[299] Gilchrist, J., *The church and economic activity in the middle ages*, London and New York, 1969.

[300] Given-Wilson, C., *The English nobility in the later middle ages: the fourteenth century political community*, London and New York, 1987.

[301] Glynne, S. R. (ed. J. A. Atkinson), *Notes on the churches of Cheshire*, Remains hist. and literary connected with the palatine counties of Lancaster and Chester, n.s. 32 (1894).

[302] Godfrey, C. J., 'Pluralists in the province of Canterbury in 1366', *JEH*, 11 (1960), pp. 23–40.

[303] Godfrey, C. J., *The church in Anglo-Saxon England*, Cambridge, 1962.

[304] Gooder, A., and Gooder, E., 'Coventry before 1355: unity or division?', *Midland hist.*, 6 (1981), pp. 1–38.

[305] Goodman, A., 'Henry VII and Christian renewal', *SCH*, 17 (1981), pp. 115–25.

[306] Goring, J. J., 'The general proscription of 1522', *EHR*, 86 (1971), pp. 681–705.

[307] Goring, J. J., 'The riot at Bayham abbey, June, 1525', *Sussex arch. collections*, 116 (1978), pp. 1–10.

[308] Gottfried, R. J., *Bury St Edmunds and the urban crisis: 1290–1539*, Princeton, NJ, 1982.

[309] Graham, R., *English ecclesiastical studies: being some essays in research in medieval history*, London, 1929.

[310] Graves, E. B., 'Circumspecte Agatis', *EHR*, 43 (1928), pp. 1–20.

[311] Graves, E. B., 'The legal significance of the Statute of Praemunire of 1353', in *Anniversary essays in medieval history by students of Charles Homer Haskins*, ed. C. H. Taylor, Boston and New York, 1929, pp. 57–80.

[312] Gray, J. W., 'Canon law in England: some reflections on the Stubbs–Maitland controversy', *SCH*, 3 (1966), pp. 48–68.

[313] Greatrex, J. G., *The register of the common seal of the priory of St Swithun, Winchester, 1345–1497*, Hampshire RS, 2 (1978).

[314] Greatrex, J. G., 'Some statistics of religious motivation', *SCH*, 15 (1978), pp. 179–86.

[315] Green, A. S. (Mrs J. R. Green), *Town life of the fifteenth century*, 2 vols, London, 1894.

[316] Green, V., *The commonwealth of Lincoln college, 1427–1977*, Oxford, 1979.

[317] Greenslade, S. L., 'English versions of the Bible, 1525–1611', in *The Cambridge history of the Bible [vol. III]: the world from the Reformation to the present day*, ed. S. L. Greenslade, Cambridge, 1963, pp. 141–74.

[318] Grierson, P., 'The origins of the English sovereign and the symbolism of the closed crown', *British numismatic j.*, 33 (1964), pp. 118–34.

[319] Grosjean, P., 'De S. Iohanne Bridlingtoniensis collectanea', *Analecta Bollandiana*, 53 (1935), pp. 101–29.

[320] Grosjean, P., *Henrici VI Angliae regis miracula postuma, ex codice Musei Britannici Regio. 13. C. VIII*, Subsidia hagiographica, 22, Brussels, 1935.

[321] Gurney, N. K. M., and Clay, C., *Fasti parochiales, vol. IV: Being notes on the advowsons and pre-Reformation incumbents of the parishes in the deanery of Craven*, YASRS, 133 (1971).

[322] Guy, J. A., *The cardinal's court: the impact of Thomas Wolsey in Star Chamber*, Hassocks, 1977.

[323] Guy, J. A., 'Henry VIII and the *Praemunire* manoeuvres of 1530–1531', *EHR*, 97 (1982), pp. 481–503.

[324] Guy, J. A., *Christopher St German on chancery and statute*, Sel., supplementary ser., 6 (1985).

[325] Gwynn, A. O., *The English Austin friars in the time of Wyclif*, Oxford, 1940.

[326] Haas, S. W., 'Martin Luther's "Divine Right" kingship and the royal supremacy: two tracts for the 1531 Parliament and Convocation of the clergy', *JEH*, 31 (1980), pp. 317–25.

[327] Haddan, A. W., and Stubbs, W., *Councils and ecclesiastical documents relating to Great Britain and Ireland*, 3 vols in 4, Oxford, 1869–71.

[328] Hahn, T., and Kaeuper, R. W., 'Text and context: Chaucer's *Friar's Tale*', *Studies in the age of Chaucer*, 5 (1983), pp. 67–101.

[329] Haigh, C., 'From monopoly to minority: Catholicism in early modern England', in *TRHS*, 31 (1981), pp. 129–47.

[330] Haigh, C., *The English Reformation revised*, Cambridge, 1987.

[331] Haigh, C., 'Introduction', in [330], pp. 1–17.

[332] Haigh, C., 'The recent historiography of the English Reformation', in [330], pp. 19–33.

[333] Haigh, C., 'Anticlericalism and the English Reformation', in [330], pp. 56–74.

[334] Haigh, C., 'The continuity of Catholicism in the English Reformation', in [330], pp. 176–208.

[335] Haines, R. M., ' "Wilde wittes and wilfulness": John Swetstock's attack on those "poyswunmongeres", the Lollards', *SCH*, 8 (1972), pp. 143–53.

[336] Haines, R. M., 'A confraternity document of St Mary Magdalene's hospital, Liskeard', *BIHR*, 45 (1972), pp. 128–35.

[337] Haines, R. M., 'Reginald Pecock: a tolerant man in an age of intolerance', *SCH*, 21 (1984), pp. 125–37.

[338] Hair, P. E. H., 'Mobility of parochial clergy in Hereford diocese, c.1400', *Trans. Woolhope naturalists' field club*, 43 (1979–81), pp. 164–80.

[339] Halcrow, E. M., 'The decline of demesne farming on the estates of Durham cathedral priory', *EcHR*, 2nd ser., 7 (1954–5), pp. 345–56.

[340] Halcrow, E. M., 'The social position and influence of the priors of Durham, as illustrated by their correspondence', *Arch. Aeliana*, 4th ser., 33 (1955), pp. 70–86.

[341] Hall, B., 'The early rise and gradual decline of Lutheranism in England (1520–1600)', in [31], pp. 103–31.

[342] Hamilton, B., *Religion in the medieval west*, London, 1986.

[343] Hanley, H. A., and Chalkin, C. W., 'The Kent lay subsidy of 1334/5', in *Documents illustrative of medieval Kentish society*, ed. F. R. H. du Boulay, Kent records, 18 (1964), pp. 58–172.

[344] Hare, J. N., 'The demesne lessees of fifteenth-century Wiltshire', *Agricultural hist. r.*, 29 (1981), pp. 1–15.

[345] Hare, J. B., 'The monks as landlords: the leasing of the demesnes in southern England', in [44], pp. 82–94.

[346] Haren, M. J., *Calendar of entries in the papal registers relating to Great Britain and Ireland: papal letters, vol. XV: Innocent VIII, Lateran registers, 1484–1492*, Dublin, 1978.

[347] Harper-Bill, C., 'Bishop Richard Hill and the court of Canterbury, 1494–96', *Guildhall studies in London hist.*, 3 (1977–8), pp. 1–12.

[348] Harper-Bill, C., 'Archbishop John Morton and the province of Canterbury, 1486–1500', *JEH*, 29 (1978), pp. 1–21.

[349] Harper-Bill, C., 'Cistercian visitation in the late middle ages: the case of Hailes abbey', *BIHR*, 53 (1980), pp. 103–14.

[350] Harper-Bill, C., 'Monastic apostasy in late medieval England', *JEH*, 32 (1981), pp. 1–18.

[351] Harrison, F. Ll., *Music in medieval Britain*, London, 1958.

[352] Harriss, G. L., 'Cardinal Beaufort – patriot or usurer?', *TRHS*, 5th ser., 20 (1970), pp. 129–48.

[353] Hartridge, R. A. R., *A history of vicarages in the middle ages*, Cambridge, 1930.

[354] Hartung, A. E., *A manual of the writings in Middle English, 1050–1500*, vii, New Haven, Conn., 1986.

[355] Harvey, B., 'The leasing of the abbot of Westminster's demesnes in the later middle ages', *EcHR*, 2nd ser., 22 (1969), pp. 17–27.

[356] Harvey, B., 'Work and *festa ferienda* in medieval England', *JEH*, 23 (1972), pp. 289–308.

[357] Harvey, B., *Westminster abbey and its estates in the middle ages*, Oxford, 1977.

[358] Harvey, J., *Mediaeval craftsmen*, London and Sydney, 1975.

[359] Harvey, J. H., 'Richard II and York', in [237], pp. 202–17.

[360] Harvey, M., *Solutions to the schism: a study of some English attitudes, 1378 to 1409*, Kirchengeschichtliche Quellen und Studien, 12, St Ottilien, 1983.

[361] Harvey, M., 'The benefice as property: an aspect of Anglo-papal relations during the pontificate of Martin V, 1417–1431', *SCH*, 24 (1987), pp. 161–73.

[362] Harvey, P. D. A., *The peasant land market in medieval England*, Oxford, 1984.

[363] Haslop, G. S., 'A Selby kithcener's roll of the early fifteenth century', *YAJ*, 48 (1976), pp. 119–33.

[364] Hatcher, J., *Plague, population, and the English economy, 1348–1530*, London, 1977.

[365] Heal, F., *Of prelates and princes: a study of the economic and social position of the Tudor episcopate*, Cambridge, 1980.

[366] Heal, F., and O'Day, R., *Church and society in England, Henry VIII to James I*, London, 1977.

[367] Heath, P., *Medieval clerical accounts*, St Anthony's hall pubs., 26, York, 1964.

[368] Heath, P., 'North Sea fishing in the fifteenth century: the Scarborough fleet', *NH*, 3 (1968), pp. 53–69.

[369] Heath, P., *The English parish clergy on the eve of the Reformation*, London and Toronto, 1969.

[370] Heath, P., 'The medieval archdeaconry and Tudor bishopric of Chester', *JEH*, 20 (1969), pp. 243–52.

[371] Heath, P., *Bishop Geoffrey Blythe's visitations, c.1515–1525*, Collections for a hist. of Staffordshire, 4th ser., 7 (1973).

[372] Heath, P., 'Urban piety in the later middle ages: the evidence of Hull wills', in [221], pp. 209–34.

[373] Heath, P., *Church and realm, 1272–1461: conflict and collaboration in an age of crisis*, London, 1988.

[374] Heffernan, T. J., 'Sermon literature', in [246], pp. 177–207.

[375] Heffernan, T. J., *The popular literature of medieval England*, Tennessee studies in literature, 28, Knoxville, Tenn., 1985.

[376] Helmholz, R. H., 'Canonical defamation in medieval England', *American j. of legal hist.*, 15 (1971), pp. 255–68.

[377] Helmholz, R. H., *Marriage litigation in medieval England*, Cambridge, 1974.

[378] Helmholz, R. H., *Select cases on defamation to 1600*, Sel., 101 (1985).

[379] Helmholz, R. H., *Canon law and the law of England: historical essays*, London and Ronceverte, 1987.

[380] Hemmant, M., *Select cases in the Exchequer Chamber before all the justices of England*, Sel., 51, 64 (1933–48).

[381] Henry, A., *The pilgrimage of the lyfe of the manhode*, EETS, o.s. 288, 292 (1985–8).

[382] Heymann, F. G., *George of Bohemia, king of heretics*, Princeton, NJ, 1965.

[383] Hicks, M. A., 'The Beauchamp trust, 1439–87', *BIHR*, 54 (1981), pp. 135–49.

[384] Hicks, M. A., 'Chantries, obits, and almshouses: the Hungerford foundations, 1325–1478', in [44], pp. 123–42.

[385] Hicks, M. A., 'The piety of Margaret, Lady Hungerford (d.1478)', *JEH*, 38 (1987), pp. 19–38.

[386] Highfield, J. R. L., 'The promotion of William of Wykeham to the see of Winchester', *JEH*, 4 (1953), pp. 37–54.

[387] Highfield, J. R. L., 'The English hierarchy in the reign of Edward III', *TRHS*, 5th ser., 6 (1966), pp. 115–39.

[388] Hill, G., *The English dioceses: a history of their limits from the earliest times to the present day*, London, 1910.

[389] Hill, R. M. T., 'A Berkshire letter book', *Berkshire arch. j.*, 41 (1937), pp. 9–32.

[390] Hill, R. M. T., *The labourer in the vineyard: the visitations of archbishop Melton in the archdeaconry of Richmond*, BP, 35, York, 1968.

[391] Hill, R. M. T., ' "A chaunterie for soules": London chantries in the reign of Richard II', in [237], pp. 242–55.

[392] Hilton, R. H., *The decline of serfdom in medieval England*, London, 1969.

[393] Hilton, R. H., *Bondmen made free: medieval peasant movements and the English rising of 1381*, London, 1973.

[394] Hilton, R. H., *The English peasantry in the later middle ages*, Oxford, 1975.

[395] Hilton, R. H., *A medieval society: the West Midlands at the end of the thirteenth century*, 2nd edn, Cambridge, 1983.

[396] Hilton, R. H., *Class conflict and the crisis of feudalism: essays in medieval social history*, London, 1985.

[397] Hilton, R. H., and Aston, T. H., *The English rising of 1381*, Cambridge, 1984.

[398] Hingeston-Randolph, F. C., *The Register of Edmund Stafford (A.D. 1395–1419): an index and abstract of its contents*, London and Exeter, 1886.

[399] Hingeston-Randolph, F. C., *The register of Thomas de Brantyngham, bishop of Exeter (A.D. 1370–1394)*, 2 vols, London and Exeter, 1901–6.

[400] Hirsh, J. S., 'Prayer and meditation in late medieval England: MS Bodley 789', *Medium Ævum*, 48 (1979), pp. 55–66.

[401] *Historical manuscripts commission: report on manuscripts in various collections*, iv, London, 1907.

[402] *Historical manuscripts commission: report on the manuscripts of Lord Middleton preserved at Wollaton Hall, Nottingham*, London, 1911.

[403] *A history of the County of Northumberland, issued under the direction of the Northumberland County History Committee*, iii, Newcastle-upon-Tyne and London, 1896.

[404] Hobbs, J. L., 'A Shrewsbury subsidy roll, 1445–46', *Trans. Shropshire arch. soc.*, 53 (1949–50), pp. 68–75.

[405] Hodgson, P., '*Ignorantia sacerdotum*: a fifteenth century discourse on the Lambeth constitutions', *R. of English studies*, 24 (1948), pp. 1–11.

[406] Hodgson, P., '*The Orcherd of Syon* and the English mystical tradition', *Proc.B.A.*, 50 (1964), pp. 229–49.

[407] Hodgson, P., and Leigey, G. M., *The Orcherd of Syon*, EETS, o.s. 258 (1966).

[408] Hogg, J., 'Mount Grace Charterhouse and late medieval English spirituality', in *Collectanea Cartusiana, III (Analecta Cartusiana*, 82:3), Salzburg, 1983, pp. 1–43.

[409] Holmes, G. A., 'Cardinal Beaufort and the crusade against the Hussites', *EHR*, 88 (1973), pp. 721–50.

[410] Holt, B., 'Two obedientiary rolls of Selby abbey', in *Miscellanea, vol. VI*, ed. C. E. Whiting, YASRS, 118 (1953), pp. 30–52.

[411] Horn, J. M., _The register of Robert Hallum, bishop of Salisbury, 1407–17_, CYS, 72 (1982).

[412] Horrox, R., and Hammond, P. W., _British Museum, Harleian manuscript 433_, 4 vols, Upminster and London, 1979–83.

[413] Horstmann, C., _Nova legenda Anglie, as collected by John of Tynemouth, John Capgrave, and others, and first printed, with new lives, by Wynkyn de Worde, a.d. MDxui_, 2 vols, Oxford, 1901.

[414] Hosker, P., 'The Stanleys of Lathom and ecclesiastical patronage in the north-west of England during the fifteenth century', _NH_, 18 (1982), pp. 212–29.

[415] Houlbrooke, R., _Church courts and the people during the English Reformation, 1520–1570_, Oxford, 1979.

[416] Housley, N., 'The Bishop of Norwich's crusade', _Hist. Today_, May 1983, pp. 15–20.

[417] Housley, N., _The Avignon papacy and the crusades, 1305–1378_, Oxford, 1986.

[418] Hudson, A., _Selections from English Wycliffite writings_, Cambridge, 1978.

[419] Hudson, A., 'Wycliffite prose', in [246], pp. 249–70.

[420] Hudson, A., _Lollards and their books_, London and Ronceverte, 1986.

[421] Hudson, A., 'Wycliffism in Oxford, 1381–1411', in [466], pp. 67–84.

[422] Hudson, A., 'Wyclif and the English language', in [466], pp. 85–103.

[423] Hudson, A., 'A Wycliffite scholar in the early fifteenth century', in [882], pp. 301–15.

[424] Hudson, A., and Wilks, M., _From Ockham to Wyclif_, SCH, subsidia 5, Oxford, 1987.

[425] Hughes, P., _The Reformation in England_, 3 vols, London, 1950–4.

[426] Hume, A., 'English books printed abroad, 1525–1535: an annotated bibliography', in _The complete works of St Thomas More_, 8/ii, ed. L. A. Schuster, _et al._, New Haven and London, 1973, pp. 1065–91.

[427] Humphery-Smith, C. R., _The Phillimore atlas and index of parish registers_, Colchester, 1984.

[428] Hunnisett, R. F., _Bedfordshire coroners' rolls_, Bedfordshire hist. RS, 41 (1961).

[429] Hunnisett, R. F., _The medieval coroner_, Cambridge, 1961.

[430] Hunt, E. W., _Dean Colet and his theology_, London, 1956.

[431] Hutton, R., 'The local impact of the Tudor Reformations', in [330], pp. 114–38.

[432] Hyams, P., 'The proof of villein status in the common law', _EHR_, 89 (1974), pp. 721–49.

[433] _Inquisitions and assessments relating to feudal aids with other analogous documents . . . A.D. 1284–1431_, vi, London, 1920.

[434] Ives, E. W., 'Crime, sanctuary, and royal authority under Henry VIII: the exemplary sufferings of the Savage family', in [10], pp. 296–320.

[435] Ives, E. W., _The common lawyers of pre-Reformation England_, Cambridge, 1983.

[436] Jack, R. I., 'The ecclesiastical patronage exercised by a baronial family in the late middle ages', _J. religious hist._, 3 (1964–5), pp. 275–95.

[437] Jackson, W. A., 'Three printed English indulgences at Harvard', _Harvard library bulletin_, 7 (1953), pp. 229–31.

[438] Jacob, E. F., _The register of Henry Chichele, archbishop of Canterbury, 1414–43_, CYS, 42, 45–7 (1938–47).

[439] Jacob, E. F., *Essays in the conciliar epoch*, 3rd edn, Manchester, 1963.

[440] Jacob, E. F., *Essays in later medieval history*, Manchester, 1968.

[441] James, M., 'Ritual, drama, and social body in the late medieval English town', *P&P*, no. 98 (February, 1983), pp. 3–29.

[442] Jenkins, D., *Legal history studies, 1972: papers presented to the legal history conference, Aberystwyth, 18–21 July, 1972*, Cardiff, 1975.

[443] Jewell, H., 'English bishops as educational benefactors in the late fifteenth century', in [221], pp. 148–67.

[444] Johnson, C., *Registrum Hamonis Hethe, diocesis Roffensis, A.D. 1319–1352*, CYS, 48–9 (1948).

[445] Johnston, A. F., 'Parish entertainments in Berkshire', in [684], pp. 335–8.

[446] Joliffe, P. S., *A check-list of middle English prose writings of spiritual guidance*, PIMS, subsidia mediaevalia, 2, Toronto, 1974.

[447] Jones, A. C., 'Bedfordshire: fifteenth century', in [362], pp. 178–251.

[448] Jones, B. R., *The royal policy of Richard II: absolutism in the later middle ages*, Oxford, 1968.

[449] Jones, W. R., 'Bishops, politics, and the two laws: the *gravamina* of the English clergy, 1237–1399', *Spec.*, 41 (1964), pp. 209–45.

[450] Jones, W.R., 'The two laws in England: the later middle ages', *J. church and state*, 11 (1969), pp. 111–31.

[451] Jones, W. R., 'Patronage and administration: the king's free chapels in medieval England', *J. British studies*, 9 (1969–70), pp. 1–23.

[452] Jones, W. R., 'Relations of the two jurisdictions: conflict and cooperation in England during the thirteenth and fourteenth centuries', *Studies in medieval and Renaissance hist.*, 7 (1970), pp. 77–210.

[453] Jones, W. R., 'The English church and royal propaganda during the Hundred Years War', *J. British studies*, 19 (1979–80), pp. 18–30.

[454] Jordan, R. M., *Chaucer and the shape of creation: the aesthetic possibilities of inorganic structure*, Cambridge, Mass., 1967.

[455] Jordan, W. K., *Philanthropy in England, 1480–1660: a study of the changing patterns of English social aspirations*, London, 1959.

[456] Kaminsky, H., *A history of the Hussite revolution*, Berkeley and Los Angeles, 1967.

[457] Kaufman, P. I., 'Henry VII and sanctuary', *Church hist.*, 53 (1984), pp. 465–76.

[458] Kedar, B. Z., 'Canon law and local practice: the case of mendicant preaching in late medieval England', *Bulletin of medieval canon law*, 2 (1972), pp. 17–32.

[459] Keen, M., 'Chaucer's knight, the English aristocracy, and the crusade', in *English court culture in the later middle ages*, ed. V. J. Scattergood and J. W. Sherborne, London, 1983, pp. 45–61.

[460] Keen, M., 'The influence of Wyclif', in [466], pp. 127–45.

[461] Keene, D., with Rumble, A. R., *Survey of medieval Winchester*, Winchester studies, 2, 2 vols, Oxford, 1985.

[462] Kelly, C., 'The noble steward and late-feudal lordship', *Huntingdon library q.*, 49 (1985–6), pp. 133–48.

[463] Kemp, E. W., *Canonization and authority in the western church*, London, 1948.

[464] Kemp, E. W., *Counsel and consent: aspects of government of the church as exemplified*

in the history of the English provincial synods, London, 1961.

[465] Kenny, A., *Wyclif*, Oxford, 1985.

[466] Kenny, A., *Wyclif in his times*, Oxford, 1986.

[467] Ker, N. R., *Medieval libraries of Great Britain: a list of surviving books*, Royal hist. soc., guides and handbooks, 3, 2nd edn, London, 1964.

[468] Kershaw, I., *Bolton priory: the economy of a northern monastery, 1286–1325*, Oxford, 1973.

[469] Kettle, A. J., 'City and close: Lichfield in the century before the Reformation', in [44], pp. 158–69.

[470] Kibre, P., *Scholarly privileges in the middle ages*, PMAA, 72, London, 1961.

[471] Kimball, E. G., *Rolls of the Warwickshire and Coventry sessions of the peace, 1377–1397*, Dugdale soc. pubs., 16 (1939).

[472] King, E. J., *The grand priory of the order of the hospital of St John of Jerusalem in England: a short history*, London, 1924.

[473] King, P. M., 'The English cadaver tomb in the late fifteenth century: some indicators of a Lancastrian connection', in [814], pp. 45–57.

[474] *The King's Book, or a necessary doctrine and erudition for any Christian man, 1543*, Church hist. soc. pubs., n.s. 10, London, 1932.

[475] Kingsford, C. L., *The Stonor letters and papers, 1290–1483*, Camden soc., 3rd ser., 29–30 (1919).

[476] Kirby, J. L., 'Two tax accounts of the diocese of Carlisle, 1379–80', *Trans. Cumberland and Westmoreland antiquarian and arch. soc.*, n.s. 52 (1953), pp. 70–84.

[477] Kirby, J. L., 'Clerical poll-taxes in the diocese of Salisbury, 1377–81', in *Collectanea*, ed. N. J. Williams, Wiltshire arch. and natural hist. soc., records branch, 12 (1956), pp. 157–67.

[478] Kirby, J. L., 'Councils and councillors of Henry IV, 1399–1413', *TRHS*, 5th ser., 14 (1964), pp. 35–65.

[479] Kitching, C., 'The prerogative court of Canterbury from Warham to Whitgift', in [613], pp. 191–214.

[480] Kitching, C., 'Church and chapelry in sixteenth-century England', *SCH*, 16 (1979), pp. 279–90.

[481] Knecht, R. J., 'The episcopate and the Wars of the Roses', *University of Birmingham hist. j.*, 6 (1957–8), pp. 108–31.

[482] Knecht, R. J., *Francis I*, Cambridge, 1982.

[483] Knight, S., 'Chaucer's religious Canterbury Tales', in *Medieval English religious and ethical literature: essays in honour of G. H. Russell*, ed. G. Kratzmann and J. Simpson, Cambridge, 1986, pp. 156–66.

[484] Knowles, M. D., *The religious orders in England*, 3 vols, Cambridge, 1948–61.

[485] Knowles, M. D., 'The censured opinions of Uthred of Boldon', *Proc.B.A.*, 37 (1951), pp. 305–42.

[486] Knowles, M. D., *The English mystical tradition*, London, 1961.

[487] Knowles, M. D., *The monastic order in England: a history of its development from the time of St Dunstan to the Fourth Lateran Council, 940–1216*, 2nd edn, Cambridge, 1966.

[488] Knowles, M. D., and Hadcock, R. H., *Medieval religious houses: England and Wales*, 2nd edn, London, 1971.

[489] Kreider, A., *English chantries: the road to dissolution*, Harvard hist. studies, 97, Cambridge, Mass., and London, 1979.

[490] Kristensson, G., *John Mirk's instructions for parish priests, edited from MS Cotton Claudius A II and six other manuscripts, with introduction, notes, and glossary*, Lund studies in English, 49, Lund, 1974.

[491] Kuttner, S., and Ryan, J. J., *Proceedings of the 2nd international congress of medieval canon law, Boston College, 12–16 August 1963*, Monumenta iuris canonici, series C, subsidia 1, Vatican City, 1965.

[492] Lagorio, V. M., and Bradley, R., *The fourteenth century English mystics: a comprehensive annotated bibliography*, New York and London, 1981.

[493] Lander, J. R., 'Council, administration, and councillors, 1461 to 1485', *BIHR*, 32 (1959), pp. 138–80.

[494] Lander, S., 'Church courts and the Reformation in the diocese of Chichester, 1500–58', in [613], pp. 215–37 (also in [330]).

[495] *La premiere part les ans du roy Henry le VI*, London, 1679.

[496] Lapsley, G. T., *The county palatine of Durham: a study in constitutional history*, Harvard hist. studies, 8, Cambridge, Mass., 1924.

[497] Lawrance, N. A. H., *Fasti parochiales, vol. V: Deanery of Buckrose*, YASRS, 143 (1985).

[498] Lawrence, C. H., *The English church and the papacy in the middle ages*, London, 1965.

[499] Lea, H. C., *A history of auricular confession and indulgences in the Latin church*, 3 vols, Philadelphia, Pa., 1896.

[500] Leach, A. F., *Memorials of Beverley Minster: the chapter act book of the collegiate church of S. John of Beverley, A.D. 1286–1347*, SS, 98, 108 (1898–1903).

[501] Leach, A. F., *Early Yorkshire schools*, YASRS, 27, 33 (1899–1903).

[502] Leadam, I. S., *Select cases in the court of requests, A.D. 1497–1569*, Sel., 12 (1898).

[503] Leff, G., *Heresy in the later middle ages*, 2 vols, Manchester, 1967.

[504] Legg, J. W., *Tracts on the mass*, HBS, 27 (1904).

[505] Legg, L. G. W., *English coronation records*, Westminster, 1901.

[506] Legge, M. D., *Anglo-Norman letters and petitions from All Souls MS 182*, Anglo-Norman texts, 3, Oxford, 1941.

[507] Lehmberg, S. E., *The Reformation Parliament*, Cambridge, 1970.

[508] Lehmberg, S. E., *The later Parliaments of Henry VIII, 1536–1547*, Cambridge, 1977.

[509] Le Neve, J., *Fasti ecclesiae Anglicanae, 1300–1540*, revised edn, 12 vols, London, 1960–7.

[510] *Les reports del cases en ley que furent argues en le temps de tres haut et puissant prince le roys Henry le IV et Henry le V*, London, 1678.

[511] *Les reports des cases en les ans des roys Edward V, Richard iij, Henrie vij, et Henrie viij*, London, 1679.

[512] *Les reports des cases en ley que furent argues en temps du roy Edward le quart*, London, 1680.

[513] Lewis, N. B., 'The last medieval summons of the English feudal levy, 13 June 1385', *EHR*, 73 (1958), pp. 1–26.

[514] Little, A. G., 'Introduction of the Observant Friars into England', *Proc.B.A.*, 10 (1921–3), pp. 455–71.

[515] Little, A. G., 'Personal tithes', *EHR*, 60 (1945), pp. 67–88.

[516] Little, A. G., 'Franciscan letters of confraternity', *Bodleian library record*, 5 (1954–6), pp. 13–25.

[517] Little, A. G. (ed. E. Stone), 'Corrodies at the Carmelite friary of Lynn', *JEH*, 9 (1958), pp. 8–29.

[518] Littlehales, H., *English fragments from Latin medieval service-books*, EETS, e.s., 90 (1903).

[519] Littlehales, H., *The medieval records of a London city church (St Mary at Hill)*, *A.D. 1420–1559*, EETS, o.s. 125, 128 (1905).

[520] Loades, D. M., 'The press under the early Tudors: a study in censorship and sedition', *Trans. Cambridge bibliographical soc.*, 4 (1964–8), pp. 29–50.

[521] Loades, D. M., *The Oxford martyrs*, London, 1970.

[522] Loades, D. M., 'The royal supremacy: a note in discussion', in [589], pp. 128–9.

[523] Loades, D. M., 'The origins of English Protestant nationalism', *SCH*, 18 (1982), pp. 297–307.

[524] Lobel, M. D., 'The ecclesiastical banleuca in England', in *Oxford essays in medieval history presented to H. E. Salter*, Oxford, 1934, pp. 122–40.

[525] Lobel, M. D., *The borough of Bury St Edmund's: a study in the government and development of a monastic town*, Oxford, 1935.

[526] Logan, F. D., *Excommunication and the secular arm in medieval England: a study in legal procedure from the thirteenth to the sixteenth century*, PIMS, studies and texts, 15, Toronto, 1968.

[527] Logan, F. D., 'The Henrician canons', *BIHR*, 47 (1974), pp. 99–103.

[528] Lomas, T., 'South-east Durham: late fourteenth and fifteenth centuries', in [362], pp. 252–327.

[529] Longley, K. M., *Ecclesiastical cause papers at York: dean and chapter's court, 1350–1843*, BTC, 6, York, 1980.

[530] Lovat, R., 'The *Imitation of Christ* in late medieval England', *TRHS*, 5th ser., 18 (1968), pp. 97–121.

[531] Lovat, R., 'A collector of apocryphal anecdotes: John Blacman revisited', in [666], pp. 172–97.

[532] Lucas, P. J., *John Capgrave's Abbreuiacion of Cronicles*, EETS, o.s. 285 (1983).

[533] Lunt, W. E., 'The collection of clerical subsidies granted to the king by the English clergy', in *The English government at work, 1327–1336*, ed. W. A. Morris and J. R. Strayer, ii, PMAA, 48, Cambridge, Mass., 1947, pp. 227–80.

[534] Lunt, W. E., *Financial relations of the papacy with England, 1327–1534*, PMAA, 74, Cambridge, Mass., 1962.

[535] Lunt, W. E., and Graves, E. B., *Accounts rendered by papal collectors in England, 1317–1378*, Memoirs of the American philosophical soc., 70, Philadelphia, 1968.

[536] Lupton, J. H., *The life of John Colet, D.D., Dean of St Paul's and founder of St Paul's school, with an appendix of some of his English writings*, London, 1887.

[537] Lusardi, J. P., 'The career of Robert Barnes', in *The complete works of St Thomas More*, 8/iii, ed. L.A. Schuster *et al.*, New Haven and London, 1973, pp. 1365–415.

[538] Luxton, I., 'The Lichfield court-book: a postscript', *BIHR*, 44 (1971), pp. 120–5.

[539] Lyndwood, William, *Provinciale, seu constitutiones Angliae* . . ., Oxford, 1679.

[540] Lytle, G. F., 'Patronage patterns and Oxford colleges, c.1300–c.1530', in *The university in society*, ed. L. Stone, 2 vols, Oxford, 1975, i, pp. 111–49.

[541] Lytle, G. F., 'Religion and the lay patron in Reformation England', in *Patronage in the Renaissance*, ed. G. F. Lytle and S. Orgel, Princeton, NJ, 1981, pp. 65–114.

[542] Lytle, G. F., *Reform and authority in the medieval and Reformation church*, Washington, DC, 1981.

[543] Lytle, G. F., 'John Wyclif, Martin Luther, and Edward Powell: heresy and the Oxford theology faculty at the beginning of the Reformation', in [424], pp. 465–79.

[544] McConica, J. K., *English humanists and reformation politics under Henry VIII and Edward VI*, Oxford, 1965.

[545] MacCulloch, D., *Suffolk and the Tudors: politics and religion in an English county, 1500–1600*, Oxford, 1986.

[546] McDonnell, E. W., *The beguines and beghards in medieval culture, with special emphasis on the Belgian scene*, New Brunswick, NJ, 1954.

[547] McFarlane, K. B., *Wycliffe and English non-conformity*, Harmondsworth, 1972.

[548] McFarlane, K. B., *Lancastrian kings and Lollard knights*, Oxford, 1972.

[549] McGrath, A. E., *The intellectual origins of the European Reformation*, Oxford, 1987.

[550] McGrath, P., 'Elizabethan Catholicism: a reconsideration', *JEH*, 35 (1984), pp. 414–28.

[551] McHardy, A. K., 'Bishop Buckingham and the Lollards of Lincoln diocese', *SCH*, 9 (1972), pp. 131–45.

[552] McHardy, A. K., 'The representation of the English lower clergy in Parliament during the later fourteenth century', *SCH*, 10 (1973), pp. 97–107.

[553] McHardy, A. K., *The Church in London, 1375–1392*, London RS, 13 (1977).

[554] McHardy, A. K., 'Liturgy and propaganda in the diocese of Lincoln during the Hundred Years War', *SCH*, 18 (1982), pp. 215–27.

[555] McHardy, A. K., 'The English clergy and the Hundred Years War', *SCH*, 20 (1983), pp. 171–8.

[556] McHardy, A. K., 'Clerical taxation in fifteenth-century England: the clergy as agents of the crown', in [221], pp. 168–92.

[557] McHardy, A. K., 'The dissemination of Wyclif's ideas', in [424], pp. 361–8.

[558] McHardy, A. K., 'Ecclesiastics and economics: poor priests, prosperous laymen, and proud prelates in the reign of Richard II', *SCH*, 24 (1987), pp. 129–37.

[559] McIntosh, M. J., *Autonomy and community: the royal manor of Havering, 1200–1500*, CSMLT, 4th ser., 5, Cambridge, 1986.

[560] McKenna, J. W., 'The coronation oil of the Yorkist kings', *EHR*, 82 (1967), pp. 102–4.

[561] McKenna, J. W., 'Popular canonization as political propaganda: the case of Archbishop Scrope', *Spec.*, 45 (1970), pp. 608–23.

[562] McKenna, J. W., 'Piety and propaganda: the cult of King Henry VI', in *Chaucer and middle English studies in honor of Rossell Hope Robbins*, ed. B. Rowland, London, 1971, pp. 72–88.

[563] McKisack, M., *The fourteenth century, 1307–1399*, Oxford, 1959.

[564] McNab, B., 'Obligations of the church in English society: military arrays of the clergy, 1369–1418', in *Order and innovation in the middle ages: essays in honor of J. R. Strayer*, ed. W. C. Jordan, B. McNab, and T. F. Ruiz, Princeton, NJ, 1976, pp. 293–314, 516–22.

[565] McNiven, P., 'The betrayal of archbishop Scrope', *BJRL*, 54 (1971–2), pp. 173–213.

[566] McNiven, P., *Heresy and politics in the reign of Henry IV: the burning of John Badby*, Woodbridge, 1987.

[567] McNulty, J., 'William of Rymyngton, prior of Sallay abbey, chancellor of Oxford, 1372–3', *YAJ*, 30 (1931), pp. 231–47.

[568] McNulty, J., 'Thomas Sotheron v. Cockersand abbey: a suit as to the advowson of Mitton church, 1369–70', in *Chetham miscellanies*, n.s. 7, Remains hist. and literary connected with the palatine counties of Lancaster and Chester, n.s. 100 (1937).

[569] McRee, B. R., 'Religious gilds and regulation of behaviour in late medieval towns', in [713], pp. 108–22.

[570] Madox, T., *Formulare Anglicanum*, London, 1702.

[571] Major, K., 'The finances of the dean and chapter of Lincoln from the twelfth to the fourteenth centuries: a preliminary survey', *JEH*, 5 (1954), pp. 149–67.

[572] Malden, A. R., *The canonization of St Osmund, from the manuscript record in the muniment room of Salisbury cathedral*, Wiltshire RS, 2 (1901).

[573] Mann, J., *Chaucer and medieval estates satire: the literature of social classes and the general prologue to the Canterbury Tales*, Cambridge, 1973.

[574] Marchant, R. M., *The church under the law: justice, administration and discipline in the diocese of York, 1560–1640*, Cambridge, 1969.

[575] Marrett, W. P., *A calendar of the register of Henry Wakefeld, bishop of Worcester, 1375–95*, Worcestershire Hist. Soc., n.s., 7 (1972).

[576] Martin, C. A., 'Middle English manuals of religious instruction', in *So meny people, longage, and tonges: philological essays in Scots and mediaeval English presented to Angus McIntosh*, ed. M. Bernstein and M. L. Samuels, Edinburgh, 1981, pp. 283–98.

[577] Marzac, N., *Richard Rolle de Hampole, 1300–1349: vie et œuvres, et édition critique, traduite, et commentée du Tractatus super apocalypsim*, Paris, 1968.

[578] Meech, S. B., 'John Drury and his English writings', *Spec.*, 9 (1934), pp. 70–83.

[579] Meech, S. B., and Allen, H. E., *The book of Margery Kempe*, EETS, o.s. 212 (1940).

[580] Melton, William de, *Sermo exhortatorius cancellarii Eboracensis hii qui ad sacros ordines petunt promoveri*, London, c.1510.

[581] Mertes, R. G. K. A., 'The household as a religious community', in [713], pp. 123–39.

[582] Minnich, N. H., 'Incipiat iudicium a domo domini: the Fifth Lateran Council and the reform of Rome', in [542], pp. 127–42.

[583] Mitchell, R. C., and Morse, L. W., *Chronicle of English judges, chancellors, attornies general and solicitors general*, Oswego, NY, 1937.

[584] Mitchell, R. J., 'English law students at Bologna in the fifteenth century', *EHR*, 51 (1936), pp. 270–87.

[585] Mitchell, R. J., 'English students at Ferrara in the XV. century', *Italian studies*, 1 (1937–8), pp. 75–82.

[586] Mitchell, W. T., *Epistolae academicae, 1509–1596*, OHS, n.s. 26 (1980).

[587] Mitchiner, M., *Medieval pilgrim and secular badges*, London, 1986.

[588] Mollat, G., *The popes at Avignon, 1305–1378*, London, 1963.

[589] Mommsen, W. J., Alter, P., and Scribner, R. W., *Stadtburgertum und Adel in die Reformation: Studien zur Sozialgeschichte der Reformation in England und Deutschland/ The urban class, the nobility, and the Reformation: studies in the social history of the Reformation in England and Germany*, Pubs. of the German hist. Institute, London, 5, Stuttgart, 1979.

[590] Moore, R. I., *The origins of European dissent*, London, 1963.

[591] Moorman, J. R. H., *Church life in England in the thirteenth century*, Cambridge, 1945.

[592] Moorman, J. R. H., *The grey friars in Cambridge*, Cambridge, 1952.

[593] Moorman, J. R. H., *A history of the Franciscan order from its origins to the year 1517*, Oxford, 1968.

[594] Moran, J. A. H., 'Clerical recruitment in the diocese of York, 1340–1530: data and commentary', *JEH*, 34 (1983), pp. 19–54.

[595] Moran, J. A. H., *The growth of English schooling, 1340–1548: learning, literacy, and laicization in pre-Reformation York diocese*, Princeton, NJ, 1985.

[596] Moran, J. A. H., 'A "common-profit" library in fifteenth-century England and other books for chaplains', *Manuscripta*, 28 (1984), pp. 17–25.

[597] Morgan, M., 'The suppression of the alien priories', *Hist.*, 26 (1941–2), pp. 204–12.

[598] Morgan, M., *The English lands of the abbey of Bec*, Oxford, 1946.

[599] Morgan, P. E., 'The effect of the pilgrim cult of St Thomas Cantilupe on Hereford cathedral', in *St Thomas Cantilupe, bishop of Hereford, essays in his honour*, ed. M. Jancey, Hereford, 1982, pp. 145–52.

[600] Muir, L., 'Translations and paraphrases of the Bible, and commentaries', in [755], pp. 350–409, 535–52.

[601] Mullett, M. A., *Popular culture and popular protest in late medieval and early modern Europe*, London, 1987.

[602] Needham, P., *The printer and the pardoner: an unrecorded indulgence printed by William Caxton for the hospital of St Mary Rounceval, Charing Cross*, Washington, DC, 1986.

[603] Neilson, N., *Year books of Edward IV: 10 Edward IV and 49 Henry VI, A.D. 1470*, Sel., 47 (1930).

[604] Neville, C. J., 'Gaol delivery in the border counties: some preliminary observations', *NH*, 19 (1983), pp. 45–60.

[605] Nolan, B., 'Nicholas Love', in [246], pp. 83–95.

[606] Nolcken, C. von, 'Julian of Norwich', in [246], pp. 97–108.

[607] Nolcken, C. von, 'Another kind of saint: a Lollard perception of John Wyclif', in [424], pp. 429–43.

[608] Northeast, P., *Boxford churchwardens' accounts, 1530–1561*, Suffolk RS, 23 (1981).

[609] Oakley, F., *The western church in the later middle ages*, Ithaca and London, 1979.

[610] Oates, J. C. T., 'Richard Pynson and the Holy Blood of Hayles', *The Library*, 5th ser., 13 (1958), pp. 269–77.

[611] O'Connor, M. C., *The art of dying well: the development of the Ars Moriendi*, New York, 1942.

[612] O'Day, R., *The debate on the English Reformation*, London, 1986.

[613] O'Day, R., and Heal, F., *Continuity and change: personnel and administration of the church in England, 1500–1642*, Leicester, 1976.

[614] Offer, C. J., *The bishop's register*, London, 1929.

[615] Ogle, A., *The tragedy of the Lollards' tower*, Oxford, 1949.

[616] Olsen, P. A., *The Canterbury Tales and the good society*, Princeton, NJ, 1986.

[617] [Ordnance Survey] *Map of Monastic Britain*, 2nd edn, London, 1954.

[618] Orme, N., *English schools in the middle ages*, London, 1973.

[619] Orme, N., 'The medieval clergy of Exeter cathedral, I: the vicars and annuellars', *Report and trans. of the Devonshire Association for the advancement of science, literature, and art*, 113 (1981), pp. 79–102.

[620] Orme, N., 'Two saint-bishops of Exeter: James Berkeley and Edmund Lacy', *Analecta Bollandiana*, 104 (1986), pp. 403–18.

[621] Orme, N., 'A medieval almshouse for the clergy: Clyst Gabriel hospital near Exeter', *JEH*, 39 (1988), pp. 1–15.

[622] Ormrod, W. M., 'An experiment in taxation: the English parish subsidy of 1371', *Spec.*, 63 (1988), pp. 58–82.

[623] Outhwaite, R. B., *Inflation in Tudor and early Stuart England*, 2nd edn, London, 1982.

[624] Owen, D. M., *Church and society in medieval Lincolnshire*, History of Lincoln-shire, 5, Lincoln, 1971.

[625] Owen, D. M., 'Bacon and eggs: bishop Buckingham and superstition in Lincolnshire', *SCH*, 8 (1972), pp. 139–42.

[626] Owen, D. M., *John Lydford's book*, Devon and Cornwall RS, 19 (1974).

[627] Owen, D. M., 'The practising canonist: John Lydford's notebook', in *Proceedings of the 4th international congress of medieval canon law, Toronto, 21–25 August 1972*, ed. S. Kuttner, Monumenta iuris canonici, ser. C, subsidia, 5, Vatican City, 1976, pp. 45–51.

[628] Owen, D. M., 'William Asshebourne's book: King's Lynn corporation archives 10/2', in *Norfolk RS*, 48 (1981).

[629] Owen, D. M., *Medieval records in print: bishops' registers*, Hist. association: helps for students of hist., 89, London, 1982.

[630] Owen, D. M., *The making of King's Lynn: a documentary survey*, Records of social and economic hist., n.s. 9, London, 1985.

[631] Owst, G. R., *Preaching in medieval England: an introduction to sermon manuscripts of the period c.1350–1450*, Cambridge, 1926.

[632] Owst, G. R., *Literature and pulpit in medieval England: a neglected chapter in the history of English letters and of the English people*, 2nd edn, Oxford, 1961.

[633] Page, C., 'The rhymed office for St Thomas of Lancaster: poetry, politics and liturgy in fourteenth-century England', *Leeds studies in English*, n.s. 14 (1983), pp. 134–51.

[634] Palliser, D. M., 'The union of parishes at York, 1547–1586', *YAJ*, 46 (1974), pp. 87–102.

[635] Pallister, D. M., 'Popular reactions to the Reformation during the years of uncertainty, 1530–1590', in [366], pp. 35–56.

[636] Pantin, W. A., 'The monk-solitary of Farne: a fourteenth century English mystic', *EHR*, 59 (1944), pp. 162–86.

[637] Pantin, W. A., *The English church in the fourteenth century*, Cambridge, 1955.

[638] Pantin, W. A., 'The fourteenth century', in [498], pp. 159–94.

[639] Pantin, W. A., 'Instructions for a devout and literate layman', in *Medieval learning and literature: essays presented to Richard William Hunt*, ed. J. J. G. Alexander and M. T. Gibson, Oxford, 1976, pp. 398–422.

[640] Parks, G. B., *The English traveler to Italy, first volume: the middle ages, to 1525*, Rome, 1954.

[641] Parmiter, G. de C., *The King's great matter: a study of Anglo-papal relations, 1527–1534*, London, 1967.

[642] Paro, G., *The right of papal legation*, Catholic university of America: studies in canon law, 211, Washington, DC, 1947.

[643] Parry, J. H., *Registrum Johannis de Trillek, episcopi Herefordensis, A.D. MCCCXLIV–MCCCLXI*, CYS, 8 (1912).

[644] Parry, J. H., *Registrum Roberti Mascall, episcopi Herefordensis, A.D. MCCCCIV–MCCCCXVI*, CYS, 21 (1917).

[645] Patterson, L. W., 'The "Parson's Tale" and the quitting of the "Canterbury Tales"', *Trad.*, 34 (1978), pp. 331–80.

[646] Peacock, E., 'Extracts from Lincoln episcopal visitations of the fifteenth, sixteenth, and seventeenth centuries', *Arch.*, 49 (1885), pp. 249–69.

[647] Pearsall, D., *Piers Plowman by William Langland: an edition of the C-text*, London, 1978.

[648] Pearsall, D., *The Canterbury Tales*, London, 1985.

[649] Pecock, Reginald (ed. C. Babington), *The repressor of overmuch blaming of the clergy*, 2 vols, London, 1860.

[650] Peers, C., and Taylor, L. E., 'On some recent discoveries in Westminster abbey', *Arch.*, 93 (1949), pp. 151–63.

[651] Percy, T., *The regulation and establishment of the household of Henry Algernon Percy, the fifth earl of Northumberland*, 2nd edn, London, 1905.

[652] Perroy, E., 'Gras profits et rançons pendant la guerre de cent ans: l'affaire du comte de Denia', in *Mélanges d'histoire du moyen âge dédiés à la mémoire de Louis Halphen*, Paris, 1931, pp. 573–80.

[653] Perroy, E., *L'Angleterre et le grand schisme d'occident*, Paris, 1933.

[654] Peters, E., *The shadow king: rex inutilis in medieval law and literature, 751–1327*, New Haven and London, 1970.

[655] Pfaff, R. W., *New liturgical feasts in later medieval England*, Oxford, 1970.

[656] Pfaff, R. W., 'The English devotion of St Gregory's Trental', *Spec.*, 49 (1974), pp. 75–90.

[657] Phillips, J., *The reformation of images: destruction of art in England, 1535–1660*, Berkeley, Los Angeles, and London, 1973.

[658] Phythian-Adams, C., *Desolation of a city: Coventry and the urban crisis of the late middle ages*, Cambridge, 1979.

[659] Pike, L. O., *Year book of the reign of King Edward the Third, year XX (second part)*, London, 1911.

[660] Plucknett, T. F. T., *Year books of Richard II: 13 Richard II, 1389–90*, London, 1929.

[661] Plucknett, T. F. T., and Barton, J. L., *St German's 'Doctor and Student'*, Sel. 91 (1974).

[662] Plumb, D., 'The social and economic spread of rural Lollardy: a reappraisal', *SCH*, 23 (1986), pp. 111–29.

[663] Pollard, A. F., *Wolsey*, London, 1929.

[664] Pollard, A. F., 'Tudor gleanings, I – the "de facto" Act of Henry VII', *BIHR*, 7 (1929–30), pp. 1–12.

[665] Pollard, A. W., and Redgrave, G. R. (rev. W. A. Jackson, F. S. Ferguson, and K. F. Pantzer), *A short-title catalogue of books printed in England, Scotland, and Ireland, and of English books printed abroad (1475–1640)*, 2nd edn, 2 vols, London, 1976–86.

[666] Pollard, T., *Property and politics: essays in later medieval English history*, Gloucester, 1984.

[667] Porter, H. C., 'The gloomy dean and the law: John Colet, 1466–1519', in *Essays in modern English church history in memory of Norman Sykes*, ed. G. V. Bennett and J. D. Walsh, London, 1966, pp. 18–43.

[668] Postan, M. M., 'Credit in medieval trade', in *Essays in economic history*, i, ed. E. M. Carus-Wilson, London, 1954, pp. 61–87.

[669] Pound, J., 'Clerical poverty in early sixteenth-century England: some East Anglian evidence', *JEH*, 37 (1986), pp. 389–96.

[670] Powell, K. G., 'The social background of the Reformation in Gloucestershire', *Trans. Bristol and Gloucestershire arch. soc.*, 92 (1973), pp. 96–120.

[671] Power, E., *Medieval English nunneries, c.1275 to 1535*, Cambridge, 1922.

[672] Pronger, W. A., 'Thomas Gascoigne', *EHR*, 53 (1938), pp. 606–26; 54 (1939), pp. 20–37.

[673] Pugh, R. B., 'Some mediaeval moneylenders', *Spec.*, 43 (1968), pp. 274–89.

[674] Pugh, R. B., *Imprisonment in medieval England*, Cambridge, 1968.

[675] Pugh, R. B., 'Early registers of English outlaws', *American j. of legal hist.*, 27 (1983), pp. 315–29.

[676] Purvis, J. S., *A mediaeval act book, with some account of ecclesiastical jurisdiction at York*, York, n.d. [1943].

[677] Purvis, J. S., 'Four antiquarian notes', *YAJ*, 42 (1967–70), pp. 52–5.

[678] Putnam, B. H., 'Maximum wage-laws for priests after the Black Death, 1348–1381', *American hist. r.*, 21 (1915–16), pp. 12–32.

[679] Putnam, B. H., 'The transformation of the keepers of the peace into the justices of the peace, 1327–80', *TRHS*, 4th ser., 12 (1929), pp. 19–48.

[680] Putnam, B. H., *Proceedings before the justices of the peace in the fourteenth and fifteenth centuries: Edward III to Richard III*, London, 1938.

[681] Raban, S., *Mortmain legislation and the English church, 1279–1500*, CSMLT, 3rd ser., 17, Cambridge, 1982.

[682] Rackham, H., *Early statutes of Christ's College, Cambridge, with the statutes of the prior foundation of God's house*, Cambridge, 1927.

[683] Radford, U. M., 'The wax images found in Exeter cathedral', *Antiquaries j.*, 29 (1949), pp. 164–8.

[684] Raftis, J. A., *Pathways to medieval peasants*, PIMS, papers in mediaeval studies, 2, Toronto, 1981.

[685] Raine, J., *Saint Cuthbert; with an account of the state in which his remains were found upon the opening of his tomb in Durham cathedral in the year MDCCCXXVII*, Durham, 1828.

[686] Raine, J., *The fabric rolls of York Minster*, SS, 35 (1858).

[687] Raine, J., *The priory of Hexham: its chronicles, endowments, and annals*, SS, 44, 46 (1863–4).

[688] Raymo, R. R., 'Works of religious and philosophical instruction', in [354], pp. 2255–371, 2466–582.

[689] Razi, Z., 'The struggles between the abbots of Halesowen and their tenants in the thirteenth and fourteenth centuries', in [19], pp. 151–67.

[690] *The records of the northern Convocation*, SS, 113 (1907).

[691] Reed, A. W., 'The regulation of the book trade before the proclamation of 1538', *Trans. of the bibliographical soc.*, 15 (1917–19), pp. 157–84.

[692] Reich, A. M., 'The Parliamentary abbots to 1470: a study in English constitutional history', *University of California pubs. in hist.*, 17 (1941), pp. 265–401.

[693] Reynolds, S., *Kingdoms and communities in western Europe, 900–1300*, Oxford, 1984.

[694] Richardson, H. G., 'Heresy and the lay power under Richard II', *EHR*, 51 (1936), pp. 1–28.

[695] Richmond, C., 'Religion and the fifteenth-century English gentleman', in [221], pp. 193–208.

[696] Richmond, C., 'The Pastons revisited: marriage and the family in fifteenth-century England', *BIHR*, 58 (1985), pp. 35–36.

[697] Richter, E. L., and Friedberg, E., *Corpus iuris canonici*, 2 vols, Leipzig, 1879–1881.

[698] Riehle, W., *The Middle English mystics*, London, Boston, and Henley, 1981.

[699] Riley, H. T., *Memorials of London and London life in the XIIIth, XIVth, and XVth centuries*, London, 1868.

[700] Riley, H. T., *Registra quorundam abbatum monasterii S. Albani, qui sæculo xv^{mo} floruere*, 2 vols, London, 1872–3.

[701] Robinson, D., *The register of William Melton, archbishop of York, 1317–1340, vol. 2*, CYS, 71 (1978).

[702] Robinson, D., 'Ordinations of secular clergy in the diocese of Coventry and Lichfield, 1322–1358', *Archives*, 17 (1985–6), pp. 3–21.

[703] Robinson, F. N., *The complete works of Geoffrey Chaucer*, 2nd edn, Oxford, 1957.

[704] Robinson, J. W., 'The late medieval cult of Jesus and the mystery plays', PMLA, 80 (1968), pp. 508–14.

[705] Rodes, R. E., jr., *Ecclesiastical administration in medieval England: the Anglo-Saxons to the Reformation*, Notre Dame and London, 1977.

[706] Rodgers, E. C., *Discussion of holidays in the later middle ages*, Studies in hist., economics, and public law edited by the Faculty of Political Science of Columbia University, 474, New York, 1940.

[707] Rogers, A., 'Clerical taxation under Henry IV, 1399–1413', BIHR, 46 (1973), pp. 123–44.

[708] Rogers, D. M., 'The "Friends of North Newington"; a new Pynson broadside', *Bodleian library record*, 5 (1954–6), pp., 251–5.

[709] Rogers, J. E. T., *Loci e libro veritatum*, Oxford, 1881.

[710] Rose, R. K., 'Priests and patrons in the fourteenth-century diocese of Carlisle', SCH, 16 (1979), pp. 207–18.

[711] Rosenthal, J. T., *The training of an elite group: English bishops in the fifteenth century*, Trans. American philosophical soc., n.s. 60, part 5 (1970).

[712] Rosenthal, J. T., 'Lancastrian bishops and educational benefaction', in [44], pp. 199–211.

[713] Rosenthal, J. T., and Richmond, C., *People, politics, and community in the later middle ages*, Gloucester, 1987.

[714] Roskell, J. S., 'The problem of the attendance of the lords in medieval Parliaments', BIHR, 29 (1956), pp. 153–204, reprinted in J. S. Roskell, *Parliament and politics in late medieval England*, 2 vols, London, 1981, i, ch.2.

[715] Ross, C., *Richard III*, London, 1981.

[716] Rosser, A. G., 'The essence of medieval urban communities: the vill of Westminster, 1200–1500', TRHS, 5th ser., 34 (1984), pp. 91–112.

[717] *Rotuli Parliamentorum*, 6 vols, London, 1767–83.

[718] Rubin, M., *Charity and community in medieval Cambridge*, CSMLT, 4th ser., 4, Cambridge, 1987.

[719] Rupp, G., 'The battle of the books: the ferment of ideas and the beginning of the Reformation', in [97], pp. 1–19.

[720] Russell, G. H., 'Vernacular instruction of the laity in the late middle ages in England: some texts and notes', *J. religious hist.*, 2 (1962), pp. 98–119.

[721] Russell, J. C., 'The clerical population of medieval England', *Trad.*, 2 (1944), pp. 177–212.

[722] Russell, J. C., *British medieval population*, Albuquerque, 1948.

[723] Russell, P. E., *The English intervention in Spain and Portugal in the time of Edward III and Richard II*, Oxford, 1955.

[724] Rymer, T., *Foedera*, vii, London, 1709.

[725] Sacks, D. H., 'The demise of the martyrs: the feasts of St Clement and St Katherine in Bristol, 1400–1600', *Social hist.*, 11 (1986), pp. 141–69.

[726] Slater, E., *Nicholas Love's 'Myrrour of the blessed lyf of Jesu Christ'*, Analecta Cartusiana, 10, Salzburg, 1974.

[727] Salter, E., 'The manuscripts of Nicholas Love's *Myrrour of the Blessed Lyf of Jesu Christ* and related texts', in *Middle English prose: essays on bibliographical problems*, ed. A. S. G. Edwards and D. Pearsall, New York and London, 1981, pp. 115–27.

[728] Salter, H. E., *Eynsham cartulary*, OHS, 49, 51 (1907–8).

[729] Salter, H. E., *A subsidy collected in the diocese of Lincoln in 1526*, OHS, 63 (1909).

[730] Salter, H. E., *A cartulary of the hospital of St John the Baptist*, OHS, 66, 68–9 (1914–16).

[731] Salter, H. E., *Snappe's formulary and other records*, OHS, 80 (1924).

[732] Salter, H. E., Pantin, W. A., and Richardson, H. G., *Formularies which bear on the history of Oxford, c.1204–1420*, OHS, n.s. 4–5 (1942).

[733] Saltman, A., *The cartulary of the Wakebridge chantries at Crich*, Derbyshire arch. soc. record ser., 6 (1976, for 1971).

[734] *Sanctuarium Dunelmense et sanctuarium Beverlacense*, SS, 5 (1837).

[735] Sandquist, T. A., 'The holy oil of St Thomas of Canterbury', in *Essays in medieval history presented to Bertie Wilkinson*, ed. T. A. Sandquist and M. R. Powicke, Toronto, 1969, pp. 330–44.

[736] Sargent, M. G., 'The transmission by the English Carthusians of some late medieval spiritual writings', *JEH*, 27 (1976), pp. 225–40.

[737] Sargent, M. G., 'Minor devotional writings', in [246], pp. 147–75.

[738] Sayers, J. E., *Original papal documents in the Lambeth Palace Library*, BIHR, special supplement, 6, London, 1967.

[739] Sayers, J. E., *Papal judges delegate in the province of Canterbury, 1198–1254: a study in ecclesiastical jurisdiction and administration*, Oxford, 1971.

[740] Sayers, J. E., 'Papal privileges for St Albans abbey and its dependencies', in [104], pp. 57–84.

[741] Sayers, J. E., 'Monastic archdeacons', in [97], pp. 177–203.

[742] Sayles, G. O., *Select cases in the court of King's Bench under Richard II, Henry IV, and Henry V*, Sel., 88 (1971).

[743] Scaife, R. H., *The register of the guild of Corpus Christi in the city of York*, SS 57 (1872).

[744] Scammell, J., 'The origins and limitations of the liberty of Durham', *EHR*, 81 (1966), pp. 449–73.

[745] Scammell, J., 'The rural chapter in England from the eleventh to the fourteenth centuries', *EHR*, 86 (1971), pp. 1–21.

[746] Scarisbrick, J. J., 'Clerical taxation in England, 1485 to 1547', *JEH*, 11 (1960), pp. 41–54.

[747] Scarisbrick, J. J., *Henry VIII*, London, 1968.

[748] Scarisbrick, J. J., *The Reformation and the English people*, Oxford, 1984.

[749] Scattergood, V. J., *Politics and poetry in the fifteenth century*, London, 1971.

[750] Scattergood, V. J., *The works of Sir John Clanvowe*, Cambridge, 1975.

[751] Schoeck, R. J., 'The Fifth Lateran Council: its partial successes and its larger failures', in [542], pp. 99–124.

[752] Searle, E., *Lordship and community: Battle abbey and its banlieu, 1066–1538*, PIMS, studies and texts, 26, Toronto, 1974.

[753] Searle, E., 'A rejoinder', *P&P*, 99 (May, 1983), pp. 148–60.

[754] Sellers, M., *The York mercers and merchant adventurers, 1356–1917*, SS, 129 (1918).

[755] Severs, J. B., *A manual of the writings in Middle English, 1050–1500*, ii, Hamden, Conn., 1970.

[756] Shaw, J., 'The influence of canonical and episcopal reform on popular books of instruction', in [375], pp. 44–60.

[757] Sheehan, M. M., *The will in medieval England: from the conversion of the Anglo-Saxons to the end of the thirteenth century*, PIMS, studies and texts, 6, Toronto, 1963.

[758] Sheehan, M. M., 'The formation and stability of marriage in fourteenth-century England: evidence of an Ely register', *Med.St.*, 33 (1971), pp. 228–63.

[759] Simpson, J. B., 'Coal mining by the monks', *Trans. institution of mining engineers*, 39 (1909–10), pp. 572–98.

[760] Simmons, T. F., *The lay folks' mass book*, EETS, o.s. 71 (1879).

[761] Simpson, W. S., *Visitations of churches belonging to St Paul's cathedral in 1297 and in 1458*, Camden soc., 2nd ser., 55 (1895).

[762] Siraisi, N., 'Introduction', in [913], pp. 9–22.

[763] Smith, D. M., *A guide to the archive collections in the Borthwick Institute of Historical Research*, BTC, 1, York, 1973.

[764] Smith, D. M., 'A reconstruction of the York "sede vacante" register, 1352–1353', *Borthwick institute bulletin*, 1 (1975–8), pp. 75–90.

[765] Smith, D. M., *Guide to bishops' registers of England and Wales: a survey from the middle ages to the abolition of episcopacy in 1646*, Royal hist. soc., guides and handbooks, 11, London, 1981.

[766] Smith, D. M., 'Suffragan bishops in the medieval diocese of Lincoln', *Lincolnshire hist. and archaeology*, 17 (1982), pp. 17–27.

[767] Smith, D. M., 'A reconstruction of the lost register of the vicars-general of archbishop Thoresby of York', *Borthwick institute bulletin*, 3 (1983–6), pp. 29–61.

[768] Smith, R. A. L., *Canterbury cathedral priory: a study in manorial administration*, Cambridge, 1943.

[769] Smith, T., Smith, L. T., and Brentano, L., *English gilds*, EETS, o.s. 40 (1870).

[770] Snape, R. H., *English monastic finances in the late middle ages*, Cambridge, 1926.

[771] Sneyd, C. A., *A relation, or rather a true account, of the island of England, with sundry particulars of these people and of the royal revenues under king Henry the seventh, about the year 1500*, Camden soc., 1st ser., 37 (1847).

[772] Spencer, B., 'Medieval pilgrim badges: some general observations illustrated mainly from English sources', in *Rotterdam papers: a contribution to medieval archaeology*, ed. J. G. N. Renaud, Rotterdam, 1968, pp. 137–54.

[773] Spencer, B., 'King Henry of Windsor and the London pilgrim', in *Collectanea Londiniensia: studies in London archaeology and history presented to Ralph Menfield*, ed. J. Bird, H. Clapman, and J. Clark, London and Middlesex arch. soc., special papers, 2 (1978), pp. 234–64.

[774] Spencer, H., 'A fifteenth-century translation of a late twelfth-century sermon collection', *R. English studies*, n.s. 28 (1977), pp. 257–67.

[775] Stargardt, V., 'The beguines of Belgium, the Dominican nuns of Germany, and Margery Kempe', in [375], pp. 277–313.

[776] *Statutes of the realm*, i–iii, London, 1816–17.

[777] Steel, A., *The receipt of the Exchequer, 1377–1485*, Cambridge, 1954.

[778] Stewart-Brown, R., *Accounts of the chamberlains and other officers of the county of Chester, 1301–1360*, RS of Lancashire and Cheshire, 59 (1910).

[779] Stewart-Brown, R., 'The Cheshire writs of Quo warranto in 1499', *EHR*, 49 (1934), pp. 676–84.

[780] Stone, E. D., and Cozens-Hardy, B., *Norwich consistory court depositions, 1499–1512 and 1518–1530*, Norfolk RS, 10 (1938).

[781] Storey, R. L., *The register of Thomas Langley, bishop of Durham, 1406–1437*, SS, 164, 166, 169–70, 177, 182 (1956–70).

[782] Storey, R. L., *Thomas Langley and the bishopric of Durham, 1406–1437*, London, 1961.

[783] Storey, R. L., 'Ecclesiastical causes in Chancery', in [104], pp. 236–59.

[784] Storey, R. L., *Diocesan administration in fifteenth-century England*, BP, 16, 2nd edn, York, 1972.

[785] Storey, R. L., 'Recruitment of English clergy in the period of the conciliar movement', *Annuarium historiae conciliorum*, 7 (1975), pp. 290–313.

[786] Storey, R. L., 'Clergy and common law in the reign of Henry IV', in *Medieval legal records edited in memory of C. A. F. Meekings*, ed. R.F. Hunnisett and J. B. Post, London, 1978, pp. 341–408.

[787] Storey, R. L., 'Gentleman-bureaucrats', in [154], pp. 90–129.

[788] Storey, R. L., 'Episcopal king-makers in the fifteenth century', in [221], pp. 82–98.

[789] Storrs, C., and Cordero Carrete, F. R., 'Peregrinos ingleses a Santiago en el siglo XIV', *Cuadernos de estudios Gallegos*, 20 (1965), pp. 193–224.

[790] Studd, R., 'A Templar colony in north Staffordshire: Keele before the Sneyds', *North Staffordshire j. of field studies*, 22 (1982–5), pp. 5–21.

[791] Sumption, J., *Pilgrimage: an image of medieval religion*, London, 1975.

[792] Sutherland, D. W., *Quo warranto proceedings in the reign of Edward I, 1278–1294*, Oxford, 1963.

[793] Swanson, H. C., 'The illusion of economic structure: craft gilds in late medieval English towns', *P&P*, 121 (November, 1988), pp. 29–48.

[794] Swanson, R. N., 'Papal letters among the ecclesiastical archives at York, 1378–1415', *Borthwick institute bulletin*, 1 (1975–8), pp. 165–93.

[795] Swanson, R. N., 'Archbishop Arundel and the chapter of York', *BIHR*, 54 (1981), pp. 254–7.

[796] Swanson, R. N., *A Calendar of the register of Richard Scrope, archbishop of York, 1398–1405*, BTC, 8, 11, York, 1981–5.

[797] Swanson, R. N., 'Thomas Holme and his chantries', *York historian*, 5 (1984), pp. 3–7.

[798] Swanson, R. N., 'Obedience and disobedients in the great schism', *Archivum historiae pontificiae*, 22 (1984), pp. 377–87.

[799] Swanson, R. N., 'Universities, graduates, and benefices in late medieval England', *P&P*, 106 (February 1985), pp. 28–61.

[800] Swanson, R. N., 'Titles to orders in medieval English episcopal registers', in *Studies in medieval history presented to R. H. C. Davis*, ed. H. Mayr-Harting and R. I. Moore, London, 1985, pp. 233–45.

[801] Swanson, R. N., 'Learning and livings: university study and clerical careers in late medieval England', *Hist. universities*, 6 (1986–7), pp. 81–103.

[802] Swanson, R. N., 'Episcopal income from spiritualities in the diocese of Exeter in the early sixteenth century', *JEH*, 39 (1988), pp. 520–30.

[803] Swanson, R. N., 'Episcopal income from spiritualities in late medieval England: the evidence for the diocese of Coventry and Lichfield', *Midland hist.*, 14 (1988), pp. 1–20.

[804] Sweet, A. H., 'Papal privileges granted to individual religious', *Spec.*, 31 (1956), pp. 602–10.

[805] *Syntomotaxia del' second part du roy Henry VI*, London, 1679.

[806] Szittya, P. R., *The antifraternal tradition in medieval literature*, Princeton, NJ, 1986.

[807] Talbert, E. W., and Thomson, S. H., 'Wyclyf and his followers', in [755], pp. 354–80, 517–33.

[808] Talbot, C. H., *Letters from the English abbots to the chapter at Cîteaux, 1421–1521*, Camden soc., 4th ser., 4 (1967).

[809] Tanner, N. P., *Heresy trials in the diocese of Norwich, 1428–31*, Camden soc., 4th ser., 20 (1977).

[810] Tanner, N. P., *The church in late medieval Norwich, 1370–1532*, PIMS, studies and texts, 66, Toronto, 1984.

[811] Tatnall, E. C., 'The condemnation of John Wyclif at the Council of Constance', *SCH*, 7 (1971), pp. 209–18.

[812] Taunton, E. L., *Thomas Wolsey, legate and reformer*, London and New York, 1902.

[813] *Taxatio ecclesiastica Angliæ et Walliæ, auctoritate P. Nicholai IV, circa A.D. 1291*, London, 1802.

[814] Taylor, J. H. M., *Dies illa: death in the middle ages. Proceedings of the 1983 Manchester colloquium*, Vinaver studies in French, 1, Liverpool, 1984.

[815] Taylor, P., 'The bishop of London's city soke', *BIHR*, 53 (1980), pp. 174–82.

[816] Templeman, G., *The records of the guild of the Holy Trinity, St. Mary, St John the Baptist, and St Katherine of Coventry*, ii, Dugdale soc. pubs., 19 (1944).

[817] Thompson, A. H., *Visitations of religious houses in the diocese of Lincoln*, LRS, 7, 14, 21 (1914–29).

[818] Thompson, A. H., 'Documents relating to diocesan and provincial visitations from the registers of Henry Bowet, lord archbishop of York, 7 Oct. 1407–20 Oct. 1423, and John Kempe, cardinal–priest of Santa Balbina and lord archbishop of York, 20 July 1425–21 July 1452', in *Miscellanea, vol. X*, SS, 127 (1916), pp. 130–302.

[819] Thompson, A. H., 'The registers of the archdeaconry of Richmond, 1361–1442', *YAJ*, 25 (1920), pp. 129–268.

[820] Thompson, A. H., 'A corrody from Leicester abbey, A.D. 1393–4, with some notes on corrodies', *Trans. Leicestershire arch. soc.*, 14 (1926), pp. 113–34.

[821] Thompson, A. H., 'The register of the archdeacons of Richmond, 1447–1477', *YAJ*, 30 (1930–1), pp. 1–132; 32 (1934–6), pp. 111–47.

[822] Thompson, A. H., *Visitations of the diocese of Lincoln, 1517–1531*, LRS, 33, 35, 37 (1940–7).

[823] Thompson, A. H., 'Diocesan organisation in the middle ages: archdeacons and rural deans', *Proc.B.A.*, 29 (1943), pp. 153–94.

[824] Thompson, A. H., *The English clergy and their organisation in the later middle ages*, Oxford, 1947.

[825] Thompson, A. H., *The abbey of St Mary of the meadows, Leicester*, Leicester, 1949.

[826] Thomson, J. A. F., 'Tithe disputes in later medieval London', *EHR*, 78 (1963), pp. 1–17.

[827] Thomson, J. A. F., 'A Lollard rising in Kent: 1431 or 1438?', *BIHR*, 37 (1964), pp. 100–2.

[828] Thomson, J. A. F., 'John Foxe and some sources for Lollard history: notes for a critical appraisal', *SCH*, 2 (1965), pp. 251–7.

[829] Thomson, J. A. F., *The later Lollards, 1414–1520*, Oxford, 1965.

[830] Thomson, J. A. F., *Popes and princes, 1417–1517: politics and polity in the late medieval church*, London, 1980.

[831] Thomson, J. A. F., *The transformation of medieval England, 1370–1529*, London, 1983.

[832] Thomson, J. A. F., ' "The well of grace": Englishmen and Rome in the fifteenth century', in [221], pp. 99–114.

[833] Thomson, J. A. F., 'Two Exeter decanal elections, 1509', *Southern hist.*, 6 (1986), pp. 36–45.

[834] Thomson, W. R., *The Latin writings of John Wyclyf: an annotated catalog*, PIMS, subsidia mediaevalia, 14, Toronto, 1983.

[835] Thorne, S. E., *Readings and moots at the Inns of Court in the fifteenth century*, i, Sel., 71 (1952).

[836] Thornley, I. D., 'The destruction of sanctuary', in *Tudor studies presented by the board of studies in history in the University of London to Albert Frederick Pollard*, ed. R. W. Seton-Watson, London, 1924, pp. 182–207.

[837] Thornley, I. D., *Year books of Richard II: 11 Richard II, 1387–1388*, London, 1937.

[838] Thrupp, S. L., *The merchant class of medieval London*, Ann Arbor, Mich., 1948.

[839] Tierney, B., *Medieval poor law: a sketch of canonical theory and its application in England*, Berkeley and Los Angeles, 1959.

[840] Tihon, C., 'Les expectatives in forma pauperum, particulièrement au XIVème siècle', *Bulletin de l'institut historique belge de Rome*, 5 (1923), pp. 51–118.

[841] Timmins, T. C. B., *The register of John Chandler, dean of Salisbury, 1404–17*, Wiltshire RS, 39 (1984).

[842] Tipton, C. L., 'The English hospitallers during the great schism', *Studies in medieval and renaissance hist.*, 4 (1967), pp. 89–124.

[843] Tittler, R., 'The end of the middle ages in the English country town', *Sixteenth century j.*, 18 (1987), pp. 471–87.

[844] Train, K. S. B., *Lists of the clergy of central Nottinghamshire*, Thoroton soc. record ser., 15, 3 vols, Nottingham, 1953–4.

[845] Trenholme, N. F., *The right of sanctuary in England: a study in institutional history*, The University of Missouri studies, 1/v (1903).

[846] Trenholme, N. F., *The English monastic boroughs: a study in medieval history*, The University of Missouri studies, a quarterly of research, 2/iii (1927).

[847] Tuck, J. A., 'Nobles, commons, and the great revolt of 1381', in [397], pp. 194–212.

[848] Tudor, P., 'Religious instruction for children and adolescents in the early English Reformation', *JEH*, 35 (1984), pp. 391–413.

[849] Twemlow, J. A., *Calendar of entries in the papal registers relating to Great Britain and Ireland: Papal letters, vol. VI, A.D. 1404–1415*, London, 1904.

[850] Twemlow, J. A., *Calendar of entries in the papal registers relating to Great Britain and Ireland: Papal letters, 1471–1484, vol.XV*, 2 vols, London, 1955.

[851] Ullmann, W., 'The development of the medieval idea of sovereignty', *EHR*, 64 (1949), pp. 1–33.

[852] Ullmann, W., *Medieval papalism: the political theories of the medieval canonists*, London, 1949.

[853] Ullmann, W., 'Thomas Becket's miraculous oil', *J. of theological studies*, n.s. 8 (1957), pp. 129–33, reprinted in [859].

[854] Ullmann, W., *Principles of government and politics in the middle ages*, London, 1961.

[855] Ullmann, W., *Liber regie capelle: a manuscript in the Biblioteca Publica, Evora*, HBS, 92 (1961).

[856] Ullmann, W., 'A decision of the Rota Romana on the benefit of clergy in England', *Studia Gratiana*, 13 (1967), pp. 451–90, reprinted in [859].

[857] Ullmann, W., *Law and politics in the middle ages*, Cambridge, 1975.

[858] Ullmann, W., 'John Baconthorpe as a canonist', in [97], pp. 223–46.

[859] Ullmann, W., *The papacy and political ideas in the middle ages*, London, 1976.

[860] Ullmann, W., 'This realm of England is an empire', *JEH*, 30 (1979), pp. 175–203; reprinted in W. Ullmann, *Jurisprudence in the middle ages*, London, 1980.

[861] Utley, F. L., 'Dialogues, debates, and catechisms', in *A manual of the writings in middle English, 1050–1500*, iii, ed. A. E. Hartung, Hamden, Conn., 1972, pp. 673–716, 834–74.

[862] Vale, M. G. A., *Piety, charity, and literacy among the Yorkshire gentry, 1370–1480*, BP, 50, York, 1976.

[863] Vauchez, A., *La sainteté en occident aux derniers siècles du moyen age, d'après les procès de canonisation et les documents hagiographiques*, Bibliothèque des écoles françaises d'Athènes et de Rome, 241, Rome, 1981.

[864] Venables, E., 'The shrine and head of St Hugh of Lincoln', *Associated architectural societies reports and papers*, 21 (1891–2), pp. 131–51.

[865] *Victoria county history: a history of Yorkshire*, iii, London, 1913.

[866] *Victoria history of the county of Cambridge and Isle of Ely*, iii, London, 1959.

[867] *Victoria history of the county of Cambridge and Isle of Ely*, iv, London, 1953.

[868] *Victoria history of the county of Chester*, iii, Oxford, 1980.

[869] *Victoria history of the county of Hertford*, iv, London, 1914.

[870] *Victoria history of the county of Northampton*, ii, London, 1906.

[871] *Victoria history of the county of Shropshire*, ii, Oxford, 1973.

[872] *Victoria history of the county of Stafford*, iii, Oxford, 1970.

[873] *Victoria history of the county of Warwick*, iii, London, 1945.

[874] *Victoria history of the county of Warwick*, viii, London, 1969.

[875] *Victoria history of the county of Wiltshire*, v, London, 1957.

[876] *Victoria history of the county of York*, ii, London, 1912.

[877] *Victoria history of Yorkshire: City of York*, London, 1961.

[878] Virgoe, R., 'The composition of the king's council, 1437–61', *BIHR*, 43 (1970), pp. 134–60.

[879] Vodola, E., *Excommunication in the middle ages*, Berkeley, Los Angeles, and London, 1986.

[880] Wagenknecht, E., *The personality of Chaucer*, Norman, Okla., 1968.

[881] Walsh, J., *Pre-Reformation English spirituality*, London, n.d.

[882] Walsh, K., and Wood, D., *The Bible in the medieval world: essays in memory of Beryl Smalley*, SCH, subsidia, 4, Oxford, 1985.

[883] Warren, A.K., *Anchorites and their patrons in medieval England*, Berkeley, Los Angeles, and London, 1985.

[884] Watson, A. G., *Medieval libraries of Great Britain, a list of surviving books edited by N. R. Ker: supplement to the second edition*, Royal hist. soc., guides and handbooks, 15, London, 1987.

[885] Watt, D. E. R., 'University clerks and rolls of petitions for benefices', *Spec.*, 34 (1959), pp. 213–29.

[886] Watt, D. E. R., 'The papacy and Scotland in the fifteenth century', in [221], pp. 115–29.

[887] Watt, J. A., *The theory of papal monarchy in the thirteenth century: the contribution of the canonists*, London, 1965.

[888] Waugh, W. T., 'The great Statute of Praemunire', *EHR*, 37 (1922), pp. 173–205.

[889] Weaver, F. W., *Somerset medieval wills (1383–1500)*, Somerset RS, 16 (1903).

[890] Wenzel, S., 'Pestilence and Middle English literature: friar John Grimestone's poems on death', in [913], pp. 131–59.

[891] Wenzel, S., *preachers, poets, and the early English lyric*, Princeton, NJ, 1986.

[892] Weske, D. B., *Convocation of the clergy*, London, 1937.

[893] Westlake, H. F., *The parish guilds of medieval England*, London, 1919.

[894] White, E., *The St Christopher and St George guild of York*, BP, 72, York, 1987.

[895] Whitfield, D. W., 'The third order of St Francis in medieval England', *Franciscan studies*, n.s. 13 (1953), pp. 50–9.

[896] Whitfield, D. W., 'An early letter of confraternity', *Franciscan studies*, n.s. 14 (1954), pp. 387–91.

[897] Whitfield, D. W., 'Conflicts of personality and principle: the political and religious crisis in the English Franciscan province, 1400–1409', *Franciscan studies*, n.s. 17 (1957), pp. 321–62.

[898] Whiting, R., 'Abominable idols: images and image-breaking under Henry VIII', *JEH*, 33 (1982), pp. 30–47.

[899] Whittick, C., 'The role of the criminal appeal in the fifteenth century', in *Law and social change in British history: papers presented to the Bristol legal history conference, 14–17 July 1981*, ed. J. A. Guy and H. G. Beale, Royal hist. soc., studies in hist. ser., 40, London, 1984, pp. 55–72.

[900] Whitton, C. A., 'The coinages of Henry VIII and of Edward VI in Henry's name', *British numismatic j.*, 26 (1949–51), pp. 56–89, 170–212, 290–332.

[901] Wilkie, W. E., *The cardinal protectors of England: Rome and the Tudors before the Reformation*, Cambridge, 1974.

[902] Wilkins, D., *Concilia Magna Britanniæ et Hiberniæ*, 4 vols, London, 1737.

[903] Wilkinson, B., 'The deposition of Richard II and the accession of Henry IV', in *Historical studies of the English Parliament*, ed. E. B. Fryde and E. Miller, 2 vols, Cambridge, 1970, i, pp. 328–53, 370–3.

[904] Wilks, M., 'Predestination, property, and power: Wyclif's theory of dominion and grace', *SCH*, 2 (1965), pp. 220–36.

[905] Wilks, M., ' "Reformatio regni": Wyclif and Hus as leaders of religious protest movements', *SCH*, 9 (1972), pp. 109–30.

[906] Wilks, M., 'Royal priesthood: the origins of Lollardy', in [143], pp. 63–70.

[907] Willard, J. F., 'The English church and the lay taxes of the fourteenth century', *The University of Colorado studies*, 4 (1906–7), pp. 217–25.

[908] Williams, A., 'Relations between the mendicant friars and the secular church in England in the later fourteenth century', *Annuale medievale*, 1 (1960), pp. 22–95.

[909] Williams, C. H., *Year books of Henry VI: 1 Henry VI, A.D. 1422*, Sel., 50 (1933).

[910] Williams, C. H., *English historical documents, 1485–1558*, London, 1967.

[911] Williams, D. H., 'Tudor Cistercian life: corrodians and residential servants', *Cîteaux*, 34 (1983), pp. 77–91, 284–310.

[912] Williams, G., *The Welsh church from Conquest to Reformation*, Cardiff, 1962.

[913] Williman, D., *The Black Death: the impact of fourteenth-century plague: papers of the eleventh annual conference of the Center for Medieval and Early Renaissance studies*, Medieval and Renaissance texts and studies, 13, Binghampton, NY, 1982.

[914] Willis Bund, J. W., *The register of the diocese of Worcester during the vacancy of the see, usually called 'Registrum sede vacante'*, part iv, Worcester hist. soc. pubs., Oxford, 1897.

[915] Wilson, J. M., *Accounts of the priory of Worcester for the years 13–14 Henry VIII, A.D. 1521–2*, Worcester hist. soc., 17 (1907).

[916] Wilson, R. A., *The registers or act books of the bishops of Coventry and Lichfield, book 5, being the second register of bishop Robert de Stretton, A.D. 1360–1385: an abstract of the contents*, William Salt arch. soc., n.s. 8 (1905).

[917] Wilson, R. A., *The registers or act books of the bishops of Coventry and Lichfield, book 4, being the register of the guardians of the spiritualities during the vacancy of the see, and the first register of bishop Robert de Stretton, 1358–1385: an abstract of the contents*, William Salt arch. soc., n.s. 10/ii (1907).

[918] Wolffe, B., *Henry VI*, London, 1981.

[919] Woodcock, B. L., *Medieval ecclesiastical courts in the diocese of Canterbury*, Oxford, 1952.

[920] Wood-Legh, K., *A small household of the XVth century, being the account book of Munden's chantry, Bridport*, Manchester, 1956.

[921] Wood-Legh, K., *Perpetual chantries in Britain*, Cambridge, 1965.

[922] Wood-Legh, K., *Kentish visitations of archbishop William Warham and his deputies, 1511–1512*, Kent records, 24 (1984).

[923] Woodruff, C. E., 'The financial aspect of the cult of St Thomas of Canterbury, as recorded by a study of the monastic records', *Arch. Cantiana*, 44 (1932), pp. 13–32.

[924] Woodruff, C. E., 'An archidiaconal visitation of 1502', *Arch. Cantiana*, 47 (1935), pp. 13–54.

[925] Woolley, R. M., *The officium and miracula of Richard Rolle of Hampole*, London, 1919.

[926] Woolley, R. M., *The York Provinciale, as put forward by Thomas Wolsey, archbishop of York, in the year 1518*, London, 1931.

[927] Workman, H. E., *John Wyclif: a study of the English medieval church*, 2 vols, Oxford, 1926.

[928] Wright, D. P., *The register of Thomas Langton, bishop of Salisbury, 1485–95*, CYS, 74 (1985).

[929] Wright, J. R., *The church and the English crown, 1305–1334: a study based on the register of archbishop Walter Reynolds*, PIMS, studies and texts, 48, Toronto, 1980.

[930] Wright, S. K., 'The provenance and manuscript tradition of the *Martyrium Ricardi archiepiscopi*', *Manuscripta*, 28 (1984), pp. 92–102.

[931] Wunderli, R. M., *London church courts and society on the eve of the Reformation*, Speculum anniversary monographs, 7, Cambridge, Mass., 1981.

[932] Wunderli, R. M., 'Pre-Reformation London summoners and the murder of Richard Hunne', *JEH*, 33 (1982), pp. 209–24.

[933] Youings, J., 'The church', in *The agrarian history of England and Wales, volume iv: 1500–1640*, ed. J. Thirsk, Cambridge, 1967, pp. 306–56.

[934] Youings, J., *The dissolution of the monasteries*, Historical problems, studies, and documents, 14, London, 1971.

[935] Zacher, C. K., 'Travel and geographical writings', in [354], pp. 1235–54, 2449–66.

[936] Zell, M. L., 'The personnel of the clergy in Kent in the Reformation period', *EHR*, 89 (1974), pp. 513–33.

[937] Zell, M. L., 'Economic problems of the parochial clergy in the sixteenth century', in *Princes and paupers in the English church, 1500–1800*, ed. R. O'Day and F. Heal, Leicester, 1981, pp. 19–43.

[938] Zika, C., 'Hosts, processions, and pilgrimages in fifteenth-century Germany', *P&P*, 118 (February 1988), pp. 25–64.

[939] Zutshi, P. N. R., 'Proctors acting for English petitioners in the chancery of the Avignon popes (1305–1378)', *JEH*, 35 (1984), pp. 15–29

UNPUBLISHED PAPERS AND DISSERTATIONS

[940] Brown, S., 'The peculiar jurisdiction of York Minster during the middle ages', D.Phil. thesis, University of York, 1981.

[941] Harvey, M. M., 'English suggestions for the reforms to be undertaken by the general councils, 1400–1418, with special reference to the proposals made by Richard Ullerston', D.Phil. thesis, University of Oxford, 1964.

[942] Lewis, F., 'Lifesize images of the wound in Christ's side and popular devotion', unpublished paper.

[943] Lipkin, J. A., 'Pluralism in pre-Reformation England: a quantitative analysis of ecclesiastical incumbency, c.1490–1539', Ph.D. thesis, Catholic University of America, Washington DC, 1979.

[944] Swanson, H. C., 'Craftsmen and industry in late medieval York', D.Phil. thesis, University of York, 1981.

Index